The
$10 TRILLION
DREAM

The

$10 TRILLION
DREAM

THE STATE OF THE INDIAN ECONOMY
AND THE POLICY REFORMS AGENDA

SUBHASH CHANDRA GARG

PENGUIN
BUSINESS

An imprint of Penguin Random House

PENGUIN BUSINESS

USA | Canada | UK | Ireland | Australia
New Zealand | India | South Africa | China | Singapore

Penguin Business is part of the Penguin Random House group of companies
whose addresses can be found at global.penguinrandomhouse.com

Published by Penguin Random House India Pvt. Ltd
4th Floor, Capital Tower 1, MG Road,
Gurugram 122 002, Haryana, India

First published in Penguin Business by Penguin Random House India 2022
This edition published in Penguin Business by Penguin Random House India 2025

ISBN 9780670095711

Typeset in Adobe Garamond Pro by MAP Systems, Bengaluru, India
Printed at Replika Press Pvt. Ltd.

www.penguin.co.in

This is a legitimate digitally printed version of the book and therefore might not
have certain extra finishing on the cover.

To Anjali, my wife, soulmate and protector

To 130 crore Indians (a number growing every day) who make up the Indian economy as consumers, 40 crore who contribute their labour and skills as workers and 8 crore who use their enterprise and capital to produce and distribute goods, services and assets

Contents

Part A: State of the Indian Economy and Policy

Prologue: Why This Book?   3

Introduction

  1. Current State of the Economy: The Trough   12

Section I: Real Economy

  2. State of the Real Economy   30

  3. State of the Agriculture Economy   43

  4. Agricultural Development Programmes
      Have Lost Their Purpose   55

  5. 2020 Agri-Reforms: More Disruption than Real   64

  6. State of the Industrial Economy   74

  7. Industrial Policy of India: Private Sector Out and In Again   79

  8. MSMEs: Small Is Not Beautiful   99

  9. State of the Services Economy   111

10. Services Have Grown without Much Policy Support   118

11. State of the Public Sector   125

12. Disinvestment without Conviction   130

Section II: Factors of Production

13. State of Land Resources   138

14. First-Generation Land Reforms   142

15. State of Labour and Employment   150

16. Consolidation Is Not Labour Reforms   161

Section III: Infrastructure

17. State of Infrastructure   172

18. Mess in Telecom, Power and Transportation Sectors   180

19. Residential Real Estate Is a Victim of Bad Policy   194

Section IV: The Digital Economy

20. State of the Digital Economy   200

21. Policy Framework Not Good Enough to Make
     India a Digital Economy   208

22. Muddled Policies in Data and E-Commerce   216

Section V: Environmental and Social Economy

23. State of Environmental Economy   224

24. Industrialization Primary Cause for Environmental Crisis   230

25. State of Education, Health and Nutrition   239

26. Education and Health Policies Not Best Suited for Economy   246

Section VI: Foreign Trade, Commerce and Investment

27. State of Foreign Trade, Commerce and Investments   258

28. Atmanirbhar Bharat: A Redux of Import Substitution Policy?   274

Section VII: The Financial Sector

29. State of Currency and Money   286

30. Two and a Half Generations of the Rupee   297

31. State of Savings and Wealth   305

32. Reserve Bank of India in the Year of the Pandemic   317

33. Economic Capital Framework: Back to Square One   323

34. Foreign Reserves in Excess of $600 Billion:
    In Service of the Nation?   337

35. State of the Financial Sector   343

36. Whither Public-Sector Banks?   358

37. Unlocking Wealth Tucked Away in Gold   364

Section VIII: Fiscal Finance

38. State of Public Finance   374

39. Public Debt Is the Achilles Heel of India   389

40. State of Public Expenditures   404

41. Assessing 'Policy' in India's Expenditures   415

42. State of Tax and Non-Tax Revenues   426

43. Two Big Tax Reforms: GST and Corporate Tax Cut   440

44. Cooperative Fiscal Federalism to Fiscal Union   455

Part B: Policy Reforms for Building a $10 Trillion Economy

Section IX: State of Policy: In Retrospect

45. Fundamental Economic Policy since Independence   474

46. Seventy-Five Years of Economic Policymaking:
    Major Lessons Learnt   480

Section X: Policy Reform Agenda

47. Fundamental Economic Policy Reforms for a
    $10 Trillion Economy   502

48. Agriculture Policy Reforms   508

49. Industrial Policy Reforms   517

50. Services Policy Reforms   538

51. Reforms of Land and Labour   551

52. Public-Sector Reforms   567

53. Infrastructure Reforms   574

54. Building India's Digital Economy   587

55. Seizing the Environmental, Social and Governance Agenda   595

56. Financial Sector Reforms   609

57. Expenditure Reforms   633

58. Taxation Reforms   646

59. Debt Reforms   677

60. Destination 2035   690

Data Sources and Other Notes   695

A Note of Thanks   697

Part A: State of the Indian Economy and Policy

Prologue

Why This Book?

Governments are all about making policies, executing these by formulating legislation and development programmes and providing public goods and services. The government comprises the political executive and civil service. The political executive is primarily responsible for making policies. Economic policymaking is of paramount importance as it plays a critical role in national income, wealth, employment, prosperity, poverty, health of people, health of environment and so much more. The civil service performs three key functions: implementing policies, laws and programmes; delivering public goods and services as well as private goods and services if the government is socialist; and assisting the political executive in making policies.

The other wings of the state—the legislature and the judiciary—also have a significant role in policymaking and implementation. The legislature, the Parliament and legislative assemblies in India, representing the people of India and the states, approve legislations and financial resources to determine and execute policies and programmes. The judiciary keeps a check on both the legislature and the government to ensure they operate according to the basic structure of the Constitution and formulate policies, approve legislations, take up programmes and spend public money within the four walls of the Constitution, the laws of the land and publicly declared policy. The judiciary also administers justice and ensures

3

that the fundamental and legal rights of every citizen are protected and all citizens are fairly treated.

The IAS Provides Invaluable Policy Experience

The Indian Administrative Service (IAS) makes up a significant chunk of India's civil services. It has a special place among India's civil services for four principal reasons. First, it is a generalist service and therefore works across the widest spectrum of the government in India. Other departmentalized civil services have a much deeper role in their specific arena.

Second, it is a service common to the Centre and states whereas the central civil services serve Central government ministries/departments and most state civil services serve the respective departments at the state level.

Third, being responsible for implementing the widest spectrum of laws and development programmes and delivering most of the public goods and services, it touches the people of India most and, therefore, is most informed of the ground realities of the country.

Fourth, as it manages most of the positions of the secretaries to the government in the states and at the Centre, it participates in policymaking most closely.

This fourfold special character of the IAS makes it an integrationist of the Union of States, which India is, and qualifies it to occupy most of the broader ministries, departments and organizations, like finance, the Cabinet Secretariat, elections, district administration and disaster management.

I joined the IAS and served for thirty-five years. The service gave me an amazing opportunity to work across many sectors of the economy and participate in policy implementation and formulation over a very wide spectrum of economic activity, culminating in a two-year stint as the Secretary in charge of the Department of Economic Affairs, Government of India.

Practitioner of Economic Management in Rajasthan

India lives in states. Constitutionally, the states are also the pivot to deliver development programmes and administer the laws of the land. As an IAS officer of the Rajasthan cadre, I implemented policies, programmes, laws and executive orders of the government in the state, many of which were in the economic space.

As a subdivisional officer in Chittorgarh, I could see agriculture land management at close quarters. As the chief executive officer of a World Bank-funded soybean processing project in Kota, I turned around a sick 'white elephant'. Later, I got the opportunity to work in the agriculture sector for many years as the director of agriculture in Rajasthan and joint secretary in the Ministry of Agriculture, Government of India.

My service in Rajasthan for the fifteen years before 2000, offered the rich experience of working in several significant infrastructure, industrial and service sectors of the economy. As chief executive of the Rajasthan Renewables Management Agency, I could participate in the development of the nascent solar and wind power generation sector, including formulation of the wind and solar policies of the state. I played a role in the unbundling of the vertically integrated Rajasthan Electricity Board into separate generation, transmission and distribution companies, which initiated my extensive association with the power sector. I participated in policy development relating to important education sector programmes, including dealing with the private and aided educational sector.

I served as secretary (finance), in charge of the Budget Division, in Rajasthan for about two years. I also served as principal secretary in charge of the entire Finance Department of Rajasthan twice: first in 2008 and then in 2014. The Finance Department provided the most wide-angled view of the entire economic, social and governance management of the state. The making of two budgets in 2006–08 and the formulation of two budgets (including one interim) in 2014 provided enormous insight into the working of the economy and the role of government finances and policy in shaping it up.

In each of these postings, I realized the difference economic policies make. While the wrong policies resulted in poor growth, losses in enterprises and a negative contribution to the economy, the right policies generated good turnover and growth in profitability, rising incomes and promotions of workers and a generally positive contribution to the economy.

My interest in pushing for the right economic policies took shape with the 2007–08 budget, where I was able to build in the

Vishwakarma contributory pension scheme for unorganized workers, the first co-contribution based pension scheme in the country. This was later adopted nationally as the Swavalamban scheme in the 2010–11 Budget. I also pushed for the creation of a rainy-day fund—Rajasthan Development and Poverty Alleviation Fund—in this budget to park a part of revenue surplus for future use. The Bhamashah scheme, which Rajasthan announced in the 2008–09 budget, was the combination of Aadhaar, Jan-Dhan and IT-accessed delivery of not just government but private services.

Central Stints Whetted My Appetite for Policymaking

I joined the Central government for the first time in the year 2000 as a director in the Department of Economic Affairs (DEA) in the Ministry of Finance. The DEA, by its very nature, dabbled in economic policymaking. Moreover, as the repository of the budgets of the Central government as well as the counterpart of the multilateral and bilateral economic and development agencies of the world, the DEA provided an excellent platform to understand and participate in national economic policymaking.

The opportunity to work as joint secretary in charge of state finances in the Department of Expenditure exposed me to the extremely important issues of the financial management of states, including their financial relationships with the Reserve Bank of India (RBI) and the Central government. This posting, including contributing to and implementing the recommendations of the eleventh and twelfth Finance Commissions, provided a solid underpinning to my understanding of fiscal federal issues, in the Indian and global settings.

As the joint secretary in charge of the newly launched Rashtriya Krishi Vikas Yojana (RKVY), I had the opportunity to work with all the Indian states in the widest amplitude of the agriculture and allied sector, which included animal husbandry and fisheries.

As the Cabinet Secretariat is the fulcrum to process all proposals going to the Cabinet and Cabinet Committees, the posting as joint secretary and, later, additional secretary in the Cabinet Secretariat provided me a ringside view of discussions in the Cabinet. Numerous CoSs held in many economic sectors during this period—telecommunication, information technology (IT), disaster management, investment promotion, environmental issues—widened my understanding of the Indian economy.

The icing on the cake came in the form of my appointment as Secretary Economic Affairs in 2017. I wrote the drafts of three budget speeches (2018–19, 2019–20 [interim] and 2019–20) and finalized the set of accompanying budget documents. National budgets are the instruments of national fiscal policy management and important vehicles to initiate economic policy reforms.

Three Key Insights

My participation in numerous economy-related engagements during my long public service and study and reflections in the past two years after my voluntary retirement in 2019 have given me three key insights into the economy.

First, an economy is all about production and distribution of goods, services and assets or the economic value added, and a correctly measured GDP is its best indicator.

When the value added grows, the GDP grows. The value added is generated by labour, machines/technology and enterprise, within the ecosystem of economic policies framed and implemented by the government.

The value added or GDP translates to income for households, profits for capital and taxes for governments. Income accumulated grows in wealth. Therefore, all income and wealth flows from GDP. If GDP grows, income, profits and taxes also grow. Wealth grows.

Households spend the income earned on consumption that drives the demand function of the economy. Entrepreneurs invest their profits/capital and the credit they avail in buildings, machines and technology to produce more goods and services. This drives investment demand. The GDP, in all its three dimensions of value added, income and expenditure, and its growth, is extremely important for the maintenance of health and nutrition standards, quality of life and prosperity of the people.

Second, human resources (labour) and capital (enterprise and technology) are the two real factors of production in today's economy. Land, natural resources and financial capital are no longer binding constraints for growing the GDP of a nation.

All human beings are endowed with two natural resources: they have organs and muscle (physical ability) and brain and mind (intelligence); though these endowments vary at an individual level. Physical abilities can be nourished or dissipated by the actions of individuals, families and societal nurturing. Intelligence can be used to acquire knowledge and skills. Human beings (labour) work to produce all goods and services with the help of tools, machines and technology using their physical abilities and intelligence. Human beings are the primary factor of production adding value in the economy and are exclusive consumers of the value added. The human resources of any society or nation are the first building blocks of the economy.

Capital in today's world is essentially made up of two factors: human enterprise and technological ability used to produce goods and services in the form of tools, machines and electronic platforms. Scientific knowledge and the technological ecosystem produce or adapt tools, machines and technology. Entrepreneurial innovation and spirit put these into action to produce and distribute goods and services. Enterprise and technological prowess can make up for deficiency of land, natural resources and financial resources. Enterprise and technological prowess constitute real capital.

Third, policy makes a material difference in the growth of the economy and distribution of the value added.

The structure of the economy, its ability to grow and the fairer distribution of income earned depends considerably on the economic policies governments choose to adopt and implement. There are fundamental or most basic structural policies, such as adoption of a communist, socialist or capitalist form of economy, openness or otherwise to global trade, investment, technology, labour and the like. As these broad policy frameworks impact incentives of entrepreneurs and labour, innovation and technology adoption, private or public-sector dominance of the economy and inflow of foreign investments and technology, they result into very different economic outcomes in terms of growth and distribution of value added. Stepped-down economic policies in different sectors and the elements of the economy also make an important contribution within the contours of broader economic policies.

The government decides the policy that creates the ecosystem for productive or unproductive use of human and capital resources and the growth and distribution of value added in the economy.

Three basic building blocks—human resources, capital and policy—determine the rise and fall of the household, societal and global economy. A country which is endowed with or develops good policy and institutions creates the right conditions for the human resources and capital to produce goods, services and assets to generate high growth and bring prosperity, and to institute fair redistribution for more equality. In such a country, the quality of life befits human dignity and rights, making nature and people live in harmony and happiness.

The Genesis of This Book

India had its national elections in May 2019 bringing economic policymaking activities to a virtual standstill.

Nripendra Misra, principal secretary to Prime Minister Narendra Modi, called some of us in late March to initiate preparations for a 100-day programme to be implemented after the elections. He also set in motion a process where different government departments would identify their priorities for inclusion in such a programme. This small group was to vet the development of the 100-day programme.

I, personally, do not set much value to such 100-day programmes as they usually tend to be built around unimplemented decisions of outgoing governments, address some short-term concerns and initiate a few new populist giveaways. As the discussions played out in April, the contents of the emerging programme convinced me that it would not address the fundamental policy issues the country India needed to work on.

I was instrumental in placing the national ambition of building a $10 trillion economy in Budget 2019–20 (interim). This goal fascinates me. It will transport India into an upper middle-income economy, make it prosperous, eliminate poverty from the face of the country and take care of concerns such as health, education and infrastructure. Budget 2019–20 (interim) had also articulated India's intention to make the economy environmentally and socially sustainable. These imperatives required a drastic shift in economic policies.

Therefore, I decided to parallelly work on a set of 100 major policy reforms (macroeconomic and sectoral) that, in my view, the country required to build an environmentally sustainable $10 trillion economy while banishing poverty in all its dimensions. I made some progress and had a draft ready. My intent was to present it to the finance minister and prime minister once the new government was formed.

My world changed drastically after the new finance minister joined. The changed equation with the political executive after May 2019 impelled me to leave the government and seek to influence policy as a member of the wider society. I continued to work on my 100 policy reforms when I was serving the three months' notice in the Ministry of Power. I did get the opportunity to present my ideas to Prime Minister Narendra Modi in September 2019.

I placed these 100 policy ideas in the public domain in November 2019. I also started writing on the state of economy and policy in India, both in the macro and sectoral contexts. These writings attracted considerable interest with many colleges, academicians, newspapers and journals reprinting and commenting on many of them. I was invited to address several colleges, industry associations and think tanks.

In July 2020, Manish Kumar from Penguin suggested I write a book on the economy and the policies India needs to enter the higher orbits of GDP growth. I found the proposal very interesting as it provided me a vehicle to explain the state of Indian economy and policy besides presenting my ideas in a more organized and coherent manner.

In the book you hold, I present my assessment of the economic policies India has pursued in its seventy-five years as an independent nation, the economy these policies have helped build, and the policies we need to build a $10 trillion economy by 2035. I hope you find the book worth your time.

Introduction

Chapter One

Current State of the Economy: The Trough

Worst First Three Years of Any Government

The present NDA government began its second term in May 2019. India's GDP grew by only 4 per cent in 2019–20. The second year, 2020–21, proved the worst ever thanks to the COVID-19 pandemic and the policy decision of imposing total lockdown, with the economy witnessing its largest-ever contraction of 7.3 per cent. The year 2021–22 was expected to be one of recovery. However, the onset of the second wave in the first quarter and its consequential impact prevented the economy from recovering fully until the end of the first half of 2021–22. India's real GDP in the first half of FY 2021–22 was still lesser than the GDP of the first half of 2019–20. As per the first advance estimates released on 7th January 2022, the economy is expected to clock growth of only 9.2 per cent in 2021–22 which would make India's GDP for 2021–22 Rs. 147.54 lakh crore.

In real terms, the Indian GDP, which was Rs 140.03 lakh crore (at 2011–12 prices) in financial year 2018–19, the year before the government's second term began, turned out to be only Rs 135.13 lakh crore in 2020–21—a loss of about Rs 5 lakh crore of income in constant prices after two years. With the Indian economy likely to be at about Rs 147 lakh crore in 2021–22 in real prices, the first three years of this term of the government will add only about Rs 7 lakh crore in GDP growth. The three-year period (2018–19 to 2021–22) appears more like a growth holiday, with an average of only 1.5 per cent per annum.

No government in the past thirty years, since the economic policy reforms began in 1991–92, has seen such a bad first half of a five-year tenure. The Narasimha Rao government produced gross national income growth of 1.0 per cent, 5.5 per cent and 4.9 per cent in its first three years from 1991 to 94. The coalition governments also produced a gross national income growth rate of 7.7 per cent and 4.2 per cent from 1996 to 1998. The Atal Bihari Vajpayee-led NDA government turned out gross national income growth of 6.2 per cent, 8.8 per cent and 3.6 per cent in the first three years of 1998–2001. Growth in the first three years of the UPA government (2004–2007) was a roaring high of 7.9 per cent, 9.3 per cent and 10.2 per cent. The first three years (2009–2011) of UPA-II also saw high growth of 8.5 per cent, 9.8 per cent and 6.9 per cent.

Indeed, the GDP growth rate of 1.5/2 per cent in the first three years of this NDA government's second term becomes a total washout if seen from the perspective of per-capita income growth when adjusted for population growth during the period.

Indian Economy Has Been Functioning Poorly Since 2019–20

2019–20: A Disappointing Year for the Economy

Indian GDP growth was in free fall since the March 2018 quarter, from a peak of 8.1 per cent in the fourth quarter of 2017–18 to 3.1 per cent in the fourth quarter of 2019–20. The Indian economy registered GDP growth of only 4 per cent in 2019–20—the slowest since 1991 in the post-reforms economic era. GDP was expected to touch Rs 225 trillion at the end of 2019–20, which at Rs 75 to a dollar was tantalizingly close to making India a $3 trillion economy. Instead, GDP at current prices turned out to be only Rs 203 trillion, making the Indian economy about $2.7 trillion.

Dark clouds had started covering the horizon from the second quarter itself when GDP growth in real terms slipped to a decade low of 4.5 per cent, bringing the growth in the first half to just 4.6 per cent. The growth collapse of gross fixed capital formation (GFCF) in the economy, which represents investments to 0.9 per cent, clearly indicated worse things to follow. Investments drive not only growth but put income in the hands of the factors of production in the years they take place in. Capital formation also enhances the capacity of the economy to produce goods and services in the years to come. This was a tell-tale sign of deepening slowdown.

When the National Statistical Office (NSO) announced the advanced GDP estimates for 2019–20 on 7 January 2020, estimating India to grow only at 7.5 per cent in nominal terms (5 per cent in constant prices), the worst fears of deepening slowdown were confirmed. From the fastest growing economy in the world, India slipped into a mediocre performance bracket. Other foreboding signs also appeared. Capacity Utilization in the manufacturing sector fell to a ten-year low at less than 69 per cent in the second quarter and averaged less than 70 per cent during the year. Electricity demand growth contracted for five months continuously during 2019–20 whereas for the fifteen-year period since 2005, it had contracted only for four months in total. Gross value added (GVA) growth of manufacturing for 2019–20 was only 2 per cent in contrast to 8.3 per cent the previous year.

Though shocking, it came as no surprise that fixed capital formation recorded no growth. In 2019–20, at Rs 45.93 lakh crore in constant prices, it grew by a paltry Rs 0.45 lakh crore over the GFCF of Rs 45.48 lakh crore in 2018–19 at a rate of just 0.01 per cent. This was one of the lowest growth rates of investment in many years. In the previous two years, the growth of fixed capital projection was projected at 16.3 per cent for 2018–19 and 9.8 per cent for 2017–18. Consequently, the rate of fixed capital formation as a proportion of GDP fell from 32.3 per cent to 31.1 per cent, a fall of 1.2 per cent in just a year.

The lockdown dealt a severe blow to the economic outcome of 2019–20. The government decided to impose lockdown with immediate effect on 24 March 2020 when there were only about 500 people infected with COVID-19. If the lockdown had been imposed from 1 April, the economy would have been saved an avoidable hit in the last week of the financial year. As it happened, the imposition of lockdown brought the economic performance for 2019–20 to its knees.

The NSO put together provisional estimates of GDP and the national income for 2019–20 on 29 May 2020. GDP in constant prices for 2019–20 was estimated to have grown by only 4.2 per cent (later revised to 4 per cent) in place of the 5 per cent advanced estimate in January. Shaving off 0.8 per cent of growth was almost entirely on account of the losses caused by the lockdown.

2019–20 turned out to be a wasted year.

2020–21: The Worst Contraction Ever

The lockdown of the Indian economy—arguably the most stringent anywhere in the world—on 24 March 2020 brought the economy to a grinding halt. The Indian economy, which produces about Rs 33 lakh crore worth of goods and services in one quarter (in constant prices), could generate GVA of only Rs 25.6 lakh crore in the first quarter of 2020–21, contracting by about 22.4 per cent. India's labour lost about 12–13 crore jobs in the immediate aftermath of the lockdown, a reduction of about 30 per cent from the normal employment of about 40 crore. The government had to announce additional market borrowing of Rs 4.2 trillion, which was about 50 per cent higher than the entire budgeted borrowing of Rs 8 trillion.

The Indian GDP contracted by a massive 24.4 per cent in the first quarter of the financial year 2020–21. Nominal GDP declined from Rs 50.04 lakh crore in the first quarter of 2019–20 to Rs 38.89 lakh crore, which amounted to a combined loss of income of over Rs 11.5 lakh crore by Indians in one quarter. There was red ink everywhere. Railways' passenger kilometres were down by 99.5 per cent, airline passengers by 94 per cent, sales of commercial vehicles by 84 per cent, cement production by 38 per cent and steel by 57 per cent. Manufacturing was down by 40 per cent, mining by 22 per cent and electricity by 16 per cent. All this was reflected in consumption reducing, in nominal terms, by over Rs 7 trillion (24.46 per cent) and capital formation by another Rs 6.82 trillion (47.9 per cent). Exports, imports or for that matter any indicator, except agriculture production and government expenditure, were down.

Second quarter GDP contraction at 7.3 per cent, in itself one of the largest contractions in India's economic history, came as a big relief against the backdrop of the slump in the first quarter of 2020–21. Nominal GDP, in current prices, was still less at Rs 47.3 lakh crore, compared to the nominal GDP of Rs 49.5 trillion in Q2 of 2019–20. India lost more than Rs 2 trillion of income in the second quarter.

NSO released advanced GDP estimates on 7 January 2021 as usual. GDP contraction for 2020–21 was estimated at 7.7 per cent. The second advanced estimates released on 26 February increased the annual contraction to 8 per cent. Finally, in the provisional estimates released on 31 May 2021, GDP contraction was printed at 7.3 per cent. This involved a little bit of adjustment as food subsidy payments for earlier years made in 2020–21 were ignored to make taxes net of subsidies somewhat higher, limiting the GDP contraction to some extent.

India has never contracted to this extent anytime in the past. In nominal terms, Indians lost an income of about Rs 6 lakh crore in absolute terms over 2019–20. Compared to the expected nominal GDP of Rs 223 lakh crore, Indians lost an income of Rs 25 lakh crore. In real terms from the consumption side, private consumption has been estimated to decline from Rs 83.22 trillion to Rs 75.61 lakh crore and GFCF from Rs 47.30 trillion to Rs 42.20 lakh crore, while government consumption is expected to register a small increase from Rs 15.4 lakh crore to Rs 15.9 trillion.

The Brahmastra Boomeranged: India Locked Down Lock, Stock and Barrel

India was not in the pink of economic health in 2019–20. Yet, by an impulsive decision, the country was placed under a twenty-one-day lockdown, without any notice or warning, on 24 March 2020 which locked up 135 crore Indians in their homes, or wherever they were stranded that evening.

Having originated in China in December 2019, the COVID-19 virus spread swiftly to all parts of the world in the next three months. In March, India had the benefit of knowing how it was effectively handled in China and South Korea and how badly it was handled in Italy and Iran. A localized total lockdown in areas where the virus had spread, to cut off contact between the infected (symptomatic or asymptomatic) and the uninfected outside the local zone, was the master key to stop the virus in its tracks. However, India decided to lock up the entire country, all its businesses and all its people.

Millions of businesses producing goods and services barring essential services were locked down and knocked down. Over 12 crore workers were rendered jobless overnight; many started walking hundreds of kilometres, as all means of transportation were also stopped, to the safety of their rural homes. The lockdown was imposed with a naive belief that India would be able to eliminate the virus in three weeks' time.

India's lockdown strategy was clearly faulty. A total economic, social and human lockdown is like the Brahmastra, the most lethal and devastating weapon. It has to be exercised with enormous care and applied with the complete precision of a nuclear option. However, India decided to use this weapon on the entire country when only tiny parts of the country (areas where visitors from infected parts of the world had landed) and very few people (about 500 in all) were actually infected, with less than ten deaths.

Lockdown 1 and 2 (the last week of March and the entire month of April) turned out to be extremely severe. Only agriculture and government expenditure, which constitute about 25 per cent of GVA, remained exempt and unaffected. The rest of the economy (mining, construction, manufacturing and services included), which makes up about 75 per cent of GVA, was massively impacted. About 70 per cent of this economy remained shuttered for the entire month of April. This meant about 50 per cent of monthly GDP output was lost in April. Lockdown 3 (the first half of May) opened up India a little and Lockdown 4 (the second half of May) allowed some more productive activities to commence. Yet the country lost about 25 per cent of monthly output in May as well.

Unlocking of India became more effective from the first week of June 2020. As time went by, most sectors were unlocked in phases. However, education, entertainment, metro and quite a few other services remained completely shuttered until August–September 2020. As a number of services are availed in close human contact, such as transportation, travel and personal salon services, they remained hugely subdued even after the economy was unlocked. It was no surprise that the Purchase Managers' Index (PMI) for services remained below thirty-five in July 2020, while PMI manufacturing crawled to about forty-six (though still in the contraction zone) in July. The PMI manufacturing and services indices returned to positive territory only in August and October 2020. The Index of Industrial Production (IIP) remained in negative growth territory for all months except one in the first nine months of financial year 2020–21 and the Index of Core Industries remained in the negative zone all through this period.

The Stimulus—More Smoke than Fire

On 12 May, Prime Minister Narendra Modi announced that the government would deliver a Rs 20 lakh crore 'stimulus package'. Finance Minister Nirmala Sitharaman unfurled the package in five instalments over the next five days (13–17 May). This package was announced at Rs 21 lakh crore on the final day of these long press conference announcements. Called the 'Atmanirbhar Bharat' package, it aimed to take care of the disruption caused by the pandemic (actually lockdown) and put India into a new orbit of 'self-reliant' growth.

Earlier on 26 March, immediately after the lockdown was imposed, the government had announced a relief package, termed Pradhan Mantri Garib Kalyan Yojana, to provide financial and food assistance to the poor and vulnerable. This package included depositing Rs 1000, in two instalments of Rs 500 each, in the bank accounts of an estimated 20 crore women, and free provision of foodgrains (5 kg of wheat/rice and 1 kg of pulses) to all ration card holders (estimated to be about 80 crore Indians). The grant of three free cylinders to 8 crore Ujjwala scheme LPG connection holders was also announced. The government claimed that these measures were to cost Rs 1.7 trillion. However, it did not provide item-wise calculations.

The Rs 21 lakh crore Atmanirbhar Bharat package was a mishmash of fiscal, monetary and liquidity interventions. In addition to liquidity measures announced by the RBI, the government had also announced several liquidity and temporary forbearance measures. There were only a few fiscal support measures and credit support measures for businesses. One set of measures were announcements of the intention to make future investments, measures that were already part of the Budget or expenditures in the domain of entities other than the Central government and its agencies.

RBI Stimulus Measures

Though quite late compared to many other central banks in advanced countries and eastern Asia, RBI was off the block solidly in the last week of March to announce a slew of liquidity measures which, as claimed by the finance minister later in her presentations in May, added up to Rs 8.1 trillion.

These liquidity measures were aimed at encouraging, in fact egging on, the banks to lend to businesses and buy corporate bonds. However, RBI did not take into account the massive credit risk averseness prevalent in the Indian banking system and the absolute inability of businesses to take any credit during the lockdown. Thus, the liquidity bazooka proved a damp squib in the first half of the financial year. The liquidity absorbed by RBI during the year 2020–21 averaged over Rs 6 lakh crore.

Credit growth remained subdued for long. In July, it fell year on year below 6 per cent. Compared to the stock of banking credit at the end of financial year 2019–20, there was a decline in the stock of credit at the end of July 2020. Credit growth refused to budge higher throughout the year. Even in November 2020, credit growth was less than 6 per cent whereas deposit growth was in excess of 11 per cent. India ended the financial year with credit growth of just above 6 per cent.

Government Measures Provided Minuscule Stimulus

The government came up with its own set of liquidity measures totalling Rs 4.45 lakh crore. These measures largely included expansion of credit by government-owned institutions to farmers and provision of loans from Central government-owned financial institutions in the power sector for the clearance of bills by the state power utilities.

Rs 90,000 credit was to be provided by the Power Finance Corporation (PFC) and Rural Electricity Corporation (REC) to bankrupt state electricity distribution companies to clear their outstanding payments of generators and other input suppliers. While state governments and state distribution companies used these funds to clear old outstanding dues to NTPC and other generation companies, the dues kept increasing throughout the year. The financial year ended with outstanding dues in March being almost at the levels of the year before. This liquidity stimulus by PFC and REC resulted in changing the creditors of state power utilities from generators like NTPC to power finance companies.

There were two specific measures to support flow of credit to non-banking finance companies (NBFCs), including housing finance companies (HFCs) and microfinance institutions (MFIs). The Rs 45,000 crore Partial Credit Guarantee Scheme 2.0 was announced to provide partial credit risk guarantee to public-sector banks (PSBs) for their subscription to the primary issuance of bonds and commercial papers of NBFCs. The scheme was actually only a modified version of the Partial Credit Guarantee Scheme under implementation since 2019. The other facility, a Rs 30,000 crore Special Liquidity Scheme for NBFCs, HFCs and MFIs, was to be implemented through a special purpose vehicle (SPV) to buy their bonds and papers in both secondary and primary markets. This scheme, which sought to provide a guarantee for ultra-short-term papers, purchased through a special vehicle funded by RBI, had insignificant demand and closed without much use. Very little liquidity actually flowed through these two initiatives.

There were three credit stimulus measures totalling Rs 3.25 trillion in the Atmanirbhar package. The largest was a Rs 3 trillion credit guarantee facility for micro, small and medium enterprises (MSMEs). The credit package also included a Rs 20,000 crore credit facility for non-performing MSMEs and a Rs 5000 crore credit facility for street vendors.

The Rs 3 lakh crore credit facility for MSMEs was initially named 'Collateral-Free Automatic Loans for Businesses', including MSMEs, and later called 'Emergency Credit Facility'. This envisaged 20 per cent additional loans automatically to about 45 lakh standard MSME borrowers with existing outstanding loans between Rs 25 crore and Rs 100 crore. These loans were to be given for a period of four years with one year of moratorium on any servicing of loans and would be backed by a 'no-questions-asked' government guarantee for 100 per cent of the loan. Later on, the scope of the scheme was expanded to many other sectors, the quantum and extent of additional credit available was increased and timelines were extended multiple times. At the close of calendar year 2021, the limit of guaranteed loans was Rs 4.5 lakh crore.

There was slow offtake under the scheme, though the additional exposure of banks was covered fully by the government guarantee. By the end of October 2020, less than half of the guarantee amount (Rs 1.45 trillion) was actually committed. The government made a provision of Rs 4000 crore in the budget of financial year 2020–21 for equity contribution to National Credit Guarantee Trustee Company Ltd. The guaranteed credit facility did not get committed even by the end of the financial year. The banks could not disburse Rs 3 lakh crore of loans even by the end of December 2021; the total amount sanctioned was Rs 2.82 lakh crore in November 2021 and disbursed amount much less at less than 2.5 lakh crore), which amount to less than 3 per cent of the overall outstanding bank credit.

For non-performing MSMEs, the government announced a Rs 20,000 crore Subordinate Debt Facility. Under this facility, banks were expected to provide loans to about 2 lakh non-performing/in-default MSMEs, which it would cover by a 20 per cent partial risk guarantee through the Credit Guarantee Fund Trust for Micro and Small Enterprises (CGTSME). The government promised to provide grant support of Rs 4000 crore to CGTMSE for this purpose. The Rs 20,000 crore Subordinate Loan Facility suffered from a birth defect. These MSEs were non-performing and in default. No provision was made in either the revised Budget of 2020–21 or the budget provisions of 2021–22 as this facility did not take off.

The last of the credit schemes was a Special Credit Facility for street vendors. Under this facility, loans of Rs 10,000 each were to be provided to 50 lakh street vendors, which would result in a flow of Rs 5000 crore to them. The scheme implemented as the PM Small Vendor Atmanirbhar Nidhi (SVANidhi) made disbursement of loans of Rs 1200 crore by the end of December 2020 to about 12 lakh street vendors. The scheme continued to perform lackadaisically. By August 2021, after about 15 months of its launch, banks could sanction only about 27 lakh applications for an amount of Rs 2696 crore.

There are about 7.5 crore MSMEs in India with over 90 per cent being microenterprises. Only about 50 lakh of MSMEs receive credit in some form from banks and non-banks. Total outstanding credit to MSEs, which RBI tracks as priority-sector loans, amounted to about Rs 15 lakh crore. Total growth of outstanding bank loans between April and September 2020 was negative at Rs 99,000 crore and turned positive only in November. This also meant that the credit disbursed under the scheme was more than offset by contraction of credit earlier provided. Clearly, there was no evidence of stock of credit to MSMEs going up despite this guarantee scheme in the first nine months of the pandemic year 2020–21. Credit flow to micro and small enterprises started showing some positive growth in 2021 and credit growth reached 9 per cent year on year in September 2021.

The government announced five measures amounting to Rs 1.295 lakh crore to make long-term investment in agriculture and allied infrastructure. A Rs 1 lakh crore Agri Infrastructure Fund to build farmgate infrastructure was the highlight of this bouquet of measures. Separately, for MSMEs, the government announced a Rs 50,000 crore 'Fund of Funds' (FOF). As part of the stimulus package, lifetime outlays were announced for two ongoing schemes: Matsya Sampada Yojana and the Viability Gap Funding Scheme.

These schemes proved to be total non-starters. The Rs 1 trillion agriculture infrastructure investment scheme did not take off in financial year 2020–21. For 2021–22, it has been approved as an interest subsidy scheme. Going by the track record of quite a few such infrastructure creation schemes in agriculture and the allied sector, there is very little likelihood of farmgate infrastructure getting created under the scheme. The FOF scheme was announced with a lot of fanfare. However, the budget outlay for the year 2020–21 was reduced from Rs 200 crore to Rs 150 crore in the revised estimates (RE) and a modest provision of Rs 250 crore was made for financial year 2021–22. Not a single investment was made in any FOF scheme during the year.

Of the Garib Kalyan package announced on 26 March, additional free foodgrains (5 kg of wheat/rice and 1 kg of dal) to 80 crore ration card holders for three months cost the government approximately Rs 30,000 crore; Rs 500 per month for three months to 20 crore women Jan Dhan account holders cost another Rs 30,000 crore; and three free cylinders to 8 crore Ujjwala scheme LPG connection holders cost about Rs 10,000 crore. Other fiscal measures—Rs 1000 to 3 crore pension holders and payment of PF contribution—cost more than Rs 5000 crore. All these added up to a maximum of Rs 75,000 crore. The fact that the government continued with the free ration scheme for the entire 2021–22 testifies to the fact of massive loss of incomes for a big proportion of India's 40 crore workers.

The government also announced a Rs 40,000 crore additional provision for the Mahatma Gandhi National Rural Employment Guarantee Act (MGNREGA) over and above the Rs 61,500 crore provision in Budget 2020–21. One-time subsidy component of the Credit Linked Subsidy Scheme (CLSS) was revived (it was closed in 2019–20) to generate an investment of Rs 70,000 crore in 2020–21. Assuming that the entire

Rs 70,000 crore of affordable housing work will be completed, Rs 14,000 crore of fiscal expenditure would be incurred by the government.

Two more Atmanirbhar packages were announced on 12 October and 11 November. The Atmanirbhar package 2.0 was modest at Rs 46,500 crore, primarily giving loans to government employees for spending on GST-paid goods, cash in lieu of leave travel concession and some loans to states. Atmanirbhar 3.0 sought to inject stimulus of Rs 2.65 trillion. It comprised additional allocation of Rs 18,000 crore and Rs 10,000 crore for the urban housing scheme and MGNREGA. It included a multi-year expected cost of the Production-Linked Incentive (PLI) scheme to promote manufacturing in India of Rs 1.45 trillion. It included additional provision for clearance of pending fertilizer subsidy bills of Rs 65,000 crore. Again, very little of this stimulus outlay got spent in 2020–21 and in 2021–22, barring the fertilizer subsidy. Clearance of the fertilizer subsidy bill represented setoff of loans taken earlier and meant no new expenditure. These packages, like the Atmanirbhar package 1.0, had big headline numbers as stimulus but very little new expenditure took place under them.

All considered, the fiscal stimulus measures announced cost the government less than Rs 2 lakh crore in financial year 2020–21 and less than 3.25 lakh crore by the end of December 2021. Considering the extent of the trauma experienced by small businesses and workers, the real Government of India fiscal package turned out to be the stingiest.

Fiscal Deficit Zoomed to 9.5 Per Cent for 2020–21 in Revised Estimates

The year 2020–21 was not a normal one in any sense; quite unprecedented fiscally. Much of the lockdown witnessed in the first half of the financial year had been rolled back by the beginning of October 2020 but fiscal impacts lingered on. While the second half of 2020–21 brought some semblance of normalcy, the fiscal performance for the year turned out to be extraordinarily bad.

In her Budget speech delivered on 1 February 2021, the finance minister had to come up with a staggeringly high number for the fiscal deficit, at 9.5 per cent for the RE of 2020–21.

For 2021–22, the fiscal deficit was projected to be Rs 15.07 lakh crore, or 6.8 per cent of the projected GDP of 2021–22. Thus, the debt would fund 54 per cent of the government's total expenditure of Rs 34.50 lakh crore (revised) for 2020–21 and 43 per cent of the total expenditure of Rs 34.83 lakh crore for 2021–22.

Stymied Privatization Push

The government announced its intention on 18 May 2020 to formulate a new coherent Public-Sector Enterprises Policy to push reforms in Central Public Sector Enterprises (CPSE). The pivot of the policy was to retain a maximum of four public-sector companies in 'strategic sectors' and privatize every other CPSE. The Budget Speech for 2021–22 outlined the policy. The policy covered all existing CPSEs, PSBs and public-sector insurance companies.

To put the new CPSE policy into action, the finance minister announced the privatization of two PSBs and one general insurance company in 2021–22. To signal the serious resolve of the government on this score, she mentioned that a bill to bring about the necessary legislative amendments would be introduced in the Budget session itself.

There was no follow-through on the ambitious reform agenda of privatization of banks until December 2021. The government did not introduce the bill to provide for privatization of banks. No action was initiated on identification and appointment of transaction advisers for privatization of two banks and an insurance company. Privatization of BPCL, Container Corporation and SCI also did not proceed to any concluding stage until December 2021. The government could complete only Air India privatization.

2021–22: V-Shaped Recovery

India's GDP contracted by 7.3 per cent in 2020–21; with negative growth of 24.4 per cent in the first quarter of 2020–21 and 7.3 per cent in the second quarter. India's GDP grew by 0.4 per cent in the third quarter and 1.6 per cent in the fourth quarter of 2020–21.

For 2021–22, India's GDP was expected to exhibit two major trends. First, the momentum of positive growth, albeit still small, witnessed in the third and fourth quarters of 2020–21 was expected to be carried on in 2021–22. Second, given the low base of 24 per cent negative growth in the first quarter of 2020–21 and return to normality in the working of the economy in the third and fourth quarters, it was expected that there would be blockbuster growth of about 25–30 per cent in the first quarter of 2021–22 and about 8–10 per cent in the second quarter.

Budget 2021–22 was made with projected growth of 11 per cent. Most institutions and analysts expected India to grow by 10–12 per cent. Economists love to describe economic growth and contractions in different shapes of the alphabet. A V-shaped recovery signifies growth contracting sharply and then recovering equally sharply, which excites many government officials for having achieved something quite commendable. A contraction of 7.3 per cent in 2020–21 followed by growth of 10–12 per cent in 2021–22 fits this characterization. That said, it should make for a sobering thought as it is quite akin to jumping out of a pit after you've fallen into one. There is really nothing to rejoice about such a V-shaped recovery.

The fierce second wave of COVID-19, caused more by a variant first seen in India (later officially termed Delta), however, upset most projections. The Government of India sensibly did not go for a nationwide lockdown this time and left it to be decided by the states. Many states did go for extensive lockdown for six to eight weeks in major cities, but applied it more judiciously. The second wave caused much deeper misery with daily reported cases exceeding 4 lakh for a few days and over 1 lakh a day for about two months. India's reported cases crossed 30 million by the middle of June 2021. There was also a massive number of deaths. At its peak in the second fortnight of April and first fortnight of May, India witnessed a massive health crisis with hospitals running out of beds, oxygen and medicines.

The second wave kept most state administrations apprehensive about the third wave and infections rising in case of a liberal opening. This kept economic activity subdued until July–August 2021. Most economic indicators suggested recovery beyond the pre-COVID levels from September onwards. Growth projections for the financial year were, however, scaled down by all institutions and analysts to 9–10 per cent.

The $5 Trillion Goal Slips Further Away

India's goal to become a $5 trillion economy was first officially stated by Prime Minister Narendra Modi at a meeting of the National Development

Council (NDC) on 15 June 2019. The target date to achieve this goal was mentioned as 2024 in the documents presented to NDC. In Budget 2019–20, however, the government, after necessary calculations of the achievable but ambitious growth trajectory, formally announced FY 2025 as the target date for making India a $5 trillion economy.

The GDP for 2018–19 was estimated at Rs 190.10 lakh crore in the provisional estimates released on 31 May 2019. As the exchange rate was Rs 69.55 to a dollar on 31 March 2019, India's GDP in dollar terms for financial year 2018–19 was $2.73 trillion. Increasing this to $5 trillion required India to grow its GDP by $2.27 trillion in six financial years. Assuming the exchange rate remained unchanged, this would have required a compounded nominal annual rate of growth of 11 per cent for the six years till 2024–25.

Considering India's track record of the previous fifteen years, this was an achievable target. Even if there was foreign exchange depreciation—about 2 per cent per annum—the country would have romped home by achieving a 13 per cent nominal rate of growth, again quite a feasible target if we were to grow at 8 per cent real and had 5 per cent annual inflation.

Unfortunately, the economy started slacking from 2019–20, the year this formal announcement was made.

India's nominal growth in 2019–20 was only 7.2 per cent. To make matters worse, the exchange rate slumped to Rs 75.3 to a dollar on 31 March 2020, depreciating by 8.33 per cent. India's nominal GDP of Rs 203 lakh crore for financial year 2019–20 was thus equal to only $2.70 trillion. In fact, the dollar GDP of India at the end of the first year (2019–20) of the announcement of the $5 trillion target was lower than the GDP of $2.73 trillion of the base year (2018–19).

The second year of the reckoning, 2020–21, proved disastrous. On account of COVID-19 and the stringent lockdown, the nominal GDP fell by about 3 per cent during the year to print only Rs 197 lakh crore. The rupee, however, appreciated a little and ended at Rs 73.2 to a dollar. A GDP of Rs 197 lakh crore at Rs 73.2 a dollar amounted to a dollar GDP of $2.69 trillion.

India's growth story could not have been more tragic in the two years since the announcement of the goal of a $5 trillion economy by 2024–25. The dollar GDP at the end of financial year 2020–21 signified that India had been virtually stagnant with a GDP of around $2.7 trillion for the past two years. There was no forward movement.

India Will Probably Reach $5 Trillion GDP by 2026–27

The goal of a $5 trillion economy by 2024–25—four years including the financial year 2021–22—will require the Indian economy to grow at 17 per cent per annum in nominal terms with the exchange rate remaining unchanged at Rs 73.2 to a dollar. If we allow 3 per cent annual depreciation of the rupee, the annual rate of growth required would get raised to about 20 per cent per annum. This is an impossible task and ask.

With a recovery growth rate of 9.2 per cent and high producer price inflation of 8 per cent in financial year 2021–22, India could achieve a nominal growth rate of 17.5 per cent. India's nominal GDP for FY 2021–22 has been estimated at Rs 232 lakh crore. Assuming the dollar–rupee foreign exchange rate settles at about Rs 75 to a dollar on 31 March 2022, India's dollar GDP for the financial year 2021–22 would come to about $3.09 trillion. In dollar terms, India's growth over 2018–19 would amount to about 4 per cent per annum. Given the weakened reform agenda and expected winding down of global stimulus, from 2022–23 onwards, at the current level of investment, inflation target and reforms, India might grow at a nominal rate of about 12 per cent per annum at best. If the average annual growth rate in nominal terms works out to be about 12 per cent per annum for three years, India's GDP will be only $4.34 trillion by 2024–25 with no depreciation of the rupee in dollar terms. And if growth slows down to 10 per cent per annum in nominal terms, even with no rupee depreciation, India will reach a GDP of only about $4.11 trillion by 2024–25. In one situation only, not a desirable one, when India witnesses high inflation leading to nominal growth of about 17 per cent with the rupee's dollar value not seeing any depreciation (unlikely to happen despite record foreign exchange reserves) can India still achieve the goal of $5 trillion by 2024–25.

The goal of a $5 trillion economy by 2024–25 is beyond India's reach.

The goal of achieving a $5 trillion economy from the level of $3.09 trillion requires five years of growth of 10 per cent per annum (without any depreciation of the exchange rate) or nominal GDP growth rate of 13 per cent with 3 per cent depreciation. With COVID-19 disruptions expected to diminish materially, global growth returning to more normal levels and India's inherent dynamism in taking advantage of the new digital economy, the goal of attaining a $5 trillion economy by 2026–27, extending the original goal by two years, would be fairly realistically reset.

India should therefore reorient its policy and steer its economy to generate a growth rate of 13 per cent nominal for the next five years (2022–23 to 2026–27)—8 per cent real and 5 per cent inflation— expecting to take in its stride even a 3 per cent annual average rupee depreciation to reach the goal of a $5 trillion economy by 2026–27.

Section I: Real Economy

Chapter Two

State of the Real Economy

Output and Gross Value Added in the Economy

When one buys a packet of potato chips, the price paid by the consumer closely equals what economists call the gross value added or GVA. Let us assume the packet of chips, to explain in simpler terms, passed through three stages of production: production of potatoes, production of the packet of chips and its distribution and sales through the distributor. At each of these three stages, there was an output that got sold as input to the next producer/distributor. The farmer sold the potato to the potato chips factory, which in turn sold the potato chips to the distributor. The distributor finally sold the packet of potato chips to the consumer. The value added by the farmer in producing potatoes equals the output of potato minus the cost of inputs like seeds, fertilizers, etc. purchased by him. For the potato chip factory, the cost of the potato that went into producing the potato chip is the input and therefore the value added by the chip factory is the output value of the potato chip minus the input cost of the potato and other purchased inputs other than the labour. Likewise, for the distributor, the cost of the potato chip is the input and the price at which the distributor sold it to the consumer is the output with the difference between the two being the distributor's value added.

Value added by all three economic agents in this example when totalled becomes the GVA of the potato chips produced and sold in the economy. Adding the output values of all the economic agents would equal the total output produced in the economy. Total output adds up the outputs produced by each of the economic agents, whereas GVA only totals the value added by the economic agents.

Governments levy taxes on output or the value added of the products produced and sold in the economy. They also provide subsidies on the output prices of a number of products; for example, the prices of fertilizers sold to farmers. Consumer prices include indirect taxes like customs duty and GST, value-added tax (VAT) or sales tax and are reduced by the subsidies on the products. Data for taxes levied and subsidies provided on each of the millions of products are not available and therefore GVA data is exclusive of taxes collected and subsidies provided. When the net of taxes minus subsidies is added to GVA, the resultant number becomes the gross domestic product or GDP.

Granular output and GVA data for numerous products and services produced and sold in the economy are available with a lag. The last set of such data available when this book was being written was for the financial year 2018–19. In the last phase of writing this book, data for the year 2019–20 became available. However, there was not much change in the basic dynamics. Therefore, this book introduces the real economy of India using the 2018–19 data.

Total aggregated output in the Indian economy, at current prices, was Rs 347.93 lakh crore, equal to $4.64 trillion at Rs 75 to a dollar. GVA was Rs 171.40 lakh crore or $2.27 trillion. GDP was estimated at Rs 190.1 lakh crore or $2.53 trillion.

Agricultural Economy Fared Better

The gross output of agriculture, forestry and fishing in 2018–19 was Rs 37.21 lakh crore in current prices out of the total output value of Rs 347.93 lakh crore in the economy. Agriculture and the allied sector contributed only about 10.7 per cent of the gross output. In terms of GVA, the contribution of the sector was Rs 29.23 lakh crore of total GVA of Rs 171.40 lakh crore, or about 17 per cent.

Crops comprise over 50 per cent of the agriculture and allied sector GVA. In 2018–19, the gross output value and GVA by crops was

Rs 19.92 lakh crore and Rs 16.15 lakh crore, constituting 54 per cent and 55 per cent of agriculture and allied sector gross output and GVA. In 2018–19, the output value of paddy was Rs 3.05 lakh crore and that of wheat Rs 1.94 lakh crore. Paddy and wheat crops have virtually finished off all other cereal crops barring maize, whose value of production in 2018–19 was still somewhat respectable at Rs 42,531 crore. All other cereals and millets—including bajra and jowar—were not even worth Rs 12,500 crore in 2018–19.

Livestock (milk, eggs, meat) has grown sizeably to Rs 8.72 lakh crore GVA in 2018–19 (54 per cent of crops and 31 per cent of agriculture and allied sector GVA). Forestry and logging (Rs 2.23 lakh crore) and fishing and aquaculture (Rs 2.13 lakh crore) were the remaining two subsectors of agriculture and allied sector GVA.

Cereals (paddy, wheat, millets and maize together) had a gross output value of Rs 5.67 lakh crore in 2018–19. The output value of pulses was only Rs 1.04 lakh crore and that of oilseeds Rs 1.58 lakh crore. Sugar's total output value was Rs 1.23 lakh crore and fibres, including cotton and jute, had an output value of Rs 0.85 lakh crore.

Fruits and vegetables have grown sizeably and contributed Rs 5.87 lakh crore in terms of output, which was in fact higher than the value of all cereal output put together. Spices contributed another Rs 1.04 lakh crore. Other outputs, including fodder, contributed the rest.

In terms of output value, the pecking order in different components of crops is fruits and vegetables (Rs 5.87 lakh crore), cereals (Rs 5.67 lakh crore), oilseeds (Rs 1.58 lakh crore), pulses (Rs 1.04 lakh crore) and spices (Rs 1.04 lakh crore), followed by the rest.

Milk, part of livestock, was the largest single group in terms of the value of output in 2018–19. It contributed Rs 7.73 lakh crore, far higher than the cereals and fruit and vegetable groups. Meat, with an output value of Rs 2.43 lakh crore, also made a substantial contribution.

Agriculture grew by 2.9 per cent in financial year 2019–20, growing at 3 per cent, 3.5 per cent, 3.6 per cent and 5.9 per cent in the four quarters. In 2018–19, too, agriculture and the allied sector had seen a quarterly growth of 3.8 per cent, 2.55 per cent, 2 per cent and 1.6 per cent. Agriculture and the allied sector have maintained good, positive growth in both the quarters of 2020–21 with a real growth rate of 3.37 per cent and 3.39 per cent recorded in the first and second quarters. Agriculture's long-term growth rate is only about 3–4 per cent; it has been 2.88 per cent from 2014–15 to 2018–19. In the post-pandemic period, agriculture has been the least affected sector and its performance is in line with the decade's growth trend.

Mining and Quarrying Moribund for Some Time

The sector's GVA was Rs 2.61 lakh crore at current prices in 2011–12. Of the total 2011–12 GVA of Rs 81.07 lakh crore, the share of the mining and quarrying sector was 3.22 per cent. In 2017–18, the sector's GVA of Rs 3.58 lakh crore was 2.30 per cent of the total GVA of Rs 155.13 lakh crore. In 2018–19, the sector's GVA was Rs 3.89 lakh crore of the total GVA of Rs 171.4 lakh crore, giving it a meagre share of 2.27 per cent.

The mining and quarrying sector comprises four subsectors: fuel minerals (coal, petroleum and natural gas); metallic minerals (iron ore, manganese ore, bauxite, copper ore, gold, etc.); non-metallic minerals (prominently limestone); and minor minerals.

The total output value of all metals and minerals produced and sold in the economy in 2018–19 was Rs 6.85 lakh crore. After deducting inputs, GVA came to Rs 3.89 lakh crore.

Fuel minerals make up the bulk of the output value of metals and minerals. In 2018–19, their output value was Rs 3.96 lakh crore, making up 58 per cent. Coal output value was Rs 1.36 lakh crore and that of petroleum and natural gas Rs 2.59 lakh crore.

The value of output of metallic minerals in 2018–19 was Rs 1.29 lakh crore. The largest contribution came from iron ore with output value of Rs 76,992 crore. Gold output contributed a niggardly Rs 1358 crore, while manganese ore and bauxite contributed Rs 6245 crore and Rs 4844 crore, respectively.

Minor minerals collectively, which include granite, marble and many others, contributed an output value of Rs 1.33 lakh crore and non-metallic minerals Rs 28,026 lakh crore, the bulk of which was limestone with an output value of Rs 22,468 crore.

India's oil and gas production has been declining for years now, increasing our dependence on imports. Coal production also seems to have reached its peak. In times to come, the paucity of fuel minerals that have been primary contributors to the sector's GVA might further reduce the share of mining and quarrying in India's GDP.

Manufacturing Sector Refuses to Leapfrog

There is almost universal long-term consensus since Independence that the growth of manufacturing is necessary to spur growth and employment in India. The teeming millions unproductively employed in agriculture need to switch over to manufacturing for employment and, in turn, lead to manufacturing contributing at least a quarter of India's GDP. However, the performance of the manufacturing sector has mostly belied this expectation.

In 2018–19, GVA by the manufacturing sector was Rs 27.67 lakh crore. This contributed 16.1 per cent to India's total GVA of Rs 171.4 lakh crore. In the eight years since 2011–12, this share has been 17.4 per cent, 17.09 per cent, 16.53 per cent, 16.32 per cent, 17.07 per cent, 16.71 per cent, 16.42 per cent and 16.1 per cent. Despite the manufacturing policy of the UPA and the 'Make in India' blitzkrieg of the NDA government, the manufacturing sector has stubbornly refused to come out of its groove of a 15–17 per cent share in India's GVA.

The National Accounts break up the manufacturing sector in five subsectors: food products, beverages and tobacco; textiles, apparel and leather products; metal products; machinery and equipment; and other manufactured goods. The subsectoral contribution in GVA in 2018–19 was Rs 2.97 lakh crore (10.7 per cent) from food products, beverages and tobacco; Rs 3.50 lakh crore (12.7 per cent) from textiles, apparel and leather products; Rs 3.64 lakh crore (13.2 per cent) from metal products; Rs 6.37 lakh crore (23 per cent) from machinery and equipment; and Rs 11.18 lakh crore (40.4 per cent) from other manufactured goods.

Manufacturing in two segments—food products, beverages and tobacco, and metal products—has been growing at very low rates this past decade. Food products, beverages and tobacco had a share of 11.8 per cent in manufacturing GVA in 2011–12, which declined to 10.7 per cent by 2018–19. Textiles, apparel and leather products had a share of 16.3 per cent in manufacturing GVA in 2011–12, which declined to 13.2 per cent in 2018–19. The share of other manufactured goods has correspondingly risen. From 37.23 per cent in 2011–12, it went up to 40.4 per cent in 2018–19.

The National Accounts provide a break-up of manufacturing output and value added in the corporate and household/informal sectors separately. GVA by the corporate sector in the manufacturing sector was Rs 24.31 lakh crore (87.9 per cent), while manufacturing GVA by the household/informal sector was much smaller at Rs 3.35 lakh crore (12.1 per cent) in 2018–19.

The manufacturing sector, which is highly diversified, uses a lot of raw material to produce industrial goods. The value of total output of the manufacturing sector was Rs 102.30 lakh crore whereas GVA was only

Rs 27.67 lakh crore. The manufacture of the coke, petroleum, rubber, chemical and related products subgroup had the largest share of output value (Rs 32.38 lakh crore of a total output value of Rs 102.30 lakh crore; 31.65 per cent) while the manufacture of machinery and equipment had an output value of Rs 22.88 lakh crore.

In terms of more specific product ranges, the largest five product groups were: coke and refined petroleum products with output value of Rs 12.62 lakh crore; transport equipment with output value of Rs 11.08 lakh crore; basic iron and steel plus casting of iron and steel with output value of Rs 9.81 lakh crore; chemical and chemical products (except pharmaceutical, medicinal chemicals and botanical products) with output value of Rs 8.21 lakh crore; and textiles plus cotton ginning with output value of Rs 7.08 lakh crore.

India is still to emerge as a significant manufacturer of IT hardware products. The total output value of computer, electronic and optical products was Rs 2.65 lakh crore in 2018–19. Manufacture of electronic components, consumer electronics, magnetic and optical media had output value of Rs 0.56 lakh crore and computer and peripheral equipment had output value of Rs 0.35 lakh crore, while manufacture of communication equipment had output value of Rs 1.28 lakh crore. To put in context the relative size of the electronic sector, the manufacture of electrical equipment had output value of Rs 3.77 lakh crore. The IT hardware sector is still smaller in output value compared to the electric equipment sector.

Evidently, India is still to discover the magic formula to push manufacturing growth.

Utilities Sector Constrained by Government Ownership and Subsidies

Utilities—electricity, gas, water supply and other utility services—is another major sector where GDP/GVA is compiled and publicly disclosed. GVA added in this sector for 2018–19 was Rs 4.56 lakh crore in current prices. This was larger than the GVA for the mining and quarrying sector (Rs 3.89 lakh crore). As sectoral inflation dynamics differ with some products witnessing higher inflation than others, in some cases, the real growth is different when calculated in terms of constant prices and current prices. This happens to be the case in the utilities sector. In constant prices, the mining and quarrying sector's GVA at Rs 3.66 lakh crore was much higher compared to Rs 2.74 lakh crore for the utilities sector. This discrepancy confirms that the mining and quarrying sector has witnessed disinflationary conditions, whereas the utilities sector, despite having been subsidized by the government, has seen higher inflation.

The total value of output generated in the utilities sector in 2018–19 at current prices was Rs 11.68 lakh crore. The largest value of output was generated in the electricity sector at Rs 8.23 lakh crore (70 per cent). Water supply (Rs 1.38 lakh crore), gas (Rs 1.15 lakh crore) and remediation and other utility services (Rs 0.92 lakh crore) were the other subsectors contributing to the value of output.

Construction, Barring Occasional Slippage, Saw Steady Growth until 2018–19

With the expansion of real estate and infrastructure, the construction sector is emerging as an important pillar of the economy. GVA by the construction sector in 2018–19 at current prices was Rs 13.44 lakh crore. In fact, the construction sector is larger than many other sectors of the economy—mining and quarrying, gas, electricity and water, transport services, financial services and even public services—in terms of GVA at current prices.

The details of output produced in the construction sector are available in the National Accounts for quite a few important subsectors, such as residential and non-residential dwellings, roads and bridges, other structures and land improvements, plantation construction and construction related to mineral exploration. The largest subsector is non-residential buildings, which generated an output of Rs 14.99 lakh crore in 2018–19, while the output value of residential dwellings was about half at Rs 7.73 lakh crore. Roads and bridges contributed a relatively small GVA at Rs 2.81 lakh crore. Other structures and land improvement contributed Rs 10.68 lakh crore of output with the output of construction related to mineral exploration valued at a mere Rs 0.69 lakh crore.

The slowdown in the economy during the second decade of the twenty-first century compared to the first decade is visible in the data on output value of residential dwellings. In current value terms, the output value of this segment was Rs 7.34 lakh crore in 2011–12. It remained almost the same, that too in nominal value, which ignores all the inflation during eight years, in 2018–19 at Rs 7.73 lakh crore. The deceleration gets fully captured in the output value at constant prices. In constant prices, the output added by the residential building segment in 2011–12 was Rs 7.34 lakh crore whereas the output added at constant prices in 2018–19 was Rs 5.75 lakh crore, an absolute decline of Rs 1.59 lakh crore over eight years. Instead of generating growth, the segment contracted by 22 per cent in real prices. This segment has seen the most severe value destruction in the years between 2011–12 and 2018–19, with the output value contracting in constant terms every single year.

The non-residential buildings or commercial real-estate subsector, however, has seen good growth. In constant prices, the output value of the segment has grown from Rs 7.17 lakh crore in 2011–12 to Rs 11.57 lakh crore in 2018–19—a growth of Rs 4.4 lakh crore or 61 per cent. In current value terms, the sector has more than doubled during this period, from Rs 7.17 lakh crore in 2011–12 to Rs 14.99 lakh crore in 2018–19.

The contrasting fortunes of the two major segments of real estate—commercial and residential—are evident from the data of output growth and value as seen above. The pandemic has altered the dynamics of the commercial real-estate sector as well with work from home (WFH) or for that matter 'work from anywhere' emerging as the preferred mode of working in the digital environment. The requirement of maintaining larger distance between individuals in offices and additional space needed in homes for conducive working may impact the demand for working space as well.

More on this later.

Trade Added Value at a Fast Clip

Trade, repair, hotels and restaurants are grouped together in one of the four services groups in the National Accounts. Trade accounts for the bulk of value added in this group and has been growing impressively. In current prices, GVA by the trade group in 2018–19 amounted to Rs 20.73 lakh crore, which was 12.1 per cent of the total national GVA of Rs 171.4 lakh crore. GVA in this group is fast catching up in terms of constant prices with the agriculture, forestry and fishing group. GVA of the trade, repair, hotels and restaurants group in 2018–19, at constant prices, was Rs 16.57 lakh crore, almost nine-tenths of the GVA of the agriculture group (Rs 18.72 lakh crore).

The total output value (not GVA) of the trade services group was Rs 30.51 lakh crore at current prices in 2018–19. Of this, trade and repair services contributed Rs 25.46 lakh crore and the hotel and restaurants group contributed Rs 5.04 lakh crore of output value. In terms of GVA, the contribution of the trade and repairs group was Rs 19 lakh crore while that of hotels and restaurants only Rs 1.72 lakh crore. More than 91.6 per cent of the value added was from the trade and repairs segment.

Indeed, the growth of the trade and repairs group, in constant prices, has been impressive during the second decade of the twenty-first century. GVA in constant prices for the group in 2010–11 was Rs 8.83 lakh crore, which rose to Rs 16.57 lakh crore by 2018–19, a growth of Rs 7.74 lakh crore or 88 per cent in eight years.

Transport, Storage, Communication and Services Related to Broadcasting

The transport, storage, communication and broadcasting services group comprises seven distinct subgroups: railways; road transport; water transport; air transport; services incidental to transport; storage; and communication and broadcasting services. The road transport group is the largest, contributing Rs 4.1 lakh crore of GVA in 2018–19 in constant prices out of a total sectoral value addition of Rs 8.31 lakh crore (almost 50 per cent). The communications and broadcasting subgroup contributed about one-fourth share (Rs 2.02 lakh crore of Rs 8.3 lakh crore). The share of railways is relatively minor: Rs 92,291 lakh crore (less than one-eighth of total GVA in the sector). Water transport and air transport are relatively insignificant, having added value of only Rs 9659 crore and Rs 9463 crore, respectively. Storage is growing but it is still the smallest component of the group, contributing only Rs 6892 lakh crore of GVA in 2018–19.

In current value terms, GVA by the transport, communications and storage group was Rs 10.69 lakh crore in 2018–19. The contribution of transport services in GVA, at Rs 7.92 lakh crore at current prices, was about 75 per cent.

The total output value of transport services was Rs 18.23 lakh crore in 2018–19 at current prices. Road transport contributed about two-thirds of this by generating an output of Rs 11.98 lakh crore. The output value of railways was Rs 1.90 lakh crore contributed by passenger services (Rs 58,053 crore) and, more significant, freight services (Rs 1,17,499 crore). Total output value of air services was Rs 1.35 lakh crore. However, as they consume a lot of inputs (Rs 1.18 lakh crore in 2018–19), the GVA is quite small.

The total value of output produced by storage, telecommunications and services relating to broadcasting was Rs 7.01 lakh crore in 2018–19 at current prices. Storage contributed a total output value of Rs 18,386 crore; the rest came from communications and services relating to the broadcasting group. In this group, there are three distinct subgroups: post and courier services, telecommunication services; and cable operators, recording, publishing and broadcasting services.

The telecommunications subgroup's output value was Rs 4.58 lakh crore; that of the cable operator and broadcasting group Rs 1.71 lakh crore; and the post and courier group Rs 0.54 lakh crore. All three groups have witnessed a healthy growth in the second decade of this century.

Financial Services Have Done Well

The financial services sector's GVA in constant prices rose from Rs 4.80 lakh crore in 2011–12 to Rs 7.63 lakh crore in 2018–19, growing by Rs 2.83 lakh crore or about 60 per cent in eight years.

The largest contribution in GVA in this group came from deposit-taking institutions (banks and some select non-banks) and money market funds, with a GVA of Rs 4.10 lakh crore out of Rs 7.63 lakh crore. Other financial intermediaries like NBFCs and mutual funds (MFs) added a value of Rs 1.36 lakh crore and various financial service providers contributed Rs 0.59 lakh crore. GVA by life insurance was Rs 40,371 crore and non-life insurance Rs 43,248 crore. Pension funds have entered the field; in 2018–19, their GVA was Rs 2408 crore.

Financial services are growing reasonably well. And with digitization increasing their reach, speed and quality, the sector is expected to grow handsomely in the years to come.

Professional Services and Leasing Nearly Doubled in Eight Years

Real-estate services, ownership of dwelling and professional services is the best performing group in terms of growth in the seven years between 2011–12 and 2018–19. Its GVA in constant terms in 2011–12 was Rs 10.51 lakh crore, which nearly doubled to Rs 20.23 lakh crore in 2018–19.

This group includes diverse service providers, from real-estate services, information and computer-related services and scientific and technical services to all remaining professional services.

The value of output generated by this group was Rs 38.79 lakh crore in current prices and Rs 30.10 lakh crore in constant prices in 2018–19. The output value of information and computer-related services in current prices was assessed at Rs 10.39 lakh crore. Ownership of dwellings services (which largely included leasing and renting services) generated an output value of Rs 11.05 lakh crore in current prices. The miscellaneous group of administrative and support services and other professional services contributed as much as Rs 13.15 lakh crore of output. The output of real-estate services was Rs 3.02 lakh crore, while professional, scientific and technical services, including R & D, contributed Rs 1.18 lakh crore.

The information and computer services subgroup has been the star performer for India. Its total value of output in current prices grew from Rs 3.44 lakh crore in 2011–12 to Rs 10.39 lakh crore in seven years, growing by an impressive Rs 6.95 lakh crore (more than 200 per cent). The value of IT services output in constant prices also grew by 150 per cent.

Increase in the value of output generated by completion of new residential units and leasing revenues has stagnated after 2014–15. The value of output in this subgroup was Rs 6.89 lakh crore in 2014–15. This grew to only Rs 7.65 lakh crore in four years by 2018–19—an increase of only Rs 0.76 crore or barely 11 per cent in four years.

Public Administration and Defence Services Reflect Inflation

Expenditure on pay and allowances of government servants, including the defence services, is covered under the public administration and defence subgroup. The GVA of this group was Rs 10.68 lakh crore in current prices and Rs 7.34 lakh crore in constant 2011–12 prices.

Value added by the Centre and states combined, including the value added by way of expenditure on public administration and defence services, was estimated at Rs 12.05 lakh crore in constant prices in 2018–19.

Other Services

The GVA of other services was Rs 9.39 lakh crore at constant prices in 2018–19. This is also a diverse group comprising value added by social sectors—education, health and social work—personal services including washing, hairdressing, custom tailoring and funeral services, the arts, entertainment and recreation, and the like.

Total value of output of this group was Rs 20.53 lakh crore in current prices and Rs 13.65 lakh crore in constant prices in 2018–19. In constant prices, education contributed an output of Rs 5.92 lakh crore, health and social work an output of Rs 3.15 lakh crore, and personal services Rs 3.48 lakh crore.

This group has also generated reasonably good growth.

Real Estate, Ownership of Dwellings and Professional Services Group Witnesses the Biggest Positive Shift in GVA Share

In constant prices (2011–12 prices), five groups out of eleven have seen a positive shift in GVA share. The largest increase has been in the real estate, ownership of dwellings and professional services group. Its share in the overall GVA increased from 13 per cent in 2011–12 to 15.8 per cent in 2018–19.

Other groups that gained share were manufacturing, from 17.4 per cent to 18.1 per cent; trade, repairs, hotels and restaurants, from 10.9 per cent to 12.9 per cent; financial services, from 5.9 per cent to 6 per cent; and other services, from 6.6 per cent to 7.3 per cent.

The largest group losing share is agriculture, which saw its share in overall GVA decline from 18.5 per cent in 2011–12 to 14.6 per cent in 2018–19, a shift of about 3.9 per cent. Other groups with a declining share in GVA include mining and quarrying, from 3.2 per cent to 2.7 per cent; construction, from 9.6 per cent to 8 per cent; and public administration, from 6.1 per cent to 5.8 per cent.

Two groups saw no change: The electricity, gas, water supply and other utility services group remained at 2.3 per cent and the transport group at 6.5 per cent.

Sectoral price movement makes shifts in the GVA share quite significant, which is reflected in the GVA share of different groups in current prices. The biggest surprise is that decline in the share of agriculture became more muted—from 18.5 per cent in 2011–12 to 17.1 per cent in 2018–19—and the GVA share of manufacturing groups declined instead of increasing, as seen above, in terms of constant prices. In current prices, the share of manufacturing in overall GVA declined from 17.4 per cent in 2011–12 to 16.1 per cent in 2018–19.

Intellectual Property, the Highest-Growing Component of Capital Formation

GFCF, which measures capital formation or investment in the economy, comprises four components in the National Accounts: dwellings, other buildings and structures (building and structures); machinery and equipment (plant and machinery); cultivated biological resources (biological assets); and intellectual property products (intellectual property/IP).

Physical assets still make up the bulk of GFCF. Of the Rs 44.61 lakh crore of fixed capital formation in 2018–19 in the Indian economy, the contribution of buildings and structures was Rs 22.02 lakh crore, almost 50 per cent. Plant and machinery was the second big block with capital expenditure of Rs 17.59 lakh crore of capital formation, making up almost 40 per cent of GFCF.

IP contributed Rs 4.89 lakh crore in terms of fixed capital formation, a little over 10 per cent of total GFCF. However, its growth rate and increasing share in overall fixed capital formation give interesting pointers about its emerging and enlarging influence in investment and growth in the economy. IP's share in fixed capital formation in 2011–12 was Rs 2.17 lakh crore out of total GFCF of Rs 29.98 lakh crore, a share of 7.24 per cent. By 2018–19, its share increased to 11 per cent.

There has been a distinct slowdown in capital formation in buildings and structures. From Rs 17.24 lakh crore in 2011–12, it grew to Rs 22.02 lakh crore in 2018–19, an increase of only Rs 4.78 lakh crore (or about 27 per cent) in seven years, clearly an evidence of slowing investment in dwellings, other buildings and structures.

Plant and machinery, despite apparent slowdown in some sectors, still had decent growth, from Rs 10.49 lakh crore in 2011–12 to Rs 17.59 lakh crore in 2018–19—an increase of Rs 7.1 lakh crore (about 70 per cent) in seven years.

Biological assets are still a nascent head of capital formation in India with the segment contributing a fixed capital of Rs 10,758 crore in 2018–19.

Chapter Three

State of the Agriculture Economy

India Was in the Forefront of Global Agriculture
for Millennia

Food, clothing and housing are the most essential goods for human survival, health, prosperity and happiness. In the pre-agriculture era, human beings depended upon nature and the wild to provide all these. Agriculture was the first organized industry created by human beings to produce food, clothing, medicine and wood for housing. Agriculture used human labour. Savings from agriculture led to the first accumulation of capital.

India has been a pioneer throughout the history of agricultural development over the past ten millennia, building on its tremendous natural advantages and innovative human spirit and ability. Surplus labour and capital from agriculture spawned handicrafts and handlooms in India and enabled the country to create highly valued products. India became the most prosperous country and remained so for centuries, creating wealth from income mostly from agriculture.

The onset of the Industrial Revolution diminished the role of agriculture as a producer of income and wealth. India lost its pre-eminence and wealth as industry advanced in the West while it was not embraced in the country. Income and wealth creation shifted to industry. In the process, India was reduced to a very poor country. By the time the British left in 1947, 80 per cent of Indians were living below the poverty line. The farmers suffered the most. The Indian farmer, who had provided all the resources for many prosperous empires to take root, had become a pauper—a malnourished soul.

Indian Agriculture at Independence

India cultivated approximately 110 million hectares of land at the time of Independence, which was the largest area under cultivation in any country in the world. It used more than 85 per cent of its area under agriculture to produce about 50 million tonnes of foodgrains. Land ownership was not evenly distributed. More than 70 per cent of the people employed in agriculture worked as peasants or labourers. They worked very small tracts of land, more often than not as unrecognized tenants. In fact, the farmers ended up typically converting their labour into food. Their lot was truly miserable. Indian agriculture was very traditional and unproductive and the country did not produce enough foodgrains to feed its teeming millions.

Droughts and famines occurred regularly. The inability of the government and people to move food from surplus regions to deficit regions made parts of India face famines in years when there was no overall shortage of food in the country. Chronic food shortages had made the British government assume control over food production, supply, trade and commerce. What we know today as the Essential Commodities Act, 1955 (ECA-1955), was first enacted in 1939 under the Defence of India Rules, which the British government converted into the Essential Supplies Act, 1946, after World War II was over.

The regulated agriculture produce markets, which we know as agriculture produce market committees (APMCs) or *mandis* today made their appearance as far back as the 1880s.

Seven states had agriculture produce marketing laws in 1950. Most agriculture produce still got consumed locally and not more than 10 per cent of foodgrains were traded in regulated markets in the 1950s.

Target to Double Food Production to 100 Million Tonnes

Food shortage was the biggest worry of Indian leaders after Independence. The country was dependent upon import of food. India imported

2.8 million tonnes of foodgrains in 1948. In the next three years (1949–51), the quantum of food imported ranged between 2 million tonnes and 5 million tonnes. Wheat was the real problem as many of the country's good wheat-producing areas had gone to Pakistan after Partition. Only about 10 million hectares of land was under wheat cultivation in 1950–51, producing just about 6.5 million tonnes of wheat.

Very early, during the First Plan period, India set a target to produce 100 million tonnes of foodgrains by the end of the Third Five-Year Plan (1961–66) to free the country from the scourge of food shortages and the ignominy of importing wheat from the US on terms that were sometimes humiliating.

India's efforts to double foodgrains production in fifteen years did not succeed with production averaging about 81 million tonnes during 1961–62 and 1963–64. In 1964–65, the rainfall was excellent and India achieved its highest foodgrains production of 89 million tonnes. The next two years were drought years. India faced its worst foodgrains crisis from 1965 to 1967. Production collapsed to just 72 million tonnes in 1965–66 and 74 million tonnes in 1966–67.

The situation had become so desperate that Prime Minister Lal Bahadur Shastri actually implored Indians to eat only once a day. About 10 million tonnes of wheat—the largest food transhipment project ever undertaken globally—had to be shipped from the US to India in 1965 to save Indians from starvation.

1947–1964: The Unproductive Years

While the first three Plans (1951–1966) talked a lot about agriculture, land and farmers, industry remained the principal object of attention and investment. A good amount of Plan funds were also allocated for agriculture, especially during the First Plan.

In the first phase, from 1947–1964, India relied on three strategic interventions to realize the goal of 100 million tonnes foodgrain production: bring in additional area under cultivation; increase irrigation; and expand availability of fertilizers and improved seeds. The first two strategic interventions were the primary focus of attention and the third intervention was more lip service.

The area expansion strategy did succeed. Almost the entire area expansion India has witnessed in the past seventy-three years took place in the 1950s and 1960s. The net area sown at the end of the Third Plan in 1966 reached 140 million hectares. Even today, the net sown area in India is about the same.

Over two-thirds of Plan outlays on agriculture during this period went towards irrigation investments. However, dam and surface irrigation proved to be a very slow moving investment. There were too many issues in building dams: acquisition of land, relocating and rehabilitating people, tough and unsuitable terrain and difficulty in taking plant and machinery to such interior and mountainous regions. Not surprisingly, despite substantial irrigation outlays, the irrigated area increased only at a snail's pace of an average 0.4 million hectares per year. The net irrigated area increased from 21 million hectares in 1950–51 to only 27 million hectares in 1966–67.

India's use of fertilizer and new seeds was pathetically low at the time of Independence. Indian farmers used a total of 66,000 tonnes of fertilizer nutrients in 1950–51. Fertilizer consumption rose to 7,85,000 tonnes in 1965–66, which was still minuscule in the context of the needs of Indian agriculture. In terms of seeds, the age of high-yielding seeds had barely taken birth by the time the Third Plan ended.

Only marginal gains were made in the agriculture and food situation from 1947 to 1964, which were also more than neutralized by the increase in India's population. On the whole, the first phase of agriculture development programmes and policy (1947–64) was a big disappointment. It did not make India self-sufficient, even for food.

India's Worst Food Crisis and PL-480

Two years of drought in 1965–67 completely exposed the weaknesses of the agriculture development strategy of the first three Plans.

The year 1965 was disastrous. Foodgrains production fell massively to 72 million tonnes in 1965–66 and 74 million tonnes in 1966–67. Ironically, while India was facing massive food shortages during the 1950s and 1960s, on the other side of the globe, Americans were wallowing in excess production of wheat.

American food aid to India, which later acquired very humiliating overtones, commenced in 1951. American President Harry Truman approved a $2 million wheat loan as part of the India Emergency Food Aid Bill in June 1951. More food aid flowed from America under the Agriculture Trade Development and Assistance Act, passed in 1954, widely known as Public Law 480 or PL-480.

It is estimated that India received total food aid of about 50 million tonnes over a twenty-year period (1951–1971), which was estimated to be worth $10 billion. This was the largest food assistance programme ever undertaken for any country. India stopped accepting food aid from America in the early 1970s. In the fifty years of PL-480 (1954–2004), it is estimated that America provided food aid aggregating $33 billion globally; India received one-third of this.

1965–1990: A Different Food Production Strategy

India changed its foodgrains development strategy fundamentally in the second phase (1965–1990). The new strategy was based on three principal planks: raise the productivity of agriculture with more crop per acre of land and more crop per drop of water; provide remunerative prices to incentivize farmers; and expand irrigation by expanding groundwater irrigation.

High-yielding varieties (HYVs) and later hybrids, nourished by fertilizers, along with the increasing use of farm equipment, helped raise farm productivity. These are the technologies that brought the green revolution to India.

To provide remunerative prices to farmers, the Indian government initiated the system of minimum support prices or MSPs in 1965. Under the system, farmers were delivered a minimum assured return/profit on agriculture as the MSP was fixed after taking into account the farmer's cost of cultivation, an imputed value for labour contributed and a profit margin. The system succeeded in incentivizing farmers at least in parts of India where foodgrain cultivation became commercial agriculture.

Expansion of groundwater irrigation provided the much needed water to foodgrain crops. Well irrigation proved far more efficient than canal-based surface irrigation, which required massive investment, large displacements and water transportation over long distances.

India's Wheat Revolution

India produced 16.5 million tonnes of wheat in 1968, an increase of 45 per cent over the previous year's crop of 11.4 million tonnes.

This revolution was engendered by the Indian crossbred variety Sonalika, which was developed in 1967 and planted on a massive scale in 1967–68. The seeds of this spectacularly performing variety were sown in 1963 when celebrated American agronomist Norman Borlaug visited India and agreed to supply seeds of Mexican semi-dwarf wheat varieties to the country. Indian scientists, actively supported by the government, worked hard and successfully demonstrated the suitability of Mexican seeds for high-yield wheat in India. They also bred Indian varieties crossing Mexican seeds with Indian varieties. Large-scale experimentations were undertaken in 1966–67 and the entire crop was saved as seeds. This scripted the 1967–68 success story.

India's wheat production never looked back thereafter, increasing to more than 25 million tonnes in 1971–72 and reaching 50 million tonnes in 1988–89. India's wheat production grew five times in twenty years since the terrible crisis of 1965–67. Wheat production had increased to 55.14 million tonnes in 1990–91 with an average yield of 2281 kg per hectares, which was more than three times the yield of 663 kg per hectares in 1950–51.

Foodgrains Production Took Off on the Back of the Wheat Revolution

Semi-dwarf varieties of rice came to India from the East. India introduced these high-yielding varieties on a large scale in 1968–69. The spread, though, was slower and less dramatic than wheat. Rice production of about 40 million tonnes in 1968–69 was not quite different than the production average recorded during 1963–65. But yields grew gradually and steadily thereafter. Rice production crossed 50 million tonnes in 1977–78 and 100 million tonnes in 2011–12.

Foodgrain production crossed 100 million tonnes in 1970–71 and 150 million tonnes in 1988–89. It was 171 million tonnes in 1990–91, having increased nearly three-and-a-half times from 50 million tonnes in 1950–51. Foodgrain yields, which were less than 700 kg per hectares in

1966–67, crossed 1000 kg per hectares for the first time in 1978–79 and had nearly doubled to 1380 in 1990–91.

MSP System Established in the 1960s

Before 1965, the government undertook no price support operations in India. Some states took sporadic measures at local levels. On 1 August 1964, the government appointed a committee under the chairmanship of L.K. Jha, secretary to the prime minister, to determine farmers' prices of rice and wheat for the ensuing 1964–65 session. The committee was also tasked to provide the terms of reference to set up an agency to provide such recommendations on a standing basis. The L.K. Jha Committee conceived of 'the producers' price as being the minimum price or a support price at which the government should undertake the responsibility for purchasing any quantities that are offered at approved assembling points'. In addition to recommending producers' prices, which were the harbinger of the elaborate MSP system, the committee recommended retail prices for the 1964–65 rice season. The roots of the ration card system also lay in the committee's recommendations, as it also recommended a 'rationing' system for some cities considering the heavy food deficit situation in the country.

The MSP system went on to become increasingly bigger, expanding from the original two crops of rice and wheat. It has also been fine-tuned over the years. Governments brought an increasing number of crops under the MSP system. However, farmers of crops other than wheat and rice did not get the benefit of MSP on account of several issues such as unsuitability of some crops like pearl-millet (bajra), which cannot be stored, and lack of procurement arrangements for pulses and other crops.

Profit margins are political decisions. Margins over cost kept increasing over the years. In 2017–18, the government decided to provide at least 50 per cent profit over cost of cultivation for all MSP crops.

Agriculture Economy 1991–2020: Production Increased but Farmers' Income Remained Stagnant

Foodgrains production crossed 200 million tonnes for the first time in 1998–99 and 300 million tonnes in 2019–2020. India's horticulture and animal husbandry production also shot up sharply. Today, India's net agriculture exports exceed $30 billion in some years.

Once India overcame its food shortage problem, policymakers lost the catalyst to drive agriculture development programmes and policy reforms despite the fact that farmers, especially landless farmers, still constituted a majority of the country's households and workforce.

In 1951, India had approximately 14 crore workers. About 70 per cent of these were dependent on agriculture as farmers and landless agricultural labourers. Unfortunately, despite the creditable growth of agriculture production, the dependence of rural workers on agriculture did not diminish significantly. In 2001, as many as 23.4 crore workers (58 per cent of total workers) eked out their livelihood from agriculture (about 13 crore as cultivators and 10.5 crore as labourers). As per the latest agriculture census data available for the year 2012–13, there are 9.02 crore agricultural households in the country.

The Indian economy started expanding rapidly after economic liberalization in 1991 and did particularly well in the past twenty years. Agriculture, however, has only been growing at about a quarter or one-third the rate of the non-agriculture economy and is, consequently, losing ground relatively. Agriculture and the allied sector make up only about 15 per cent of India's GDP now. As the share of income accruing to about 40 per cent of the population dependent upon agriculture is not even 15 per cent of the national income, farming households have a very low income. The largest proportion of poor people in the country comes from landless labour working as farm labour.

No Path-breaking Agriculture Development Strategy after the Green Revolution

No new agriculture development strategy has been deployed in the country in the past three decades. Today's agriculture development programmes are mostly repackaged versions of the programmes initiated during the green revolution phase (1965–1990). The HYV programme of the 1960s–1970s was reorganized as the Mini-kit Programme for Rice, Wheat and Coarse Grains and Integrated Cereals Development Programme—Rice/Coarse Cereals/Wheat-Based Cropping System and Development of Pulses. These programmes became part of the Rashtriya Krishi Vikas Yojana

(RKVY) and the National Food Security Mission (NFSM) in 2007–08. Horticulture programmes were converted into the National Horticulture Mission in 2003. In 2015, the agriculture and allied sector production and productivity programmes were reorganized under the three umbrellas of green revolution, white revolution and blue revolution programmes, without really changing anything. In effect, production and productivity enhancement programmes in the past three decades have been nothing but old wine in new bottles.

That said, agriculture development programmes did witness a differentiated approach to achieve productivity gains during this period. Eastern India had a much better water regime but relatively poor productivity of foodgrain crops. Agriculture development programmes were focused on this region in this phase. Agriculture in Bihar turned around. There have also been notable gains in other eastern and north-eastern states. More attention was paid on pulse cultivation, horticulture and proteins (milk, meat) as the food crisis receded. India achieved 90 per cent self-sufficiency in pulses and became the largest milk producer. The production of fruits and vegetables also went up considerably.

Well irrigation expanded to about 60 million hectares (almost thrice that of canal irrigation). Programmatic interventions to popularize the use of sprinklers, drips, water-efficient seeds and farming practices have been set in motion. Likewise, increased chemical residues in food, fruits and vegetables have led to interventions in organic agriculture.

Agriculture has been growing at a low but reasonably steady growth rate, in excess of 3 per cent, in the past twenty years. The demand-and-supply situation for most crops has changed for the better on account of population growth at a much lower rate than agriculture. However, farmers' incomes have stagnated.

Reforms of 1990s Bypassed Agriculture

The foreign exchange crisis of 1991 did not have its roots in agriculture. The reforms of 1991 were essentially industrial sector reforms, though the depreciation of the rupee did benefit agriculture exports as well.

In 1991, despite the slew of industrial, trade and FDI reforms, no new agriculture policy was announced. Agriculture continued to be protected and no FDI was permitted in the sector. India negotiated the largest protection for agriculture when the World Trade Organization (WTO) was set up in the 1990s. The 1991–92 Budget promised continued protection of agriculture and rural development outlays at 50 per cent of Plan resources.

All agriculture development programmes were continued with varying degrees of emphasis in the post-1991 period. Though there was some minor upward adjustment of fertilizer prices, the reforms largely ignored the agriculture sector.

Direct Income Transfers Make an Entry in 2018

The government initiated a number of programmes to protect income from agriculture, including different crop insurance programmes, disaster relief and rehabilitation assistance programmes and MSPs. However, these were indirect income protection programmes.

Launched in 2018–19, PM-Kisan is the first direct benefit transfer scheme in agriculture. It was launched to protect farmers' incomes in the face of a steep fall in agricultural produce prices since 2016–17. It provides Rs 6000 per annum in three instalments of Rs 2000 each to about 9 crore farmers. The programme has continued despite farm prices recovering in 2019–20. From a political viewpoint, it is quite unlikely that this programme will be withdrawn any time soon. In a manner, it has become an income transfer programme to farmers as it has no linkage to anything other than the beneficiary being registered as a landholder and consequently treated as a farmer.

PM-Kisan has become the largest and the biggest programme of the Ministry of Agriculture. Its outlay exceeds the total outlay of all other schemes of the Department of Agriculture and Farmers' Welfare for the year 2020–21.

Agriculture Has Ceased to be the Driver of Global Growth, Employment and Prosperity

From 1.6 billion in 1900, the global population crossed 6 billion in the year 2000. The population of the US went from 76 million in 1900 to over 282 million in 2000. In 1900, the US produced 599.315 million bushels of wheat (16.3 million tonnes); in 2000, it produced 2228.160 million bushels (60.6 million tonnes). The US produced 2661.978

bushels of corn in 1900, which went up to 9915.051 bushels in 2000. In 1900, 41 per cent of the US workforce was employed in agriculture; this fell to just 1.9 per cent in 2000. While agriculture contributed 8 per cent of the US GDP in 1930, it was less than 2 per cent in 2000.

In the twentieth century, the production of wheat and corn increased four times in the US, which was more or less equal to the increase in the population. However, the share of labour force dependent upon agriculture declined from roughly 40 per cent to 1 per cent. The share of agriculture in GDP also declined from an estimated 10 per cent to 1 per cent. Labour productivity in agriculture rose more than 40 times; 2 per cent of the labour force produced enough cereals and other agricultural products for the population to feed itself and export. The value addition in the non-agriculture economy—industry and services—became 99 per cent of GDP, which made the agriculture economy an almost negligible contributor to employment and value addition from the viewpoint of economic prosperity.

The same story has played out in most other countries of the world. There are as many as sixteen countries today where the share of agriculture in GDP is less than 1 per cent. This includes small nations such as Singapore, Qatar and Luxembourg, and also fairly big economies like the UK, Belgium, Germany and Switzerland. There is a large number of countries where the share of agriculture is between 1 per cent and 5 per cent, including populous countries like Brazil (4.4 per cent), Romania (4.1 per cent), Greece (3.6 per cent), Chile (3.5 per cent), Russia (3.4 per cent), Spain (2.6 per cent), Poland (2.4 per cent), Australia (2.1 per cent), Italy (1.9 per cent), Netherlands (1.6 per cent), South Korea (1.6 per cent), France (1.6 per cent) and Denmark (1.3 per cent). In 2019, the entire European region had about 1.55 per cent of GDP from agriculture. Many of these countries are, in fact, leaders of agriculture in the world and the largest exporters of agricultural produce. And China, now, has less than 7 per cent of GDP coming from agriculture.

There is a very clear correlation in the income level of the economy and the proportion of people employed in agriculture. The richer countries have less than 5 per cent of people employed in agriculture and the poorest countries have more than 50 per cent. In 2019, global GDP from agriculture was only 4 per cent of the total GDP of $87.7 trillion. The GDP growth rate in agriculture has been less than 1 per cent.

Data from the International Labour Organization (ILO) indicates that the proportion of people employed in agriculture has come down globally from 44 per cent in 1991 to 27 per cent in 2019.

The agriculture sector has been able to meet the global requirement of food and clothing even though it is growing at less than 2 per cent globally. Agriculture has long ceased to be a driver of global prosperity.

Chapter Four

Agricultural Development Programmes Have Lost Their Purpose

Farmers primarily produce foodgrains, pulses, oilseeds, milk, eggs, meat and the like. Food is the primary need and principal desire of humans. Therefore, it is quite natural for everyone to get emotional about food. Farmers have been elevated to the pedestal of food-givers or *annadata*.

Farming is a tough enterprise. It is also a highly risky enterprise. Rains may play spoilsport. Other natural calamities—flood, drought, hailstorms—can occur. As there is no invisible market hand playing a balancing role by bringing equilibrium in demand and supply of different agricultural products, prices may crash in the event of overproduction. Farming involves working exposed to the elements in place of the comfort of a factory or office. Finally, as food constitutes a greater part of the consumption expenditure in developing countries like India, governments do not allow farmers to get high prices for their produce. Farming is a low-return enterprise, not a business.

A partial explanation for elevating the farmers in our country to annadata or semi-godly status flows from the self-interest of governments and consumers. Farmers are made to suffer the economic consequences of small and uncertain incomes from their produce as producing food for consumers becomes part of discharging their duty as annadata.

55

Adam Smith, the father of economics, sought to disabuse both consumers and food-providers of their emotions when he said: 'It is not from the benevolence of the butcher, the brewer, or the baker that we expect our dinner, but from their regard to their own self-interest. We address ourselves not to their humanity but to their self-love, and never talk to them of our own necessities, but of their advantages.' Smith was seeking to convert the relationship of producers of food and consumers of food into an economic and business relationship where both parties act in their self-interest.

Agriculture has done well in India in the past seventy-four years. However, the lot of farmers in general still remains miserable. Governments have tried numerous agriculture development and input subsidization programmes and provided price and output protection. Yet, the largest proportion of the poor in India comes from the farming community: small and marginal farmers and landless farm labour. Government programmes have totally missed heeding the advice of Adam Smith to make farmers work in self-interest. Farming needs to become a business for farmers to have any chance of becoming prosperous.

Let us look at how the economics of onions works in India.

Oniononomics: Once in Two to Three Years, Onion Prices Bring Tears to Consumers

In December 2019, the price of onions crossed Rs 100, on average, in many retail markets; they were even sold at over Rs 200 per kg in some places. Prices fell soon and onions were selling at just Rs 10 per kg after a few months. Once every two to three years, onion prices bring tears to the eyes of consumers. However, such episodes do not last for more than two to three months at best.

After Prime Minister Indira Gandhi exploited the onion price rise to topple the Janata government in 1980, the price of onions has become a political hot potato! The high prices of onions, which India produces in surplus and exports, lead to much breast-beating, breaking news in the media and chart-topping memes on social media. Invariably, the government panics as if the country were in the midst of a major economic crisis. This leads to the government putting a ban on the exports of onions, imposition of storage and other controls under the ECA and a few raids, including by income tax authorities, on onion traders.

Considering that such episodes are invariably short-lived, why do we fret so much over onion prices?

Low Incomes for Onion Farmers

India produces around 230 lakh tonnes of onion, on average 18 kg of onion per person, a year. This is a little over 20 per cent of the total world onion production, making us the second largest producer of onions after China, which produces about 25 per cent. Egypt and the US come in third and fourth, each with about 3–4 per cent of the global share. India consumes only about 60–70 per cent of the onions produced. The rest is either exported, used otherwise or wasted. In fact, India is the largest exporter of onions in the world, earning over Rs 3000 crore in 2018 alone. China, the US and Egypt are the next three largest exporters, earning about less than half of what Indian exporters earn every year. India is also the lowest cost producer of onion and prices in India are usually the lowest in the world.

India has three crops of onion a year. The Rabi crop, which is harvested between March–May, is the largest. A little over 150 lakh tonnes of total onion production of 235 lakh tonnes in 2018–19 was produced in this crop season. The crop is quite stable in terms of production with very little variation from year to year (except in years when farmers decided to cut down on planting on account of extremely low prices the year before). This crop is also 'storable' and farmers have developed on-farm storage to stock it and release it gradually every month until September–October. India has two smaller crops of onion: Kharif sown between July–August and harvested between October–December contributing about 30–35 lakh tonnes or 15 per cent of the annual crop production and late Kharif, sown between December–January and harvested between January–March, producing 40–50 million tonnes on average or about 20 per cent of annual production. These two crops see varying production depending upon monsoons, floods, droughts or other climatic catastrophes.

Onion Price Gyrations

While the bulk of the onion crop is produced in Maharashtra, Madhya Pradesh and Karnataka (almost two-thirds of the annual crop), the shrillest cries are heard in Delhi and other northern cities when prices shoot up. Wholesale onion prices in Delhi in the first five months (March–July) of the flush season (March–September) in the four years ending in 2019 averaged less than Rs 10 per kg, recording less than Rs 8 per kg in almost half of these months. Onion prices start rising from August (Rs 35 per kg in 2015, Rs 20 in 2017, Rs 17 in 2019) in the wholesale markets of Delhi if trouble is anticipated in the Kharif crop or the farmers decide to cut down on Kharif sowing, having received very low prices for their preceding Rabi crop. As the demand-and-supply situation gets disturbed for ensuing months (the situation gets more difficult if the late Kharif crop also suffers), prices start rising more acutely. If the Kharif turns out to be better than anticipated between September–October or there is good sowing for late Kharif, prices start reverting to their lower levels from November–December itself.

The pattern of onion prices over the years is predictable. The primary reason for the price rise from August to December is the vagaries of the weather. Traders might take advantage of the situation to make some quick money, but they are not responsible for the demand-supply gap in the months of shortages, which is entirely weather-related, sometimes accentuated by farmers receiving very low onion prices in the previous season.

Onion is not the most nutritionally rich or essential food. It contains about 90 per cent of water and some flavour. Consumers should ride through these short episodes of price volatility by paying higher prices briefly or cutting down consumption temporarily. Let us remember that Indian farmers receive, on average, the lowest prices in the world for their onion produce.

Banning Exports is Not the Solution

Our distorted policies to handle production, storage, exports and imports are primarily responsible for this state of affairs.

Politicians are primarily driven by the instinct and intent to keep consumers happy and offer them onions at less than Rs 15–20 per kg. To ensure this, India has adopted a very restrictive and ad hoc export policy. Two instruments are used: fixing a minimum export price (MEP) and banning exports outright. The MEP instrument is deployed as soon as there is a feeling that onion prices might shoot up beyond Rs 20 a kg in wholesale markets. An MEP towards the higher end of global prices is fixed to discourage farmers/traders to export. Whenever wholesale prices go beyond Rs 30–50, an outright export ban is put in place. When prices crash, and it happens usually as soon as the new Rabi crop arrives, these restrictions are relaxed.

ECA-1955 was amended in 2020 and it sought to place higher hurdles in terms of minimum price rise before the government resorts to imposing of storage and export controls. However, with a small rise in onion prices immediately after the ECA was amended in September 2020, the government imposed a ban on onion exports.

Unnecessary and ad hoc restrictions imposed through foreign trade policy and under the ECA are quite often at the root of the onion price crisis. And control on production, transportation, trading and exports of agricultural commodities are at the root of farmers' poverty.

Farming Policies Perpetuate Sickness in Agriculture Business

The agriculture policy of India rests on three principal pillars. First, provide farmers with agriculture inputs (seeds, fertilizer, electricity, insurance, etc.) free of cost or at subsidized prices. Second, support output prices by fixing MSPs (minimum support prices) at the cost of cultivation and a minimum 50 per cent margin. Third, extend liberal credit almost free of interest and write off principal loans due from time to time.

These policies are responsible for keeping more than 50 per cent of India's enterprises and workforce trapped in low-income agriculture, which keeps rural India poor and unskilled, unable to improve their lot.

Subsidization of Inputs Does Not Contribute to Farmers' Incomes

The principal agriculture development strategy adopted by India was to provide inputs free or at highly subsidized rates. Surplus land was allotted free. Irrigation water was provided free. Electricity was heavily subsidized generally, with some states providing electricity free as well. Seeds, fertilizers, loans, insecticides, farm equipment, or every other input was provided free of cost or at highly subsidized prices. These free or highly subsidized inputs were expected to help the farmers earn income. Unfortunately, that has been the biggest falsehood. Free and subsidized inputs either cover the high cost of inputs, get lost in inefficient application or end up subsidizing consumers. The farmers rarely gain.

Free distribution of land and virtually free provision of canal water did not help a majority of farmers as the expansion of irrigation took some time. Only about 10 per cent of land could be irrigated even after many years of works undertaken by the government at public expenditure. Allocation of canal irrigation water to farms was made at very liberal rates and was used by the farmers by flooding their fields. While 1 kg of rice can be produced in less than 100 litres of water, Indian farmers use an average 2500 litres of water to produce 1 kg of rice. Excessive allowance of water from canals for flood irrigation did not contribute anything to the productivity of crops on the margin. Instead, it gave India a lot of problems related to water-logging.

Green revolution technologies—high-yielding varieties of seed, later hybrid seeds—required intensive agriculture with the support of fertilizers, pesticides and farm equipment for planting, harvesting and other agricultural operations.

These farm inputs were produced inefficiently mostly in the public sector at much higher cost. Indian farmers, mostly small and marginal, were neither capable nor willing to bear this cost. Moreover, they were unfamiliar with the new agri-technologies and needed to switch over from traditional low-input, low-yield agriculture to high-input, high-yield agriculture. For all these reasons, the government decided to supply most of the new agriculture inputs, including seeds, fertilizers, agriculture equipment, weedicides and insecticides, either free of cost as part of the agriculture demonstration and mini-kits programmes or at highly subsidized prices. It did this by subsidizing the producers of the agriculture inputs; for example, the fertilizer and tractor companies.

Finally, the remaining inputs in agriculture also caught the attention of the government. Free canal water made it harder for the government to refuse subsidizing the use of pump-sets run with electricity to draw underground water in non-canal irrigated areas. The fact that electricity had been nationalized by the 1960s and that its use to draw groundwater facilitated the irrigation of crops in areas underserved and unserved by canals made the case for subsidy still stronger. Further, electoral politics also played a significant role in not charging farmers for the electricity they used. Free electricity led to farmers pumping water from very high depths and also indiscriminately using it to flood the fields, like the canal water farmers. In due course, the electricity subsidy started costing the government so much that its finances suffered and electricity utilities were rendered bankrupt. Yet, the farmers continued to get subsidized or, in many states, free electricity.

Input subsidies do not benefit farmers. The cost of production of most farm produce in India is higher than the global cost despite free and subsidized inputs. The benefit to farmers of free and subsidized prices gets lost in overapplication of inputs, inefficient application of inputs and artificially higher cost of production of such inputs.

MSPs Have Not Helped Either

Taking care of input costs is one side of the farmers' income equation. The other side is prices. The government established the system of regulated markets where farmers were expected to get remunerative prices of their produce brought into the APMCs and sold in a system of transparent bidding.

Agricultural produce is bulky, perishable and usually non-standard. All these factors ensured that farmers did not get a good price for their produce even in the regulated markets. In any case, most of them, being small and marginal farmers, have no ability to sell produce at the time when the prices are good for them. Rather, most farmers tend to offload their produce in mandis or elsewhere immediately after harvest and end up getting very low prices as the demand-supply position at the time of harvesting gets acutely distorted.

Considering this reality, the government came up with the idea of assuring a minimum price for agricultural produce. It stood as a guarantor that farmers' produce would be bought at a minimum price declared beforehand if market prices fall lower than this price.

However, to really succeed, the MSP system required the government to have the ability to buy the entire surplus quantity of agricultural produce, store it for the time required, and then either export it or deliver it at consumption points when market supplies dwindle. If the government lacks this ability, the MSP system does not work. This is precisely what has happened.

Barring some parts of the country and for only a few crops, the government could not create the requisite system of procurement, storage and disposal. As a result, despite MSPs being declared for almost every agricultural crop (not horticulture and animal husbandry products), very few crops, other than wheat and rice, get procured under the MSP system. Some studies have estimated that only 6 per cent of agricultural produce gets sold at MSPs in India.

Subsidized Credits, Evergreening and Loan Write-Offs Have Led to No Real Working Capital or Investments

The government first provided cheaper credit to farmers for their crop loans through agriculture credit cooperative societies. However, as these societies delivered credit effectively only in a few states, the government roped in the nationalized banks and established a network of regional rural banks to channel the credit to farmers. Very soon, the interest cost also got taken care of by the Centre and the states. In many instances, even the principal loan was paid off by the government in what has come to be known as loan waivers or write-offs.

The total aggregate agriculture credit outstanding exceeds Rs 12 lakh crore. The bulk of this is for farming of crops. As value addition of crop cultivation is only about Rs 18 lakh crore, the credit to agriculture value addition exceeds more than two-thirds. These loans are largely short-term loans for working capital purposes. The repayment period for short-term loans runs into the next season of crops and most of the time to the next year's crops. As a result, there is no change in month-to-month outstanding agriculture credit. Practically, agriculture loans are literally loans in perpetuity. These have been availed of and remain consumed or used up. Farmers obtain agriculture inputs on credit or they take credit needed from the commission agents and input suppliers.

Goal of Doubling Farmers' Income Has Not Been Realized

Ever since Independence, India's agriculture programme strategy focused only on increasing production and productivity. The income of farmers was not a real policy goal. Only in 2014 did the government specifically mention the doubling of farmers' income by 2022 as a policy goal. However, programmes and policies did not change much to attain this goal.

Farmers' income is the net sales price farmers get of their agricultural produce minus the cost of cultivation incurred to produce the same. As their operational holdings are small—less than a hectares on average—they end up earning very low profits/income as such small landholdings only deliver a very small agri output for sales. Farmers' incomes in India on average are about one-fifth of other workers and about 30 per cent of the national average income.

The goal of doubling farmers' income has not been very well defined by the government—whether it meant gross value added (GVA) of crop sector would need to double or if the entire agriculture and allied sector GVA was aimed to be doubled or it was to be measured in terms of per capita income in nominal prices or in real prices. A committee appointed by the government for this purpose ended up recommending more government investment for production and productivity growth. The lack of a coherent policy and strategy has ensured that there is no yardstick to even measure progress made to achieve this. Farmers' income needs to be raised at least five times to bring about a worthwhile change in their lives. This requires a multipronged strategy. Primarily, it requires agriculture to be made into a business for farmers to make decent profits out of their hard work and enterprise.

Chapter Five

2020 Agri-Reforms: More Disruption than Real

The MSP system distorts the market for field crops. There are other mechanisms that also impact markets in agricultural produce.

ECA, by conferring administrative and discretionary authority on the Centre and states to place restrictions on trade, distribution and storage of agricultural commodities, does result in altering the market in agricultural produce. Adjustment in the customs duty levied on import and export of agricultural products is another instrument that enables the government to upend the markets.

The APMC laws of state governments makes the agriculture market an administered market rather than a free market. They create perverse incentives for state governments to tax agricultural produce transactions, ostensibly to pay for creation of infrastructure for agriculture. These laws also create perverse incentives for licensed traders and agents. All these interests disrupt the market.

Farmers must get good and remunerative prices for their produce. By nature, agricultural produce, especially if sold fresh or unprocessed, is a very difficult commodity. Developing the right market infrastructure, regulatory institutions and a regulatory system to handle it is tough, but necessary.

Indian agriculture is essentially small-holder agriculture. Farmers have no real pricing power. They mostly dispose of their produce instead of selling it. Mostly, farmers sow their field without any good idea of what prices they will receive or the prevalent demand-supply situation upon harvesting. The absence of a developed futures market in India exacerbates the situation. Farmers are usually guided by hindsight, what they got for their last crop. It is not unusual to witness alternate bouts of increased and reduced sowing by farmers depending upon the prevalent price at the time of sowing. Often, farmers end up betting wrong.

Agriculture Marketing Regulation Started in the Nineteenth Century

Agriculture marketing regulatory interventions in India started from the other end: the protection of consumer interests and streamlining supplies of agricultural raw materials to industries.

The first regulated market, called Karanja, was established in 1886 in Hyderabad to ensure availability of pure cotton at reasonable prices for the textile mills of Manchester. The first legislation to provide for regulation of agriculture markets was the Berar Cotton and Grain Market Act, 1887, which empowered the British Resident to declare any place in the assigned district a market for sale and purchase of agricultural produce and constitute a committee to supervise the regulated markets. This law seeded the agriculture produce mandis and APMC of today.

This Act became the model for enactment of similar legislations in other parts of the country. Quite a few states enacted such legislations in the sixty-year period before Independence.

Adoption of APMCs and Legislation for Regulation of Markets

Independent India liked the approach of regulated APMCs.

The First Plan promoted the concept and encouraged more states to go in for such regulated agriculture produce markets. The Second Plan rued the insufficient progress made in this regard. Noting the rationale of the regulated APMCs, it encouraged the states to set up such markets and laid targets for their expansion in the country.

Globally, agriculture produce is traded more in forwards than in terms of spot. Spot markets do not eliminate the price risk while forward markets provide a mechanism for income assurance. This was the rationale for India to legislate the Forward Contracts (Regulation) Act, 1952 (FCRA). For forward markets, India adopted a diametrically opposite regulatory model than the APMC Acts. APMCs provided for hardcoded regulations by state governments and were implemented in a totally decentralized mode. Meanwhile, FCRA provided for a centralized body, the Forward Markets Commission (FMC), to regulate forward markets.

APMCs Turned into a Strangleho'd over Farmers

APMCs, which are essentially spot wholesale marketplaces for agricultural produce, were designed to serve three broad functions:

First, create a marketplace for agriculture produce where sellers (farmers) and buyers (government organizations, industries and traders) can transact with the assistance of market infrastructure and agents.

Second, regulate contracts, practices and intermediary payments to create a fair and low-cost trading regime for farmers who, on account of being disadvantaged, were vulnerable to market abuse.

Third, generate resources for the government to invest in infrastructure to facilitate packaging, transportation, storage and marketing of farmers' produce.

The development of APMCs in the first fifty years after Independence seemed to serve all these objectives. Thousands of market yards were created all over the country and APMC laws hardcoded contracts, commissions and other market practices to make these systemic and known to farmers. The fees levied (popularly known as mandi fees) under the APMC laws generated substantial resources, which were administered by marketing boards to create market infrastructure. Indian farmers kept increasing marketable surplus, which was transacted in APMCs across the country. APMCs successfully converted the totally disorganized wholesale agricultural produce marketing of the 1950s into a largely streamlined and organized marketing system by the end of the twentieth century.

A big structural mistake, however, turned APMCs into a stranglehold over the sellers (farmers) over a period of time. The fundamental mistake was the monopolistic nature of the system. Every APMC was legislated to have a physical market-yard and a market catchment area. This resulted in only one mandi/market for the agricultural produce of a defined market area. The produce grown in the market area was to be brought only to the designated market yard. The farmer had little choice but to comply.

The other law, the ECA, placed restrictions over industrial and wholesale buyers. They were subjected to stock limits. Having a shop became an essential prerequisite for traders and commission agents to buy produce from the mandi. This restricted purchasers to a small band of buyers and agents who, more often than not, colluded with each other to get the better of the farmers. Farmers were at the mercy of this small number of traders to sell their produce. The reform had turned into deform.

APMC Reforms Initiated in 2003

Recognizing the problems in the APMC marketing system, the government set up a committee in 2001. A task force examined these recommendations in 2002. This resulted in the Model APMC Law, 2003. While some states carried out these recommendations over the next decade, the progress was not considered satisfactory. A group of state agriculture ministers, appointed by the Union Ministry of Agriculture on the direction of Prime Minister Manmohan Singh, reviewed the progress in 2011–2012. The group's main recommendation was that the Model APMC Act, 2003, should be adopted by all states in its entirety.

The Model APMC Act, 2003, and subsequent amendments in the model law diluted the monopoly of APMCs only a little. The market area for each APMC was sought to be increased to the entire state and traders' licences were to be converted into pan-state licences. These reforms were carried out by some states, but remained more on paper. As the regulatory regime and fee structure remained the same in every mandi, it made no difference to the farmer. The monopolistic character of APMCs remained unaffected even in the states where the Model APMC Act, 2003, was legislated.

Some more choices were offered to farmers. Farmers' markets could be established in addition to APMCs. Contract farming was allowed to enable farmers to enter into direct contracts with processors. However, it is difficult for farmers to set up markets as they do not have the resources, time and ability to do so. Contract farming contracts were very highly regulated. Again, the result was not encouraging. Only a limited number of farmers' markets were set up in seventeen years of these market reforms and a negligible number of contracts were registered under the contract farming facility.

Though exemptions were provided in some states on horticulture products, the mandi fee regime essentially remained intact. In effect, mandi fees generate very small resources these days to take care of market infrastructure. Most market infrastructure in the past two decades has been constructed under central schemes like RKVY, the Market Infrastructure Scheme, Warehousing Scheme of Food Corporation of India (FCI), and the like.

The APMC reforms of the past two decades did not address the principal flaws in agriculture produce marketing: the absence of competitive markets; a one-size-fits-all approach of overregulation of markets implemented in a decentralized manner by organized vested interests; lack of standardization and aggregation of farmers' produce; leasing of land not being legally permitted; and exclusion of processors and wholesalers on account of storage restrictions. Consequently, the APMC reforms did not make much of a difference.

Farmers' Produce Trade and Commerce (Promotion and Facilitation) Act, 2020, Designed to Disrupt and End the Monopoly of APMCs

The Farmers' Produce Trade and Commerce (Promotion and Facilitation) Act, 2020, promulgated in September 2020 (later repealed), struck at the root of the APMCs' monopoly over wholesale agricultural produce trading. It also virtually abolished the system of mandi fees. The law was truly revolutionary with respect to these two fundamental deformities of India's agricultural produce trading system. While it did not directly dismantle the APMC system (APMCs continued to survive as they were currently within the confines of their physical market yards), it had the potential to massively disrupt these by taking away their business.

The Act granted complete freedom to farmers to sell at the regulated market yards of AMPCs or outside. It enfranchised almost every business entity (under a very wide definition) to set up a physical trading station outside the APMC market yard or establish an electronic trading system anywhere in the country. Farmers and traders could undertake interstate and intrastate transactions without any restrictions. As there is a distinct comparative advantage to set up shop outside APMCs to trade in agriculture produce—both in terms of trading freedom and non-payment of mandi fees—it was expected that trading of produce would have commenced outside APMC market yards.

The states had three options before them when this law was enacted. First, not to do anything and slowly see the regulated APMCs suffer a slow death as trading in APMC market yards would become defunct over a period of time. Second, to amend their APMC laws to abolish or drastically reduce mandi fees and permit APMC traders to undertake intrastate and interstate transactions as the Act allowed the non-APMC traders to do. Third, agitate directly or indirectly with the Central government to repeal or substantially dilute the Farmers' Produce Trade and Commerce (Promotion and Facilitation) Act, 2020.

Most state governments chose the first option. Surprisingly, no state, including the BJP governments, went for the second option although that would have been the most constructive. While there was no overt use of the third option by any particular state, the farmers' agitation launched in November 2020 was in that direction.

A key objective of establishing the APMC system was to provide a fair and level playing field to farmers in trading practices, charges and payments. The Farmers Produce Act 2020 literally created anarchy. No regulated marketing regime was made applicable to trade transactions undertaken under the 2020 Act. There was no regulator either. Electronic trading platforms were supposed to, on their own, 'prepare and implement guidelines for fair trade practices such as mode of trading, fees, technical parameters, including interoperability with other platforms, logistics arrangements, quality assessment, timely payment, dissemination of guidelines in the local language of the place of operation of the platform and such other matters'. The Central government had indicated that it might frame some of these regulations if it wished to.

For physical trades, there was no requirement of such self-regulation at all. With respect to agricultural produce, there is an uneven relationship between farmers and traders, which this Act did not recognize or safeguard.

Implementation of the Act was expected to have been chaotic and bumpy, but the reform was likely to do a lot of good in the long run.

The final outcome, however, was a big let-down. Farmers' Produce Trade and Commerce (Promotion and Facilitation) Act, 2020 was simply repealed, undoing its reform elements as well. It would have to resurface at some stage again with the core reforms remaining intact—maybe on the lines of how FDI in multi-brand retail was handled—the Parliament passes an enabling law under which the states enact the agriculture trade liberalization laws.

Farmers (Empowerment and Protection) Act, 2020, Would Not Have Changed Contract Farming Much

The land revenue and tenancy laws of most states do not permit leasing of agriculture land. Leasing of land is outlawed in the country. Informal leasing of land for farming, however, is widespread. The arrangement of share-cropping/contract farming, based on leasing of land, is almost universally informal in India.

The 2003 APMC Model Act institutionalized contract farming. The law required a sponsor to register the farmer and a contract farming agreement with an APMC. The contract was prescribed by the government. It also stipulated that no title, rights, ownership or possession in land could be transferred, alienated or vest in the sponsor. The law also exempted contract farming from the mandi tax.

However, this regime did not make much progress. Over the years, APMCs came to be viewed more as culprits rather than facilitators of contract farming. The Central government drafted a specialized Model Contract Act in 2018 to exclude APMCs from contract farming. The Act enacted in 2020 built on the Model APMC Act, 2003, and Draft Model Contract Act, 2018, and intended to mainstream contract farming.

Excluding the jurisdiction of the APMCs, the Act conferred authority on the Central government to issue directions for effective implementation of the provisions. Dispute settlement authority lay with subdivisional magistrates.

The contract farming as envisaged in the Act was essentially the continuation of the same artificial construct of the past seventeen years reflected in state laws. It was also excessively intrusive, regulatory and centralized. It unnecessarily provided for various aspects that are part of normal contracts anyway and do not need to be mandated by law.

This law would have met the same fate as the contract farming provisions in the Model APMC Law, 2003 even if it was not repealed.

Essential Commodities Act, 1955, is an Unnecessary Relic of the Past

ECA-1955 was actually founded in 1939 as part of the Defence of India Rules, which was replaced by the Essential Supplies (Temporary Powers) Act, 1946. The provisions of ECA when enacted in 1955 were similar to the 1946 law.

ECA-1955 conferred powers on the Central government to 'regulate or prohibit' 'production, supply and distribution' of an 'essential commodity' and 'trade and commerce therein'. These powers were to be exercised for 'maintaining or increasing supplies of the commodity', or 'securing their equitable distribution' and 'availability at fair prices'.

ECA-1955 had an extensive list of essential commodities. Clause 2 (a) included foodstuffs, including edible oilseeds and oils, cotton, jute and cattle fodder from the agriculture commodities universe. It also had a number of industrial goods like iron and steel, petroleum products, parts of automobiles, paper and drugs. An omnibus clause authorized the Central government to declare the product of any industry, the control of which has been declared expedient by the Parliament in the public interest, as an essential commodity. Quite a few products like cement and sugar were brought under ECA-1955 using this power.

At one point in the 1980s, as many as seventy commodities were under these control orders. It was a licence-permit, price-control raj at its zenith.

As the industrial economy expanded and shortage of industrial goods disappeared after the 1980s, control orders for most industrial goods were rescinded. In 2006, ECA-1955 was amended to omit Section 2(a), which included the list of essential commodities, to include a new Section 2A to define essential commodity as a 'commodity specified in the Schedule' and to confer power on the Central government to add or remove any commodity from the Schedule. In the Schedule, all commodities other than drugs and petroleum products were from the agriculture world: fertilizers, foodstuffs, hank-yarn, jute and seeds. Cottonseed was added to the seeds list in 2009.

Food was the main reason why ECA was brought in and sustained over several decades. While the production of agricultural commodities and supply of foodstuffs had increased substantially by this time, the law still held sway.

However, the Government of India resorted to a roundabout way to defang ECA-1955 once food shortages had become a thing of the past and to prevent abuse of the law. In 2002, the Removal of Licencing Requirements, Stock Limits and Movement Restrictions on Specified Foodstuffs Order was issued. It removed all controls on buying, stocking, selling, transporting, distributing, disposing, acquiring, using or consuming of a long list of foodstuffs: wheat, paddy/rice, coarse grains, sugar, edible oilseeds and edible oils. In November 2004, the 1999 order declaring 'onions' as an essential commodity was rescinded as well.

However, there is too much vested interest in keeping foodstuffs under control. Policymakers do not want to get on the wrong side of consumers even if that meant hurting farmers' interests. Any fall in production or rise in prices provided an excuse to reverse the gear. The process of unravelling the liberalization order began in 2006. The 2002 order was first placed in abeyance with regard to wheat and pulses for a period of six months on 29 August 2006. Most of the commodities over which ECA-1955 was rendered inapplicable by the 2002 order were brought back under control by issuing such abeyance orders.

In 2014, the new NDA government decided to bring liberalization back. It consolidated all orders issued earlier under the Foodstuffs Order, 2002, and issued the new Foodstuffs Order in September 2016, superseding the 2002 Order. Worded similarly to the 2002 order, it included some additional foodstuffs: wheat products (maida, rava, suji, atta, resultant atta and bran), gur (jaggery), and hydrogenated oils or vanaspati. The NDA government was also not willing to go the whole hog, however. The order was placed under abeyance for varying periods of time for pulses, sugar, edible oilseeds and oils. Onions were also removed from the scope of the 2016 order in August 2017.

ECA Reforms Undertaken in 2020 as Part of Farm Laws Were Meaningless

The Essential Commodities (Amendment) Act, 2020, promulgated in September 2020, modified the regulatory and control regime for foodstuffs.

It did not, however, exclude agricultural commodities from the Schedule of ECA-1955. Nor did it delete Section 2 Subsection 4, which conferred jurisdiction on the Central government to exercise the powers of ECA-1955 over foodstuffs. The Act only modified the circumstances in which the regulatory and control authority was exercised in case of foodstuffs, more specifically in the matter of specifying stock limits, by building in some additional exclusions.

To exercise regulatory authority for fixing the stock limit only, extraordinary price rise was defined as 100 per cent price rise in case of horticulture produce and 50 per cent price rise in case of other crops over the price prevailing the previous year on the same day or five years' average retail price, whichever is lower. A 100 per cent price rise year on year for onions and other horticulture produce is very common. Terms like extraordinary price rise and natural calamity were too nebulous to be determinants in the application of ECA-1955.

Chapter Six

State of the Industrial Economy

India Late to the Industrial Revolution

The Industrial Revolution began in the late 1780s in the West. Over the next 150 years, industrialization transformed predominantly stagnant agricultural economies into high-growth industrial economies. However, India, who became and remained one of the richest nations globally for many centuries on account of its leadership in the agriculture era, did not adopt industrial technologies for many decades.

The first successful commercial steam engines made their presence felt in the last decade of the seventeenth century. New technologies, such as the flying shuttle, drop box and spinning frame, with the use of steam power in factories, transformed clothmaking in the middle of the eighteenth century. The Industrial Revolution was born. The industrialization of economies created an enormous amount of income and wealth. Production and trade of industrial goods enriched many countries. India did not gain as it was a latecomer on the industrialization bandwagon.

Beginning in the late nineteenth century, India did witness some industrialization, largely in consumer industries such as sugar, cotton and jute. That said, India was a predominantly agricultural, low-income and stagnant economy at the dawn of Independence. When India became independent, only 6 per cent of its GDP was contributed by manufacturing or industrial goods.

Pre-Independence Industrialization

Basking in the riches of its agricultural economy or steeped in the traditions of an agricultural economy, India ignored the industrial revolution in much of the eighteenth century and first half of the nineteenth century.

The country's large, thriving clothmaking industry had been operating successfully for centuries and its exquisite handlooms and handicrafts were renowned the world over. India's pre-industrial textile industry faced its first real challenge only in the early nineteenth century when cheaper mill cloth started arriving at Indian ports from Britain.

As the cloth that came from Britain used cotton from India, it dawned on British entrepreneurs, as well as some Indian ones, that it would make economic sense to make yarn in India. The first Indian cotton yarn-making factory is said to have been established in 1818. Gradually, Indian entrepreneurs progressed along the value chain; India's first cotton textile mill was established in 1854 in Bombay (now Mumbai). From then on, India's cotton textile industry started growing.

Though some other consumer industries did develop in the pre-Independence period, the First Plan rightly noted the 'relative backwardness of industrial development in India' judged by the fact that 'in 1948–49, factory establishments accounted for only 6.6 per cent of the national income'. It further noted that prior to World War I, the only major industries that had developed substantially were cotton and jute textiles.

At the time of Independence, it is estimated that India's share of global GDP had declined to only about 4 per cent from close to 20 per cent during the Mughal period, and the share of Indian industry as a proportion of global industrial output was less than 2 per cent.

Industrial Economy Grew in the First Twenty-Five Years of Industrialization

As per the back series of the National Accounts published by the Ministry of Statistics and Programme Implementation (MOSPI), India's GDP at factor cost at 1960–61 prices was Rs 14,071 crore in 1960–61.

Industrialization, which is best represented by the GDP in the secondary sector (manufacturing, construction and utilities), had a GDP share of Rs 2721 crore. The larger industrial economy of India had grown up to a little higher than 19 per cent by 1960–61.

Manufacturing constituted the bulk of GDP at factor cost in the secondary sector with a GDP of Rs 1994 crore out of Rs 2721 crore; construction at Rs 641 crore, and utilities (electricity, gas and water supply) at Rs 86 crore making up the rest. Manufacturing GDP formed 14.2 per cent of the overall GDP. India's manufacturing GDP more than doubled in the first fifteen years.

Both the secondary sector and manufacturing, per se, kept growing for the next fifteen years as well. In 1974–75, the secondary sector's GDP contribution of Rs 5217 crore, at 1960–61 prices, made up 24.7 per cent of the Rs 21,670 crore GDP of India. The share of manufacturing (Rs 3810 crore) had also risen somewhat higher to 17.6 per cent in 1974–75.

Gross domestic capital formation (GDCF) was small at 16.9 per cent in 1960–61. The rate of capital formation remained in the range of 16.5 per cent to 17.7 per cent in most years until 1974–75. In 1966–67 and 1974–75, it crossed 19 per cent and in 1961–62 and 1968–69, it fell below 15.5 per cent.

Gross value of output at current prices recorded in 1974–75 for registered manufacturing was dominated by food and textiles. Food manufacturing gross value of output was Rs 3.4 lakh crore in 1974–75, which was about 18 per cent of the total gross value of manufacturing (registered) output of Rs 19.03 lakh crore. Textiles was another big sector with a total value of output of Rs 3.58 lakh crore contributing about 19 per cent.

The basic metal industry, which had been assigned so much importance and investment by the government, contributed a total value of output of Rs 2.30 lakh crore only.

Industrial Output Stagnated since the 1970s

According to the data provided in the latest Economic Survey 2020–21, at constant prices (2004–05 series), the real GVA of India's secondary sector (manufacturing, construction and utilities comprising electricity, gas and water supply) was Rs 1.36 lakh crore in 1974–75. With total GVA being Rs 6.28 lakh crore, the secondary sector made up 21.7 per cent of India's GVA. The secondary sector's GVA grew to Rs 3.25 lakh crore in 1990–91 (24.1 per cent of the overall GVA of Rs 13.47 lakh crore) and to Rs 5.71 lakh crore in 2000–01 (24.3 per cent of total GVA of Rs 23.48 lakh crore). In 2011–12, the last year of the data as per the 2004–05 series, the GVA of India's secondary sector at Rs 13.7 lakh crore made up 26.1 per cent of the total GVA of Rs 52.48 lakh crore. The GVA of India's secondary sector has hovered around 25 per cent of the total GVA for the past thirty years.

The new series 2011–12 data also reflects much the same situation. For 2011–12, the GVA of the secondary sector of Rs 23.73 lakh crore made up 29.3 per cent of the total GVA of Rs 81.07 lakh crore. Provisional estimates of 2019–20 place the secondary sector's GVA to be Rs 36.59 lakh crore, which turns out to be 29.65 per cent of the total GVA of Rs 133.01 lakh crore. Data at current prices, however, reveals a smaller share of the secondary sector. The GVA of the secondary sector as per provisional estimates of 2019–20 is Rs 46.47 lakh crore, which is only 25.33 per cent of the total GVA of Rs 183.43 lakh crore.

Substantial Compositional Change in Industrial Output over Fifty Years

The textile industry was India's most dominant industry at Independence. In 1950–51 (at 1999–2000 prices), to make the comparison meaningful, the industry's domestic value of products was Rs 2631 crore out of total manufactured products of Rs 8659 crore, an impressive 30 per cent. In fact, in current prices (prices prevailing in 1950–51), the share was as high as 42.5 per cent (Rs 210 crore out of the total value of manufactured products of Rs 494 crore).

Over the years, the textile industry lost its dominance in India's manufacturing basket. In 1975–76 (in constant 1999–2000 prices), the value of products was only Rs 5799 crore, making up 16.25 per cent of the total value of manufactured products of Rs 35,694 crore. In 1990–91, when India was about to turn the page by dismantling the licence permit raj, the output of the textile industry was valued at Rs 13,019 crore (1999–2000 prices), 12.9 per cent of the total value of manufactured products of Rs 1,01,467 crore.

Metal products and machinery and chemicals and chemical products, the focus of industrialization after Independence, saw their share go up in India's manufacturing. At constant 1999–2000 prices, the value of metal products and machinery, which was Rs 450 crore in 1950–51 (5.2 per cent), went up to Rs 19,314 crore in 1999–2000 (11.2 per cent). Likewise, chemicals and chemical products, which had a total value of products (in constant 1999–2000 prices) of Rs 601 crore (6.9 per cent), went up to Rs 42,690 crore (24.7 per cent).

Indeed, the decline of the traditional textile industry and expansion of new industries by the end of the twentieth century are apparent from the National Accounts numbers.

Chapter Seven

Industrial Policy of India: Private Sector Out and In Again

1947–1991: Industrial Policy 1.0

Government Takes Charge of Industry

Immediately after Independence, the government decided to take charge of India's industrialization. It decided to evict the private sector from many industrial sectors. Wherever it was not barred, the private sector was to be controlled.

The Industrial Policy Resolution, 1948, was the first policy resolution to enunciate this policy.

The resolution classified industries in four broad categories and paved the way for the government's exclusive or discretionary entry in all the segments.

First, government monopoly: the Policy Resolution laid down that the government would have exclusive monopoly of establishing industrial establishments in specified areas; arms and ammunition, atomic energy and railway transport were to be made the monopoly of the Central government.

Second, exclusive preserve for new investment: The Policy Resolution laid down that the government would be exclusively responsible for the

79

establishment of new undertakings in six basic industries—coal, iron and steel, aircraft manufacture, shipbuilding, manufacture of telephone and telegraph wireless apparatus and mineral oils. It was left to the government to decide to provide some stake to the private sector if it found it necessary to secure the cooperation of private enterprise in the national interest.

Third, control and regulate private enterprise: The Policy Resolution specified eighteen industries of national importance, including automobiles, heavy chemicals, heavy machinery, machine tools, cement, sugar and cotton, which were to be controlled and regulated.

Fourth, open for government intervention: The Policy Resolution decided to leave the rest of the industrial field open to private enterprise, though it was made clear that the state would also progressively participate in this field. Such industries could also be nationalized.

1956 Industrial Policy Resolution Drives the Nail Deeper

The Industrial Policy Resolution, 1956, announced the intent of the government to place 'commanding heights' of industries in the public sector, which was a way to achieve 'a socialist pattern of society'. This was to be done to accelerate the rate of economic growth and speed up industrialization, by developing heavy and machine-making industries, expanding the public sector, and building a large cooperative sector in India.

The 1956 Resolution provided primacy of place in industrialization to the public sector. It stipulated that all industries of basic and strategic importance, or in the nature of public utility services, were to be only in the public sector.

The resolution classified industries into three categories:

First, industries where the state would be exclusively responsible for future development were listed in Schedule A. All new units in these industries, except those whose establishment in the private sector had already been approved, were to be set up by the state. It was reiterated that railways and air transport, arms and ammunition, and atomic energy would only be developed as Central government monopolies.

Second, industries listed in Schedule B were to be progressively state-owned. The government was to take the initiative in establishing new undertakings in such industries and private enterprise was expected to only supplement the effort of the state.

Third, for all remaining industries, future development was, in general, left to the initiative and enterprise of the private sector. However, the state could start any industry in this category as well.

The policy expressed through these two resolutions and the Industrial Development and Regulation Act (IDRA) 1951 was very clear in intent, content and implementation mechanism. Industrialization, more particularly the establishment of basic industries and utilities, was exclusively reserved for the public sector. The government was to increasingly expand investments in other industries. The private sector was excluded from all industrial sectors and was permitted to invest and operate industries largely in the field of consumer goods. Even where permitted, the private sector would operate under the heavy hand of the government for which a very elaborate system of regulation and control was put in place.

While India did not adopt an outright communist model of production (total government ownership of industries), the 1948 and 1956 Industrial Policy resolutions, IDRA-1951 and many other legislations like the Control of Capital Issues, 1947, ensured that it would be near total governmentalization of industrialization in India.

Industrialization Model Based on Five Key Assumptions

India wanted to industrialize rapidly to escape the low growth of decades and build a socialist society. The country wanted to build basic industries, to make machines to fully exploit its mineral resources and build utilities and an industrial base. The model it adopted was built on the belief that the government would lead industrialization and the private sector would play a subordinate role.

India's industrialization model was based on five key assumptions:

First, industrialization flows from the capital employed and there is a certain fixed relationship between capital deployed and output generated. This relationship is captured in what is known as the 'incremental capital output ratio' (ICOR). The government assumed that the ICOR would remain constant for an industry and the capital investment made in the public sector would generate a defined amount of output or value added.

Second, the ownership of capital did not matter. It was assumed that it does not matter whether a steel mill is set up by the government or by a private entrepreneur. The amount of capital invested would produce the same amount of output, irrespective of ownership. In other words, business was the business of the government and the government was as efficient an industrialist as a private entrepreneur.

Third, all forms and kinds of entrepreneurship—large or small, company or cooperative or unincorporated entities—were equally effective for industrialization. A linked assumption was that large private entrepreneurship was socially bad as it led to concentration of wealth and increase in inequality.

Fourth, there is no difference between risk capital (equity) and debt capital (credit). It is the quantum of total capital that matters, not the type of capital. The government would fund industrial projects through surplus from its budgetary revenues and the debt would be raised on the budget and off budget (in the balance sheet of the enterprise established). Equity was merely a cheaper form of capital and not risk capital. No interest was paid on equity and, as profits were not the objective of investment, receiving return on equity investment as dividends was not the goal.

Fifth, the social and fringe benefits of industrialization, such as employment, backward area development and utilization of natural resources, are the most desirable objectives of industrialization. These benefits were thought to outweigh the commercial advantages of markets and location of industry. The economic rate of return and social benefit were seen as more valuable than financial rate of return as a guide for investment decisions.

These assumptions in the 1950s–1970s led to the design of inappropriate policies, legislations and regulations that made industries produce costly, non-competitive and poor-quality products. An increasing number of controlling measures were required to protect these enterprises with high tariffs and directed credit. These assumptions ultimately failed India's foray into industrialization.

Government Investment Goes Bust Even in Basic Industry

The First Plan, which devoted more resources to agriculture and irrigation than industrialization, was considered reasonably successful. The Second Plan, which was heavily focused on industry, especially heavy industry, did not succeed as much. The Third Plan was a disaster, also because of two wars and two massive droughts.

At the onset, the planning apparatus assumed the government would be able to raise tax revenues in surplus of revenue expenditure and would thus be able to generate surplus from current revenues for making large investments for India's industrialization.

The First Plan outlay was Rs 2069 crore for the Centre and state governments over the period 1951–56. This outlay was planned to be financed to the extent of Rs 1414 crore from surplus normal revenue and capital receipts of public authorities, including loans and grants received from abroad. From the Third Plan onwards, surplus from current revenues disappeared and borrowings were raised not only to finance Plan expenditure but also to fund the current revenue gap.

The Plans started relying on borrowings and 'deficit financing' right from the beginning to fund 'planned investment'.

The paucity of resources led to underinvestment. Unproductivity of investment in the public sector led to cost overruns and deteriorating ICORs. By reserving basic industries, mining and utilities only for the public sector as well as new investments in most other capital-intensive industries (Schedule A and Schedule B of the Industrial Policy Resolution, 1956) for the public sector, the government actually bit off more than it could chew.

Industrial projects suffered from both ends. Project costs kept going up and means of financing kept getting increasingly stressed. Smaller availability of resources led to thinner allocations, which led to time and cost overruns. India had severe under-capacity in all basic industries, such as iron and steel, cement, capital goods and even cars, scooters and telecom equipment. No wonder many of these commodities had to be placed under control orders issued under ECA-1955 and rationed. By the 1970s, these shortages reached extremes. Instead of controlling the commanding heights of industry, the public sector was struggling to meet even minimum demand of several products.

Private Sector Debarred from Many Industries

The industrial policy regime instituted in the 1950s muzzled the private sector by grossly limiting its entry and presence in industry in four major ways:

First, the private sector was debarred from entering into basic goods, capital goods, utilities and mining of major minerals—iron and steel, heavy castings and forgings of iron steel, heavy plant and machinery, heavy electrical plants, coal and lignite, mining and processing of copper, lead, zinc, tin, molybdenum and wolfram, atomic minerals, aircraft, air transport, railway transport, shipbuilding, distribution of electricity and many more. By and large, in this reserved field, private-sector presence became minuscule or completely non-existent.

Second, in other important industrial sectors—like minerals not in Schedule A, aluminium, machine tools, ferro alloys, basic and intermediate products of chemical industry, antibiotics, fertilizers, etc.—the private sector was treated as a stepchild and reluctantly tolerated with a distinct preference for the public sector. While Bharat Aluminium Company Ltd (BALCO) and National Aluminium Company Ltd (NALCO) got preferential mining leases, private-sector entities had to struggle.

Third, the rest of the industrial space was split up between large and small industry. Many sectors, at one time exceeding 700, were reserved for small industry. There were artificial limits of investment in plant and machinery to distinguish the large and small sectors, leading to stunted development of the items reserved for the small sector.

Finally, the dynamic part of the industry—large industry—was placed under a strangulating control regime. No new industrial unit or expansion of an existing unit was allowed without the permission of the government. Investment decisions were made by civil servants, not businessmen.

The ICOR kept rising menacingly, from 2.95 in the First Plan to an extremely high 6.63 in the Sixth Plan (1976–77 to 1980–81).

Private Sector Muzzled in Its Limited Space

Industrial registration and licencing began with IDRA-1951. Section 10 of the Act provided that the owner of every private industrial undertaking shall register the undertaking. The registration certificate issued mentioned the production capacity of the undertaking besides other particulars.

IDRA-1951 further provided that a licence would be required for establishing a new undertaking; manufacturing a new article by an existing undertaking; effecting substantial expansion by an existing unit; changing the location of an existing undertaking; and carrying on the business of an existing undertaking.

Consequently, an industrialist could not establish any new manufacturing facility, adopt any new technology or expand a factory without a licence from the government. Thus, businessmen stopped doing genuine business. Lobbying for licences became the big business. As the economy was operating under shortages and manufacturing units were protected from imports from abroad and competition from inside, licences generated profits. Crony capitalism, not a competitive industry, flourished in the country.

Tightening the Noose over the Private Sector

The industrial policy of the 1950s was based on a hugely flawed understanding of the institutions and incentives that make the industry perform. The policy disregarded enterprise and excluded entrepreneurs from a considerable area of manufacturing. It was based on the incorrect notion that capital functions in a linear manner. The fundamental belief was that capital formation, i.e., deployment of more machines, would produce output and that the government could create the resources necessary for industrialization.

Very soon, the lack of dynamism of the government as an entrepreneur became all too apparent. The failure of the Third Plan slowed capital formation as well. The private sector got used to the rules of the game of licence and permit raj. As the private sector controlled the credit resources of the banking industry, large business houses successfully became partners in crony capitalism using their persuasion and money power to obtain licences and credit. Some Indian businessmen thrived while most Indian businesses and economic growth suffered.

The collapse of industrial growth by the middle of the 1960s became a cause of concern for policymakers.

The Hazari Committee was appointed in 1966 to enquire into the working of the licencing system and its role as an instrument of industrial planning. It pointed out several defects in the prevailing licencing system.

The Dutt Committee Report, published in 1969, concluded that the 'licencing system as it actually worked, had by and large failed to achieve its objectives, and that the complexities and delays of the licencing system operated in favour of larger industrial houses'.

Instead of correcting the fundamental illogic of industrial policy, the government went on a spree to further tighten licencing policies over the next fifteen years (1965–1980) and also enacted other legislations like the Monopolies and Restrictive Practices Act (MRTP Act). These measures compounded the original sin.

The Industrial Licencing Policy of 1970 imposed additional severe restrictions on 'large industrial houses'. A new concept of 'core' industries was evolved—similar to the Schedule A industries of the 1956 Policy—and new investment of Rs 5 crore or more was categorized as 'heavy investment'. The government tightened the policy further in the space in which the private sector was earlier allowed to invest by mandating that heavy investment in core industries could be made only in the joint sector. Further, for all industrial investments in the middle sector (Rs 1 crore to Rs 5 crore), it was decided to give special consideration to the 'licence applications of parties other than undertakings belonging to the larger industrial houses'. Essentially, the ostensible intent was to tweak and tighten the country's licencing system in a way to control and contain existing industrial houses.

Controlling Monopolies and Dominance Another Weapon against Private Industry

The government appeared more worried about the 'concentration of economic power' by the end of the 1960s rather than the industrialization of the economy. To stop the concentration of economic power, the MRTP Act was enacted in 1969. The motivation was to control monopolies and restrictive trade practices 'injurious to the public welfare'.

Every undertaking which, by itself or with interconnected undertakings, controlled not less than one-third of production, supply or distribution of a commodity or provided or otherwise controlled not less than one-third of any services rendered in India with aggregate assets of Rs 1 crore or more was considered a 'dominant undertaking' and was required to register with the MRTP Commission. Likewise, large undertakings (by themselves or with interconnected undertakings) with assets of Rs 100 crore or more, even if these were not dominant undertakings, were also required to register. The dominant and large entities were also required to obtain the approval of the MRTP Commission, besides taking due licence, to undertake any substantial expansion.

The Foreign Exchange and Regulation Act (FERA) was enacted in 1973, which tightly controlled foreign investments in the Indian industry. Raising capital by making capital issues was further tightened.

Reviews of the industrialization and working of the licencing policy undertaken in the early 1970s revealed that the government was not able to develop an efficient public sector; and had fettered the private sector in the country. Responding to this sad state of affairs, some relaxations in the operation of the licencing system were granted in the Revised Licencing Policy, 1973, and Industrial Licencing Policy, 1975. However, old habits die hard. The Licencing Policy, 1977, tightened the controls again.

Sick Industry Not Allowed to Die

Industrial sickness in India was the direct result of the defective industrial policy. Industry was unable to invest in new technology on account of the highly restrictive licencing policy that did not permit new investment and expansion. Crony capitalism ensured that licences were cornered by the few who could find a market for their shoddy products as demand outstripped supply. For many industrial operators, it was profitable to make money by driving the industry sick rather than operating an undertaking profitably.

In tune with the times, the government believed it was a better industrialist. IDRA-1951 empowered the Central government to authorize a government officer to take over the management of an industrial undertaking if, after an investigation, it believed it was being managed in a manner highly detrimental to the industry concerned or the public interest. IDRA-1951 also empowered the Central government to restart a sick industry if it was of the opinion that the finances as well as condition of the plant and machinery could be properly utilized in production.

IDRA-1951 could not prevent industrial sickness. The government came up with special legislation to address industry-specific sickness such as the Cotton Textile Companies (Management of Undertakings and Liquidation or Reconstruction) Act, 1967; the Sick Textile Undertakings (Taking Over the Management) Act, 1972; and the Sick Textile Undertakings (Nationalization) Act, 1974. Later in 1985, an omnibus Sick Industrial Companies Act (SICA-1985) was enacted to detect industrial sickness in general and provide for revival.

The government takeover by nationalization proved to be no solution. The government was not a better entrepreneur than the private industrialist. In some cases, the special legislations and SICA-1985 were used to benefit some friends of the ruling party (crony capitalism) by socializing the private sickness at a public cost. In general, neither the taking over of the private industry by the government nor the special and general legislations to cure industrial sickness yielded any positive results.

The sickness kept spreading. As per information tabled in the Parliament in response to a question in 1985, it was reported that there were over 60,000 sick undertakings in the country in 1982. With the number rising by several thousand a year, the count of sick industries reached close to 1 lakh by 1984.

Incipient Reforms Began in the 1980s

The fact that the industrial policy resolutions of 1950s, the monopolization of investments in heavy industry in the public sector, the restrictive industrial licencing regime, perpetuation and nationalization of sick industries and increasing control over the large private industrial sector were not working had become quite apparent to policymakers in the 1970s. The success of East Asian and South-east Asian countries with liberal industrial policies and open foreign investment made the contrast very stark.

The year 1980 marked the beginning of the reversal of failed industrial policies pursued from 1947 to 1979.

The government issued a new Industrial Policy Statement on 23 July 1980. While the Industrial Policy issued in July 1991 dismantled the 1956 Industrial Policy Statement and marked the end of Industrial Policy 1.0 and the beginning of Industrial Policy 2.0 in the country, the 1980 Industrial Policy Statement initiated the process of dismantling.

The significant liberalization measures to roll back the excesses of the licencing regime were as follows:

First, automatic expansion of capacity was permitted in all industries by 5 per cent per annum or 25 per cent in a Five-Year Plan period.

Second, favourable policy dispensation was created for 100 per cent export-oriented units and expansion of existing units for purposes of export by establishing a fast-track pathway for such proposals.

Third, industrial processes and technologies aimed at optimum utilization of energy or exploitation of alternative sources of energy were given special assistance, including finance on concessional terms.

There were quite a few other announcements that merely amounted to tinkering but had a positive signalling effect. These included raising investment limits to Rs 2 lakh for tiny units, Rs 20 lakh for small units and Rs 25 lakh for ancillaries.

Many more liberalizing measures followed in the 1980s. Gradually, a number of industries were delicenced. Licences for large investments in backward areas were abolished. Broad-banding of licences was permitted in 1986. Industrial undertakings were allowed to switch over their assembly lines from one product to another in the same industry group. Automatic regularization of capacity increase was permitted for higher limits. MRTP permissions were done away with for several industries as were distribution controls over a number of industries.

The 1980 Industrial Policy Resolution opened the door for private sector-led industrialization of India. Additional measures taken during the 1980s strengthened the private industrial sector. India delivered a satisfactory industrial performance in the 1980s. The manufacturing growth was over 7 per cent from 1980 to 1990. Share of manufacturing in GDP grew from a little less than 14 per cent to about 17 per cent in 1990. Exports grew handsomely in the second half of the 1980s, recording a growth rate of over 14 per cent.

Industrial Policy 1.0 Delivered Anaemic Growth

India grew poorly in the 1950–1980 period, with the GDP rising by hardly 3 per cent to 3.5 per cent annually on average. Many Asian countries, such as Japan, South Korea, Singapore and Taiwan, and later other South Asian countries like Malaysia and Thailand raced ahead to generate much higher growth during this period.

Indian industry put on an equally disappointing show despite considerable investment by the government. Growth rates of the secondary sector plummeted, most particularly in the 1965–66 to 1974–75 period, when the licence permit raj was at its peak and investments in public-sector investment had slowed down considerably. During this ten-year period, except for two years (1969–70: 5.1 per cent and 1969–70: 7.8 per cent), the secondary sector grew only at sub-4 per cent rates. Manufacturing growth rate averaged only about 5 per cent during the thirty years from 1950 to 1980.

Some relaxations in the restrictive policy regime from 1973 onwards led to a pickup in industrial growth in the next five years (1975–1980). The process of dismantling mindless constraints on industrial capacity creation commenced with the Industrial Policy Resolution of 1980, which gathered further pace in the 1980s. Private-sector industry started delivering higher growth of over 7 per cent.

On the whole, the period of Industry Policy 1.0 (1947–1991) was one of low industrial and overall economic growth. It was a suboptimal performance by any standards.

1991 Marks a Watershed: Industrial Policy 2.0

The industrial and licencing policies pursued for more than forty years (1947–1990) conclusively failed in industrializing India. The policies, however, succeeded in stymieing and stunting the private sector in the country, which was the objective of the industrial policies after Independence.

The balance of payments crisis of 1990–1991 forced the hand of the government and made reforms in trade, foreign exchange and industrial policy unavoidable. These reforms were inevitable to save India from the ignominy of defaulting on its international payment obligations and living a hard life on account of its inability to import even crude oil to meet minimum energy needs. The crisis and trade and exchange reforms provided a good opportunity to undertake reforms of industrial policies as well.

Industrial Policy Reforms in 1991 Were Initiated Apologetically

The first nineteen paragraphs of the Statement on Industrial Policy presented by the government in the Parliament on 24 July 1991 paid lip service to the Industrial Policy Resolutions of 1948 and 1956 and the socialist pattern of society.

It began with an apology. 'In 1956, capital was scarce and the base of entrepreneurship not strong enough. Hence, the 1956 Industrial Policy Resolution gave primacy to the role of the state to assume a predominant and direct responsibility for industrial development,' went Paragraph 3 of the Industrial Policy Statement 1991 (IP-1991). The argument defied logic. If private entrepreneurship in India was weak in the 1950s, why exclude it from so many basic and key sectors and subject it to the tight leash of licencing and control? IP-1991 did not mention IDRA-1951 and the Licence Policy of 1967, which created the strangulating licencing regime. Instead, it mentioned the licence policies of 1973 and 1980, whereby some relaxations were given.

IP-1991 wrongly claimed that the industrial policies of the 1950s, 1960s and 1970s created a climate for rapid industrial growth. India was one of the most industrially laggard countries during this period. It claimed that broad-based infrastructure had been built up, which was not the objective of industrial policy and also factually incorrect. It also claimed that basic industries had been established, whereas India was still importing most of its capital goods and whatever basic industries were set up were based on imported technology.

The lip service and apology were, however, necessary to make the reforms optically acceptable and palatable to the lawmakers who had lived on the diet of the stifling controls. The government could successfully pull the wool over their eyes by styling the change as a continuation of existing policies—the beginning of re-privatization of industrial sectors but in the garb of the old socialist pattern of society.

IP-1991 initiated fundamental reforms in key areas such as industrial licencing, foreign investment, foreign technology acquisition and economic dominance. It made minor reforms in public-sector policy but barely touched small industry policies, including reservations of small scale.

IP-1991 Dismantled Reservation for the Public Sector

The most important reform of IP-1991 was to terminate reservation for the public sector, thereby permitting the entry of the private sector in almost every industrial activity. This opened the doors for re-privatization of industry in the country.

IP-1991 reserved only eight industries for the public sector (Annexure I): arms and ammunition and allied items of defence equipment, defence aircraft and warships; atomic energy; coal and lignite; mineral oils; mining of iron ore, manganese ore, chrome ore, gypsum, sulphur, gold and diamonds; mining of copper, lead, zinc, tin, molybdenum and wolfram;

minerals specified in the Schedule to the Atomic Energy (Control of Production and Use) Order, 1953; and railway transport. By separate notifications over the years, the reservation of these industries for the public sector has almost been completely abolished. Only two industries are currently reserved: railway operations (private investment is permissible in construction, operation and maintenance activities) and atomic energy (production, separation and enrichment of special fissionable materials and substances and operations of the facilities). Even for railway operations, under public-private partnership (PPP) arrangements, private-sector entry has been permitted in the operation of both freight and passengers.

The most myopic industrial policy—the exclusive reservation of the public sector and exclusion of the private sector—was completely reformed. This has led to private-sector investment far exceeding public-sector investment in many hitherto reserved industries, including iron and steel, oil and gas, major minerals and power. This is proof that the policies of 1948 and 1956 deprived the country of the benefit of private enterprise and investment in a large segment of manufacturing and industries.

IP-1991 Abolished the Rapacious Licencing Regime

The havoc that industrial licensing policies instituted in the 1950s–1970s created became apparent in the 1970s and 1980s. While some liberalization measures were initiated in the 1980s, IP-1991 pushed out the rapacious licencing regime.

It noted correctly that Indian entrepreneurs needed to be actively encouraged to exploit and meet emerging domestic and global opportunities and challenges. It was necessary to 'let the entrepreneurs make investment decisions on the basis of their own commercial judgement'. 'The attainment of technological dynamism and international competitiveness requires that enterprises must be enabled to swiftly respond to fast changing external conditions that have become characteristic of the industrial world'. The policy statement rightly argued that the role played by the government had to be 'changed from that of only exercising control to one of providing help and guidance by making essential procedures fully transparent and eliminating delays'.

The statement in the matter of abolishing the licencing regime was unequivocal. It said, 'Industrial policy will henceforth be abolished for

all industries, except those specified, irrespective of levels of investment.'
Annexure II specified eighteen industries for which compulsory licencing
was continued; the list included major industries like coal and lignite,
petroleum, alcoholic drinks, sugar, motor cars, drugs, paper and newsprint.

IP-1991 started the process of unravelling licencing policies. Over
the years, most compulsory industrial licencing has gone. Only four
items currently require industrial licence, that too more for safety reasons
considering the nature of these industries: cigars and cigarettes; electronic
aerospace and defence equipment; industrial explosives and three specified
hazardous chemicals.

Indeed, Indian industry is breathing free since 1991.

IP-1991 Opened the Door for Foreign Direct Investment

At the time of Independence, India was flush with foreign reserves in
the form of sterling balances. India followed a reasonably liberal foreign
investment policy during the First Plan period. However, by the time the
Second Plan (1957–1962) was under implementation, the foreign exchange
situation started deteriorating and India jumped on the bandwagon of
self-reliance—with the intent of manufacturing everything in the country.
The foreign exchange situation became very bad in the Third Plan and
India made its first substantive devaluation in 1966.

FERA-1973 shut the door on foreign investments and foreign
technology imports. The Janata government made even invested foreign
companies like IBM leave the country by tightening the FERA regime.
While foreign direct investment (FDI) globally was galloping in the
1980s, India's performance was pathetic. The worldwide flow of FDI was
increasing at rates higher than 20 per cent in the four years prior to 1991.
The annual growth rate of FDI between 1983 and 1989 was 29 per cent;
India's growth of FDI was 0.1 per cent in 1980–82 and 0.2 per cent from
1985 to 1987.

The government initiated blockbuster FDI reforms through IP-1991.
A long list of high-priority industries was drawn up (Annexure III of IP-
1991 contained thirty-four industries) and FDI with controlling interest
of 51 per cent was permitted in automatic approval mode. The Foreign
Investment Promotion Board (FIPB) was created and FERA-1973 was
amended to deliver bottleneck-free approvals. Other liberalization measures

included freeing up components, raw materials and intermediate goods; allowing knowhow fees and royalties to be paid liberally; and permitting the establishment of trading companies.

IP-1991 led to the steady liberalization of the FDI regime in India. Progressively, most industries were opened for automatic FDI inflows. Currently, more than 95 per cent of all FDI flows are under automatic route. Global FDI growth continued to be very strong in the 1990s and India joined the ranks of high FDI-receiving countries, becoming part of the top category of FDI recipients—countries that recorded over 30 per cent rate of growth between 1986 and 2000, as per the World Investment Report, 2000. In the past few years, India has become one of the ten highest FDI recipient countries in the world.

IP-1991 Signalled Technology As Key to Competitiveness

India initially accepted international technology to build steel plants, power machinery and other basic industries in the 1950s. However, we gradually developed an acutely short-sighted approach towards technology in the name of self-reliance. Import substitution became the key industrial policy in 1960s and 1970s. In line with this mindset, the country became averse to foreign technology imports. By 1980s, we had one of the most obscurantist and closed technology import regimes. Meanwhile, East Asia was building its industrial muscle by importing technology and reverse engineering the same.

IP-1991 signalled a complete change of mindset. India decided to grant automatic permission for foreign technology imports in high priority industries (Annexure III) and liberalized payment rules for royalties and technical fees. Payment of technology imports—lumpsum Rs 1 crore or limited to 5 per cent royalty for domestic sales and 8 per cent for exports—were permitted freely. Even for non-Annexure III industries, royalties could be paid at these rates if no free foreign exchange was required for payment. Likewise, no permission was required for hiring foreign technicians and foreign testing of indigenously developed technologies. The lumpsum payment limit was raised to $2 million in the early 1990s.

There was an attempt in 2015–2018 to roll back India's free technology import regime on account of the misplaced perception that there was a large outgo in the form of royalty payments. Fortunately, the proposal got shelved.

Doing Away with Artificial Division of Industries between Small and Large Sectors

IP-1991 did not touch the artificial division of industries between the small and large sectors. It merely said, 'Industries reserved for the small-scale sector will continue to be so reserved.' A separate policy statement was issued that increased the investment limits in different segments of the small sector and announced some financial measures for supporting small-scale industry (SSI). However, the winds of liberalization and deregulation had begun to blow. It was only a matter of time that reservations for the small-scale sector would also blow away.

The reservation of some items for manufacture by SSI only started sometime in the late 1960s. Section 29B was inserted in IDRA-1951 sometime in the early 1970s. More and more items were added to the list of items reserved. The notification issued on 25 July 1991, immediately after the announcement of IP-1991, listed all the items reserved for the small sector in Annexure III. Only a few more items were added to the list in the post-liberalization period. At its peak in 1997–98, there were about 840 industrial products reserved for manufacture exclusively in the small sector.

The process of de-reservation started in 1997–98 when the first notification was issued in April 1997 de-reserving about fifteen items, including ice-cream, vinegar, rice milling, dal milling, biscuits, hairdryers and ashtrays. This process of removing items from the list continued over the next eighteen years. Finally, through a notification issued on 10 April 2015, the twenty remaining items were de-reserved. With this, the saga of SSI reservations came to a close.

SSI manufactured about 7000 industrial items in India in the late 1990s, with about 850 items on the reservation list. It is argued that even at the peak of small scale reservation, the share of output of reserved items was only about 30 per cent of the manufacturing goods output of SSI.

Small-scale reservation was based on the misinformed notion that it did not matter whether an industrial product is manufactured on a small or large scale. Scale economies were not clear to policymakers. Most items reserved for the small-scale sector were labour-intensive industries. If these were manufactured at scale, they would be competitive while small-scale manufacture could compromise competitiveness and quality.

Small-scale enterprises are quite competitive in several businesses, and these do not need reservation to thrive. Ultimately, the short-sightedness of the policy of reserving items exclusively for small-scale manufacture dawned on policymakers and finally in 2015, the nonsensical policy ended.

Manufacturing Policy 2011, Industrial Corridors and Make in India

The makeover of policy focus from restraining and containing the private sector in Industrial Policy 1.0 (1947–1991) to promoting and facilitating the private sector during Industrial Policy 2.0 (from 1991) has been continued with two major policy initiatives taken by the government in the twenty-first century.

To enhance the share of manufacturing in GDP to 25 per cent and create 100 million manufacturing jobs, the government announced the National Manufacturing Policy in 2011. It intended to create an enabling policy environment, in partnership with the states, and proposed incentives for infrastructure development on public-private partnership (PPP) basis.

The policy pioneered the concept of National Investment and Manufacturing Zones (NIMZs) for focused, cluster-based development of manufacturing. The instrumentality of NIMZs was designed to create large, integrated industrial townships with state-of-the-art infrastructure. To facilitate politics-free governance, these zones were to be designated as self-governing townships. However, not much progress has been made in creating NIMZs. Only three NIMZs have been given final approval so far at Prakasam (Andhra Pradesh), Sangareddy (Telangana) and Kalinganagar (Odisha). Actual industry is yet to move in there.

The government took up the integrated development of industries using the industrial corridor approach when the Delhi-Mumbai Industrial Corridor (DMIC) project was initiated in 2006. The DMIC is taking up the development of several NIMZs and investment zones along with a dedicated freight corridor. The progress of DMIC has also been quite slow. Further, the government has announced four more corridors: the Amritsar-Kolkata Industrial Corridor (AKIC); Chennai-Bengaluru Industrial Corridor (CBIC); East Coast Economic Corridor (ECEC), which is backed by a dedicated freight corridor; and Bengaluru-Mumbai Industrial Corridor (BMIC). These corridors are also making progress, though at a very slow pace. The finance minister announced some parts of these large corridors as flagship projects in her Budget speech for 2021–22.

Launched in 2014, the 'Make in India' programme combines strategies of the new manufacturing policy, industrial corridors, cluster approach, infrastructure building, and encouraging technology, FDI and ease of doing business to focus on twenty-five selected sectors. It seeks to create the right policy environment, infrastructure and competitiveness to give the Indian industry an edge in these sectors. The number of sectors has been increased to twenty-seven under what is called 'Make in India (MII) 2.0'. A sectoral review of policies and supportive programmes for boosting these twenty-seven sectors can really help. However, if the reassessment of overall and sectoral policies does not result in a drastic change of policies and programmes, MII 2.0 may remain just talk rather than materially changing the situation on ground.

Manufacturing Is Going the Agriculture Way Globally

The share of manufacturing in GDP of sixteen advanced countries in 1950 was 31 per cent. Developing countries were industrially backward at that time and the share of manufacturing in the GDP of the twenty-nine largest developing countries was only 11 per cent. According to data from the UN, the share of manufacturing in global GDP was still high at 25 per cent in 1970 but had started plateauing. From then on, there has been a constant decline, with the share of manufacturing in global GDP falling to about 16 per cent in 2017.

The world has seen the shifting of manufacturing from advanced countries to developing countries in the past thirty years, which is reflected in the declining share of manufacturing in the GDP of advanced economies. As per UN data, in case of the US, share of manufacturing in GDP has declined from about 23 per cent in 1970 to about 11 per cent in 2017. According to World Bank data for high-income countries, the share of manufacturing in GVA has declined from 17.5 per cent in 1997 to 14 per cent in 2018. In case of low-income countries, the trend demonstrates a different path but the long-term direction is unmistakable. The share of manufacturing in their GDP was 16 per cent in 1998. This peaked at 27 per cent in 2007 and has since then steadily declined to come down to 20 per cent in 2019.

There is now global overcapacity in most manufacturing industries. The demand for most manufactured goods has peaked. There is a clear decline in per-capita consumption of many industrial goods for various reasons, including limited capacity to consume and the environmental overload. Efficiency in production and lower consumption of raw materials (more product per unit of input) have also led to decline in growth of demand for many manufactured products and their raw materials.

Industry is viewed as a major employment provider in the world, especially in developing countries. However, global employment in industry has been stagnating for quite some time. As per the modelled estimates of the International Labour Organization (ILO), global employment in industry increased from 20.5 per cent to just 23.5 per cent, albeit with a variable trend, in the past thirty years. Employment in agriculture saw a secular decline during this period and virtually halved from 44 per cent in 1990 to 27 per cent in 2020. Employment in services, however, has seen a steady increase from about 34 per cent in 1990 to 51 per cent in 2020.

These employment trends unmistakably portray the past and future pattern of employment in the three large constituents of the economy: agriculture, industry and services. Agriculture is in a terminal decline phase as far as employment is concerned. The share of agriculture in global employment would keep going further down and might become less than 10 per cent in the next fifty years. Employment in industry will stagnate for a while and then start declining to reach less than 10 per cent in the next fifty years. Services are now getting impacted by digitalization, yet the services space is likely to keep evolving and generating new opportunities and may maintain its share in global employment at 50 per cent of employable workforce.

Chapter Eight

MSMEs: Small Is Not Beautiful

The MSME Universe

The Micro, Small and Medium Enterprises Development Act, 2006 (MSME Act), was amended on 26 June 2020. Before the amendment, manufacturing enterprises with less than Rs 10 crore investment and service enterprises with less than Rs 5 crore investment in plant and machinery were collectively referred to as MSMEs. Where capital investment did not exceed Rs 25 lakh and Rs 10 lakh, respectively, in manufacturing and services, enterprises were categorized as micro-enterprises. Manufacturing and services enterprises with capital investment higher than micro-enterprises but less than Rs 5 crore and Rs 2 crore, respectively were categorized as small enterprises.

The largest category of enterprises in the MSME space, called medium enterprises, had an investment limit of Rs 10 crore and Rs 5 crore, respectively for manufacturing and services enterprises. These limits were fixed in 2006 and had remained unaltered for fourteen years.

The 2020 amendment in the MSME Act introduced two major changes in the classification system. First, the investment limits for manufacturing and service enterprises were combined into one limit and, second, an additional turnover criterion was added. The investment limit for micro-enterprises was raised to Rs 1 crore and a turnover ceiling of Rs 5 crore was prescribed. For enterprises to be considered small, it was necessary not to have investment in excess of Rs 10 crore and turnover in excess of Rs 50 crore. For medium enterprises, investment and turnover limits were fixed at Rs 50 crore and Rs 250 crore, respectively.

These new limits would result in 'large enterprises' with investments between Rs 10 crore and Rs 50 crore being classified as MSME.

How Many MSMEs Do We Have?

How many enterprises operating and doing business in the country are MSMEs? Nobody really knows. There is no system of registering all MSMEs. There is no national or state database of MSMEs.

India conducts an Economic Census periodically to collect data on 'non-farm businesses', i.e., counting all businesses other than agriculture businesses. These business entities are termed establishments. The Economic Census is conducted on a sample basis. The last Economic Census, the sixth, was conducted in 2013.

The Economic Census 2013 found that there were about 5.85 crore business establishments in operation in the country, of which more than 60 per cent were in rural areas. The Census 2013 reported that there was good growth in the number of such business establishments in the period between the Fifth and Sixth Economic Census; the Fifth Economic Census was conducted eight years earlier in 2005. The number of establishments in the country increased by more than 40 per cent during this period, which roughly provides a growth rate of about 5 per cent a year. The Economic Census 2013 also reported that there were thirteen crore workers employed in these businesses.

The National Sample Survey 73rd Round (NSS 73rd Round) conducted in 2015–16 substantiated the data and findings of the Economic Census 2013. It found that there were 6.34 lakh unincorporated non-agricultural MSMEs in the country. It also reported that over 99 per cent of these enterprises (as many as 6.30 crore out of total 6.34 crore establishments) were micro-enterprises. Only a little over 3 lakh enterprises were small. Medium enterprises numbered 5000.

Taking the annual growth rate of 5 per cent in the number of MSMEs between 2013 and 2020, the number of non-farm agricultural, industrial and service establishments in India should be about 8 crore in 2020.

MSMEs Are Predominantly Private, 'Own Account', Proprietary and Unincorporated Businesses

The 2013 Economic Census revealed very useful information about the nature, ownership, employment and other features of non-farm small enterprises in the country.

More than 96 per cent establishments were found to be owned by private entrepreneurs. Over 70 per cent of establishments were classified as 'own account' establishments that did not employ any workers. About 90 per cent were owned by a single person; in other words, these were proprietary establishments.

A significant proportion of establishments (36 per cent) were home-based or without any fixed structure or workplace to operate from. About 20 per cent of establishments, operating from outside the home, did not have any fixed structure or a permanent place to work from. This means that there are about 1.5 crore businesses in the country that operate more like 'hawkers' having no fixed place to produce and sell goods or services.

Business enterprises are categorized in different ways depending upon the form of organization, ownership and liability: companies, sole proprietorship, partnership, association of persons, self-employed persons and many other forms of non-formal arrangements. However, there are essentially two basic forms of business organizations from an ownership and liability perspective: incorporated (essentially businesses that are incorporated as companies) and unincorporated (all other forms of businesses). Mostly, bigger businesses are incorporated as companies while small businesses operate as unincorporated entities. The requirement to raise capital from others and keep business and personal financial affairs separate makes the difference while choosing to organize a business as an unincorporated entity or an incorporated one.

Incorporated businesses, mainly companies, are organizations where the liability of each owner is limited to the capital contributed by such a person in the business venture. Unincorporated businesses, in whatever form whether proprietorships or partnerships (except the limited liability partnerships or LLPs, which are closer to companies in terms of liability of the owner-partners), are organizations where the liability of each business owner is unlimited and thereby extends beyond the capital contributed by such businessmen in the venture to their personal property as well.

There are over 17 lakh registered companies in India. And the balance 800 lakh-odd businesses are unincorporated businesses, mostly MSMEs.

MSMEs Lack Identity

India uniquely identifies each of its over 130 crore resident individuals. All these individuals are assigned a unique ID number. The country also identifies all its incorporated entities uniquely. Each one of about 17 lakh companies has a unique name and ID. However, India does not uniquely identify and recognize each of its unincorporated businesses entities, which happen to be the MSME universe. MSMEs do not have a unique business identity number.

MSMEs have a ministry to look after their interests, like companies have the Ministry of Corporate Affairs (MCA). The MCA has a well-developed system through the Registrar of Companies to not only register companies but to seek out all necessary details of their business operations. There is no authority under the MSME Ministry to recognize and maintain a register of MSMEs, which mostly happen to be unincorporated enterprises.

The system of registering unincorporated entities in India is fragmented in parts and non-existent generally. Some forms of unincorporated business entities have different authorities to register them; most do not. Proprietorship concerns, which a majority of MSMEs effectively are in the legal sense, are not registered by anyone as a business entity, though their shops (where applicable) are registered by labour department officials in most states. Partnerships are voluntarily registered in a Register of Firms by designated state government authorities; mostly cooperative departments are assigned this responsibility though partnerships are not cooperative enterprises. Registration of partnership firms is not mandatory and most partnership firms do not register. Societies are registered by the Registrar of Societies, and so on. All these registers are disjointed and usually maintained manually.

No authority in India really recognizes MSMEs. There is no national business register of unincorporated MSMEs in India. The Udyog Aadhaar Number (UAN) assigned by the MSME Ministry from 2015 to MSMEs on a voluntary basis is good for nothing. The architecture of the UAN scheme is also fundamentally flawed. It essentially assigns an enterprise number to an individual, not to the business. UAN is based on the individual's Aadhaar ID.

MSMEs are large in number but small in scale of business. These businesses are everywhere but the existence of most of them is not recognized formally as they do not have a business identity. They are publicly lauded for the value of their services to society, but their own cause is not served in a worthy manner. Micro businesses, in fact, are *vyavsaik anaath*, or business orphans.

Policy Assumes Small Business is Inherently Weak

The MSME policy has evolved in India with the objective of promoting SSI to serve the goal of the socialist pattern of society. Large private industry was viewed as bad from the standpoint of a socialist society whereas small private industry furthered the notion of the socialist pattern of society. Very early after Independence, the large private industry was subjected to much exclusion whereas small industry was favoured with reservations. Basic industries were reserved for the public sector and a lot of consumer industries were reserved for SSI.

The policy of SSI reservation remained a favourite for many decades. At its peak, more than 900 products were reserved for manufacturing exclusively in SSIs. A majority of these items, such as textiles, were most competitively produced at large scale. India lost the global export battle in manufacturing these items competitively at the altar of SSI reservations. Most reserved items were also low-tech, high labour-intensive products. As they could not be produced at scale to meet global demand, their potential to create jobs was also lost.

The policy always believed that small businesses, later on further divided into micro, small and medium, are inherently weak compared to large-scale enterprises and would survive only with government exemptions, concessions and financial support. Many exemptions under tax, labour and other laws have been prompted by this basic policy assumption.

Small businesses are not fundamentally unprofitable. These are different businesses that meet vital economic needs and, therefore, should be treated as normal businesses. It is not crutches but the right policy support that these businesses need to thrive.

MSMEs Lack Access to Equity Capital

Any business needs equity to get started. Equity is the risk capital necessary to bring in debt capital as well. MSMEs, most particularly micro-enterprises, badly lack equity. Most micro-entrepreneurs have only their skills/knowledge and time as equity. Some may have some savings, a parcel of land or loans taken from friends and relatives.

It is a stark fact that the Indian governmental and financial ecosystem does not provide any equity support to MSMEs. It does not even talk about it.

The Ministry of MSMEs, Government of India, operated more than forty schemes with a total outlay of about Rs 7500 crore in 2020–21. There are schemes to support credit, technology upgradation, market support, employment, and so on. But there is not a single scheme that supports the provision of equity. The Ministry of MSMEs does not even recognize equity as important. In fact, the Annual Report of the Ministry of MSMEs for 2018–19 does not feature the word 'equity' even once in the entire 150-page report!

Only one study conducted for India's MSMEs makes some estimate of their equity requirement. In 2018, the International Finance Corporation (IFC), an affiliate of the World Bank, published a comprehensive study of requirements and availability of finance for MSMEs in India. It estimated demand for equity finance by MSMEs at Rs 18.4 lakh crore out of total required finance of Rs 87.7 lakh crore. Unfortunately, after estimating the requirement of equity finance in its initial part, the rest of the report did not talk about equity and concentrated only on credit finance.

Small Industries Development Bank of India (SIDBI), the apex development finance institution for MSMEs, which had outstanding Rs 95,000 crore of credit finance at the end of financial year 2017–18, directly and indirectly through refinance, did not provide any equity support to MSMEs. Its balance sheet does not even include provision of equity in the list of its assets. It only provides a small and negligible amount of venture capital support to some start-ups under some lines of credit.

Small and medium companies have an option to raise equity on the SME exchanges of the BSE (formerly the Bombay Stock Exchange) and NSE (National Stock Exchange of India). This exchange allows companies with post-issue face value capital up to Rs 25 crore, which is far higher than the maximum Rs 10 crore investment permissible for medium enterprises in plant and machinery. Still, only about 300 companies are listed on both the BSE and NSE SME exchanges. These companies raised a total of about Rs 6000 crore until 2020 in equity capital since the inception of these exchanges in 2012. Details of how many of these companies are MSMEs are not available.

There are specialized institutions like small finance banks and NBFCs that focus on small businesses. Unfortunately, these institutions also neglect the provision of equity.

Credit Support is Available Only to a Fraction of MSMEs

The government and financial system profess to provide a large chunk of credit to MSMEs. Yet, there is a big gap between the credit required and credit being made available to them. This forces MSMEs to remain credit-starved or to fall into the clutches of informal sources of credit.

The IFC report published in 2018 concluded that the overall demand of MSMEs for debt finance was an estimated Rs 69.3 lakh crore of debt. The report focuses on debt financing. Recognizing that the debt requirement of MSMEs is met only to a very small extent by formal sources of financing, it stated that 84 per cent of the debt demand of Rs 69.3 lakh crore, i.e., Rs 58.4 lakh crore, was met by informal sources. Only about Rs 11 lakh crore of debt demand was met by all the formal sources put together: banks, regional rural banks, urban cooperative banks, non-banks, SIDBI and the government.

RBI provides data about total bank credit outstanding in the country. At the end of financial year 2018–19, there were 88.87 lakh loan accounts of industrial enterprises in the banking system. There were also 1.43 crore accounts of traders, of which 1.3 crore were retail trade accounts. Transporters had 31.84 lakh crore accounts and all other service enterprises had 68.97 lakh accounts. Even in absolute numbers, total business bank accounts were 3.33 crore in all. This is only about 40 per cent of the total 8 crore businesses in the country. Several businesses have bank accounts in more than one bank. The data of unique bank account numbers is not available.

According to RBI data on the credit advanced to micro and small sectors (as these are covered under priority sector lending), for the year ending March 2020, total credit outstanding against MSEs from scheduled commercial banks (which covers about 90 per cent of total credit advanced by the banking system) was Rs 11.63 lakh crore. RBI separately provides details of credit outstanding towards medium enterprises (but not medium service enterprises)—the amount was Rs 1.06 lakh crore.

RBI or any other official institution in the country does not provide data about total credit advanced to MSMEs by banks, non-banks and other financial institutions. TransUnion CIBIL is the only agency that provides information on credit advanced to MSMEs from banks and non-banks. However, its definition of MSME is based on the amount of loan advanced, not the legal definition of MSME, which is based on investment in plant and machinery.

Government Grants Support is Meagre

By their very nature, grants can only be provided by the government and charities. The MSME Ministry has an annual budget of about Rs 7500 crore. While no case can be made for the government to provide support to every MSME, for 7.5 crore MSMEs in the country, the total budget provision works out to Rs 1000 per enterprise. This is spread over forty schemes and the average allocation per scheme is less than Rs 200 crore.

The government provides credit-linked capital grant support for the establishment of MSMEs under two different schemes, which happen to be the largest schemes of the ministry as well.

The largest scheme is called the Prime Minister Employment Generation Programme. Under this, establishment of micro-enterprises is encouraged by provision of 25 per cent of project cost as capita subsidy in rural areas and 15 per cent of project cost as capital subsidy in urban areas for projects with a maximum cost of Rs 25 lakh in manufacturing and Rs 10 lakh in service enterprises. Thus, this scheme is restricted to micro-enterprises. The total allocation under this programme for 2020–21 was Rs 2500 crore. Assuming an average capital subsidy of Rs 5 lakh, the scheme can provide capital subsidy support to only 50,000 enterprises a year, not even 0.1 per cent of the micro-enterprises in the country.

Under the technology upgradation scheme, credit-linked capital subsidy is provided for technology and quality upgradation. With an allocation of a little over Rs 650 crore, the scheme is meant to assist micro and small enterprises to upgrade their manufacturing and processing technologies. Technology is costly. Even if we assume that the cost per unit assisted is, again, about Rs 5 lakh, the benefit will reach only about 12,000 micro units. Once more, a very shallow reach.

There are numerous other schemes with separate thematic objectives.

The short point is that the entire financial support of Rs 7500 crore budgeted by the government for a year for MSMEs is quite minuscule compared to the requirement of Rs 88 lakh crore estimated by IFC. The government support turns out to be less than 0.1 per cent of the estimated need.

Helping MSMEs with Alternative Investment Funds—a False Promise

The MSME Ministry intends to use the expertise of private equity funds and management to make investments in MSMEs. The idea is good in its intent but deficient in inspiring confidence.

There were two line items in the MSME Ministry's Budget 2020–21 about such alternate investment funds (AIFs). One is the MSME Fund and the other is the Fund of Funds.

The government had conceived the idea of an MSME Fund in the year 2017–18. A token provision of Rs 0.01 crore was made for the same. Next year, it provided Rs 100 crore in Budget 2018–19 under the head 'MSME Fund'. No fund was however utilized. Again, in 2019–20, a provision was kept for Rs 100 crore. This was reduced to Rs 0.01 crore in revised estimates. Provision for the year 2020–21 was also reduced to Rs 50 crore. Three years have gone by since the idea of the MSME Fund emerged, yet not a single rupee has been used. In fact, the budgetary documents do not even describe the purpose or structure of this provision, which is usually stated for every line item in the Ministry's Expenditure Budget.

In 2020–21, a Fund of Funds was proposed and a provision of Rs 200 crore made. As part of the Atmanirbhar Bharat stimulus package announced by the Finance Minister in May 2020, the Government of India's contribution to the Fund of Funds was raised fifty times from

Rs 200 crore to Rs 10,000 crore. However, this appeared to be more in the nature of building castles in the air rather than anything concrete. The FoF has not seen the light of day.

There is a specific class of funds called SME funds approved by the SEBI as part of the alternative investment channel. SME funds are placed in Category I of AIFs. A Fund of Funds for MSMEs would invest in the SME funds promoted by private equity firms.

According to information from SEBI, SME funds acquired total commitments of Rs 542 crore at the end of December 2019. The actual funds raised were only Rs 121 crore and the actual funds invested amounted to Rs 63 crore cumulatively.

As investing in MSMEs through a Fund of Funds would not require the government to set up an AIF and appoint an investment manager, the Fund of Funds announced in the Budget might see better traction. However, it was difficult for the government to invest Rs 200 crore in the financial year 2020–21. The provision for the Fund of Funds was reduced to Rs 100 crore in the revised budget for 2020–21. Likewise, investing Rs 10,000 crore over the next few years, when the total investment made by SME funds was only a little over Rs 60 crore, was nothing but a daydream. It would be advisable to have a more realistic ambition for the Fund of Funds rather than announcing grandiose but unattainable goals.

MSMEs Were Hit Hard in the Lockdown

The economic lockdown imposed in India on 24 March shuttered about 70 per cent of the economy for five weeks. As everyone was asked to stay home and no non-essential manufacturing or service businesses were allowed, small businesses or MSMEs suffered the most. More than 90 per cent of MSMEs, or about 7 crore MSMEs, could no longer carry on with business across sectors, from mining, construction and manufacturing to providing services through shops and roadside establishments. All small entrepreneurs delivering personal services, where MSMEs are mostly engaged, had to close their doors, rendering entrepreneurs and workers redundant.

MSMEs suffered in many ways: First, most could not produce and sell any goods and services during the first forty-day lockdown period. At least 90 per cent of MSMEs, numbering over 7 crore, simply shut shop. For a period of at least forty days, they received no income. Though they could avoid the cost of inputs, they had to bear several fixed costs, such as rents, interest payments (moratorium even when granted is only postponement of interest payment, not waiver), some wage payments, and maintenance expenditure. Most MSMEs were not in a position to live with this liability. Unless supported, millions were in danger of simply closing down and defaulting on their obligations.

Second, these 8 crore MSMEs employed about 15 crore workers. Barring a few medium and small industries, most were not able to pay wages. For the self-employed/own-account micro-entrepreneur, net income from the business amounted to wages. Initial estimates in March and April suggested that over 10 crore MSME workers lost their jobs and wages. Job surveys by the Centre for Monitoring Indian Economy (CMIE) confirmed that more than 13 crore jobs were lost in the month of April.

MSMEs produce about 30 per cent of GVA. However, the losses suffered by MSMEs are much greater than the losses suffered by either farmers, larger industries or larger service-providing organizations. MSMEs suffered 50 per cent of the overall contraction suffered by India in 2020–21. As India's economy contracted by nearly 8 per cent in 2020–21, 4 per cent of overall contraction would be only for the MSMEs. 4 per cent of Rs 200 lakh crore GDP of India means Rs 8 lakh crore. MSMEs together suffered losses of at least Rs 8 lakh crore of GVA in 2020–21.

MSMEs have a larger share of wages in GVA. For micro-enterprises, share of wages in value added is in the range of 75–90 per cent. On average, if we take the share of wages to be about 80 per cent of MSMEs' GVA, this meant that the MSME workers who lost their jobs would have suffered a wage loss of about Rs 6 lakh crore in 2020–21.

A Missed Survival Package for MSMEs

The right stimulus for MSMEs could have been for the government to extend grant support for their lost wages and committed expenditures. Additionally, it could have used the opportunity to place the entire ecosystem at ease of doing business for MSMEs on a stronger footing. Unfortunately, it did not offer any direct package of support, nor did it create a strong, facilitative and supportive business ecosystem for MSMEs.

The government should have offered a grant-financed financial relief package to MSMEs, including compensation for two elements of losses and cost suffered during the lockdown: a normative payment to cover at least 50 per cent of the lost earnings/wages of MSME owners/workers and some relief to cover fixed and unavoidable costs like rent, instalment payment of hired equipment, etc. If the government had paid Rs 20,000 per MSME owner/worker for the estimated number of 10 crore MSME worker-months and Rs 6000 per MSME for about 8 crore MSMEs for operational expenses, it would have cost the government only about Rs 2.5 lakh crore during 2020–21. Instead of providing this grant-based fiscal support, the government offered to underwrite loss on 20 per cent additional loans to existing MSME borrowers of the banking system, amounting to Rs 3 lakh crore.

While the loan guarantee package was not expected to finally cost the government Rs 3 lakh crore as all the forty-five-odd loanee MSMEs were not likely to default, the loan guarantee package turned out to be enormously deficient with regard to helping the cause of MSMEs mainly for two main reasons. One, the loan package ended up assisting only about 5–7 per cent of MSMEs and that too the ones which are relatively better off; the grant-based package would have served the interest of all the 8 crore micro and small businesses. Two, the loan guarantee package compromised the credit culture massively and would probably end up impairing the banking system much more than the benefit it would provide to small businesses. It is also likely to create a very bad functional relationship between the government and banks, by bringing the credit policies of banks under direct government interference as is evident in the case of Public Sector Banks (PSBs), functioning under an owner-owned relationship.

The fiscal package could have provided a golden opportunity to bring the MSMEs in the formal business fold and create a good administrative relationship between them and the government through a formal registration and business operations depository system. Using the opportunity of distress caused by the COVID-19 crisis, the Central government could have announced a survival package conditional on MSMEs registering for a unique business ID and filing a return of business operations with the government linked with a unique ID.

Chapter Nine

State of the Services Economy

Services Economy Was Small and Highly Disorganized at Independence

India did not have any system worth the name to estimate GDP and income at the time of Independence. The National Income Committee, appointed in August 1949, made the first estimates of national income for 1948–49, which were released in April 1951.

The Committee estimated India's national GDP/GVA/income in 1948–49 at Rs 8710 crore. Of this, agriculture's contribution was the largest at Rs 4150 crore, which was close to half the income at 47.6 per cent. Mining, manufacturing and hand trades (handicrafts and handlooms) economy were estimated at Rs 1500 crore or 17.2 per cent of the total economy. Services were organized in two broad groups of commerce, transport and communications and other services.

Communications (post, telegraph and telephone) contributed GDP of only Rs 30 crore (0.3 per cent). Railways made a contribution of Rs 200 crore or 2.3 per cent of the economy. The share of organized banking and insurance was also quite small at Rs 50 crore, contributing 0.6 per cent of GDP. Other commerce and transport, which grouped all the unorganized trade and transport services including services of

111

indigenous moneylenders, contributed a large amount of Rs 1420 crore or 16.3 per cent of GDP. The services of professions and liberal arts were recognized as a separate group and contributed Rs 320 crore of national income (3.7 per cent). Domestic service was also recognized as a separate group and contributed Rs 150 crore of income (1.7 per cent). The house property group, essentially rental income, contributed Rs 450 crore (5.2 per cent) and the contribution of government services (administration) to GDP was valued at Rs 460 crore (5.3 per cent).

Together, services, though quite disorganized and fragmented, contributed Rs 3080 crore of national income in 1948–1949, which formed 35.4 per cent of the national GDP.

Services Have Been Contributing More than 50 Per Cent of Growth since the 1970s

India placed huge emphasis on industrialization in the 1950s and 1960s. The share of services in India's GDP averaged 28.2 per cent in 1950s with services contributing 32.2 per cent of the growth taking place during this period. The contribution of services improved in the 1960s with services GDP rising to 31.4 per cent in the decade and contribution of services improving to 38.1 per cent in the growth of GDP during this decade.

The 1970s saw services taking off in a major way. Their contribution to GDP growth in this decade crossed 50 per cent and has been measured at 52.7 per cent. This enhanced the share of services in India's GDP to 34.4 per cent. The decade of the 1980s saw the share of services in growth falling to less than 50 per cent at 43.6 per cent. As it was still higher than the share of services in GDP, the share of services in GDP improved to 38.6 per cent in the 1980s.

At the time India abandoned the policies of nationalization and de-privatization and adopted the policies of re-privatization of the economy in 1991, the services GDP at factor cost was Rs 81,260 crore (1980–81 prices), which made up 38.7 per cent of India's GDP.

Rising formalization of the services economy saw the share of trade, hotels, transport and communication group of services improving from 44.3 per cent in 1950s to 48.7 per cent in 1980s. On the contrary, the share of the finance, insurance, real estate and business services group declined from 23 per cent in 1950s to 20.4 per cent in the 1980s. The share of the social and personal services group also declined somewhat from 32.8 per cent in the 1950s to 30.9 per cent in the 1980s.

Services Economy Crossed 50 Per Cent Mark by the Turn of the Century

In 1999–2000, India's GDP at factor cost (at 1993–94 prices) was Rs 11.48 lakh crore.

The trade, transport, storage and communication group of services contributed Rs 2.56 lakh crore of GDP, the financing, insurance, real estate and business services group contributed Rs 1.46 lakh crore of GDP, and the public administration and defence and other services group contributed Rs 1.53 lakh crore of GDP at factor cost. Together, the services group contributed Rs 5.55 lakh crore of GDP. India's services GDP in 1999–2000 had commanded 48.3 per cent of GDP.

As GDP estimates get revised from time to time depending upon the series of prices adopted, the share of services in 1999–2000 came very close to 50 per cent at 1999–2000 prices. At these prices, services contributed Rs 8.88 lakh crore, which was 49.69 per cent of India's GDP at a factor cost of Rs 17.87 lakh crore.

India's services GDP crossed the 50 per cent mark the next year in 2000–01, the first year of the new millennium. India's GDP at factor cost was Rs 18.64 lakh crore in 2000–01. The trade, hotels, transport and communication group contributed Rs 4.16 lakh crore, the financing, insurance, real estate and business services group contributed Rs 2.43 lakh crore, and public administration and defence and other services contributed Rs 2.79 lakh crore. Together, services contributed Rs 9.38 lakh crore and services GDP, at 50.03 per cent, crossed the halfway mark for the first time.

Services Contribute More Positively than Goods in the External Trade Account

India has fared far better in terms of the services trade than goods trade for many years now. From 2013–14 to 2019–20, India's export of services rose from $151.8 billion to $213.2 billion in 2019–20, increasing by $61.4 billion. India's export of services in 2013–14 was 48.3 per cent of India's goods exports; in 2019–20, it improved to 68 per cent. While exports of goods declined even in absolute terms by $1.3 billion (from $314.46 billion in 2013–14 to $313.14 billion in 2019–20), export of services increased by as much as $61.4 billion. The share of services has risen to as much as 40.5 per cent of total export of goods and services of $526.34 billion in 2019–20. This heralds a significant transformation of India's exports. While goods exports have stagnated, services exports have maintained smart growth in the past seven years despite the fact that India's trade policy continues to lay emphasis on goods exports.

Though the import of services has also been rising at a fast clip (from $78.7 billion in 2013–14 to $128.3 billion in 2019–20), growth in export of services was much higher in absolute amounts. India had a surplus on account of services in 2013–14 of $73.1 billion, which increased by $11.9 billion to $84.9 billion in 2019–20.

India exported $96.1 billion worth of telecommunication, computer and IT services in 2019–20. The country's import of such services amounted to $10.2 billion. India thus had an impressive surplus of $85.9 billion in the IT segment of services, which was greater than the total surplus on the services account of $84.9 billion. In fact, the country's IT services exports make up 45 per cent of the total services export. IT services have been playing a stellar role in cushioning the pressure on India's foreign exchange account.

The largest trade deficit in the services group was recorded with respect to royalties at $6.8 billion in 2019–20. India is majorly dependent on foreign technology and FDI. As the benefits of foreign technology import and FDI far outweigh the cost in terms of royalties, this should not be a cause of concern.

In 2019–20, India recorded a deficit of $157.5 billion in the goods account and a surplus of $84.9 billion in the services account. Surpluses on services covered more than half of India's trade deficit on account of goods.

Services Exports Are Rising

The income generated by national GDP, inclusive of export income, can be augmented further by the income domestic factors of production can earn by investing and working abroad. Capital investments made by national enterprises abroad earn income in the form of dividends, retained earnings and capital gains. National labour working abroad earns wages and other work-related remunerations that adds to the national income. A country that makes higher direct investment abroad and can make its non-immigrant labour work abroad is much better off. This income, also referred to as primary income earned abroad, is not export income but akin to income earned from exports.

Being a capital and technology-deficient country, India has received far more Foreign Direct Investment (FDI), foreign portfolio investment (FPI) and other investments than it makes. In 2019–20, income earned by non-residents from India amounted to $49 billion, whereas Indian residents earned investment incomes of only $15.4 billion. There was a transfer of $33.6 billion from India to the rest of the world on this account. Compensation earned by Indian residents in the employment of non-residents at $5.6 billion was, however, much higher than the compensation paid by resident employers to non-resident labour, at $2.7 billion, resulting in a positive contribution of $2.9 billion to India's national income. In the primary account, India was in a deficit of $27.3 billion on the whole.

Labour-surplus countries tend to witness export of labour as well. Such labour immigrates to other countries in search of better employment and income. However, their familial and emotional connections last for many decades after they have immigrated. Many of these people send part of their income as remittances for family and relations. Globally, Indians settled abroad as non-residents transferred as much as $75.7 billion in 2019–20, which added to the national income of India. As immigrant labour earns income by and large by delivering services, this income is another variant of the export of services.

If we take a wider view of the services exported from India, we can add incomes earned by export of services ($213.2 billion), incomes earned as compensation by Indian resident employees ($5.6 billion) and remittances made by the Indian diaspora ($75.7 billion) as services. Together, India earned $294.5 billion from these different modes of export of services. The country's total current account income was $642.1 billion ($533.6 billion of goods and services, $25.2 billion of primary income of factors of production and $83.4 billion of secondary income, mainly remittances). The income earned by services was virtually half (45.9 per cent) of the total income in 2019–20 from the rest of the world.

The day when services will contribute about half the total income of Indian residents from abroad does not appear to be far away. The day when export of services exceeds the export of goods will also occur in the not-so-distant future if we plan and focus on our services export strategy better.

Growing Share in Services Export but Presence in Only a Narrow Range of Services

The export of services takes place, as agreed by the global community in the General Agreement on Trade in Services, in four modes: cross-border supply (services flow from one country to another, mostly electronically); consumption abroad (the customer physically travels to the country of the service provider, such as a tourist for pleasure or medical treatment); commercial presence (by establishing a business establishment in the country of service delivery and consumption); and presence of natural persons (where the service provider physically moves to the country where the service is consumed).

The export of services in three modes—cross-border supply, consumption abroad and presence of natural persons—is included in the current account statistics. The service delivered by commercial presence does not form part of the current account statistics but is captured to measure the full extent of export of services. The data for export of services through commercial presence abroad is captured as part of the Foreign Affiliates Trade Statistics (FATS) generated by the World Trade Organization (WTO). WTO produces a report called 'Trade in Services by Mode of Supply' (TISMOS), which combines the current account statistics of export in services and FATS to produce a full account of the global trade in services.

India's share of services in the basket of export of services in 2018 was the third highest among major exporters. Singapore, with about 31 per cent share of services, had the largest share of services in total exports, followed by the European Union (EU), which had a share of a little over 29 per cent. India had a share of about 28 per cent. The US, which has 80 per cent share of services in its GDP, had a share of export of services of 25 per cent in its total exports.

With services dominating global GDP today, exports reflect the developed state of the economy. Developed/advanced countries account for over two-third of global export of services, developing countries about 32 per cent, and least developed countries only 0.8 per cent.

According to data from the United Nations Conference on Trade and Development (UNCTAD), global trade in services (excluding services delivered in commercial presence abroad) was $5.8 trillion in 2018. It increased at a lower rate of about 2.7 per cent in 2019 (over 7.5 per cent in the previous two years), rising to $6 trillion. The US was the largest exporter of services at $828 billion in 2018. It had a positive trade balance in services of $269 billion. Three European countries, the UK, Germany and France, occupied the next three positions with exports of $376 billion, $331 billion and $291 billion, respectively.

With a share of 3.51 per cent in global exports in services, India exported $205 billion of services in the three modes. The country imported $177 billion worth of services, which gave us a surplus of $28 billion on the services trade.

The World Trade Report 2019—The Future of Services Trade of the WTO takes a wider view by including services delivered through subsidiaries/branches of companies in other countries. According to this report, trade in services grew at a faster rate than the trade in goods between 2005 and 2017, at 5.4 per cent, and was worth $13.3 trillion. Commercial presence in the form of subsidiaries and branches was the most dominant mode accounting for about 59 per cent of export of services, with cross-border services amounting to about 28 per cent, consumption abroad about 10 per cent, and the balance 3 per cent in the form of presence of individuals in another country.

Like the UNCTAD data, even in terms of the wider definition adopted in this report, the share of developing countries was smaller at 25 per cent of global exports and 35 per cent of global import of services. The least developing countries had a minuscule share of 0.3 per cent of global exports and 0.9 per cent of global imports. The report expects the share of services trade to rise to 50 per cent of total global trade by 2040.

Chapter Ten

Services Have Grown without Much Policy Support

India Develops a Plan for Champion Services

The Union Cabinet approved a plan to raise India's share in global service exports from 3.3 per cent in 2015 to 4.2 per cent in 2022. It focused on twelve identified 'champion service sectors': IT and ITeS; tourism and hospitality; medical value travel; transport and logistics; accounting and finance; audio-visual; legal; communication; construction and related engineering services; environmental; financial; and education. The government proposed the creation of a dedicated fund of Rs 5000 crore to promote the development and realization of the export potential of these services.

In September 2019, the Ministry of Finance approved an umbrella scheme, the Champion Services Sector Scheme (CSSS), along with sectoral schemes of six ministries in charge of the identified services—human resources; telecommunication; Ayurveda, Yoga and Naturopathy, Unani, Siddha and Homeopathy (AYUSH); housing and urban affairs; tourism; and IT—for a total commitment of Rs 3370 crore from 2019–20 to 2023–24.

The Services Export Promotion Council (SEPC) publishes an annual report to chart progress and provide data on export of services as well as implementation of CSSS. The 2019–20 report throws no positive light on the gains made by the country in this regard. Nor does the annual report of the Department of Commerce.

As Indian firms have not established much commercial presence abroad, the country's share in global exports of all services, including by commercial presence abroad, has fallen from 3.3 per cent in the balance of payments exports of services to 1.6 per cent in total global exports of $13.3 trillion in 2019 according to the TISMOS database.

Distribution or E-commerce Services Have Remained Stunted

The largest constituent of global services exports is distribution services with a share of about 20 per cent, which translates to exports of $2.64 trillion. These services, provided by wholesalers and retailers, have now been increasingly overtaken by digital platforms like Amazon, Alibaba and Walmart–Flipkart. These services are also provided by establishing a commercial establishment in the countries of consumption of the goods.

CSSS does not pay attention to distribution services, despite this being the largest exportable service segment globally.

Indian entrepreneurs invested in export of IT services from the very early period of globalization and digitalization of services, around the turn of the millennium. A few start-ups like Flipkart ventured into distribution services. Unfortunately, the country got into two major policy muddles in the past twenty years that inhibited our growth in distribution services. First, we entered a large but wholly unnecessary debate in the platform versus inventory model of building e-retailers, including multi-brand versus single-brand e-stores/e-delivery. This was intended to stop the likes of Amazon from finding their feet in India. The result was the opposite. Not only has Amazon built a large franchise in distribution, the other American giant, Walmart, has gobbled up Flipkart, resulting in India becoming a major importer of distribution services and an almost nonentity in export of distribution services.

The second unnecessary and harmful policy muddle has been the handling of data privacy and data localization. Today, the capability to deploy artificial intelligence (AI) is the key to a successful distribution business, whether wholesale or retail, single or multi-brand, for groceries or discretionary items. Data is critical for both AI and building a basic electronic distribution business.

By choosing to define private data very broadly and placing major restrictions on the use of critical and non-critical personal data (expanded to even non-personal data in the recommendations of the Parliamentary Committee on the data privacy law), India has not only restricted global businesses from investing in the country but also, by default, excluded Indian businesses from building global businesses using the data of their people. The same is the case with localization.

First, RBI created a very inward-looking and restrictive data localization policy for the entire payment space (nothing happens in the distribution business if payments cannot be made effortlessly). And then the Department of Industrial Policy and Promotion came up with a poorly drafted and deeply flawed data policy as part of the e-commerce policy. Later, this entire approach was embedded in the draft Data Protection Law.

If India is to have a good shot at the export of distribution services and our entrepreneurs to dream of building global digital distribution businesses, we will have to junk the approach of favouring only a platform model of e-commerce and adopt a more open data privacy and data localization policy.

Financial Services Have Remained Neglected

With a share of 18.6 per cent, financial services is the second largest component of export of global services, amounting to earnings of nearly $2.5 trillion in 2017. Global integration of finance and financial services riding on the back of technology (fintech) is providing a major fillip to financial services business and exports. Financial services have been primarily delivered for many decades by the establishment of branches and subsidiaries abroad. This is now being threatened by digital platforms.

India has not witnessed much export of financial services thus far. Indian banks, insurance companies and other financial service providers hardly went abroad to establish branches and subsidiaries. Not surprisingly, the country's share in export of financial services has been negligible. However, the digitalized integration of financial services in the world offers an excellent opportunity for Indian start-ups and businesses to get a piece of the pie.

Digitalized financial service businesses are akin to e-commerce in distribution of goods. Indians have a natural affinity to both financial services and Information and Communication Technology (ICT) businesses. The fact that most large digital technology firms and many big financial firms globally are headed by Indians is testament to this.

The right policies for data handling are as important, if not more, for financial businesses and exports as they are for distribution services. The growth of India's financial services businesses has been stifled on account of the dominance of PSBs, barring State Bank of India (SBI), which have not moved beyond the traditional business model.

Telecommunications, Computer Services and Audio-Visuals

For this group of services, where India has a substantial share, global exports in 2017 amounted to $1.75 trillion (13.2 per cent). Cross-border services are primarily delivered through electronic and telephonic means. Such services, in all, totalled $3.7 trillion, of which almost half was contributed by telecommunication, computer services and audio-visuals. ICT services expanded at a very high annual rate of 11 per cent from 2005 to 2017. Within the overall group of ICT services, export of IT services amounted to $438 billion in 2017, of which India's share was $52 billion.

India has not shifted the policy focus on expanding the ICT export basket beyond bread-and-butter IT services. Cloud-based ICT services are emerging as a big business, as is Software as a Service (SaaS). There are many other areas within the ICT space where Indian firms are just finding their feet. As cloud-based ICT services require enormous data storage and processing capacities, India's IT infrastructure promotion scheme has not focused on building these in the private sector.

Transport

The transport group is the fourth largest group of services with the TISMOS database accounting for exports of $1.57 trillion in 2017.

The globalization of goods consumption requires transportation of goods from the countries of export to the countries of import. Likewise, the emergence of global value chains in the production system, combining the advantages of cheaper labour in one place, raw materials in another, industrial complexes in a third place and specialization in production of parts, has led to the use of an enormous amount of transport services globally. There has also been a big upsurge in passenger travel for business, leisure and tourism.

India has seen some good e-commerce businesses being built in the domestic transport sector. However, a lot of transportation of goods and passengers still remains in small hands or in the public sector. India will need to get its domestic transportation business right to become a meaningful global exporter of transportation services.

Tourism

Tourism is the last of the five groups of services that had exports worth over $1 trillion with a share of 7.8 per cent. An estimated 1.3 billion tourist arrivals were recorded in India in 2017.

Services consumed by travelling to other countries had a total share of 10.4 per cent in total service exports, 60 per cent of which is generated by tourism.

India's tourism potential is enormous. Export revenues from tourism are earned by tourist arrivals in the country. Therefore, to build a big tourism export revenue business, India will require to adopt requisite policies and programmes, develop infrastructure of airlines, roads, hotels and eateries, and invest in soft services.

France used to receive about 90 million tourists a year until 2019; Spain around 83 million; the US 80 million; and China and Italy about 65 million. Turkey and Mexico used to see between 40 and 50 million tourist arrivals a year. Several countries, including Thailand, Germany and the UK, saw tourist arrivals exceeding 35 million a year.

Tourist arrivals in India in 2019 were about 17–18 million, much less than five other Asian countries: Japan (32 million), Malaysia (26 million), Hong Kong (24 million), Macau (19 million) and Vietnam (18 million).

India has liberalized e-visas for tourists from most countries as part of its focus on the CSSS for tourism and hospitality services. While this is significant, much more needs to be done to aspire to over 50 million tourists a year. This challenge has become tougher after COVID-19.

Other Services

Globalization is driving the growth of business and consulting services. Digitalization is enabling the delivery of business and professional services in the form of cross-border trade and numerous firms now work practically in virtual mode.

IP services, which include royalties and fees for reproduction and distribution of copyrights, although small in size for the present, are growing quite well. IP services exports primarily flow from advanced countries to the developing countries; 92 per cent of exports of IP services of about $400 billion originated from developed countries.

There were over 5 million international students in 2017.

The size of environmental services was estimated to be about $20 billion in 2017.

Services delivered through the presence of persons abroad form a relatively minor part of the total export of services, totalling only $0.4 trillion in 2017.

Construction services are estimated to have grown at 7 per cent annually since 2005, with China emerging as a major construction services exporter ($188 billion in 2017 accounting for over 37 per cent of construction exports).

The three services that recorded an annual growth rate higher than 10 per cent since 2017 included research and development (R & D) services and health services, though with a smaller base.

India does not have any significant presence in these areas.

Services Exports More Concentrated in Developed and a Few Developing Countries than Goods Exports

While developed countries have ceded manufacturing to developing countries since the 1980s, they have monopolized the export of services. In 2005, developed countries had a share of over 85 per cent in global export of services. That said, developing countries gained a notable share of over 10 per cent from 2005 to 2017; this grew to over 25 per cent in 2017. Among the developing economies, five countries, all from Asia (China, Korea, Hong Kong, Singapore and India), accounted for over half (56.7 per cent) of the developing countries' export of services. Their share of global export was 14.5 per cent whereas the rest of the 125 developing countries could manage to export 10.7 per cent.

These five developing countries are expanding services export in construction; financial, professional, business and distribution services; and ICT and transport by establishing a commercial presence abroad. However, India is not a leader in establishing a commercial presence abroad in these areas, except in ICT services.

India's Services Export Basket is Very Narrow

The global trade system monitors exports and imports for fifteen groups of services. According to data of 2019–20 from Services Export Promotion Council (SEPC) there are only four major service groups that account for as much as 90 per cent of exports in India: IT services; business services; travel; and transport. In the areas of top global services export (distribution services and financial services) and rapidly growing new areas (IP services, construction, education, etc.), India has an insignificant presence and share. ICT services (45 per cent), business services (21 per cent), travel (14 per cent) and transport (10 per cent) were the four largest service exports of India.

CSSS covers twelve sectors that traverse nine of the fifteen groups in which export of services is classified globally. These are tourism and hospitality (part of the tourism group with a global share of 8 per cent); medical value travel and healthcare services (0.4 per cent); transport and logistics including maritime transport (part of transport, 12 per cent); accounting and finance, including auditing and book-keeping; legal; construction and related engineering including architectural services; business services and maintenance and repair (part of other business services, 4 per cent, and professional services, 3.4 per cent); audio-visual and entertainment services; IT/BPM and other services (telecommunications, computer services and audio-visuals, 13 per cent); environmental services (0.2 per cent); financial services (19 per cent); and education (0.8 per cent).

CSSS has not identified even a small service area to focus on in six of the fifteen groups of services included in the TISMOS report accounting for roughly 40 per cent of global services export. These six areas are distribution (global share of 20 per cent); construction (3.4 per cent); IP-related services (3 per cent); R & D (1.4 per cent); recreational, cultural and sports (0.9 per cent); and rental and leasing (0.5 per cent).

If one deconstructs nine groups for export of services identified for CSSS, it becomes apparent that even among these, the ground covered by the identified twelve sectors/subsectors is only a smaller part of the portfolio of services that together make up 60 per cent of global services export. A broad estimate would indicate that India's twelve identified champion services do not cover more than 25 per cent of the $13.3 trillion global export of services.

Chapter Eleven

State of the Public Sector

Universe of Central Public Sector Enterprises (CPSEs)

There are two sets of CPSEs: non-financial or real-sector CPSEs, and financial sector CPSEs. The Department of Public Enterprises publishes an annual survey of CPSEs; the 2018–19 edition was placed in the Parliament in February 2020. There were 348 CPSEs at the end of 2018–19, with 249 operating, eighty-six 'under construction' and thirteen under closure/liquidation.

The total capital employed in all CPSEs as on 31 March 2019 was Rs 26.34 lakh crore. The CPSEs had total 'financial investment' of Rs 16.41 lakh crore, including total paid capital of Rs 2.76 lakh crore. The accumulated reserves and surpluses of CPSEs at Rs 9.93 lakh crore made up the difference between the total capital employed and total financial investment. Total net worth amounted to a little over Rs 12 lakh crore. As on 31 March 2019, 56 CPSEs were listed with a total market capitalization of Rs 13.71 lakh crore, which comprised 9.08 per cent of total BSE market capitalization on that day.

The 249 operating CPSEs earned gross revenues of Rs 25.43 lakh crore; 178 CPSEs aggregated net profits of Rs 1.75 lakh crore while 70 reported losses of Rs 0.32 lakh crore. On the whole, CPSEs returned a net profit of Rs 1.43 lakh crore and 121 operating CPSEs declared and paid dividend of Rs 0.72 lakh crore.

Total GVA of CPSEs in 2018–19 amounted to Rs 5.60 lakh crore as reported in the survey. Adding back indirect taxes paid of Rs 1.84 lakh crore, GVA was Rs 7.14 lakh crore. In terms of GVA, CPSEs contribute only about 4 per cent of the total.

Workers earned wages of Rs 1.53 lakh crore, the government got taxes of Rs 3.25 lakh crore and the remaining Rs 2.36 crore belonged to capital contributors (dividend, interest and retained earnings).

Market Capitalization of CPSEs

At the close of the stock exchanges on 16 September 2020, the fifty-eight listed non-financial CPSEs had a total market capitalization of Rs 9.46 lakh crore, 6 per cent of the total market capitalization of Rs 157.63 lakh crore on that day. None of them had market capitalization in excess of Rs 1 lakh crore and only 20 had market capitalization over Rs 10,000 crore; ten CPSEs had market capitalization of less than Rs 1000 crore. Meanwhile, market capitalization of the topmost private company in India, Reliance Industries Ltd, was close to Rs 15 lakh crore, exceeding the market capitalization of all the 58 listed non-financial CPSEs.

In the financial space, twelve PSBs were listed on the stock exchange in the middle of September. In addition, there were two NBFCs (PFC and REC) and two insurance sector companies, GIC and New India Assurance. The market capitalization of the banks was Rs 3.32 lakh crore in the middle of September and the two NBFCs and insurance companies had a total market capitalization of Rs 45,800 crore and Rs 41,397 crore respectively. All the sixteen financial sector companies put together had a market capitalization of Rs 4.19 lakh crore, with the market capitalization of the largest private-sector bank, HDFC Bank, alone exceeding Rs 5.92 lakh crore.

Market capitalization of SBI was respectable at Rs 1.74 lakh crore. For the remaining eleven PSBs, it was only Rs 1.58 lakh crore collectively. The PSB with the next highest market capitalization was the scam-ridden Punjab National Bank (PNB) with a market capitalization of Rs 30,930 crore. The desperate state of PSBs can be gauged by the fact that the market capitalization of the technically private IDBI Bank, which has the highest ratio of non-performing loans, at Rs 38,564 crore, exceeded the market capitalization of PNB in September 2020.

Putting things into perspective, the market capitalization of the seventy-four CPSEs (financial and non-financial) was Rs 13.65 lakh crore. The market capitalization of one company, Reliance Industries Ltd, exceeded this.

Government is No Longer Investing in Growth through CPSEs

As per the information provided in the expenditure profile 2020–21, the Government of India provided equity support of Rs 2,09,687 crore to public enterprises in financial year 2018–19. In addition, loans of Rs 16,178 crore were also provided. Equity support was provided to as many as twenty-eight public enterprises. The three largest investments made included Rs 1,06,000 crore of capital support to PSBs, Rs 35,819 crore of equity support to NHAI and Rs 52,838 crore of equity support to Indian Railways. Together, these three types of enterprises—banks, railways and national highways—got budgetary support for equity investment of Rs 1,94,657 crore. These three entities claimed 92.83 per cent of the entire equity investment made by the Government of India in financial year 2018–19.

What is significant to note is that all the three sets of enterprises are sick. They do not contribute anything significant to GVA and earn very little or no profits and, consequently, do not provide any return to the Government of India in the form of dividends or capital gains.

The Railways used to pay, at least in accounting terms, a dividend at the rate of 3 per cent of eligible assets until 2015. The Lok Sabha discussed a recommendation of the Railway Convention Committee in 2016 to the effect that the Railways should not be asked to pay any dividend to the general exchequer. The Minister of Railways at the time also argued that the Railways was a 'strategic asset' but 'in deep trouble for long'. The Lok Sabha adopted the resolution. The Railways has not paid any dividend for the past four years. The year 2020–21 turned out to be the worst, with the Railways forced to keep its passenger business largely suspended on account of COVID-19. Instead of expecting any dividend on investments of over Rs 10 lakh crore made in the Railways, the government had to give a special loan of Rs 90,000 crore to keep the Railways afloat.

National Highways Authority of India (NHAI) is also a continuously loss-making organization. As it keeps its own commercial system of accounting, the loss it incurs every year remains unknown. Every expenditure incurred in constructing roads is capitalized and no depreciation is charged. NHAI has been monetizing some road assets through the Toll, Operate and Transfer (TOT) system. It has stated that it would also adopt the system of transferring road assets to infrastructure investment trusts (INVITs). However, how much capital loss it makes on each TOT or INVIT transfer remains completely opaque. The government funds NHAI by transferring part of the infrastructure and road cess collected. What is quite clear is that fund transfer to NHAI has been a one-way street. NHAI has never and is never expected to pay any dividend on the equity provided by the government.

PSBs used to make dividend payment to the Government of India until 2015–16, in the days when the practice of evergreening NPAs was the norm. After the asset quality review in 2016, when the true state of non-performing loans came up, PSBs went into large losses. They have paid no dividend to the government since 2017–18. Instead, the government has been putting more and more money into them by using the recapitalization route.

The short point is that the equity investments made by the government in the past couple of years are going to public enterprises that are neither generating growth for the country nor any returns to the government. These equity investments are more like grants to cover losses and expenditures than investment.

CPSEs Are in Terminal Decline

CPSEs are commercial enterprises owned by the government. Most have been entrusted to non-civil servant managers, though some are run as departmental undertakings directly by civil servants.

The British organized the first government enterprises, the Railways and Post Office, which are still run as departmental undertakings. India had only five undertakings that could be called Central government enterprises at the time of Independence. However, that number grew massively in pursuance of a socialist pattern of society after Independence, which muzzled the private sector and saw the public sector growing in the most significant and capital-intensive segments of the economy.

CPSEs grew organically and inorganically (by nationalization) from the 1950s to 1980s. The 2018–19 survey classifies them in four major sectors—agriculture; mining and exploration; manufacturing, processing and generation; and services—and twenty industry/services groups. More than half the over Rs 25 lakh crore of gross turnover is contributed by petroleum (refinery and marketing) at Rs 13.84 lakh crore. Almost all operating CPSEs were set up before 1990.

The year 1991 marked a watershed for CPSEs. With every sector of the economy being opened again for the private sector, the government did not establish new CPSEs, except in financial and some other services. The CPSEs are losing share of value added every year.

There are a few sectors where CPSEs still have a share of more than 50 per cent, such as coal mining, crude oil exploration and extraction, petroleum product marketing, railways and banking. Even in these sectors, their share is fast contracting. In banking, CPSEs are losing market share at the rate of about 3 per cent a year. In oil exploration, almost all new finds are in the private sector and if the plans to privatize BPCL go through, the presence of CPSEs in oil marketing will fast recede.

In a nutshell, CPSEs are in terminal decline.

Chapter Twelve

Disinvestment without Conviction

From Investment to Disinvestment

In the 1990s, once the era of economic liberalization started, the policy on public-sector enterprises got reset from investment to disinvestment. In 1991–92 itself, minority stakes in thirty-one Public Sector Undertakings (PSUs) were disinvested for an amount of Rs 3038 crore. The policy of minority stake sale continued throughout the 1990s, with some amount being raised in eight out of nine years until 1999–2000.

The first Disinvestment Commission was established in 1996 to place the process on a more serious footing, including considering cases for 'strategic sale' (another name for real privatization, with the government selling majority stake in the CPSE and it becoming a private entity thereafter). A separate Department of Disinvestment was set up in 1999.

The first strategic sale/privatization transaction took place in 1999–2000 when the government realized the first consideration of Rs 105.45 crore. The strategic sale was the policy of the government during the first NDA term when the bulk of privatization that has taken place until today was concluded. Major CPSEs like Bharat Aluminium (BALCO), CMC Ltd, Hindustan Zinc, Indian Petrochemicals Corporation Ltd (IPCL), Maruti Suzuki and Videsh Sanchar Nigam Ltd (VSNL) were privatized. This policy was stalled when the UPA government came to power in 2004 with the government reverting to minority stake sale. No privatization transaction took place in the ten years of the UPA government (2004–2014).

The NDA government reverted to the policy of strategic sale in 2015 and has attempted a few transactions. However, there has not been a single success in the past six years other than sales of government stake in a CPSE to another CPSE or a group of CPSEs. In 2018–19, HPCL was sold to ONGC. In 2019–20, REC was sold to PFC. In 2019–20, there were three strategic sale transactions (Tehri Hydro, North East Power and Kamarjar Port Ltd). All three companies ended up being bought by other CPSEs. These transactions did not lead to any privatization; in fact, the government did not even transfer management control to the buyer CPSEs. In a way, for the buyer, it was only a financial investment with real management control still remaining with the government.

The government signalled a real intent for strategic sale in November 2019 when it announced the sale of three CPSEs: BPCL, CONCOR and SCI. However, it could not complete these transactions in financial year 2019–20.

2020–21 Proved to Be a Washout for Disinvestment

The government had decided upon the highest-ever target of Rs 2.1 lakh crore to be raised from proceeds of disinvestment in 2020–21. This was set at over four times the actual receipts of only Rs 50,304 crore in 2019–20. In fact, the 2020–21 targets are way above the best performances of Rs 1,00,045 crore in 2017–18 and Rs 94,727 crore in 2018–19.

The first six months literally got washed out in the lockdown with crash of equity prices, complete disarray in CPSE valuations and general distraction in the government.

The government resumed minority stake sale with a 15 per cent stake sale in Hindustan Aeronautics Ltd in August 2020 and Bharat Dynamics Ltd in September 2020. These issues garnered about Rs 5700 crore. The Bharat Dynamics stake sale was not fully subscribed and the government could only offload 12.82 per cent. These were the only two transactions conducted in the first six months of financial year 2020–21.

Four strategic sales were announced in financial year 2019–20: BPCL, Air India, CONCOR and SCI. The Air India sale was mainly to stop the operating sclerosis, with the government likely to write off much of equity and almost all the debt. However, BPCL, CONCOR and SCI were expected to garner more than Rs 75,000 crore from their stake sale. The Expression of Interest (EOI) for BPCL was first invited on 7 March 2020 and was postponed quite a few times. The last postponement was until 30 September 2020. Finally, the government received EOI for BPCL on 1 December 2020, though only three parties submitted their interest. These EOIs remained awaiting evaluation until December during financial year 2020–21. The EOI for CONCOR could not be issued during the year, while the invitation for SCI was issued in August 2020. EOI for Air India was also received in December. The government did not disclose the interested parties during the financial year. None of these strategic sales could proceed beyond issue of the preliminary memorandum and receipt of EOIs in two of the companies during the year.

The stake sale of LIC, though only a minority stake sale, was another major item on the disinvestment agenda during the year. This required quite a few amendments in the LIC Act. There are also some major issues connected to the valuation of LIC. The government placed the requisite amendments in the LIC Act by way of the Finance Bill, 2021. The issue of valuation could not be sorted out during the year. The LIC issue also remained on hold during 2020–21 and did not make any meaningful progress.

The government could realize only Rs 5781 crore until September 2020 against the mammoth target of Rs 2.10 lakh crore and Rs 18,896 crore until December 2020. Faced with the ground reality, the strategic sale in BPCL, CONCOR and SCI not proceeding very well and the LIC stake sale unlikely to materialize during the year, the target of Rs 2.10 lakh crore was scaled down to Rs 32,000 crore in Budget 2021–22 for revised estimates of 2020–21. Finally, the government realized only around Rs 38,000 during the year, inclusive of sales of evacuee property shares and the Specified Undertaking of Unit Trust of India (SUUTI) shares sale.

The year 2020–21 proved to be a washout for privatization and disinvestment of public-sector enterprises and banks.

Minority Stake Sale Strategy Policy Has Not Worked

Assuming that about two-thirds of the share capital of the seventy-four listed CPSEs is held by the Government of India, the value of the shares attributable to it is about Rs 9 lakh crore. At 80 per cent of shares held by the government, the value attributable goes up to a little less than Rs 11 lakh crore.

The first major realization that needs to be accepted while designing a divestment strategy is that there is not much juice left to be extracted if the government were to retain a 50 per cent shareholding—this would bring the value of its shareholding to Rs 6.82 lakh crore. If the total value of government shares is about Rs 9 lakh crore, only about Rs 2 lakh crore can be realized at best even if all government stake beyond 50 per cent in the seventy-four companies is sold.

The actual situation is much worse. Government shareholding in ONGC, the company with the largest market capitalization of about Rs 92,000 crore, is only 60.41 per cent. In PowerGrid Corporation, which comes in second with market capitalization of Rs 90,000 crore, government shareholding is only 51.34 per cent. In NTPC, too, it is only about 51 per cent. In SBI, with market capitalization of Rs 1.74 lakh crore, government stake is only 57.64 per cent. It is in the dud stocks with low market capitalization where the government's share is large, in many cases exceeding 90 per cent.

These shareholding patterns starkly reveal that the government is not left with much shareholding above 50 per cent in the most capitalized CPSEs—the four companies mentioned above share over 35 per cent of total market capitalization. However, in these companies, the government is left with only about 5 per cent of total market capitalization, or about Rs 25,000 crore.

The policy of minority stake sale is not getting us anywhere.

Selling Stakes Below 50 Per Cent and Retaining Management Control Has Not Worked Either

The government announced in Budget 2019–20 that it would be 'open' to retaining management control 'to below 51 per cent to an appropriate level on a case-to-case basis' where deemed necessary. Further, it also 'decided to modify the present policy of retaining 51 per cent government stake to retaining 51 per cent stake inclusive of the stake of government-controlled institutions'.

This announcement marked a threefold deviation from the earlier policy of selling only minority stake. First, the government was open to make a strategic sale or privatize by going below a 51 per cent stake, which included selling complete stake as well. Second, wherever it was necessary to retain management control, it could go below 51 per cent but retain management control. Third, it was also agreeable in policy to apply the 51 per cent threshold taking the composite stake of the government and the government-controlled institutions into consideration.

By announcing a total stake in BPCL, after taking out the Numaligarh Refinery, a stake sale of 30.8 per cent of a total stake of 54 per cent in CONCOR and its entire stake of 63.75 per cent in SCI, the government has rolled out the first part of the policy: stake sale with management control by divesting total stake or retaining less than 26 per cent.

The other two components of the policy—considering the stake of the government and government-controlled institutions together for the purpose of a 51 per cent stake, and going below 51 per cent but retaining management control—seem to have been abandoned. Instead, the policy seems to be shifting to total stake sale without retaining management control.

Proposal to Privatize Non-Strategic PSUs in May 2020

In May 2020, Finance Minister Nirmala Sitharaman spoke about a new PSU privatization policy as part of her announcements under the Atmanirbhar stimulus package of Rs 21 lakh crore. She stated that the government would privatize public-sector enterprises in 'non-strategic sectors'. She further announced that a list of strategic sectors would be announced soon and that even in these sectors, only one to four public-sector enterprises would remain. The government did not follow up on the announcement for quite some time. In August 2020, there was speculation in the media that the government had identified eighteen sectors as strategic.

The debate about strategic and non-strategic sectors of the economy, in a certain sense, is phoney. In the heydays of policy preference for the socialistic pattern of society during the 1950s to 1980s, the industrial policy resolutions enforced by IDRA and licencing policies had identified several sectors as 'strategic'. As only the public sector was permitted to establish new enterprises in these large sectors of economy, investment and operational performance of the economy in these sectors suffered massively. These policies and laws, which produced the so-called low Hindu rate of growth and had an adverse impact on growth and development, have been gradually done away with after liberalization in 1991. From the vast list of several sectors identified as strategic in 1951, only two sectors remain currently classified as strategic under the industrial policies and laws of the country.

The CPSE survey classifies the CPSEs into four sectors and twenty cognate groups. The twenty groups are agro-based industries in the agriculture sector, coal, crude oil and 'other minerals and metals' in the mining and exploration sector, steel, petroleum (refinery and marketing), fertilizers, chemicals and pharmaceuticals, heavy and medium engineering, transportation vehicle and equipment, industrial and consumer goods, textiles and power generation in the manufacturing, processing and generation sector and power transmission, trading and marketing, transport and logistics, contract and construction and technical advisory services, hotel and tourist services, financial services and telecommunication and IT in the services sector.

The phoney nature of the strategic and non-strategic sector debate becomes apparent when one looks at the first question: Is any sector truly strategic from the perspective of the economy or CPSEs? The economy-wide approach to identify strategic sectors has been abandoned in the past thirty years, with good results. In each of the twenty groups recorded in the CPSE survey, the private sector has emerged strongly with the public sector fast losing market share. Therefore, the presence of CPSEs cannot serve any exclusive national objective in any of these economic sectors. Therefore, there cannot be any further classification of any sector as strategic from the economy's perspective.

Can some sectors be strategic from the CPSE perspective? No CPSE wants to be privatized. If you ask the management of CPSEs and the administrative ministries that control them, they would like their sector to be classified as strategic, not from any strategic angle but simply to ward off the possibility of sale. The Ministry of Power would argue that power generation, power transmission and even power distribution are all strategic. PSBs, even when they have been lending to industry and infrastructure and are increasingly getting drowned in non-performing loans, would also argue that banking is a strategic sector. They would be duly supported by the Department of Financial Services. When the government has permitted private-sector refiners and is offering BPCL, which has considerable refinery and distribution capacity, for privatization, can oil refining and marketing be called strategic? When power-sector generation is primarily taking place in the renewable sector and the private sector, how can power generation be strategic? Is telecom strategic enough to retain MTNL and BSNL in the public sector when the proportion of subscribers they serve is less than 10 per cent?

There is no sector in which CPSEs are operating that is strategic; no CPSE that is strategic; and no objective criterion that can be evolved to define any sector or CPSE as strategic. It leads nowhere. Of course, if you do not want to privatize a particular CPSE, you can always take the shelter of calling it strategic. If you don't want to privatize, don't do it but do not take shelter under the excuse of calling any sector or CPSE strategic.

Section II: Factors of Production

Chapter Thirteen

State of Land Resources

Land is the First Asset Class

An asset produces an income or saves expenditure. Most real assets like land, buildings and machines are employed in the production of goods and services. Real assets contribute to value addition, which is part of the GVA and GDP. Financial assets like equity and debt generate financial income. Some real assets like house property not used for one's own residential purposes also behave like financial assets. Financial assets also contribute income by their rising valuation.

Earth was a silent factor of production before human labour made it an active factor of production by converting forests and grasslands into agricultural fields to produce crops, vegetables, fruits and clothing to sustain human life and make it better. Land is the first asset humanity thus 'created'. Wild land got turned into agricultural land and residential land where humans built houses/shelters to live in and keep their domesticated animals. In due course, the ownership of agricultural and residential land got recognized as private assets owned by individuals, families, estates and communities. Land became the basis of human settlements; it provided food and produced income from surplus crops. Human civilization took root.

Over the millennia, agricultural lands got concentrated in fewer hands. Estates symbolized the concentration of the asset in a fewer number of people. The majority of people, in many countries, turned to work on lands owned by others in their estates or farms and got transformed into another factor of production: labour. Land and labour were the two principal factors of production in preindustrial societies. Over time, ownership of land, being the only real asset, became the manifestation of wealth.

Buildings constructed over land became the new real asset class. Industrialization led to further accumulation of capital in even fewer hands. In fact, land and buildings still remain a dominant part of the assets and wealth portfolio of the rich.

Land Use in Agriculture

The Ministry of Agriculture conducts land use surveys. As per the data available for the year 2015–16, the reporting area for land utilization was 307.75 million hectares of the total geographical area of India of 328.73 million hectares.

Land utilization is classified in nine broad categories.

The largest amount of land is used for sowing crops. The net sown area was reported to be 139.51 million hectares in 2015–16, which is in line with the decadal average of a little over 140 million hectares. There are two other categories of land considered fit for agriculture. These are fallow lands (agricultural lands that are kept uncultivated) and other uncultivated lands, excluding fallow lands. Fallow lands were reported to be 26.72 million hectares in 2015–16 and other uncultivated lands excluding fallow lands were counted as 25.64 million hectares. If we add up the net area sown, fallow lands and other uncultivated lands excluding fallow lands, total 'agriculturable' land becomes 191.87 million hectares, which is over 62 per cent of the reporting land mass of India.

The reporting land mass is also classified in two other categories: forest and land not available for cultivation. Forest land was recorded to be 71.87 million hectares, 23.35 per cent of the total reporting land mass.

The land classified as not available for cultivation was recorded at 44.02 million hectares, a share of 14.30 per cent. This land is further subdivided into two categories: area under non-agricultural uses and barren and unculturable land. The area under non-agricultural use was recorded at 27.08 million hectares, or about 8.8 per cent.

Built-Up Land is Still Much Smaller

Total built-up area—factories, roads, buildings—represent the land used by the non-agricultural economy. According to a satellite-based study titled 'History of Land Use in India during 1980–2010', published in the journal *Global and Planetary Change* in 2014, the total area occupied by buildings, roads and railways (all the built-up area) was only 2.04 million hectares—the area under crops was stated to be 140 million hectares in the study. Total built-up area under buildings was less than 0.7 per cent of the country's reporting land mass.

The Ministry of Agriculture, as we noted above, places about 27 million hectares as 'area under non-agricultural uses'. The definition of 'area under non-agricultural uses' is however much wider than the definition of 'built-up area' as it covers lands under rivers, water bodies, parks, social forestry and so on. As the land statistics published by the Ministry of Agriculture do not specifically carve out built-up land, we can assume India's built-up area is somewhat higher than the 2.04 million hectares confirmed by satellite data—let's say about 3 million hectares or about 1 per cent of total land area of the country.

Meanwhile, according to the land use statistics published by the Ministry of Agriculture and the satellite imagery-based numbers quoted in the study, agricultural crops occupy about 140 million hectares, which is 45 per cent of reporting land area. Land under cultivation has expanded from about 115 million hectares in 1950. As irrigation facilities have expanded, including double-cropped area, total cropped area is approximately 200 million hectares now.

Agriculture, mining and other directly land-based productive activities contribute only 20 per cent of India's GDP. The rest of the economy, which uses 1 per cent of the land mass, contributes 80 per cent. The productivity of land use in non-agriculture and agriculture thus gives a ratio of approximately 1:200.

The Government of India Owns More than a Million Hectares of Land

The Government of India created a system of collecting information about the land owned and controlled by different ministries, departments, PSUs and other public entities. In October 2017, it released information about such owned and controlled land. It revealed that the Government of India owned 13505.44 sq. km. of land, or 1.35 million hectares.

The Railways owned 2929.6 sq. km., the Ministry of Coal and related companies owned 2580.92 sq. km., the Ministry of Power and its enterprises owned 1806.69 sq. km., Heavy Industries and Public Enterprises owned 1209.49 sq. km. and Ministry of Shipping owned 1146 sq. km. The Ministries of Steel, Agriculture, Home Affairs, Human Resources Department and Defence owned lands between 300 and 600 sq. km.

That the land owned by the government is substantial can be gauged by the fact that built-up land in India, as per satellite surveys, was only 2.04 million hectares in 2010. While a good part of the land said to be owned by the Government of India or central public-sector undertakings is for mining leases, the land owned by the Ministry of Railways and Ministry of Heavy Industries and Public Enterprises, which is good for industrial and residential development, exceeds 0.4 million hectares.

Chapter Fourteen

First-Generation Land Reforms

India at Independence: A Poor Country with Low Per-Capita Land

The Indian population was 360 million in 1951. That year, net land area sown was a little less than 120 million hectares of a total reporting area of about 305 million hectares. On average, Indians had only 0.85 hectares of land per capita. Compared to any other part of the world, the country had a very small per-capita availability of agricultural land.

More than 82 per cent of Indians (295 million of a total counted population of 357 million in the 1951 Census) lived in rural areas. The Census counted 104 million Indians as self-supporting—those who depended on income generated by themselves. About 70 per cent of self-supporting persons (71 million) derived their income from cultivation of land. Thus, land was the principal source of livelihood for about 75 per cent of Indian households.

In the 1951 Census classification, these 71 million people dependent upon cultivation of land were classified in three categories: 'owner-cultivators', 'unowned-cultivators' or cultivators cultivating lands of others, and 'cultivating labourers'. About 46 million (64 per cent) cultivated land wholly or primarily owned by them. These were owner-cultivators. Only 8.8 million (12 per cent) people were cultivating lands that were wholly or primarily owned by others—they were 'tenant cultivators'. There were 15 million (21 per cent) cultivating labourers. There was one more class of people dependent on land. There were 1.6 million (2.3 per cent) self-supporting persons who depended on the rent incomes from the land. These were 'non-cultivating owners of land', also described as 'agricultural rent receivers'.

Real GVA at factor cost in agriculture, forestry, mining and quarrying at current prices was Rs 5274 crore in 1951 (53 per cent of total GVA of Rs 10,036 crore). The per-capita income of 295 million people living in rural areas in 1950–51 was only about Rs 180. Too many people living in rural areas dependent upon land cultivation and earning a very low income was the root cause of India's abject poverty at the time of Independence. Poverty, malnutrition and disease were rampant in rural India.

The country also inherited a highly lopsided distribution of land. A great majority of people, the peasants, worked on lands controlled by relatively fewer landlords. They earned a pittance as wages and small share in produce for their backbreaking work. Much of the crop or proceeds of the crop went to the landlords and the government as revenue. Too little per-capita availability of land, also unevenly distributed, provided fertile ground to create widespread sentiments of class injustice in the country.

Land Reforms Find No Mention in the Constitution

As the ruling party the Indian National Congress (INC), the Constituent Assembly and the leadership did not develop a commonly shared understanding of the land reform agenda even in the years immediately following Independence, no land reform agenda was built into the Constitution. There was no declaration about the abolition of the zamindari system and establishing a direct relationship between the state and the tiller of the land in the document. Nor were there any provisions about agriculture ceiling or converting tillers' tenancy rights into ownership.

The Constitution only incorporated two related aspirations in the directive principles of state policy—even these did not refer to land reforms and agriculture directly. Article 39 (b) enjoined the state to direct its policy towards securing 'that the ownership and control of material resources of the community are so distributed as best to subserve the common good'. And Article 39 (c) expected the state to ensure 'that the operation of economic system does not result in the concentration of wealth and means of production to the common detriment'.

Land was a provincial subject in the 1935 Government of India Act. It was continued as a state subject in the Constitution. The placement of land in the State List and lack of assignment of any specific role to the Central government with respect to land reforms in the Constitution resulted in the Centre not having any formal leadership role in matters concerning land reforms.

It Took Twenty-Five Years to Build Consensus on Land Ceiling Reforms

A Congress Agrarian Reforms Committee was appointed in 1947 with J.C. Kumarappa as chairman. It made clear recommendations on removal of intermediaries and conferring tenurial rights, but not explicitly on land ceilings.

The Planning Commission appointed a Panel on Land Reforms under the chairmanship of Gulzarilal Nanda in May 1955. It recommended that the family be taken as the real operative unit in land ownership; for this purpose, the aggregate area held by all members of a family should be taken into account. The panel defined family widely to consist of husband, wife, dependent sons and daughters and grandchildren, and exclude land held by married daughters and earning sons.

This Commission was, however, quite generous in recommending exclusion of several categories of landholders from the ceiling: sugarcane farms owned by sugar factories, orchards, plantations, special farms such as cattle breeding and dairy farms, farms in a compact block, efficient, mechanized farms and farms with heavy investment. The appropriate basic unit for land ceiling, definition of family, exemptions from the ceiling and related issues remained undecided for a long time.

In August 1971, a Central Land Reforms Committee (CLRC) was constituted with Fakhruddin Ali Ahmed, then minister of food and agriculture, as chairman. It recommended that the ceiling on landholding should be applicable to the family as a whole; the term 'family' being defined to include husband, wife and minor children only. CLRC recommended fixing a ceiling for a family of five within a range of

10 to 18 acre for various categories of land. It recommended an absolute ceiling for a family of five at 54 acre. It also recommended withdrawal of exemptions in favour of mechanized and well-managed farms.

These recommendations of CLRC were reviewed by another high-powered committee (HPC), which disagreed with CLRC on the crucial issue of definition of family. The HPC was of the view that ceiling should be applied to a family of five as a unit, consisting of husband, wife and three children, whether major or minor. Major sons were to be included in the family unit of five. It also recommended that if the members in a family were less than five, the ceiling should be reduced by one-fifth per person. Going with the CLRC's broad thrust, the HPC recommended that exemptions be further restricted by rigidly defining plantations and withdrawing blanket exemptions in case of lands held by trusts, institutions, etc.

Land Ceiling Finally Implemented

The Government of India finally released its guidelines to the states on land ceiling in 1971–72. The Constitution was also amended in 1971 to replace the requirement of paying 'compensation' for acquiring land in excess of ceiling by an 'amount' to be fixed by laws, which were also made non-challengeable by putting such laws in the Ninth Schedule of the Constitution. The states enacted their land ceiling laws building on these guidelines and aligning their laws with the new constitutional mandate regarding compensation. States that had enacted land ceiling laws earlier modified them.

For determining the level of ceiling, the guidelines suggested broad principles and left actual determination to the states. They proposed that a 'family holding' may be considered from two aspects: as an operational unit, and as an area of land that can yield a certain average income. If the states found it difficult to correlate a family holding to a given level of income adjusted to a supposed level of prices, they could exercise their judgement to decide the area of land that might be declared a family holding. They were also delegated the authority to decide whether the ceiling should apply to individual holdings or to holdings of families; and, especially in the latter case, the basis on which the size of the family should be allowed in the application of the ceiling.

These guidelines paved the way for implementation of agricultural land ceiling in the country. The Punjab Land Reforms Act was enacted in 1972 and The Rajasthan Imposition of Ceiling on Agricultural Holding Act in 1973. Many other states followed. States that had enacted land ceiling laws earlier brought these in line with the new guidelines and constitutional provisions. The Tamil Nadu Land Reforms (Fixation of Ceiling on Land) Act, 1961, was modified in 1970 and ceilings made applicable from 1970. Maharashtra had also adopted land ceilings in 1961, which were extensively modified in the 1970s.

In all, the states declared 2.7 million hectares land as surplus, i.e., the land in excess of land ceiling. Of this declared surplus, 2.3 million (87 per cent) hectares were possessed and 1.9 million hectares distributed to 5.5 million households (37 per cent to scheduled castes [SCs] and 16 per cent to scheduled tribes [STs]).

The land ceiling issue was largely forgotten after the 1980s. A Committee on Land Reforms appointed by the United Progressive Alliance (UPA) government in 2008 last reviewed the matter. It quoted estimates made by the Lal Bahadur Shastri National Academy of Administration (LBSNAA), which reckoned that the potential ceiling surplus land in India was about 21 million hectares. If these estimates are taken as accurate, the land in excess of ceilings acquired and distributed was less than 10 per cent of the potential. Lamenting the lack of progress in the implementation of land ceiling after the 1980s, the Committee on Land Reforms vigorously argued for taking up the ceiling reform agenda again. However, its report did not make any progress.

The Planning Commission captured the policy flipflop in designing and implementing land reforms most poignantly. In its report in 1973, its Task Force noted: 'In no sphere of public activity in our country since Independence has the hiatus between the precept and practice, between policy pronouncements and actual execution, been as great as in the domain of land reforms.'

Conferring 'Ownership' Rights on Tillers and Abolition of Intermediaries, By and Large, Completed in the 1950s and 1960s

Traditionally, land belonged to the king or his latter-day replacement, the republican state. In olden times, peasants had the permission of the state to till the land on the pain of paying tax, usually a part of the produce. As agriculture grew, kings and states started granting ownership/rights to landlords to get the land tilled, collect taxes and pay it to the treasury.

Two systems defining the relationships of the tillers of the land with the states were quite prominent in India at the time of Independence.

First, in large parts of the country, especially under what came to be known as the zamindari system (prevalent in West Bengal, Orissa and a few other states), the intermediary or zamindars enjoyed considerable ownership rights in the land given by the state. Farmers were given permission to till assigned lands and pay the tax to the zamindar, who would in turn pay a part of it to the state at the rates specified by the government. These farmers had no ownership of the land they tilled; they did not have any permanent right of tenancy and could be ejected at the will of the zamindar. These peasants, thus, had no direct relationship with the state in any manner.

Second, in the rest of the country, under the ryotwari system, there was no formal intermediary and the farmer was ostensibly in a direct relationship of tax payment with the state. However, in practice, there were numerous intermediaries, acting under different authorities granted and assumed, who lorded over the farmers. The tenurial standing of the farmer was also not very clear and coded in laws.

States started enacting their land tenancy laws in 1948. Erstwhile Bombay State passed its land tenancy law in 1948, which later became applicable to Maharashtra and Gujarat. Rajasthan passed its law in 1955 and the longstanding Bihar Tenancy Act, 1885, was amended in the 1950s and 1960s to provide for tenancy, land consolidation and other reforms.

West Bengal, under the Left Front government, went one step further. Sharecropping was a very common arrangement in rural India.

The farmer would take land from the recorded landowner and pay a share of the produce to the owner; the share depended on several factors, such as who would provide inputs, etc.

As land leasing was illegal in almost the entire country, the sharecropping system was completely informal. West Bengal decided to convert sharecropper cultivators (called *bargadars*) into permanent tenants. About 1.5 million bargadars were provided permanent tenancy in Operation Barga in the state, which concluded sometime in the 1980s.

The legislations abolishing the zamindari system and intermediaries achieved a significant transformation of the countryside by enlarging the base of land ownership. As a result of the implementation of these laws, ownership of nearly 40 per cent of cultivable land was transferred to direct producers. Further, under the tenancy laws, nearly 12.4 million tenants obtained secured rights or ownership rights over an area of 6.16 million hectares (i.e., about 4.4 per cent of cultivated area).

Agricultural Land Situation at the End of the 1980s

Bringing more land under agriculture was the stated policy of the government in the first forty years after Independence. In the enthusiasm to distribute as much land as possible, land that was not quite suitable for agriculture was also allotted to farmers and landless labourers in the hope that these lands would expand agriculture in the country.

On the eve of Independence, the state owned vast tracts of land, to which were added large areas of uncultivated wastelands taken over during abolition of intermediaries. These lands were classified as 'lands which are degraded and cannot fulfil their life-sustaining potential'. The total area of wastelands was estimated to be 63.85 million hectares, 20.17 per cent of total geographical area. Some of these wastelands were also allotted to the landless. Till March 2002, 5.97 million hectares of wastelands have been distributed to the landless poor.

Agricultural land grew by about 20 million hectares to reach an average of about 140 million hectares in the 1970s. It has pretty much stayed at that level for the past four decades. Net irrigated area was smaller at 21 million hectares in 1950; it grew to 48 million hectares at the end of 1990. India's population increased to about 900 million in 1990. Per-capita availability of agricultural land came down to about 0.15 hectares in 2011.

First-Generation Land Reforms Were a Mixed Bag

India's track record of land reforms in the period 1947–1990 was mixed.

While impressive land reforms took place in the matter of conferring tenancy/ownership rights to tillers and abolition of intermediaries, the land ceiling laws failed to meet their objectives.

Under the tenancy laws passed by all the states, farmers were conferred permanent tenancy rights over the lands they tilled or possessed. And the abolition of intermediaries marked the end of an iniquitous era.

Meanwhile, the agriculture land ceiling laws were at best a partial success. Only a small amount of land in excess of the ceiling (the surplus land) was actually acquired and distributed. The entire matter was almost relegated to the background by the end of the 1980s. On the other hand, the urban land ceiling laws were an abject failure.

The first generation of land reforms, with whatever successes they achieved and failures encountered, were mostly over by the end of the 1980s.

Chapter Fifteen

State of Labour and Employment

Human labour produces all economic goods and services, using skills, tools and technology. Thus, labour plays a preeminent and critical role in the economic system, production of GDP and consumption of all goods and services sold in the economy.

In the agricultural age, the labour force used physical energy and manual skills, both natural endowments, to work the land. Acquisition of more skills and invention of some tools enabled the labour force to be more productive and branch out into the handicraft and handloom segments. After the invention of the steam engine and electricity, machines became more powerful and expanded the range of goods produced, leading to a transfer of labour from agriculture to industry. At some stage, machines started to substitute human labour. However, the advancement of the industrial economy gave rise to the requirement of numerous services: retail, finance, construction, and so on. Labour started plateauing in industry and getting absorbed in services. In the latest edition of technological advancement, especially the onset of digital technologies, a lot of service work is being done more efficiently and productively by digital programmes and applications and through the Internet. There has been a significant substitution of human labour in traditional services as well on account of increased use of digital technologies.

The requirements of the digital age are leading to several new services for consumption and investment. However, with agriculture, industry and services requiring much less human labour, we are likely to witness an epochal change. There is a lot of concern and debate about the future of work. Questions are being raised about the availability of work for all the labour in the world.

We should look at the emerging situation carefully. If necessary, humanity should get ready to accept that the full employment of the labour force would not be needed to produce all the goods and services required for human consumption. It might become necessary for governments to frame policies to deal with excess labour.

Understanding Employment

In 1947, all member countries of the ILO agreed (some upgradation was made in 1982) on certain basic definitions and understandings of labour. A broad construct of employment and unemployment was created. All people above the age of fifteen are now (earlier people in the age group of fifteen to sixty-four) considered part of the 'working age' population. This working age population is divided into two broad sub-groups of being 'in the labour force' and 'not in labour force'. The working age population recorded as being in the labour force is considered the 'economically active population'. Those in the labour force or the economically active population who get jobs are considered employed and those who do not get jobs are considered unemployed or 'not employed'. The labour force thus comprises two sets of workers: 'employed' and 'not employed or unemployed'.

These definitions enable understanding of key relationships of labour, employment and jobs in the economy. The definitions of total population, working age population, population in labour force, population employed and population unemployed depict the state of labour, employment and unemployment in the economy. The ratio of population of age fifteen and above to the total population gives the working age population ratio.

Let us take India's population as on 31 December 2020 to be 138 crore and the population aged fifteen and above at 103 crore. In such a case, the working age would be 103 crore and the ratio of working age population to total population 74.63 per cent. The ratio of population in the working age willing to work to the working age population gives the ratio of population in the labour force. If we further assume that 41 crore out of 103 crore working age people in India were willing to work in December 2020, the labour force would be equal to 41 crore and the ratio of labour force to working age population would be 39.8 per cent. This also implies that 60.2 per cent of the working age population is not interested in working, for whatever reasons. The people in the labour force may get employment or they may not. The proportion of the workforce not employed gives the unemployment rate. In our example, if 3 crore out of the labour force of 41 crore did not get employment in the month of December 2020, the unemployment rate would be 7.3 per cent. The employment rate is computed with reference to working age persons. In our example, 38 crore persons got employment in December (41 crore labour force; 3 crore unemployed). The proportion of 38 crore (labour employed) and 103 crore (working age population) gives the employment ratio. In this example, the employment rate would be 36.89 per cent.

The unemployment rate is the proportion of the unemployed to the labour force, not working age population. This signifies the proportion of people in the active labour force who are not able to find employment. The number of people in the working age population but not in the active workforce indicates the reservoir of employable people not interested or able to join the workforce.

ILO measures another important relationship. All workers who are able to find some work—even an hour a week—are considered employed as per the definition of employed and unemployed. There are many workers who want to work longer hours than the employment they get. Such workers are 'underemployed'. Similarly, there are quite a few workers who are not currently seeking work on a temporary basis and therefore not part of the workforce but are otherwise interested in working. These are 'potential' workers. These two categories of workers—those who are underemployed and the potential labour force—when added to the unemployed offer the measure of total underutilized labour.

The universe of workers comprises all economic spheres of production and all workers, whether in paid employment or self-employment.

ILO counted the global working age population at 5.7 billion in 2019; 3.5 billion or 61 per cent of this population was in the labour force and 2.3 billion, or 39 per cent, were not. Of the 3.5 billion workers in the labour force, 3.3 billion were employed (57 per cent of the working age population) and 188 million were unemployed (4 per cent). The unemployment rate (unemployed/workforce) was 5.4 per cent. Total labour underutilized was 473 million, about 14 per cent.

The employment to population ratio is gradually reducing worldwide for the past twenty-five years. It reduced 0.8 per cent during 1994–99, and 1 per cent during 1999–2004, 2004–09 and 2009–14. The reduction rate declined to 0.6 per cent in 2014–19. Even before COVID-19, the ILO expected the employment rate to reduce by 1.1 per cent in 2019–2024. The proportion of population to total working age population has declined by about 4.5 per cent in the past twenty-five years.

India Measures Labour Employment and Unemployment Quite Poorly

The country's official data collection on labour and employment status is abysmal. India used to conduct large sample-sized, five-year employment and unemployment surveys as part of the National Sample Survey (NSS) rounds. This quinquennial employment survey started in the twenty-seventh NSS round (1972–73) and the ninth survey was conducted in 2011–2012. That survey has been discontinued; no such survey took place in 2016–17.

These five-year surveys were replaced by an Annual Employment-Unemployment Survey. The first such survey was conducted in 2010 and the last, the fifth, in 2015. The last survey reported labour force participation rate as 50.3 per cent, employment rate of 47.8 per cent and unemployment rate of 5.0 per cent.

These annual surveys were replaced in 2017 by the Periodic Labour Force Survey (PLFS), which was designed to estimate three key ratios of employment (worker-population ratio, labour force participation rate and unemployment rate) at an interval of three months in urban areas only. Employment status is measured on a daily, weekly and yearly basis.

PLFS was intended to measure these three key ratios on a weekly basis. The ninth quarterly PLFS was released on 9 September 2021 for the quarter October–December 2020.

The Centre for Monitoring Indian Economy (CMIE) conducts regular labour surveys called the Consumer Pyramids Household Survey, or CPHS. There is a key difference between PLFS and CPHS. While PLFS uses the international definition of treating workers as employed even if they worked for an hour any day in the past seven days, CPHS uses a more stringent definition of employment: working for not less than three hours on the day of the survey.

CPHS is the only survey in India that brings out three key labour ratios on a regular basis every week: worker participation rate, employment rate and weekly unemployment rate. This data is also provided on a monthly, quarterly and yearly basis. In India, we do not have official employment data for the COVID-19 period even at the end of March 2020, whereas very comprehensive data sets are available from CMIE.

Labour Participation Rate Peaked in the 1970s

Data from the Second Labour Commission on the labour participation rate (LPR) until 2000 suggests that it was the highest in 1977–78 in both rural and urban areas. LPR for men in rural and urban areas was recorded at 56.5 per cent and 54.3 per cent respectively in 1977–78. For women, it was recorded at 34.5 per cent and 18.3 per cent, respectively, in rural and urban areas. Combined LPR was 45.8 per cent in rural areas and 37.2 per cent in urban areas.

LPR has gradually declined from this level in the late 1970s. By 1999–2000, LPR for rural areas had declined to 42.3 per cent and 35.4 per cent for urban areas, a decline of about 3 per cent in rural areas and 2 per cent in urban areas. The decline in female LPR was more pronounced, falling by 4.1 per cent in rural areas to 30.2 per cent and by 3.6 per cent in urban areas to 30.2 per cent and 14.7 per cent, respectively.

GDP has been rising continuously, at a much higher rate in the 1980s and 1990s, indicating the expansion of economic activities. However, LPR has been declining. While this indicated an improvement in productivity, the potential of the economy to absorb labour was going down.

Women's Participation in Labour Force One of the Lowest in the World

In 2020, the global participation of women in the labour force (women who are either working or unemployed but seeking work) represented by female LPR was 46.9 per cent, as per the database maintained by ILO/World Bank. India's female LPR is merely 20.2 per cent. This means that only one in five women in the working age of over fifteen participates in the labour force. There are only a handful of countries—Algeria, Syria, Yemen and a few other Arab countries—that have a female LPR lower than India.

Indeed, female LPR in India has been declining significantly in the past fifteen years. From a peak of 31.9 per cent in 2005, it declined rapidly to 22.8 per cent in 2012. It has continued to decline thereafter, although at a slightly lower rate.

How long and to what level will LPR decline in India? Will we attain the dubious distinction of being the worst country where women do not work in the economy? Why have we confined our women to their homes? Will this not hold back India's growth, poverty reduction and population control? Should the trend not be reversed?

It is clearly time for Indian society and the government to adopt proactive policies to promote the participation of women in the workforce.

Another Disturbing Trend: NEET is Rising

Given rapid technological developments, both mechanical and digital, and the requirement to invest more in education and training, the youth (in the age group of fifteen to twenty-four) are expected to be in educational and training institutions or joining the labour force as and when they complete their relevant education. Youth who are neither in the workforce nor in educational and training institutions are measured as Not in Employment, Education and Training (NEET). This, in a manner, measures wasting youth in a country.

ILO's Annual Report 2020 counted 1.2 billion young persons in the age group fifteen to twenty-four in 2019; 429 million (36 per cent) of them were assessed to be in employment and 509 million (42 per cent) were found to be studying in educational and training institutions. The remaining 267 million (22 per cent) were in the NEET category. This is quite a worrying proportion. More young women (31 per cent) were in NEET than men (14 per cent).

For India, based on data available for 2018, NEET was as high as 30.4 per cent, implying that three out of every ten young men from fifteen to twenty-four were not in employment, education or training. While many were probably in preparation for examinations for government service or other pursuits, many others were probably idling away or even involved in unsocial activities. This also includes a large number of young women sitting idle at home, married or unmarried. There were 24.75 crore youth in India in 2019. This meant 7.5 crore young Indians were wasting themselves in unproductive activities that year.

Difficult Labour Situation Worsened after the Pandemic

As per PLFS 2019–2020 (July-June), the only available official data for the pre-pandemic period, labour force participation rate (LFPR) in India (rural and urban areas combined) was only 38.3 per cent as per current weekly status (CWS), employment ratio or worker population ratio (WPR) 35 per cent and unemployment rate only 3.4 per cent. This report covers the April–June period of the year 2020–21 when the first wave was at its peak. The report does not specifically bring out the impact on the labour situation in this period.

According to CMIE, the unemployment situation worsened drastically following the lockdown in March 2020. In the week ended 29 March 2020, the unemployment rate spiralled to 23.8 per cent. As the lockdown was rolled back over the next few months, the unemployment rate returned to a more normal level of 7 per cent by September 2020. LPR declined from 41.9 per cent in March 2020 to 35.6 per cent in April 2020; it was 42.7 per cent in 2019–20. LPR also recovered to rise to 40.5 per cent in July 2020, but still remained uncomfortably low at about 40 per cent in September 2020.

The ILO-modelled database, using the international definition, informs us that LPR in India has declined from 58.4 per cent in 1990 to a little over 49 per cent in 2020. Female LPR declined sharply from about 30 per cent in 1990 and 32 per cent in 2005 to a little over 20 per cent in 2020.

Proportion of Wage and Salaried Workers Also Low, Affirming Large-Scale Informality of the Economy

ILO classifies workers in four broad categories: wage and salaried workers; own account workers; contributing family workers; and employers. Own account workers are self-employed people who are not paid by any employer and who also do not employ any paid workers. They mostly work alone or sometimes with partners, like other family members. A contributing family worker typically works on a self-employment basis and not as a partner in an establishment of a family member. Employer-workers are self-employed but also employ one or more paid workers.

In 2019, 53 per cent of workers in the global workforce were wage and salaried workers, 34 per cent own account workers, 11 per cent contributing family members and only about 2 per cent were employers. The proportion of workers in wage and salaried employment in the world has been going up constantly. It rose from 44 per cent in 1990 to 48.5 per cent in 2010 and is near 53 per cent now.

India lags far behind the global average on these indicators. Only about 24 per cent of Indian workers were in wage and salaried jobs in 2020 as against the global average of 53 per cent. The share of workers with wage and salaried jobs, however, is rising at a good clip, having gone up from a measly 14.5 per cent in 1990 to 24 per cent in 2020. There has been an accelerated increase after 2010—it was only 16.7 per cent in 2010; in a decade, it rose to 24 per cent, virtually rising by 0.7 per cent every year.

Average Wage is Low

Official data on the wage profile of India's workers is not available after the 2011–12 National Employment and Unemployment Survey. Average wage in 2011–12 was assessed to be only Rs 247 per day, which was, at the average exchange rate of Rs 53 to a dollar in that year, a little less than $4.7 a day. A large part of India's labour force comprises own account workers and contributing self-employed family members. Their wages are simply not ascertainable. A good part of wage and salaried workers are also casual workers. The average wage of casual workers in 2011–12 was Rs 143 per day, or about $2.7.

In the lockdown imposed after COVID-19, the unemployment ratio fell quickly from about 25 per cent in April to about 7 per cent in September 2020. While LPR was somewhat lower in September 2020 compared to April 2020, the fact that the unemployment ratio fell to 7 per cent indicated that most of the over 10 crore labour who had become jobless after the lockdown had returned to work between July and September.

However, there was clear evidence of low wage distress among those who were employed. Millions are estimated to have lost salaried jobs and become casual workers. Even those who worked as casual workers earlier were reemployed at much lower wages. The spike in jobs under the Mahatma Gandhi National Rural Employment Guarantee Act (MGNREGA) programme also indicated the lowering of worker income.

Only Two Major Schemes Accounted for the Bulk of Labour Budget until 2018–19

The Ministry of Labour and Employment (MoLE) is primarily in charge of Central government schemes for welfare of labour. In all, it operated twenty-nine schemes in 2018–19 and spent Rs 9291 crore on them.

Two schemes—the Pradhan Mantri Rozgar Protsahan Yojana (PMRPY), with expenditure of Rs 3499 crore, and government contribution to the Employees' Pension Scheme, 1995 (EPS), with an expenditure of Rs 4900 crore—accounted for a total expenditure of Rs 8399 crore, which consumed 90 per cent of the entire budget expenditure of MoLE.

There was only one other programme—the umbrella labour welfare scheme—with an outlay of over Rs 100 crore, with the expenditure on welfare schemes amounting to Rs 236.26 crore. It provides for the welfare of *beedi* workers, cine workers and labour working in mica mines, iron/chrome/manganese ore mines and limestone and dolomite mines. It also includes funds allocated for the North-east and the SC and ST components. These allocations are funded from industry-specific cesses or are mandatory allocations for SCs and STs.

The remaining twenty-six programmes/heads of expenditure were too small to make any significant dent even on any particular aspect of labour welfare.

Contributory Pension Schemes for Unorganized Sector for Workers and Traders Unravelling

In financial year 2019–20, the government introduced two contributory new pension types of schemes for all unorganized sector workers (Pradhan Mantri Shram Yogi Mandhan or PM-SYM) and small traders and farmers (Pradhan Mantri Karma Yogi Mandhan or PM-KYM). The amount spent on these two schemes in 2019–20 was Rs 355.20 crore and Rs 155.87 crore. For financial year 2020–21, revised allocations of Rs 500 crore and Rs 180 crore have been made for these two schemes.

PM-SYM was launched on 5 March 2019, just before the announcement of the general elections for the Lok Sabha, after the provision for the scheme was made in the revised Budget for 2018–19. It provides for a monthly pension of Rs 3000 to unorganized sector workers in the age group of eighteen to forty, on self-declaration basis, provided they make a monthly contribution depending upon the age at which they join. For a worker who is twenty-nine, the monthly contribution is fixed at Rs 100 per month. The monthly contribution for the youngest worker (18 years) is Rs 55; for the oldest (forty years of age), it is Rs 200 per month.

The government has assumed major financial responsibility under the scheme. It is administered by LIC, which makes the investment of the corpus as per the investment pattern approved by the government. The government makes a contribution equal to that of the worker. It has also an underwritten shortfall, if any, in the corpus to discharge its pensionary obligations.

The government had stated that there were about 50 crore workers in the unorganized sector at the time of launching the scheme. By the end of the first full year of the operation of this scheme, a total of 43.64 lakh informal sector workers were registered under the scheme, a little less than 1 per cent of the targeted 50 crore. Enrolments under the scheme slowed down in financial year 2020–21. By 30 June 2020, enrolments increased to only 44.14 lakh and by 30 September 2020 to only 44.53 lakh. In six months, not even 1 lakh new workers registered for the PM-SYM. This might have been on account of the larger distress caused by COVID-19 and job losses caused by the lockdown. Even in the third quarter of 2020 (October–December) and fourth quarter (January–March), the enrolments did not pick up. The number of workers enrolled as on

31 March 2021, as per the numbers released by MoLE, was only 44.96 lakh. The scheme has completely stalled as additions in the first eight months of year 2021–22 were less than 15,000 a month.

It has been over two and a half years since the scheme was launched—total registrations are only about 45 lakh, less than 1 per cent of targeted workers.

The Labour and Employment Challenge is Massive

India's policymakers face a massive labour and employment challenge. The dimensions of these daunting challenges are as follows.

First, a very large proportion of people of working age (fifteen-plus) is not in the workforce. About 60 per cent of Indians of working age are neither employed, nor underemployed, which means three-fifth of our labour does not contribute to the formal economy of India by not participating in the production of goods and services at all. It is indeed a huge loss of growth potential.

Second, about 80 per cent of Indian women of working age are not in the labour force, making India one of the worst countries in this regard globally.

Third, more than 30 per cent of about 25 crore Indian youth (from fifteen to twenty-four years) are not in employment, educational institutions or training. This indicates that a massive number (over 7.5 crore) of Indian youth is literally wasting away.

Fourth, only less than 25 per cent of the jobs in India are wage or salaried jobs. Three-fourth of jobs are either own account jobs (mostly single-person enterprises) like vegetable vendors or *pakora* makers, or contributing family members. The country's proportion of wage and salaried jobs is one of the lowest in the world, indicating a huge informality of production in India.

Finally, though the nominal unemployment rate, at about 7 per cent, is relatively higher than many other countries, the real problem is the low wage of those who are employed. Indian workers earn pitiably low wages on average.

Policymakers are trying to address some of these challenges like low wages by fixing minimum wages but all the other challenges mentioned above have not received their attention.

Chapter Sixteen

Consolidation Is Not Labour Reforms

Fair Conditions of Workplaces and Employment are
Principal Objectives of Labour Laws

The issues that have received the largest attention of politicians, labour leaders and policymakers relate to pay and allowances, working conditions, employee-employer disputes and the social security of mostly those in the organized sector. Lately, attention has shifted to those in the unorganized sector.

There is no legal and standard definition of what constitutes the organized sector and the unorganized sector. The organized sector was defined indirectly for the first time in the Unorganized Workers' Social Security Act, 2008 (UWSSA-2008) to mean 'an enterprise which is not an unorganized sector'. The unorganized sector was defined to mean 'an enterprise owned by individuals or self-employed workers and engaged in the production or sale of goods or providing service of any kind whatsoever, and where the enterprise employs workers, the number of such workers being less than ten'. These definitions are based on the definition of 'factory' in the Factories Act, which treats all places where manufacture of goods takes place with ten workers or more, if power is used, and twenty or more, if no power is used as a factory. This meant that all manufacture with less than ten workers was not a factory and therefore was unorganized.

UWSSA 2008 expanded this concept of less than ten workers to services enterprises as well. It also, by implication, expanded the organized sector to all factories and other enterprises employing more than ten workers, removing the element of using power or manufacturing only.

There is no system of registering all enterprises in India. Unorganized enterprises are mostly informal and the official system has no data on them. Ironically, as the definition of 'organized sector' is negatively defined and the fact that there is no system of registering the unorganized sector, if you go by the above definitions, you will neither know the unorganized or organized enterprises of India! The official system in India calls unorganized enterprises by another name: MSMEs.

Numerous Laws to Deal with Labour Issues

When factories started coming into existence after the invention of power-driven machines, labour faced poor working conditions as well as exploitative terms and conditions of employment. The conditions were highly iniquitous compared to the profits that factories generated for their owners.

There was a wave of legislations across the world to create acceptable working and employment conditions for workers. India was no exception. In the twentieth century, India enacted several legislations to improve the terms of engagement for workers. Later, attention started shifting to workers in the unorganized sector and many laws have been enacted in the past three decades to improve their lot.

That said, these labour laws concern only a small fraction of workers. The base law dealing with working conditions is the Factories Act. It applies to establishments/enterprises that employ over ten workers with the use of power or more than twenty workers without the use of power. The annual survey of industries collects statistics for all factories and establishments with over 100 workers. In 2018, there were 2.38 lakh such factories and establishments in the organized sector in India, which employed a total of 1.22 crore workers. This is less than 2.5 per cent of the country's estimated 50 crore labour force.

The Labour Code on Wages was passed by the Parliament in 2019. This Code consolidates four dimensions of pay and allowances by bringing four laws—the Minimum Wages Act, 1948; Payment of Wages

Act, 1936; Payment of Bonus Act, 1965; and Equal Remuneration Act, 1976—under a single Code. The central rules prepared under the Code on Wages were notified on 24 August 2020 as the Draft Code on Wages (Central) Rules 2020. These rules were still in the process of finalization by the end of financial year 2020–21.

The other three Codes—the Occupational Safety, Health and Working Conditions Code, 2020, which deals with workplace conditions; the Industrial Relations Code, 2020, which deals with different laws relating to organization of labour and resolution of labour disputes; and the Code on Social Security, 2020, dealing with various aspects of social security for workers of organized and unorganized sectors—were passed by the Parliament on 23 September 2020.

The Draft Occupational Safety, Health and Working Conditions Code (Central) Rules 2020 were notified on 19 November 2020 and the Draft Rules on Industrial Relations Code were notified by the Central government on 29 October 2020. The Draft Rules on Social Security were published on 13 November 2020.

Four Codes Consolidate Concepts and Definitions

The four Labour Codes have consolidated twenty-nine laws on labour. These laws had variously described and defined labour in different ways: workman, worker, employee, organized worker, unorganized worker, and so on in the context of the respective laws.

The Factories Act, the principal law for governing workplace conditions in manufacturing, defined labour as 'worker' to mean a person employed directly by or through any agency in any manufacturing process, in any kind of work incidental to or connected with the manufacturing process, or subject to the manufacturing process. The Mines Act does not use the expression 'worker' or 'miner' for labour working in mines; rather, it uses an expansive expression: 'a person working or employed in or in connection with a mine is said to be working or employed'. The Industrial Disputes Act used the expression 'workmen' for labour and defines this as a person employed in an industry to do any manual, unskilled, skilled, technical, operational, clerical or supervisory work, for hire or reward. The Payment of Wages Act uses 'employee' to mean any person who is employed for hire or reward to do any work, skilled or unskilled, manual or clerical, in scheduled employment with respect to the minimum fixed rate of wages.

The new Code on Wages has come up with a common definition. 'Worker' in the Code on Wages means any person (excluding an apprentice) employed in any industry to do any manual, unskilled, skilled, technical, operational, clerical or supervisory work for hire or reward, whether the terms of employment are express or implied, and includes working journalists and sales promotion employees. It also uses a definition of 'employee' similar to worker except that it includes administrative and supervisory workers as well. The Industrial Relations Code and Workplaces Conditions Code use exactly the same definition of employee and worker as the Wages Code. The Social Security Code uses almost the same definition of employee and worker but also brings in additional types of workers, like 'platform worker', 'home-based worker' and 'gig worker' within the broad framework of worker and employees.

Bringing greater uniformity in key definitions of different forms of labour in different kind of occupations is the most significant contribution of the consolidation exercise in labour laws. The Social Security Code understandably uses the widest definitions of workers/employees, making it applicable to the largest proportion of labour.

Occupational Safety and Health Code is Old Wine in New Bottle

The Occupational Safety, Health and Working Conditions Code, 2020, brings within its fold thirteen different laws relating to workplaces/working conditions/working relationships operating in the country. It describes different workplaces as 'establishments' and uses a single definition to define an establishment and to which establishments it applies.

The Code prescribes that every employer of any establishment shall apply for registration with the registering officer appointed by the appropriate government. It defines an establishment to mean a place where any industry, trade, business, manufacturing or occupation is carried on in which ten or more workers are employed. The use of the expressions 'business', 'occupation' and 'trade', which are not defined in the Code, are wide enough to bring within its scope every workplace, whether a motor transport undertaking, newspaper establishment, audio-video production, building and other construction, plantation, factory or mine or industry that are separately defined in the Code or specifically included in the definition of 'establishment' and 'shops', warehouses, malls, logistics, railways, IT centres or data centres, which are not either specifically defined or included in the definition of an establishment.

The Code is essentially a patchwork of thirteen laws into a single one and does not really go the whole hog to use an omnibus definition to bring all workplaces within the scope of registration. This will lead to several problems in translating the vision of creating one nation with one database of businesses.

Reproducing most provisions of earlier laws does not constitute reform, or even consolidation. It is more like the creation of an umbrella scheme by reorganizing about 200 centrally sponsored schemes (CSSs) in twenty-five flagship umbrella schemes. Nothing really changes—all the CSSs continued to operate as they were, as sub-schemes.

Many provisions in the Occupational Safety Code relate to wages and social security. They have been carried from earlier laws dealing with specific occupations. There are wages and social security provisions for contract workers, interstate migrant workers and a few others. These issues should be dealt with in the Code on Wages and Code on Social Security.

Workplaces have been transformed in the twenty-first century. The Code does not address this reality, most prominently in modern workplaces like malls, warehouses, logistic centres, airports, IT and data centres.

Wage Code Perpetuates the Status Quo

The Wage Code displays the least dynamism of the consolidation exercise. While seeking to merge four laws into one, it continues with all pre-existing deformities.

The preamble merely notes that it is an act to 'amend and consolidate the laws relating to wages and bonus and matters connected therewith or incidental thereto'.

The Code recognizes only one form of wages: wages to be paid to employees who work on a salaried basis. It does not provide for all the newer forms of labour provision, like the gig economy, contractor-employee relationship, and so on. And as it doesn't concern itself with establishments that employ less than ten workers, it leaves out 99 per cent of the businesses in India.

The Code also continues with a fragmented approach to deal with wages. It does not recognize the 'cost-to-company' approach or the total package cost. Instead, it continues with elaborate enumeration of numerous components of wages and how establishments are supposed to deal with the same.

The Wage Code stipulates that the appropriate government 'shall' fix the minimum rate of wages payable to employees. It also obligates the appropriate government to fix the minimum rate of wages for 'time work' and 'piece work'. Minimum wages can be fixed by the hour, day or month. The Payment of Minimum Wages Act, 1948, which the Wage Code subsumes, required the appropriate government to fix minimum wages for establishments included in the two schedules to the Act. The Code seems to stipulate that minimum wages need to be fixed for all establishments covered.

The factors of inflation and skills have serious implications on wages. The Code continues with the practice of obligating appropriate governments to take into account 'skills of workers required for working under the categories of unskilled, skilled, semi-skilled and highly-skilled', 'geographical areas', 'variation in the cost of living index number applicable to such workers' and 'cash value of the concessions in respect of supplies of essential commodities at concession rate' while determining minimum wages for different kinds of establishments and jobs therein.

The Schedule to the Minimum Wages Act lists hundreds of varieties of establishments. Every type of establishment employs workers with different skill sets and at different levels of managerial responsibility. There are thirty-odd states in India. Consequently, we have thousands of minimum wage rates in the country. Establishments have to file detailed returns regarding wages paid to their employees.

The Code authorizes the Government of India to prescribe a national minimum wage rate as was the case before the consolidated Wage Code was brought in. The government prescribes a minimum wage for four skill categories and three different regions of India and also fixes a variable rate (to take care of inflation) for different types of establishments. State governments cannot fix a minimum wage lower than the national minimum wage rates fixed by the Centre.

The government cannot understand the variations of skills and behavioural aspects of the employer-labour engagement to be able to decide appropriate wages for millions of jobs and the variations therein. It is even more complicated in emerging economies where fixed and stable jobs are becoming increasingly fewer.

Social Security Code Merely Expands the Intent

The Social Security Code 2020 not only consolidates the existing nine laws dealing with social security but expands the coverage of workers for benefits. In terms of intent, the Code is progressive. However, while it expands eligibility of labour for additional coverage and benefits, the government needs to develop programmes and schemes to do the needful. The history of social security legislations, especially those that attempt to provide coverage to workers outside the large and organized sector, is testament that intended benefits are not translated into action. Therefore, the key to the success of the Social Security Code lies in its implementation.

The Social Security Code materially expands coverage and benefits in five principal ways. First, it allows non-covered establishments to voluntarily join Employees' Provident Fund (EPF) and Employees' Pension Scheme (EPS). This will expand the choice of non-covered establishments to choose between National Pension Scheme (NPS) or Employees Provident Fund Organisation (EPFO), if they decide to provide such retirement savings-related benefits to employees. Second, the Code defines new forms of employment, such as aggregator, gig worker and platform worker, to include them within the ambit of the law. It also defines an establishment, without adding the condition of a minimum ten employees. Thus, in law, it includes all establishments in the country within its scope. Third, the Code seeks to establish an electronic system of registration of establishments. This has the potential to create the largest database of establishments in the country. Fourth, it makes employees on fixed-term contracts eligible for gratuity. Fifth, the Code provides for registration of every unorganized worker, including gig workers and platform workers, on the basis of self-declaration electronically.

There is a great deal of confusion with regard to registration of enterprises/establishments in the country. Now, the Social Security Code proposes registration of every establishment (equivalent of enterprise or business) and labour. However, it has been proposed only as one more system of registration, and not as a unique system of registering every business/enterprise/establishment and assigning a unique business number to it.

The Social Security Code continues with institutional arrangements for the social security system almost as it exists. The EPF system continues without any change in its trustee board, organization and provident fund commissioner. The same is true of the Employees State Insurance Scheme system or the institutional system under the Building and Construction Workers' law. Even the almost non-operational system of the Unorganized Workers Social Security System with its board continues as is. The same applies for the systems of gratuity, maternity benefit, employees' compensation, etc., which have been merged in a single law.

There is no integration in the institutional, administrative, scale of subscription and benefit, investment pattern or any other aspect of schemes/funds as they operate currently. The Code incorporates all the definitions that exist in different laws and most key provisions of these laws remain almost unchanged. In this sense, it is more of a patchwork than the creation of an integrated system of social security.

The Social Security Code creates two structural templates for social security schemes: one for unorganized sector workers and the second for gig and platform workers. The Code mandates the Central government to formulate and notify, from time to time, 'suitable welfare schemes' for unorganized workers on matters relating to life and disability cover; health and maternity benefits; old age protection; education; and any other benefit it may determine. Such schemes, when notified, might be funded by the Centre, partly by state governments, partly by contributions from beneficiaries and the establishments concerned, and partly by corporate social responsibility (CSR).

For gig and platform workers, the entire responsibility has been cast on the Centre to formulate welfare schemes for life and disability cover, accident insurance, health and maternity benefits, old age protection, creche, and any other benefit determined. These schemes are also envisaged to be funded in a manner similar to the funding of Central government schemes for the welfare of unorganized workers. While the Code offers mandates to formulate and fund welfare schemes for unorganized workers and gig and platform workers, no specific entitlements have been created, nor has any specific scheme been announced. The workers will have to trust the good intentions and abilities of the Centre and the states in this regard.

No welfare schemes for gig and platform workers have been formulated at the close of calendar year 2021.

Industrial Relations Code Brings Reforms for Factories of Bygone Era

The Industrial Relations Code merges three labour-related laws: the Trade Unions Act, 1926; Industrial Employment (Standing Orders) Act, 1946; and Industrial Disputes Act, 1947.

The industry has been asking for freedom to 'hire and fire' workers and close factories when it is no longer economically viable to carry on production. The Code has brought in significant changes with respect to this traditional ask. First, it includes the concept of fixed-term employment as a regular mode of employment and building of provisions relating thereto in the law. Second, it eliminates the misuse of casual leave as a weapon of industrial action by bringing the same within the scope of 'strike'. Third, it eliminates multiplicity of negotiating trade unions in an establishment by mandating that only a trade union with the support of 51 per cent or more workers would be allowed to participate in negotiations. Further, it eliminates strong-arm tactics by providing for a seat on the council for the support of every 20 per cent of workers. Fourth, it makes the life of enterprises employing less than 300 workers simpler, by making certain restrictive conditions—mandatory certification of complete standing orders and taking prior permission before layoff, retrenchment and closure—applicable only to industrial establishments that have over 300 workers on their rolls. Fifth, it prohibits strikes and lockouts in all industrial establishments without fourteen days' notice.

These changes tilt the balance in favour of entrepreneurs as there are only a few thousand industrial establishments in India with over 300 workers. However, it is difficult to understand why government permission is needed for factories that employ more than 300 workers. Starting and closing an enterprise should be the decision of entrepreneurs, depending on economic factors and their financial conditions.

Implementation of Labour Laws Progressing Very Slowly

The first labour code—the Code on Wages—after approval of the Parliament and the President, was published on 8 August 2019 in the e-Gazette of India. The notification to bring the law into force was still to be issued at the end of March 2021. The same has been the fate of the three other laws, though these were notified later in September–November 2020.

Labour laws use the concept of appropriate government. The Codes need detailed rules to implement the provisions of the Code. The rules are framed by the 'appropriate government'. The Central government is the appropriate government for establishments of the Central government, railways, mines, oil fields, major ports, air transport service, telecommunication, banking and insurance company or a corporation or other authority, established by a Central Act or CPSEs or their subsidiaries or autonomous bodies owned and controlled by the Central government, including contractors for any of these establishments. The state government is the appropriate government for the rest of the establishments. Almost 99 per cent of the establishments/enterprises/bodies to whom the labour codes would apply would have state governments as the appropriate government.

It is therefore essential that state governments frame the rules for implementation of the Codes to make any real and meaningful move towards their implementation. While the Central government has notified draft rules under the four Labour Codes, very few state governments had done so by the end of financial year 2020–21. They seem to be in no hurry to do so.

In September 2021, the Ministry of Labour sought applications from experts to frame the rules for the four Labour Codes. These experts have not been hired at the time this book went into print.

The Government of India seems to have put the implementation of consolidated Labour Codes on the slow burner. None of the Codes were notified for implementation by the end of calendar year 2021.

Section III: Infrastructure

Chapter Seventeen

State of Infrastructure

Infrastructure is a poorly understood concept. Essentially, whether publicly or privately built and operated, it is made up of physical assets or 'facilities' that provide 'service'. Roads and railways are facilities that provide the service of transportation. Power plants provide electricity service. Airports provide service for the operation of airlines. Most infrastructure comprises physical facilities. However, in the IT age, there are technology-based facilities that are more virtual than physical. The Internet is the mother of technology-based facilities. Infrastructure services should be distinguished from services provided by human beings. Numerous services are provided by humans, directly or using machines and technology. A hairdresser doing your hair or an accountant who writes your company's accounts are rendering what is typically and normally understood as service. These services are simply 'services'. The difference between normal business services and infrastructure services is that businesses services are produced and provided by workers whereas infrastructure services are primarily provided by the facility created.

Infrastructure services are vital and intrinsic to development and growth. When habitations get connected by roads, the interactions of their inhabitants with the rest of the world improve. Transportation provided by roads enables people to reach workplaces, education centres, hospitals, airports, markets and numerous other providers of goods and services. Roads are essential for the development of unconnected areas. The same applies to other infrastructure services, whether electricity, telecom, the Internet or other infrastructure. The country or locality where infrastructure is not commensurate with the requirement of the people, government and businesses remains underdeveloped and poor.

As infrastructure is a facility, it is characterized as being 'commonly used'. Many times, the characteristic of being commonly used is so strong that it is quite difficult to measure the use of an infrastructure facility by a specific person or business. A road is used by so many people and vehicles that it is generally quite difficult to measure and charge for an individual's or vehicle's use. This characteristic usually results in making consumption of infrastructure non-excludable (no person can be excluded from using the service) and non-rivalrous (use by one person does not come in the way of use by another). These two characteristics make most infrastructure a public good. Public goods and services have usually been entrusted to the government by society. Thus, governments and other public authorities have taken the responsibility and lead in constructing infrastructure facilities.

Advancement of technology and regulatory practices have made it possible to measure the consumption of some high-value infrastructure services by individuals, vehicles and businesses. Tolling a road or bridge can allow measurement of road use by a particular vehicle. It is simpler to measure the time for which an incoming aircraft has used an airport. Use of electronic metering can measure consumption of electricity, water and other liquids and flows. This is enabling the conversion of infrastructure businesses from being purely public utilities/facilities to privately owned/operated facilities, in turn giving an enormous boost to private investment in infrastructure.

In fact, infrastructure is becoming as viable and common a business as any other manufacturing undertaking, service or business.

Infrastructure Comprehensively Defined by the Ministry of Finance

The Department of Economic Affairs, Ministry of Finance, notified a harmonized master list of infrastructure for the first time in 2006. This has been expanded from time to time. The notification in August 2020 included affordable rental housing complexes in the list. The harmonized list of infrastructure is divided into five subsectors: transport and logistics; energy; water and sanitation; communication; and social and commercial infrastructure. In all, thirty-four specific types of infrastructure are mentioned in the master list. However, it still excludes technological or non-physical infrastructure.

There is a direct relationship between economic growth and infrastructure investment as a country graduates from low income to middle income status. Several ministries and departments in the Government of India deal with different types and aspects of infrastructure. There is no overarching ministry or department responsible for infrastructure. Some coordination in approach has been done by the Planning Commission (now NITI Aayog) and the Ministry of Finance.

Infrastructure Investment Rose Sharply from 2005–06

According to the 2014 version of Infrastructure Statistics, India's investment in infrastructure as well as private-sector investment rose significantly from 2005–06 onwards.

India's investment in infrastructure was barely 4–5 per cent of GDP in the years 1999–2000 and 2005–06. As the GDP itself was small, this translated into infrastructure investment of Rs 1–2 lakh crore per annum during this period. As growth took off, infrastructure investment also rose. Infrastructure investment exceeded 5 per cent of GDP in 2005–06, 6 per cent in 2007–08 and 8 per cent in 2010–11.

In rupee terms, infrastructure investment crossed Rs 2 lakh crore in 2005–06, Rs 3 lakh crore in 2007–08, Rs 4 lakh crore in 2008–09 and Rs 6 lakh crore in 2010–11. In less than five years between 2005–06 and 2010–11, infrastructure investment trebled in terms of rupees and by more than 60 per cent in terms of ratio to GDP. Investment in infrastructure during the first decade of the current millennium was on a roll.

Private investment in infrastructure also took off notably from 2006–07. From a little less than 1.5 per cent of GDP in 2006–07, it grew massively to rise to a little less than 4 per cent of GDP by 2010–11. Public investment kept pace with the growth in GDP and ranged between 4 per cent and 5 per cent of GDP all through this period, which coincided almost entirely with the Eleventh Plan period.

The CSO/National Statistical Office (NSO)/Ministry of Statistics and Programme Implementation (MOSPI) has stopped publishing Infrastructure Statistics after 2014.

Investment Slackening for Some Time

Infrastructure Statistics 2014 noted that investment started falling from the year 2011–12. In rupee terms, it fell to less than Rs 5.5 lakh crore; in terms of ratio to GDP, it declined to less than 7 per cent.

With the stoppage of Infrastructure Statistics by the Planning Commission/NITI Aayog, there is no authentic and comparable data available for infrastructure investment in India—it has to be estimated indirectly. All infrastructure investments are part of GFCF, or gross fixed capital formation. In particular, the Dwellings, Other Buildings and Structures (DOBS) part of GFCF (the other three parts are Machinery and Equipment, Cultivated Biological Resources and Intellectual Property Products) is a close proxy for infrastructure investment although some part of this component also represents fixed investment in manufacturing and other sectors of the economy.

In 2018–19, GDP, GFCF and DOBS (at 2011–12 prices) were Rs 140 lakh crore, Rs 44.6 lakh crore and Rs 22 lakh crore, respectively. GFCF was 31.9 per cent of GDP and DOBS 15.7 per cent of GDP in 2018–19. In 2014–15, GDP, GFCF and DOBS (at fixed 2011–12) prices were Rs 98 lakh crore, Rs 32.8 lakh crore and Rs 17.7 lakh crore. The ratio of GFCF to GDP and DOBS to GDP was 33.5 per cent and 18 per cent, respectively. Compared to 2014–15, GFCF (represented by ratio of GFCF to GDP) and investment in fixed dwellings, buildings and structures (represented by ratio of DOBS to GDP) declined from 33.5 per cent and 18 per cent to 31.9 per cent and 15.7 per cent respectively. In 2011–12, these two ratios were 34.3 per cent and 19.8 per cent. In eight years, the GFCF and DOBS declined by about 2.4 per cent and 4.1 per cent. These are quite sharp, large declines.

The stagnation in infrastructure investment is also corroborated by bank credit to the infrastructure segment. RBI data indicates that infrastructure investment (classified further in four subsectors of power, telecommunication, roads, and other infrastructure) was Rs 10.56 lakh crore at the end of March 2019 and Rs 10.54 lakh crore at the end of March 2020. Infrastructure bank credit outstanding at the end of financial year 2015–16 was Rs 9.65 lakh crore, which declined in absolute terms to Rs 9.06 lakh crore and Rs 8.90 lakh crore in the years 2016–17 and 2017–18. As a proportion of GDP at current prices, infrastructure lending by banks declined from 7 per cent in 2015–16 to 5.6 per cent in 2019–20. The infrastructure lending segment also had the highest proportion of non-performing loans.

National Highways Have Grown in Fits and Starts

In 1951, 19,811 km of roads were designated as national highways. This increased to 23,798 km in the next 10 years and stayed almost unchanged a decade later (23,838 km in 1971). The 1970s saw the first major spurt when the designated national highways increased to 31,671 km in 1981.

The 1980s saw no real activity and the number stayed at 33,650 km in 1991. The real upsurge came in the 1990s when more than 24,000 km of other roads were upgraded to national highways. India had 57,737 km of national highways at the commencement of the new millennium in 2001. The number increased at a steady pace to 70,934 km in 2011.

There has been a rush to declare more roads as national highways in the second decade of the twenty-first century, more pronouncedly after the NDA government took over in 2014. From a length of 79,116 km at the end of 2013, national highways grew to 91,287 km in 2014. As per the annual report of the Ministry of Road Transport and Highways (MoRTH), the length of national highways stood at 1,32,500 km at the end of 2020. Essentially, the number grew from just about 80,000 km at the end of the UPA's second term to 1,32,500 at the end of 2020, an increase of 52,500 km in less than seven years—an annual increase of over 7500 km per year!

What is the right length of national highways in India? What should be the criterion for declaring a highway a national highway? What explains these spurts and fits and starts in growth? The current phase of national highways expansion is quite instructive in this respect.

The NDA government, more specifically MoRTH, decided sometime in 2014 that as many state highways as possible should be converted into national highways. The criterion for declaring a highway a national highway was relaxed. A new class of 'in-principle' declaration of national highways commenced in 2014. As a result of this policy, as per the note issued by PIB in July 2019, as many as 71,898 km of state highways were approved as 'in-principle' national highways since April 2014, 'subject to the outcome of their Detailed Project Reports (DPRs)'. Of these, highways of 19,170 km length were declared national highways until July 2019.

National highways should be viewed as a national grid of large interstate carriageways connecting major ports, production centres and human habitation, requiring movement of goods and passenger vehicles of more than a specified number. The rest of the major roads should remain intrastate and state highways connecting at major points to national highways.

No such load study has been carried out and presented to the public about the national highways' length of over 1.3 lakh km and the candidate ('in-principle') national highways of over 60,000 km. If one were to take into account a number of low-volume highways declared as national highways, there does not appear to be a good justification for the claim of such a large network of national highways.

Share of Industry in Power has Been Constantly Declining

The share of industry in electricity consumption in India was quite high at 71 per cent in 1947. As India industrialized during the First and Second Plan periods (1951–61), industry's share in total power consumption went up further, peaking at 75 per cent at the end of 1960–61, when the Second Five-Year Plan ended. The share of industry in power consumption was still high at 72 per cent at the beginning of the 1970s.

Expansion of electricity supply to agriculture and later, from the early 1980s, to residential consumers, led the relative share of industry to fall steadily in the 1970s and 1980s. By the end of the 1970s, industry's share in electricity consumption had fallen to 62 per cent, and to a little over 51 per cent in 1989–90. Industry's share of electricity consumption fell by more than 20 per cent in twenty years. This trend continued unabated with industry consuming only 46 per cent at the end of the Tenth Plan in 2006–07.

The share of industry as a consumer of electricity in India was only marginally above 40 per cent in 2018–19. The share would fall below 40 per cent any time soon.

Not only does industry have a paltry share in total electricity use, it is voting with its feet in buying electricity from distribution companies

(DISCOMs). It has been steadily building captive generation capacity and, of late, buying power from energy exchanges.

Industry started investing in captive power generation in the 1970s, the time when State Electricity Boards (SEBs), the predecessors of DISCOMs, were diversifying towards agriculture and residential consumers, favouring them with lower tariffs. For the first time, industrial enterprises built about 2600 megawatts (MW) of captive power-generation capacity (1849 MW thermal and 559 MW diesel) during the Fifth Plan period in the 1970s. Captive power capacity had grown to around 17,000 MW by the end of the Ninth Plan in 2001–02. Investment in captive power plants received a big boost thereafter with capacity reaching as high as 58,000 MW at the end of financial year 2018–19.

Having installed large captive power generation capacity, the industry is buying a smaller share of power for manufacturing from DISCOMs. In 2017–18, captive power generated reached 180 billion units. Industry used a total of 469 billion that year, of which captive power comprised about 40 per cent. In fact, captive power generated by industry accounted for 16 per cent of the total power consumed in India in 2017–18. Excluding power captively produced and consumed in 2017–18, only 289 billion units of power were supplied by state utilities to industry, which was only about 25 per cent of total power supplied and used in India in 2017–18.

Electricity purchase from DISCOMs by industry is fast tapering off.

Two Major Transformations: From Fossil Fuels to Renewables, and Public to Private Sector

Total installed power-generation capacity in India (grid connected; not including power generated by gensets and renewable home lighting systems) at the end of October 2020 was 3.73 lakh MW or 373 GW. The generation capacity owned by the private sector was 1.75 lakh MW, over 47 per cent of the total power-generation capacity of the country.

Thirty years ago, there was hardly any private-sector power-generation capacity in India. Power generation was opened for private-sector investment in 1991. There were many policy problems in the initial years. Only 1430 MW of power-generation capacity was added in the private sector in the Eighth Plan (1992–1997), more than half of which was in the gas power plant segment (762 MW). Power generation in the private sector started assuming notable proportions by the end of the 1990s. At the end of financial year 2011–12, India had a total power-generation capacity of 2.11 lakh MW—the private sector's share was 29.11 per cent with 61,409 MW of capacity. Very soon, this share will exceed 50 per cent as most new generation is coming up in the private sector.

India's renewables-based power-generation capacity (primarily hydro, solar and wind) at the end of October 2020 was 1.35 lakh MW, comprising hydro (45,699 MW) and renewables (89,636 MW), which made up over 36 per cent of total installed capacity. At the turn of the millennium, solar and wind power-generation capacity was quite insignificant. Today, the largest addition every year is from the renewables segment.

The only renewable power generation taking place in India in 1990 was hydropower. The country had total hydro and renewable power generation-capacity of 18,307 MW at the end of financial year 1990. The first wind power-generation capacity started coming on stream in 1993–94 and India's installed renewable power (other than hydro) grew to 902 MW by financial year 1997. This then grew, primarily driven by wind power generation, to 7760 MW by 2007. Once solar power became competitive (initially with government subsidy support and after 2015 without such support), renewable power generation (other than hydro) really took off. India's renewable power capacity (other than hydro) was 24,503 MW by the end of 2012; it reached about 87,000 MW by the end of financial year 2020.

From 2017 to 2020, while thermal power-generation capacity from all sources (coal and gas) grew by only about 12,000 MW, renewable power capacity (other than hydro) grew by as much as 30,000 MW. Hardly any new thermal power plants have been announced in the past three to five years; only ongoing projects are being taken up for completion. Almost all new capacity being planned is renewable-based. One can expect (in terms of capacity installed) that renewables, including hydro, will cross thermal power-generation capacity by 2030.

Chapter Eighteen

Mess in Telecom, Power and Transportation Sectors

Telecom

India's future as an economy is critically linked with telecom infrastructure. The economy is fast digitalizing and needs to digitalize even faster. Digitalization runs on telecom and fibre. In India, digitalization is riding the mobile revolution. Almost every Indian is connected with a mobile device. The country connects and interacts on telecom infrastructure and devices. Voice telephony, the Internet, social media and businesses all run on telecom today.

Indians love visual content on their mobiles. We consumed 12 gigabytes (GB) of data per person per month in 2019, the highest in the world. This reached 13.5 GB in December 2020, recording over 20 per cent annual growth. It has been estimated that individual data consumption is likely to exceed 25 GB per month by 2025. The average revenue per unit or subscriber of mobile telephone companies was around Rs 150 or about $2 per subscriber for voice, messaging and data in 2020. These rates are the lowest in the world; compared to many advanced markets, they are actually twenty-five to fifty times lower. Indian consumers have the best deal in the world.

When an industry creates so much value and enjoys so much demand, it should be rolling in profits. Yet, the Indian telecom industry has been in dire straits for quite some time. Only three telecom players are left standing, not counting the public-sector sick duo of BSNL and MTNL. One of the three companies, Vodafone Idea, reported a loss of Rs 73,878 crore in 2019–20, the highest ever loss recorded by any Indian company ever.

Fluctuating Fortunes of the Telecom Business in India

The cellular telecom business in India was born in failure in 1995 when fourteen companies bid for mobile service licences and quoted atrociously high fixed licence fee (spectrum came bundled with licence). The market was not known and it required large investment to put in place the infrastructure for providing mobile telecom services. In those days, a call on a cellular phone cost over Rs 16 per minute. The annual fixed licence fee was calculated at the auction-determined fixed licence fee or at Rs 6000 per subscriber, whichever was higher. Almost all companies defaulted on the payment of the licence fee.

The 1995 auction proved to be a winner's curse and brought the industry to its knees. There was a real danger of licensees downing their shutters fully and India missing the mobile revolution. The government took a courageous decision in 1999 and allowed telecom companies to migrate from a fixed licence fee regime to one based on revenue share.

This decision transformed the fortunes of the industry. Falling technology prices and India's fascination for mobile telephony contributed further. The cost per subscriber declined massively as the subscriber base grew by leaps and bounds. By 2001–02, telecom companies had started reporting profits. This made telecom licences very valuable and the share prices of companies galloped. Some telecom licensees could sell their stakes, raking in billions of dollars in profit. The overwhelming profits made by some operators gave birth to scandals and scams. The industry, however, got disrupted when the Supreme Court cancelled 122 2G licences in 2012, making several companies (including a number of foreign investors) lose billions of dollars paid in licence fees and investments made in establishing networks.

The prices of voice calls had started drifting lower from 1999 itself. The price of a voice call dropped from Rs 16 a minute in 1995 to Rs 3 a minute in 2004 and Rs 0.47 a minute in 2012 to virtually zero by

2016–17. The voice call, which was the bedrock of profitability of telecom companies for the first fifteen years of their existence, started contributing almost nothing towards revenues from 2017. Data became the principal contributor of revenue. Yet, the ARPU, which was about Rs 1600 in 1998, came down to only Rs 72 per month in March 2018. The profitability of telecom companies tanked.

From 2009 to 2019, all private telecom companies, barring Jio, Airtel and Vodafone–Idea, abandoned their operations. Government entities BSNL and MTNL are also a pale shadow of the past, with less than 7 per cent of actual operational market share in November 2019.

The saviour of 1998—the revenue-sharing regime—is ironically proving to be the principal reason for their woes in 2020. The root of their woes lies in the fact that the telecom companies did not pay licence fee and spectrum charges on what they claimed were non-telecom revenues, whereas they had signed on to pay fees on the entire gross revenue, adjusted only for three items: interconnection charges paid to other service providers; roaming charges paid to other service providers; and service tax collected. While there are no firm estimates of these arrears, along with penalties and penal interest, an estimate placed in the Supreme Court estimated these arrears to be about Rs 1.47 lakh crore, more than the annual revenue of the telecom companies in 2019–20.

Wider Telecom Crisis

The telecom crisis in India was not limited to adjusted gross revenue (AGR)-related issues; it ran larger and deeper.

There are four major dimensions of the present crisis.

First, the business—both voice and data—might be headed towards becoming a duopoly (Jio and Airtel) with the remaining players, Vodafone–Idea and BSNL–MTNL, losing their market share continuously which may lead to their eventual shutdown. This has enormous consequences for consumers, investments in the sector, and competitiveness in the industry.

Second, all other telecom licensee companies, such as Reliance and Aircel, have already shut shop and are mostly in insolvency proceedings. Their networks and spectrum licences are getting wasted and not being put to any active service. Further, they are not paying their dues to the government. Putting the valuable spectrum these companies have on sale and facilitating their orderly resolution has not been possible because of our messed up policy regime.

Third, the government is pumping in billions of dollars (over Rs 70,000 crore) to 'revive' BSNL and MTNL. With the country facing a massive economic slowdown and a tough fiscal situation, is it advisable to throw scarce good money after a hopeless cause as it is quite unlikely that these two companies can be revived?

Fourth, telecom technology continues to advance with the arrival of 5G, which has the potential to connect machines and deliver much faster digital services. The policy conundrum caused by very high reserve prices recommended by TRAI is likely to make India miss the 5G bus as well.

All four issues needed to be resolved in the larger interest of the country.

Sector is Clutched Back from Precipice

Better sense dawned on the government in September 2021 which has pulled back the telecom sector from the precipice. The Union Cabinet in its meeting of 15 September 2021 approved a set of measures and procedural reforms to address both short-term and long-term issues of the sector.

The package included immediate relief measures of reducing the requirement of bank guarantees substantially (the government released about Rs 9000 crore worth of guarantees in December 2021), reducing interest rates, removing penalties and permitting 100 per cent FDI in the sector. Structural reform measures which would put the industry on a stronger footing included exclusion of non-telecom revenues from the definition of AGR on a prospective basis, increasing the tenure of spectrum allocation from twenty years to thirty years, permitting surrender of spectrum after ten years in future auctions, levying no spectrum usage charges (SUC) in future spectrum auctions and encouraging sharing of spectrum by removing additional 0.5 per cent SUC earlier levied on spectrum transfers.

These measures have brought back confidence in the telecom operators. The operators could hike the charges for prepaid customers in November–December 2021. The churn of subscribers is also nearing the end.

It looks as though the sector would see operations becoming profitable for all the three operators soon.

BSNL–MTNL on Ventilator Support

The BSNL–MTNL duo is on its deathbed. There were 96.09 crore active wireless/mobile telephone subscribers in India (according to VLR, or visitor location register, data) at the end of September 2019. Of this, active subscribers of BSNL and MTNL were only about 6.44 crore and 10 lakh, respectively. Thus, the public-sector duo enjoyed a princely share of 6.71 per cent. BSNL–MTNL largely offer 2G services and consequently their ARPU is also low. Little wonder then, that BSNL reported a loss of over Rs 14,000 crore on revenues of Rs 19,300 crore in 2018–19. MTNL, a listed company, reported a net loss of Rs 3390 crore for the year 2018–19. The loss of MTNL widened to Rs 3694 crore in 2019–20. BSNL accounts for 2019–20 are still not available. These are estimated by market sources to be Rs 15,500 crore.

The government announced a 'revival' package of Rs 69,000 crore in October 2019. Budget 2020–21 made a provision of Rs 37,640 crore to provide support to BSNL and MTNL, including Rs 14,115 crore of equity infusion in BSNL and Rs 6295 crore for MTNL. A further provision was made for making ex-gratia payment to voluntary retiring employees of BSNL/MTNL of Rs 9860 crore and Rs 3295 crore. The government also provided for Rs 2541 crore and Rs 1133 crore as grant-in-aid to BSNL and MTNL, respectively, for payment of GST on 4G licences.

Private telecom companies are getting crushed under the weight of AGR-related demands and public-sector telecom companies are crushing the government under the weight of their accumulated losses and infructuous investments. There is virtually no likelihood of these two companies garnering even one-tenth of the share of the telecom market. They are terminally ill and will eventually have to be put to rest.

The only justification offered publicly by the government for such a massive revival package is that these two companies are 'strategic'. No more details have been provided about what strategic interest these two companies serve and why and how such a mammoth revival package will serve this strategic interest. If providing secure lines of communications to government officials is the strategic interest in mind, there are surely better technical solutions to ensure this at a fraction of the cost of proposed investment.

A significant part of the revival package is to be funded from sale of land and building assets of BSNL and MTNL. The government's track record of selling land is dismal. It was quite unlikely that BSNL and MTNL's land

and buildings would get sold and this has been proven by the experience of the past fifteen months. BSNL and MTNL have not been able to sell any piece of land. These companies have gone back to the government citing low valuations being offered for their lands and buildings. The same has been the experience elsewhere. The recapitalization package of PSBs had a component of sale of non-core assets, like asset management companies and housing loan companies. Despite three years having gone by, not a single such non-core company, which is relatively easier to sell than land and buildings, has been sold.

A major element of the revival package is that these two companies will create a 4G network and acquire new customers. 4G networks were built by private-sector companies quite some time ago. These are deeply entrenched and much more efficient than anything BSNL–MTNL could ever build. It would take some time for the BSNL–MTNL 4G network to come alive, and may never even happen. Even if it does, the chances of BSNL–MTNL acquiring the customers of the three existing private-sector players are next to nothing.

5G Spectrum Auction Keeps Getting Delayed

After a gap of nearly five years, the Government of India put a total of 2308 megahertz (MHz) of spectrum on sale in an auction that took place in March 2021, which, at reserve prices, was valued at Rs 3.92 lakh crore. Only three telecom companies—Jio, Bharti and Vi (Vodafone–Idea after its rebrand)—participated in the auction and purchased a total of 855.66 MHz of spectrum, which will fetch the government Rs 77,815 crore, with about Rs 27,600 crore paid upfront and the rest spread over sixteen equated instalments.

The frequency bands in which the spectrum was bought—800, 900, 1800, 2100 and 2300 MHz—were essentially for the purpose of renewing the expiring spectrum licence, not for rolling out 5G services.

There was no bidder for the 700 MHz band, which is considered to be quite efficient, as the reserve price for the same was perceived to be very high. The government realized only 20 per cent of the reserve price of the spectrum put on sale. The auction proved very clearly that there is no interest in international players any longer to come and set up telecom and data services in India and that the reserve prices the government is demanding are atrociously high.

There was no auction or allotment for 5G spectrum during the first nine months of financial year 2021–22. The indications from the government were that these auctions would most likely take place in the middle of year 2022–23.

Power Sector

The electricity business in India was completely confined to the private sector before Independence. Its only issue of concern was safety, as it was a difficult commodity to handle. Initial electricity laws, including the Indian Electricity Act, 1910, therefore dealt only with safety and licencing aspects, with local authorities entrusted with licencing. At the end of calendar year 1947, India had generation capacity of a little under 1400 MW, almost all in the private sector. A number of electricity distribution companies had been licensed, beginning with CESC in Calcutta.

The electricity sector shifted almost completely to the public sector in the 1950s. Electricity generation, transmission and distribution companies were all nationalized and bundled into regional and later state electricity boards. Only a handful of distribution companies remained private. Until 1990, the private sector was completely banished from the power sector. Independent private producers (IPPs) were first permitted to invest in generation in 1991. Under the 1990s version of the power-sector reforms, state electricity boards were reorganized into separate generation, transmission and distribution companies, which led to the privatization of a few distribution companies in Odisha, Delhi and a few other places. Private-sector generation companies invested massively, first in conventional thermal power generation and hydro-generation and, later, in renewable power generation. The private sector was permitted in transmission as well later.

As things stand today, the bulk (over 90 per cent) of power distribution is in the public sector, almost entirely state government-controlled enterprises. Both the Centre and state government enterprises still have a massive presence in generation, with a collective share of more than 80 per cent of the power generated. While the private sector is growing in transmission, owing to the sector opening up late, over 90 per cent of the transmission lines have been built and are run by the public sector.

Power Sector is in a Mess

On an annual turnover of about Rs 6 lakh crore, the power sector loses about Rs 2 lakh crore every year. State governments subsidize power-sector entities heavily, spending over Rs 1 lakh crore every year in cash subsidies. All the cash is collected at the distribution end. Insufficient cash collections by the DISCOMs result in non-payment, delayed payment or partial payment across the chain. Generators suffer as do fuel and other suppliers to generators. Most generators have assured legal returns of about 15 per cent on equity, but insufficient payments by DISCOMs stresses them as well. Both DISCOMs and generating companies have been defaulting on bank loans as well. Every now and then, the government comes up with a package, the last one dubbed Ujjwal DISCOM Assurance Yojana (UDAY), to restructure the finances of the power sector. The state governments pick up the bill of restructuring, taking a considerable part of the accumulated liabilities on their books. Banks and other suppliers also take a hit.

There have been at least three major bailouts in the past twenty years that may have temporarily improved finances. However, the underlying rot, the gap of about one-third in the cost and realization of power produced and distributed, remains unresolved. DISCOMs have not paid over Rs 1.5 lakh crore of generators' bills. Two power-sector capital investment financing CPSEs, Power Finance Corp (PFC) and Rural Electrification Corporation (REC), have been recently asked to provide loans of Rs 1 lakh crore to DISCOMs to pay the outstanding bills of generators.

The private sector, which has entered generation in a big way, has found to its chagrin that the power it supplies is not fully paid for. This has made many thermal power plants set up by private-sector companies go sick. Renewable power companies had become the darlings of foreign investors as such power is both green and competitive. However, the flurry of investments in renewables has also stopped on account of payment concerns.

Policy of Overcharging and Forcibly Retaining Industry to Pay for Losses in Other Segments Has Failed India

Can a business that fleeces its highest paying and most valuable customers thrive, or for that matter even survive for long? The electricity supply business in India is essentially in the hands of DISCOMs. These utilities have been pursuing a policy of excessively overcharging their industrial and commercial consumers, while providing no assurances of supplying reliable and uninterrupted power. The sector has been, until very recently, in major supply deficit, only recently shifting to excess supply mode. Despite this fundamental shift, DISCOMs have not changed their policy of fixing above-market power supply rates for industry.

The strategy by DISCOMs to overcharge industrial customers to cross-subsidize their other buyers has also been responsible for making Indian industry non-competitive. It seemed to work for some time in partly sustaining the convoluted model of electricity supply and pricing in India. But with captive power-generation capacity reaching critical mass and industry no longer remaining a dominant buyer, the last chapter in the existence of DISCOMs may well be written soon.

The average cost of power generation is around Rs 4 per unit. The average cost of power to industries in India is Rs 7–10 per unit, varying among states, depending upon the type of industrial customer and so on. Power is sold to agriculture at less than Rs 1 per unit; in many states, it is cheaper or even free. Most states also keep electricity rates around the average cost of power generation or lower for residential customers. Industry has borne the brunt.

State DISCOMs do not want to let their 'creamy' customers go. So they have designed and implemented several policies to retain them—by force.

One such policy is the levy of a cross-subsidy charge on industries and businesses for the power they buy from private-sector producers or other cheaper sources. Most state DISCOMs levy a heavy surcharge ranging from Rs 1 to Rs 3 per unit of power purchased using open access. Rajasthan levies Rs 2.63 per unit on industrial consumers of 132 KV and above. The objective is clear. DISCOMs want to make the net cost of such electricity for the industrial entity as close to, if not higher than their own rates, thus making industrial entities 'captive' to them.

Many industry and business enterprises, especially MSMEs, do not have the scale to justify investing in a captive power plant. Consequently, all these entities—and there are millions of them—are not able to escape the clutches of DISCOMs.

There is another policy measure that makes the lives of industrial units establishing captive power plants difficult. The effective cost of captive power plants goes up if capacity utilization falls for any reason. Therefore, these units wish to sell their surplus power to other industrial consumers. However, they are not allowed to sell to anyone other than the state DISCOMs. Thus, DISCOMs become monopoly power purchasers for the surplus power of these units and offer them a pittance.

Despite all these constraints and extortionary policies, DISCOMs are finding it increasingly difficult to retain industrial customers and sell to them full quota of their electricity demand.

Power Continues to Remain Hostage to the Mess in Distribution

Most electricity produced in the country, thermal, hydel, renewable or any other mode, reaches consumers, whether businesses or households, through DISCOMs, which are owned and controlled by state governments barring a few exceptions. DISCOMs are almost invariably bankrupt.

The Ministry of Power has created a portal, Payment Ratification and Analysis in Power Procurement for Bringing Transparency in Invoicing of Generators (PRAAPTI), which captures the state of desperation in the power sector. DISCOMs hardly pay current bills. They only clear overdues from their current revenues and any extraordinary borrowings. For the month of October 2020, as disclosed on the PRAAPTI portal, DISCOMs were billed for Rs 15,545 crore by private generators and third-party suppliers (other than the generating companies of the same government). They paid only Rs 1979 crore against current bills within the forty-five days given to them to make the payment, and paid Rs 11,923 crore of overdue payments. As Rs 13,081 crore of current bills became overdue during the month, the outstanding overdues at the end of the month increased from Rs 1,24,940 crore to Rs 1,26,098 crore. Total overdues of DISCOMs, if you include the amount outstanding to generators owned by the same government and loans taken by special purpose companies to provide liquidity, would easily exceed Rs 3 lakh crore. Clearly, the power distribution sector is in a complete mess.

Some states and cities have privatized DISCOMs. For instance, Delhi did this about fifteen years ago and its transmission, distribution and billing losses are on a par with the best in the world now. There has not been any real increase in the cost of electricity, yet the two private-sector companies that manage power supply and distribution are neither dependent upon the state government for subsidy nor are they in losses. Similar experiences are playing out in a few other states, such as Odisha, where electricity distribution has been privatized.

Passenger Transport

Government-Owned and Operated after Independence

The transport industry contributed Rs 9.1 lakh crore of the total GVA of Rs 171.4 lakh crore, at current prices, in 2018–19. This amounted to 5.3 per cent of total GVA. Road transport contributed GVA of Rs 5.31 lakh crore and Railways Rs 1.24 lakh crore, which made up roughly 59 per cent and 14 per cent of transport sector GVA. Road transport is the dominant transport sector in India.

The GVA contribution of the public sector in road transport amounted to Rs 0.37 lakh crore; in railways, it was Rs 1.24 lakh crore. The public-sector share in road transport came almost entirely from state transport undertakings (STUs). The share of all the STUs was less than 7 per cent of road transport GVA. The Railways had almost 100 per cent of GVA contributed by the public sector.

The current state of affairs of STUs and the Railways is very different from what was envisaged in the heydays of socialism and the public sector 'controlling the commanding heights of the economy'.

For inexplicable reasons, India opted for government ownership and control of all public passenger transportation after Independence. The Railways was a Central government department while bus transport was decided to be established under the ownership and control of state governments, leading to the creation of STUs. Air passenger transport, which was under a private company, was nationalized soon after Independence. In due course, city bus services were also run and managed by government undertakings.

Some animal-driven vehicles (like *tongas*) and human-powered vehicles (like cycle-rickshaws) and motor-driven small city transport like auto-rickshaws were privately operated. Personal transport—cycles, scooters, motorcycles, cars—were, of course, privately owned and used. Almost all long distance and most other public transport was owned and operated by the government.

Railways Remains a Government Undertaking

The railway network in India was initially built by the British, beginning with the first 34 km railway line between Bombay (Bori Bunder) and Thane, which opened for passenger transport in 1853. A number of privately owned railway companies were set up between 1855 and 1880 to build railway lines and establish rail transport in different parts of the country. The railway network in India had reached 9000 km by 1880. The British government started purchasing private railway companies in the beginning of the twentieth century; it is reported that by 1907, the entire major railway network was purchased and owned by the British India government. The Railway Board was established in 1901 and railway finances were separated from general finances in 1924.

By 1930, the Indian railway network had become one of the largest in the world with an overall length of 66,000 km carrying about 620 million passengers and 90 million tonnes of goods annually. Partition in 1947 divided this network. In 1950, India's railway network was 53,596 km long, which rose to 64,600 km by 2012 and exceeded 67,500 km in 2020. Many railway lines have been converted to double tracks after Independence. Total railway tracks (counting double lines as two tracks) exceed 96,000 km now.

The Railways continued to operate as a department of the Government of India with the Railway Board interposed as a kind of corporate structure and government secretariat to manage the system. The Railway Budget retained a separate identity until September 2016 when it was merged with the General Budget.

Railways Not Able to Cover its Operating Costs

The policy decision after Independence to retain railways as a 100 per cent government monopoly and nationalize all road transporters and national and state highways has proved extremely costly across parameters—cost of service, quality of service and access to service.

It has been tellingly observed that both railways and roadways existed for employees, not passengers/consumers. At one point in time, the Railways employed over 16 lakh semi-literate and poorly trained staff with only 3000 officers to manage and supervise the operations of a network of over 65,000 km. State roadway undertakings had a national ratio of six staff to a single bus, whereas private buses were operated with one staff per bus.

The roadways in almost all the states remained confined to national and state highways and did not provide service to a large swathe of rural areas. State roadway corporations could provide city bus services only in some states. It was not unusual for people living in rural areas to remain unserved or hugely underserved. Later, illegal services operated by unauthorized buses and small vehicles came up to fill the void in many states, at least to connect nearly rural and suburban areas with cities.

The Railways was mostly unable to recover its operating cost from operating revenues as it kept passenger fares subsidized. This policy had another unintended consequence. Freight rates were kept relatively very high, making the Railways lose freight traffic to freight road transport— the only component of the transport system that was not nationalized. The Railways lost both passengers and freight. The Railways' share of passenger traffic and goods traffic exceeded 70 per cent and 90 per cent respectively after Independence; it is down to 7 per cent and under 30 per cent now. The share of STUs in passenger road transport is also only about 7 per cent. Both the Railways and state roadways have become marginal players despite the policy of making them monopoly operators.

Realizing this, the government started building some elements of private operations in the Railways. A few years ago, private investment was invited in goods wagons under an 'Own Your Wagon' scheme; in container management by allowing private container depots to be set up; and lately in passenger traffic by offering certain routes for private operations. These initiatives have not made a significant difference in the value addition made by the private sector—more than 99.5 per cent of the value addition in the Railways is made by the public sector.

STUs Unravelling but Not Fading Out

The First Five-Year Plan describes the state of road transport services in the country. There were reported to be as many as 47,575 operators in the country; twenty-five of these owned a fleet of vehicles exceeding 100. As many as 46,000 operators had less than five vehicles to provide transport services. In pre-Independence India, some princely states had established bus transport undertakings owned and operated by their governments.

The Road Transport Corporation Act, 1950, had been enacted to enable state governments to 'establish a Road Transport Corporation for the whole or any part of the state'. It also provided for acquisition of private road transport undertakings on payment of compensation and for the Central government to participate in the equity capital of these road transport corporations.

The first Five-Year Plan noted that state-operated services existed in varying scales in Assam, Bihar, Bombay, Madhya Pradesh, Madras, Orissa, Punjab, Uttar Pradesh, West Bengal, Hyderabad, Madhya Bharat, Mysore, Rajasthan, Saurashtra, Travancore–Cochin, Kutch, Himachal Pradesh, Manipur, Bilaspur and Delhi. The First and Second Five-Year Plans 'encouraged' states to consolidate small operators in the larger STUs and provided for equity stakes to be taken, first by the Railways and later by the Government of India, in these STUs.

By 1960, road transport undertakings were established in all the states. The service of transportation of passengers by road also did not escape the winds of socialism. The nationalization of private operators and establishment of monopoly state-owned corporations to establish and operate bus services were achieved through two basic policy instruments.

One, only operators with permits could lawfully ply bus services on routes declared by the government. Second, permits were denied to private operators and routes were nationalized by giving permits only to STUs. By the end of the 1980s, only STUs were plying buses on national and state highways.

Mismanagement and inability to operate commercial services made the state transport business bleed very soon. In 2015–16, the combined revenues of forty-seven STUs out of the fifty-four 54 STUs that were reporting results were Rs 51,748 crore and their combined losses during the year amounted to Rs 11,350 crore (after accounting for all subsidy and other supports) with forty of the forty-seven STUs incurring losses.

Some states like Madhya Pradesh, Chhattisgarh, Jharkhand and West Bengal do not have state road transport corporations any longer or their undertakings are completely defunct. Many others are also quickly going down the hill. Private operators have now assumed almost the entire space in road transport with 93 per cent of the share of road transport GVA.

Chapter Nineteen

Residential Real Estate
Is a Victim of Bad Policy

India's Real-Estate Landscape

If you surveyed the residential real estate sector in India during the pre- and post-COVID-19 period, you would notice that home sales in metros were falling, new housing projects all over the country had slowed down or come to a trickle, and the housing price index was showing negative real price increase. While housing loans were growing at a healthy rate, the housing loans to GDP ratio was relatively very low, indicating late commencement of the housing loan business in India and lower base. A few housing finance lenders were facing a problem while most builders were stressed, and many simply insolvent. India's residential real estate was in deep crisis which began well before COVID-19.

Commercial real estate, however, was on a good growth trajectory before the pandemic. With an estimated size of about 700 million sq. ft of commercial real estate in India in 2019, growing at about 20 per cent per annum, the segment was expected to grow to over 2000 million sq. ft by 2025. Commercial real estate has attracted considerable interest from big foreign alternate asset investors. It has also seen financing innovation in the form of Real Estate Investment Trusts (REITs), which allow commercial real-estate companies to free up their capital and smaller investors to build a high-yield-return portfolio. With expansion of the IT and ITES sector, financial industry, logistics and organized retail, the commercial real-estate market was booming.

COVID-19 has changed real-estate market dynamics massively for both residential and commercial real estate. Owing to the perceived high risk of contracting infection if strangers work in closed spaces, a large chunk of office real estate occupied by IT, finance and other industries remained unused, with managers and workers being asked to work from home. While offices may see some normality when the risk of COVID-19 abates, working from anywhere, from home or the office, has likely become the new normal. This will reduce demand for commercial office space and the industry might not see double-digit growth in times to come. The hospitality segment of commercial real estate might also witness similar downward demand. However, thanks to e-commerce and digital working rising rapidly, there is likely to be much higher growth for data centres, warehousing and local common co-working spaces. The demand for better and bigger homes—to live and to work from—has grown over since the onset of COVID-19 while the demand for affordable housing has slowed down. On the whole, it appears the pandemic might have a long-term positive impact on residential real estate as millions of white-collar workers reshape their homes to make them suitable for work.

It must be noted that the real-estate industry is extremely important for India's economic growth with construction contributing about 6 per cent of GVA and the industry providing millions of jobs.

Fundamental Cause of Crisis in Residential Real Estate

In the past three decades, most spectacularly after 2003, residential real-estate markets and businesses in India were built on steroids of large capital gains and black money. From 2003 to 2011, stories of residential plot prices doubling every three to four years and residential houses/flats giving 20–30 per cent returns per annum in most urban markets were common and driving the frenzy of investing in real estate. This bull market invited all kind of finance—individual savings; speculators borrowing as much as possible from banks and others; politicians and officials deploying proceeds of corruption and black income; and businessmen diverting funds from legitimate businesses—to buy and book plots, houses and flats. Only a fraction of this demand was for the real need of owning a home;

most of it was to make a quick buck. This runaway demand unleashed the 'animal spirits' of builders, who cared two hoots about the price of land. Land parcels were bought, many times even without caring for the right title, at whatever prices available, and houses and flats sold for cash in 'pre-launch roadshows', often even when the land was not in physical possession. All prices were zooming without anybody worrying about the bubble eventually bursting. Prices of Indian real estate, in many places, put real-estate prices in developed economies to shame.

Real-estate prices have a bad habit of going out of sync with their fundamental value, especially in such frenzied situations. The primary use of a house/flat is for living. Whether you live on rent or in your own house, you get the same economic value as far as the basic service of living is concerned. Therefore, interest payable on the amount of capital invested in a house/flat should be equal to the rental it earns/can earn. However, fundamental valuation was not driving demand, but the lure of capital gains. The rental value became a sideshow. If capital appreciation materialized, it did not matter whether the house remained unoccupied for five years without earning any rental income. The moment this kind of capital appreciation disappears from the equation, the house/flat people invested in becomes a liability rather than an asset.

Following the global financial crisis, which also had its origin in real estate, Indian real-estate prices stated stabilizing/correcting somewhere around 2011–12. Since then, there has been no significant increase in plot/house/flat prices in most places in India. Once real-estate prices stopped growing at high rates, speculative interest flagged. This brought down demand for residential real estate materially. Builders started feeling the pinch but chose to believe it was a short-term phenomenon and that the boom would soon return.

It did not. Demonetization in 2016 delivered the final blow, taking away the major driver of speculative demand. Misreading the situation, many NBFCs and HFCs decided to throw a lifeline to many builders in this beleaguered industry, by lending to projects at very high rates of interest. Excessive borrowing and stalled offtake of constructed houses made residential real-estate builders and companies suffer more. As a result, many accumulated loan liabilities far in excess of the value of assets they held. Builders became insolvent, which transferred the stress of loans taken to NBFCs, HFCs and banks, which funded them by raising funds from mutual funds (MFs) and banks riding on cheap liquidity available after demonetization. As the demonetization largesse reduced and the IL&FS crisis happened, these lenders of last resort also sputtered, cutting off all liquidity (ILFS, the largest infrastructure and infra-financing conglomerate in India, collapsed in 2018 under the weight of overvalued projects and excessively leveraged finances, with considerable sharp and unethical practices hidden behind the debacle). The residential real-estate industry collapsed in 2018.

Lakhs of completed units had no buyers in 2019–20 and most part of 2020–21. Lakhs of incomplete units are still stuck at end-2021 and not getting completed on account of project companies and promoters becoming insolvent. DHFL, a major housing finance company with assets exceeding Rs 1 lakh crore, was admitted under the Corporate Insolvency Resolution Process (CIRP). It had loans in excess of Rs 40,000 crore outstanding towards real-estate developers. Later, the law was amended to allow resolution of financial companies like DHFL through the Insolvency and Bankruptcy Code (IBC) process. DHFL was finally sold to an NBFC with lenders and investors suffering a massive haircut.

Did the Rs 25,000 Crore AIF Work?

Rightly concerned about the state of residential real estate, the government has also been fully aware of the backward and forward linkages of the real-estate sector with economic growth, employment and wages and the health of core industries like steel and cement.

Trying to find a solution for the crisis, it announced the establishment of an alternate investment fund (AIF) of Rs 25,000 crore in November 2019 to provide a lifeline to stressed real-estate developers. The government promised to contribute Rs 10,000 crore to the corpus of this fund and noted that there were about 4.58 lakh housing units stuck in India with over 1,600 stalled realty projects. The AIF, to be managed by a professional agency, was expected to attract investments of about Rs 15,000 crore (later pegged at Rs 12,500 crore) and provide debt financing, with first right to recovery, to relieve the funding stress of these stalled projects.

This AIF was registered with SEBI and SBI Caps was appointed its investment manager.

The AIF has existed for over two years now. However, nothing much has really come out of it. About fifty projects have reportedly been approved. The Fund does not disclose how much has been disbursed.

The fact is that the Rs 25,000 crore AIF has virtually flopped. No real capital contribution, other than from the government, SBI and LIC, has come to the Special Window for Affordable & Mid-Income Housing (SWAMIH) Fund. The fund has not been able to disburse much funds worth the name. This is quite in line with what was expected given the inherent contradictions in the scheme.

There were fundamental design problems in the financing model of the AIF. It was set up to provide debt to stalled projects with the condition that repayment and interest payment got the security of an escrow, which the cash-starved builders were in no position to offer. Loading more debt on already overleveraged residential real-estate developers was not the right financial prescription. The financing arrangement did not solve the issue of the basic unviability of stalled projects.

There was also an inherent conflict between the interests of the AIF and existing lenders. With the AIF designed to demand first right to be serviced and the security of an escrow, the interests of existing lenders would suffer. This would pit them against the AIF, which would lead to stalling of financing.

Section IV: The Digital Economy

Chapter Twenty

State of the Digital Economy

Digital technologies are transforming economies the world over. The global digital economy is estimated to be about $5 trillion or about 5–6 per cent of global GDP. However, there is still a lot of non-standard measurement of global digital GDP. Microprocessor chips by Intel are unquestionably digital hardware. So are laptops produced by Dell or desktops by Lenovo. Likewise, written code and business process management (BPM) services by TCS and Infosys are also clearly part of the digital economy. However, is the turnover of an e-commerce platform like Amazon or Flipkart digital economy? Or payments made through unified payments interface (UPI)?

The difference between digital economy and digitalization of economy has to be clearly understood. The sale of goods is trade, whether performed by a mom-and-pop store, malls or on e-commerce platforms. Likewise, providing credit by banks is banking, whether delivered by processing a manual file or digitally. Production processes are getting increasingly digitalized across all sectors of the economy by building in integrated circuits and software programs. The capex incurred on digitizing a manual or agricultural or industrial process gets counted as value added by the supplier of digital technology but that does not make the digitalized process digital value added or digital GDP. There should not be double counting of digitalized services like trading, banking or entertainment as digital economy.

A good metric is to assess the digitalization of different sectors of the economy if we want to understand how much of the economy or parts of the economy are becoming digital. Digitalization can be measured by developing a good index taking into account factors like the extent of digital hardware and software capex out of total capex. The capex incurred by PowerGrid and other transmission companies on computers, fibre optics, scanners and other digital hardware and all the code/programs purchased as a proportion of total capex incurred would indicate, in a broad measure, the level of digitalization of power transmission. Other factors like proportion of consumers reached digitally or turnover achieved digitally would also indicate digitalization of the sector. An index of all relevant factors can be built to gauge the extent of digitalization of the economy.

The state of the digital Indian economy can be best figured out by assessing how much of the GVA/GDP comes from the production of digital goods and services. Digitalization of the economy should be separately assessed by developing an appropriate metric for it.

Size of the Indian Digital Economy

All economic activities are organized into five-digit codes and in twenty-one sections, eighty-eight divisions, 238 groups, 403 classes and 1304 subclasses for compilation of GDP and other statistical purposes.

One specific division captures manufactured digital goods. This is Division 26—the manufacture of computer, electronic and optical products. This division organizes digital goods into eight groups. We can therefore measure India's GVA from manufactured digital goods by looking at the data of Division 26. Digital services are more dispersed in a number of divisions. Section J, among others, contains all the divisions that capture value added from digital services. There is Division 58 in Group 582, which measures the value added from software publishing. Division 62 is made up of computer programming, consultancy and related activities. Division 63 measures value added from information service activities with two groups: Group 631 (data processing, hosting and related activities; web portals) and Group 639 (other information service activities). Further, in this section, Division 59 (motion pictures, video and television programme production, sound recording and music publishing activities); Division 60 (broadcasting and programming activities); and Division 61 (telecommunication) are also substantially digital value addition services.

Total GVA in the manufacturing sector is measured in two subsectors: corporate manufacturing and household manufacturing. Data in the National Accounts Statistics 2021 inform that in 2017–18, 2018–19 and 2019–20, at current prices, the GVA of manufacturing in the corporate sector was Rs 22.49 lakh crore, Rs 24.57 lakh crore and Rs 23.75 lakh crore, respectively. GVA of IT products manufactured (computer, electronic and optical products; electronic components, consumer electronics, magnetic and optical media; and optical and electronic products put together) was only Rs 1 lakh crore, Rs 1.09 lakh crore and Rs 1.08 lakh crore in the corporate sector in these three years. This indicates that digital manufacturing GVA in India was less than 4.4 per cent of manufactured GVA.

In the household sector, the manufacturing GVA of IT products manufacturing is still smaller. Of the total manufacturing GVA of Rs 3.17 lakh crore, Rs 3.47 lakh crore and Rs 3.37 lakh crore in these three years, the share of IT products was only Rs 0.056 lakh crore, Rs 0.054 lakh crore and Rs 0.043 lakh crore yielding a share of only about 1.6 per cent a year on average.

Together, the digital products manufacturing was only about 3.5 per cent of manufacturing GVA. Evidently, India's manufacturing of digital technology products is quite small.

The size of GVA by digital services in India is much larger. In the three years of 2017–18, 2018–19 and 2019–20, GVA at current prices under 'information and computer-related services' was Rs 6.61 lakh crore, Rs 7.70 lakh crore and Rs 8.70 lakh crore out of the total GVA of Rs 155.06 lakh crore, Rs 171.61 lakh crore and Rs 184.61 lakh crore respectively. The information and computer related services made up 4.26 per cent, 4.49 per cent and 4.71 per cent of the total GVA at current prices.

Two stylized facts are unmistakable. First, digital manufacturing in India is very small and its share in manufacturing is fluctuating. Second, digital services have a respectably large share and their share is growing.

GVA/GDP of the Indian digital economy thus makes up less than 5 per cent of the total economy. When you break this up in digital manufacturing and digital services value added, GVA from digital manufacturing in total GVA works out to be only 0.5 per cent, with the other 4 per cent being contributed by digital services. Global digital manufacturing GVA is about 5 per cent and the size of the digital economy, comprising digital manufacturing and digital services, is much larger. India has a long way to go despite our proven prowess in producing and delivering digital business services and writing software programs.

Digitalization of the Indian Economy

Agriculture and industrial economies began getting digitalized when their manual and mechanical processes improved with the addition of digital capital stock (hardware and connection to digital networks) and embedding of IT services. The capital expenditure of all traditional sectors of economy—agriculture, mining, manufacturing, construction and different services—on IT equipment is a good indicator of digitalization taking place in any of these sectors. Likewise, the operational expenditure on IT services by these traditional sectors can be an additional indicator of digitalization underway.

Data of capital expenditure is available for each sector of economic production, divided in four broad categories: dwellings, other buildings and structures; machinery and equipment; cultivated biological resources; and IP products. Capital expenditure on digital hardware and software is part of machinery and equipment.

Unfortunately, the disaggregated data on capital expenditure made on digital hardware, network connections and software out of the total capital expenditure on machinery and equipment is not separately available.

Services are getting far more digitalized than goods, especially financial, accounting, communication, entertainment and transportation services. More than 90 per cent of payments by value are now made digitally. Most banking services are consumed digitally. Many movies and television and sports programmes are produced and delivered digitally.

As the digital equipment and machinery to produce and deliver these services are not produced domestically, there is a heavy dependence on imports. Electronic imports exceed $50 billion and are the second largest item of imports, comprising over 10 per cent of total import bills. India has been good at delivering software services but even basic software for digitalizing economic processes is imported in large quantities.

The digitalization of the economy is progressing, but is still at a relatively nascent stage.

India Yet to Arrive in the Digital Age

UNCTAD publishes an annual Digital Economy Report. In the 2019 edition, the report states that 'the world is only in the early days of the data-driven economy', despite stellar progress. A perusal of the report indicates that India is still a relatively minor player. Look at these numbers.

First, global internet protocol traffic, which was only 100 GB per day in 1992, grew to 100 GB per second in 1992 and a little under 50,000 GB per second in 2017.

Second, the digital economy is highly concentrated in two countries: the US and China, which enjoy 90 per cent of market capitalization value of the world's seventy largest digital platforms.

Third, 40 per cent of colocation data centres in February 2019 were in the US; India had only 3 per cent.

Fourth, e-commerce sales exceed 80 per cent in South Korea, 60 per cent in Japan and 45 per cent in the US. India's share of e-commerce sale is much smaller. Cross-border B2C sales from India are almost non-existent whereas they exceed 5 per cent for quite a few countries.

Fifth, the top 100 websites located in South Asia, including India, are hardly requested outside the region. In contrast, the top 100 websites located in the US–Canada are requested almost everywhere in the world.

Sixth, not a single top seventy global platform providing different e-commerce services—transportation, delivery, financial services, entertainment, media, search—is Indian.

We do have a dominant presence in the business process outsourcing (BPO) services industry with more than 50 per cent share of the global market. However, this is more on account of our productive digital labour than digital entrepreneurship, capital or technology prowess.

Programmatic Initiatives for Promoting Digital Economy

The Government of India has undertaken several programmes to promote digitalization of governance and digital empowerment of the common man. However, there is no coherent and well-directed strategy for digitalization of the economy. This is hurting India's growth potential.

The government undertook a number of small standalone programmes in the 1980s–1990s to advance the objective of electronic governance. In the middle of the first decade of the new millennium, it adopted the National E-governance Programme, bringing together thirty-odd discrete programmes. Further consolidation and additions have led to the programme being rechristened as 'Digital India'.

Digital India also focuses on digital governance and citizens' empowerment and organizes the government's programmatic interventions in nine pillars. Though there is an element of digital infrastructure creation, it is not a Make in India programme to manufacture hardware and software or create digital networks and platforms, which are the real growth engines. The Make in India programme focuses on twenty-five sectors; IT and BPM sector is one of them. However, there is no focus on hardware.

India's $1 Trillion Digital Opportunity

In February 2019, the Ministry of Electronics and Information Technology (MEITY) published a report titled 'India's Trillion Dollar Digital Opportunity'. It presents a detailed, albeit mixed-up, strategy for India to seize the trillion-dollar digital economic opportunity by 2025.

Let us get one crucial factor cleared first. Does the report talk about $1 trillion GVA opportunity for India or a digitalized Indian economy of $1 trillion? To be fair, the report does not project the goal of $1 trillion as GVA in 2025 from the ICT sector. In fact, it does not use the concept of digital economy loosely used worldwide, which includes entire e-commerce as digital economy. MEITY uses a much wider concept of the 'digital ecosystem', which includes recognized parts of the ICT/digital economy comprising IT–BPM, digital communication services (including telecom) and domestic electronics manufacturing, which are the recognized sectors of the GVA metric, as well as turnover from e-commerce, but also adds digital payments and direct subsidy transfers, which only have a fraction of their turnover and value added attributable to digital economy. The report makes a valuable contribution as it focuses attention on sectors with excellent potential of mainstreaming digitalization, but has to be understood correctly in its context as otherwise it can mislead people into believing that India might be at the threshold of generating GVA from hardware, software and digital services of about 20–25 per cent of total GVA in another four to five years.

India's Scanty Fibre and Satellite Infrastructure

In 2019, market analysis group IDATE conducted a survey ranking countries on the basis of homes and buildings connected to fibre

(Fibre to the Home [FTTH] and Fibre to the Building [FTTB]). The cut-off criterion was a minimum 1 per cent of homes and buildings connected to fibre. The survey found sixty-four countries in the world meeting this minimum threshold; these countries had 1.2 per cent to 95.7 per cent of homes and buildings connected to fibre. UAE, Qatar, Singapore, China, South Korea, Hong Kong, Japan, Mauritius and New Zealand were the top nine countries with fibre penetration exceeding 53 per cent. Unfortunately, India did not even make the 1 per cent cut, a sad reflection of the state of optical fibre penetration in India.

The IDATE report for Asia Pacific 2020 indicated the same status of India. There were 459 million homes and buildings connected to fibre at the end of December 2019 in the Asia and Pacific. And there were sixteen countries in the Asia and Pacific with more than 1 per cent penetration of FTTH/B. India was not one of these countries. Singapore with 94.8 per cent penetration, China with 80.1 per cent and Hong Kong with 74.9 per cent led the pack. Japan also had a healthy 72.6 per cent penetration rate. In South Asia, Sri Lanka with 1.2 per cent was the only entry in the list.

There are two imperatives that make fibre the choice of digital infrastructure creation. First, the cost of digital services delivered through fibre should be competitive to the cost of digital services delivered through spectrum. Second, it should be possible to make fibre reach homes and buildings.

While the cost of fibre is a pittance, laying fibre in Indian conditions is time-consuming and expensive. Piped natural gas (PNG) had the same disadvantage compared to LPG cylinders. However, two policy decisions smoothened the transition to PNG in Indian cities. First, the transition of buses and other modes to transport to compressed natural gas (CNG) by the same concessionaire brought in considerable business and the pricing of PNG was just about the same as LPG. Most important, the laying of PNG and CNG infrastructure, which is far more demanding than optical fibre, was administratively facilitated. Likewise, appropriate policy incentives in the form of all digital services being delivered through fibre, reducing the cost of laying fibre infrastructure and facilitating its laying, would be vital to realize the policy goal of 'Fibre to All' expressed in the National Digital Communications Policy, 2018 (NDCP-2018).

The satellite business is not reserved for the public sector under IDRA-1951. However, only the Space Commission and Government of

India organizations were allowed to develop and launch satellites. What was not done by law was achieved by administrative fiat. ISRO and other public institutions, however, have done a fabulous job of making and launching satellites, providing excellent quality at most competitive costs. However, not allowing the private sector has constrained the use of satellites in the expansion of digital infrastructure.

The Government of India permitted the private sector to enter the satellite business in 2020 by revoking the administrative decision. One hopes this decision is implemented without any constraints and backroom controls. Indian entrepreneurs have the potential to make the country a global satellite manufacture and launching hub.

All considered, the combination of fibre to every building (home and business), 5G spectrum and satellites for all digital applications should help India create world-class digital infrastructure and pave the way for digitalization of the Indian economy, businesses and households.

Chapter Twenty-One

Policy Framework Not Good Enough to Make India a Digital Economy

National Policy on Electronics, 2012 (NPE-2012)

Chip design, producing integrated circuits for manufacturing computers and embedding consumer and other products, also called electronic system design and manufacturing (ESDM), or simply electronics, is the first of the three big digital technologies: hardware, software and platforms.

Recognizing that it was losing the electronics hardware game, India announced the National Policy on Electronics (NPE) in 2012. The policy recognized explicitly that the electronics industry was the largest and fastest growing manufacturing industry in the world with a turnover of about $1.75 trillion. It also recognized that the domestic electronics industry was quite small at only $20 billion with 'actual value-addition in domestically produced electronic product' being very low, ranging between 5 per cent and 10 per cent in most cases. It presented an ominous scenario of Indian demand for electronics reaching $400 billion by 2020 and the country importing about $300 billion of electronics, which 'may far exceed oil imports', unless the government took action.

NPE-2012 articulated the vision of creating 'a globally competitive electronics design and manufacturing industry to meet the country's needs and serve the international market' and the specific objective of achieving a turnover of about $400 billion by 2020, involving investment of about $100 billion and employment to around 28 million.

NPE 2012 proposed a slew of measures, like providing 'attractive fiscal incentives across the value chain of the ESDM sector through a Modified Special Incentive Package Scheme (M-SIPS) to eliminate disability costs in manufacturing on account of infrastructure gaps relating to power, transportation, etc., and mitigate the relatively high cost of finance'. It also spoke of 'setting up of semiconductor wafer fab facilities and its ecosystem for design and fabrication of chips and chip components'. All the usual measures of 'giving preference to domestically produced electronic products', 'incentives for setting up over 200 electronic manufacturing clusters (EMCs)', 'development of appropriate infrastructure', a 'fairly stable tax regime conducive to attract global investments and encourage the electronics sector' and a 'Fund of Funds' were also promised.

The policy did not achieve its objectives though the share of India in global electronics manufacture went up from 1.3 per cent in 2012 to about 3 per cent in 2018. Electronic imports exceeded $50 billion in 2019–20 with 40 per cent coming from China. Though there has been notable progress in mobile handset manufacturing, the domestic electronics industry is still not worth $75 billion.

National Policy on Electronics, 2019 (NPE-2019)

NPE-2019 is largely an updated version of NPE-2012 with some refinement. The target of $400 billion turnover in electronics manufacture, which was to be achieved by 2020, has been pushed to 2025. The policy relies heavily on the manufacture of mobile handsets (1 billion handsets; $190 billion turnover).

NPE-2019 chronicles the poor progress in most measures initiated under NPE-2012. For instance, 134 units assisted under the M-SIPS made a capital investment of $1.3 billion and achieved a turnover of about $10 billion. Though twenty greenfield EMCs and three brownfield clusters were 'sanctioned', none seem to have become functional. The amount committed by the Electronics Development Fund, the Fund of Funds set up to encourage venture capital, could commit only Rs 857 crore or about $130 million totally to as many as thirteen 'daughter' funds.

There are some modifications. The fabless chip design industry is to be promoted now, while the semiconductor fab facilities proposed in NPE-2012 did not get established in India.

NPE-2019 does not offer anything new to promote electronic hardware production. The government is supplementing the policy with other measures, like PLIs, or production-linked incentives, to encourage the establishment of industries that use a substantial amount of electronics.

PLI Scheme for Large-Scale Electronics Manufacturing

Both the editions of the NPE were more focused on scale of electronics manufacturing than electronics manufacturing. Other than the proposal of semiconductor fab manufacturing, all other proposals were effectively targeted towards small-scale enterprises in the electronics sector. Small-scale enterprises do not have any electronics technology and make only a few electronic components. As the producers of some small-value electronic products, small-scale enterprises mostly use second-hand/recycled components in consumer electronic products. Even larger enterprises in India are not manufacturers of basic electronics, like the chips made by Intel or solar wafers. Nor are they large enough to reap the advantage of scale manufacturing like Samsung or Apple in the mobile segment.

Recognizing the limitation of NPE-2019 in incentivizing large-scale manufacturing, the new PLI scheme focuses on value addition in assembling and manufacturing some components, and notes the need for a mechanism to compensate for manufacturing disabilities that are to the tune of '8.5 per cent to 11 per cent vis-à-vis other major manufacturing economies'.

The PLI scheme offers incentive of 4–6 per cent on incremental sales of mobile phones and eight specified electronics components (e.g., discrete semiconductor devices like transistors, printed circuit boards) manufactured in India to approved companies. It aims to bring iconic mobile set manufactures to India and is expected to cost a total of Rs 48,000 crore over the next five years.

An Assessment of Electronics Manufacturing Policies

The global electronics hardware industry is the largest growing manufacturing industry as it produces electronics that are change agents to transform the production of all goods and the delivery of services. The hardware industry has grown to be over $2.5 trillion and is expected to be the biggest growing industry for many more years.

However, we have not been able to jump on the electronics manufacturing bandwagon. India's 3 per cent-odd share is in turnover of electronic products. If the value added in the electronics hardware industry is taken into account, the country's share in global value added in electronic hardware alone is still smaller.

The largest value addition in the electronics hardware industry is concentrated among a few manufacturers who own most patents and are master designers. The personal computers and devices segment is dominated by Apple, IBM, Lenovo and HP, while Samsung, Huawei, Apple and Oppo enjoy over 60 per cent share globally in mobile manufacturing. In 5G technology-based instrument manufacturing, Ericsson, Nokia, Qualcomm and Huawei dominate the world, while among semiconductor manufacturing companies, Intel, SK Hynix, TSMC, Micron Technology and Qualcomm enjoy preeminent status. It is unfortunate to note that there is not a single Indian company among the global top ten in any of these segments. It is a sobering thought. This is possibly recognized by Indian policymakers as both NPE-2019 and PLI-2020 do not talk about creating Indian electronics manufacturing behemoths.

National Policy on Software Products, 2019 (NPSP-2019)

India has strong IT companies and is the largest exporter of IT services in the world. However, when it comes to software products, the country's performance is as bad as electronic products manufacturing. The National Policy on Software Products, 2019 (NPSP-2019), the first policy targeting software products as such, makes a telling statement that the contribution of software products to IT and ITES was only $7.1 billion of the total estimated revenue of $168 billion. The export of software products was worse at only $2.3 billion of total exports of $126 billion, giving the country only a 0.5 per cent share of the global software market. The worst part was that India imported software products worth $10 billion, making us a net importer of software products.

Software or coding is the second pillar of the digital revolution—a skill at which Indians excel. Most companies in Silicon Valley employ Indian engineers for coding. Indian companies have also developed some world-class software products. In the banking space, Indian companies have developed products like Finacle and TCS BaNCS, which rank among the top ten software products. Yet, when it comes to the top ten or even twenty-five software companies of the world, Indian companies do not figure anywhere.

NPSP-2019 applies the hackneyed formula of promoting industrialization in India by customizing it to the software industry. It talks about nurturing 10,000 technology start-ups; creating a talent pool of 1 million IT professionals; setting up a single-window platform for facilitation of the software product industry and allowing set-off of tax payment on the investment made. The policy proposes no interventions to make India a software products giant.

Today, electronics manufacturing and software industries are the best value creators in the world of manufacturing and development. These industries are promoted by iconic technology entrepreneurs and only need an enabling environment from governments. The top companies dominate the world of electronics manufacturing and software development and employ the best brains. The type of interventions and support offered in NPSP might help some small enterprises to write software for local use. This is important but any hope that such enterprises can produce world-beating software products would be misplaced.

Policies to Promote IT Services

IT services are business services performed from a remote location or by stationing the personnel of the IT services company in the premises of the outsourcing company. We captured the opportunity offered by fast and cheaper data transmission over distances, which allowed business services to be delivered in the US and other countries by IT companies located in India.

India's cheaper and educated workforce provided the killer advantage. Many new technocrat entrepreneurs helped seize this moment for India, such as Infosys and HCL Technologies. Some traditional economy companies—TCS and Wipro, for example—also diversified into the IT services space.

The government created the right policy environment for this success. The software technology parks set up provided faster data transmission facility, the biggest differential for establishing successful enterprises, as well as other technological infrastructural services like data storage facilities. One big fiscal concession was income-tax profit exemption.

These policies were adequate to empower Indian entrepreneurs to set up world-class companies and capture one-third of the global business for the country.

If the government had provided the policy and infrastructure support of the type offered under NPSP and NPE for IT services export promotion, we may not have seen the development of our IT services giants. As the IT services business is suited to both large and small businesses, software technology parks offered their services to both and small businesses thrived equally. Electronics hardware and software products, by nature, are more suited to large-scale enterprises.

Policies for IT Infrastructure

Digital infrastructure is built on whatever medium—fibre optics, satellites, spectrum—can carry and store data fast and in huge volumes. In India, digital infrastructure has developed most on spectrum using mobile telephony. Most data is transmitted on spectrum in India as fibre optics has got a relatively short shrift, though it seems to be receiving attention now. Likewise, we have constrained the use of satellites in moving data.

We have fallen into another trap by unimaginatively using digital infrastructure for digitalizing the economy. Just as excessive pricing of land became a constraint on development of industries, excessive pricing of spectrum, especially after the 2G scam, is coming in the way of adoption of digital technologies and would most likely constrain the use of 5G technologies as well.

National Digital Communications Policy, 2018 (NDCP-2018)

The government adopted NDCP-2018, recognizing that 'digital infrastructure and services are increasingly emerging as key enablers and critical determinants of a country's growth and well-being'. The policy is vital to achieve two major goals: transforming the economy into a digital one by digitalizing production and distribution of goods; and transforming society, comprising individuals and households, into a digital one.

NDCP-2018 focuses on the second objective and by and large ignores the first one. Its vision statement aims to 'fulfil the information and communication needs of citizens and enterprises through the establishment of ubiquitous, resilient, secure, accessible and affordable Digital Communication Infrastructure and Services and, in the process, support India's transition to a digital empowered economy and society'. It sets its goals in terms of providing digital infrastructure services to people: universal broadband connectivity at 50 Mbps to every citizen; 1 Gbps connectivity to all gram panchayats; 100 Mbps broadband on demand to all key development institutions; fixed-line broadband access to 50 per cent of households; unique mobile subscriber density of fifty-five by 2020 and sixty-five by 2022; deployment of public Wi-Fi hotspots; and connectivity to all uncovered areas. There is no mention of enabling businesses to get digital infrastructure services to transform the production of goods and services.

NDCP-2018 talks about establishing a National Broadband Mission, but securing universal broadband access through four different nets: BharatNet, GramNet, NagarNet and JanWiFi. It also talks about the Fibre First Initiative to take fibre to the home and key development institutions in Tier 1, 2 and 3 towns and rural clusters. Grudgingly, it mentions 'every enterprise' as well.

NDCP-2018 is welfare-oriented, not business-oriented. Global enterprises that have developed and own their digital technologies are making an enormous amount of money. Indian corporates do not have these digital technologies. The policy should have focused on getting these technology majors to invest in India to create the most advanced and functional digital infrastructure in the country. The goal of attracting $100 billion of foreign investment is mentioned. Merely making such a general statement will not bring FDI. We need to create customized solutions, like the PLI initiative, to get electronics manufactured in India. In fact, if we make our auction terms more business-like, getting world-class, cutting-age digital infrastructure constructed in India would cost the government nothing.

Chapter Twenty-Two

Muddled Policies in Data and E-Commerce

Fundamentality of Data Creation, Storage and Use for the Digital Economy

All numbers, words, pictures, sounds, information, expressions and everything else constructed in bytes are data. Data has been described as the new oil. This is an incorrect description. Data is more like matter. All the agriculture and industrial goods produced are made of matter. All digital goods and services produced are made of data. Some matter works better as fuel or energy. Oil is more of a fuel and not building block matter. For the digital economy, data does not work like fuel, semiconductors perhaps do. For the digital economy, data is everything: it is the input, the process of production and the output. The economy cannot be digitalized without extensive creation and use of data. Data is the matter for the digital economy and semiconductors are fuel.

Humans are factors of production and consumers of most goods and services produced in the economy. Digitalization offers the opportunity of a fundamental reset from the production systems of the industrial economy. The industrial economy was most competitive and productive producing goods at scale. This led to mass production of almost every product. Though humans have innumerable subtle variations in physical parameters, mass production could only afford a few. For instance, shirts could be produced only in three or four sizes. With more variations, scale and competitiveness were lost. In the process, products could not be customized precisely to each individual. Customization was a lost cause in the Industrial Revolution.

The digital revolution brings back customization as a key differentiator of products and services for every individual.

Customization requires personal data: for example, the precise measure of all dimensions of the foot for making the best fitting shoes for each individual; individual preferences for delivering the products desired; even producing a car that meets the specific needs of an individual or family. The digital economy works, thrives and prospers by using personal data.

However, personal data can be misused to target or manipulate a person or a group with similar attributes. Personal data on identity, health and other information of a sensitive nature can be hacked or misused to cause financial and other harm to the person concerned. It is absolutely necessary that such misuse, manipulation and harm be prevented.

The absolute indispensability of personal data for digitalization of the economy and the uncompromisable state obligation of preventing the misuse of this data represent the most intricate conflict in the march of the digital economy. How a nation or society arrives at a solution that achieves a balance between both objectives will determine its success or failure in reaping the advantages of digitalization of the economy.

Data Legislation and Regulation in India

Unfortunately, the value and critical advantage of data for digitalization of the economy did not get much appreciation in India. Instead, protection of personal data got all the policy attention, specifically after 2016.

Protection of sensitive personal data (SPD) was sought to be ensured by the Information Technology (Reasonable Security Practices and Procedures and Sensitive Personal Data or Information) Rules 2011 framed under the IT Act, 2000. These rules defined personal data and set out the obligations of body corporates in the collection, use and transfer of such data. There were no serious restrictions on the use of personal data by body corporates in the SPD Rules.

In July 2017, the government constituted a committee of experts under the chairmanship of Justice B.N. Srikrishna to deliberate upon a data protection framework for India. While the preamble to the terms of reference (ToR) of the Srikrishna Committee referred to the 'need to ensure growth of the digital economy', the ToRs were governed by the utmost importance of 'keeping personal data of citizens secure and protected'. The aim was also 'to study various issues relating to data protection in India' and 'to make specific suggestions for consideration of the Central government on principles to be considered for data protection in India and suggest a draft data protection bill'.

The report of the Srikrishna Committee did not make a single recommendation on how to seize the opportunity to digitalize the Indian economy by using data as the critical advantage. All its recommendations related on how to define and deal with personal data. The Committee also recommended a comprehensive Personal Data Protection Bill, 2018.

The Bill recommended by the Srikrishna Committee was examined by the government taking into consideration feedback from people and institutions. After certain changes, it introduced the Personal Data Protection Bill, 2019, in the Parliament for adoption. The 2019 Bill is far more restrictive in the use of personal data than the 2018 Bill.

There are four major concerns with the way the government has chosen to deal with the issue of data.

First, the world of data is being viewed from a very narrow lens of personal data. The larger world of data, which includes non-personal data as well as non-personal aspects of personal data, is being given short shrift.

Second, all the energy and efforts are focused only on protection of personal data at every stage—collection, storage and use—as a matter of privacy and private property. There is no thought and strategy for using data as a matter of critical advantage for building a competitive and rich digital economy and seizing the opportunity offered by digitalization of production of goods and services.

Third, the fundamental construct of the Constitution to protect the privacy of citizens from the government, which is part of our fundamental rights, is being sought to be turned on its head by seeking to exclude private businesses from the use of personal data while giving overriding access to the government to not only personal data of persons but also non-personal data of businesses.

Fourth, in today's virtual world, there are no national boundaries for storage and access to stored data. An overnationalistic view on localization of data would only hurt our interests.

For example, the US does not restrict the use of personal data for business purposes, except where it is really a matter of privacy defined precisely. The EU has also developed extensive regulations to encourage free use of non-personal data. It is time India, too, considers a law for the use of data, including personal data, by businesses to provide a competitive advantage to our businesses. Sensitive or critical personal data needs to be defined narrowly, the access to which can cause real harm to the person concerned. There is nothing sensitive about a bank account number, caste or religion of a person. There is no need to define these as sensitive personal data.

The bill proposes massive administrative machinery and elaborate procedures to obtain the consent of the 'data principal' for use of personal data. If enacted, it would usher in a regime worse than the licence permit raj that destroyed private enterprise in industrialization. There should be a more liberal and easier process to obtain the consent of a person for use of personal data. Willingly provided information while filling up an application or an interaction should suffice to obtain a consent that is 'free, informed, specific, clear and capable of being withdrawn'. That said, misuse of private data must be as punishable as breach of privacy.

The bill has been examined by the Joint Committee of the Parliament. The committee's recommendations did not change any of the contested provisions. Instead, it muddied the water further by doing away with the difference between personal and non-personal data, indirectly subjecting non-personal data to the same privacy protection. The Committee also expanded the authority of the government to use personal and non-personal data and grant exemptions. Fundamental right of life and liberty, from which the right to privacy is derived, which is actually against the government, has been turned on its head completely. The committee's recommendations do not seem to be in the interest of building the digital economy of India. The government would need to examine the entire matter afresh.

E-commerce Policy Proposal Continues to Queer the Pitch

Trade and commerce, like any other service sector, are an economic service and extremely amenable to digitalization. Transacted digitally, e-commerce has enormous advantages of cost, time and distance, owing to which it is disrupting traditional trade and commerce the world over.

There is no legitimate rationale for a separate law or policy for e-commerce, just as there is no logic in a separate law or policy for e-banking, e-accounting or BPO. However, Indian policymakers have been very sensitive to foreign companies selling products in India through both the brick-and-mortar model and e-commerce mode. Likewise, they have been averse to permitting foreign companies to invest in the trade and commerce business segment in India, again both in traditional and e-commerce mode.

The Department for Industrial Policy and Promotion (DIPP), renamed Department of Promotion for Industry and Internal Trade (DPIIT), has been in charge of FDI policy. India has evolved a restrictive FDI policy for trade and commerce over the years. There are distinctions in terms of wholesale trade and retail trade; multi-brand and single-brand stores; brick-and-mortar trade and commerce and e-commerce; and platform e-commerce companies and own product inventory/direct selling e-commerce companies. There are also numerous conditionalities on local content, minimum investment amount, export obligation, localities where the business can be established and extent of foreign ownership. The policy is quite complex.

For no good reason, DPIIT decided to take over the mantle of controlling digital aspects of e-commerce as well, notably data. In February 2019, it announced a Draft National E-Commerce Policy with the theme, 'India's Data for India's Development'. It is hardly an e-commerce policy. Rather, it is clearly a trade data control and regulation policy. It aims to 'regulate cross-border data flow'; lays down 'conditions to be adhered to by business entities which have access to sensitive data of Indian users stored abroad'; bans 'sharing of such data with third-party entities, even with customer consent'; mandates 'e-commerce companies to ensure that all product shipments from other countries are channelized through the Customs route'; and proposes creation of industrial standards for smart devices and IoT (Internet of Things) equipment.

The proposed e-commerce policy transgresses the mandate of MEITY as data regulation, irrespective of sector, is its domain. Excessively restrictive, it amounts to the worst form of protectionism in trade and commerce that India successfully demolished in 1991.

The inherent contractions and excessive protectionism proposed in the policy have not allowed it to progress much. The government has indicated that it is working on another draft, which is still in the works.

There is absolutely no need for the government to frame an e-commerce policy to regulate data and digitalization of trade and commerce services. The policy draft should simply be scrapped.

Consumer Protection (E-Commerce) Rules Another Protective Attempt to Shield Declining Physical Distribution

The government used powers under the Consumer Protection Act 2019 to frame amendments to the Consumer Protection (E-Commerce) Rules 2020 and released its draft for public comments on 21 June 2020. The draft rules seek to impose several unnecessary and onerous obligations on e-commerce entities operating in India.

Quite unrelated to the objectives of the Consumer Protection Act, the draft rules contained several provisions relating to the listing of related parties and associated enterprises as sellers, prohibitions on sale of its own goods and services by the e-commerce entity on its e-commerce platform, prohibition of flash sales, etc. The proposals of the draft rules hurt not only the foreign e-retailers but also domestic e-commerce entities. In this sense, the Consumer Protection draft rules went beyond the approach adopted for many years for achieving these objectives under the FDI regulations.

Quite predictably, the draft rules were opposed both by the foreign-controlled e-commerce companies and also by the domestic e-commerce companies. The draft rules are so widely framed that these rules, if finally notified, would become the bane of not only e-commerce companies in trading but would hurt the fintech, health-tech and other technology companies being established by start-ups in India.

These rules are an attempt to stop the march of e-commerce and digital technology-driven services, which are creating enormous business value, by disrupting the entire distribution and retail businesses being more efficient, less costly and delivering better service experience.

The draft rules should be withdrawn.

Section V: Environmental and Social Economy

Chapter Twenty-Three

State of Environmental Economy

Low Per-Capita Total Emissions, but Rising

India's total greenhouse gas (GHG) emissions were estimated to be the equivalent of 3.202 million tonnes of carbon dioxide (CO_2) in 2014, which made our per-capita GHG emissions about 2.48 tonnes of CO_2 equivalent per person. The country's share was 6.55 per cent of total global GHG emissions of 48.89 billion tonnes of CO_2 equivalent. India's per-capita emissions were far lower than global emissions of 6.73 tonnes of CO_2 equivalent.

The country's total GHG emissions of 3.202 million tonnes of CO_2 equivalent for a \$2.131 trillion economy meant that the energy intensity of India's GDP, measured in tonnes of CO_2 equivalent per million dollars of GDP, was 1503 tonnes of CO_2 equivalent. Global energy intensity was 665 tonnes. In this metric, India's energy intensity was 2.26 times the global average.

CO_2 forms the largest component of GHGs. India reportedly emitted 2.299 million tonnes of CO_2 in 2018, 4.8 per cent more than the previous year.

That said, India made impressive environmental commitments as part of nationally determined contributions. In fact, the global Climate Action Tracker has rated the country's efforts as '2 degree compatible'—

this means such efforts could limit average global temperature rise to 2°C by 2100.

India Breathes Bad Air

India has a National Air Quality Index (AQI) since 2014 that takes eight pollutants into account: particulate matter less than 10 micrometre (PM_{10}); particulate matter less than 2.5 micrometre ($PM_{2.5}$); nitrogen dioxide (NO_2); sulphur dioxide (SO_2); carbon monoxide (CO); ozone (O_3); ammonia (NH_3); and lead (Pb). Their individual values over a twenty-four-hour or eight-hour period are placed in six categories depending upon safety levels: good (0–50), satisfactory (51–100), moderately polluted (101–200), poor (201–300), very poor (301–400) and severe (401–500). The most severe value of any of these eight elements indicates the AQI for that place and day.

Particulate matter, especially $PM_{2.5}$, enters the lungs and can cause aggravated asthma, decreased lung function, respiratory difficulties like irritation of airways, coughing and difficulty in breathing, and even premature death in people with heart or lung disease. NO_2 also contributes to particulate pollution and chemical reactions that produce ozone. Its impact on health is largely similar to the effects of PM. SO_2, besides causing health problems like NO_2, is also linked to cardiovascular disease. CO causes headache, dizziness, vomiting and nausea; if the levels are very high, it may lead to unconsciousness and even death. Ozone can trigger chest pain and coughing and harm lung tissues, besides worsening bronchitis and asthma. A large presence of ammonia in the air causes burning of the nose, throat and respiratory tract. It can also cause bronchiolar and alveolar oedema. Exposure to lead causes anaemia and may damage the kidneys and brain.

Air is life-giving and life-sustaining. However, the AQI readings tell us how injurious life-giving air has become to life itself. 'Delhi's AQI Reads 450 and Reaches Most Severe Zone'—we've all seen screaming newspaper headlines like this, especially at the onset of winter in the national capital. India is breathing bad air.

Released in October 2020, *The State of Global Air* report assesses air quality on three important parameters: people's exposure to $PM_{2.5}$ (which represents ambient outside air pollution), ozone exposure and indoor pollution. The report found a marginal decline in the global level of $PM_{2.5}$ exposure over the period 2010–2019. However, the presence of ozone has increased over this period. Likewise, the use of solid fuels in homes for cooking and heating, which is a primary reason for indoor pollution, has also declined globally.

India fares badly with respect to two of the three metrics: exposure to $PM_{2.5}$ pollution and increase of ozone. However, the country has done quite well in reduction of use of solid fuels in homes, although the proportion of households using solid fuels still continues to be quite high. In 2019, India had the highest population-weighted annual average $PM_{2.5}$ exposure in the world at 83.2 micrograms per cubic metre ($\mu g/m^3$) of air. WHO's safe limit for weighted annual average $PM_{2.5}$ exposure is only 10 $\mu g/m^3$. India was in the least healthy category of exposure, between 75 and 85 $\mu g/m^3$. Over the period 2010–2019, the country saw the third highest increase in exposure after Nigeria and Bangladesh at 6.5 $\mu g/m^3$ over this period; Nigeria had an increase of 7.5 $\mu g/m^3$. A number of countries saw decline in exposure during this period. India's general quality of air suggests a state of emergency.

We also fared poorly with regard to ozone exposure.

India performed well in handling indoor pollution. South Asia, which has the second highest use of solid fuels—coal, charcoal, wood, agriculture waste, animal dung and kerosene—in the world, recorded the largest decline in the proportion of households using solid fuels from 2010 to 2019, from close to 74 per cent in 2010 to about 60 per cent in 2019. In India, about 54 million households stopped using solid fuels to meet their cooking and heating needs. This was the second largest decline in the world after China, which saw a tremendous reduction to the tune of 220 million households.

About 3.8 billion people (49 per cent of the global population) are still exposed to indoor pollution on account of using solid fuels. The number is the highest in Sub-Saharan Africa where several countries have almost every household using solid fuels. India's good performance is partly explained by the expansion of schemes like the Ujjwala Yojana, which has led to the provision of an LPG connection to over 80 million families, most of whom were earlier using solid fuels, including kerosene. There has been a remarkable decline in the use of kerosene in the country.

That said, India needs to urgently attend to the matter of the worst quality of air in the world, which continues to deteriorate. In fact, the situation in several pockets is even more dire than what the national average conveys.

Water Quality is Also a Matter of Serious Concern

Quality of water is extremely important for both human and aquatic life. India monitors about 3500 locations for water quality. This network of monitoring stations covers over 1800 locations on rivers, about 475 lakes/ ponds/tanks, about fifty canals, about fifty creeks and seawater locations, fifty drains, fifty sewage treatment plants, ten water treatment plants and about 1000 wells.

Biological, chemical and physical aspects of water impact its quality in terms of fitness for bathing, drinking and supporting aquatic life. Water quality aspects to be assessed include temperature (impacts life and reproduction of aquatic organisms); turbidity (impacts light penetration that affects productivity of plants in waterbodies); bacteria (pathogens coming from human and animal waste are a health risk); dissolved oxygen (concentration of dissolved oxygen necessary for aquatic life); pH (balance between acidic and alkaline ions); organics (carbon-based industrial chemicals that are toxic and carcinogenic); and a few others, like the presence of metals, ammonia, etc.

There is no water quality index in India that provides a numeric value to capture the overall quality of water like the AQI. The Central Pollution Control Board (CPCB) has identified four parameters to calculate water quality. These are dissolved oxygen, which should be higher than 4 mg per litre; biological oxygen demand (BOD), which should be lower than 3 mg per litre; faecal coliform which should be lower than 2500 most probable number (MPN) per 100 ml; and total coliform, which should be fewer than 5000 MPN per 100 ml. Essentially, it boils down to two parameters: BOD, as higher demand indicates lower availability of dissolved oxygen; and coliform count. Water is evaluated for these aspects. If any value is not met, the water is considered unsatisfactory.

CPCB classifies all unsatisfactory river stretches in five priority categories depending upon BOD.

In May 2019, CPCB announced that the entire water from the Ganga was unfit for direct consumption. Of the 86 live stations monitored, only seven areas were found to have water fit for drinking after disinfection; the rest was not fit for drinking even after disinfection. It is estimated that 70 per cent of surface water in India is unfit for consumption. Another estimate suggests that as much as 40 million litres of wastewater enters rivers, lakes and other water bodies without being treated.

A 2015 CPCB report announced that the number of polluted rivers (whose water is not fit for drinking) in India increased from 121 to 275. In terms of polluted stretches, it found 302 polluted stretches on 275 rivers. This number increased to 351 in 2018. The problem is becoming quite acute in the case of groundwater as well. Besides availability going down, the quality of water, owing to the presence of chemicals and other harmful substances, has also been consistently falling.

There is a water quality emergency in India.

India's Environmental Laws Have a Broad Sweep

India participated in the first international environment conference in Stockholm in June 1972. Realizing that the state of the environment was fast deteriorating, the country decided to enact a law. The Environment (Protection) Act, 1986, referred to the decisions taken at the United Nations Conference on the Human Environment held in Stockholm and the need to implement these decisions insofar as they relate to the 'protection and improvement of environment and prevention of hazards to human beings, other living creatures, plants and property'.

The Environment Act, 1986, defines 'environment' widely to include 'water, air and land and the interrelationship which exists among and between water, air and land, and human beings, other living creatures, plants, micro-organism and property'. It also defines 'environmental pollutant' widely to mean 'any solid, liquid or gaseous substance present in such concentration as may be, or tend to be, injurious to environment'. The law treats 'the presence in the environment of any environmental pollutant' as environmental pollution. In a nutshell, any solid, liquid and gaseous substance present in water, air and land in such concentration that it is injurious to the natural state of relationship between water, air and land and human beings, other living creatures, plants, micro-organisms and property becomes environmental pollution.

The Environment Protection Act also deals with hazardous substances in quite a comprehensive manner.

The Act confers immense powers on the Central government. It empowers it 'to take all such measures as it deems necessary or expedient for the purpose of protecting and improving the quality of the environment and preventing, controlling and abating environment pollution'. The powers conferred are more extensive and intrusive than any other law has conferred in India. The Centre can lay down standards for the quality of environment, standards for emission or discharge of environmental pollutants from any source whatsoever, and prepare and prescribe manuals, codes or guides relating to prevention, control and abatement of environmental pollution. It can also place restrictions on areas in which any industries, operations or processes shall not be carried out or be carried out subject to safeguards prescribed. In the exercise of these powers, the Central government can bring in industrial licensing or impose any kind of prohibitory orders on production of goods and services. It also has sweeping powers under Section 5 of the Act to issue directions to 'any person, officer or any authority' that they would be bound to comply with. There are apparently no constraints on the authority of the Central government to issue directions.

Every person carrying on any 'industry, operation or process' has been prohibited to 'discharge or emit or permit to be discharged or emitted any environmental pollutant in excess of such standards as may be prescribed'. In case the discharge of an environmental pollutant occurs in excess of prescribed standards, the person responsible is bound to take necessary action to mitigate the environmental pollution caused as a result. Wherever such a discharge is expected to occur, the person responsible has to take necessary action to prevent and mitigate such discharge. There is a clear responsibility imposed by the law on the person in charge of any process or establishment that might lead to discharge of environmental pollution.

The government and authorities have also been empowered to act in situations where such occurrence of pollution takes place. There is an obligation on the person carrying on the industry, operation or process to intimate the fact of such an occurrence or apprehension to the authorities. The authorities have been empowered to take remedial measures. The person responsible for occurrence of the pollution is bound to render all assistance and pay the expenses incurred by authorities on remedial measures along with interest. The authorities have the right to enter, inspect and search such premises. An offender under the Act is liable for a fine and jail up to a period of five years, which in certain cases can increase to seven years.

Chapter Twenty-Four

Industrialization Primary Cause for Environmental Crisis

Increasing Awareness of the Impact of Development on the Environment

Humans were, in general, not conscious of the adverse impact of their agricultural and industrial progress till about fifty to sixty years ago. This was because the tipping point in the use of nature's products and her capacity to absorb noxious gases, emissions and pollutants had not been reached. We enjoyed many free lunches. No more, however.

Humans have become far more aware of the adverse impacts of energy use, industrialization and excessive consumption. In the past fifty to sixty years, governments the world over have started controlling adverse environmental impact by regulating the use of fossil fuels, chemicals and certain materials. Industry has also invested in using materials and energy more efficiently and controlling emissions. The use of coal, the father of industrialization, is being reduced everywhere and the day is not far when its use becomes history.

Innovation of digitalization is enabling less use of materials and energy in production and distribution of goods and services. The use of several materials has peaked. Digitalization has introduced enormous efficiencies. Efficient industrialization and increasing universalization of digitalization will help humans bring the environment back to a sustainable state.

Environmental Impacts are Personal, Local and Global

The use of fuels, improper disposal of agricultural and human waste, use of inorganic materials and the by-products of agriculture, industrial and digital production and distribution alter the sustainable balance of nature and her bounty—clean air and water, green earth, blue skies, ambient temperatures, natural forests, wetlands and other ecospheres—harming both the environment and the people who inhabit it.

Adverse environmental impacts operate at three levels: individual or personal, local or social, and global.

Many impacts affect individuals. For instance, workers in a slate-producing industry can get silicosis; workers in chemical factories are exposed to health hazards in the form of leaks; and women cooking with dung or wood are exposed to noxious fumes and black carbon. There are numerous production and consumption processes for both goods and services that expose millions of people to adverse impacts.

Most impacts are local, confined to an area that may be large or small but is localized. A thermal power plant spewing smoke sends out particulate material of small sizes (2.5 mm and 10 mm), which affects human health, and noxious gases such as nitrogen oxide, sulphur oxide and mercury. These pollutants spread over a certain area and settle down, or get blown to another area nearby. The burning of paddy stubble by farmers in Punjab in September–October every year to clear their fields to sow wheat spreads black carbon, particulate matter and other pollutants over a larger local area of India. Delhi bears the noxious consequences every year of such stubble burning.

Some environmental impacts are global. Coal-based power plants produce CO_2 while burning carbon in coal. Rotting of agro-waste or growing of paddy in water produces methane. CO_2 and methane are GHGs. Once produced, they remain in the atmosphere forever until sequestered or converted into basic elements again. Their impacts do not remain localized. GHGs prevent the escape of heat into the outer atmosphere. They act like traps and contribute to heating up the planet; the eventual consequence is 'global warming', which, as the name suggests, affects the entire world. Likewise, chemical substances used in air-conditioners and other cooling devices can cut into the ozone layer and deplete it. This again has a global impact as the ozone layer acts as a shield to prevent harmful rays coming in from outer space.

Global Response to Environmental Deterioration Has Evolved since the 1960s

There were episodes of severe environmental distress in the world before global awareness developed to treat environmental deterioration as a serious threat to mankind. The notorious London smog caused by burning of coal and acid rains in some parts of the US and Europe caused not just severe discomfort and health issues but also fatalities. However, these episodes were treated as local and the rest of the world was not unduly concerned or alarmed.

Rachel Carson's book *Silent Spring* (1962) is credited with bringing the adverse effects of uncontrolled chemical discharges in water streams to global consciousness. The impact of use of fossil fuels, discharge of chemicals and other industrial pollutants in water and air, and expanded production of non-biodegradable products began to assume serious proportions in the 1960s. The atmospheric discharge of GHGs also assumed a significant scale by then. This was the tipping decade when mankind began to understand the impact of development on the well-being of people and the environment.

Legislations for controlling environmental pollution started appearing in the 1960s. The US passed the Clean Air Act in 1963 to control air pollution; it adopted a comprehensive Clean Water Act in 1972. The Basic Law on Environmental Pollution Control was adopted in 1967 in Japan, which was concerned about the food poisoning caused by consumption of fish with traces of mercury discharged by the gold mining process. India passed the Water (Prevention and Control of Pollution) Act in 1974 and the Air (Prevention and Control of Pollution) Act in 1981.

The Stockholm Conference, the first international conference on environmental issues, was convened in 1972. It spurred global consciousness on the consequences of the development and industrialization model and the need to take corrective steps. The UN Environment Programme (UNEP) was launched in 1972, around the same time.

The world has come a long way since. In 1992, the Earth Summit drew up a major agenda and set of agreements to protect the environment. The last major milestone was the Paris Agreement in 2015. There have also been numerous conventions on different chemicals and materials causing pollution and global warming.

Use of Fuels and Chemicals in Production and Distribution of Goods and Services Is at the Root of Environmental Crisis

The use of fossil fuels—oil, coal and natural gas—and materials, especially chemicals, as sources of energy and inputs, creates almost all the impacts, whether personal, local or global.

Formation of CO_2 takes place from the use of fossil fuels in myriad processes of production and distribution (in agriculture, industries and transportation). CO_2 is the largest factor/agent that impacts the global climate. CO_2 and a few other gases, when released in the environment, act as GHGs.

Other gases can be equated in terms of CO_2. The totality of CO_2 equivalent gases has been growing massively since industrialization spread all over the world. The world generates about 30 million metric tonnes of CO_2 equivalent per year. There are a few chemical substances, like ozone-depleting substances, that also impact the global environment.

Numerous metals and minerals are used as raw materials in the production of industrial goods and machines. Many minerals when used as inputs lead to production of chemicals. These chemicals are used in different ways in the production and distribution chain. Fertilizers and insecticides are chemicals that are extensively used in the production of food and other agriculture produce. Several chemicals are used to produce consumer products for use in industry, construction and households. Paints, adhesives and plastics are all products of minerals and metals. Some heavy metals, materials like plastics and noxious gases like nitrogen oxide can impact air, water and soil to create bad local environmental impacts. Some fuels and chemicals can be poisonous or otherwise bad for the health of individuals.

Most adverse environmental impacts, whether global, local or personal, can be traced to the use of fossil fuels, chemicals and heavy metals.

The environment gets adversely impacted in carrying out processes that are incidental or essential to production of fossil fuels and materials and processes deployed to allow the release/disposal of by-products of the products manufactured.

Fossil fuels, metal and minerals are extracted from the womb of the earth. The process of extraction involves disturbing tree and soil cover and disturbs the carbon balance in nature and nutritional balance of soil.

It also releases soil and other substances in water and air. The dumps of overburden in coal and other mining areas are stark reminders of the local pollution caused by the processes of excavation and extraction.

The disposal of plastics and other solid wastes, products made of materials and chemicals, chokes local sewage disposal systems, sullies lakes and rivers and finally pollutes the seas.

The solution for all adverse environmental impacts lies in handling fossil fuels and materials better.

CO_2 the Largest Culprit

The UN system and international treaties identify seven gases as GHGs, as included in Annex A to the Kyoto Protocol. These are CO_2; methane (CH_4); nitrous oxide (N_2O); hydrofluorocarbons (HFCs); perfluorocarbons (PFCs); sulphur hexafluoride (SF_6); and nitrogen trifluoride (NF_3). The last gas, NF_3, was added by the Doha Amendment.

All parties to the UN Framework Convention on Climate Change, 1994 (the Climate Change Convention), have committed to publish and make available to the Conference of Parties, 'national inventories' of anthropogenic emissions (largely the result of industrial production and urbanized living) 'by sources and removals by sinks of all greenhouse gases' except the 'gases controlled by the Montreal Protocol'.

There are different reporting obligations for the industrialized countries that are further divided in three broad categories: first, the countries responsible for much of the GHG emissions until 1990; second, industrialized countries that are not considered Economies in Transition (EIT); and third, the remaining industrialized member countries. There are, in all, forty-three such countries, and are collectively known as Annex I countries. These include the EITs, which are also separately named in Annex II of the Convention. The Convention has adopted comprehensive guidelines on reporting requirements and processes.

CO_2 is the largest GHG emitted every year. In 2018, total GHG emissions from anthropogenic sources were 51.8 gigatons of CO_2 ($GtCO_2$) equivalent. Including land-use related emissions, total GHG emissions were 55.6 $GtCO_2$. CO_2 made up 72 per cent of global GHGs, followed by methane (CH4) at about 19 per cent and nitrous oxide (N_2O) at about

6 per cent. Together, these three gases contributed 97 per cent of GHGs. The remaining gases, basically those monitored under the Montreal Protocol on Substances that Deplete the Ozone Layer, also called F-gases, contributed 3 per cent. CO_2 is primarily generated by burning of fossil fuels in the industrialization and transportation processes. Therefore, industrialization and transportation are the primary cause of GHG emissions, which in turn contribute to raising global temperatures and causing most of the ill-effects of climate change.

Global Priority is to Control GHG Emissions

While climate change is a complex phenomenon and a result of myriad forces (natural and human) working on the environment, the global community has been able to subsume the impact of all GHG emissions on global warming.

A reasonably steady relationship has been defined for the quantity of GHGs in the atmosphere in the pre-industrial period (1850–1900), the increase in this pre-industrial GHG inventory over a longish period of thirty years, and the total inventory of GHGs at which average global temperatures will rise by a specified percentage.

Experts believe incalculable damage would be done to the earth and its residents if temperatures were to rise by more than 2 per cent over the pre-industrial average. The world can avoid the most pernicious consequences if it can limit the global temperature rise in the twenty-first century well below 2° Celsius above pre-industrial levels and further pursue concerted efforts to limit the temperature increase to 1.5° Celsius.

Global consciousness, which started emerging in the 1960s, saw its first manifestation at the Earth Summit in Rio in 1992 to commit to an agenda for the twenty-first century: Agenda 21. Finally, global concern transformed into global resolve in the form of the Paris Agreement in 2015.

Though former US President Donald Trump withdrew from the agreement in 2017, the new US President Joe Biden re-entered the agreement soon after his inauguration and the global community is committed to roll back and modify processes to control global GHG emission to the extent necessary to limit the temperature rise to agreed levels.

Carbon Budget and Emissions Gap

CO_2 in the earth's atmosphere reached 409.8 parts per million (ppm) in 2019. From 287 ppm, it reached 296 ppm in 1900 and increased to 311 ppm in 1950. Thereafter, it rocketed thanks to heavy industrialization and urbanization all over the world, reaching 331.11 ppm in 1975 and 369.55 ppm in 2000. In the past nineteen years, the CO_2 level has increased by 40.3 ppm, an increase of over 2 ppm every year.

The pre-industrial level of CO_2 is approximately assumed to be 280 ppm, a little below the level of 287 ppm for 1850. While it is a complex science with many influencing factors, scientists broadly agree that doubling of pre-industrial CO_2 in the atmosphere will likely cause average global surface temperatures to rise between 1.5° and 4.5° Celsius. Doubling of the pre-industrial level of CO_2 of 280 ppm means CO_2 levels rising to 560 ppm.

Global temperature records are available since 1880. In line with a certain relationship between the rise in CO_2 levels in the atmosphere and rise in the earth's surface temperatures, an increase of 1.1° Celsius has been observed since 1880. As the rise in surface temperature leads to severe consequences, the Paris Agreement aims to keep global temperature increase well below 2° Celsius, hoping to limit it to 1.5°.

There is a certain relationship between the weight of carbon burnt and CO_2 emissions—in the process of burning, one atom of carbon combines with two atoms of oxygen to form CO_2, which makes the weight of CO_2 3.6667 times the weight of carbon. Releasing 1 kg of methane is equivalent to releasing 84 kg of CO_2 whereas releasing 1 kg of nitrous oxide is 298 times. Approximately 36.81 billion tonnes of CO_2 was released in the atmosphere in 2019.

Using the relationship between the increase in CO_2 concentration in the atmosphere (ppm) and increase in temperatures, it is possible to estimate the quantum of CO_2 emissions for every 1° rise in average temperatures. Various estimates have been made of the quantity of CO_2 emissions that might be released to keep the rise of temperature over pre-industrial temperatures to 2° Celsius, the aim of the Paris Agreement.

This is the maximum permissible 'carbon budget' or 'GHG emissions budget'. Referenced to a particular point in time, the difference between the maximum permissible budget and the emissions already made until then is the 'remaining carbon budget'.

The parties to the Paris Agreement have committed to bring down GHG emissions by a certain level over a period until 2030. At the rate at which emissions are currently taking place, the level of CO_2 in the atmosphere would be higher than the maximum permissible budget. This difference is the ask or the extent of emissions reduction required. The commitments made by countries will reduce emissions by a certain amount but a gap will still remain.

Various estimates have been made of the remaining carbon budget by different scientists and institutions. Some estimates opine that there is no carbon budget left as the world has already exceeded the threshold. The UNEP has compiled these estimates, which range from -192 $GtCO_2$ to 779 $GtCO_2$.

India Faces a Major Dilemma in Coal

India has the third largest reserves of coal and generates more than 70 per cent of its electricity at present by using coal. Coal was the cheapest, easily available and most reliable source of power generation for the country for decades. All other fossil fuels—gas, crude oil—were in short supply. It was a no-brainer that India went after constructing large coal-based thermal power plants to generate electricity for its power-starved industry, agriculture and households.

However, coal has created a major pollution problem in the country. While black soot coming out of coal-fired power plants was visible and therefore got a quicker policy response, the more dangerous emissions of nitrogen oxides, sodium oxides, lead and mercury, being invisible, were practically ignored by policymakers until very late in 2015. India has now established standards for their emission and the thermal power generation industry is in the process of installing requisite technology to capture these pollutants and control their emissions within permissible limits. The work is progressing very slowly.

In the past few years, renewable technology has advanced significantly, bringing down the cost of generating electricity to levels lower than coal power. Grid technology is also advancing to manage the volatility of renewable power. Battery technology is improving as well, which provides the option of storing renewable power. Advancement in hydrogen-based power generation is likely to provide good options for mainstreaming the volatility caused to the grid by renewables.

While the historical carbon contribution of India is low, today the country is the third largest emitter of carbon in the environment. India faces a big dilemma in persisting with coal power generation.

Chapter Twenty-Five

State of Education, Health and Nutrition

Economy of Education

Imparting education is an important economic service that serves two basic functions. First, it make people learn about self, society and geophysics to live a quality life. Second, it imparts skills and knowledge to optimize inherent talent to produce goods and services to add maximum economic value. The economy of education revolves around the institutions, teachers and infrastructure that enable and deliver these two services.

The first kind of education, often called 'general education', has a lot of externality in that it not only benefits the recipient but society at large, as such an educated person can harmonize their life with other members of society and become a responsible and contributing member of the community. The tools to deliver general education are language, literacy and computing. Such education services, especially to children, are usually paid for by the government or community. The economy of general education is more part of the public and charitable economy although in many parts of world, and India, general education has also become a private economic function.

The second kind of education is more a private service. It involves imparting and obtaining skills and knowledge to produce economic goods and services. Different skill and knowledge sets equip the recipient to deliver very different quantum of value added, which leads to differential payment. More common skills where supply is more than demand tend to deliver lower compensation. Skills that deliver higher value get higher compensation. As such education (skills and knowledge) primarily determines the economic value of the person, the investment in acquiring such skills and knowledge and their use is a private economic activity and function.

Size of India's Education Economy

Education services are accounted for in 'Other Services' in the National Accounts. The value of the output produced in the form of education services was Rs 9.30 lakh crore in 2018–19. In constant terms (2011–12 prices), the value of education output was assessed at Rs 5.92 lakh crore. The value of education services output in 2011–12 (in constant terms) was Rs 3.38 lakh crore. The value of education output has grown steadily since 2011–12 with annual growth rates ranging from 5.5 per cent to 11.3 per cent. Inputs, including financial services, consumed by the education sector in India in 2018–19 were Rs 1.22 lakh crore and accordingly the sector's GVA was assessed at Rs 4.70 lakh crore in constant prices. In current prices, in 2018–19, the sector's GVA was Rs 7.41 lakh crore. As total GVA in the economy in 2018–19 was Rs 128.03 lakh crore at constant prices and Rs 171.4 lakh crore at current prices, the share of education in the GVA of the Indian economy was 3.67 per cent in constant prices and 4.32 per cent in current prices. Education is a significant economic sector.

The National Accounts do not provide a break-up of different segments of the sector in terms of value added, such as elementary, secondary, higher education, technical education, and so on.

Economy of Health

Healthy individuals and families are essential for any nation to be economically productive and prosperous. While many health-related matters are private in nature, public health has a major role to play in every nation. The economy of health, the world over, has been shaped by struggles of policymakers in managing the private and public elements of health management.

There are countries that consider health a completely or largely private matter and therefore to be delivered by private-sector health providers and paid for from the incomes of individuals/families or by buying insurance. On the other hand, there are countries that consider health an entirely public concern and build a large public-sector health system to provide services to citizens. Most countries, of course, lie amid these two extremes, with a mix of public and private-sector contributions.

India has built a large public-sector healthcare system from villages to district levels—a network of health sub-centres, primary health centres (PHCs), community hospitals at selective block levels and district hospitals—funded entirely by public resources. We have also built top-class national public healthcare institutions like the All India Institute of Medical Sciences (AIIMS). Further, the country has launched a large publicly funded health insurance programme called Ayushman Bharat to take care of the medical needs of about 50 crore poor Indians.

In the private domain, India has developed a large network of hospitals and health clinics in the country. Most sophisticated medical services are available in private hospitals, in addition to top-end public institutions like AIIMS and state-level speciality hospitals.

The sector is a very large employer with doctors, paramedics and other healthcare workers.

Size of India's Health Economy

The National Accounts provide data on the output generated, inputs used and GVA by 'health and social work', which is mainly health services. In 2018–19, the value of output produced by the health and social work sector was assessed at Rs 3.16 lakh crore at constant 2011–12 prices and Rs 4.70 lakh crore at current prices. Inputs used by the sector were Rs 1.20 lakh crore at constant prices and Rs 1.78 lakh crore at current prices. The GVA of the health and social service sector was therefore counted at Rs 1.92 lakh crore at constant prices and at Rs 2.86 lakh crore at current prices. The health economy was 1.5 per cent in constant terms and 1.67 per cent in current prices.

There is considerable debate in the country and among policymakers about the percentage of GDP and public expenditure that should be spent on health. The National Health Policy, 2017 (NHP-2017), aims to increase health expenditure by government to 2.5 per cent of GDP by 2025.

The National Accounts do not specifically capture national expenditure on health. The GVA of health and social work as available in the statistics is the closest estimate we have.

The World Bank and many other multilaterals use a different definition of health expenditure developed by the WHO as part of the System of Health Accounts (SHS). This classification includes expenditure on healthcare goods and services consumed by people during a year. However, it does not include capital expenditure on buildings, machinery, IT and vaccine stocks. According to this definition, India's healthcare expenditure in 2018 was 3.6 per cent of GDP. It was 4.3 per cent in 2001, declining to 3.2 per cent by 2011, after which it picked up to reach 3.75 per cent in 2013. It has been marginally declining and has been in the range of 3.5 per cent to 3.6 per cent since then.

The Government of India compiles details of health expenditure by the Centre and the states. According to its statistics, estimated government health expenditure, including capital expenditure, in financial year 2016–17 was Rs 1.88 lakh crore, or 1.2 per cent of GDP. The government also estimates the expenditure made by households directly (in addition to the expenditure made by the government). Such expenditure, termed 'Out of Pocket' expenditure, was Rs 3.4 lakh crore in 2016–17, or about 2.2 per cent of GDP. Another separate category of expenditure in government statistics is private expenditure on health insurance. In 2016–17, this was estimated at Rs 0.27 lakh crore, or about 0.2 per cent. According to government estimates, total health expenditure (by the government and households), including capital expenditure by the government, was 3.6 per cent of GDP in 2016–17.

Health Situation Remains Grim

The Ministry of Health published a document titled 'Situational Analysis—Backdrop to the National Health Policy-2017' before NHP-2017 was adopted. The document candidly acknowledges the economic, financial and fiscal challenges in the health sector.

On fiscal capacity, the document states: 'the fact however remains that inability to cover the entire spectrum of healthcare needs through increased public investments has led to a rise in out-of-pocket expenditure and consequent impoverishment.' The fact that rising health costs are borne privately by poor Indians is acknowledged candidly: 'Over 63 million persons are pushed to poverty every year due to healthcare costs. In 2011–12, the share of out-of-pocket expenditure on healthcare as a proportion of total household monthly per capita expenditure was 6.9 per cent in rural areas and 5.5 per cent in urban areas. This led to an increasing number of households facing catastrophic expenditures due to health costs (18 per cent of all households in 2011–12 compared to 15 per cent in 2004–05).'

It recognizes that the coverage of publicly funded health insurance programmes, the central Rashtriya Swasthya Bima Yojana (RSBY) programme and state-funded trust model programmes, did expand quite well but still remained inadequate: 'The population coverage under these various schemes expanded from almost 55 million in 2003–04 to 370 million in 2014 (almost one-fourth of the population).'

On the private healthcare industry, the document grudgingly admits: 'The private healthcare industry is complex. It includes insurance and equipment which account for about 15 per cent, pharmaceuticals over 25 per cent, diagnostics 10 per cent and hospitals and clinical care about 50 per cent. The private healthcare industry is valued at $40 billion and is projected to grow to $280 billion by 2020 as per market sources. The current growth rate of the healthcare industry, at 14 per cent, is projected to be 21 per cent in the next decade . . . Over 70 per cent of the ailing population in rural areas and almost 80 per cent in urban areas utilize private facilities. The private healthcare sector is highly differentiated. Majority of private healthcare enterprises are Own Account Enterprises (OAEs), which are household-run businesses without hiring a regular worker.'

Expenditure on Nutrition

The nutrition economy is not separately measured in the National Accounts. There is no data on GVA added by nutrition services. The expenditure by the Government of India on child development programmes was Rs 16,800 crore in financial year 2018–19.

India did quite well in meeting the targets set by the Millennium Development Goals (MDGs) for child and maternal mortality rates.

However, the MDG goal of eradicating hunger, measured by reduction in proportion of underweight children below five years of age—the MDG target was 26 per cent of underweight children by 2015 from the base level of 52 per cent in 1990—has proved more elusive. The Backdrop to the Health Policy Document, 2017, estimated that India was able to reduce malnutrition/hunger to only 29 per cent by 2015. Recent surveys have indicated that the situation has actually worsened since.

The Ministry of Women and Child Development (WCD) is the government ministry primarily responsible for nutrition programmes for children and women. The Ministry of Education also runs a Midday Meal Programme for schoolchildren while the Ministry of Food and Public Distribution procures and allocates food (principally rice and wheat) to support nutrition through the public distribution system.

Poor Ranking on the Global Hunger Index

The 2020 Global Hunger Index (GHI) ranks India ninety-fourth out of 107 countries. It also classifies countries in categories of low, moderate, serious, alarming and extremely alarming based on their state of nutrition severity. With a score of 27.2, India falls in the serious category.

GHI determines the state of hunger in a country by assessing indicators that measure malnutrition. There are four components: general undernourishment, measured by share of population with insufficient calorific intake; child wasting, measured by lower weight for height for children under five years of age; child stunting, measured by lower height for age for children under five; and child mortality, measured by mortality rate of children dying before completing the age of five.

India has done reasonably well in reducing the child mortality rate; the country's indicator value is only 3.7. Likewise, there is a steady improvement in general undernourishment with malnutrition in the general population going down from 19.8 per cent in 2006 to 14 per cent in 2020. However, malnutrition among children continues to be worrisome. The indicator of wasting in children has gone up from 15.1 per cent in 2012 to 17.3 per cent in 2020. Similarly, the indicator of stunting among children continues to be extremely high (though falling gradually) at 34.7 per cent.

According to the Global Nutrition Report 2018, India is home to 46.6 million stunted children, one-third of the world's total. The 2020 edition of the report, which tracks the state of nutrition based on ten criteria, noted that India's performance deteriorated in six out of ten indicators in 2019, much before the onset of the coronavirus crisis, and that the country did not have data for three of the indicators. India's performance improved only on one indicator.

Chapter Twenty-Six

Education and Health Policies
Not Best Suited for Economy

Education

India's Education Policies Have Addressed Mostly Quantitative Aspects

India laid emphasis on higher education in the first twenty years after Independence. Primary education was neglected. It led to the production of well-educated persons from institutions of higher learning, many of whom went abroad. The general masses remained by and large uneducated.

India promulgated its first Education Policy in 1968, followed by the second in 1986. Both these policies laid emphasis on compulsory school education and spread of literacy. The Government of India also initiated several path-breaking programmes. By the turn of the century, almost every eligible child was in school and the 'gross enrolment ratio'—the ratio of students in elementary schools to the number of students in the age group of six to fourteen—crossed 100 per cent. Literacy also spread. Most states were declared as fully literate.

Thereafter, universal enrolment for secondary education and creation of government school infrastructure became the major policy objective.

Secondary school gross enrolment ratio rose to a high level of about 75 per cent by 2015. It remains at that level, as per World Bank data.

The gross enrolment ratio was achieved by constructing schools, appointing teachers and bringing students to schools with no charge for tuition, books and meals. The inputs produced attendance. However, enrolment and attendance did not equal learning and quality of education.

New Education Policy, 2020 (NEP-2020) Brings about Some Structural Changes

The government adopted the New Education Policy in 2020 (NEP-2020).

The Policy proposes 'revision and revamping of all aspects of the education structure, including its regulation and governance, to create a new system that is aligned with the aspirational goals of twenty-first century education, including SDG4 [Sustainable Development Goal 4], while building upon India's traditions and value systems.'

The largest structural change planned is in the school system.

The current system of 10+2 (ten years of common school education and two years of selective subject education) is to be replaced by a four-tiered 5+3+3+4 education system. The new system proposes to integrate three years of early childhood education delivered in the *anganwadi/preschool/balvatika* system with two years of current primary education into 'foundational' education. The remaining three years of current primary school (1–5 grade) is being broken into two years of foundational and three years of 'preparatory' schooling. The envisaged third tier of three years of schooling (6–8 grade) corresponds with present-day upper primary schooling. Two years of education (currently part of secondary education in 9–10 grade) and two years of senior secondary education (11–12 grade) are being combined in the fourth tier of secondary education. The new system formalizes early childhood education by combining the present informal educational arrangement for preschool (before a child turns six) in playschools, anganwadis and other miscellaneous arrangements with two years of formal schooling.

The second structural change is to create a system of school complexes/clusters to group one secondary school with all other schools offering lower grades in its neighbourhood, including anganwadis, in a radius of 5–10 km. This is to address the concern of thinly spread teaching and infrastructural resources by creating an educational complex with shared resources. A government survey in 2016 found that 28 per cent of India's public primary schools and 15 per cent of upper primary schools had less than thirty students. On the other hand, over 1 lakh schools were single-teacher schools. The creation of school complexes/clusters will be able to address these deficiencies.

NEP-2020 also proposes creation of a State School Standards Authority (SSSA) to 'establish a minimal set of standards based on basic parameters (namely, safety, security, basic infrastructure, number of teachers across subjects and grades, financial probity and sound processes of governance)'. NEP-2020 directs every state to establish 'an independent, state-wide, body' (SSSA).

The goal of policy and regulatory arrangements like SSSA is to assess and accredit all 'public and private schools (except the schools that are managed/aided/controlled by the Central government on the same criteria, benchmarks, and processes'. The objective is to hold all educational institutions 'to similar standards of audit and disclosure as a "not-for-profit" entity'.

NEP-2020 also proposes to create 'a higher educational system consisting of large, multidisciplinary universities and colleges, with at least one in or near every district, and with more HEIs [higher educational institutions] across India that offer medium of instruction or programmes in local/Indian languages'. HEIs include universities, autonomous colleges and other similar institutions. The Policy looks unfavourably at specialized HEIs that focus on a single or a few disciplines and makes no bones about its objective of phasing out 'single-stream HEIs'. The 'main thrust' of NEP-2020 'is to end the fragmentation of higher education by transforming higher education institutions into large multidisciplinary universities, colleges and HEI clusters/Knowledge Hubs, each of which will aim to have 3,000 or more students'.

There is Limited Opening for Foreign Universities

NEP-2020 addresses the internationalization of education to promote India as 'a global study destination providing premium education at affordable costs, thereby helping to restore its role as a Vishwa Guru'. India led the world in the agriculture age and was indeed at the forefront of knowledge creation at that time. Indian institutions of higher learning, like Nalanda, Taxila and Vikramshila, attained global glory in that age.

India missed out on the advancement of technology and knowledge in the second millennium, most spectacularly when the Industrial Revolution was sweeping the world. And the country is not in the forefront of knowledge creation in the current information age. Thus, aiming to be a 'Vishwa Guru' should not merely be a slogan.

We have the right human resources and minds to catch up with the world and assume leadership status. It is also notable that Indians constitute the second largest community of immigrant students in North America and Europe, and that one of the largest segments of foreign exchange expenditure is expenditure on education abroad.

The Policy has a two-pronged approach to open education for foreign universities and develop Indian institutions to set up campuses abroad. It envisages opening an International Students Office at each HEI to host overseas students. Research/teaching collaborations and faculty/student exchanges with high-quality foreign institutions will be facilitated, and mutually beneficial MoUs with foreign countries signed. High-performing Indian universities will be encouraged to set up campuses in other countries. 'Selected universities' from the top 100 global universities will be encouraged to operate in India. A legislative framework facilitating this entry has been promised and such universities will be given special dispensation regarding regulatory, governance and content norms on a par with other autonomous institutions in India.

NEP-2020 Persists with All 'Education' Being a Not-For-Profit Activity

Education essentially serves two major societal and personal needs: first, it brings every individual familiarity, knowledge and understanding of self, society and the geophysical world to develop as a healthy, happy and responsible human being; second, it equips every individual to work productively and contribute to the economy.

The first type of education is a pure 'merit good' with enormous externalities, while the second type is essentially skills and deeper knowledge, which is largely a private good with limited externalities. Let's call the first type general education and the second, technical education. A clearer understanding of these two different forms of education has enormous implications for designing the correct policies.

As a classic merit good, general education is a community responsibility and should be delivered and funded as a community/state enterprise. On the other hand, as a private good, technical education should be delivered and funded as a private enterprise.

In India, all educational institutions can be established only as a 'society', 'trust' or 'not-for-profit' company. Educational institutions, including technical education institutions, cannot be established legally as proprietary or partnership companies or any other 'for-profit' entity. This policy is incorporated in all the education-related laws of the Centre and states. The mindset of all educationists is informed by the requirements of general education and it makes no distinction between general and technical education. The courts, including the Supreme Court, have upheld this. NEP-2020 also carries forward the same idea.

Technical education institutions—management, engineering, medical, teaching, paramedical, diploma engineering, industrial training or any others—at any level of learning (secondary, college or postgraduate) have all been set up by private entrepreneurs as 'not-for-profit' institutions. However, this is only on paper. As these enterprises cannot charge freely determined fees, all kinds of distortionary and corrupt practices have been employed to make their profit while keeping the 'not-for-profit' facade in place.

Sponsors of such institutions have eaten away money from procurement. They have charged extraordinary amounts in capitation fees, when there was large demand for these courses. They have bribed regulators to get seats sanctioned for their institutions without having the requisite facilities. They have also paid their teachers much less in reality than what they showed on paper. These practices made students pay much more than the true market cost of obtaining such technical education and the entrepreneurs made good profits, but in 'black' money. The government got no taxes on their incomes/profits. In the process, the education environment became vitiated, with corrupt and compromised regulatory institutions, fly-by-night operators as educationists and poor quality of technical education for students.

The situation has changed marginally in the past few years. For some streams of technical education, like engineering and management, supply increased in a huge measure with the entry of a slew of fly-by-night operators. As the standard of education was worthless in most of these institutions, demand evaporated. A large number of such engineering colleges, universities and management institutions have been closing in the past few years.

The government brought in regulators to control fees charged by private educational institutions. All kinds of complications went into determination and enforcement of fees. Different quotas came up. Institutions designed different responses. Still, the ground situation for technical institutions in the country remains the same.

There is massive demand for admissions in government-funded institutions. While the government has tried to expand capacity, budgetary considerations come in the way. Therefore, the ratio of seats to applicants remains 100 times or more for many institutions. Barring some reputed private institutions, there is no demand for technical education in private institutions, except where the availability of government jobs in relation to the supply of requisite number of degree/diploma/certificate holders is high.

The NEP-2020 brings no change in the fundamental education policy construct.

Health

Current National Health Policy Recognizes the Changing Health Economy

NHP-2017, the latest in a series of health policies adopted by the government (earlier editions were in 1983 and 2002), recognizes the changing health management priorities and health economy in India.

Moving on from the concerns of child and maternal mortality and communicable diseases, which have been rapidly declining, the Policy shifts focus to non-communicable and infectious diseases and the catastrophic health expenditure pushing households into poverty. It also recognizes the rapid expansion of the private health industry, which is growing at double digits.

The primary aim of NHP-2017 is 'to inform, clarify, strengthen and prioritize the role of the government in shaping the health system in all its dimensions', which includes investment in health, organization of healthcare services, developing better financial protection strategies and strengthening regulation and health assurance.

Despite This Realization, NHP-2017 Essentially Remains a Public-Sector Health Policy

NHP-2017 sets its goals in most ambitious, and general, terms. It envisages the 'attainment of the highest possible level of health and well-being for all at all ages' and 'universal access to good quality healthcare services without anyone having to face financial hardship as a consequence'. That said, the background document made it evident that this was not the reality in the healthcare sector and that the government was in no position to achieve these goals through public-sector expansion of healthcare services.

The Policy also sets specific targets to be achieved by 2025, including life expectancy of 70, reduction of the total fertility rate (TFR) to 2.1; under-five mortality rate to twenty-three; maternal mortality rate (MMR) to 100 (by 2020); and infant mortality rate to twenty-eight (by 2019); as well as increasing the utilization of public health facilities to 50 per cent and the government's healthcare expenditure to 2.5 per cent of GDP. In addition, it mentions many more disease-specific and health infrastructures.

The largest health policy goal is to raise public health expenditure to 2.5 per cent of the GDP 'in a timebound manner' and allocate resources to the states linked to state development indicators, absorptive capacity and financial indicators. According to NHP-2017, the increased expenditure will be financed by 'general taxation' and the government would consider imposing taxes on specific commodities like tobacco, alcohol, junk food, the extractive industry and pollution.

The Policy proposes a significant shift in the organization of public healthcare delivery. Primary healthcare would be substantially expanded with the policy goal being changed from 'selective care' to 'assured comprehensive care with linkages to referral hospitals'. The secondary and tertiary care policy goal would be changed from 'input-oriented to output-based strategic purchasing'. The strategy of 'user fees and cost recovery' is slated to be abandoned in favour of 'assured free drugs, diagnostic and emergency services to all'. Urban health services are to be expanded substantially from 'token interventions' to 'on-scale assured interventions' of 'primary healthcare delivery and referral support for urban poor'. This marks a massive shift to comprehensive public health services funded by the exchequer.

Comprehensive primary healthcare services would be delivered through 'Health and Wellness Centres' established on geographical and population norms to provide convenient access to every household. Secondary healthcare services would be expanded at the district and sub-district levels to provide specified secondary services like caesarean sections and neonatal care with the provision of at least two beds per 1000 population such that 'it is accessible within the golden hour'.

Public hospitals are to be repositioned as a tax-financed, single-payer healthcare system, where care is prepaid and cost-efficient, quality of care is imperative and facilities undergo periodic measurements and quality certification. Public hospitals would provide universal access to a progressively wide array of free drugs and diagnostics.

The Policy prioritizes the primary healthcare needs of the urban population with special focus on poor populations living in slums and other vulnerable populations such as the homeless, ragpickers, street children, sex workers and temporary migrants. It also seeks to achieve convergence among wider determinants of health, such as air pollution, solid waste management, water quality, occupational safety, vector control and urban stress.

It advocates resource allocation of a major proportion (up to two-thirds or more) to primary care, followed by secondary and tertiary care, and proposes some realignment in the financing of public healthcare facilities. Operational costs would be reimbursed for care provision and on a per capita basis for primary care. Infrastructure, maintenance and salary expenditure of staff and administrative expenses will be funded on an actuals basis. A vague notion of incentivizing the performance of primary healthcare facilities has also been expressed.

Interventions for Expanding Supply of Doctors and Paramedics Unspecific and Inadequate

While addressing the most critical constraint in expanding healthcare facilities in the country—rapidly increasing the supply of well-trained doctors and paramedics—the Policy relies only on generalities. 'Strengthening existing medical colleges and converting district hospitals to new medical colleges to increase number of doctors and specialists' has been 'recommended'. It drifts when it only seeks to recognize 'the need to increase the number of postgraduate seats', or when it supports 'expanding the number of AIIMS-like centres' or when it 'advocates a common entrance exam for UG entrance at the all-India level' or when it 'recognizes the need to improve regulation and quality management of nursing education'.

Similar ambiguity is on display in the case of paramedical skills. 'Training courses and curriculum for super speciality paramedical care would be developed,' it says. 'The Policy recognizes the role played by physiotherapists, occupational and allied health professionals keeping in view the demographic and disease transition the country is faced with and also recognizes the need to address their shortfall'.

It also talks about the creation of a 'Public Health Management Cadre' in all states based on public health or related disciplines, as an entry criterion. But no rationale has been provided for this proposal.

Private Sector Largely Ignored

The policy only 'suggests' exploring collaboration for primary care services, with 'not-for-profit' organizations with a track record of public service where critical gaps exist. It offers only limited collaboration with private-sector healthcare providers, 'especially those working in rural and remote areas or with under-served communities' who could be 'offered encouragement through provision of appropriate skills to meet public health goals'.

The policy only deals with charitable private-sector providers. It further notes that it supports 'voluntary service in rural and under-served areas on a pro-bono basis by recognized healthcare professionals under a "giving back to society" initiative'. Another form of collaboration sought to be encouraged is 'engagement in public goods, where the private sector contributes to preventive or promotive services without profit—as part of CSR work or on contractual terms with the government'.

It seeks to use strategic purchasing as stewardship to direct investment for the commercial health sector. Critical gaps in public health services would be filled with strategic purchasing, which would encourage the private sector to invest in capacity creation to provide these services. The main mechanism of strategic purchasing would be insurance and through trusts. The government also proposed to buy in the private sector in urban primary healthcare by building partnerships to address specific gaps like diagnostic, ambulance, safe blood, rehabilitative and palliative services, mental healthcare and telemedicine.

Section VI: Foreign Trade, Commerce and Investments

Chapter Twenty-Seven

State of Foreign Trade, Commerce and Investments

Foreign Trade Promotes GDP Growth and National Income

GDP, the sum of all value added in the goods and services produced in an economy, is also the source of income of the three major factors of production: labour (salary/wages), capital/entrepreneur (profits) and the government (taxes). It therefore makes eminent sense to produce goods and services and export the same to other countries to earn wages, profits and taxes for the labour, capital and government of the exporting country. Additional income brings higher prosperity.

No country produces all the goods and services its residents need for consumption and investment. That's why most essential imports take place. The residents of a country may also prefer to consume goods and services produced elsewhere for better quality, novelty or other reasons. There may also be a need for machine and technology imports owned/patented by others.

Imports can be paid for by export income, importing capital or paying gold/other precious metals. Transferring gold and silver, which used to be the primary mode of settling the export-import deficit until the middle of the twentieth century, is no longer in practice. A country either pays from export income or by importing capital—debt, equity or both. An excessive export-import deficit, also called current account deficit, made good by importing portfolio capital, especially debt, brings the country concerned to grief sooner or later as debt servicing becomes impossible after some time and equity portfolio inflow reverses quite often for various reasons.

India's policies on exports, imports, foreign investment, external debt and exchange rate management have seen many changes since Independence. These have had a tremendous impact on the country's GDP, growth, external debt and exchange rate.

Goods' Exports Were Stagnating

Financial year 2020–21 was unusual on account of the surge of COVID-19 across the world, upending production of goods and services. Therefore, it should be ignored for any meaningful analysis of long- or medium-term trends.

Data from the previous seven years, however, unmistakably points out that India's exports are stagnating. In 2013–14, the country exported $314.46 billion worth of goods. In 2019–20, after six years, our goods exports amounted to $313.14 billion, a shade lower than 2013–14 in absolute terms. No growth in six years! In fact, exports of goods had gone down to an embarrassingly low level of $262.29 billion in 2015–16. Only in the year 2018–19 did India's exports, at $330.08 billion, exceed the nominal level of exports made in 2013–14. In the six years from 2014–15 to 2019–20, goods exports averaged only $299.06 billion. Consider the fact that in the six years from 2007–08 to 2013–14, exports grew from $162.90 billion to $314.46 billion. From 2013–14 to 2019–20, exports were flat at $314.46 billion in 2013–14 and $313.14 billion in 2019–20. The stagnation is apparent.

Thirty commodities account for about 94 per cent of India's exports. All other commodities and commodity groups contributed only $25.3 billion exports in 2013–14 and $21.04 billion in 2019–20.

In 2013–14, the three largest commodity groups were engineering goods ($63.9 billion), petroleum products ($63.2 billion) and gems and jewellery ($41.4 billion). These three accounted for 54 per cent of exports ($168.5 billion out of $314.4 billion). Four more groups of commodities had exports of over $10 billion: readymade garments ($15 billion); drugs and pharmaceuticals ($14.95 billion); organic and inorganic chemicals ($12.29 billion); and cotton yarn/made-ups ($11.02 billion).

While overall exports in 2019–20 were completely flat at the level of 2013–14, there were significant changes at the commodity group level.

The largest increase took place in the case of engineering goods, which saw an increase of $14.8 billion over the level of $63.9 billion in 2013–14, or about 23 per cent.

India's exports were stagnating in nominal terms as noted above. They have been declining in real terms for the past six years. As a proportion of GDP, exports were 16.9 per cent in 2013–14. They have declined continuously and steadily to 15.2 per cent in 2014–15, 12.45 per cent in 2015–16, 12.03 per cent in 2016–17, 11.46 per cent in 2017–18, 12.16 per cent in 2018–19 and 10.89 per cent in 2019–20. This has definitely hurt India's growth.

India's Imports Continue to Grow, Though at a Lower Rate

India's imports resumed their growth journey from the year 2016–17. From a tremendously high level of $490.74 billion in 2012–13, imports declined to $450.21 billion in 2013–14 and continued to do so for the next three years, bottoming out at $381.01 billion in 2015–16. Thereafter, they increased at a good clip, reaching $514.08 in 2018–19, crossing the $500 billion mark for the first time, and ended up lower at $474 billion in 2019–20.

Thirty commodities/commodity groups account for 95 per cent of India's imports. All the remaining commodities/commodity groups accounted for imports of only $22.5 billion in 2013–14 and $21.2 billion in 2019–20.

Oil and petroleum products comprise the largest segment of India's imports. Petroleum products cost India $164.8 billion in 2013–14, as much as 36.6 per cent of India's total imports of $450.2 billion. To India's good fortune, oil and petroleum prices started declining from 2014–15. Prices of petroleum products bottomed in 2015–16 and India's import bill declined to $82.9 billion, which was nearly 50 per cent of petroleum products import bill in 2013–2014. Foreign exchange spent on import of petroleum products went up thereafter every year: to $87 billion in 2016–17, $108.7 billion in 2017–18 and $140.9 billion in 2018–19, before declining to $130.5 billion in 2019–20. In 2019–20, the import cost of petroleum products was still lower by $34.3 billion compared to 2013–14.

There were nine products/product groups—coal ($16.4 billion); organic and inorganic chemicals ($17.4 billion); artificial resins and plastic material ($10.5 billion); pearls, precious and semi-precious stones ($24 billion); iron and steel ($12.7 billion); machinery–electricals and non-electricals ($27.1 billion); transport equipment ($19.3 billion); electronic goods ($32.4 billion) and gold ($28.7 billion)— that cost more than $10 billion in imports each in 2013–14. In aggregate, the import bill of these nine items was $188.5 billion. In aggregate, these nine items cost $240.4 billion in 2019–20, an increase of $51.5 billion over the import cost in 2013–14.

The government has taken several initiatives to increase manufacturing in India, especially in electronics. Yet, imports have continued to rise. Import of electronic items in 2019–20 were to the tune of $52.5 billion, increasing by $20.1 billion or 62 per cent during this period. India continues to be overly dependent on electronic items from the rest of the world. The next largest increase in absolute amount is seen in the case of plant and machinery ($12.4 billion; 46 per cent), again indicating India's dependence on the world for capital goods.

A Serious Goods Trade Deficit Problem

India has recorded a trade deficit (excess of imports over exports) in every one of the past forty years. The largest trade deficit of $184 billion was recorded in 2018–19 and the smallest, $1.07 billion, in 1993–94. India's trade deficit in 2019–20 was $160.86 billion.

Import of crude oil and oil products is the most significant reason for the persistent trade deficit. During the forty-year period from 1981–82 to 2019–20, the country had a deficit on the oil account (excess of oil imports over oil exports) of $1.25 trillion. Our aggregate non-oil trade account deficit during the same period was only $850 billion. The oil deficit of $1.25 trillion made up nearly 60 per cent of the total trade account deficit during this entire period of $2.09 trillion of aggregate deficit.

India is Faring Better in Services

Over the same period of 2013–14 to 2019–20, India fared better in terms of services. The export of services rose from $151.8 billion in 2013–14 to $213.2 billion in 2019–20, increasing by $61.4 billion. In 2013–14, India's export of services was 48.3 per cent of goods exports; in 2019–20, it had improved significantly to 68 per cent. While total exports of goods in absolute terms declined marginally by $1.3 billion (from $314.46 billion in 2013–14 to $313.14 billion in 2019–20), the export of services increased by $61.4 billion.

The export of services making up as much as 40.5 per cent of total export of goods and services of $526.34 billion in 2019–20 is a significant transformation that is yet to be fully recognized.

The import of services has also been rising at a fast clip—from $78.7 billion in 2013–14, it rose to $128.3 billion in 2019–20, recording an increase of $49.5 billion or 62.9 per cent, slightly higher than the increase of 61.4 per cent recorded in case of export of services.

In 2013–14, India had a surplus on account of services of $73.1 billion. This increased by $11.9 billion to $84.9 billion in 2019–20.

IT Services the Bulwark of Foreign Trade

India exported $96.1 billion worth of telecommunication, computer and IT services (essentially IT services) in 2019–20. We also imported some amount of such services to the tune of $10.2 billion. Thus, the country had an impressive surplus of $85.9 billion in the IT segment of services. This was greater than the total surplus on the services account of $84.9 billion. The stellar role of IT services in cushioning the pressure on India's foreign exchange account is evident.

After the IT services and telecommunications segment, the next largest surplus was recorded with respect to travel services at $7.99 billion. Travel services have also been consistently providing a surplus despite the fact that Indians spent over $22 billion on consumption of travel services as income from travel services recorded $30 billion in 2019–20. Another notable surplus was in the case of financial services at $1.8 billion, though the total size of financial service exports was small at $4.7 billion.

On the deficit side, the largest negative income was recorded with respect to charges for the use of IP not included elsewhere—essentially, royalties at $6.8 billion. India is dependent on foreign technology and FDI support. As the benefits of foreign technology import and FDI far outweigh the cost in terms of royalties, this should not be a real cause of worry. Transport services at a negative balance of $3.3 billion was the next highest amount of deficit. Other negative contributing services were more balanced as their deficits were much smaller at less than $1 billion.

Inflows/Incomes of Factors of Production and Investment Flows

Three other important segments of the current account reflect trade in factors of production: compensation of resident employees working abroad or working digitally for residents of other countries; investment income from investments made in equity and debt in any form (FDI, portfolio investment and income on investment of foreign exchange reserves deployed abroad); and transfers by NRIs to resident Indians. These are all positive inflows for India and help meet the deficit on the goods and services trade account. Meanwhile, such payments/transfers made by resident Indians to the rest of the world reduces the positive flows on the account.

Indian resident workers received compensation payments of $5.6 billion in 2019–20, whereas Indian employers paid $2.7 billion of compensation to foreign workers. Thus, Indian workers earned a net compensation of $2.9 billion.

India has been importing capital from abroad. This results in net negative investment income. The country paid $15.4 billion in dividends, interest and accrued incomes to non-residents for the stock of FDI in 2019–20, whereas Indian businesses earned $6.9 billion on their FDI abroad. India has a large stock of foreign portfolio investment (FPI) on both debt and equities as well. The country paid $11 billion of interest, dividend and capital gains on FPI in 2019–20 while India's portfolio investment earned a negligible amount of $216 billion as our stock of portfolio investment abroad is meagre. There is one more investment income category called 'Other Investment Income' which includes income on equity and investment fund shares that are not classified as FDI or FPI as well as income attributable to policyholders in insurance, pension and other guarantee schemes. India had negative income inflows with respect to this category, too, $14.3 billion (income $1.4 million and expenditure $15.7 billion), exceeding the net negative income on FPI of $10.8 billion.

Finally, the income on investment of reserve balances of the central bank was positive for India. The country earned a net income on investment of reserve assets of $6.9 billion (income $6.945 billion and expenditure only $53 million) thanks to the large foreign exchange reserves we hold and deploy abroad. It is a matter of consideration how much India pays for capital imported and how much it earns on the investment of foreign exchange reserves abroad.

Transfers from the Diaspora

Financial transfers are received from people of Indian origin settled abroad. The government also receives grant transfers from multilateral, bilateral and other institutions. Over the years, transfers from NRIs have grown substantially whereas grant receipts by the government have come down significantly.

In 2019–20, personal transfers, primarily from NRIs, amounted to $80.8 billion whereas non-Indians resident in India transferred only $5.1 billion, resulting in a net positive inflow of $75.7 billion to India. On the government account, there was a net negative grant inflow of $903 million with the Indian government transferring $1.01 billion and receiving only $156 million.

Primary and Secondary Income Made the Current Account Deficit Smaller

India's goods and services trade account resulted in a deficit of $72.8 billion in 2019–20. The country's primary income (sum of flows on account of compensation of employees and investment income, including on foreign currency reserves) was in a negative of $27.3 billion. India's secondary income (primarily on account of transfers by the Indian diaspora abroad) was in a positive of $75.3 billion. On aggregate, the current account was in a deficit of only $24.6 billion, or 0.86 per cent of GDP.

India's current account deficit at $24.6 billion in 2019–20 was lower than the deficit of $48.7 billion in 2017–18 and $57.2 billion in 2018–19.

India is a capital and technology-deficit country that exports a large amount of labour. This is mirrored in India's trade and current account.

Four Types of Capital and Financial Flows

The integration of the global market for production of goods and services and the difference in the capital and financial resource bases of countries have led to the movement of capital and investment internationally. This movement is now primarily in private flows.

Capital and financial account flows not only serve the purpose of financing the current account deficit, but also contribute to capital formation in recipient countries.

There are four important types of capital/financial flows.

First, direct investments by foreign corporations and investors in companies and other business entities producing goods and services. In India, we describe these as FDI and outward direct investment (ODI).

Second, purchase of securities—equity and debt—on stock exchanges or bilaterally under what is described as the over-the-counter (OTC) market by non-residents. In India, such financial investments are called FPI, which, at the broader level, includes such investments by NRIs in securities.

Third, the investments other than FDI and FPI or 'Other Investments'. This includes other equity (American depository receipts and global depository receipts, or ADRs and GDRs); currency and deposits, primarily NRI deposits in India's case; loans that include external assistance availed by the government; ECBs taken by corporates and banking capital; insurance, pension and guarantee investments; trade credit and advances; other receivables and movements in special drawing rights (SDRs).

Fourth, reserve assets, which include the movement of monetary gold (gold bought, sold and retained by central banks for monetary purposes), and reserve assets held in other jurisdictions.

If we take the movement in reserve assets as part of the capital and financial account, the surplus or deficit in this account would broadly mirror the deficit and surplus in the current account. In other words, the combined effect of the surplus and deficit in the current and capital/financial account would more or less equal the addition/reduction in reserve assets.

FDI Has Seen Steady Accretion

India received a net increase of $56 billion in FDI in 2019–20. Of this, the net increase in equity and investment fund shares was $47.7 billion and in debt instruments $8.3 billion. In case of equity FDI, $65.9 billion of FDI came in, whereas $18.2 billion of FDI investments was redeemed and repatriated, resulting in a net FDI addition of $47.7 billion. This comprised two major components: fresh net inflows of $33.5 billion and reinvested earnings of $14.2 billion.

Net equity FDI addition was in the order of $43.3 billion in 2018–19, $36.7 billion in 2017–18, $39.7 billion in 2016–17, $41 billion in 2015–16, $31.3 billion in 2014–15 and $29.5 billion in 2013–14. Equity FDI has increased from addition of $29.5 billion in 2013–14 to $47.7 billion in 2019–20. In fact, it saw an increase in all the six years since 2013–14 except in 2016–17 and 2017–18.

Direct investment in debt securities has seen a sharper increase during this period. In 2013–14, direct investment by non-residents in Indian debt securities was in the order of only $1.3 billion. Debt investments increased by about 150 per cent in 2014–15, rising to $3 billion. In 2015–16, FDI in debt securities increased to $3.9 billion. It fell in 2016–17 to $2.49 billion and remained subdued in 2017–18 and 2018–19 at $2.69 billion and $3 billion respectively. Then, it jumped to $8.3 billion in 2019–20 raising total FDI (both equity and debt) to $56 billion ($43 billion in 2018–19).

Net direct investment by Indians in other countries were in the order of $9.2 billion, comprising $6.1 billion of equity (new investments of $4.9 billion and reinvestments of earnings of $1.2 billion) and $3.1 billion of direct investment in debt instruments. Direct investments by Indians (or ODI) in 2019–20 rose to $13 billion, comprising $7.3 billion of equity investments ($4.2 billion of new investments and $3.2 billion of reinvested earnings) and $5.7 billion of direct investment in debt instruments.

ODI has followed a more volatile journey since 2013–14. In 2014–15, it fell to $4 billion, then rose to $8.89 billion in 2015–16 to fall again to $6.6 billion in 2016–17. ODI started rising again from 2017–18 ($9.1 billion) to $12.6 billion in 2018–19 and $13 billion in 2019–20.

Net of ODI, FDI was at $43 billion in 2019–20, 50 per cent over the level of $30.7 per cent in 2018–19. Net FDI was $21.6 billion in 2013–14, which rose smartly to $31.3 billion in 2014–15 and $36 billion in 2015–16. It remained stuck at $35.6 billion in 2016–17 and then fell to $30.3 billion in 2017–18 and $30.7 billion in 2018–19.

Portfolio Investments are Excessively Volatile

Portfolio investments—investments in shares and debt securities in stock markets or OTC markets—are hot money. These investments are made with a view to make profits using opportunities provided by rising stock prices, which happen on account of numerous factors and movement in yields of debt securities. India has a large stock of portfolio investments by foreigners, whereas Indians are still to make any notable investments in financial assets abroad.

The six years since 2013–14 have witnessed excessive volatility. The year 2013–14 witnessed a net inflow of portfolio investment in India in the order of $5 billion. The next year, 2014–15, saw a tremendous increase in FPI coming to India at $40.9 billion, while 2015–16 saw a net outflow of $4 billion. The year 2016–17 was again positive and saw FPI inflows of $7.7 billion. This was followed by another blockbuster year in 2017–18 with net FPI inflow of $22.2 billion. However, 2018–19 flipped with negative FPI of $2.2 billion and 2019–20 saw marginal positive inflows of $552 million.

FPI flows comprise both equity and debt. Debt flows are far more volatile. In 2013–14, while total inward portfolio investments were positive at $5 billion, debt flows were negative at $8.5 billion, whereas equity inflows were positive at $13.5 billion. In 2014–15, debt inflows at $26.2 billion were far higher than equity inflows at $14.8 billion, fairly similar to the previous year. The year 2015–16 again saw negative foreign portfolio debt at $483 million; this increased to a negative $828 million in 2016–17. In 2017–18, the tide turned again substantially with foreign portfolio inflows again being exceedingly high at $20.6 billion. The years 2018–19 and 2019–20 have also been volatile with 2018–19 recording a net outflow of $3.7 billion and 2019–20 recording a positive flow of $990 million. This big volatility in foreign debt portfolio investments accentuates the pressure on the Indian rupee. RBI has to undertake operations to mop up excessive inflows and sell dollars in the market when foreign portfolio investors cause larger outflows by selling debt securities in the market. India needs to find a solution to reduce this volatility for orderly functioning of the foreign exchange markets.

With only restricted permission for Indians to invest in foreign securities (equity and debt), net foreign portfolio inflows and outflows to the country on this score are relatively small. In the past four years, such net outflows have only been $154 million in 2016–17, $50 million in 2017–18, $213 million in 2018–19 and negative outflow or return of $851 million in 2019–20.

Other Investment Flows—Essentially NRI Deposits and Loans—Are Quite Sizeable

Equity raised on stock exchanges abroad in the form of ADRs and GDRs, NRI deposits, loans raised by the government abroad and by private entities in the form of ECBs and funds raised by banking institutions (banking capital) and funds transferred under insurance, pension and standardized guarantee schemes all get classified under other investment flows.

Other investment flows (net) at $35.7 billion in 2019–20 were higher than net direct investments ($33.5 billion) and net portfolio investments ($0.6 billion). These flows have also been quite volatile, largely on account of the behaviour of NRI deposits and ECBs. The other equity from GDR and ADR has been practically non-existent as India has not been able to notify rules for these for the past five years.

NRIs deposited $55.6 billion in 2019–20 and withdrew/redeemed deposits of $47.6 billion during the year, resulting in a net inflow of $8 billion. The previous year, in 2018–19, NRIs deposited $60.3 billion and withdrew $49.6 billion. a net inflow of $10.7 billion. NRI deposits have been exhibiting tendencies similar to foreign investment in debt securities. There was a massive inflow of $38.9 billion in 2013–14 and $15.8 billion in 2014–15, and a net outflow of $12.4 billion in 2016–17.

Investment in the Indian economy has been cooling down since 2010–11. ECB inflows reflect two factors: the strength of new investments and relative availability and cost of loan financing for Indian corporates in India and abroad. In 2013–14, there was a net outflow of loans to India (including external assistance, ECBs and banking capital) of $2 billion. Much of this was on account of ECBs. The net inflow of loans to India continued to be minus $1.9 billion in 2014–15, $9.1 billion in 2015–16 and minus $10 billion in 2016–17. Because of the changed dynamics of availability of loans in India (largely on account of the risk-averse nature of PSBs after burgeoning non-performing loans from 2015–16) and cost differential, ECB flows turned positive from 2017–18, resulting in net inflow of loans of $8.7 billion. These flows continued to be positive for the next two years, resulting in net inflow of loan capital of $10 billion in 2018–19 and $12.3 billion in 2019–20.

Change in RBI Reserves Sums Up Net Flows

The current account deficit balance of India at $24.6 billion was more than compensated by higher positive inflows on the capital and financial account in 2019–20. FDI had a positive inflow of $43 billion, FPI had positive inflows of $1.4 billion and other investments had positive inflows of $35.7 billion. There was also smaller movement in other minor heads of the capital and financial account. On financial derivatives (other than reserves) and employee stock options account, India got a positive inflow of $4.1 billion in 2019–20 while there was a negative flow of $1.1 billion on the capital account of general acquisition/disposal of non-produced non-financial assets. The capital and financial account produced a surplus of $83.06 billion. After adjusting the current account deficit of $24.6 billion, there was an overall balance of payment surplus of $58.5 billion in 2019–20.

RBI's Reserve Assets (foreign exchange reserves) went up by $59.5 billion during 2019–20. The remaining was explained as Net Errors and Omissions of $974 million or about $1 billion.

Different components of the current, capital and financial accounts behave differently each year depending upon larger economic forces, Central government budget balances and borrowings, international financial flows, policies pursued by different countries, and so on. The current account has almost always been in the negative for India. However, on aggregate, different components of the financial and capital account, despite moving in different directions in some years, have generally been so positive that, in most years, they have been able to overcome the current account deficit. In the past seven years, barring 2018–19, RBI was able to increase its foreign exchange reserves every year.

Reduction in foreign reserves was in the order of $3.34 billion in 2018–19. In all other years, there was an increase: $43.57 billion in 2017–18; $21.55 billion in 2016–17; $17.91 billion in 2015–16; $61.41 billion in 2014–15; and $15.51 billion in 2013–14.

FDI Flows Exceeded $700 Billion in Twenty Years

India started compiling FDI data systematically and consistently from the year 2000. FDI data has three components: equity inflows, reinvested earnings and other capital. FDI is primarily equity flows from the rest of the world to India. Such equity flows are primarily in companies and other incorporated bodies. However, small FDI flows are also received by unincorporated bodies like partnerships and individual proprietorship concerns. FDI equity inflow data is available for incorporated and unincorporated bodies separately. The profits earned on the foreign equity investment already in the country and not repatriated abroad are counted as reinvested equity earning. Some inflows with quasi-equity characteristics, such as foreign currency convertible bonds, are accounted for as 'other capital'.

India has received total FDI of $721.78 billion until September 2020. Of this, $502.88 billion was new equity inflows in incorporated bodies and $18 billion in unincorporated bodies, bringing the new equity FDI inflow total to $520.88 billion. Reinvested earnings amounted to $161.71 billion while other capital inflows were $39.19 billion.

DPIIT, in the Ministry of Industry and Commerce, maintains detailed data, such as countries of origin of FDI, sectors in which FDI is flowing and states where FDI landed. As per this comprehensive database, which is published every quarter, pure equity inflows until September 2020 stood at $500.12 billion (as against $520.88 billion, according to RBI data).

Fifty per cent of these pure equity inflows of $500.12 billion have come from two countries: Mauritius ($144.71 billion; 28.94 per cent) and Singapore ($105.97; 21.19 per cent). The US, the Netherlands, the UK and Japan are other significant exporters of FDI to India, contributing more than 5 per cent of equity inflows. US investors pumped in equity FDI inflows of $36.9 billion (7.38 per cent), the Netherlands $35.35 billion (7.07 per cent), Japan $34.15 billion (6.83 per cent) and the UK $29.56 billion (5.91 per cent).

According to DPIIT records, India has received FDI equity inflows from as many as 166 countries, including small inflows from countries like Bangladesh ($0.08 billion) and Venezuela ($.01 billion). DPIIT has not been able to trace the origin of $6.98 billion of FDI equity inflows. NRIs have also been accorded a separate classification for the purpose of FDI that has not been allocated to any country. FDI equity inflows contributed by NRIs are not very large, amounting to $4.68 billion until September 2020.

DPIIT classifies FDI equity inflows in about sixty different sectors. The five largest sectors individually account for more than 5 per cent of equity inflows and together about half the total FDI stock (47.67 per cent). The largest FDI receiving sector is services that, as per DPIIT's grouping, includes financial services and some non-financial services: finance, banking, insurance, non-finance/business outsourcing, R & D, courier services, technical testing, etc. The services sector has received FDI of $84.25 billion so far, which is 16.85 per cent of total FDI flows of $500.12 billion.

The next four highest FDI receiving sectors are computer hardware and software with $62.46 billion (12.49 per cent), telecommunications $37.54 billion (7.46 per cent), trading $28.54 billion (5.71 per cent) and construction development $25.78 billion (5.16 per cent).

In all, twenty-one sectors have received FDI of more than $5 billion each, or more than 1 per cent of the total FDI flow.

In terms of the destination of FDI, there is a lopsided distribution. Gujarat, with $185.96 billion, leads the pack with a share of more than one-third of FDI inflows (34.97 per cent). Maharashtra has a share of 20 per cent ($108.82 billion). Karnataka ($79.48 billion; 14.69 per cent) and Delhi ($66.35 billion; 12.20 per cent) are the next two. Together, these four states account for more than 81 per cent of FDI inflows. Jharkhand (4.85 per cent), Tamil Nadu (3.61 per cent), Haryana (2.6 per cent) and Telangana (2.5 per cent) are the other states with a share of more than 1 per cent.

The computer software and hardware sector received as much as $17 billion.

In terms of countries of FDI origin, Mauritius seems to be losing its pre-eminence. In 2019–20, inflows from Mauritius were only $8.14 billion whereas Singapore had a share of $14.67 billion. It was the same the previous year (2018–19) when FDI received from Singapore amounted to $16.2 billion and Mauritius $8.08 billion.

India's Global FDI Rank Improving

Global FDI flows peaked at $2 trillion in 2015. In the next three years, they declined to $1.54 trillion in 2018 and stayed much the same in 2019 ($1.495 trillion) before COVID-19 struck. Following the pandemic, FDI flows are likely to fall to about $1 trillion in 2020. FDI flows are likely to suffer in all geographies and economies in the range of 25 per cent to 40 per cent.

Asia has emerged as the largest FDI destination in recent years, receiving about one-third of global FDI flows, or around $500 billion, of FDI flows of a total $1.5 trillion. Europe and North America are declining as FDI-receiving geographies with their economies maturing. North America's FDI flows were stagnant at $297 billion in both 2018 and 2019. FDI declined in Europe from $429 billion in 2018 to $364 billion in 2019.

The US remains the largest single country as far as FDI inflows are concerned, having received around $250 billion of FDI (about 16 per cent of global inflows) in both 2018 and 2019. China has continued with a solid second position with FDI inflows in the range of $140 billion a year.

India improved its position in 2019 to rank ninth, receiving $51 billion in new FDI flows behind the US, China, Singapore, the Netherlands, Ireland, Brazil, Hong Kong and the UK.

Foreign Investment Regime is Anchored in FEMA (Non-Debt Instruments) Rules, 2019

India does not have capital account convertibility and FDI inflows and outflows are capital account transactions. FDI inflows are governed by the Foreign Exchange Management (Non-Debt Instruments) Rules, 2019, notified by the Department of Economic Affairs, Ministry of Finance, in the exercise of powers conferred by the amendment in the Foreign Exchange Management Act (FEMA) in 2015.

DPIIT is entrusted with FDI policy and notifies changes in the policy by way of press notes. The policy is updated and consolidated annually into a Master Circular. The latest FDI Circular was issued on 15 October 2020.

FDI Policy, contained in the Master Circular, now operates within the limits of the capital account convertibility permitted by the Foreign Exchange Management (Non-Debt Instruments) Rules 2019.

FPIs are investments made by non-residents to buy shares of Indian companies for returns in the form of dividends and capital gains. The investors do not seek to participate in the management of the company; they make their money by buying and selling shares or derivatives thereof.

FPIs are also capital account transactions like FDI. They have to be specifically permitted by the government or RBI, as per the authority conferred by FEMA.

After the amendment in FEMA in 2015, the authority to frame regulations for the portfolio lies with the Government of India, which is required to be exercised in consultation with RBI. Before the amendment, the authority to regulate portfolio investment was bestowed on RBI. The amendment divided the authority to regulate capital account transactions between the government and RBI. The government was given the authority to regulate non-debt transactions and RBI the debt transactions, both in consultation with the other for respective sphere of authority.

After a long tussle between the government and RBI, the government finally notified the Non-Debt Regulations in 2019, laying down the broader rules for portfolio investments as well as other non-debt capital account transactions.

SEBI is the market regulator. The participation of FPIs in the stock markets is regulated by SEBI, within the contours of FEMA and non-debt regulations framed by the government.

Chapter Twenty-Eight

Atmanirbhar Bharat: A Redux of Import Substitution Policy?

Policy of Import Substitution Led to a Steady
Loss of Export Share until the 1980s

Ironically, India was more open to trade with the world before 1947 than for the next thirty-five years thereafter. Openness in trade brings competitiveness in exports. The country's share of global exports was about 2 per cent in 1947; it reached its lowest level of 0.6 per cent in 1983. We followed an import substitution policy for much of this period in an attempt to become self-reliant or *atmanirbhar* in the production of all manufactured goods.

India's merchandise trade surplus in 1937 was a positive $47 million, whereas in 1948 it turned into a negative balance of $122 million. According to the UN World Economic Report 1948, the Index of India's merchandise trade had fallen to 75 in 1946 (base year 1937: 100). The Index recovered to between 81 and 92 in the four quarters of 1947. Still, India's merchandise trade was about 15 per cent lower in 1947 compared to 1937.

India's share in global exports kept falling after Independence. In 1984–85, GATT's World Trade Report offered data on value and share of global exports for major exporting countries for 1953, 1963, 1973 and 1983. With exports of $1.1 billion in 1953, India had a share of 1.3 per cent of global exports and was the sixteenth largest exporting country in the world. In 1963, we exported $1.6 billion worth of goods and services but came down to twentieth place with 1 per cent share. In 1973, the country did not even figure in the twenty-six top exporting countries listed. It was the same in 1983.

In 1980, India's global exports at $5.9 billion, of total exports of $1.97 trillion, gave us a share of only 0.3 per cent. The country was almost closed to the world in terms of trade as our imports at $12.6 billion were also only 0.63 per cent of total global imports of $2.01 trillion. India's share of global trade (imports and exports together) was $18.5 billion of the total trade of $3.98 trillion, a share of just 0.46 per cent. In terms of share of exports of goods and services as a percentage of GDP, India's performance was the worst in 1965, when the exports of goods and services as a proportion of GDP amounted to only 3.31 per cent. The country had a very small rise in share of exports of goods and services to GDP until 1991, when it was 7.05 per cent. After liberalization, exports took off and rose to the highest exports of goods and services to the GDP ratio of 25.43 per cent in 2013. Again, it has been falling steadily since then and reached only 18.4 per cent in 2019.

Trade Self-Reliance is Usually Disguised Trade Nationalism

No human being, household, village, city or state in India can produce the goods and services needed for sustenance and consumption by itself. This was extremely difficult even in the pre-agricultural period when people lived in tribes. It is impossible in the modern era of specialization and technological and economic integration. Further, if everyone could produce and consume all goods and services, there would be no income generation to buy from anyone else. Such a world is nothing but a chimera.

The same rationale applies to sovereign nations as well. No nation can hope to produce all the goods and services needed for the consumption and welfare of its people. Nations are endowed with different natural resources. For instance, India is deficient in energy fuels and has to import them for growth and development. Differences in skill endowments and abilities make nations competitive in the production of certain goods and services.

This serves humanity well by engendering trade in different products and services produced by different people. There is also a difference in the development of technologies that provides a comparative advantage. Not every nation can hope to produce all technologies at the same level of competence and master the production of all goods and services.

True self-reliance, in the context of international trade, should only mean that a country is able to earn enough export revenues (on a medium/long-term basis) to pay for the import of the goods and services it needs to meet necessities, and capital goods and consumer requirements. There is no real self-reliance in attempting to manufacture local goods and services as a substitute to meet these requirements.

More often than not, such efforts result in domestic manufacturers being deprived of the right capital goods and technology, leading them to produce shoddy substitutes at high costs. To enable the sale of such poor-quality substitutes, the government ends up spending a lot of money in subsidies and protection of high tariffs. The consumers suffer most.

The belief that a 'strong' currency and domestic manufacturing of every good and service is optimal for the national interest is nothing but trade nationalism. Such nationalism appeals to many politicians and political parties, and also strikes a chord with the general populace. Most people are willing to make a sacrifice to serve what they perceive as the national interest, including boycotting foreign goods and consuming poorer and costlier domestically produced goods. This emotion is exploited by the politicians and results in the adoption of policies like the import substitution of the 1950s–1980s and the recent Atmanirbhar Bharat.

Control of Import was India's Trade Policy Choice in the 1950s

At the time of Independence, India had a good amount of pound sterling reserves. Our planners were also quite aware of the need to import capital goods and food to boost domestic manufacturing and meet minimum food consumption requirements.

To quote from the First Plan Document:

'We shall have to provide not only for more food and raw materials to meet the additional demands generated by the expenditure but also for additional machinery, equipment and other producer goods—but a deficit of about Rs 180–200 crore per annum in balance of payments seems likely and even necessary in the remaining years of the Plan. About Rs 50 crore of the balance of payments deficits in this period could be financed each year from the sterling releases.'

India had instituted severe import controls in the 1940s to manage the situation arising from World War II and global shortages of commodities for non-military consumption. There was some liberalization in 1946–48 to meet pent-up demand for consumption and capital goods. The Government of India appointed an Import Control Inquiry Committee in 1950. Its recommendations were basically guided by the realization that the availability of foreign exchange was smaller than the consumption and investment requirement. It is instructive to note the basic objectives set by the Committee for Import Control Policy of India for the 1950s was: to limit aggregate imports on the government and commercial accounts to the total available foreign exchange earnings from different sources, including sterling releases; and to distribute available foreign exchange resources in the most equitable manner among the commodities required for planned development of agriculture and industry and essential requirements of consumers.

Import Substitution and Self-Reliance Defined Trade Policy from the 1960s

The Government of India appointed an Import and Export Policy Committee in 1961 for a fresh review of the general import and export control policy, including export promotion measures, as well as the system of priorities for import of raw materials, machinery and capital goods. This Committee brought the policy of import substitution clearly to the fore.

The Fourth Five-Year Plan (1969–1974) brought up self-reliance as a major economic plank. It spoke specifically of 'the need to achieve speedy self-reliance'. Recognizing that the economy's requirements of capital equipment, metals, petroleum products and chemicals were growing fast and dependence on imports was especially large, the plan document argued for 'progressive movement towards self-reliance' realized by a relatively faster expansion of domestic production in these industries over the next decade or so.

The policy of self-reliance, guided by the strategy of import substitution, was implemented most fiercely from the time Indira Gandhi assumed the leadership of the country. In the 1970s, India used all trade policy levers to shut out imports: very high tariff walls (average import tariffs exceeded 200 per cent); severe quantitative restrictions (almost all imports required licence); and non-allocation of foreign exchange (limited exchange quotas for imports). As a consequence, the country's non-oil and non-cereal imports were less than 3 per cent of our consumption in 1975–76.

Import Substitution Slowed Growth

Beginning in the second half of the 1960s, many developing countries (Japan, Taiwan, South Korea) embarked on export-led growth strategies. This required an open attitude to FDI and import of foreign technology, fuels and raw materials. It also required openness to import consumer goods, both for consumption and reverse engineering to produce the same products at competitively lower costs to build exports using cheaper labour and skills. In the middle of the 1960s, a number of ASEAN countries joined the export bandwagon. As the industrial world (North America and Europe) had gotten rich and there was large consumption demand, these East Asian countries built a large export base and generated very good growth to benefit their countries and people.

Unfortunately, India went in the reverse direction, literally shunning imports and foreign investments. From the 1960s, we did try to promote exports but it was a feeble and fearful export strategy. Some preferences and relaxations were made in importing raw material for the purpose of exporting goods. These reluctant import permissions were completely undone by the lack of technology imports and onerous procedural requirements to use imported materials, claim duty refunds and obtain permits and foreign exchange. The consequences were predictable.

According to World Bank data, exports of goods and services from South Africa rose from 2 per cent in 1960 to about 30 per cent in 1980. Export of goods and services from Indonesia increased from 11 per cent of GDP in 1960 to 31 per cent in 1980. Goods and services exports of East Asia and the Pacific as a group rose from 5 per cent of GDP in 1960 to 20 per cent in 1980. Meanwhile, India's exports stagnated from 5 per cent of GDP in 1960 to only about 6 per cent in 1980. The export of goods bottomed at 3 per cent of GDP in 1983–84 (Rs 9866 crore; 3 per cent of GDP, according to *Economic Survey* 1984–85).

India paid a heavy price for the policies followed from the 1950s to the 1980s. We lost out on exports and a valuable source of paying for import of capital and consumption goods. This loss, coupled with the policy of discouraging foreign investment, led to enormous deficiency of foreign exchange to pay for even the most essential imports. Consequently, India was always running a large trade deficit and became dependent on foreign aid from bilateral and multilateral sources. This effectively mortgaged our policy choices to other powerful nations. The country was impelled to make a hefty devaluation in 1966 and suffered the ignominy of going with a begging bowl to Aid India Consortium and other foreign donors to stay afloat. The policy of self-reliance effectively made India dependent on others. What appeared emotionally appealing and galvanizing proved economically disastrous and made the country poor and desperate.

Rollback of Import Substitution and Self-Reliance from 1991

Realizing the futility of the import substitution policy, India started making changes in the 1980s. The first Export-Import Policy (EXIM Policy) was announced in 1985, which contained some trade liberalization measures. Technology imports and capital goods imports were liberalized. Some monetary incentives for registered exporters were announced, which came to be known as REP scrips. We moved from an ad hoc and restrictive trade policy to a predictable multiyear policy framework. EXIM Policies were thereafter announced at three-year intervals.

The economic reforms of 1991 transformed trade policy, abandoning import substitution. Besides liberalizing foreign investments and technology imports, which contributed enormously by raising the quality of domestically produced goods and range of export products, the country used foreign currency adjustment to boost export competitiveness. We also adopted the EXIM Policy under a statutory framework in 1992.

Export performance improved dramatically; foreign exchange reserves shot up and a considerable amount of foreign investment came in. From catering for just four weeks of imports, India's foreign exchange reserves rose to exceed import requirements of over fifty weeks in the next twenty-five years. Several global crises came and went—like the oil crisis of 1988–89, the East Asian crisis of 1998 and the global financial crisis of 2008—but we never found ourselves short of foreign exchange reserves to import capital and consumer goods. The country could completely open its current account and removed almost all restrictions on import. Licencing was given up. Yet, India remained total self-reliant in the matter of dealing with imports. This was true self-reliance. India was really atmanirbhar in terms of its trade and foreign investment account in the 1990s and the first decade of the twenty-first century.

Trade Policy Developments since 2015

India's export performance since 2012–13 has been quite poor. Exports declined from 2013–14 for the next two years and then gradually recovered only to achieve the 2013–14 level in nominal dollars only in 2018–19. Imports, however, grew, though at a much smaller rate.

EXIM Policy 2015–2020 went along the lines of EXIM policies followed for the previous two decades. The only new element of note was the introduction of incentive schemes for goods and services exports. These schemes—the Mercantile Exports from India Scheme (MEIS) and Services Exports from India Scheme (SEIS)—promised a percentage of export value as duty-free scrips, which could be used freely for payment of import duty or sale to other importers and exporters. The MEIS incentive kept getting liberalized in terms of items covered and the rate of incentive. In 2018–19, the estimated liability of the incentive was about Rs 1 lakh crore. The scheme became a major drag on customs revenue and its impact on promoting exports was hardly visible.

The government started raising tariffs on several import items more systemically and comprehensively from 2018. Budget 2018–19 raised import tariffs on consumer items (processed foods, toiletry, footwear, watches, toys and games, etc.), electronic items (mobile phones, printed circuit boards, LCD/LED panels, etc.) and even some items that are exported after processing (diamond, precious stones, etc.). These increases were viewed by many as a protectionist move. Budget 2019–20 increased import tariffs on seventy-five items, including industrial intermediates (PVC, propylene, metal fittings, etc.), electronics (digital recorders, CCTV cameras, optic fibre cables, etc.) and consumer items (cashew nut kernels, ceramic tiles, etc.). Quite surprisingly, the high duty on gold of 10 per cent was further raised to 12.5 per cent. Budget 2020 continued with the tradition and import duty was raised on several items, such as fans, water heaters, shoes, mattresses, refrigerators, air-conditioner compressors, electric vehicles, and so on. Effective import duties have gone up substantially in the past three to four years.

Relying on Self-Reliance Again

The promotion of Make in India has been provided as the rationale for continuously raising import duties. In addition, our trade policies have sought to achieve certain specific objectives, such as discouraging/stopping imports from China, taking on the US in the tariff war launched by former US President Donald Trump and protecting Indian industry from global dumping. Finally, Prime Minister Modi announced the goal of Atmanirbhar Bharat in his address to the nation on 12 May 2020, following it up with his speech on Independence Day on 15 August 2020.

In his address on 12 May, the Prime Minister called for achieving self-reliance to win the war against the novel coronavirus outbreak and 'emerge as a global leader'. In his speech on Independence Day, he exhorted the nation to be 'vocal for local' to achieve the goal of Atmanirbhar Bharat by using local products.

A few other policies were also taken up to encourage Make in India, such as a phased manufacturing programme for mobile phones and the major initiative on PLI schemes for as many as thirteen sectors.

Trade policy developments in the past six years (2014–2020) mark a distinct reversal of the policies pursued since 1991. While the external situation in the 2020s is markedly different than the situation prevalent in the 1950s or 1970s, the call for self-reliance is the same.

Is Atmanirbhar Bharat Import Substitution 2.0?

Emerging from 100 years of colonial rule, India had largely missed the Industrial Revolution although some industrialization in cotton and jute textiles, processing of tea and manufacture of steel had started taking place after 1920. India was dominantly a rural agricultural country with very little to export except commodities, handicrafts and minerals. However, our policymakers had lofty ambitions of industrializing India and producing everything 'from a needle to a ship'. It was a mistaken assumption. India did not have the requisite technology or capital goods. The second mistake was to undertake all basic manufacturing in the public sector. The industrialization strategy was motivated by the notion of self-reliance, which we now call Atmanirbhar Bharat.

The situation is entirely different today. The world is virtually post-industrial. Global manufacturing value chains have a larger capacity to produce almost all required manufactured goods. Supply now exceeds demand, the reverse of the situation prevailing from the 1950s to 1980s. While it was far easier to build manufacturing for exports at that time, today a country can hope to raise its export share only by outpacing another country, and that's possible only when it can produce better quality goods at relatively lower international prices. Manufacturing today is led by IT. The multinational owning technologies and design for digitalization decides where to manufacture components and final products. In the absence of cutting-edge IT and design, India can only offer to manufacture components and products for these global multinationals. It is a challenge to gain export share by following a doctrine of self-reliance.

That said, we have no constraint of foreign exchange today. India has foreign exchange reserves exceeding $650 billion, the fourth largest in the world. Thus, we don't need to follow an import substitution policy to conserve foreign exchange.

Then, what can the call for Atmanirbhar Bharat achieve?

Since May 2020 when the goal of self-reliance was announced, the government has been at pains to explain that this is not a policy of import substitution or an attempt to shut down FDI or ban imports. In fact, more efforts have been taken to explain what Atmanirbhar Bharat isn't, than what it is!

Interpreting the follow-up action taken, the policy seems to have three core objectives: to reduce imports and investments from China; provide protection to domestic manufacturing; and get the Make in India policy to work.

The government is using all the tools—higher tariff, outright ban and technical barriers—to reduce imports and investments from China. While there was some evidence of imports from China reducing initially, it proved too temporary. In fact, in 2020-21, the imports from China rose to be 16.6% of India's total imports, which was not only much higher than the previous two years (13.7% each), but the highest share since 2014–15. China and ten other countries also joined a mega trade pact, Regional Comprehensive Economic Partnership or RECP, which India decided to forgo at the last hour. It is quite likely that Chinese imports and investments will find their way to India via other member countries of RCEP.

The intent to provide protection to domestic industry is partly to offset the cost disabilities Indian manufacturers encounter and partly to offer them a price advantage. Indian manufacturers face a substantial disadvantage in terms of higher tax, higher power costs and higher interest. The PLI scheme is also meant to offset some of these cost disadvantages, as is the reduction in the corporate tax rate in 2019. Protection against anti-dumping on account of global surplus of manufactured goods is another requirement. While these measures are likely to have success in some products, such as mobile handsets and some medical devices, they will not improve general competitiveness. Moreover, the implementation of these schemes is sure to have its challenges.

The Make in India objective flows partly from the second objective. The government has been proactive and committed to FDI, though sometimes the ambivalence towards foreign technology imports becomes apparent. This provides a major contextual difference from the 1950s. This policy encourages foreign companies to set up manufacturing facilities in India, partly to serve rising domestic demand as well. Some investments will definitely flow to India to take advantage of PLI schemes and import duty differentiation.

The goal of self-reliance has not been spelt out in specific targets or timelines in terms of import reduction, export increase or current account surplus. Such targets may not be essential but there should be some specified anchors to judge the success of the policy.

All considered, the vocal campaign for self-reliance is unlikely to have a major impact on the trajectory of India's import dependence or export growth. It appears that this slogan, too, will be another entry in the history of India—hopefully, without causing negative consequences for the economy.

Section VII: The Financial Sector

Chapter Twenty-Nine

State of Currency and Money

Aggregate of Currency Supply and Bank Deposits is 'Money'

Economic agents, whether producers or consumers, hold currency to undertake transactions, make payments and transfers, and to retain for future purchasing power. They can also keep currency with banks as deposits to be withdrawn and used when needed. The central bank issues currency and usually manages its circulation through banks. All the currency with the public and banks, all deposits held with the banks and bankers' deposits with the RBI, together, constitute the stock of money.

There are three levels of the stock of money.

First, paper currency held by people (including all non-monetary or non-banking institutions, whether individuals, unincorporated firms or companies); if currency held by the banks on their account is added to this (not counting the currency owned by RBI held in the chest-branches of some agency banks), it is called the currency in circulation.

Second, the central bank or the monetary authority is liable to provide currency to banks and other institutions that hold deposits. The currency held by people and banks (i.e., currency in circulation plus the deposits of banks with the central bank, usually called reserve money) becomes the second level of stock of money.

Third, currency in circulation and all deposits held by people in banks together is the total stock of money. This is the broadest measure of the stock of money.

The stock of money is distinguished in terms of its 'moneyness'—the ability to be used for payments instantaneously. Currency or paper notes and coins are perfect money as these are used to make payment by simple transfer. Likewise, current account deposits and most savings bank deposits are also instantaneously usable for making payments. By differentiating deposits in terms of their being demanded or their instantaneousness, central banks like RBI describe different variation of broad money stock in terms of M1 (currency in circulation plus demand deposits), M2 (M1 plus deposits in post office savings bank accounts), M3 (M1 plus time deposits held by banks) and sometimes M4 (M3 plus time deposits held in post offices). RBI used the money classification system to accommodate post office deposits that were quite material till twenty-five to thirty years ago. This is no longer the case. The global monetary system has two broad classifications: M1 (currency in circulation and demand deposits with the banks) and M2 (M1 plus time deposits with banks/monetary institutions). M1 is also described as narrow money and M2, broad money.

With the spread of digitalization, the rigidity in using deposits for payments has been increasingly diminishing. Today's savings accounts are literally current accounts in the hands of account holders. Even fixed deposits held in banks are convertible into savings or being withdrawn prematurely, as term deposits become increasingly digital. The currency held by the public and total deposits in the banks effectively comprise the total stock of money.

This stock of money can be used to make payments for goods and services produced and exchanged in the economy. Currency circulates and, over a period of time, coins and notes can get used many times over. The frequency of use of currency in economies differs on account of several factors. If some currency is stashed away, that amount does not circulate. If some coins become debased, they go out of circulation. Term deposits with banks with stiffer penalties or in non-electronic mode are unlikely to get used for payments.

Rise in prices is inflation. Seen another way, inflation is essentially the measure of reduction in the value of money. If money stock goes up without increase in GDP or less increase in GDP with the velocity of money remaining unchanged, the economy would witness inflation or reduction in value of money to bring equilibrium back in GDP, money and velocity of money. If the money stock goes up and the GDP also goes up correspondingly without the velocity of money changing, there is unlikely to be any inflation, which will continue to maintain stability of money. If the stock of money goes up but the velocity of money comes down correspondingly, even if there is no change in GDP, there is unlikely to be any inflation.

Currency Notes Make Up One-Seventh of Money in India

At the end of financial year 2019–20, total 'currency in circulation' or CIC was Rs 24.47 lakh crore. Of this, Rs 0.98 lakh crore was in the form of cash with banks. Therefore, the currency with the public was Rs 23.50 lakh crore.

At the end of 2019–20, banks held Rs 5.44 lakh crore as bankers' deposits with RBI, largely to comply with the obligation of cash reserve ratio (CRR). In addition, there were 'other deposits' with RBI amounting to Rs 0.39 lakh crore. These two types of deposits with RBI added to the currency in circulation, amounting to Rs 30.30 lakh crore, was the stock of reserve money in India.

Finally, demand deposits (which the depositor can withdraw any time without any notice to the banks; mostly balances in current accounts) were Rs 17.38 lakh crore and time or fixed deposits (which can be usually withdrawn only at the end of the term) were Rs 126.74 lakh crore.

Broad money is a measure of currency and deposits of the public. This measure excludes the cash held by banks and the deposits of banks with RBI. Narrow money is currency with the public and demand deposits (the other deposits with RBI are also added). The measure of broad money adds term deposits to narrow money.

In India, narrow money (also called M1) at the end of 2019–20 was Rs 41.26 lakh crore and broad money (M3) was Rs 167.80 lakh crore. Currency notes with the public, at Rs 23.50 lakh crore, made up approximately one-seventh of the broad money stock of Rs 167.80 lakh crore at the end of the year.

Velocity of Money Also Matters

Money is used to make payments for goods traded or services availed. If all payments made in a year are added and the number is divided by the stock of money, one gets the velocity of money in an economy. As crores of payments are made every day in numerous cash and digital modes (UPI alone was used to make more than 450 crore payments in December 2021 in India exceeding Rs 8 lakh crore), it is difficult to add up all the payments. GDP is an inaccurate but closer proxy for value of goods and services paid for and therefore the ratio of GDP to stock of money works as a rough estimate of the velocity of money in an economy.

Using this crude measure, with India's nominal GDP being Rs 203 lakh crore in 2019–20, the velocity of money in India was a low 1.21. In effect, the GDP measures total value added, whereas transactions take place for all inputs and outputs, which is a multiple of the value added. The real velocity would be much higher.

The velocity of money is coming down all over the world, most noticeably in advanced countries. The velocity of money is trending lower even in India.

For inflation, it is not only the quantum of increase in money supply relative to increase in GDP that matters but changes in velocity of money. If the quantum of money goes up but the velocity correspondingly goes down, there is likely to be no impact of increased money supply on inflation, with other things being equal.

Fiat Currency Incubated Monetary Instability

Every good and service produced and consumed in an economy gets exchanged/traded at a value/price expressed in terms of money. As long as gold and silver, valuable goods in themselves, doubled up as currency, the role of money in the exchange of other goods and services was quite straightforward. All goods and services were valued relative to the value of the gold/silver and the gold/silver coin acted as a stable medium of exchange. There was no notable instability in the value of money and no need for any 'monetary policy' to control inflation and maintain the value of money.

Similar stability of money continued to exist when paper currency notes were introduced as money but were kept aligned to the value of gold/silver by being freely convertible in gold/silver coins. In the era of gold/silver currency or even when the gold/silver standard was prevailing, it did not matter which country's gold/silver coin/note was used, as every coin/note was exchanged for the quantity of pure gold or silver or both and there was a stable exchange ratio between gold and silver.

Much of the global currency system until the 1960s operated on this basis, including during the Bretton Woods era (the agreement was signed in 1944) as every currency was expressed to be equivalent to a certain weight in gold and its relative value to the US dollar was fixed accordingly. The fact that the US dollar was convertible in gold at a fixed ratio of $35 to an ounce of gold made all international currencies virtually convertible in gold.

When countries, one after the other, went off the gold/silver standard and the US refused to convert $35 into an ounce of gold in 1971, only paper currency was left to discharge the function of money. That's when the situation got complicated. Paper currency, whether dollars, sterling or rupees, not backed by gold/silver, had no value of its own. It became necessary to determine the real monetary value of the currency issued and maintain the stability of that value for the currency to continue to function as money.

An era of inflation ensued, starting in the late 1960s. The US had more than twenty-five years of acute inflation until the early 1990s. This phenomenon played out the world over. India also experienced the worst of inflation in the 1970s, 1980s and 1990s. Inflation and the stability of money became a major policy problem.

Runaway inflation caused unprecedented harm to growth and employment. In the 1970s, monetarists reasoned convincingly that stability in the value of money could be achieved by controlling the excessive quantum of money. Inflation targeting became the policy choice globally. India also adopted inflation targeting formally as the monetary policy instrument in 2015. Besides a few other structural factors, monetary management under the inflation-targeting regime ensured containment of the inflation demon in most parts of the world.

In the paper currency era, monetary stability and inflation management are significant policy issues.

Inflation's Negative Impact on Value of Money

For the period 1861–1957, inflation in general was quite low thanks to the gold/silver standard ensuring constrained money supply. The adoption of fiat currency removed the restraint on money supply. Inflation also did not seem to work effectively to create growth and employment. In fact, while inflation raged in the 1970s and 1980s, unemployment also soared. The relationship of unemployment and inflation, which was postulated to be inverse by noted economist Phillips, made famous by the well-known Phillips Curve, proved to be direct. Both the Keynesian model and Phillips Curve lost their justification. For policymakers, the lure of monetary-based expansion of public expenditure was too intoxicating a brew, but by the late 1980s, it was becoming apparent that the party would not last forever.

India also unleashed the monetary purse beginning in 1955. The government effectively directed RBI, which meekly complied, to provide it unrestrained credit. The mechanism was simple but lethal. The government would issue ad hoc treasury bills and RBI would put an equal amount into the government's account. The unproductivity of a lot of expenditure ensured that there was no commensurate growth. Inflation was the manifestation of unproductive expenditure and excessive monetary expansion. In October 1974, India recorded inflation of 34.7 per cent.

American economist and monetarist Milton Friedman pointed out the obvious connection between the excessive supply of money and inflation. He famously said, 'Inflation is always and everywhere a monetary phenomenon in the sense that it is and can be produced only by a more rapid increase in the quantity of money than in output.'

The World Doused Inflation to Restore Value of Money

In 1979, economist Paul Volcker took over as chair of the US Federal Reserve (Fed) when consumer price inflation was 13 per cent. Recognizing the reason for it, he pursued a policy of controlling credit expansion and money supply by raising the Fed's benchmark interest rates. Interest rates were raised to a record high of 20 per cent. Inflation came under control, to less than 5 per cent.

Indeed, inflation was everywhere and inflation targeting (to bring it down to tolerable levels) by restraining supply of money became the policy choice globally. New Zealand was the first country to formally adopt inflation targeting in 1990. Canada followed suit soon. Others did so over the next twenty-five years. India also adopted inflation targeting, though informally, in the late 1990s. In 2015, the country formally adopted the inflation-targeting framework, mandating RBI to maintain consumer price inflation in the corridor of 2–6 per cent.

Inflation-targeting frameworks succeeded. Other factors like ageing of societies leading to demand stagnation, increase in production of goods and services making supply outpace demand, and increase in productivity and cost of services thanks to digitalization also helped. These days, inflation is not a major global concern, barring a few rogue states. In fact, the lack of inflation is a concern in some countries.

Overweighted Food Creates Impression of High and Volatile Inflation in India

The wholesale price index number of manufactured products in India rose from 121.9 in 1972–73 to 270.6 in 1981–82, a simple average of 14.87 per cent a year. The same wholesale price index number in the next series rose from 103.5 in 1982–83 to 243.2 in 1993–94, at the rate of 11.64 per cent. Inflation in manufactured products was quite high in the 1970s and 1980s.

Moderation started somewhere in the early 1990s. The wholesale index number (1993–94 base series) rose from 112.3 in 1994–95 to 166.3 in 2004–05, registering a simple annual increase of 4.91 per cent. The same type of moderation was noticed in the next series (base 2004–05) when the wholesale price index rose from 102.4 in 2005–06 to 139.5 in 2011–12, recording a rise of 5.3 per cent annually. Inflation in manufactured products collapsed in the 2010s with the wholesale price index increasing from 105.3 in 2012–13 to 118.3 in 2019–20, an annual increase of only 1.62 per cent.

India is still young. There is every reason to believe that consumption and investment demand in India must rise in double digits. However, global supply excess in many commodities and scaling up of production capacities in many manufactured goods have seen shortages of manufactured products disappear. For manufactured products, there is no real inflation issue in the country.

The GDP deflator, which measures economy-wide inflation, is also relatively low. It rose from 100 in 2012 (the 2011–12 series) to 138.8 in 2020, an average of 4.3 per cent.

In January 2011, the government established the Consumer Price Index-Combined (CPI-C), a composite all-India index. Earlier, there were consumer price indices for specific consumer segments, like industrial workers, agriculture labourers and so on. The inflation target, given as a legislative mandate for RBI in 2015, is also set in terms of the CPI-C.

The CPI-C rose from 93.3 in 2011–12 to 146.3 in 2019–20, registering an annual increase of 5.9 per cent, way above the average annual increase of 1.62 per cent recorded in the wholesale price index or 4.3 per cent in the GDP deflator.

The CPI-C represents a much lower proportion of goods and services produced and consumed in India. Therefore, it is not really a good measure of inflation of overall consumption. It also does not represent inflation in investment goods. Moreover, it gives excessive weightage to food and beverages (54.18 per cent). Food items are also quite volatile as well, especially vegetables. The CPI-C is the wrong index to target in India's effort to control inflation.

RBI has adopted CPI-C and the inflation as recorded in CPI-C has to be kept within the tolerable range. The CPI-C design systemically over-projects inflation. As a result, RBI also tends to overreact to control inflation. Unfortunately, the monetary actions of RBI cannot effectively target inflation in food items. This ends up depressing the prices of manufactured goods and overall price levels. Thus, India's efforts to achieve monetary stability by targeting inflation has proved to be quite a poor exercise.

Collapse of Inflation Makes Monetarist Theory Redundant

Japan entered no-inflation territory in the early 1990s. Most of Europe has not seen inflation of more than 2 per cent in the twenty-first century. Americans have, for long, set 2 per cent as the minimum inflation target but have not succeeded for two decades despite adopting all kinds of quantitative easing and ballooning of the Fed's balance sheet. Over $3 trillion of money and reserves have been injected in the US after the outbreak of COVID-19 and supply chains collapsed for some time, yet there is no sign of inflation. The Fed has now adopted an average of 2 per cent as the inflation target.

According to monetarist theory, massive monetary expansion in developed countries should have resulted in runaway inflation, but it has not. There are three principal reasons for the collapse of inflation in developed countries.

First, a very stable and longer-term demand and supply equilibrium—where supplies are outpacing demand for reasons like demographic change, construction of infrastructure and global integration—has taken the wind out of the sails of suppliers. They are just not in a position to increase prices for most goods and services.

Second, integration of global supply chains, global trade, massive reduction in transportation costs, rush of interest rates towards zero and the growth of e-commerce have lowered producers'/suppliers' cost of production and distribution, thus protecting corporate profits, while reducing consumers' costs at the same time.

Third, household and corporate savings, including monetary and credit expansion, are increasingly feeding into asset prices in place of consumption and investment, leaving very little or no impact of monetary expansion on inflation.

When developing countries start moving into the upper middle-income or high-income brackets, they start exhibiting the same tendencies. In any case, a supply-demand equilibrium is taking place on a global level for many commodities and the advantages of cost reduction are also available to many developing countries.

There have been numerous episodes of very sharp and big monetary expansions. In the calendar year 2020, the money supplied expanded massively in most countries. However, there was no real inflation in any advanced country. Most developing countries did not see any real inflation. Monetary expansions have tended to get leaked into wealth with demand for purchase of or investment in assets of all classes (equity, bonds, gold, real estate and the like) going up. In 2021, expansionary fiscal policies and supply disruptions led to inflation coming to the fore, which provided necessary justification to start rolling back ultra-easy monetary policies by the end of the year.

In most of the world, inflation is no longer a monetary phenomenon as Freidman wanted us to believe. Circumstances change; theories also have to change. In most countries today, monetary expansion does not cause a rise in prices of goods and services any longer. Instead, it raises wealth/assets prices.

MMT is Repackaged Keynesian Stimulus

A number of economists, most actively in the US, are arguing that governments, especially in advanced countries, can monetize as much deficit as necessary to finance full employment or serve any other public policy objective—such as investing in health for all or old-age social security—without worrying about fiscal deficits. These economists place only one caveat to this unabashed expansion of fiscal expenditures: inflation should not rise. This theory is being touted as the Modern Monetary Theory (MMT).

Most high-income countries have not witnessed inflation despite their central banks using all sorts of monetary tools, such as driving down interest rates close to zero, quantitative easing, purchase of private corporate bonds, expanding the central bank balance sheet and managing the interest rate curve. Proponents of MMT believe that stimulus/monetary expansion from the monetary authority is useless in pushing up real economic activity, i.e., in generating real demand or reducing unemployment. These objectives could be achieved only if governments expand expenditure to bring in an economy-wide balance in demand and supply. This would generate growth, take care of social security and other re-distributional objectives, and achieve full employment.

The expansion of fiscal expenditures by printing more currency or creating more money can work, like the original Keynesian hypothesis, only if it results in increased production of goods and services. However, delivering helicopter money that does not result in increased consumption and new investment in productive capacity is as ineffective as monetary stimulus. In economies where this is not the outcome, there would neither be growth, nor inflation. Such fiscal expansion would also leak into an increase in asset prices.

The MMT does not work for an economy like India. In fact, it is similar to what the country used to do from the 1960s to the 1980s: runaway expansion of fiscal expenditure financed by automatic monetization of money. India witnessed excessive inflation during this period. The country still has unsatisfied demand but constrained supply. If the MMT were to be applied in India today, the results would be very close to what we witnessed until 1990: low growth and high inflation.

Chapter Thirty

Two and a Half Generations of the Rupee

First Generation of the Rupee—the Standard
Silver Rupee Debuts in 1835

The rule of the East India Company (EIC) had spread over large tracts of India by 1835. This included the three Presidency Towns of Calcutta, Bombay and Madras, as well as many other territories. The Presidency Towns were minting silver coins that circulated in their areas, performing the function of currency. Many princely states also minted coins, which contained different quantities of pure silver. There was considerable confusion about the relative value of the different coins in circulation.

The EIC decided to accept the silver coin circulating in Bombay Presidency as the standard coin, gave it the name of 'Rupee' and declared the 'Silver Rupee' as the legal tender across the territories of India it controlled.

The Indian rupee was a metallic coin with a standard weight of 180 grains and standard content of 165 grains of pure silver and fifteen grains of alloy. This was the standard currency minted and circulated by the government of the day: the EIC. Central banks did not exist in the world at that time. Banking itself was nascent in India then.

The silver rupee became standard currency all over India soon. The Calcutta Mint minted silver rupees as per demand. The value of coins of other princely states got fixed with reference to the relative pure silver contained therein.

Indian mints also issued a gold coin: the mohur. Its value was fixed in terms of the silver rupee—Rs 15 to a gold mohur reflecting the gold-silver ratio of 15:1.

The silver rupee operated on the classical metallic standard. It contained 165 grains of pure silver. Conversion of bullion into silver rupees and vice versa was freely permitted. A mint charge was levied whenever anyone wanted to get silver bullion minted into rupees to cover the cost of minting. It was also no crime if rupees were melted and converted into bullion.

The quantum of rupees in circulation was determined by the demand for coins needed for smooth conduct of trade and other financial transactions.

Limitations of Silver Rupee Gave Birth to Paper Notes in 1861

The limitations of the silver rupee soon became apparent, including inconvenience in use for large value transactions and payments to be made over distances. India is a vast country. It was also primarily an agricultural economy. Peasants preferred to sell their crops upon receipt of silver coins. The weight and volume of the silver rupee posed problems in transportation. Thus, respectable merchants started taking silver coins and issuing paper promissory notes convertible in equal value of silver rupee. Traders who trusted the merchant or banker would exchange silver rupees with such promissory notes on paper.

The government realized the need for paper currency notes convertible in silver or silver coins on demand. In 1861, it decided to issue paper rupees, fully convertible in silver rupee, which continued to be the primary currency. The first paper rupee was issued in 1862.

Issuance of paper currency was backed by the Paper Currency Reserve consisting of silver and gold coins. The 1861 Indian Paper Currency Act provided for only a small part of paper currency reserves to be held in the form of securities issued by the Government of India—only Rs 2 crore.

Rupee notes equal in value to silver rupees came into circulation and their prevalence increased. The government kept its promise of converting rupee notes into silver rupee coins.

However, as the invested portion started rising on account of various factors, it started becoming difficult for the government to honour its promise.

The penny dropped in 1893. The government decided to close the mints to free coinage of silver. People could no longer bring any bullion to mint it into silver coins. Likewise, there was no more conversion of paper rupees into silver coins.

India decided to go off the metal standard. This heralded the end of the first-generation currency in India.

Second Generation of Rupee is Essentially Fiat Money

India started on the second generation of money—token currency—in 1893. Silver coins continued to be minted in India even after 1893. However, the proportion of paper currency kept increasing. The invested portion of the Paper Currency Reserve, which was fixed at Rs 2 crore in 1961, was raised gradually to Rs 120 crore in 1920. The absolute maximum limit of the invested portion was indirectly done away with in 1920 by prescribing that the metal portion of the Reserve would not be less than a proportion of the total reserves.

Minting of silver coins was gradually reduced. Paper currency became the main currency in circulation. In 1940, the silver content in the silver rupee coin was reduced to half the full weight of the coin, i.e., ninety grains. Finally, in June 1947, minting of silver coins was totally stopped. From then on, paper currency has been the exclusive currency of India.

The minimum metal portion of currency reserves was abolished at some stage. There is no requirement of minimum gold or silver to be kept as part of the reserves. At the end of December 2020, currency notes of about Rs 27.5 lakh crore were in circulation in India. The value of gold with RBI was less than Rs 2.7 lakh crore.

Indian Currency is Primarily the Paper Rupee

Exactly 100 years after the first standard pan-India silver rupee was issued, RBI was formed as a privately owned central bank in 1935.

Note issuance, which was carried out by the government in the Department of Issue and through Reserves Treasuries and Circles in the country, was taken over by the central bank. RBI has an Issue Department, which manages and accounts for the currency in circulation.

Coins are still minted in government mints. After the stoppage of the silver rupee, coins were of small denominations. Later, coins were introduced for relatively larger denominations: the Re 1 coin held fort for long. Coins of Rs 2, Rs 5 and Rs 10 were introduced. In 2019, the government introduced a Rs 20 coin as well. People don't find coins convenient for transactions. Only about 1 per cent of the currency in circulation—about Rs 6500 crore (all small and rupee coins together) against notes in circulation—is in coin form.

Physical currency in circulation and currency as deposits in saving and current accounts are as good as currency in circulation. In the digital world, deposits perform payments faster than paper currency payments. However, there is a difference between the two. The currency note is the currency. Deposits can perform payments, which is the main function of currency. Deposits are money but not currency. Deposits can be converted into currency while the rupee banknote remains the currency.

Digital Payments are Making Money Digital

Money or currency intercedes to complete trade and other financial transactions. Paper currency is lightweight and easy to carry. It can also be assigned any monetary value. India had a Rs 10,000 note in 1947.

Paper currency, though, suffers from a major drawback; it has to be physically delivered. This shortcoming was overcome substantially by the arrival of banks. You can deposit your paper currency or cash in your bank account. Thereafter, you issue a cheque to make a payment.

However, cheques have to go through a long process for realization. The banker of the issuer had to send it to the banker of the recipient or a clearing house. If the parties are in two different cities or in different countries, the process of realization was still longer and more tortuous.

The advent of digital technologies has resolved this problem. The adoption of core banking technologies has allowed every bank account to become a digital one. Creation of market infrastructure like the National Payment Council of India (NPCI) has converted all digital bank accounts in India into digital wallets in a single bank.

You can now make all payments on your mobile phone or computer. Most payments are instantaneous. Digital technologies have removed all the limitations of paper currency.

It is estimated that more than 90 per cent of all payment transactions in value in India take place digitally now. However, over 80 per cent of transactions in volume are still estimated to be conducted in cash—by way of exchanging currency notes.

Digital payment has a number of advantages over physical payment. It costs money to print paper currency and manage the system. It is also easy to counterfeit, posing a threat to national security and impelling central banks to constantly upgrade the security features embedded in currency notes. Paper notes have a limited life and replacing paper with plastic or any other material is expensive. Physical movement of paper currency notes costs money, as does storing them, stuffing them in ATMs or delivering them on the counter of banks. Digital transactions, relatively, have almost no cost. That said, they can be hacked and central banks have to build appropriate security systems. However, comparatively, digital money management is cheaper and more hassle-free than the paper currency system.

There Is a Problem in Global Payments

There has been considerable expansion in the linking of banks globally. Banks establish correspondent banking relationships to facilitate transfer of money and payments. The evolution of messaging systems like SWIFT and digital payment platforms have expedited global payments and reduced the cost of money transfer over the past few years. Digital payment systems like UPI and Internet banking are very efficient and cost nothing—but these are only available for domestic payments and transfers.

There are, however, still problems with the global payment architecture.

It is difficult to order and pay for goods and services on e-commerce platforms located in other countries. It is more difficult to raise loans and credit from lenders outside the country. Even transferring incomes as remittances costs a lot. A World Bank study estimated this cost to be in the order of about $30 billion or about Rs 2.1 lakh crore in 2017. The Indian diaspora ends up paying about 2.5 per cent or more for $500 remittance transfers. Immigrant workers of some countries lose 15–20 per cent of their earnings while transferring funds to their homeland.

All this happens because there is no integration of bank accounts and balances internationally. In fact, most developing countries, and even many advanced countries, have not been able to do so even domestically.

Burst of Private Cryptocurrencies Globally

Bitcoin, the most well-known, used and traded private cryptocurrency, burst on the global scene in 2014 with a market cap of about $10 billion. The market cap of bitcoin crossed $1 trillion in February 2021.

Unlike a currency that has a stable value/price, bitcoin prices have varied phenomenally—from less than $500 per bitcoin in most of 2014–2015, it peaked at about $15,000 in December 2017 and fell below $3500 by December 2018. In 2021, bitcoin rose to its lifetime-high levels though there was quite a bit of volatility as well. From the level of about $35,000 on 11 January 2021, it touched $55,600 on 20 February 2021 rose to $63,000 in April, fell to less than $40,000 in September, rose again to $67,000–70,000 levels in October–November before ending the year at around $43,000. Bitcoin's market cap in March 2021 exceeded one-third of India's total GDP.

All currencies in the world are issued by sovereign or central banks, on behalf of the sovereign. Official/sovereign currencies carry a sovereign guarantee to pay equal value in gold or silver or simply fiat money. Private cryptocurrencies have no such guarantees. Central banks manage the issuance and circulation of money to maintain the value of official currencies. Issuers of cryptocurrency make no claim or effort to maintain the value of cryptocurrencies.

Most operating cryptocurrencies in the world have been created by private entrepreneurs/speculators by creating blocks of coins using blockchain technology in the distributed ledger technology (DLT) mode. There is no preassigned nominal or real value of private cryptocurrencies. Their prices fluctuate depending upon demand and supply. While there has been some use of cryptocurrencies in payments, including in international transfers, private cryptocurrencies have not been successful in becoming a significant means of payment primarily on account of a lack of fixed/stable value.

Blockchain technology can also be used by central banks to issue official currency. A few countries have initiated steps to develop models of official cryptocurrency but no central bank has launched one so far. The World Economic Forum and IMF have come up with some models of official cryptocurrencies under the broad rubric of 'Central Bank Digital Currency' or CBDT.

Facebook announced its intention to launch a stable cryptocurrency called Libra in 2019. It released a white paper in June 2019 and created an organization in partnership with others interested in the payment ecosystem to configure the design. The central architectural aspect of the design was that Libra would have a stable relative value in terms of major currencies. It is still to be launched.

Cryptocurrencies Seek to Change the Basic Form of Currency

The innovators of cryptocurrencies intended to solve the problem of international payments by creating a digital network of crypto-coin holders who can lend, borrow or pay using crypto-coins anywhere in the world at a fraction of the cost of conventional transfer. Cryptocurrencies in the form of stable-coins are a more refined version of this effort.

Everyone who owns cryptocurrencies in the distributed ledger knows which computers own how many bitcoins. In the world of cryptocurrencies, you know how much is in your crypto-wallet, what is the total size of all the wallets and which computer holds how much in its wallet.

Cryptocurrencies mark a revolutionary departure in the evolution of money. From the metal coin to paper, you now have the prototype of a digital currency with no physical form, which exists in the form of computer codes and not any fiat printed on a piece of paper.

Cryptocurrency is different from digital payment in paper currency. Digital applications are used to make payments in currency that continues to be in paper form. Cryptocurrency is digital currency, which by its very nature is used to make payments in digital form. Digital currency is different from digital payment.

Cryptocurrencies Have an Identity Crisis

In India, of late, most cryptocurrency enthusiasts are at pains to explain that the idea of cryptocurrencies is not to replace or substitute official currencies. It's called a currency but is not supposed to replace the rupee or any other official currency?

A currency serves the purpose of payment when buying and selling a commodity. A commodity, which has some inherent value, is bought and sold for consumption or retention as an asset. Currency and commodity are two different things.

A cryptocurrency is not a commodity with any intrinsic or commonly acceptable value. Thus, it does not satisfy the normal definition of a commodity.

Normally, commodities are consumed. Commodities derive their value as meeting consumer demand of consumption. Their prices are determined by the interplay of the forces of demand and supply, which is not necessarily based on utility to the consumer. Cryptocurrencies are not consumed.

Cryptocurrencies do exhibit the character of being an asset—a non-physical asset like goodwill or a brand. The value of the asset has no definite relation to the underlying utility from the use or retention of the asset. Asset valuation is the function of demand and supply of that asset.

In view of this, it is apparent that no cryptocurrency is a currency. Cryptocurrencies are not commodities either. They can at best be viewed as an asset.

Maintaining the value of currency and money is complex. Blockchain technology is designed to keep a decentralized record, but it has no algorithms or program that can manage, maintain or move the value of currency with the real economy and ensure stable conversion with real/official currencies.

Pureplay cryptocurrencies have no interface with the real economy and, therefore, cannot maintain any value relationship with the wider economy.

Cryptocurrencies are unlikely to make any headway in becoming a significant part of the digital payment system.

Chapter Thirty-One

State of Savings and Wealth

Savings

Savings Finance Investments

Investments are broadly of two kinds: creation of new assets and purchase of existing assets. Investment in new assets builds the productive capacity of the country; purchase of existing assets does not add to productive capacity but it might raise the value of the assets. The national savings deployed to make new investments amount to capital formation, which adds to the national capacity of goods and services for consumption or investment, thereby increasing GDP. Savings invested in purchasing existing assets do not add to GDP. Assets created and accumulated form the wealth of a nation, which is usually measured in monetary terms. The wealth of a nation can increase by creation of fresh assets as well as increased valuation of existing assets. Increase in wealth may not necessarily indicate an increase in the productive capacity of a nation.

Savings are mostly made by households and corporations. Governments are net dissavers, almost invariably in developing countries. Households, however, usually do not make productive investments directly. They invest in bank deposits, government deposits, insurance products, currency, gold, listed shares and occasionally in primary issuances and new firms. Many households do set up proprietary and partnership firms that undertake productive investments, but the majority of their investments go in the portfolio of assets: deposits, shares, bonds, currency and gold.

Capital formation and FDI represent investment in the creation of fresh productive capacity, whereas investment in the portfolio of existing assets, including by FPIs, generally represent investment in existing assets, impacting wealth but not productive capacity.

Independent India Was Born a Poor Nation, With Low Income and Low Savings

The First Plan noted the abysmally low level of investment in capital formation prevalent in India—about 5 per cent—and the poor availability of data.

With an estimated high rate of population growth (about 2.75 per cent per annum), despite assuming a very favourable capital output ratio (incremental units of capital required to generate additional one unit of output) of 3, the First Plan estimated that it would take twenty-five years to double the per-capita income in India by raising the national income of Rs 9000 crore in 1950–51 by 160 per cent by 1975–76. This would require, according to the Plan, raising the savings and investment rate substantially from 5 per cent to about 20 per cent over this period.

India's savings rate did improve slowly but steadily in the second half of the twentieth century. The 1999–2000 Economic Survey noted that the savings rate (gross domestic savings comprising savings of all players: households, the private corporate sector and government) was 10.2 per cent of GDP in 1950–51 and fixed capital formation was 9.3 per cent (public and private sector combined). The savings rate fluctuated between 8.1 per cent and 13.9 per cent during the decade, recorded 12.7 per cent in 1960–61 and averaged a little more than 10 per cent. Capital formation fared better with inflow of some foreign savings and averaged over 11.5 per cent.

India's domestic savings rate crossed 15 per cent in 1959–60, 20 per cent in 1976–77 and 25 per cent in 1994–95. Financed largely by the domestic savings rate, the GFCF rate crossed 15 per cent for the first time in 1965–66 and 20 per cent in 1982–83. As India pursued self-reliance and import substitution policies in the first forty years after Independence, fixed capital formation lagged behind the domestic savings rate during this period.

National Savings Rose to Highest Levels Between 1990 and 2010

The 2013–14 Economic Survey reported that India's gross domestic savings rate was 22.9 per cent in 1990–91. The savings rate fell for the next two years and then steadily rose to 25 per cent in 1999–2000. The first decade, until 2007–08, saw a sharp rise in the savings rate. It jumped from 25.9 per cent in 2002–03 to 29 per cent in 2003–04 and again to 32.4 per cent in 2004–05, an increase of 6.5 per cent in two years, the highest jump ever recorded in the history of India. After increasing by about 1 per cent annually for the next two years, it crossed 35 per cent and rose to 36.8 per cent, the highest savings rate recorded to date in the country, before peaking.

In the 1990s, India started opening up to foreign savings and investments. Fixed capital formation rose sharper than the domestic savings rate. India's capital formation went past 25 per cent in 1995–96, 30 per cent in 2004–05 and peaked at 38.1 per cent in 2007–08. GFCF was also higher than 30 per cent every year since 2005–06 till the end of the decade, with the peak rate of 32.9 per cent recorded in 2007–08. In 2007–08, the year of the global financial crisis, India witnessed its highest savings rate, highest gross capital formation rate and highest GFCF rate. Savings supported a massive investment binge.

Domestic Savings Rose Steadily Over Sixty Years

There are statistical base revisions almost every decade. The 2019–20 Economic Survey provides details of gross savings rate, gross capital formation and GFCF since the commencement of the Republic in 1950. It confirms a slow rise in the savings rate in the 1960s thanks to a low-income base, which was not even enough to support adequate nutritional consumption. The savings rate rose steadily from a low base in the 1960s to 2000. Savings jumped massively in the first decade of the twenty-first century and then started tapering off. The current savings rate is akin to what we saw in the late 1990s and the early part of the first decade of the twenty-first century.

As per the 2019–20 Economic Survey, India's gross saving rate was 9.5 per cent in 1950–51, 11.6 per cent in 1960–61, 14.3 per cent in 1970–71, 17.8 per cent in 1980–81, 22.9 per cent in 1990–91, 23.7 per cent in 2000–01 and 33.7 per cent in 2010–11. In 2007–08, India recorded a gross savings rate of 36.8 per cent. In 2013–14, it was 32.1 per cent. It fell to 30.3 per cent in 2016–17 and stayed around the same level (30.5 per cent) in 2017–18. In 2018–19, it was close to falling below 30 per cent (recorded 30.1 per cent). And in 2019–20, it actually went below 30 per cent, ending a fifteen-year streak of relatively high savings rates.

Where Are India's Household Savings Deployed?

Households saved about Rs 20 lakh crore (Rs 19.96 lakh crore) in 2018–19. These savings were invested in several financial assets. The largest chunk was deployed in deposits: Rs 7.8 lakh crore with banks; Rs 7.3 lakh crore with non-banks, Rs 0.3 lakh crore with cooperatives and Rs 0.2 lakh crore with other financial institutions. The second most preferred mode of savings was provident and pension funds (Rs 3.96 lakh crore) followed by increase in currency (Rs 2.8 lakh crore), insurance funds (Rs 2.6 lakh crore) and claims on government through small savings and other deposits (Rs 1.99 lakh crore). Savings in shares and debentures (Rs 0.8 lakh crores) was the smallest of the major savings avenues for households.

Households made investments in physical assets of about Rs 21.8 lakh crore in 2018–19. These assets primarily comprised property and included consumer durable assets. Savings in gold, shown separately in the National Accounts, amounted to Rs 0.36 lakh crore in 2018–19.

Gross household savings in all three principal modes—financial savings, savings in physical assets and gold—amounted to Rs 42.1 lakh crore or about 22.4 per cent of GNI.

Households did not finance all their financial savings and investments from their incomes. They also borrowed. Total incremental borrowings of households in 2018–19 amounted to Rs 7.66 lakh crore. Net of financial borrowings, financial savings were Rs 12.3 lakh crore. Net of financial borrowings, gross household savings (financial savings, investment in physical assets and gold) were Rs 34.5 lakh crore, or 18.4 per cent.

The household savings deployment pattern of 2018–19 is representative of the long-term savings deployment pattern in India, though there are significant variations with respect to certain asset classes from year to year. In 2016–17, when the government carried out a large-scale demonetization exercise, households shed currency of Rs 3.33 lakh crore instead of the usual additional deployment. The subsequent two years saw remonetization, which was reflected in a higher than trend yearly deployment of savings in currency. The shrinking of currency held by the public was reflected in a much higher deployment in bank deposits, insurance funds and shares and debentures.

Global Savings Rate Constant at around 25 Per Cent for the Past Fifty Years

In 2020, the Asian Development Bank (ADB) published an excellent report, *Asia's Journey to Prosperity*. Table 7.2 summarizes the global savings phenomenon for the period 1960–2018. The global gross domestic savings rate was 26 per cent between 1970 and 1979. This declined marginally to 24.8 per cent during 1980–89 and then rose somewhat in the next two decades—to 25.1 per cent during 1990–99 and 2000–09. In the second decade (2010–2018), the domestic savings rate fell slightly to 25.1 per cent. Global domestic savings rates have averaged 25 per cent, almost unchanged, for the past fifty years.

However, growth engines have shifted dramatically from 1960 to 2018. The report divides Asia in two blocks: Developed Asia (Japan and Australia) and Developing Asia (the rest of Asia). Developing Asia had a domestic savings rate of only 18 per cent in 1960–69, whereas Developed Asia had a domestic savings rate of 30.5 per cent. Asia, inclusive of China and India, was hardly saving and investing in the 1960s although some smaller countries like South Korea and Taiwan had started their investment-led growth journeys.

In the 1970s, Japan had a sterling savings rate of 37 per cent and the Organisation for Economic Co-operation and Development (OECD) countries had a strong rates of 25.2 per cent. Besides Developing Asia, other developing regions, like Latin America, also had a low domestic savings rate of about 20 per cent. Developing Asia started taking off in the 1970s; by the 1990s, the global growth engine had shifted to Asia, reflected in very high domestic savings and investment rates. Developing Asia recorded a domestic savings rate of 24.9 per cent in 1970–1979, 27.4 per cent in 1980–1989, 32.9 per cent in 1990–1999, 36.6 per cent in 2000–2009 and 41.0 per cent in 2010–2018.

These blockbuster rates, exceeding 40 per cent in the second decade of the twenty-first century, were almost double the savings rate of all other regions during this period (23.4 per cent Developed Asia; 21.4 per cent OECD; 20.2 per cent Sub-Saharan Africa; and 19.8 per cent Latin America). Not surprisingly, Developing Asia contributed more than 60 per cent of global growth in 2019 in terms of purchasing power parity (PPP).

The Asia Prosperity Report also documents the phenomenal rise in the savings rate of India and China. India had a domestic savings rate of 8.4 per cent during 1960–1969, which increased steadily to 12.6 per cent, 15.8 per cent, 23.9 per cent, 29.9 per cent and 31.5 per cent in the next five decades. China had a higher starting point—a domestic savings rate of 27 per cent in 1960–69—which jumped to 36.6 per cent in the 1970s. It stagnated to 35 per cent during 1980–1989 when the country started opening up. China's domestic savings rate rose steadily thereafter to 39.7 per cent during 1990–1999, to 44.5 per cent during 2000–2009 and 48.3 per cent during 2010–2018. China literally saved half its income for investment in the current decade. As per-capita income had risen to high levels, the Chinese people enjoyed better consumption standards despite saving such a large proportion of their incomes for investment in growth.

Other regions decelerated in terms of domestic savings; both the developed OECD countries and the non-Asian developing countries (Latin America and Sub-Saharan Africa). The global growth engine has shifted from the rest of the world to Asia.

Why is the Savings Rate Falling in India?

It is important to diagnose why the domestic savings rate is falling in India before attempting to provide solutions for the situation.

Households, the primary savers, save from their incomes for two primary reasons: building a nest egg for their old age or future unemployment; and for better returns from their savings for improved future consumption. Households save in financial instruments if they believe they can get better returns than expected inflation. They also make investments in property and other tangible and intangible non-financial assets if the returns from such investments exceed returns from financial investments.

Indian households got outstanding returns in the first decade of the twenty-first century from savings invested in both financial instruments and real estate. Inflation was low and returns on bank deposits typically exceeded inflation (wholesale inflation index was the benchmark). As stock markets were booming after 2003, fuelled by global investment flows and excellent returns for corporates, households also made investments in shares and quasi-share instruments, such as MFs, unit-linked insurance plans (ULIPs) and insurance products. House property prices rose over 200 per cent in the first decade in many markets. The frenzy drove massive household investments in real estate, for both occupational and speculative purposes.

The housing bubble burst in the second decade. Speculative purchases petered out, leaving large unsold inventories in most cities. New launches are few and far between. The fall in savings of Indian households in the second decade of the twenty-first century is almost entirely explained by this. A massive reduction of over 5 per cent in the overall household savings rate is explained by the collapse of their investment in real estate.

A rebound in the domestic savings rate will come from restructuring the residential real-estate market.

Wealth

Contrasting Fortunes of Indians: The Super-Rich and Stunted Children

On 26 December 2020, a headline in *Business Standard* shrieked: 'Super-Rich Club Sees 10 entrants; Wealth Up 33 per cent'. In the year of COVID-19 and the lockdown when the economy was projected to witness the largest ever contraction of national income by about 7–10 per cent, the super-rich club of India grew to an all-time high membership of ninety billionaires, adding ten new billionaires in the year; their combined wealth was over Rs 35 lakh crore, or about 17.5 per cent, of the country's national income.

Only a week earlier, the results of the National Family Health Survey (NHFS) 2020 were published for twenty-two states and union territories.

It highlighted India's poor nutritional status with widely prevalent child malnutrition, captured in the proportion of children who are stunted (lower height than standard for the age) or getting wasted (lower weight than standard for the height). Several states saw their proportion of stunted or wasted children below the age of five increasing compared to NHFS 2015. Over 10 per cent of India's population still lives in extreme poverty. Poverty and malnutrition have worsened in 2020 owing to widespread job and income losses on account of the slowing economy, lockdown and declining government expenditure.

The contrast between the country's privileged and poor could not be starker. It is heart-rending. In a weird way, the rise of billionaires and increasing number of stunted children in India depicts what has been touted as K-shaped recovery—where one part of the economy sees high growth despite the overall economy going down, whereas the other part of the economy sees much worse economic contraction than the overall contraction depicts.

Wealth and Income (GDP)

GDP broadly measures domestically created income. It is the result of all the work put in and value addition created during the year. Income grows with the growth of GDP.

GDP is a measure of flow that is earned during a period of time by contributing to value addition. Wealth, in contrast, is a stock measure. It is the value of assets, financial and non-financial, owned by a household, corporation or government at any particular point in time.

A part of GDP is spent in capital formation or investment. Households buy property and invest in financial assets like shares and bonds. Corporations invest in new projects and ventures. The part of GDP invested in capital formation creates assets. The aggregate value of assets owned by a household or corporation is the wealth of the concerned household or corporation.

In the final analysis, the wealth of corporations is owned by shareholders. The final beneficial owners of stocks in corporations are individuals and households. The wealth of a nation is thus equivalent to the wealth of all its households.

GDP or the flow of income has been measured for quite some time now. The wealth of a nation is a relatively new phenomenon. The twentieth century saw enormous expansion in GDP, which created enormous amounts of wealth. Valuation of wealth has fuelled further growth of wealth. While the national accounts of most countries still do not measure national wealth, many organizations/institutions have started computing and assessing the wealth of nations.

State of Global Wealth

The Credit Suisse Research Institute publishes a Global Wealth Report (GWR); the GWR 2020 edition was published in October 2020. According to GWR 2020, the size of global wealth at the end of 2019 was about $400 trillion ($3,99,179 billion). Global GDP in 2019 was $87.55 trillion, according to the IMF. While the global wealth estimates are for sixty-five countries, they encapsulate almost the entire global wealth. Thus, global wealth is about four-and-a-half times the size of global GDP.

Asia-Pacific is the wealthiest of the five continental regions (Asia-Pacific, North America, Europe, Latin America and Africa) with wealth of $164 trillion, a little over 40 per cent of global wealth. China's wealth has been estimated at about $78 trillion, India's $15 trillion and the rest of the Asia-Pacific (including Japan and South Korea) about $70 trillion.

The US was the wealthiest country (in aggregate terms, nation as a whole) in 2019 with wealth of $115 trillion of the total North American wealth of $137 trillion. Europe's total wealth was estimated at $94 trillion.

Africa is still struggling to make both ends meet and much of its income/GDP is spent on consumption or illicit transfer abroad—very little goes into building wealth. Consequently, Africa's wealth is estimated to be a little less than $5 trillion. Latin America is the next least wealthy continental region with aggregate wealth of $12.4 trillion at the end of 2019.

Global wealth per person (global wealth divided by the number of adults) was estimated at $77,309 in 2019. North Americans were the wealthiest with an average adult wealth of $4,46,638 per person. Switzerland was the wealthiest country in the world (barring the small countries of Liechtenstein and Monaco) with average adult income kissing

$6,00,000. Chinese wealth per adult was estimated at $70,962, while for India, it was $17,299.

Global wealth has been rising at a reasonably fast clip in the twenty-first century. In 2000, it was estimated at about $118 trillion (in 2019 dollars). It rose by a compounded growth rate of 6.6 per cent in the twenty-year period. The period 2000–2007 saw the fastest rise in global wealth at over 10.3 per cent per annum. There was a decline of 7.5 per cent in 2008 and thereafter it grew at an average of 5.7 per cent per annum.

State of Wealth in India

GWR 2020 has a section narrating India's wealth story. The country's per-adult wealth was estimated at $17,299 in 2019. India's per-capita wealth grew at a rate of 9.7 per cent per annum, about one-and-a-half times the global average. According to the report, there were about 9.12 lakh 'dollar millionaires' in the country. It also noted the unequal distribution of wealth with 72.8 per cent of Indian adults owning less than $1,00,000 of assets/wealth; the global average is about 56 per cent.

Forbes magazine publishes a list of global billionaires virtually on a real-time basis on its dashboard. At the end of 2020, there were four Indian billionaires in the top 100, eight in the top 200, thirteen in the top 300, sixteen in the top 400, twenty-two in the top 500, forty-two in the top 1000, sixty-seven in the top 1500, ninety-five in the top 2000, and 118 in the entire list of about 2250 billionaires. India's fairly large presence in the list also vindicates GWR 2020's conclusion of excessive inequality.

Bloomberg, too, publishes a list of the top 500 global billionaires, which is also updated on a real-time basis. This list is similar to the *Forbes* list with only some minor variations. As per this list, the number of Indian billionaires at the end of December 2020 was nineteen.

No Indian institution, official or unofficial, provides estimates of the wealth of India and Indians.

What is Driving Global Wealth Creation?

Primarily, two forces drive wealth creation. First, savings from the current income invested in real productive assets to grow incomes or save expenditures (factories, infrastructure, house property). Second, credit creation by central banks and banking companies. Central banks conduct monetary policies in a manner that releases additional currency and reserve money in the system, which helps banking and other depository institutions create credit to enable businesses and households to invest in productive assets. A good part of household savings also becomes available to businesses and investors, directly or through intermediation of financial institutions, to be invested in equities. Most of the banking system's support reaches businesses as debt. Together, debt and equity help create productive assets, which build national wealth.

There is another manner in which wealth creation takes place. This is increase in valuation of assets, without making any direct impact on the working and contribution of the underlying productive assets. Bonds are valued at mark to market. If the interest rate goes up, the value of an existing bond goes down and if the interest rate goes down, the value of an existing bond goes up. Additional demand for equity shares listed on a stock exchange from FPIs makes their prices go up, which raises market capitalization (the measure of valuation of shares). The COVID-19 scare in March 2020 made investors in equity sell their shares, which crashed share prices from 15 per cent to 40 per cent all over the world. That did not change the available investment to the companies. Later, hopes of recovery and a vaccine brought share demand back and equity prices rose. In fact, they were higher at the end of December 2020 than December 2019 in most stock exchanges. Inflow of over $22 billion of FPI in the Indian equity market in calendar year 2020 saw the markets not only recover about 30 per cent of lost value but end the year on a record high. The availability of ultra-cheap money thanks to loose/accommodative monetary policies was followed by central banks driving up the valuations of financial and non-financial assets.

Real investment and valuation are the two primary forces that drive up or down (mostly up) the wealth of a country. The size of GDP and savings behaviour of households and existing stock of investments/capital formation determine the pace of growth of real wealth. When the existing stock of savings turns into a savings glut and is further supplemented and enlarged by loose monetary policies, the valuation of assets gets driven up and the wealth of nations gets jacked up by valuations.

The Valuation Game is a Distraction

There is a lot of temptation in valuations. Asset holders are happy if the valuation of their house, shares, gold or any other financial or non-financial assets goes up. The urge to drive up asset prices, driven by greed, the real characteristic of animal spirits, often takes over the mind.

Indian share markets have seen this many a time since Independence, with outright fraud often used to play the valuation game—from the Mundra affair in the 1950s where LIC was conned for a higher valuation of shares sold and pledged and Harshad Mehta, who defrauded SBI to lend crores of rupees without any collateral or security, to Ketan Parekh, who manipulated the stock market. Insider information, false tips, driving up prices of penny stocks, fake pledge of shares and many other dirty tricks have been employed to manipulate the markets and valuation of shares for gains. Such gains never help channel investment to productive ventures.

Similar valuation games have been played in the real-estate market. House prices have been manipulated to generate extraordinary returns on residential properties. Such returns attracted a lot of speculative interest from individuals, households and even businesses, who diverted their business resources into land and house investments. Fraud has been used to achieve this objective as well.

Developed countries are acutely in the grip of the valuation game. As their economies have matured and much of the required infrastructure, manufacturing, technology and real estate have been constructed, there are not enough opportunities to channel savings in these productive activities. Rising incomes have made household savings rise significantly. This situation is driving down interest rates. So many bonds in Japan, Europe and other industrialized countries are negatively priced, indicating that there is no real investment demand or that supply of funds exceeds demand. Further, the central banks in these countries play the game of easing up money supply, quantitative easing and many other instruments. The real effect of all these is to throw costless money to businesses and households. Not finding a good opportunity to invest in the host countries, these businesses and households take these cheap funds to emerging market countries, aiming to make money at the cost of people there.

India needs to avoid getting caught in this valuation game, whether run by domestic manipulators or foreign investors.

Chapter Thirty-Two

Reserve Bank of India in the Year of the Pandemic

Monetary Stability is the First Responsibility of RBI

'Whereas it is expedient to constitute a Reserve Bank of India to regulate the issue of Bank notes and for keeping of reserves with a view to securing monetary stability in India . . .', begins the Preamble of the Reserve Bank of India Act, 1934 (RBI Act). RBI was established for the purpose of issuing banknotes maintaining the monetary stability of India 'to operate the currency and credit system of the country to its advantage', the Preamble added. Monetary stability is measured by depreciation in the value of money. Inflation is the obverse of depreciation in value or the stability of value of money.

RBI did a good job, more by default than deliberate policy action, until 1955. Money supply remained quite restrained despite India adopting a planned economy model with expanding expenditure to be funded by debt. However, RBI gave in to the Centre in 1955 when it decided to accept ad hoc government treasury bills to issue money. Soon the trickle of ad hoc treasury bills became forceful enough to open the tap of money issuance. The investments made in the economy funded by this excessive money supply and debt did not raise the productive capacity of the economy. The result was acute inflation. By the 1970s,

India regularly encountered episodes of double-digit inflation, sometimes exceeding 20 per cent. The rupee depreciated and monetary stability was heavily compromised.

Similar inflationary tendencies were seen in many other countries. Monetarists propounded the theory that money supply was the cause of inflation. Most economies and central banks started pursuing tighter money policies, generally described as inflation targeting. Inflation was tamed and monetary stability restored in much of the world through such policies as well as development and ageing, particularly in advanced countries.

The Government of India and RBI formally adopted the inflation-targeting regime in 2015. The Preamble of the RBI Act was further amended/expanded to explicitly and unequivocally state 'AND WHEREAS the primary objective of the monetary policy is to maintain price stability while keeping in mind the objective of growth'.

Maintaining monetary stability is the first responsibility of RBI.

Exchange Rate Stability is an Extension of Monetary Stability

The Indian economy is intricately linked and integrated with the rest of the world. Exports and imports of goods and services together comprise about 40 per cent of GDP. These imports and exports, though produced and consumed in Indian currencies, are paid for and settled in international currencies. This leads to exchange of Indian currency with foreign currencies.

It is not trade alone that requires to be settled in terms of external currencies. India imports a lot of capital, both in the form of direct foreign investments and portfolio investments. India makes some direct foreign investments as well. Capital flows tend to be bulky and volatile, especially portfolio inflows. To the extent that capital inflows are offset by the deficit in the current account (goods and services), capital flows help meet demand and supply of foreign currencies. Excessive capital flows put excessive pressure on the external value of the rupee.

There are quite a few other important items related to receipts and payments of foreign currencies. Indian workers work abroad. There is a large Indian diaspora settled abroad. These people transfer a considerable amount of foreign currencies to India.

All these exchanges take place at a price, which for all practical purposes is the external value equivalent of Indian currency. If dollar trades are settled at Rs 74 for every rupee, the rupee's external value is 1/74th of the dollar. When the price of the dollar goes up or down, the value of the rupee depreciates or appreciates accordingly.

Maintaining stability in the external value of the rupee is as important as maintaining stability in its internal value.

Credit or Financial Stability is the Other Major Function of RBI

RBI creates money by extending credit to the government and banks. This created/manufactured money, usually called reserve money, is the base of credit creation in the economy.

Credit fuels government expenditure and private investment, which funds growth and redistribution. Correct and calibrated credit expansion generates the right amount of growth and keeps the financial system stable. Excessive credit expansion overheats the economy and disturbs stability. Excessive and indiscriminate credit expansion also leads to failure of businesses, frauds and waste. This generates non-perming loans and non-payment of credit extended, which disturbs stability. The stability of the credit system is the biggest insurance for the stability of the financial system.

RBI is also the regulator of banks, the primary vehicle of credit creation and management. The Banking Regulation Act, 1949, confers it considerable regulatory authority, including licencing, control over management and closure of banks. RBI's regulatory authority over PSBs, the nationalized banks owned by the government, is somewhat constrained by the two Bank Nationalization Acts. There is also some diffusion of regulatory authority over cooperative banks, including urban cooperative banks.

By exercising its sole authority of creation of reserve money and considerable regulatory authority over the banking system, RBI manages and maintains the stability of the credit system, also referred to as the financial system.

Other Non-Core Functions Entrusted to RBI

Though it need not be, RBI is the banker to the Government of India. By entering into agreements, it is also the banker to state governments. It manages the issuance and extinguishment of the market debt of the Government of India as well as state governments. Being the banker and debt manager of the Government of India and the state governments is a non-core function of RBI.

India followed quite a restrictive foreign exchange system after Independence. By now, India has instituted an almost free current account convertibility but has still not gone for capital account convertibility. FEMA confers considerable authority on RBI in the matter of permitting capital account transactions, recording such transactions and regulating the system of authorized agents to manage foreign exchange transactions. After the recent amendment in FEMA in 2015 and notification of rules by the Government of India in 2020, RBI is the primary policymaker for debt issues (in consultation with the government), whereas the government is the primary policymaker for non-debt issues (in consultation with RBI).

Management of foreign exchange reserves is another non-core function entrusted to RBI. To a considerable extent, management of monetary policy function, especially maintaining the external value of Indian currency, also affects management of foreign exchange reserves.

There are quite a few other small non-core functions that RBI manages in India.

Currency Management in 2021

At the end of December 2021, total notes in circulation were Rs 29.69 lakh crore or about 14.6 per cent of the pre-COVID projected GDP of Rs 203 lakh crore. As the GDP is expected to increase to about Rs 223 lakh crore in nominal terms in 2021–22 and currency might grow by another Rs 0.3 lakh crore by the end of March to be about Rs 30 lakh crore, the currency to GDP ratio for 2020–21 is likely to turn out to be about 13.5 per cent. This ratio is a full 3 per cent higher than the ratio of currency to GDP prevalent in 2016–17 before demonetization was ordered to reduce cash in the system.

Reserve money aggregates in India broadly follow currency aggregates. At the end of December 2021, total reserve money was Rs 37.44 lakh crore comprising Rs 29.96 lakh crore of currency in circulation (80.1 per cent), Rs 6.97 lakh crore of bankers' deposits with RBI (18.6 per cent) and the rest classified as 'other' deposits with RBI (Rs 0.5 lakh crore).

Credit Management and Regulation

Outstanding bank credit as on 26 March 2021 (financial year end) was Rs 109.51 lakh crore. It grew by 5.6 per cent year on year. In financial year 2019–20, compared to the outstanding credit at the beginning of the financial year, growth was a lowly 6.1 per cent. As on December 17, 2021, the outstanding bank credit rose to Rs 113.14 lakh crore, which in terms of credit growth year on year and credit growth during the financial year, 2021–22 was: 7.3 per cent vis-à-vis 6.0 per cent the previous year, and 3.3 per cent vis-à-vis 1.7 per cent the previous year.

RBI had unleashed liquidity ever since the pandemic struck and lockdown was imposed in March. The government had also offered guarantees and other supports under many schemes as part of the stimulus package. Through the National Credit Guarantee Trustee Company, the government provided 100 per cent guarantee coverage on the outstanding amount for the credit facility provided under the Emergency Credit Line Guarantee Scheme (ECLGS) as on the date of the non-performing asset. Guarantees totalling Rs 3 lakh crore had been extended for both MSMEs as per the original mandate as well as the stressed sectors of the economy identified by RBI.

Loans amounting to Rs 1.58 lakh crore were reportedly disbursed under ECLGS by 4 December 2020, which made about 1.2 per cent of bank credit outstanding at the beginning of the financial year. Total increase in outstanding bank credit until 4 December 2020 in the financial year was Rs 1.34 lakh crore. Putting these two together meant that, excluding the guaranteed credit growth, there was negative credit growth of about Rs 25,000 crore in India in the first nine months of COVID-19 impacting India despite full implementation of liquidity and stimulus measures of the RBI and Government of India.

Financial year 2021–22 turned out to be somewhat better though there was nothing spectacular about it. Credit grew by 3.65 lakh crore in first nine months or about 3.3 per cent.

A number of new innovations were used to infuse liquidity in the system: Long Term Repo Operations (LTRO—RBI provides funds for one to three years at a fixed rate), Targeted Long Term Repo Operations (TLTRO—RBI mandates that LTRO funds would have to be invested in specified securities or specified type of loans), Special Liquidity Facility for Mutual Funds (SLFMF—special liquidity to banks for lending to mutual funds), Special Liquidity Scheme for NBFCs/HFCs (special liquidity to banks for lending to NBFCs and HFCs), etc. A number of open-market operations (OMOs—RBI buys government securities from banks for cash or vice versa) with variants like Operation Twist (RBI exchanges securities, e.g., buys one set of securities, say, a ten-year paper by selling another maturity paper, say, three-year security to bring down the yield of the ten-year paper using lower short rates) were also tried.

However, in the face of great credit averseness of the banking system—especially PSBs—nothing worked.

The great liquidity infusion came to naught and RBI could not instil any stimuli or interest in the banking system to lend to ensure credit growth.

Chapter Thirty-Three

Economic Capital Framework: Back to Square One

RBI Act Provides Only Rs 5 Crore as Capital

Section 4 of the RBI Act is very short and straightforward. It says, 'The Capital of the Bank shall be five crores of rupees.' This section has remained unchanged since 1 January 1949, the date with effect from which the RBI was nationalized from a private company by the Reserve Bank of India (Transfer to Public Ownership) Act, 1948. Section 5, which provided for increase and reduction of share capital before RBI was nationalized, was repealed from the RBI Act in 1948.

The capital of RBI is Rs 5 crore and it cannot be increased or decreased. In the past seventy-two years, it has discharged all its obligations and run up a portfolio of assets of Rs 50 lakh crore. Evidently, capital has never been a constraint on the ability of RBI to carry out its functions.

Accumulated Capital of RBI

RBI's balance sheet for 2019–20 ending on 30 June 2020 correctly notes that its 'Capital' is Rs 5 crore. It has three other entries, which together with this capital, amount to total accumulated capital. First, the 'Reserve Fund' of Rs 6500 crore. Second, 'Other Reserves' of Rs 232 crore.

And, finally, under a somewhat misleading heading, 'Other Liabilities And Provisions' of Rs 15,16,621 crore. All these added up make RBI's capital, as on 30 June 2020, Rs 15,23,358 crore.

The Other Liabilities and Provisions section has 12 items (Schedule 3 of RBI Balance Sheet).

Four of these items represent valuation gains on securities, foreign exchange contracts and gold (Currency and Gold Revaluation Account or CGRA with balance of Rs 9,77,141 crore; Investment Revaluation Account—Foreign Securities with balance of Rs 53,834 crore; Investment Revaluation Account—Rupee Securities with balance of Rs 93,415 crore; and Foreign Exchange Forward Contracts Variation Account with zero balance). Together, these valuation gains amounted to Rs 11,24,390 crore.

Six items represent provisions for actual or contingent liabilities of RBI. These include transfers to the Asset Development Fund of Rs 22,875 crore, Provision for Forward Contracts Valuation Account of Rs 5925 crore, Provision for Payables of Rs 2600 crore, Provisions for Gratuity and Superannuation Fund of Rs 25,639 crore, Bills Payable of Rs 2 crore and Miscellaneous Obligations of Rs 14,028 crore. Together, these provisions amount to Rs 71,069 crore.

The payment of Rs 57,128 crore to be made to the Government of India out of the surplus earned of Rs 1,30,743 crore was shown as Surplus Payable to the Central government.

The last item in the Other Liabilities and Provisions is titled 'Contingency Fund'. This had a balance of Rs 2,64,034 crore as on 30 June 2020, which included a surplus of Rs 73,615 crore transferred from the surplus earned of Rs 1,30,743 crore in 2019–20.

A clearer way of looking at the non-monetary liabilities or accumulated capital of RBI is to divide the fifteen items mentioned in the Balance Sheet and under Other Liabilities and Provisions and consider the overall capital of Rs 15,23,358 crore in three parts: the capital that represents largely valuation gains; the capital that represents provisions made for actual/contingent real liabilities; and the capital that represents accumulated profits or surpluses retained and not transferred to the Government of India.

Accumulated valuation gains were Rs 11,24,390 crore. Realized and retained profits amounted to Rs 2,93,646 crore (Contingency Fund of

Rs 2,64,034, Capital of Rs 5 crore, Reserve Fund of Rs 6500 crore and Other Reserves of Rs 232 crore). The remaining amount of Rs 1,05,322 crore (including Rs 57,128 crore to be transferred to the Government of India) represented provision for liabilities.

RBI was holding Rs 15.23 lakh crore of capital, including accumulated retained profits of Rs 2.94 lakh crore, as against the capital of Rs 5 crore provided by the law.

RBI's Economic Capital Framework

The RBI Act has no provision for an Economic Capital Framework (ECF). RBI, however, did adopt the ECF in 2016, which was reviewed and a fresh ECF was recommended by the Jalan Committee in 2019. Shorn of its complex terminology, ECF essentially decides how much of its annual surplus RBI will retain with the remaining transferred to the Government of India.

As seen above, the accumulated capital of RBI is essentially made up of two parts: valuation gains/provisions and realized and retained surpluses/ profits. The ECF deals with both these aspects of accumulated capital.

Foreign exchange securities, domestic rupee securities and gold holdings make up practically the entire investment assets of RBI. The value of all these assets keep fluctuating according to market movement in prices. The valuation provisions (principally the CGRA in Other Liabilities and Provisions) represent the difference in market value of these securities and gold on the day of the Balance Sheet and the cost at which these securities were purchased or are recorded in the books of RBI.

The first part of the ECF determines how much of the valuation provisions should be there to provide for market risk in case there is downward movement in the value of securities and gold in future.

The Committee recommended a methodology described as 'expected shortfall under stressed conditions with target of 99.5 per cent confidence level and lower risk tolerance limit of 97.5 per cent' for measuring the market risk of RBI's assets portfolio. This complex formula leads to determination of valuation provisions required as a proportion of the total Balance Sheet of RBI.

The second part of the ECF relates to how much 'realized equity' or retained profits RBI needs to keep. The Committee determined that to meet 'monetary, financial and external stability risks' and also to cover 'credit and operational risk', RBI should maintain a contingent risk buffer of 5.5 per cent to 6.5 per cent of its Balance Sheet.

The Committee linked the transfer to the government primarily to the availability of realized equity compared to required realized equity. If the 'available realized equity including the surplus of the year' is lower than the minimum 'required realized equity', no transfer will be made to the government. If the 'available realized equity before including the surplus of the year' is higher than the 'maximum required realized equity', all the surplus would be transferred. If the 'available realized equity including the surplus of the year' is higher than the 'minimum required realized equity' but lower than the 'maximum required realized equity', the Board will take a decision on how much to transfer to the government and how much to retain.

As far as the complex market risk provision is concerned, no transfer was recommended even if the available valuation provision is higher than the higher range of the provision required. If the available valuation provision is lower than the lower range of the provision required, the surplus would not be distributed even if the available realized equity is higher than the maximum required realized equity.

RBI Assets Suffer No Real Valuation or Market Risk

RBI defines market risk related to assets it holds in terms of likelihood of their rupee value depreciating. Depreciation in value of three principal assets—rupee securities, foreign securities and gold—is the valuation risk for RBI. At the end of September 2020, the largest assets were foreign securities at approximately $500 billion (about Rs 37 lakh crore). Rupee securities came in second at about Rs 12 lakh crore, followed by gold at about Rs 2.75 lakh crore.

Market risk related to foreign currency assets of RBI is defined in terms of the rupee value depreciating. The rupee value of dollar assets depreciates when the rupee appreciates. Therefore, if RBI expects the rupee to appreciate, it would be required to hold provisions for foreign securities. The ECF requires RBI to hold large provisions to cover this risk. It might seem strange that while strengthening of the rupee vis-à-vis foreign currency indicates a stronger nation, for RBI it is a loss of valuation.

Market risk related to the government securities RBI holds is more conventional. Whenever the interest rate of government securities goes up, the value of RBI's holding goes down. The reverse occurs when interest rates go down. Setting interest rates in the economy is one of the primary functions of RBI. Normally, it raises interest rates to cool down inflation and such action takes interest rates towards more neutral territory, but the capital framework mandates RBI to hold provisions for interest rate risk until it fixes it.

Gold is held by RBI as a currency reserve asset and also as it is an evergreen and secular standard of value. RBI has never sold gold for rupees; in fact, it buys gold by issuing rupees. RBI's gold is 'held to maturity', which is essentially forever. Yet, the capital framework mandates it to hold provisions for potential loss of gold value in rupee terms.

None of RBI's assets actually suffer any real market or valuation risk.

Complex Formulae Designed to Ensure All Surplus Remains with RBI

The formula recommended by the Jalan Committee and accepted by RBI results in required provision for market risk of about 17 per cent of the assets—17 per cent of the RBI Balance Sheet amounted to about Rs 9 lakh crore of provision required at the end of financial year 2019–20. That's a massive provision for non-existent risk!

Before the RBI Act was amended in 1955, it permitted the central bank to make provisions for 'such other contingencies . . .'. This was deleted and the Act since provides that RBI can make provisions that bankers normally make. Central banks are not expected to make any provision for possible erosion in the value of reserve assets.

However, in a desire to hold these provisions, RBI has leaned on different formulae over the years. In 2016, the RBI Board decided to measure market risk by adopting a super complex formula built around three elements.

The first element is the measure of Value at Risk (VaR). The traditional model of determining VaR is to treat it equal to the maximum asset value, which had historically suffered loss. A variation of this is Stressed Value at Risk (S-VaR), which measures the value at risk under select 'stressed conditions', which are mostly defined subjectively. Another variant is called the Estimated Loss (EL) method, which takes into account all possible defaults. In other words, it also takes into account the remaining amount of assets (tail risk) after taking into account stressed value at risk. The first element is the value at risk.

The second element is the confidence level you choose at which events that put value at risk might occur. This is the probability element.

The third element is the interval adopted at which the loss might take place.

RBI decided to adopt StressedVaR.9999 confidence level and a ten-day interval. This formula, in its opinion, was supposed to give it the best credit rating—a rating better than the best AAA-rated sovereigns like the US. While no central bank has ever been rated by the credit rating agencies in the world, RBI wanted to be internally assessed as having the best credit rating in the world, only for the purpose of retaining as much of the surplus as possible!

The formula yielded a value of about 24 per cent of assets (total assets of RBI comprising its foreign currency reserves, government securities and other assets) as required reserves/provisions for the supposed valuation loss in the assets. The RBI Board was further talked into deciding to hold additional provisions up to 4 per cent of the size of the Balance Sheet as cash reserves. In sum, 24 per cent of the assets for possible valuation losses as provisions and another 4 per cent to be held in cash, also termed as realized equity.

RBI adopted the toughest and most conservative formula that yielded an amount of provisions and reserves that would almost always be greater than the available reserves and surplus generated in a year. This provided the RBI requisite justification to hold all the profits/surplus for itself.

As it turned out, if RBI was allowed to go by this formula of determining provisions and reserves, it was not required to transfer any surplus to the government during the financial years 2016–17 and 2017–18. Quite naturally, the government took exception to this and raised questions about the appropriateness of the formula. These questions led to the constitution of the Bimal Jalan Committee.

The Committee could not find any justification for the need to have the highest AAA credit rating for RBI and also for holding the high degree of valuation reserves. Accordingly, in its recommendations, it accepted dilution in the rigour of the market/valuation risk formula. The modified formula for market risk as given in its report reduces requirement of holding valuation provisions from 24 per cent of assets to 17–18 per cent of the size of assets. However, what the Committee gave away with one hand, it took away with the other. The Committee recommended that cash reserves or realized equity be raised from 4 per cent to 5.5–6.5 per cent.

The Committee further stipulated that the available provisions, if these are in excess of required provisions, would not be distributed as surplus. However, if the available provisions are less than the required provisions, the shortfall would be made up from the realized equity reserves and the surplus generated during the year.

This meant that recommended valuations reserves of 17–18 per cent would act as the minimum required before any surplus is distributed to the government.

What the ECF designed in 2015 achieved by fixing the level of provisions required for market risk at a very high level of 24 per cent, the Bimal Jalan Committee formula achieved by making valuation provisions undistributable. The whole purpose of the complex exercise of designing unnecessarily complex formulae for determining required market/valuation provisions was only one: to prevent distribution. The net result of these intellectual gymnastics is that valuation provisions are not to be touched. Period.

RBI Needs No Capital for 'Monetary, Financial and External Stability Risks'

The RBI Board decision accepting the Bimal Jalan Committee report cites 'monetary, financial and external stability risks' in view of its role as 'the monetary authority' and the 'lender of last resort' as the rationale for retaining realized equity. Realized reserves or equity are accumulated non-distributed surpluses.

A reading of the long report of the Committee makes it evident that it invented every possible excuse to hold on to as much realized equity/reserves as possible.

The role of RBI as monetary authority requires it to issue currency and manage the reserve currency base (currency with public and bankers' deposits with RBI). The supply of money is managed by modulating currency issuance and determining the appropriate level of deposits that bankers are required to keep with RBI. Both these are currency issuance and regulatory functions. These functions are discharged by increasing or decreasing money supply. This requires RBI to hold no capital or provisions. In fact, holding capital and provisions are 'non-monetary' in nature. Any funds held by RBI as capital or reserves have to be invested in some assets. Monetary supply cannot be influenced by capital and reserves. The capital, reserves or realized equity have no role whatsoever in the discharge of RBI's function as the monetary authority.

Being the bankers' regulator (not under the RBI Act but under the Banking Regulation Act; in many countries, central banks are not banking regulators) vests RBI with an important role in maintaining credit and financial stability. It is also a 'lender of last resort'. As a central banker, it can provide liquidity/credit to banks even when the credit system has frozen and banks are in danger of collapsing on account of a liquidity squeeze. RBI discharges this function by creating more money—by issuing more currency or increasing banks' deposits with itself—to be used whenever banks need. Both these measures of coming to the rescue of bankers, however, do not require RBI to use any capital. It uses its monetary authority, not capital, to discharge these functions.

An argument has been made in the Bimal Jalan Committee report that RBI might suffer loss on the credit it provides to banks as a lender of last resort in case banks default. Banks never default to the central bank. Even when banks go bankrupt, while equity holders and depositors may suffer, the central bank is unlikely to face default. The government might have to pump in capital but the central bank never suffers. RBI has never faced such a default and is unlikely to see such an eventuality. Offering the function of lender of last resort as a reason to hold realized surpluses is nothing but an intricately designed excuse.

The last of the arguments offered relates to foreign exchange management. RBI buys foreign currency assets using funds arising from two basic resource pools: funds generated by the issuance of currency/reserve money, and funds retained as capital (both realized and unrealized equity).

The reserve money supply, nominal value of currency in circulation and bankers' deposits do not change on account of any change in the value of the reserves' assets procured against money supply. Therefore, even if there is a change in the rupee value of foreign currency assets, the money supply remains unchanged. There is no need for RBI to use realized equity to provide for valuation change in foreign currency assets held as reserve assets.

The argument to provide for valuation change in foreign currency assets by using provisions out of realized equity is a poor one. It posits that RBI first uses accumulated capital/reserves to buy foreign currency assets and then requires accumulated reserves to provide for a loss in their valuation. If there are no accumulated profits/equity to buy the foreign currency assets, there would be no loss in valuation of such assets and consequently no need to provide for provisions for such losses!

Any way you see it, there is no justification or requirement for RBI to hold any reserves/provisions to manage its key functions of being the monetary authority and lender of last resort or for foreign exchange management. All these arguments are nothing but hogwash, created only to justify retention of profits.

National Savings for a Rainy Day or National Wastage?

The final justification used by the Bimal Jalan Committee was that such provisioning is like 'the country's savings for a 'rainy day' [a monetary/financial stability crisis]'.

Implicit in this phraseology is that realized equity/accumulated surpluses are national savings that can be used in times of major monetary or financial crisis. It is prudent for individuals, households and businesses to set aside some profits for investments or for use during difficult times. In the same vein, possibly, the argument was offered that if surpluses generated are distributed to the government, they would get used up to meet some public expenditure. Governments do not save and therefore if RBI retains the surplus, it would constitute 'national savings'.

There are two issues connected with this reasoning. First, whether it is advisable to use the surplus to meet legitimate public expenditure needs now or retain it with the RBI to meet legitimate public expenditure needs in future during a crisis. Second, whether deploying such savings in foreign currency assets is the most prudent means of growing savings.

The Central government is acutely short of fiscal resources to meet legitimate public expenditure needs. The Centre borrows and services debt. Therefore, if RBI saves its surplus and does not distribute it to the government, an equal amount is borrowed by the government to meet its deficit. Therefore, taken together, there are no national savings when RBI retains surplus.

RBI invests these savings primarily in foreign currency assets. These assets have yielded less than 1.5 per cent return in 2019–20. In 2020–21, they are expected to yield only about 1 per cent. The government's borrowing cost in 2019–20 was about 7 per cent. In 2020–21, it is expected to be about 6 per cent. Therefore, the nation loses 5–6 per cent of returns on RBI retaining its surplus as savings and investing it in foreign currency assets. A 5 per cent loss on Rs 15 lakh crore of retained equity is Rs 75,000 crore. A 5 per cent loss on realized equity balance of Rs 2.6 lakh crore as on 30 June 2020 was over Rs 11,000 crore. The government would have saved this much if it had borrowed less, equal to surplus retained as savings by RBI.

So, even when you take into account investment of accumulated capital as 'national savings', the nation loses a minimum Rs 11,000 crore and a maximum Rs 75,000 crore. Clearly, it is a national waste, not national savings, when RBI retains its surplus.

RBI Capital Framework was a Bad Deal for the Government

RBI needs no capital for its monetary, banking and foreign exchange policies and regulation. Retained profits yield excessively poor returns. Therefore, whether functionally or from an investment perspective, retaining surplus is an unnecessary and poor policy option.

Almost all profits RBI makes come from the discharge of the sovereign function of currency issuance: the difference in the returns earned on currency reserve assets and the cost of printing and managing currency.

The governing law makes it abundantly clear that RBI will have capital of only Rs 5 crore and all surpluses would be transferred to the government.

Yet, the RBI has successfully manoeuvred to keep Rs 15 lakh crore of provisions with it; roughly Rs 12 crore of valuation provisions and Rs 3 lakh crore of cash realized surpluses.

The Bimal Jalan Committee again worked out a bad deal for the government. It used two stratagems to achieve this objective.

First, it took valuation reserves completely out of the government's reach. The recommendation that if the required valuation reserves are less than the available valuation reserves, the excess, even if of durable nature, would not be available for distribution meant that accumulated profits in the form of valuation gains would not be available to the government as surplus.

It is, incidentally, only a matter of accounting that valuation gains are 'realized' or 'unrealized'. In 2019–20, when RBI wanted to give a higher distribution to the government to make it look that the Bimal Jalan Committee had been favourable to it, it simply swapped foreign securities with accumulated profits with new securities at current prices. The difference, over Rs 50,000 crore of valuation gain, got converted into realized gain and RBI paid that as a dividend to the government. Therefore, as far as the ECF recommended by the Bimal Jalan Committee is concerned, valuation gains of over Rs 12 lakh crore are out of reach of the government. However, if you want to distribute some part of it, you just need to swap old securities with accumulated gains with the same securities at current prices.

Second, in terms of functional requirement, RBI needs no capital reserves for monetary, financial and external liabilities management. Yet, in 2016, it decided to maintain balance equal to 3–4 per cent of assets as realized equity in the Available Contingency Fund. Instead of lowering this unnecessary requirement, the Committee raised it to 5.5–6.5 per cent.

The Available Contingency Fund/realized equity balance exceeded 7 per cent of assets as on 30 June 2018. The logic of the Committee's recommendation was to deprive the government of as much as possible of the accumulated realized profits of about Rs 2.4 lakh crore.

As the requirement of realized equity would rise every year at 5.5–6.5 per cent for the increased assets of RBI, the surplus would have to be retained to this extent by it. If the assets base rises by Rs 10 lakh crore, Rs 55,000–65,000 crore of surplus would be retained.

The net effect of both recommendations is that the government would never get 100 per cent of surplus in future. And in most years, about 50 per cent or more of the surplus would be retained by RBI to be invested in low-yielding foreign currency assets. That's a really bad deal for the government—and the nation.

Like the ECF of 2015–16, which resulted in transfer of 100 per cent surplus of 2015–16 to the government despite being very hawkish and designed to retain surplus for RBI, the ECF of 2019–20 delivered 100 per cent surplus for 2018–19 to the government. However, like the 2015–16 framework, which started hurting the government in 2016–17, the 2019–20 framework struck in the distribution of surplus of 2019–20.

RBI retained Rs 73,615 crore of the surplus of Rs 1,30,747 crore of financial year 2019–20. There was no public protest by the government. However, the retention of 56 per cent of the surplus, amounting to Rs 73,615 crore, is quite a large amount, more so in a year when the economy was hit hard by the pandemic.

Undoubtedly, the battle will begin again and the government will seek a review of the ECF recommended by the Bimal Jalan Committee.

RBI Buried Jalan Committee in 2021

RBI reported massive increase in its total income for 2018–19, the first year of the Jalan Committee, of Rs 1,93,036 crore (as against total income of Rs 61,818 crore in 2016–17 and Rs 78,281 crore in 2017–18). Total income for 2019–20 was reported at Rs 1,49,672 crore. For the nine-month financial year 2020–21, total income reported is Rs 1,33,273 crore.

RBI uses the head 'exchange gain/loss from foreign exchange transactions' to book abnormal income by selling or buying securities simultaneously. For 2018–19, the first year of implementation of the Jalan Committee recommendations, RBI's abnormal income under this head was Rs 28,998 crore. In the same year, RBI used excess realized income reserves of Rs 52,618 crore ('provision no longer required and miscellaneous income') to distribute surplus. Thus, an income of Rs 81,616 crore was 'abnormal income' in 2018–19; the normal total income for the year being only Rs 1,11,420 crore. For 2019–20, RBI's abnormal income was Rs 29,993 crore and normal/real total income for 2019–20 was Rs 1,19,679 crore. For the truncated 2020–21, RBI's abnormal income is as much as Rs 50,629 crore and normal income Rs 82,644 crore. With RBI earning normal income on an assets base of only 2.72 per cent, 2.24 per cent and 1.93 per cent for these three years, its normal income has declined consistently.

Excluding transfers to the provisions account, the Contingency Fund, RBI's expenditures in these three years were Rs 16,981 crore, Rs 18,925 crore and Rs 13,437 crore (annualized Rs 17,916 crore).

Taking into account the real normal income and real normal expenditure of RBI, the real surplus earned by RBI during these three years was Rs 94,439 crore, Rs 1,00,754 crore and Rs 69,207 crore (annualized Rs 92,276 crore) respectively. RBI transferred Rs 1,75,991 crore to the government for 2018–19, Rs 57,132 crore for 2019–20 and Rs 99,126 crore for 2020–21. RBI effectively transferred 186 per cent of the normal surplus for 2018–19, 57 per cent of normal surplus for 2019–20 and 143 per cent of normal surplus for 2020–21.

For the three years of 2018–2021 together, RBI earned normal surplus of Rs 2,64,400 crore, whereas it transferred Rs 3,32,249 crores to the government. In fact, it has ended up transferring 125.66 per cent of the normal surplus earned to the government during the three-year period.

RBI was faced with a major dilemma in 2020–21. It required Rs 39,634 crore to keep the Contingency Fund at the level of 5.5 per cent of the average Balance Sheet assets. It earned only Rs 69,207 crore during the truncated nine months. If it retained Rs 39,634, RBI could have transferred only Rs 29,573 crore to the government. Such a small transfer would have riled the government. Non-maintenance of the realized reserves at 5.5 per cent of the assets would have violated the Jalan Committee recommendation completely.

The only way RBI could have got over this impossible situation was by fiddling with this recommendation. This is what it did. As per the RBI annual report, RBI booked Rs 50,629 crore of unrealized valuation gains into realized profits in 2020–21 by selling the foreign exchange securities it held and simultaneously bought the same or different securities at the current prices. The booked valuation gains of Rs 50,629 crore raised the transferable income from Rs 29,573 crore to Rs 80,202 crore. RBI actually transferred Rs 99,126 crore. The balance of about Rs 19,000 crore was made up by under-transferring an equal amount to the Contingency Fund.

With these acrobatics, RBI could manage to keep the facade of the ECF as recommended by The Jalan Committee. RBI has also reached to the end of the revaluation corridor recommended by the Jalan Committee. If the rupee appreciates on 31 March 2022 a little higher than what it was on 31 March 2021, the valuation buffers to maintain even the lower limit of valuation corridors would get breached. There is a good likelihood that the RBI will not be able to defend the valuation corridor in 2021–22 unless the rupee depreciates by a good measure or the government settles for a very low transfer, as in 2019–20. The Jalan Committee has been de facto buried for 2020–21 transfers. It will most likely be formally buried when it comes to deciding the 2021–22 surplus transfer.

Chapter Thirty-Four

Foreign Reserves in Excess of $600 Billion: In Service of the Nation?

India is the Fourth-Largest Holder of Foreign Currency Reserves in the World

The IMF provides detailed data on foreign exchange reserves held by different countries. Gold is treated as part of foreign exchange reserves.

In December 2021, global holdings of foreign exchange reserves amounted to $12.8 trillion. India's holdings were $650 billion, about 4.96 per cent of global foreign currency reserves. The country achieved the milestone of holding the fifth largest reserves in the world in 2020 and the fourth largest reserves in 2021.

With holdings of $3399.9 billion, China has the largest hoard, followed by Japan with holdings of $1387.4 billion. Switzerland's stash of $850.8 billion defies the relationship of foreign exchange reserves with the size of economy and exports. Russia, with $562.3 billion, has fallen behind India now.

India left oil exporter Saudi Arabia and Hong Kong behind. Saudi Arabia's foreign currency reserves amount to $501.8 billion while Hong Kong has a little under $475 billion. Taiwan, South Korea and Brazil are the three other countries with the largest foreign currency reserves in the world.

India faced its worst foreign exchange crisis when it was left with reserves of only $5.8 billion at the end of March 1991 and had to hypothecate about 47 tonnes of gold to raise about $400 million to avert payment default. These reserves were sufficient to pay for only four weeks of import. Today, India has foreign exchange reserves adequate to pay for fourteen months of imports.

India's situation has dramatically changed as far as foreign exchange reserves are concerned.

RBI Sources for Accumulating Foreign Exchange Reserves (Investible Funds) are Essentially Two: Reserve Money and Accumulated Capital

Like other currency-issuing central banks, RBI is both the product and regulator of fiat currency. Its main function is to issue currency, which constitutes its primary liability. In addition, RBI keeps bankers' and 'other deposits' of a monetary nature, which when added to the currency with the public makes the currency base of the country, also called reserve money.

The reserve money is the principal and only real liability of RBI. Like all other central banks managing fiat currency and enjoined by the law, it is required to keep reserves, made up of permissible assets, equal to its currency and reserve money liabilities. The reserves, at least as legal fiction, provide an assurance to the public that in the unlikely event of the public/depositor demanding 'value' of the currency issued and other deposits held by RBI, it would pay up by 'encashing' the reserves.

The remaining net liabilities of the RBI are nothing but its accumulated capital. Thus, there are two real parts of the liabilities side of the RBI Balance Sheet: reserve money liabilities and accumulated capital.

RBI does not present its Balance Sheet in such a clear manner. It is divided in two parts: the Balance Sheet of the Issue Department, responsible for issuing 'currency', not full 'reserve money' and the Balance Sheet of the Banking Department, which basically records the assets and liabilities of the banking function RBI discharges. RBI's banking function relates to its role as a banker to the Central and state governments and a banker to banks.

The RBI Balance Sheet as on 30 June 2020 on a net basis, after taking out reverse repo and other liquidity-related deposits of the banks of Rs 6.68 lakh crore, was Rs 46.7 lakh crore.

RBI's reserve money at the end of FY 2019–20 was Rs 31.63 lakh crore—currency in circulation of Rs 26.60 lakh crore, bankers' deposits of Rs 4.64 lakh crore and 'other deposits' of Rs 0.39 lakh crore. The net accumulated capital of RBI at the end of 2019–20 was Rs 15.1 lakh crore largely hidden under the head 'Other Liabilities and Provisions'. The three items shown more explicitly—Capital of Rs 5 crore, Reserve Fund of Rs 6500 crore and Other Reserves of Rs 232 crore—are too small to be counted.

In a nutshell, RBI's net Balance Sheet of Rs 46.7 lakh crore comprises two principal liabilities: reserve money liabilities of Rs 31.6 lakh crore and accumulated capital of Rs 15.1 lakh crore. Its accumulated capital of Rs 15.1 lakh crore is 3,00,000 times the Rs 5 crore of capital invested by the government.

Insurance against Raids by Speculators is the Principal Benefit of Foreign Exchange Reserves

The daily turnover in foreign exchange markets was estimated to be over $6 trillion a day in 2019, more than twice the annual GDP of India. As traders and capital providers are faced with temporal mismatches in their foreign exchange requirements, there is considerable forward buying and hedge trading. There is too much at stake in this market and stability of currency exchange prices in the spot and future is extremely important. A lot of money can be made by traders and speculators if they can foresee or manipulate exchange prices in the future.

After currencies moved off the gold standard with the advent of the Bretton Woods system in 1944 and the indirect gold standard moving off the dollar standard in 1971, they have no single or common anchor. The price of the exchange is mostly determined by the demand and supply position of the foreign currency and the ability to keep currency prices stable and orderly depends upon the reserves central banks hold to balance the demand and supply of foreign exchange.

Currency speculators can launch a successful run on the currency of a country if the central bank does not have enough power or ability to keep the wolves under control. Most of the currency crises the world has seen since the 1960s—Chile, Mexico, South-east Asia, Russia—took place under a vulnerable foreign exchange position.

Adequate foreign exchange reserves act as insurance or guarantee against any adventure or misadventure by currency manipulators.

India was short of foreign exchange reserves in much of the twentieth century. This forced the first major devaluation of the rupee in 1966 and was primarily responsible for the 1991 crisis. The perception of vulnerability in 1998, 2013 and 2018 also led to similar attempts but did not succeed as India not only had adequate reserves but bolstered them by issuing bonds/deposits, such as India Development Bonds, Millennium Bonds and India Resurgent Bonds.

Insurance protects but over-insurance is an unnecessary cost. If an asset valued at $1 billion is insured for $5 billion, it does not offer protection beyond $1 billion. The premium paid for insurance beyond $1 billion is simply a waste.

RBI Earns a Paltry Return on its Investment

RBI earned a surplus of Rs 1.50 lakh crore (including profits from sale of investments) in 2019–20 on an asset base of Rs 53.35 lakh crore, giving a return of 2.8 per cent. In the previous year, the return was higher at 3.42 per cent (Rs 1.40 lakh crore over the asset base of Rs 41.03 lakh crore, thanks to very large income on account of sale of investments yielding large capital gains). In the previous three years, the rate of return was only 2.49 per cent, 1.87 per cent and 2.16 per cent, respectively. On average, RBI earns a gross income of about 2.5 per cent on its assets.

In 2018–19, RBI earned Rs 61,022 crore of interest on its domestic investments and Rs 45,815 crore of interest income on its foreign investments. In addition, it received profits of Rs 28,998 crore by selling foreign securities. RBI's domestic investments were Rs 9.9 lakh crore and foreign investments Rs 27.9 lakh crore. The amounts of interest earned on domestic and foreign assets and the size of such assets in 2019–20 were Rs 60,957 crore and Rs 48,376 crore and Rs 11.72 lakh crore and Rs 35.45 lakh crore, respectively.

The interest earned on domestic assets amounted to 6.16 per cent and 5.20 per cent in 2018–19 and 2019–20, respectively. The interest earned on foreign assets amounted to 1.64 per cent and 1.36 per cent for these two years respectively.

RBI's low returns on its investment portfolio are largely explained by foreign securities constituting the bulk of its investment portfolio and these securities earning small returns.

It chose to invest about 75 per cent of its investible funds in foreign securities (it was 74 per cent in 2018–19 and 75 per cent in 2019–20). The 75 per cent investments yielded only 1.5 per cent returns in the two years together. International investment returns were trending much lower in 2020–21. RBI may end up getting only about 1 per cent returns on its foreign investments.

The interest earned on foreign securities is only about 25–30 per cent of the interest earned on domestic assets. The foreign assets portfolio pulls down RBI's overall earning, although its earnings from domestic assets was also lower than the interest earned by other financial players, including public-sector players like NPS and EPFO.

RBI's Low Return on Investment Is a Large Cost to the Nation

RBI's 2019–20 foreign assets portfolio was worth Rs 35 lakh crore yielding a 1.36 per cent return, whereas the domestic assets portfolio earned 5.2 per cent, which was lower than the returns earned by other public-sector asset managers. This 3.86 per cent lower return on the foreign assets portfolio amounted to an income loss of Rs 1,35,100 crore. The cost of maintaining RBI's reserve assets and investing accumulated capital in low-yielding foreign currency assets is indeed staggering.

RBI is expected to have foreign currency assets of Rs 40 lakh crore in 2020–21. The returns environment on foreign currency assets has further deteriorated and is likely to be only about 1 per cent. Therefore, RBI is likely to earn only about Rs 40,000 crore of interest income on its foreign assets in 2020–21. If we assume an interest return of 6 per cent on its domestic portfolio, the loss of interest on the foreign assets portfolio would amount to Rs 2,00,000 crore.

RBI's surpluses are meant to be transferred to the Government of India. The loss of investment returns effectively amounts to corresponding lower income of the government. This is a large national loss.

Chapter Thirty-Five

State of the Financial Sector

The specific contribution of the financial sector to the national income is captured under the category 'financial services' in the National Accounts. In 2018–19, gross output value of financial services, at current prices, was assessed at Rs 13.14 lakh crore out of a total gross output value of Rs 347.93 lakh crore. In terms of GVA, the contribution of financial services was Rs 9.52 lakh crore in the total GVA of Rs 171.4 lakh crore. Financial services made up 3.78 per cent of gross output produced in India's economy and 5.55 per cent of GVA. In other words, 5.55 per cent of total income accruing to the factors of production in India in 2018–19 originated in the financial sector.

While the direct contribution of financial services in the national income might look smaller, the financial sector is all pervasive in the economy. It runs the wheels of the entire economy as it enables production, distribution and consumption of all goods and services. The financial sector manages all investment and capital: savings, equity, debt, or other financial assets. Every economic activity involves payment. The sector handles payments and helps collect taxes, other fiscal income and borrowings. Governments have stopped managing their finances. There is no real treasury in governments today; it only keeps accounts and makes and receives payments.

Economic growth and development depend greatly on investments in factories, infrastructure and workplaces to produce goods and services. Usually, entrepreneurs and investors do not have the funds for such investments. The financial industry has evolved to provide and procure the requisite funds. Investors require different kinds of finance—equity, debt, grant support—and the financial sector has grown to meet all these requirements. The growth and development of a country is dependent upon the development of its financial sector.

Equity Markets in India

The rise of corporations or companies gave birth to equity markets. Limited liability is a crucial feature of companies. Share in equity stock of a company, now universally measured in terms of face value of shares held by any investor (promoter or non-promoter), is the maximum liability of the investor in the liabilities of the company. If the issued equity capital of a company is Rs 1 crore, divided in 10 lakh shares of Rs 10 each, and a person holds 1000 shares, their liability is limited to Rs 10,000.

Limited liability turned into a big advantage as it became possible to raise large amounts of equity capital without worrying about the risk of the unknown or unlimited liability. While equity capital was initially raised from friends, acquaintances and relatives, equity stock exchanges soon developed to enable entrepreneurs and businessmen to raise capital from any investor.

The Bombay Stock Exchange, now known as BSE, was formed as the Native Share and Stock Brokers' Association in July 1875. It was the first stock exchange not only in India but all of Asia. BSE functioned as an unregulated association of stockbrokers until 1956, when the Security Contracts (Regulation) Act (SCRA) was enacted. BSE was granted permanent recognition under SCRA in 1957.

Stock exchanges were gradually demutualized (stockbrokers ceased to be the owners) to strengthen regulation and stop equity manipulation. The National Stock Exchange (NSE) was incorporated as a demutualized stock exchange in 1992 after the infamous Harshad Mehta scam. Today, it is India's premier equity stock exchange with about 95 per cent of equity trade turnover. In October 2020, of a gross turnover of Rs 12.93 lakh crore, it recorded a turnover of Rs 12.23 lakh crore; BSE's turnover was only Rs 0.70 lakh crore.

The primary rationale for equity stock exchanges to exist is to enable entrepreneurs to raise capital. Equities are important assets and, therefore, wealth and savings managers trade in equity to manage investors' wealth. The function of raising equity capital is served in what is known as the primary market and the function of asset investment and management is served more by trading in what is known as the secondary market.

Indian equity stock exchanges served the purpose of enabling entrepreneurs to raise capital for many decades. However, for the past two decades, stock exchanges are increasingly becoming asset management vehicles. The regulatory environment has also become biased against raising equities for new ventures. A company needs a record of at least three years of profit to list on the mainboard, the principal stock exchange platform of NSE/BSE.

Equity issuances (all types: initial public offers or IPOs, follow-on public offers or FPOs, and rights issues) in India were a minuscule Rs 23,722 crore in 2018–19. The previous year, in 2017–18, the highest equity issuances of the decade were recorded at Rs 99,765 crore. The lowest equity capital raised through the stock exchanges was Rs 9434 crore in 2014–15. A total of Rs 3,47,672 lakh crore (data for nine months for 2019–20) was raised through equity issuances in the decade ending 31 March 2020, an average of Rs 34,767 crore per annum. For an economy of the size of Rs 200 lakh crore, Rs 30,000–40,000 crore of equity on average per annum is peanuts, less than 0.2 per cent of GDP.

There are virtually no equity funding institutions in India. Banks do not provide equity. There are no public financial institutions (the erstwhile IFCI, IDBI, ICICI are either closed or defunct) to provide equity. The problem for the start-up world is still more acute. Start-ups cannot list until their businesses mature and, therefore, cannot raise equity funds from the market or public.

Such small amounts of equity capital being raised through stock exchanges/public markets is symptomatic of an acute equity deficiency or equity crisis in India. This has not only emasculated the growth of industry and businesses but also led to many malpractices, including fraud, to convert loans taken into equity or by padding up equipment purchases to create equity.

In 2021–22, start-ups started raising capital from equity markets by listing. Most start-ups listed were at the stage of building their businesses. In that sense, the capital markets served the purpose of raising risk capital for new and growing businesses. As most of these start-ups were loss-making in the conventional sense, there was no good valuation metric for assessing the right capitalization value of these issues. Most issues also include a good part of the equity sold by existing shareholders to monetize their stakes.

Debt Markets in India

Debt is raised by all the economic agents: governments, businesses and households. It is also provided by many financial agents: banks, non-banks, asset-managing institutions and people in general directly. India has mostly developed as a debt-financed economy. Debt is raised in various forms with loans and bonds being the most prominent. The debt market is much larger than the equity market.

No single public agency in India keeps track of all the debt raised in India. The RBI keeps an account of the amount lent by banks as loans and cash credit. SEBI monitors debt raised in the form of debt securities. No one keeps track of amounts lent by savings management institutions like LIC, EPFO and NPS.

According to the RBI, banks expanded credit to businesses and households by an amount of Rs 6 lakh crore in 2019–20 (Rs 11.46 lakh crore the year before), recording a growth of 6.1 per cent. And SEBI tells us that an amount of Rs 6.10 lakh crore was raised in the form of corporate bonds by various issuers.

As per RBI's statement, *Trends in Flow of Financial Resources to Commercial Sectors from Banks and Non-Banks*, banks credit flow to businesses and households in 2019–20 was Rs 5.81 lakh crore (Rs 5.89 lakh crore of non-food credit and Rs -0.08 crore of non-SLR investments by banks). The year 2019–20 marked an abrupt deceleration of bank credit to businesses and households; it slid from Rs 9.16 lakh crore in 2017–18 and Rs 12.29 lakh crore in 2018–19.

Credit from non-banks also decelerated in 2019–20. The RBI statement further reveals that the flow of resources from domestic non-banks was only Rs 3.21 lakh crore in 2019–20 as against Rs 8.86 lakh crore in 2017–18 and Rs 7.35 lakh crore in 2018–19. NBFCs' total credit outstanding rose from Rs 23.16 lakh crore at the end of 2018–19 to Rs 23.61 lakh crore at the end of 2019–20, increasing by only Rs 45,000 crore. MFs, financial institutions and other non-banks contributed the rest of the flow of resources to businesses and households from non-banks.

Debt flow from abroad in the form of ECBs was the one source of financing to businesses that expanded in 2019–20 thanks to lower cost of borrowings abroad. ECBs contributed Rs 1.54 lakh crore of credit flows to businesses against Rs 0.70 crore in the previous year and negative Rs 5129 crore in 2017–18.

While there is some overlap in the data (banks lend to non-banks and non-banks also raise corporate bonds), it should be fair to assume that even in the lacklustre year of 2019–20, incremental credit growth to businesses and households exceeded Rs 10 lakh crore or about 5 per cent of GDP.

Asset Management

With global wealth at about $400 trillion (GWR 2020), a large and sophisticated wealth/asset management industry has developed. This is broadly divided into two classes: asset management and alternative asset management. Financial firms that manage wealth/assets by investing in well-developed investment products like equity and fixed income securities and their offshoots like index funds and derivatives are part of the asset or investment management industry. Financial firms that manage wealth by investing in newer and developing asset classes like real estate, private equity and venture capital are categorized as alternative asset management firms.

The global asset management industry is estimated to be about $90 trillion and the alternative asset management industry about $10 trillion. Total assets under management of the main and alternative asset management industry globally are about $100 trillion, which exceeds the global GDP of about $85 trillion.

The Indian asset management industry is relatively small. Forty-odd companies that have set up MFs to invest savings/profits in different equity, debt and other assets have about $400 billion of assets under management in 2020. All types of pension, superannuation and provident funds together manage about $1200 billion of assets. The alternative asset management industry is more nascent with about $50 billion of assets under management. In all, the asset management industry in India is estimated to be under $2 trillion.

Payments and Other Financial Services

The National Accounts classify financial service providers in three categories: Monetary Financial Institutions (comprising the central bank, deposit-taking corporations and money market funds); Other Financial Corporations (comprising other financial intermediaries, non-money market funds, financial auxiliaries and captive financial institutions); and Insurance and Pensions Funds (comprising life insurance funds, non-life insurance funds and pension funds).

The value of services provided by different financial service providers can be measured in terms of the incomes they receive for services rendered. Monetary financial institutions contributed the largest chunk of GVA of Rs 4.98 lakh crore of the total GVA of Rs 9.52 lakh crore (52 per cent) under the financial services category. Other financial corporations added a GVA of Rs 3.32 lakh crore (35 per cent). The retirement and pension fund industry contributed a GVA of Rs 1.23 lakh crore (13 per cent).

The payment industry has expanded enormously and is currently undergoing a massive transformation. Many other financial services have also expanded. The financial services industry grew at over 12.5 per cent in current prices for two years after 2016–17.

Retirement and Long-Term Savings

There are three large organizations that manage the savings of millions of Indians to provide them an income after retirement and help them create long-term assets like a home. These are the Life Insurance Corporation of India (LIC), Employees Provident Fund Organization (EPFO) and National Pension Scheme (NPS).

LIC had a life fund of Rs 37.28 lakh crore as on 31 March 2021, which rose by as much as Rs 6.05 lakh crore over the Fund of Rs 31.24 lakh crore at the end March 2020. The EPFO presents accounts separately for the unexempted establishments and exempted establishments. The investment of the Employees Provident Fund (EPF) (unexempted), in the financial year 2019-20, was Rs 7.66 lakh crore. The corpus of the Employees' Pension Scheme (EPS) operated by EPFO at the end of financial year 2019–20 was Rs 4.76 lakh crore. There is a small corpus of Rs 0.28 lakh crore for the Employees Deposit Linked Insurance Scheme (EDLI). The corpus of funds managed by EPFO at the end of financial year 2019–20 thus exceeded 12.70 lakh crore. In addition, the corpus of exempted funds was Rs 83,640 crore at end 2019–20. The New Pension Scheme (NPS) had Rs 6.57 lakh crore of assets under management at the end of October 2021. These three long-term/retirement savings organizations had over Rs 40 lakh crore of assets under management at the end of financial year 2018–19. Currently, their assets under management exceed Rs 55 lakh crore.

EPFO had 13.50 lakh contributing establishments, 23.43 crore contributing members and 66.83 lakh pensioners as on 31 March 2020. NPS had 140.10 lakh contributing subscribers at the end of October 2021. And LIC had 27.97 crore policies in force at the end of financial year 2020–21.

All the three behemoths invest primarily in government securities. Regulatory policies prescribe the investment pattern and these organizations have very little leeway in managing their investments. While LIC uses its inhouse investment management capability, both EPFO and NPS have virtually given their investment corpus to fund managers who abide by the regulatory policies prescribed for investments.

Investment guidelines for EPFO are focused on government securities. A minimum of 45 per cent and up to 65 per cent of the corpus is required to be invested in government securities, other securities guaranteed by the government and units of MFs investing in government securities. As on 31 March 2020, EPFO had invested Rs 2.09 lakh crore in Central government securities, Rs 5.09 lakh crore in state government securities and Rs 2.16 lakh crore in securities of public sector financial institutions/undertakings. Further, Rs 0.54 lakh crore is lying in the Centre's special deposit scheme. More than 60 per cent of the overall debt portfolio of EPFO is in government securities and deposits. It invests the remaining amount in PSU bonds and a little in private-sector companies' bonds. The investment pattern permits up to 15 per cent investment in equity and equity-oriented schemes, but a very small proportion goes in the same.

NPS investment guidelines prescribe a maximum exposure of 50 per cent of the corpus in government securities and related investments, including state development loans. There is another category of debt instruments and related investments that can have up to 45 per cent investments. Whichever way the guidelines have been interpreted, as on 31 March 2021, of the total corpus of Rs 5.78 lakh crore, Rs 1.81 lakh crore was invested in Central government securities and Rs 2.92 lakh crore in state government securities. In all, 81 per cent of the total corpus of NPS and other pension schemes regulated by the Pension Fund Regulatory and Development Authority (PFRDA) was invested in government debt.

The Centre made a transformational move in 2004 when most new Central government staff were brought into the defined benefit system. The system was gradually adopted by all state governments, public-sector non-industrial entities and state government entities.

This move, in fact, brought the retirement savings industry to India. However, the conservatism applicable on EPFO investments was more or less replicated in NPS; as mentioned above, NPS, too, invests almost its entire corpus in government securities. There is no forward thinking about retirement fund managers setting up investment desks and building inhouse capability to invest in alternative assets like direct investment in infrastructure and real estate.

Government Pre-empts Bulk of Credit: Government Held Half the Credit Stock of Rs 300 Lakh Crore in 2020

Three groups of borrowers—governments, businesses and households—are the final consumers/users of credit. Credit/financial flow that takes place between different kind of players of the financial system does not constitute the final credit outstanding from the financial system to the real economy.

Combined outstanding credit/borrowing/debt of governments, businesses and households in India was Rs 300 lakh crore. In dollar terms, outstanding credit stock amounts to $4 trillion (at Rs 75 to a dollar).

Governments borrow to meet the gap in their expenditures and revenues. The Centre and states are the largest group of debtors. Together, they had a built-up debt stock of about Rs 150 lakh crore by 2020. The

Central government owed, mostly to Indian residents, roughly Rs 100 lakh crore and the states, collectively, another Rs 50 lakh crore.

Non-financial/real sector businesses of all types (agricultural, industry or services, micro, small, medium or large, public sector or private sector) borrow from all types of lenders (banks, non-banks and others) in different forms (loans, advances, bonds, etc.). They had an outstanding credit of about Rs 100 lakh crore.

While households are primarily savers, many borrow to finance the acquisition of assets, such as houses, vehicles and other consumer durables. Many households, especially the poor, also borrow for current consumption. The stock of credit availed by households or household debt was about Rs 50 lakh crore.

India's GDP was about Rs 200 lakh crore in 2020. The outstanding credit stock of Rs 300 lakh crore owed by governments, businesses and households amounted to 150 per cent of GDP. It was too large a stock of debt for comfort.

Banks are Principal Credit Providers

There are five broad classes of lenders or creditors: banks, NBFCs; long-term saving funds, the central bank (RBI); and the rest of the world. There is a wide variety of NBFCs, including HFCs, long-term saving funds, including retirement funds like EPFO and NPS funds as well as life-insurance companies.

Banks are the largest suppliers of credit. Outstanding bank credit to final users (businesses, governments and households) was about Rs 130 lakh crore. Including credit funded indirectly through non-banks, the outstanding credit of banks was close to Rs 140 lakh crore.

The law permits RBI to provide credit to businesses as well. However, at present, it lends only to the government. The outstanding credit of RBI, almost entirely to the Central government, was about Rs 10 lakh crore. Inclusive of RBI's credit, the credit of the banking system to ultimate borrowers amounted to Rs 150 lakh crore, or about half the total credit of Rs 300 lakh crore.

NBFCs, including HFCs, raise their funds from banks, other financial entities handling savings (MFs, insurance companies) and savers directly in deposits and investment in bonds. NBFCs and HFCs had about Rs 50 lakh crore of credit outstanding primarily to businesses and households.

Long-term savings institutions, like the LIC, MFs, EPF and NPS, provide credit primarily to governments. Their exposure to businesses and households in India is relatively insignificant. Households keep some of their savings directly with the government through the system of small savings. The credit contribution of these savings institutions in the overall outstanding credit was around Rs 70 lakh crore.

The remaining credit—about Rs 30 lakh crore—came from the rest of the world. This included investment by foreign institutional investors (FIIs) in government securities and other corporate bonds and loans by financial institutions in the form of ECBs of businesses.

Non-Banks Provide about Two-thirds of Credit to Governments

A little over Rs 100 lakh crore of total government debt was in the form of securities. At the end of March 2020, the outstanding stock of Central government-dated securities was Rs 65 lakh crore, that of state government securities was Rs 33 lakh crore and outstanding treasury bills were in the order of about Rs 5 lakh crore. A little less than 50 per cent of Central government securities, more than 67 per cent of state government securities and over 50 per cent of treasury bills were held by investors other than banks. In all, about Rs 60 lakh crore of credit in government securities was provided by non-banks.

The most prominent investors were insurance companies, which held approximately Rs 30 lakh crore of the government debt of Rs 150 lakh crore, or about 20 per cent. Retirement and savings funds like LIC and EPFO look for more secure yields—they held about a quarter of the entire stock of the state government securities. Their investment in government securities (Centre and states) approximated Rs 10 lakh crore. The balance Rs 20 lakh crore credit was held by MFs, foreign investors, primary dealers and other non-bank players.

As the total debt of the Central government was about Rs 100 lakh crore at the end of March 2020 and market borrowings were about Rs 70 lakh crore (dated securities Rs 65 lakh crore and treasury bills

Rs 5 lakh crore), the rest of the Centre's debt of about Rs 30 lakh crore came from non-financial market sources. About Rs 15 lakh crore was contributed by small savings, about Rs 6 lakh crore by external loans (from multilateral and bilateral organizations), over Rs 2.5 lakh crore by way of recapitalization bonds subscribed to by PSBs and about Rs 1.5 lakh crore by non-market securities like oil bonds. Together, these non-market borrowings contributed about Rs 26 lakh crore. The balance Rs 4 lakh crore comes from provident fund deposits, public account surplus and numerous other small heads.

FIIs were permitted to invest in debt securities of the Government of India in 1993. FPIs held about Rs 4 lakh crore of Central government securities. They had almost no investment in state government securities. The policy relating to their investment has undergone several changes.

Bankers are Shying Away from Lending to Businesses

The credit provided by banks to businesses and households is captured as outstanding bank credit whereas the credit provided to governments is shown as investments. Total outstanding bank credit (other than to governments) was Rs 103.72 lakh crore as on 27 March 2020, the last reporting Friday of financial year 2019–20. Though there was a growth of Rs 2.67 lakh crore in the month of March 2020 alone, total bank credit to businesses and households increased by about Rs 6 lakh crore in the entire year of 2019–20. Annual credit growth turned out to be only 6 per cent. This was one of the lowest rates of growth of bank credit in India in many years.

The data of sectoral deployment of bank credit is available only for 'about 90 per cent' of outstanding bank credit. At the end of financial year 2019–20, sectoral deployment details of Rs 92.12 lakh crore of outstanding non-food gross bank credit are available. RBI provides data for four sectoral groups of borrowers: agriculture (which includes allied sectors), industry (micro, small, medium and large), services and personal loans. The first three categories are businesses; the last, household loans.

Household loans were in the order of Rs 25.54 lakh crore. Outstanding loans to businesses, of the total Rs 92.12 lakh crore of credit, were

Rs 66.58 lakh crore. Business credit included agriculture and allied sectors' credit of Rs 11.58 lakh crore, credit to industry of Rs 29.05 lakh crore and credit to services of Rs 25.95 lakh crore.

Services loans included credit of Rs 8.07 lakh crore to NBFCs. Excluding credit to NBFCs, banks' credit to real economy businesses amounted to Rs 58.51 lakh crore. If we keep aside credit of Rs 11.58 lakh crore to agriculture, manufacturing and services, credit was only Rs 46.93 lakh crore.

A good chunk of credit to businesses—over 15 per cent, or Rs 10 lakh crore—was non-performing. Banks also have about 3 per cent of their business loan portfolio stigmatized as frauds. Loans to households have a very low default rate.

Credit outstanding at the end of financial year 2020 to real businesses (all loans excluding loans to NBFCs and the retail sector) of Rs 58.51 lakh crore as a proportion of total outstanding credit was 63.5 per cent. If we apply this ratio to total bank credit outstanding at the end of March 2020, banks' outstanding credit to non-financial businesses would be Rs 65.84 lakh crore.

RBI classifies outstanding credit in two big groups: food credit and non-food credit. Outstanding food credit was a measly Rs 0.52 lakh crore with non-food credit amounting to Rs 103.1 lakh crore. It is difficult to understand why bank credit is still presented in two major groups of food credit and non-food credit, when food credit is not even 0.5 per cent of the outstanding bank credit.

Bankers Did Not Lend During Much of Pandemic Period

Provision of credit is the raison d'être of the banking system. Banks primarily source their funds from savers but also create credit. Banks, especially PSBs, have become quite risk-averse in the face of mounting non-performing loans and frauds. Lenders feared another wave of non-performing loans.

Banks and non-bank lenders turned to RBI to help manage mounting non-performing loans, raise additional resources and deal with this grossly unusual situation. RBI allowed the banks to grant a moratorium for three months on servicing loans initially; this was later extended to August 2020. Finally, it announced a liberal scheme for banks to restructure 'COVID-19 affected standard loans'. RBI also opened up a facility for banks to acquire lending resources for periods as long as three years at very low rates: Targeted Long-Term Repo (TLTRO). It reduced the reverse repo rate (where banks park excess cash) to as low as 3.75 per cent to 'force' banks to lend and not park. It also reduced CRR by 1 per cent. This package was expected to make Indian banks, especially PSBs, lend to businesses. Unfortunately, this didn't happen.

Many businesses categorized as non-essential suffered a body blow. Some of these loans, for instance, loans to tourism, hotels, restaurants and recreation service businesses, were expected to become non-performing as their business could be lost or severely affected. Many others, like textiles and organized retail, were likely to become non-performing if they did not receive some grant support from the government and additional working capital support from banks.

In addition to RBI allowing banks to grant a moratorium on loans and classification of NPAs, the finance minister announced raising of the threshold of default under the IBC to Rs 1 crore from Rs 1 lakh to exclude most MSMEs from its ambit and save companies from insolvency on account of the pandemic. SEBI also asked rating agencies to hold off for a time.

While these measures provided much needed breathing space to fundamentally strong businesses, bankers feared that these measures only provided a facade of solvency to businesses that were fatally wounded in the turmoil. Banks granted moratorium to all credits irrespective of the nature of impact on their businesses and credit quality. Moratorium was also allowed to mortally wounded businesses. In their case, the moratorium and suspension of insolvency were only a temporary reprieve.

Credit expansion during much of financial year 2020–21 remained below 6 per cent, even lower than the very low growth recorded in financial year 2019–20 despite the crying need of businesses to get credit support to carry on with their pandemic-impacted businesses. RBI provided enormous liquidity support. The government pitched in with a liberal guarantee scheme. Yet, bankers did not lend.

They preferred to push the can down the road.

Non-Banks and Credit to Businesses in India

Outstanding credit to businesses from all non-banks was around Rs 30 lakh crore, less than half the credit provided to businesses by banks.

Among non-banks, NBFCs are major providers of credit to businesses in India. Gross outstanding credit by NBFCs as on 30 September 2020 to businesses was in the order of Rs 25.5 lakh crore. About two-thirds of non-bank credit to businesses comes from NBFCs. The rest flows from HFCs (to real-estate companies/builders), LIC (loans to some companies and investment in their corporate bonds), MFs (loans against shares, etc.) and investment by retirement-savings organizations, FPIs and savers directly in corporate bonds.

HFCs primarily provide loans to households with some accommodation to real-estate businesses. Total loans and advances of HFCs amounted to Rs 11.97 lakh crore as on 31 March 2020.

The insurance companies, mostly LIC, find much more comfort in routing their credit to public-sector entities and authorities like NHAI, HUDCO and others.

NBFCs' credit to businesses was growing at a much faster rate than banks before the IL&FS blowout. They were able to leverage cheaper resources from mutual funds. They are also able to reach businesses that mainstream banks find difficult or costlier to reach. Further, NBFCs are not restrained in providing credit to certain sectors like real estate, unlike banks. What's more, they are digitally nimble and have a much lower cost of doing business.

NBFCs do not have access to a steady resource of deposits from households. They do raise some borrowings in the form of long-term debentures. However, the bulk of their resources comes from credit provided by banks and other players in the financial landscape, like MFs. NBFCs had seen their access to such funds becoming costlier (spreads had risen sharply) and in some cases totally denied in the wake of the ILFS crisis. Now, they are facing a kind of ILFS replay in the wake of COVID-19.

NBFCs are also dependent upon constant reflows from their existing portfolio of loan assets. If reflows get affected, their ability to service their resource providers and provide fresh loans suffers. The moratorium granted by RBI on the servicing of loans given by NBFCs created a lot of problems, particularly owing to the lack of clarity on the applicability of moratorium on loans that NBFCs have to service.

NBFCs faced a double whammy during the pandemic year. Their loans to businesses turned bad in greater proportion. They had to give a moratorium to all businesses and were not able to enforce their security or approach the IBC courts. On the other hand, they had to service their loans to banks, pay regularly on debentures issued and saw their funding from MFs getting diminished.

Chapter Thirty-Six

Whither Public-Sector Banks?

PSBs Losing Market Share in Credit at a Fast Clip

Barring SBI, all other commercial banks were private banks in India in 1969. Prime Minister Indira Gandhi nationalized fourteen private banks as a political act and, in one move, transformed over 80 per cent of India's banking assets into public-sector assets. She came back to power in 1980 and nationalized six other private banks to bring 90 per cent of banking credit under the umbrella of government control.

This dominance, however, did not last long. The inefficiencies and inadequacies of public-sector banking started showing up soon. In less than twenty-five years, the government decided to bring back private-sector banks (PVBs). New private banks were licenced in 1994. With this began the decline of the market share of PSBs.

At the end of 2019–20, PSBs had 9.27 crore credit accounts with a total amount of Rs 60.7 lakh crore of outstanding credit. PVBs held 12.71 crore open credit accounts with outstanding credit of Rs 36.13 crore. PSBs maintained 87,576 offices whereas PVBs maintained 33,464 offices.

While PSBs had a smaller share of credit account holders (34 per cent versus 46.6 per cent held by PVBs), their share of outstanding credit was higher at 57.7 per cent (versus 34.3 per cent share of PVBs). The share of PSBs in credit is still over 50 per cent, but it is declining rapidly.

In 2002, RBI did not recognize the PVBs as a class. Private banks were bundled together as 'Other Scheduled Commercial Banks'. PSBs had two separate classes of banks: SBI Group and Nationalized Banks.

SBI Group and nationalized banks had 72.3 per cent of credit outstanding (SBI group 25 per cent and nationalized banks 47.3 per cent). Other scheduled commercial banks had a share of only 17.5 per cent. In 1995, SBI Group (29.2 per cent) and nationalized banks (53.4 per cent) had 82.6 per cent share of credit, while other scheduled commercial banks had only 6.9 per cent share of credit outstanding.

Before the onset of economic reforms in 1991 and licencing of new private banks in 1994, the share of private banks was only 3.7 per cent in 1990. SBI Group (27.2 per cent) and nationalized banks (59.6 per cent) together had a share of 86.8 per cent in outstanding credit. The rest of the outstanding credit (9.5 per cent) was held by foreign banks or FBs (6.2 per cent), and regional rural banks (3.3 per cent).

PSBs have lost 29 per cent of share in credit in the past thirty years, at the rate of 1 per cent a year.

At the end of financial year 2013–14, PSBs had a 73.2 per cent share (SBI Group 22.1 per cent and nationalized banks 51.1 per cent). PVBs had only 19.4 per cent. In the past six years, PSBs have lost 15.5 per cent share at the rate of 2.6 per cent per year. They are hurtling down at a fast clip.

This downfall is likely to slow down but it seems fairly certain that by 2025, the share of PSBs (including SBI Group) in outstanding credit will fall below 50 per cent in India.

It's Better to Treat SBI Group and Other PSBs Differently

SBI Group was analysed separately in banking returns until 2016–17. The share of the group in deposit and credit was 22 per cent and 21.4 per cent in 2015–16, whereas the share of nationalized banks was 48.6 per cent and 46.7 per cent, respectively. In 2016–17, when its share was shown separately for the last time, SBI Group had a share of deposit and credit of 22.8 per cent and 21.3 per cent, respectively. The share of nationalized banks was 46.6 per cent in deposits and 44.5 per cent in credit. Their combined share in credit was 65.8 per cent.

In 2017–18, the combined share of SBI Group and nationalized banks was reported at 63.2 per cent in the banking returns statistics published by RBI. This was 2.6 per cent less than the combined share of 65.8 per cent in 2016–17. In 2016–17, while SBI Group had lost only 0.1 per cent share in credit compared to the previous year, the remaining PSBs (the erstwhile nationalized bank group) lost 2.2 per cent.

While RBI data does not provide a separate share of SBI Group and the remaining nationalized banks, the annual report of SBI (now a single entity as all associate banks have been merged in SBI) states that SBI's share of advances in the country was 19.7 per cent in 2019–20. As the combined share of PSBs in outstanding credit was 57.7 per cent in 2019–20, the share of the rest of the PSBs works out to 38 per cent. Juxtaposing against the share in credit in 2013–14, SBI Group has lost only 2.4 per cent market share of credit (19.7 per cent vis-a-vis 22.1 per cent), whereas the rest of the PSBs (essentially twenty nationalized banks now consolidated into twelve) had lost as much as 13.1 per cent market share in outstanding credit.

SBI and the rest of the nationalized banks had a different origin, evolution and banking culture. SBI was effectively always a state-controlled bank but with a private-sector banking culture, which did not change much after it was nominally nationalized in 1955. The other twenty nationalized banks were promoted by princes, private individuals and industrial houses. They worked as private banks and went through the shock of government ownership and control in 1969 (fourteen banks) and 1980 (six banks). Their culture and management changed completely and they became pretty much carbon copies of each other and very close to government departments over the years.

Thus, it is advisable to treat SBI and the other PSBs separately.

PSBs are Sick

PSBs reported a net loss of Rs 66,608 crore in 2018–19 and Rs 26,015 crore in 2019–20.

All other kinds of banks (barring payments banks, which are congenitally flawed) made a profit in both these years. PVBs made a profit of Rs 27,621 crore in 2018–19 and Rs 19,111 crore in 2019–20.

Profitability of FBs was the highest; they reported profits of Rs 14,508 crore and Rs 16,180 crore in these two years.

The accumulated capital, reserves and surpluses (net worth) of PSBs were Rs 6.53 lakh crore and the aggregate assets size was Rs 107.83 lakh crore at the end of 2019–20. While the aggregate assets to GDP ratio exceeded 53 per cent of estimated GDP (indicating the enormous systemic value of PSBs), the net worth was only 6.06 per cent of aggregate assets. PVBs, on the other hand, had a net worth of Rs 6.19 lakh crore on aggregate assets of Rs 58.32 lakh crore, a ratio of net worth to assets of 10.61 per cent. FBs had a net worth to assets ratio as high as 15.35 per cent. The net worth of PSBs is fast depleting despite large capital infusion by the government on account of deeper sickness.

The capital to risk-weighted assets ratio (CRAR) is the lowest for PSBs among the three large components of the banking industry: PSBs, PVBs and FBs. PSBs' CRAR was 12.9 per cent (12 per cent in the previous year) in 2019–20 whereas the CRAR of PVBs and FBs was 16.5 per cent and 17.7 per cent, respectively.

PSBs are writing off NPAs in a big way. In 2019–20 as well, they wrote off Rs 1.78 lakh crore worth of NPAs. Gross NPAs outstanding for PSBs at the end of 2019–20 were as large as Rs 6,78,317 crore (despite some moderation on account of standstill on recognition of NPAs), which was 10.3 per cent of their gross advances. The outstanding gross NPAs of PVBs at the end of 2019–20 were Rs 2.10 lakh crore, 5.5 per cent of gross advances. The gross NPAs of PSBs were twice as much as those of PVBs. The gross NPAs of FBs were still lower at 2.3 per cent of gross advances.

The intensity of fraud taking place in PSBs is much greater than PVBs and FBs. In 2018–19, 88.5 per cent of the value of fraud reported occurred in PSBs, which declined somewhat to 79.9 per cent in 2019–20.

Continuous losses, high NPAs, and the majority of frauds clearly underline that PSBs are sick.

Banks are For Lending; PSBs are Not Lending

Outstanding bank credit of scheduled commercial banks was Rs 52.6 lakh crore at the end of financial year 2012–13. Outstanding bank credit crossed Rs 100 lakh crore and reached Rs 103.7 lakh crore at the end of financial year 2019–20. It doubled in seven years. In the previous seven years, from 2005–06 to 2012–13, it had risen by more than three-and-a-half times from Rs 15.07 lakh crore in 2005–06 to Rs 52.6 lakh crore.

According to the RBI database, PSBs' loans outstanding were Rs 60.70 lakh crore at the end of 2019–20 whereas PVBs' loans outstanding were Rs 36.13 lakh crore. The credit outstanding of PSBs was Rs 40.71 lakh crore at the end of 2012–13; for PVBs, it was only Rs 10.54 lakh crore. In seven years, the outstanding credit of PSBs grew by Rs 20 lakh crore whereas that of PVBs grew by Rs 15.6 lakh crore. The credit growth of PSBs was less than 50 per cent in seven years while the PVB loan book grew by about 150 per cent.

Outstanding credit of PSBs was Rs 52.04 lakh crore at the end of 2016–17, whereas that of PVBs was Rs 21.27 lakh crore. In 2017–18, 2018–19 and 2019–20, the PSB loan book grew by only Rs 8.66 lakh crore whereas the outstanding credit of PVBs grew by as much as Rs 14.86 lakh crore. Credit growth of PSBs was less than 37 per cent of their aggregate loan growth of Rs 23.52 lakh crore.

PSBs are not lending these days. If banks do not lend, why do they exist?

Consolidation of PSBs is No Reform

In all, the Government of India nationalized the twenty largest private banks: fourteen in 1969 with deposits of over Rs 50 crore and six in 1980 with deposits of Rs 200 crore. One of the nationalized banks, the New Bank of India, was merged with Punjab National Bank in 1993. IDBI Bank (promoted by IDBI in 1994, in which IDBI itself merged later in 2002) was the twentieth government-owned bank. IDBI Bank was 'privatized' by the government selling a majority stake to LIC. The remaining nineteen nationalized banks were categorized as nationalized banks/PSBs until 2017.

SBI was incorporated in 1955. The entire undertaking of the Imperial Bank, which was the mega government-controlled bank from the nineteenth century and in which quite a few other banks promoted by different principalities were merged from time to time, was transferred to SBI in the 1950s. After merger of all its subsidiaries, SBI is one of the twenty PSBs.

The government has been consolidating the twenty PSBs by merging them. Vijaya Bank and Dena Bank were merged with Bank of Baroda in 2019. In 2020, Oriental Bank of Commerce and United Bank of India were merged with Punjab National Bank. Allahabad Bank was merged with Indian Bank. Syndicate Bank was merged with Canara Bank. Andhra Bank and Corporation Bank were merged with the Union Bank of India. Thirteen PSBs thus stand consolidated in five banks: Bank of Baroda, Punjab National Bank, Canara Bank, Union Bank and Indian Bank. Besides SBI, these PSBs are relatively bigger banks.

There are six smaller PSBs as well: Central Bank of India, Indian Overseas Bank, Punjab and Sind Bank, UCO Bank, Bank of Maharashtra and Bank of India. In terms of size of business (credit plus deposit put together), these six banks together had an aggregate business of Rs 24.68 lakh crore at the end of March 2019, whereas SBI alone had a business of Rs 52.05 lakh crore, Punjab National Bank Rs 17.94 lakh crore, Bank of Baroda Rs 16.13 lakh crore and Canara Bank Rs 15.20 lakh crore. Some of these banks are really pygmies (Punjab and Sind Bank with a business size of Rs 1.71 lakh crore and Bank of Maharashtra with Rs 2.34 lakh crore).

PSBs have the same owner: the Government of India. They have the same mindset and policies, similarly recruited personnel, and the same incentives and disincentives. When two or more PSBs are merged into one, practically nothing changes. There were some expected gains in terms of saving expenditure by rationalizing branches and staff as many PSBs had branches close to each other. However, under union pressure or otherwise, the government has not taken up rationalization measures seriously. As a result, except the fact that the number of PSBs has come down from twenty to twelve, there is not much change in their functioning or record. This is reflected in their credit and deposit performance in 2020–21.

Chapter Thirty-Seven

Unlocking Wealth Tucked Away in Gold

India's Great Gold Wealth

Global stocks of gold are estimated to be close to 2 lakh tonnes. Estimates of the World Gold Council (WGC) suggest that the total quantity of gold mined until the end of 2019 was 1,97,576 tonnes. As gold is indestructible, the entire gold ever mined in human history exists in one form or another. According to WGC, this stock of gold is used/available in one of four broad forms. Jewellery has the largest share of 92,947 tonnes (47 per cent), followed by gold held as investment by individuals and households (private investment), which is estimated at 42,619 tonnes (21.6 per cent). Monetary authorities (mostly central banks) of the world, despite moving away from using gold as currency or as backup/reserve for gold standard currency, still hold 33,919 tonnes of gold. The rest of the gold, used in various applications like technology, dentures, etc., classified as 'others', is estimated at 28,090 tonnes (14.2 per cent).

WGC estimates that gold is mined at the rate of about 800–1000 tonnes per quarter or about 3000–4000 tonnes a year. In 2010, global gold stocks were estimated to be 1,68,348.5 tonnes, which have grown by 29,337.2 tonnes in nine years, or by 3247 tonnes a year. Two-thirds of current above-ground gold stocks, or about 1,32,350 tonnes, have been mined since 1950.

There are various estimates of gold stocks in India. In a speech delivered by economist and retired IAS officer Y.V. Reddy in 1996 at the Gold Economic Conference, organized by WGC in New Delhi, he quoted WGC numbers to state that estimated gold stocks in India were 9016 tonnes, which was about 7 per cent of the global stocks of 1,28,800 tonnes at the time. In 2017–18, following a study, WGC estimated the stock of gold held by Indian households at around 23,000–24,000 tonnes. It estimates that the country currently holds stocks of about 25,000 tonnes of gold, which is over 12 per cent of global gold stocks. As India has been bringing in about 700–1000 tonnes of gold every year and the country would have conceivably brought in about 15,000–16,000 tonnes of gold in the twenty-five years since Reddy spoke, we can assume gold stocks of about 25,000 tonnes in different forms as a credible estimate.

Gold was priced at about $60 million per tonne in December 2020. At about Rs 75 to a dollar, this translates into Rs 450 crore a tonne. India's holdings of 25,000 tonnes would thus be worth about Rs 112.5 lakh crore (about $1.5 trillion). Taking the GDP at Rs 200 lakh crore, the country's gold wealth is valued at over 55 per cent of GDP. Assuming annual global production of gold to be around 3200 tonnes and India's imports on an average at about 700–800 tonnes of gold every year, India imports about 20 per cent of annual global production. This makes our gold wealth grow by about $45–50 billion every year. The country uses foreign exchange reserves of approximately $30–50 billion every year in importing gold, which is quite substantial. Thus, this amount of expenditure in importing gold is more than the fresh inflow of annual FDI in the country.

Seen another way, India's fascination with gold has caused us to spend virtually the entire FDI flow in purchasing gold and, then, converting the gold into jewellery. Consider the fact that wealth equivalent to more than 50 per cent of India's GDP is tucked away in gold and we virtually convert all our FDI flows into purchasing gold from the rest of the world. Is this the right recipe to finance growth and development? Does it serve any private or public interest? Can't this great wealth be unlocked for more productive use?

Gold: Store of Value or Investment?

Gold has been used as currency or standard of currency for centuries. It was effectively the underlying currency of the world in most countries for over 2000 years. Silver, which also worked as currency, was always valued in terms of gold and in that sense reflected the derived value of gold. Until 1970, gold (and silver) served to clear international balance in imports and exports. A country importing more than exporting shipped gold and the country exporting more received gold in payment and settlement. India was a net exporter during the last two millennia and received considerable payments in gold. Gold was valued by Indians as the real store of value and they happily traded their handicrafts, handlooms and agriculture produce for it.

When the world moved to paper currency and the inability of governments and central banks to manage inflation caused by indiscriminate issue of currency became a pandemic, Indian households found gold a protector of real value. Gold prices beat the inflation caused by depreciation of currency—against both external currencies and internal over-issuance. Financial instruments did not protect savings; there were times when the interest yield on government bonds and bank deposits were lower than the interest received. Gold was considered the ideal hedge by most Indian households. As gold was stocked mostly in the form of jewellery, it served an additional purpose without much extra cost (making charges in India have been almost insignificant) of meeting the family's need for ornaments. The fascination of Indian households for gold is quite understandable.

However, the gold holdings of households are no better than wads of currency notes stuffed into mattresses. The enormous gold savings of Indians serve no purpose as far as financing investments are concerned. For a country starved of financial capital, storing over Rs 112 lakh crore of equity in the form of jewellery in almirahs and lockers is nothing but a monumental waste of resources. With central banks and governments getting a good handle on inflation and financial instruments and derivatives protecting value and providing good returns, stashing away such a vast investible resource is not in the national or individual interest.

The time has come for a change of mindset and gold to emerge as a massive resource of investment—without, of course, compromising on the needs of households to protect against inflation and the use of ornaments for social purposes. India must unlock the wealth tucked away in gold.

Development of Gold as a Financial Asset Class

Transactions and holdings of gold can be classified into two categories: commodity gold, gold as goods, inventories or valuables; and financial gold (including monetary gold). Gold in India is mostly held by households, jewellers, temples and trusts. RBI holds about 700 tonnes of gold. Banks in India do not keep gold though some NBFCs (gold finance companies) buy gold for cash and lend against deposit of gold. Gold is a common possession of most families and temples in India, in the form of jewellery and coins. While holding jewellery as ornaments is important, it is also purchased with an investment objective.

Development of gold as a financial asset class can provide a better alternative to people than holding jewellery as a financial asset to manage inflation risk. This would require gold to serve two objectives. First, to protect the value of investment, with gold as the underlying asset, equal to the value of gold at the time of disposal/maturity of investment. Second, to earn positive financial returns over and above covering the cost of using jewellery for ornaments. If these two objectives are served by the investment with gold as the underlying asset, it should be possible to convince people to convert gold as a financial asset instead of keeping it as a commodity in the form of jewellery. That said, it won't be easy and quick as using gold as a default asset for savings is deeply ingrained in the Indian psyche.

The good news is that there has been a shift in the mindset of millennials and Generation Z, who do not share the fascination of their elders for gold. They find gold jewellery an unnecessary accessory and managing gold as a commodity inconvenient. Gold as an asset class would appeal to them much more. The beginning of the end of physical gold as a default asset can be made with this new generation of Indians.

Steps Taken to Promote Gold as a Financial Asset Class

The Government of India has taken several measures to develop gold as a financial asset. In 2015, the NDA government launched a number of schemes: the Gold Monetization Scheme (GMS), Sovereign Gold Bond

Scheme (SGB) and India Gold Coin (IGC). These schemes did not succeed as expected but could still mobilize about 30 tonnes of gold in a three-year period. The SGB scheme made some impressive gains in 2020 when gold prices shot through the roof, with international gold prices crossing $2000 an ounce in August 2020. Though it appears counterintuitive, evidence suggests that SGB schemes attract more investment when gold prices are high and rising and less investment when they are low and falling.

A Comprehensive Bouquet of Gold-Based Financial Assets

The simplest and most effective strategy for drawing out gold from household almirahs, lockers and temple vaults is to provide all financial investment products with gold as an underlying asset/currency and design returns that partly share the profits the financial resources generate by unleashing gold.

The first such class of financial assets is banking products. Banks provide savings accounts and fixed deposits as investment options for savers. These are denominated in monetary rupees and earn returns in rupees. Banks return the original investment in nominal rupees along with interest on maturity or at due periodicity. If banks were to provide gold savings accounts and gold fixed deposits, returning the same amount of gold at maturity and paying some interest in rupees for the period of deposit, savers/investors would continue to be protected for the value of gold as gold (like saving in physical gold). Over and above, they would get some financial returns in the form of gold. For investors who store jewellery as an investment alone, such gold savings/fixed deposit accounts would save the cost of making charges and keep their gold safe. Therefore, the banking system should offer gold savings accounts and fixed deposits.

These gold accounts can be opened with either households/temples surrendering idle gold to the banks or even making deposits in rupees equivalent to the day's price of gold. The investor should have the assurance and option to receive the equivalent value of gold or physical gold on the day of maturity. This would build confidence and trust. The bank receiving the gold deposit can, of course, convert it into a financial resource by selling/transferring it to gold traders, jewellery manufacturers or gold vaults offering such services. The funds so raised would earn returns like all other deposits. With appropriate risk management practices, banks can not only hedge the price risk on gold but offer a financial return to the savers. This is precisely the logic of the SGB scheme. A special class of non-banks—gold NBFCs—can also be created/licensed to offer these savings and fixed deposit products. It should be fair to assume that if the government can offer a financial return of 2.5 per cent per annum in addition to protecting the value of gold, banks and non-banks can do better.

Second, the SGB scheme should be revamped to make it work better. The Government of India offers several certificates and bonds schemes, such as National Savings Certificates, Kisan Vikas Patra and RBI Savings Bond Scheme. These are all fixed period products that return the original value of investment on the maturity and pay interest, usually at a fixed rate, during the period of investment that may be paid at regular intervals or maturity.

Retaining the principal features of the current SGB scheme, the government should offer the facility to invest in these bonds on tap through designated post offices, banks, stock exchanges and RBI counters. The two-way prices (for selling and buying) of gold bonds should be declared every day. The bonds should be marketed/sold through investment bankers/intermediaries like brokers and agents who market small savings products with the same commission payable on financial products. The bonds should be held only in demat accounts and be transferrable much the same way as equity shares are transferred today with the National Securities Depository Ltd (NSDL) and Central Depository Services India Ltd (CSDL) working as the depositories of these bonds.

Third, LIC, MFs and other asset managers should also be permitted, with appropriate regulations, to offer gold-denominated insurance policies, MF units and similar investment products ensuring two key features: redemption/payment in gold of original investment quantity and additional financial returns.

Development of Spot and Future Markets for Gold

Gold derivatives are permitted to be traded in all exchanges regulated by SEBI. However, there is no organized spot market in the country for gold. India should set up an India Gold Exchange (IGE) for spot and forward gold trading, regulated by an independent gold regulator. SEBI regulates gold derivatives as securities but physical gold is a commodity. Some commodity exchanges have come up in the country like electricity exchanges and, more recently, a gas exchange. This offers three possibilities for regulation of spot and future markets for gold: SEBI regulates both spot and future markets; a specialized gold regulator regulates both spot and future markets; and SEBI regulates the future market while a specialized gold regulator regulates the spot market. The optimal arrangement would probably be a specialized gold regulator who regulates both the spot and future markets.

This platform will incentivize trading across the country based on a nationwide vaulting infrastructure network, with significant benefits of greater formalization of the gold economy. Gradually, the IGE can also allow trading of other precious metals like silver and platinum, and commodities currently under the jurisdiction of the Central government. Necessary market infrastructure arrangements like clearing and settlement institutions can be made, leveraging on existing market infrastructure for the equity, bonds and derivative markets.

Efficient and functional market infrastructure for gold storage, delivery, purification, standardization and pledging are sorely lacking in the country. Making gold a financial asset and development of an efficient exchange would require enormous investment in building market infrastructure. A bullion bank facilitates gold trading, borrowing and lending; overdrafts; vaulting; hedging; inventory or consignment management; broking and futures trading; collateral management; swaps; precious metals research; mine or project finance and physical precious metals distribution/logistics. Specialized banks like payments banks have been established by RBI. Likewise, a few bullion banks should be developed, either as specialized banks or existing banks and non-banks being given such licences.

Currently, SEBI regulates bullion vaults by laying down guidelines for custodial services with regard to securities, including for gold derivatives. The regulation of warehouses and extension vaults is actually the responsibility of the Warehouse Development and Regulatory Authority of India (WDRAI) under the Warehouse (Development & Regulation) Act, 2007. The gold regulator should be provided with the authority to develop and regulate bullion vault infrastructure in the country.

A Hassle-Free System to Convert Stashed Gold into a Financial Asset

There is considerable amount of gold with households, institutions and temples, lying without a purpose or as an inefficient avenue of financial security. Current schemes, besides having structural flaws, are not consumer-friendly. The process and time taken to convert gold in the form of jewellery or in other physical form to the standard form before it is accepted by banks under these schemes is tortuous. Likewise, there are severe flaws in the entire process of banks handing over the gold to the Metals and Minerals Trading Corporation of India (MMTC) and MMTC selling it to the highest bidder.

A revamped bouquet of schemes making gold a financial asset class should make it hassle-free for households and temples to convert their jewellery and other forms of physical gold into financial gold or equivalent physical gold certificates. Bullion banks, other authorized banks and regulated vaults should work with transparency to verify the actual gold in standard gold units and give it instant credit in their bank accounts or provide gold certificates to take back equivalent physical gold at the end of the desired period.

Section VIII: Fiscal Finance

Chapter Thirty-Eight

State of Public Finance

Raising Taxes to Finance Public Expenditures is the Core of Public Finances

The institution of government has been created by society to produce public goods and services such as law and order, defence, currency, maintaining relations with foreign countries, administration of justice and the like. The institution of government, in times of social welfare, has also expanded to deliver merit goods like education, health and nutrition and also to redistribute wealth and income from the haves to the have-nots.

Discharging all these functions adequately and satisfactorily requires finance. Tax revenues, borrowings and printing money are the three sources for governments to raise the necessary fiscal resources to fund requisite public expenditures.

Printing money to fund government expenditure led to prolonged episodes of high inflation. India also used this to its utter dismay from the 1950s to 1990s. The government has been cautious in resorting to this temptation even in the pandemic year. Though advanced economies resorted to this device very heavily in 2020–21, most developing countries stayed away from monetizing deficits by creating money.

Borrowing funds is the third source of financing expenditure.

Governments make revenue and capital expenditures on public goods and services. Governments also make revenue and capital expenditures on merit goods and services. They spend on redistribution by giving subsidies, grants, scholarships and support to the poor and other deserving sections of society. Governments pay interest on debt raised earlier. They also incur capital expenditure on making investments in producing private goods and services and revenue expenditure on subsidizing these products and services.

Governments get some revenues in the form of dividends and other pay-outs from investments made in the public sector. Sometimes, they also get capital payments by disposing of these public-sector undertakings and capital works. All these expenditures net of non-tax revenues and capital receipts constitute the expenditure of governments.

Net government expenditure minus tax revenues results in fiscal deficit. This fiscal deficit is met by raising borrowings. This is net fiscal deficit or fiscal deficit as commonly understood. Governments also incur expenditure every year in repaying old borrowings/debt.

The borrowings raised to fund the fiscal deficit and the borrowings raised to repay old debt together are described as gross borrowings. While gross borrowings would be higher than the fiscal deficit, net new borrowings equal fiscal deficits.

Occasionally, governments use sharp practices to understate fiscal deficit. Expenditure on providing equity to banks by issuing recapitalization bonds is one such practice. The equity is funded by the banks subscribing to the bonds issued by the governments. The whole transaction is accounted as one transaction with zero expenditure by reducing the bond amount received from the equity expenditure. This results in artificially suppressing fiscal expenditure. In such a case, while the borrowings received from the bonds issued may be counted for the purpose of public debt, the same is not shown as part of the fiscal deficit.

Debt is Serviced by Future Taxpayers

Borrowings raised by governments become their debt, which is serviced and repaid by future revenues and borrowings. In essence, borrowings represent the shortfall between government expenditures and revenues in any year and the debt of the government represents accumulated borrowings. The more governments accumulate debt, an increasing share of future revenues and borrowings gets used in servicing the debt instead of public expenditure.

Excessive borrowings by governments results in two consequences sooner than later. First, borrowings become a zero-sum game when new borrowings get used up to serve accumulated debt, leaving no real resource to undertake public expenditure. Second, the private sector gets starved of investible funds with adverse consequences for growth of the country.

Article 292 confers power on the Government of India to borrow on the security of the Consolidated Fund of India (CFI), which receives all revenues and borrowings. The Article subjects this executive power to 'such limits, if any, as may from time to time be fixed by the Parliament by law'. The Parliament has chosen not to fix any borrowing limits specifically thus far. No debt limit law has ever been passed in India.

Public Debt and Liabilities

All receipts of the government are accounted for in the CFI. The government makes expenditures from the CFI. It also raises debt on the strength and security of the CFI and accounts for it in the CFI. The Government of India has executive authority to raise debt in domestic markets (internal debt) and overseas markets (external debt). State governments can raise debt only in domestic markets. Internal and external debts together make up public debt.

The Constitution allows the Centre and the states to maintain non-government accounts in what is called the Public Account. Funds belonging to persons other than the Government of India—small savings raised from people, provident fund and other deposits of government servants, GST Compensation Cess for compensating state governments, etc.—are to be kept in the Public Account.

Governments use the surplus in the Public Account to borrow from it. For example, the surplus in the National Small Savings Fund (NSSF), an account in the Public Account of India, is used to subscribe to the special securities issued by the Government of India. Even after such deployment, some more cash balance remains available in the Public Account and is used by the government as its cash balance.

The debt/borrowings/liabilities raised thorough the CFI with or without the security of the CFI is the public debt. These debts/borrowings/liabilities may be raised domestically or abroad. They may be raised by issuing securities/debt to an account maintained in the Public Account like NSSF. These debts and liabilities constitute the public debt of India. These liabilities are accounted for as public debt in the Budget, Accounts and other publications of the government.

There are two other kinds of public debt, which, however, are not accounted as public debt.

The first kind of liabilities arise when the balances in the accounts maintained in the Public Account are used to provide loans to government agencies, and thereby not accounting for such loans in the CFI, to fund the expenditure of the government.

The accumulations in NSSF are used to fund the government's expenditure (food subsidy) by giving loans to organizations like FCI.

The other kind of real liability is when the account used to borrow funds is accounted for neither in the CFI nor the Public Account but some entity outside the government. When the government used Housing and Urban Development Corporation (HUDCO) to raise loans to pay for affordable housing subsidies programme or National Bank for Agriculture and Rural Development (NABARD) to provide finance to a society created outside the government system to finance subsidy support for a rural housing programme, these liabilities do not figure in either the CFI or the Public Account. These loans raised were fully serviced by the government. The interest and principal repayments were paid by the Government of India. These liabilities are true off-budget liabilities of the Government of India.

The true debt of the Government of India is the sum of debt and liabilities raised and accounted for in the CFI, the resources of the Public Account used to fund the government/fiscal expenditure and the liabilities created outside the CFI and the Public Account to fund government/public/fiscal expenditure.

The government reports its public debt and liabilities as part of the Budget papers. A Statement of Liabilities of the Central government is always published as part of the Receipt Budget.

The Finance and Accounts of the Government of India, prepared annually by the Controller General of Accounts (CGA), also publish the details of debt and liabilities. These are actual accounts and available in the public domain only after the CAG has audited the accounts and the same are placed in the Parliament.

Further, the Ministry of Finance annually publishes a 'Status Paper on Government Debt'.

Government Started Counting its Fiscal Deficit in 1991–92

The Government of India did not recognize the concept of fiscal deficit until the 1980s. Earlier, the government used to treat all receipts, whether tax, non-tax or debt, as the same kind of receipt without any difference relating to their implications for its debt. The difference between total receipts and total expenditures was treated as budget deficit or residual deficit, which was left as uncovered to be bridged by ad hoc borrowing from the RBI. For example, in the Budget speech of 1980–81, the finance minister, in para 62, said, '. . . the total receipts in 1980–81 are estimated at Rs 19,827 crore as against Rs 18,980 crore in the interim Budget. Total expenditure is estimated at Rs 21,467 crore. The deficit at existing rates of taxes will thus be Rs 1640 crore.' After accounting for additional resource mobilization through tax effort, the finance minister noted in para 120: 'The tax effort net of reliefs proposed in the Budget will on the whole bring in about Rs 282 crore for the current year, of which Rs 223 crore will accrue to the Centre. There will be a residual deficit of Rs 1417 crore which I propose to leave uncovered.' What was left uncovered was supposed to be made up either by reducing the expenditure from the Budget levels during the course of the year, by borrowing additional amounts from somewhere, or if the tax effort shows up unexpected gains, or a mix of any or all of these. Or, better still, by the increase in RBI credit to the Government of India.

In the regular Budget presented for financial year 1990–91, the overall deficit was shown to be Rs 7206 crore. The *Budget at a Glance* duly notes at the bottom: 'Increase in net RBI Credit to Central government—Rs 7206 crore'.

Recognition of the concept of fiscal deficit in India's budgeting system took place in the most unusual circumstances. In the 1991–92 Interim Budget, which was not really presented but just approved by the Parliament as the Chandra Shekhar government had fallen, Finance Minister Yashwant

Sinha recognized the concept of fiscal deficit. The *Budget at a Glance* of the Interim Budget 1991–92 proposed revenue deficit for financial year 1991–92 at Rs 17,766 crore, budgetary deficit at Rs 9977 crore and fiscal deficit at Rs 38,475 crore. The fiscal deficit equalled the borrowings and other liabilities of Rs 28,498 crore and the net increase in RBI credit to the Central government (which equalled budgetary deficit) of Rs 9977 crore.

All Budgets thereafter have presented fiscal deficit numbers. At some point in time, the concept of budgetary deficit went out and only fiscal deficit, which equalled borrowings and other liabilities, remained as the depiction of the gap between total expenditure of the government and total non-debt receipts.

India Adopts a Law to Limit Fiscal Deficits in 2003–04

While India started recognizing fiscal deficits from financial year 1991–92, there was no check on limiting it to any particular level. Globally, two rules were getting increasing traction. One, the so-called golden rule: limiting revenue expenditures to revenue receipts. This rule enjoined governments not to borrow for revenue or current expenditures. Second, the fiscal deficit rule: limiting fiscal deficits to a certain fraction of GDP. This rule enjoined governments to take only a limited amount of savings for expenditures beyond revenue receipts. Europe had adopted a 3 per cent fiscal deficit rule under the Maastricht Treaty for the countries joining the EU. Many countries enacted fiscal responsibility and budget management laws to give statutory backing to these two rules.

The Indian government also adopted the Fiscal Responsibility and Budget Management Act (FRBM Act) in 2003–04. It did not specify any particular revenue and fiscal deficit target but left it to be determined by the government under the rules to be framed under the Act. After some deliberations, 3 per cent fiscal deficit was proposed.

All state governments in India also followed suit, most expeditiously after the Twelfth Finance Commission made it mandatory for them to enact the FRBM laws to claim benefits of debt waiver and consolidation. The Government of India also linked approvals for borrowing ceilings and market borrowings for the states to the fiscal deficit targets recommended by the Finance Commission as part of the fiscal consolidation path and the passing of FRBM laws.

The Government of India found it hard to achieve the fiscal deficit target. The turmoil caused by the global financial crisis in 2008–09 was used to suspend and reset the fiscal consolidation and fiscal deficit path. The NDA government designed its own fiscal consolidation glide path in 2014–15 to attain the 3 per cent fiscal deficit target by 2018–19.

The government decided to hardcode the fiscal deficit target in the FRBM law. The FRBM Act was amended via the Finance Act 2018–19 to prescribe that the fiscal deficit of 3 per cent of GDP would be achieved by financial year 2020–21 and thereafter would not be exceeded. Further, the amended FRBM Act provided that the Government of India would attain the target of Central government debt and liabilities to GDP ratio of 40 per cent by 2024–25.

Fiscal Deficit Goes out of Shape in 2019–20 and Crossed All Limits in 2020–21

The fiscal deficit was Rs 6.49 lakh crore in 2018–19. Fiscal deficit, in nominal terms, was Rs 5.03 lakh crore in 2013–14, the year before the NDA government took over in May 2014. The increase in fiscal deficit in five years, the first term of the NDA government, was very small. It rose to Rs 5.11 lakh crore in 2014–15 (an increase of only Rs 0.08 lakh crore), Rs 5.33 lakh crore in 2015–16 (an increase of Rs 0.22 lakh crore), Rs 5.36 lakh crore in 2016–17 (an increase of Rs 0.03 lakh crore), Rs 5.91 lakh crore in 2017–18 (an increase of Rs 0.55 lakh crore) and Rs 6.49 lakh crore in 2018–19 (an increase of Rs 0.58 lakh crore).

The fiscal deficit for 2019–20 (actual), as per the details presented in Budget 2021–22, rose to Rs 9.34 lakh crore, an increase of Rs 2.85 lakh crore. This was a massive increase of 43.9 per cent over the fiscal deficit of 2018–19. And 2019–20 was not the year of the pandemic.

The revised fiscal deficit of 2020–21, as presented in Budget 2021–22, was a humungous Rs 18.49 lakh crore. The fiscal deficit of 2020–21 increased by Rs 9.13 lakh crore, almost a 100 per cent increase. Compared to financial year 2018–19, the fiscal deficit in financial year 2020–21 rose by Rs 12 lakh crore, an increase of 185 per cent. The fiscal deficit of the Government of India trebled (from Rs 6.49 lakh crore in 2018–19 to Rs 18.49 lakh crore in 2020–21) in two years.

Not to be left behind in financial year 2021–22, the government proposed a fiscal deficit of Rs 15.07 lakh crore, 230 per cent of the fiscal deficit of 2018–19.

The fiscal deficits of 2020–21 and 2021–22 are partly explained by the rolling back of massive off-budget borrowings resorted to in the previous four years. The sharp practices of managing fiscal deficits do show up at some point in time.

Share in Central Taxes is Dominant Source of Resource Transfers to States

Before the institutionalization of GST in 2016, the Constitution of India had a neat arrangement of taxation powers being divided between the Centre and the states. While the Centre had full authority to levy, collect and administer income taxes, both personal and corporate (barring income tax on agriculture incomes), and levy production taxes (excise duties, later called value-added tax, or VAT) on all commodities (except alcoholic and medicinal preparations), the states had the authority to levy, collect and administer taxes on sale of goods, excise duties on alcohol and medicinal preparations, property tax and transportation taxes.

For financial year 2018–19, the gross tax revenues of the Central government were Rs 20.80 lakh crore, comprising Rs 6.64 lakh crore of corporate income tax (CIT), Rs 4.73 lakh crore of personal income tax (PIT), Rs 1.18 lakh crore of customs duty, Rs 2.31 lakh crore of union excise duties, Rs 5.82 lakh crore of central GST and other small revenues. The share of central taxes transferred to the states amounted to Rs 7.61 lakh crore with the Central government retaining Rs 13.17 lakh crore. The states got 36.59 per cent of the gross tax collection of central taxes as against a broadly stipulated share of 42 per cent by the Finance Commission.

According to the government's *Budget at a Glance,* which provides details of all the transfers to the state governments, total transfers to the states were Rs 11.95 lakh crore for the financial year 2018–19. The states' share in central taxes (Rs 7.61 lakh crore) thus amounted to 63.68 per cent of total transfers from the Centre to the states.

The Finance Commissions also recommend some specific grants to states. Grants for local bodies, both urban and rural, have been a permanent feature of the Finance Commissions' recommendations after constitutional amendments in the 1980s. For 2018–19 (actuals), the states were provided with grants of Rs 35,064 crore for rural local bodies and Rs 14,400 crore for urban local bodies.

The other significant grant to the states based on the recommendations of the Finance Commissions is the Centre's contribution to state disaster relief funds (SDRFs). The Finance Commissions determine specific amounts of annual contribution to SDRFs for each state for the five years covered by their recommendations. These contributions were made in the ratio of 75:25 by the Centre and states until the Thirteenth Finance Commission. The Fourteenth Finance Commission recommended that the Central government transfer 90 per cent. However, despite accepting this recommendation, the Centre transferred only 75 per cent of the state-specific contribution recommended for SDRFs. For financial year 2018–19, the Central government transferred Rs 9658 crore as its share. For the 'Post Devolution Revenue Deficit Grants' for states, recommended by the Finance Commissions to take care of the uncovered gap in the budgets post devolution, the Centre transferred Rs 34,582 crore in 2018–19.

In all, Rs 93,704 crore of Central government funds were transferred to states in 2018–19 under various schemes of non-discretionary transfers. This amounted to 4.5 per cent of the gross tax revenues of 20.80 lakh crore of the Central government in 2018–19. Together, with tax transfers of 36.6 per cent and grants transfer of 4.5 per cent, the Central government transferred 41.1 per cent of the gross tax collected.

Largest Discretionary Source of Transfers to States is CSSs

According to the statement recording central transfers to states in *Budget at a Glance* (2020–21), Rs 2.71 lakh crore was transferred to the states under Centrally Sponsored Schemes (CSSs) as revenue expenditure in 2018–19. This amounted to 13.03 per cent of the gross central tax revenues of Rs 20.80 lakh crore, a substantial share. The Central government also publishes a Statement as part of the Budget papers, Statement 4A, titled Centrally Sponsored Schemes, which informs us that the total revenue expenditure on CSSs in 2018–19 was Rs 2.96 lakh crore. The difference is accounted for by Central government establishment expenditure on administering CSSs as well as some small transfers to central agencies, who in turn spent it on administering or transferring to state governments.

The largest CSS in 2018–19 was the Mahatma Gandhi National Rural Employment Guarantee Programme (popularly known as MGNREGA), which provides wages and unemployment allowance to labour seeking employment from the government. The National Health Mission, which partly funds infrastructure creation, services of health staff in subcentres and primary health centres and expenditure on medicines and other disposables, cost the government Rs 31,502 crore.

Other significant CSSs include Green Revolution (an umbrella scheme of agricultural interventions) at Rs 11,748 crore, Pradhan Mantri Gram Sadak Yojana (building of rural roads as per minimum norms laid down) at Rs 15,414 crore, Pradhan Mantri Awas Yojana (construction of affordable houses for the rural and urban poor) at Rs 25,442 crore, Swachh Bharat Mission—Gramin (building of toilets in rural areas and spreading awareness to make rural India free of open defecation) at Rs 12,913 crore, National Education Mission (an umbrella scheme for creation of school infrastructure and to fund salaries of new teachers and other staff) at Rs 30,830 crore, Integrated Child Development Scheme (an umbrella scheme of interventions to improve nutritional and health standards of children below the age of five) at Rs 21,612 crore and the Urban Rejuvenation Missions, which include two schemes (AMRUT and Smart Cities Mission) to fund urban infrastructure at Rs 12,085 crore.

Fifteenth Finance Commission Recommended Same Share of Central Taxes for the States

The Fifteenth Finance Commission submitted its report to the President on 9 November 2020. The government placed the Explanatory Memorandum on the Action Taken on the recommendations made by the Fifteenth Finance Commission on 1 February, the day the Budget was presented for financial year 2021–22.

The Fourteenth Finance Commission had recommended states' share in central taxes, after excluding cess and surcharges, at 42 per cent. The Union government was not very comfortable about it, which was reflected in the terms of reference of the Fifteenth Finance Commission as presented above.

The states had demanded a 50 per cent share in the central taxes. The Fifteenth Finance Commission did not accept this demand arguing that the states had received 50.2 per cent of gross revenue receipts (GRR) of the Central government during the Fourteenth Finance Commission period despite noting that in 2019–20, the share of total transfers in the GRR of the Central government was only 48.6 per cent and the share of states in central taxes had precipitously fallen to only 27.9 per cent out of this. It also did not accept the contention of the Central government to reduce share in central taxes on the same argument that the overall share of the transfers to the states during 2015–2020 (at 50.2 per cent) had remained almost similar to that during the Fourteenth Finance Commission period (48.2 per cent).

After taking note of all these demands and contentions, the Fifteenth Finance Commission decided to recommend the same percentage of 42 per cent as states' share in the divisible pool as recommended by the Fourteenth Finance Commission. It only made a technical revision of taking out the share of Jammu and Kashmir as the erstwhile state had been converted into two union territories in the meantime. The Commission expressed the hope that there would be no further decline in the divisible pool as a proportion of gross revenue receipts.

Fifteenth Finance Commission Recommends Several Grants, but Many Not Accepted by the Centre

The grant package of the Fifteenth Finance Commission is more comprehensive than that of the Fourteenth Finance Commission. The Commission recommended the following:

First, revenue deficit grants of Rs 2,94,514 crore to seventeen states as it judged these states to remain short of the revenues required to meet their justified expenditures even after factoring in devolution. The Commission did not accept the suggestion of the Central government of considering to discontinue the system of revenue deficit grants.

Second, a total of Rs 4,36,361 crore of local bodies' grant delinking the grants package from performance-based grants. Performance-based grants were reduced to only Rs 8000 crore for incubation of new cities and Rs 450 crore to promote the concept of shared municipal services. While grants of Rs 2,36,805 crore were earmarked for rural local bodies and Rs 1,21,055 crore for urban local bodies, the Commission recommended health grants of Rs 70,051 crore to be spent through local governments.

Third, grants of Rs 1,22,601 crore for disaster management.

Fourth, bringing back the concept of sector-specific grants, which also included recommendations on performance-based grants, which the terms of reference required the Commission to consider extensively. In all, sector-specific grants of Rs 1,29,987 crore were recommended, which included three performance-based grants: Rs 4800 crore for incentivizing the states to enhance educational outcomes, Rs 6143 crore for online learning and development of professional courses (medical and engineering) in regional languages for higher education and Rs 45,000 crore for performance-based incentives for carrying out agricultural reforms of amending land-leasing laws, maintaining and augmenting groundwater stock, growth in agriculture exports and encouraging production of oilseeds, pulses and wood and wood-based products. The sector-specific grants also included grants for health (Rs 31,755 crore), maintenance of Pradhan Mantri Gram Sadak Yojana (PMGSY) for roads (Rs 27,539 crore), judiciary (Rs 10,425 crore), statistics (Rs 1175 crore) and aspirational districts and blocks (Rs 3150 crore).

Finally, bringing back the old concept of state-specific grants with a total of Rs 49,599 grants for states. All states have been recommended to receive these grants with Karnataka getting the largest share of Rs 6000 crore. The total grants package was estimated at Rs 10,33,062 crore by the Commission.

The Explanatory Memorandum laid before the Parliament informed that the government, for the grants recommended by the Fifteenth Finance Commission, had accepted the recommendation of the post-devolution deficit grants amounting to Rs 2,94,514 crore, including the amounts recommended for each of the states and the manner of providing the grants as contained in the report of the Commission. It also accepted the recommendations with respect to local bodies' grants and disaster-related grants as recommended by the Commission.

The government, however, did not accept the recommendations of the Commission for the grants to states for specific sectors and stated, 'The government will give due consideration to sectors identified by the Commission while formulating and implementing existing and new Centrally Sponsored and Central Sector Schemes.' It also did not accept the recommendations of the Commission for state-specific grants as well and instead stated, 'Keeping in view the untied resources with the state governments and the fiscal commitments of the Central government, due consideration will be given to the above recommendations.'

The Commission had also recommended a fiscal consolidation roadmap for states and higher limit for net borrowings of 4 per cent of the gross state domestic product (GSDP) for financial year 2021–22, 3.5 per cent for 2022–23 and to be maintained at 3 per cent of GSDP from 2023–24. The Commission had also recommended an additional annual borrowing space of 0.5 per cent of GSDP for the period 2021–22 to 2024–25 for the power sector based on a performance criterion. The government accepted 'in principle the recommendations in respect of the quantum as a per cent of GSDP of net borrowing ceilings for the States'. However, the Action Taken Report stated, 'other recommendations related to the fiscal road map for the States and amendments to the FRBM Act will be examined separately'.

The government did not, in the Budget 2021–22, except the health sector grants, deliver sector-specific and state-specific grants to the states. The additional borrowing space is also more likely to be used to fund states' investments in public-sector power companies and to pay their bills to the central agencies and private sector.

The Government Continues Diluting the Devolution Pool for Reducing Effective Share of States

The Fifteenth Finance Commission recommended 'retaining the vertical share of 41 per cent of the divisible pool of taxes for the States during the award part of this Commission'.

The 'divisible pool' is the most critical part for operationalizing recommendations regarding share of states in central taxes. Article 270 of the Constitution, after the Eightieth Constitutional Amendment, defines the divisible pool. It prescribes that 'all taxes and duties referred to in the Union List', 'except the duties and taxes referred in articles 268 and 269' and 'surcharges on taxes and duties referred to in article 271' and 'any cess levied for specific purposes' shall be shared between the Union and the states. As articles 268 and 269 refer to marginal taxes like tax on stamp duty and consignment sale, all union taxes, including income tax, corporation tax, central GST and excise duties are shareable with states. Article 280 makes 'net proceeds of taxes' shareable, which allows the Central government to exclude the cost of collection of taxes from shareable tax proceeds. Likewise, tax proceeds attributable to union territories are not part of the net proceeds of taxes.

The Central government can, however, keep union taxes outside the divisible pool by levying surcharges, which Article 271 permits the Parliament to levy by increasing any of the union duties and taxes. It can also levy any cess for any specific purpose. Surcharges are usually meant to serve any extraordinary needs and cesses to service any specific purposes.

The Central government has increasingly reduced the effective share of states in union taxes and duties. Gross tax revenues (including the states' share) in 2018–19, 2019–20 and 2020–21 have been Rs 20.80 lakh crore, Rs 20.10 lakh crore and Rs 19.00 lakh crore, respectively, whereas the Centre appropriated Rs 13.17 lakh crore, Rs 13.57 lakh crore and Rs 13.45 lakh crore, respectively. This gives it a share of 63.3 per cent, 67.5 per cent and 70.8 per cent in these three years. Correspondingly, states got a reduced share in taxes of 36.3 per cent, 32.5 per cent and 29.2 per cent in these years. Thus, the Centre has been effectively chipping away at the states' share in central taxes determined by the Finance Commissions. For financial year 2021–22 (BE), the Central government has estimated the share of states at Rs 6,65,572 crore, whereas the gross tax receipts are estimated at Rs 22,17,059 crore. This gives the states an effective share of only 29.6 per cent, much less than the share of 41 per cent mandated by the Finance Commission.

The feat of reducing the states' share sharply in financial year 2020–21 (to 29.2 per cent from 32.5 per cent in 2019–20) was achieved by increasing non-shareable special additional excise duties and road and infrastructure cess on petrol and diesel from time to time, in the most accentuated manner after 6 May 2020. The government imposed an additional levy of a whopping Rs 13 per litre on diesel and Rs 10 per litre on petrol, which raised the incidence of excise duties on diesel to Rs 31.8 per litre and Rs 32.9 per litre on petrol (these duties were Rs 3.56 per litre on diesel and Rs 9.48 per litre on petrol in 2014, when the NDA government had taken over). With such a large imposition of

The $10 Trillion Dream

non-shareable special additional excise duties and road and infrastructure cess on diesel and petrol, the shareable basic excise duty was only Rs 2.98 per litre on petrol and Rs 4.83 on diesel. The rest was all non-shareable components.

The consequence of this policy choice by the Government of India has been amply reflected in the gross collection of excise revenues and the share of the states therein. The revised estimates of excise duties for financial year 2020–21 are Rs 3,61,000 lakh crore. The estimated share of states in the excise duties revenues for 2020–21 are only Rs 19,578 crore. All the states get only 5.4 per cent of the share of all the excise duties and cesses collected by the Central government as against the Finance Commission-recommended share of 41 per cent.

The process of diluting the 'divisible pool' continued in Budget 2021–22 as well. A new cess—agriculture infrastructure and development cess—has been levied by bringing a necessary law through the Finance Act 2021. Customs duties have also been made more non-shareable by converting existing basic customs duties into agriculture infrastructure and development cess on several items.

For financial year 2021–22, estimated excise duties revenues are Rs 3,35,000 crore whereas the states' estimated share is Rs 19,475 crore, which is only 5.81 per cent. The states have effectively been deprived of their share in union excise duties. For customs, the net tax receipts for RE20–21 are Rs 1,12, 000 crore, whereas the share of states estimated for the year is Rs 36,592 crore—a share of 32.67 per cent. For 2021–22, the estimated collection of customs revenues is Rs 1,36,000 crore whereas the estimated share of states is Rs 40,216 crore, which brings the share of states down to 29.57 per cent. The levy of agriculture infrastructure and development cess on select imported goods may have started the process of weaning the states away from customs revenues from financial year 2021–22.

Therefore, while the Central government accepted the recommendation of the Fifteenth Finance Commission to continue with providing states a share of 41 per cent in central taxes, by reducing the divisible pool by transferring shareable tax revenues to non-shareable cesses and surcharges, the effective share of states in central taxes continues to decline. It is slated to fall to less than 30 per cent in financial year 2021–22.

Chapter Thirty-Nine

Public Debt Is the Achilles Heel of India

Size of Debt and Liabilities of the Government of India

The Budget 2020–21 Statement of Liabilities of the Central government, published as part of the Receipts Budget, stated that the public debt of the government was Rs 73.45 lakh crore at the end of 2018–19. In addition, there were other liabilities of Rs 17.39 lakh crore. Together, the total debt and liabilities of the Government of India, as per the Budget Papers, was Rs 90.83 lakh crore in financial year 2018–19. India's GDP, as per the first revised estimates published by NSO on 29 May 2020, for financial year 2018–19 was Rs 189.71 lakh crore at current prices. India's public debt as a proportion of the GDP was 38.72 per cent and total debt and liabilities 47.88 per cent.

The Budget 2021–22 Statement of Liabilities states that the public debt of India in 2019–20 was Rs 83.20 lakh crore, comprising internal debt of Rs 80.20 lakh crore and external debt of Rs 2.99 lakh crore. In addition, according to the Statement, the Government of India had other liabilities of Rs 19.27 lakh crore. Public debt together with other liabilities aggregated the net liabilities of the Central government at Rs 102.47 lakh crore. As a quick estimate of GDP places India's nominal

GDP for financial year 2019–20 at Rs 203 lakh crore, the public debt to GDP ratio for 2019–20 works out to be 40.99 per cent. The total liabilities of the Government of India as a proportion of GDP worked out to be 50.47 per cent of GDP.

The Status Paper on Government Debt 2018–19 reports that the Central government's liabilities were Rs 86.73 lakh crore at the end of 2018–19. This comprised the public debt of Rs 75.88 lakh crore, other liabilities of Rs 9.96 lakh crore and extra-budgetary resource liability of Rs 0.90 lakh crore. The Status Paper presents the Government of India's debt and liabilities in three buckets. First, 'Public Debt', which is debt accounted for in the CFI. Second, 'Public Account—Other Liabilities', which is liability arising out of the non-government or de facto government accounts maintained in the Public Account. Third, introduced very recently, is 'Off-Budget Liabilities'. The debt to GDP ratio of the government's debt and liabilities as per the Status Paper comes to 45.71 per cent.

Public debt and liabilities, as presented in the Budget papers for the year 2018–19, were Rs 90.83 lakh crore. There is a difference of Rs 4.1 lakh crore between the numbers reported in two different publications of the Government of India. There is a difference in all the components of the debt and liabilities. The public debt as per the Budget papers is Rs 73.45 lakh crore, whereas as per the Status Paper it is Rs 75.88 lakh crore. The other liabilities, as per the Budget papers, were Rs 17.39 lakh crore, whereas as per the Status Paper, these were only Rs 9.96 lakh crore. The Budget papers did not explicitly include any number for off-budget liabilities, whereas the Status Paper puts it at Rs 0.9 lakh crore.

Different treatment of three liabilities—external debt, NSSF in the Public Account and extra budgetary resources/off-budget borrowings—explains the difference.

External debt in the Budget papers is stated in historical values, i.e., at the conversion rates of the year when the external debt receipts came in. The Status Paper restates the external debt at current values. External debt at historical values was Rs 2.70 lakh crore whereas at current rates it was Rs 5.13 lakh crore. The Budget papers, effectively, understated the debt and liability of the Government of India by Rs 2.43 lakh crore.

There was an outstanding NSSF investment of Rs 4.71 lakh crore in state government securities and Rs 2.72 lakh crore represented loans given to public agencies. Together, Rs 7.43 lakh crore of NSSF liabilities have been excluded from the debt and liabilities of the Government of India. The NSSF loans to FCI for covering the food subsidy have also been excluded from the liability of the Government of India, which does not appear to be correct. However, in terms of pure difference in the estimation of debt and liabilities of the Government of India, the Budget papers overestimate the liabilities.

Finally, the Status Paper adds liabilities of Rs 0.9 lakh crore represented by fully serviced bonds, or FSBs, to the government's liabilities. The government did acknowledge in the Budget papers that there were some liabilities outside CFI and the Public Account. The Statement on Liabilities, in a footnote, stated, 'In addition to above, government liabilities on account of Extra Budgetary Resources (government fully serviced bonds), at the end of FY 2018–19 were Rs 89,864.10 crore, which was about 0.47 per cent of GDP.'

The net effect of these three adjustments—addition of Rs 2.43 lakh crore for undervaluation of external debt, reduction of Rs 7.43 lakh crore of NSSF investments in state government securities and loans to other public agencies and addition of Rs 0.9 lakh crore of FSBs—totals Rs 4.1 lakh crore, which is the exact difference between the debt and liability as per the Budget papers and the Status Paper.

Government of India Debt is Almost All Domestic

India's public debt is primarily domestically funded. Internal debt in 2018–19 was Rs 70.75 lakh crore, or as much as 96.32 per cent of the public debt. External debt, the debt raised by the government from all non-residents, including multilateral and bilateral institutions, was only Rs 2.70 lakh crore, or 3.68 per cent. Even if one takes into account the current value of external debt, which was Rs 5.13 lakh crore in 2018–19, the proportion of external debt in the public debt of India goes up to only 6.76 per cent.

The debt and liabilities of the Government of India on the Public Account and as extra-budgetary resources are entirely in domestic currency. Therefore, if we relate the external liabilities at current prices to the total debt and liabilities (as per the Status Paper), the ratio of external debt to total debt and liabilities falls to 5.9 per cent.

There is no reason to continue to depict external debt in government accounts and Budget papers at historical values. The government maintains accounts for each external bilateral and multilateral agency in foreign currency and Indian rupees in the separate accounts maintained by the Controller of Aid, Accounts and Audit in the Department of Economic Affairs.

The government can easily pass an accounting entry at the end of the year bringing outstanding balance at the current values by crediting an equal amount in an External Aid Reserve. This way, it would not only be able to present current valuation of external liabilities in the Budget papers but would also have some reserve to fall back on when repaying these liabilities.

This would align the external debt and public debt numbers in the Status Paper and the Budget papers.

Government Built Up Large Off-Budget Expenditure from 2016–17

Expenditure not met from the revenues of governments leads to incurrence of liability to be repaid from future revenues. Expenditure over revenues results in fiscal deficit. Fiscal deficit is financed by raising debt and incurring liabilities. When the expenditure and debt/liability incurred are both accounted for in the CFI, they are transparently and correctly accounted for in the Budget and accounts. There are certain contrived ways in which expenditure and liabilities can be accounted for in the Budget and accounts to understate the level of expenditures and fiscal deficit.

One method of lowering the real fiscal deficit is to deduct a revenue or capital receipt from expenditure. This brings down the headline aggregate expenditure and fiscal deficit. Equity investment expenditure in PSBs, for example, has been accounted for in the Budget and accounts in the last four years (from financial year 2017–18) by deducting the funds raised by issuing bonds to the banks from equity investment expenditure. Equity infusion in PSBs is a legitimate expenditure of the government and bonds issued are like any other borrowings made by the government. This investment should have fiscal deficit implications equal to the investment made. However, by treating it in this manner, the fiscal deficit is artificially reduced.

The reverse implication arises when a government claims to have incurred expenditure on a public welfare measure by transferring funds to the personal deposit (PD) of a department of the government, illegally maintained in the Public Account. Several state governments resort to this kind of manufactured expenditure by transferring budgeted funds to such PD accounts to claim reimbursement from the Centre or simply to 'save the funds from lapsing'.

Even bigger skulduggery takes place when public expenditure is carried out entirely outside the CFI. This may be done by raising debt/ liabilities in accounts maintained in the Public Account, in deposit accounts of departments maintained with banks, in SPVs created to meet specific expenditures, or by entering into special arrangements with government-owned organizations to finance government expenditure from their own fund or funds raised for such expenditure. Some examples of such practices are food subsidy paid for by the NSSF account kept in the Public Account, the toilet programme and housing subsidies met from FSBs raised by SPVs of the government, and expenditure from the Agri Infra Fund and Animal Husbandry Fund raised by NABARD.

Off-budget borrowings have been around for the past fifteen years. In the years between 2004 and 2010, the government had issued special securities to oil marketing companies (OMCs) and fertilizer companies in lieu of its subsidy obligations. These transactions were carried out through the Public Account. Subsidy paid to FCI through loans from NSSF are transactions similar to subsidy paid to OMCs by issuing oil bonds. These liabilities are reflected as other liabilities of the government in the Statement of Liabilities. There is a liability of Rs 1,62,827 crore towards the oil and fertilizer bonds issued during this period. The repayment of these bonds would start in financial year 2021–22. Accordingly, Budget 2021–22 informs us that the outstanding liability towards special securities issued in lieu of subsidies to OMCs, fertilizer companies and FCI would come down to Rs 1,52,828 crore.

The government resumed the practice of incurring expenditures by way of off-budget liabilities from the fiscal year 2016–17. Development expenditures of various ministries and departments began to be met by issuing FSBs. Such FSBs are raised by SPVs, organizations or financial institutions owned by the government. The government issued a commitment to service such bonds fully by paying interest and principal liabilities. The practice to fund the FCI food subsidy bill partly by lending NSSF funds to FCI also commenced in the year 2016–17.

For the year 2017–18, the government incurred expenditures aggregating about Rs 1.6 lakh crore, or about 1 per cent of GDP, outside the Budget and the CFI. Rs 80,000 crore of investment in the equity of PSBs was made by deducting the expenditure from the corresponding debt receipt of Rs 80,000 crore from the same PSBs by issuing special securities. Rs 65,000 crore of food subsidies was paid by giving loans to FCI from NSSF.

In all, total expenditures of Rs 15,095 crore were met off-budget by issuing these FSBs in 2017–18. FSBs were issued to pay Rs 3105 crore for irrigation projects under the Ministry of Water Resources, River Development and Ganga Rejuvenation; Rs 4000 crore for paying for the government's grant portion under the Deen Dayal Gram Jyoti and Saubhagya schemes; Rs 7330 crore of subvention support under the Pradhan Mantri Awas Yojana (PMAY); and Rs 660 crore for covering the liabilities of Inland Waterways Authority of India (IWAI) under the Ministry of Shipping. Finally, an expenditure of about Rs 5000 was incurred by way of incurring additional annuity payments liabilities, largely for road projects.

The phenomenon of off-budget expenditure by excluding these from the computation of fiscal deficit continued in the next three financial years of 2018–19, 2019–20 and 2020–21.

The government issued special securities to PSBs of Rs 1,06,000 crore in financial year 2018–19 and another Rs 65,443 crore in financial year 2019–20. As per the revised estimates of financial year 2020–21, the government issued recapitalization bonds of Rs 20,000 crore to PSBs and proposes to issue another set of Rs 20,000 crore in 2021–22. While the recapitalization bonds of Rs 2,91,443 crore at the end of financial year 2021–22 (if the government sticks to budgeted amounts) would be part of the debt and liabilities of the Government of India, fiscal deficit would stand understated to the extent of issue of recapitalization bonds in the respective years. The government has also issued recapitalization bonds of EXIM Bank, IDBI Bank and IIFCL. The total amount of these bonds issued up to financial year 2019–20 was Rs 14,705 crore.

Loans of Rs 97,000 crore and Rs 1,10,000 crore were extended from NSSF to FCI for 2018–19 and 2019–20, respectively, making outstanding

NSSF loans to FCI rise to Rs 2,54,600 crore at the end of financial year 2019–20. FSBs of Rs 65,602 crore were issued in 2018–19 and Rs 22,006 crore in 2019–20. In 2020–21, FSBs of Rs 49,500 crore were proposed to be issued in the Budget estimates, which was reduced to Rs 31,459 crore in the revised estimates.

NSSF had become a large off-budget vehicle. As on 31 March 2019, net accumulated inflows/deposits in NSSF were in the order of Rs 15.02 lakh crore. The investment in Central government securities was Rs 6.09 lakh crore, in state government securities Rs 4.71 lakh crore and in public agencies Rs 2.72 lakh crore, aggregating Rs 13.52 lakh crore. There were accumulated losses/shortfall of Rs 1.14 lakh crore and a cash balance of Rs 0.36 lakh crore. The largest component of NSSF investment in public agencies—Rs 1.91 lakh crore out of Rs 2.72 lakh crore—was loan to FCI in lieu of payment of food subsidy.

This arrangement allowed the government to exclude revenue expenditures of Rs 1.91 lakh crore from its expenditures, fiscal deficit and debt and liabilities numbers. The practice to shove food subsidy off-budget is continuing. Loans from NSSF to FCI increased to Rs 2.55 lakh crore (by Rs 64,000 crore) in 2019–20 (revised estimates) and Rs 3.23 lakh crore (by Rs 68,000 crore) in 2020–21 (Budget estimates). The majority of other loans from NSSF are also in the nature of government expenditure and liabilities of the government. Loans to NHAI (which has no revenue to service the loans; toll receipts are accounted for as non-tax receipts of the government), Air India and the Building Materials and Technology Promotion Council (BMTPC) for affordable housing subsidies are all real liabilities of the government.

Government Vows to Clean Up Off-Budget Borrowings

After highlighting the efforts of the government in improving disclosures for off-budget borrowings in previous budgets, the finance minister, in her Budget Speech 2021–22, proposed 'to discontinue the NSSF loan to FCI for food subsidy'. This marked the winding down of the harmful practice initiated in financial year 2016–17.

In Annexure VI of the Budget Speech 2021–22, the details of extra-budgetary resources, commonly called off-budget borrowings, included lesser issuance of FSBs (Rs 31,459 crore in RE2020–21 against

Rs 49,500 crore planned in BE20–21—actual in 2019–20 only Rs 22,006 crore) and lesser lending from NSSF to fund the revenue expenditure of the government (Rs 94,636 crore in RE20–21 against planned Rs 1,36,600 in BE20–21).

As no issuance of FSBs was proposed for financial year 2021–22, this meant discontinuation of this mode of raising off-budget borrowing, initiated for the first time in India's fiscal management armoury and vocabulary in 2016–17. The Annexure also stated that funding from NSSF would be reduced to only Rs 30,000 crore in financial year 2021–22.

The off-budget expenditure of Rs 94,636 crore (as given in the Annexure to the Budget Speech) through NSSF in RE20–21 comprises two items: Rs 84,636 crore to FCI for food subsidy and Rs 10,000 crore to BMTPC, a special purpose vehicle (SPV) under the Ministry of Urban and Housing Affairs, for affordable housing subsidies.

Separately, the government revised the allocation for food subsidy to FCI (from Rs 77,983 crore in BE20–21 to Rs 3,44,077 crore in RE20–21) and for decentralized procurement (from Rs 37,337 crore in BE20–21 to Rs 78,338 crore in RE20–21). Taking all the provisions of food subsidy made in NSSF and the demands of the Department of Food and Public Distribution, the government enhanced the provision from Rs 2,51,920 crore in BE20–21 to Rs 5,07,051 crore in RE20–21, recording an increased food subsidy provision of Rs 2,55,131 crore. For financial year 2021–22, budget provision of Rs 2,42,616 crore has been provided for food subsidy.

The NSSF accounts presented further details about the loan payment from NSSF to FCI for food subsidy and the repayment of the NSSF loan. There was an opening balance of outstanding loans from NSSF to FCI for food subsidy of Rs 2,54,600 crore as on 1 April 2020. Further loans of Rs 84,636 crore were provided for in RE20–21 and repayments of Rs 2,20,524 crore were also included in the NSSF accounts. This would leave a balance of NSSF loans to FCI of Rs 1,18,712 lakh crore at the end of financial year 2020–21. Collation of this information available in NSSF accounts suggests that Rs 55,000 crore would be repaid in 2021–22, which would leave a balance Rs 63,712 crore, to be repaid in 2022–23 or after.

Putting together all these pieces of information reveals that the government provided an amount of Rs 2,42,616 crore in BE21–22 for food subsidy as revenue expenditure in the demands of the Department of Food and Public Distribution. There is no provision for payment of any food subsidy to FCI in the NSSF estimates for 2021–22 but there is a provision for repayment of Rs 55,000 crore. Therefore, the estimated food subsidy for 2021–22 is Rs 1,87,616 crore.

The estimated food subsidy bill for 2020–21 is the amount of food subsidy provision in the RE budget of the Department of Food and Public Distribution minus the net repayment from FCI in the NSSF accounts. As the NSSF accounts record repayment by FCI of Rs 2,20,524 crore and disbursement of Rs 84,636 crore, the net repayment to NSSF for food subsidy is Rs 1,35,888 crore. As the total food subsidy provision in the RE budget of the Department of Food and Public Distribution is Rs 4,22,415 crore (Rs 3,44,077 crore for FCI and Rs 78,338 crore for decentralized procurement), the estimated food subsidy bill of 2020–21 works out to Rs 2,86,527 crore. The government provided for clearing the outstanding NSSF food subsidy loan of Rs 2,54,600 crore in the beginning of 2020–21 by repaying net Rs 1,35,888 crore in 2020–21, Rs 55,000 crore in 2021–22 and the remaining Rs 63,712 crore in 2022–23 or later.

With the government providing for the full food subsidy bill of Rs 2,86,527 crore for 2020–21 and Rs 2,42,616 crore for 2021–22 and beginning the process of repaying outstanding NSSF loans to FCI, it turned a new leaf in the transparent payment of food subsidy expenditure. Further, while it was expected to take two more years (2021–22 and 2022–23) to clear off past food subsidy obligations, the government did clear the NSSF liabilities budgeted to be cleared in 2021–22 in financial year 2020–21 itself by taking advantage of higher taxation receipts in the last quarter of 2020–21. Let's hope India does not have to resort to the skulduggery of paying food subsidy bills by giving loans to FCI from NSSF again.

Is India's Debt a Big Reason to Worry?

India has high public debt among the emerging market and middle-income economies.

As per information provided in the Fiscal Monitor, published by the IMF, the public debt of the emerging market and middle-income countries at the end of calendar year 2019 was 54.3 per cent of their combined GDP. The public debt to GDP ratio of low-income developing countries was lower at 43.3 per cent. As advanced countries have much higher public debt to GDP ratio of 104.8 per cent, the global public debt to GDP ratio in 2019 was 83.5 per cent.

India's public debt to GDP ratio in the year 2019 was 73 per cent. It was the highest among the major emerging market and middle-income countries, only after Brazil, which had a higher ratio of 87.7 per cent. Brazil's ratio includes the public debt owed by the general government and also other firms in the non-financial sector. The ratio of public debt to GDP for China was 56.5 per cent; for Indonesia, it was only 30.6 per cent. While the emerging market and middle-income countries of Europe had a combined public debt to GDP ratio of only 28.7 per cent, Turkey's ratio was 31.7 per cent. In the low-income developing country space also, Nigeria's public debt to GDP ratio was only 29.1 per cent and that of Bangladesh 35.7 per cent.

The Budget 2021–22 informs that the Central government's total debt and liabilities were estimated at Rs 102.47 lakh crore at the end of year 2019–20. The revised estimates of the total debt and liabilities for the year 2020–21 were placed at Rs 121.22 lakh crore and the budget estimates for 2021–22 at Rs 135.87 lakh crore. A press release on India's GDP in May 2021 placed India's GDP, in current prices, for 2019–20 at Rs 203.5 lakh crore and for 2020–21 at Rs 197.5 lakh crore. If India's nominal GDP grows by 12 per cent in 2021–22, it is likely to be around Rs 221.2 lakh crore. This results in the debt to GDP ratio of Central government debt and liabilities to be 50.4 per cent for the year 2019–20, 61.4 per cent for the year 2020–21 and almost the same 61.3 per cent in 2021–22.

Total liabilities of the Central government were Rs 4.27 lakh crore in 1991–92, as per the data in the *Handbook of Statistics on Indian Economy*, published by RBI. These liabilities rose to Rs 114.4 lakh crore in 2019–20. Total liabilities of the state governments were Rs 1.28 lakh crore in 1990–91. These reached Rs 52.58 lakh crore by 2019–20. The combined liabilities of the Centre and states were Rs 5.58 lakh crore in 1991–92, which rose to Rs 146.90 lakh crore in 2019–20. The Central government's liabilities rose by about twenty-seven times during this period, state governments' liabilities rose by about forty-one times and combined liabilities rose by twenty-six times. The combined liabilities are after cancelling the loans from the Centre to the States.

Central government debt and liabilities have been rising mostly in double digits during the past three decades, with a rise of under 10 per cent limited to only three out of twenty-nine years. The lowest growth in debt and liabilities was recorded in 2016–17 (7.42 per cent) and the highest in 2001–02 (15.62 per cent).

India's GDP has also been rising at a fair pace since 1991–92. IMF data indicates that India's general government gross debt to GDP ratio was 68.3 per cent in 2011. This ratio came down to 66.8 per cent in 2014, declining in all the three years in between. It then started rising to reach 69.6 per cent in 2018 and 72.3 per cent in 2019. Taking into account the impact of COVID-19 on GDP contraction and rise in public expenditures, the IMF projects the ratio to shoot up to 89.3 per cent in 2020, rise to 89.9 per cent in 2021 and then stabilize around this level till 2025.

Is Borrowing for Capital Expenditure Intrinsically Good?

In 2019–20, the government had budgeted a fiscal deficit of Rs 7,03,760 crore while capital expenditure budgeted was only Rs 3,38,569 crore. This is only about 48 per cent of the fiscal deficit. As fiscal deficit represents borrowing, more than half the borrowings, even in terms of budgeting, were spent on consumption expenditure. The situation was similar in 2018–19. Less than half the borrowings were intended to be used for capital expenditure. The actual position is still worse. In 2017–18, the actual amount spent on capital expenditure was Rs 2,63,140 crore of the fiscal deficit of Rs 5,91,062 crore, just 44.5 per cent.

What exactly constitutes capital expenditure of the Government of India? The largest item of capital expenditure in Budget 2019–20 was the provision of Rs 1.03 lakh crore for defence expenditure. While weapons and other means of warfare are extremely important for national security, they don't raise the productive capacity of the economy. This expenditure is a little less than one-third of the entire capital expenditure. There were funds budgeted for supporting infrastructure construction by government agencies. For instance, equity contribution for metro projects (Rs 17.7 thousand crore), capital contribution to the Railways (Rs 65.8 thousand crore), capital works of national highways (Rs 36.7 thousand crore) and other roadworks of MoRTH (Rs 35.4 thousand crore) fall in this category and certainly appeared quite justified. The capital outlay of Rs 21.01 lakh crore budgeted for Nuclear Corporation (Rs 3000 crore), FCI (Rs 1000 crore), investments in multilateral financial institutions (Rs 5500 crore), other financial institutions like NIIF (Rs 4000 crore), construction of police housing (Rs 1900 crore under Police Research) and for contribution of Rs 12.60 crore to CPSEs was partly for the creation of productive economic capacity and partly to support current operations.

Capital expenditure under the two broad heads of 'Establishment' (Rs 7.5 thousand crore) and 'Other Transfers' (Rs 7.5 thousand crore) were entirely meant for assistance provided by the Centre to the states, mostly North-eastern and other Himalayan states for aid/establishment support. Therefore, only a little more than half the expenditure budgeted as capital expenditure was actually capital expenditure.

Does Fiscal Deficit End Up Only Financing Massive Interest Payments?

The Government of India, on its own account, is a very large debt issuer. A large stock of debt securities have now been built with its total debt and liabilities exceeding 45 per cent of GDP. A large pre-emption of savings and credit created in the economy by the government leads to high interest rates. All this has led the interest expenditure of the government to balloon. The government classifies interest payments in five broad heads: internal debt, external debt, provident funds and other specific accounts in the Public Account, reserve funds, and other liabilities. Interest on internal debt constitutes the bulk of interest payments today. In 2017–18, interest on internal debt amounted to Rs 4,87,527 crore, which was 89.71 per cent of total interest paid (Rs 5,43,404 crore). Interest on market loans (the usual dated long-term market securities issued by the government) amounted to Rs 4,04,132 crore (74.37 per cent of total interest paid). Interest on external debt is quite small as such loans on the Government of India account are stabilized and will decline going forward. An amount of only Rs 5951 crore was paid on this account. As provident fund deposits grow at a steady rate, interest payments under this head are also small and growing slowly. In 2017–18, these amounted to Rs 33,135 crore, a negative growth rate of 2.48 per cent over 2016–17. The government usually earns some money as premium on government securities issued. Likewise, it also earns some interest on market loans. Finance and Accounts place this income on the revenue side, whereas the Budget papers and analytical reports display the interest payment net of these incomes. In 2017–18, such net receipts were about Rs 14,755 crore, which put the net interest expenditure at around Rs 5,28,600 crore.

Interest on 'other obligations' actually represents the result of the bypass on fiscal deficit financing attempted from time to time by the government. Interest paid on this head in 2017–18 was Rs 15,975 crore. This included interest on petroleum bonds (Rs 9583 crore), special securities issued to FCI (Rs 1319 crore), OMCs (Rs 407 crore), bonds issued to fertilizer companies (Rs 1174 crore) and interest paid to SBI for the government bonds subscribed to by SBI to enable the Government of India to invest in the rights issue of SBI (Rs 835 crore). Almost all these obligations were taken on by the UPA government between 2004–05 and 2012–13. The NDA government has also resorted to this route to recapitalize the PSBs and other financial institutions like EXIM Bank and IIFCL. These bonds were first issued in 2017–18. The first interest obligations for them came up for payment in 2018–19. As further bonds were issued in 2018–19 and 2019–20, and by then the amount of bonds issued exceeded Rs 2,15,000 crore, interest payment on these obligations exceeded the entire interest payment made in 2017–18 in this head.

In 2017–18, interest payment at Rs 5,28,900 crore of the total budgetary expenditure of the government of Rs 21,41,973 crore was 24.6 per cent of total expenditure. This saw a minor decline in 2018–19 according to the provisional numbers released. This year, net interest payments amounted to Rs 5,82,675 crore of a total expenditure of Rs 23,11,422 crore, exceeding 25 per cent of total expenditure.

Expenditure on interest payments is the largest head of payment and constitutes as much as about 25 per cent of the government's total expenditure. About a quarter of all the resources the government raises every year—tax, non-tax and debt taken together—only goes to service interest on the debt and liabilities undertaken in previous years. This is an extraordinary pre-emption of resources.

The combined expenditure of the Central government (actuals) in 2017–18 on interest payments (Rs 5,28,952 crore) and establishment

(Rs 4,73,031 crore) was Rs 10,01,983 crore, which turned out to be in excess of 45 per cent of the total expenditure of Rs 21,41,973 crore incurred. Whenever we talk about the ability of the Central government to adjust its expenditure, we need to remember that close to half its expenditure is beyond its control. It is the first charge on revenues and debt raised, and has to be paid.

The gargantuan burden of interest payment is a good enough reason to consider moderating fiscal deficit and debt overhang.

Is India's Credit Rating Affected by the Large Deficit and Debt Overhang?

Sovereign credit ratings are material in determining access to internal credit and the price at which such credit can become available to sovereign, sub-sovereign and private corporates. Indian corporates—in the public and private sectors—borrowed close to $30 billion in 2019 from international debt markets. The country has an investment-grade sovereign debt rating from all the major rating agencies. Sovereign credit rating works as the base of credit rating for corporations. No corporate from India can get a rating better than this.

Global market intelligence provider S&P uses two key measures while assessing the fiscal performance of the governments it rates. One relates to change in net general government debt as a percentage of GDP. This is nothing but fiscal deficit. On a scale of one to six, where one is assessed as the strongest and six the weakest, fiscal deficit of 0–1 per cent of the GDP gets a rating of one, fiscal deficit of 2–4 per cent gets a rating of three, and fiscal deficit of above 6 per cent gets a rating of six.

With respect to debt levels, keeping the cost of debt in consideration, S&P's matrix provides the highest ranking of one to a country with general government debt level of less than 30 per cent of GDP and cost of debt (effective interest) below 5 per cent. A country with general government debt level of 60–80 per cent with cost below 5 per cent gets a ranking of three and a country with the same level of debt but with cost of debt from 5–10 per cent gets a ranking of four. A country with debt level exceeding 100 per cent, with cost of debt below 5 per cent gets a ranking of five but with cost of debt higher than 5 per cent gets the worst ranking of six. Likewise, a country with 60–80 per cent debt level with cost of debt exceeding 15 per cent or a country with debt level of 89–100 per cent but cost of debt of 10 per cent or more gets a rating of six.

India performs quite poorly in both these metrics.

According to credit rating agency Moody's, fiscal strength is one of the three major rating parameters that determines a government's financial strength. India's financial strength has been rated consistently for quite some time at M+ level, i.e., medium strength. The biggest weakness in the metric of fiscal strength is a large debt burden. India's general government debt and liabilities (a little less than 70 per cent) are among the highest in comparably rated sovereigns. Deterioration in fiscal metrics is considered one of the largest negative credit events.

India's sovereign credit rating, upgraded in 2017–18, was brought back to the lowest investment grade by Moody's in June 2020–21. After the second wave of the pandemic hit India, Moody's has placed India's credit rating on a negative outlook on account of diminishing prospects of high growth and rising deficits and debt levels. While the Government of India still does not issue sovereign bonds to borrow in foreign currencies, a number of sub-sovereigns and private parties do. For these borrowers, India's sovereign rating acts as the ceiling. Their cost of borrowings are likely to rise notably if India's ratings were to be downgraded to non-investment category.

Chapter Forty

State of Public Expenditures

The Budget papers divide total expenditures into two broad divisions: the Centre's expenditure and transfers. The Centre's expenditure is made by the Central government ministries, departments and its organizations and bodies. Transfers are expenditures incurred by state governments, grant-in-aid institutions and bodies and organizations with independent legal structures.

The Centre's expenditure is broadly classified in three parts: establishment expenditure i.e., expenditure on salaries, pensions and other administrative expenditure; expenditure on central-sector schemes and projects; and expenditure classified as other central-sector expenditure, which includes investments in public-sector enterprises.

Expenditures treated as transfers also comprise three broad categories: expenditure on centrally sponsored schemes (CSSs), expenditure incurred on grants recommended by the Finance Commissions and expenditure classified as other grants/loans/transfers.

Budget 2019–20

The actual expenditures of the Government of India for financial year 2019–20, without counting the off-budget expenditure, were Rs 26.86 lakh crore. The expenditure on the revenue account was Rs 23.50 lakh crore and that on the capital account Rs 3.36 lakh crore. The first revised estimates of GDP at current prices for financial year 2019–20 are placed at Rs 203.51 lakh crore. India's Central government expenditure for the year 2019–20 was 13.2 per cent of GDP, revenue expenditures were 11.5 per cent and capital expenditure 1.7 per cent of GDP.

The Centre's expenditure, in total, was Rs 20.54 lakh crore. Establishment expenditure was Rs 5.70 crore, expenditure on central-sector schemes and projects was Rs 5.75 crore and other central-sector expenditure was Rs 7.27 lakh crore. Expenditure on interest is part of other central-sector expenditure; it was Rs 6.12 lakh crore in 2019–20.

Transfers included expenditure of Rs 3.10 lakh crore on CSSs, Rs 1.24 lakh crore on grants recommended by the Fourteenth Finance Commission and Rs 1.99 lakh crore on other grants, loans and transfers.

In terms of specific thematic heads of expenditures, the largest heads of expenditure were as follows. First, expenditure on interest payments: Rs 6.12 lakh crore. Second, expenditure on defence: Rs 3.19 lakh crore. Third, expenditure on subsidies: Rs 2.28 lakh crore, comprising food subsidy of Rs 1.09 lakh crore, fertilizer subsidy of Rs 0.81 lakh crore and petroleum subsidy of Rs 0.39 lakh crore. Fourth, expenditure on pensions: Rs 1.84 lakh crore. Fifth, expenditure on tax administration, including GST compensation transfers: Rs 1.54 lakh crore. Sixth, transfer to states: Rs 1.49 lakh crore. Seventh, expenditure on schemes of development departments: rural development Rs 1.42 lakh crore, agriculture and allied activities Rs 1.12 lakh crore, education Rs 0.89 lakh crore, energy Rs 0.44 lakh crore, urban development Rs 0.42 lakh crore, and so on.

In terms of expenditures on specific schemes, the largest scheme was the Mahatma Gandhi National Rural Employment Guarantee (MGNREG) scheme, with expenditure of Rs 71,687 crore. Other significantly large schemes included the Jal Jeevan/National Rural Drinking Water Mission (Rs 10,030 crore), National Education Mission (Rs 33,654 crore), National Health Mission (Rs 35,155 crore), Pradhan Mantri Awas Yojana, or PMAY (Rs 24,964 crore), Pradhan Mantri Gram Sadak Yojana, or PMGSY (Rs 14,017 crore), Integrated Child Development Scheme (Rs 22,032 crore), Crop Insurance Scheme (Rs 12,639 crore), interest subsidy to farmers for short-term credit (Rs 16,219 crore), Pradhan Mantri Kisan Samman Nidhi (Rs 48,714 crore), urea subsidy (Rs 54,755 crore), nutrient-based subsidy (Rs 26,369 crore), food subsidy to FCI under the National Food

Security Act (Rs 75,000 crore), food subsidy for decentralized procurement (Rs 33,508 crore), police infrastructure (Rs 18,162 crore) and support to NHAI (Rs 31,691 crore) and roadworks (Rs 46,292 crore).

Budget 2020–21

Government Planned for Expenditures of Rs 33.53 Lakh Crore

The Central government's budgeted expenditure for 2020–21, as approved by the Parliament, though without much discussion on account of the COVID-19 scare in March 2020, was Rs 30.42 lakh crore, or a little over $400 billion at Rs 75 to a dollar.

Estimated public expenditures of Rs 3.11 lakh crore were designated off-budget. Off-budget expenditures are effectively incurred from funds and vehicles outside the CFI.

Off-budget expenditure for 2020–21 included Rs 73,147 crore of net funding from NSSF, Rs 49,500 crore by way of issuance of FSBs outside the CFI by various government agencies, though fully serviced for interest and repayment by the Central government from the CFI; Rs 10,000 crore of recapitalization bonds for infrastructure from IIFCL, and Rs 1,78,121 crore of borrowings by three non-commercial organizations: Air India Asset Holdings (an SPV that houses Air India's debt taken over by the government), the Railways (for capital expenditure serviced from government revenue) and NHAI, which has no revenues worth its name to service the debt incurred from toll revenues.

Budgeted expenditures amount to about 15 per cent of India's estimated pre-COVID-19 GDP for 2020–21 of Rs 210 lakh crore. Inclusive of off-budget expenditure, the Central government's public expenditure for 2020–21 was estimated to be in the order of Rs 33.53 lakh crore or a little less than $450 billion, which makes up 16.5 per cent of GDP.

Budget 2020–21 Started Unravelling Even Before the Year Began

Even before financial year 2020–21 commenced, COVID-19 struck India. The government imposed a complete lockdown in the last week of March 2020. With all businesses and factories shut down, the economy went into a tailspin.

Budget 2020–21 started falling apart even before financial year 2020–21 actually began. The lockdown imposed in the last week of March 2020 struck a massive blow to people, the economy and the Budget. Both sides of the Budget—revenues and expenditures—started unravelling right at the start of the financial year.

There was no provision for the Rs 1.7 lakh crore Atmanirbhar Bharat package announced on 26 March in the 2020–21 budget. The measures announced entailed an additional expenditure of about Rs 75,000–80,000 crore beyond what was budgeted.

As the government did not want fiscal expenditures to go out of control, it opted for strategies to cut down some budgeted expenditures or undertake expenditure commitments such that the actual outgo was postponed for later.

The government had to take emergency measures to support people's livelihood, putting growth objectives in the background. Revenue estimates were feared to fall very badly. The government decided to enhance the borrowings programme by over Rs 4 lakh crore.

Government Clamped Down on Expenditure on 8 April

The Ministry of Finance issued instructions on 8 April 2020, citing the stressed cash position in the first quarter, to regulate and control government expenditure. For the purpose of expenditure control, the ministries and departments of the Central government were placed in three categories, without specifying the rationale of the classification. No quantification of expected savings was explained either. In addition, large expenditures require prior clearance of the Ministry of Finance. No specific item of expenditure to be cut was specified in the order. It was left to the ministries and departments concerned.

Category A included seventeen demands. The ministries and departments controlling these demands were exempted from any cut. This category included apex institutions of the state like the President and the Supreme Court; the primarily rural-focused departments of Rural Development, Agriculture and Food and Public Distribution; departments engaged in delivering health services like the Department of Health, Ayush and Health Research; mandatory expenditures like interest payments; and some economic ministries and departments like Textiles,

Civil Aviation and Pharmaceuticals. These seventeen demands had a budgeted expenditure of Rs 14.38 lakh crore, or 46.62 per cent of the total budget expenditure of Rs 30.42 lakh crore.

Category B included thirty-one demands. This category was subjected to limiting first quarter expenditure to 20 per cent with a further condition that expenditure would not exceed 8 per cent in any single month. This category included most departments that discharge sovereign functions, including public goods functions. Demands controlled by the ministries of Home Affairs, Police, Defence, Cabinet and Union Territories fall in this category. Three important economic and infrastructure ministries and departments fall in this category as well: Road Transport and Highways, Petroleum and Natural Gas, and Fertilizers. Budgeted expenditure for 2020–21 in this category was Rs 11.45 lakh crore, or 37.14 per cent of budgeted expenditure.

Category C had the maximum number of fifty-two demands. This category included most economic, infrastructure and social development ministries and departments but were subjected to the minimum ceiling of total expenditure of 15 per cent of the annual budget in the first quarter, with expenditure in any single month not exceeding 5 per cent. The ministries and departments directly concerning labour and small businesses like Labour and Employment, Skill Development and Entrepreneurship and MSMEs are also part of this group. Budgeted expenditure for 2020–21 in this category amounted to only Rs 5.01 lakh crore, or 16.24 per cent.

Of the budgeted discretionary expenditure of Rs 30.42 lakh crore for financial year 2020–21, a budget of only Rs 14.39 lakh crore was of a discretionary nature; the rest being of a mandatory nature like interest, establishment expenditure, etc. Discretionary expenditure under Category B was Rs 4.69 lakh crore and under Category C Rs 4.50 lakh crore. As only categories B and C were subjected to cuts, the ministries and departments controlling eighty-three of the 100 demands actually had only Rs 9.19 lakh crore of discretionary budget to achieve their targeted cuts. Most of these discretionary expenditures were growth-oriented; the axe fell hardest on these.

The 8 April order remained in force during the entire first half of the financial year.

Government's Contractionary Stance Post COVID-19 Worked in First Half 2020–21

The Central government has been able to spend about 25–30 per cent of annual Budget expenditure in the first quarter since 2017–18, the year when the Budget was presented on 1 February for the first time. At a rate of 30 per cent, actual expenditure in the first quarter would have been Rs 9.25 lakh crore; at 25 per cent, it would have been Rs 7.60 lakh crore. If the ministries and departments in the B and C categories were able to limit their expenditures to 20 per cent and 15 per cent, respectively, as mandated, the total expenditure in the first quarter would have been only Rs 7.35 lakh crore.

The expenditure restrictions imposed by the government on 8 April worked, but only to a certain extent. According to numbers released by the Controller General of Accounts (CGA) on 29 July 2020, actual expenditure for the first quarter came to Rs 8.16 lakh crore, which at 27 per cent, was lower than the normative 30 per cent. This was despite the government releasing additional funds for health and other required expenditures to deal with the pandemic.

The growth slump on account of COVID-19 and the lockdown led to more than 10 crore workers losing their jobs and growth contracting by over 15 per cent in the first half of the financial year. There was persistent demand for fiscal stimulus to address the misery of workers and help small businesses revive. The government, however, remained steadfastly tight-fisted in the first half. Perhaps it was more worried about inflation, which was rising on account of supply disruptions.

As a result of the contractionary policies pursued by the government, total expenditure at the end of September 2020 was only Rs 14.79 lakh crore, which was lower than the expenditure in the first half of financial year 2019–20 of Rs 14.89 lakh crore, even in absolute numbers.

Government Started Talking about Expanding Expenditure from October 2020

In October, the government signalled its intention to loosen up the purse strings, the impact of which was visible from November. Total expenditure in November and December—Rs 6.18 lakh crore—exceeded total expenditure of Rs 4.55 lakh crore the previous year.

Despite this, the Government of India's total expenditure (Rs 22.8 lakh crore) in nine months was 74.9 per cent of BE–21 (Rs 30.4 lakh crore). This was marginally less than the expenditure of 75.7 per cent incurred in first nine months of the year 2019–20. Both revenue expenditure and capital expenditure were quite close to the expenditure levels of the previous year.

There was, however, a distortion in capital expenditure. The government had disbursed Rs 0.84 lakh crore as loans against disbursement of only Rs 0.21 lakh crore last year. These loans, given to the Railways and the states, were exceptional and meant to cover revenue expenditures, and therefore not the Centre's real capital expenditure. Excluding these loans, the Centre's capital expenditure was only Rs 2.25 lakh crore (54.5 per cent) in the first nine months, which was lower than the Rs 2.34 lakh crore incurred the previous year.

Expenditures in Revised Estimates 2020–21 Jumped to Rs 34.50 Lakh Crore

Revised estimates placed as part of Budget 2021–22 heralded a big jump in expenditures. Total budgeted expenditure went up from Rs 30.42 lakh crore in budget estimates to Rs 34.50 lakh crore in revised estimates, recording an increase of Rs 4.08 lakh crore.

Revenue expenditure estimates were revised to Rs 30.11 lakh crore against the budget estimate of Rs 26.30 lakh crore. While there was an increase in capital expenditure estimates as well (from Rs 4.12 lakh crore in the budget estimates to Rs 4.39 lakh crore in revised estimates; at 6.55 per cent), the increase in revenue expenditure of Rs 3.71 lakh crore was much higher at 14.1 per cent.

Major Window-Dressing in Capital Expenditure

The government gave a loan from the general revenues to the Railways (both the accounts are otherwise part of the same CFI) of Rs 89,000 crore for covering revenue losses on account of COVID-19 and the lockdown. Excluding this window-dressing, there was a net decrease of Rs 58,000 crore in the capital expenditure in the revised estimates.

The Ministry of Railways had a capital expenditure provision of Rs 70,000 crore in BE20–21. In the revised estimates, it went up to Rs 1,08,398 crore which, on the face of it, is a decent increase of Rs 38,398 crore. A closer scrutiny of capital expenditure of the Railways for financial year 2020–21, however, revealed large revenue expenditure disguised as capital expenditure.

Capital expenditure, under all the regular heads of the Railways for 2020–21, has heavily underperformed during the year. Capex for the construction of new lines has reduced from Rs 12,000 crore to only Rs 929 crore, for gauge conversion from Rs 2250 crore to merely Rs 26 crore, for rolling stock from Rs 5787 crore to Rs 2004 crore, for track renewals from Rs 10,599 crore to nil, and so on. However, the government from the General Budget gave a 'Special Loan for Covid-Related Resource Gap' of Rs 79,398 crore to the Railways to provide liquidity support to meet its losses in the current year and also for 'liquidating adverse balance in the public account' of the Railways for the year 2019–20.

If the 'capital expenditure' of 'Special Loan for Covid-Related Resource Gap', is eliminated from capital expenditure, the actual capital expenditure of Railways for financial year 2020–21 comes down to only Rs 29,000 crore. Railways infrastructure from government support got reduced from Rs 70,000 crore from the Budget to Rs 29,000 crore in the revised estimates. Railways' expenditure reduction, effectively, was the largest contributing reduction to the capital expenditure.

Increased Expenditure of Rs 4.08 Lakh Crore Was Not Really an Increase

There are quite a few adjustment entries in the revised expenditure budget of financial year 2020–21. To highlight a few:

First, the government will be repaying Rs 1,35,888 crore to NSSF in financial year 2020–21 by using the excess inflows in the NSSF account. FCI owes this amount to NSSF having taken the loans in previous years in lieu of due food subsidy. The government uses surplus cash in NSSF either by issuing special securities to NSSF or by using it as a cash balance as NSSF accounts are in the Public Account. The government will provide budgetary funds to FCI to repay NSSF and, in turn, issue special securities to NSSF to receive back the payments made by FCI to NSSF. The whole transaction would amount to no real expenditure but will transform the accounting entries.

Second, the government had also increased the food subsidy payment for the current year by providing for full subsidy due of Rs 2.87 lakh crore, whereas budget estimates were only Rs 1.09 lakh crore earlier. The rest of the food subsidy was to be paid through NSSF. As per the provisions made in the revised estimates, the entire food subsidy for 2020–21 of Rs 2.87 lakh crore will be paid through the Budget. This increases government expenditure by about Rs 1.8 lakh crore, though there is no effective increase in overall expenditure on the food subsidy account.

Third, the entry of Rs 89,000 crore in case of the Railways is only an accounting treatment. It amounted to no real expenditure.

Likewise, the arrears of fertilizer subsidy cleared and many other such items make their contribution to show that expenditure would be going up by Rs 4.08 lakh crore, though effectively there is little expenditure going up.

Budget 2021–22

Budget 2021–22 is Smaller than RE2020–21

Total expenditure through the Budget of the Government of India in RE20–21 is Rs 34.50 lakh crore. Total expenditure through the Budget for BE21–22 is Rs 34.83 lakh crore. It represents an increase of Rs 33,000 crore in Budget expenditure. As there are no off-budget public expenditures proposed either in the RE20–21 or the BE21–22, the door-to-door increase in the budgetary outlay for 2021–22 over RE2020–21 amounts to a princely 96 per cent. This certainly is no budgetary expenditure push.

Public expenditure through resources of public enterprises is Rs 6.45 lakh crore in RE20–21 and Rs 5.83 lakh crore in BE21–22. There is a reduction of Rs 62,000 crore in the resources of public enterprises for the year 2021–22, which largely represents capital expenditure through the public sector and public authorities. This reduction amounts to 9.6 per cent.

Total Central government expenditure through budgetary resources and the resources of public enterprises is slated to go down from Rs 40.96 lakh crore in RE20–21 to Rs 40.66 lakh crore in BE21–22, which represents an absolute decrease in the nominal levels of expenditure. It is no comfort that the reduction is less than 1 per cent.

At the aggregate level, there is no planned/budgeted fiscal expansion in 2021–22.

Capital Expenditure in Budget 2021–22

In her Budget speech, the finance minister highlighted a massive increase in the capital expenditure budget estimates of year 2021–22 by comparing it with the budget estimates of the year 2020–21. She claimed that the capital expenditure in the 2021–22 Budget had expanded to Rs 5.54 lakh crore from Rs 4.12 lakh crore in the budget estimates of 2020–21, recording a jump of 34.5 per cent!

Capital expenditures increased from Rs 4.12 lakh crore in BE20–21 to Rs 4.39 lakh crore in RE20–21 and to Rs 5.54 lakh crore in BE21–22. Increase in BE21–22 over RE20–21 is Rs 1.15 lakh crore, which is also an impressive increase of 26.2 per cent! As overall, budget expenditure has gone up by only Rs 33,000 crore, in terms of overall fiscal expansion, this implies a corresponding reduction in demand push represented by revenue expenditure as overall expenditures are not rising.

Considering that capital expenditure is assumed to be better expenditure than revenue, it is necessary to see where the capital investment push has been directed.

Major increases have been provided for in the budget of MoRTH (from Rs 92,051 crore in RE20–21 to Rs 1,08,230 crore), Ministry of Housing and Urban Affairs (from Rs 10,309 crore to Rs 25,759 crore), Department of Financial Services (from Rs 13,650 crore to Rs 25,800 crore) and the Department of Economic Affairs (from Rs 17,943 crore to Rs 56,607 crore). For the Railways, which has a very large capital budget, there is no increase as Rs 1,07,100 crore has been budgeted against RE of Rs 1,08,398 crore. Likewise, the capital outlay of the Defence Services has also seen marginal increase (from Rs 1,34,510 crore to Rs 1,35,071 crore).

Almost the entire increase of Rs 1.15 lakh crore in the capex of BE21–22 over RE20–21 is accounted for by four large provisions. Rs 20,000 crore has been provided for investing as equity in the proposed new DFI (development finance institution) in the budget of the Department of Financial Services. A lumpsum provision of Rs 44,715 crore has been made under the Department of Economic Affairs to support the infrastructure pipeline. Provision of Rs 20,490 crore has been made under DOT in the name of support to PSUs. A provision of Rs 18,998 crore for metro projects (against Rs 6484 crore in RE20–21) has been made in the budget of Ministry of Housing and Urban Affairs. There is also an increase of Rs 16,173 crore for NHAI and other roadworks in BE20–21 of MoRTH. Together, these four heads account for an increase of Rs 1,01,378 crore out of a total increase of Rs 1,15,073 crore in the capex budget of BE20–21 over RE20–21, a share of over 88 per cent.

Chapter Forty-One

Assessing 'Policy' in India's Expenditures

The purpose of government expenditures and economic policymaking is almost always three-fold: deliver public goods and services; stimulate growth and even out economic cycles; and redistribute wealth and incomes. These expenditures reveal the economic policy of the government. The government also incurs considerable expenditure that serves none of these policy purposes, e.g., payment of interest and pensions. For assessing policy expenditures, it is necessary to identify the total policy expenditure in the Budget, classify the total policy expenditure into these three broad categories and then assess whether the expenditures in any particular year are in line with the policy imperatives of that year.

Government accounts and budgets are presented in a highly straitjacketed manner in myriad heads and subheads. Expenditures are also not classified and presented in policy expenditure and non-policy or maintenance expenditures. The Central government presents its expenditures in four broad categories: central-sector schemes, Centrally Sponsored Schemes or CSSs, other central expenditures and transfers. All the four broad categories may have any of all the three types of policy expenditures and also purely maintenance expenditures. The government secures the approval of the Parliament for incurring expenditures under roughly 100 grants. Making sense of government expenditures from the policy perspective requires looking at each and every line item presented in these four broad categories and under 100-odd grants.

Centre's Discretionary Expenditure is Less than Half Its Budgeted Expenditure

More than half of India's budgeted expenditure is of a non-discretionary or mandatory nature. The Central government has virtually no discretion or control to reduce or enhance it to deal with the economic cycle or effect better redistribution.

Such non-policy and non-discretionary expenditures include four broad types of expenditures in Budget 2020–21: salaries, pensions and the rest of establishment expenditure (Rs 6.10 lakh crore); interest payments on debt and other fiscal liabilities of the government (Rs 7.08 lakh crore); grants to the states mandated by the Finance Commission, including disaster-relief and local bodies grants (Rs 1.50 lakh crore); and GST compensation (Rs 1.35 lakh crore). These four items added up to Rs 16.03 lakh crore in Budget 2020–21, which was 52.69 per cent of total budgeted expenditures of Rs 30.4 lakh crore.

A good part of such non-policy or mandatory type of expenditure is outrightly unproductive as well. Of Rs 30.42 lakh crore of Budget expenditure in 2020–21, as much as Rs 9.03 lakh crore (30 per cent) is unproductive in nature and therefore does not serve any public purpose in the present. Such unproductive expenditures included provision for interest payments (Rs 7.08 lakh crore) and pensions (Rs 1.34 lakh crore defence pension and Rs 0.61 lakh crore civilian pension).

Total outlays of Rs 14.39 lakh crore (47.31 per cent) in Budget 2020–21, intended to be spent on four kinds of development and non-development schemes and services, was in control of the Central government and thus could be considered discretionary expenditure of the Centre that could be spent on the three broad policy-based expenditures in the year 2020–21 (public services, growth and redistribution).

First, the central-sector schemes directly implemented by the ministries and departments of the Central government (Rs 8.31 lakh crore in Budget 2020–21). This expenditure also accounted for most of the capital expenditure, subsidies and schemes directly implemented by the Centre.

Second, budget for the CSSs (Rs 3.40 lakh crore), which provide grants to state governments to undertake schemes of delivering public services like health and education, growth like MGNREGA and redistribution like old-age pension and food security scheme. CSSs finance subjects reserved constitutionally for states.

Third, 'other central expenditure' (Rs 1.80 lakh crore of a budgeted Rs 8.88 lakh crore after excluding interest payments) provided for expenditures incurred though agencies like University Grants Commission (UGC) and investment made in and other assistance provided to PSUs, like equity support to BSNL.

Fourth, 'other transfers' (Rs 0.88 lakh crore) basically accounted for transfer of loans and discretionary grants to state governments.

Some of these formally discretionary expenditures also tend to be non-discretionary in practice. For example, the central-sector schemes included capital outlay for Defence of Rs 1.14 lakh crore. Such expenditures are hardly effective from the economic and social policy perspective. However, taking into account the fact that such expenditures also result in production and purchase of goods and services, these could be treated as part of policy-oriented expenditures.

Policy Expenditures in Budget 2020–21

All Central government discretionary expenditures and some part of non-discretionary expenditures incurred through state governments, like the Finance Commission grants, etc., make up the policy expenditures in Budget 2020–21. Thus, policy expenditures are larger than the discretionary expenditures of the Central government.

The Central government Budget allocated Rs 6.88 lakh crore (23 per cent) of expenditure to deliver public goods and services (about one-fourth of the total budget). Most of it was on the budget. Including off-budget expenditure, public goods and services expenditure allocation amounted to Rs 6.96 lakh crore in 2020–21. Outlays for public goods and services were spread over about sixty of the 100 demands.

The expenditure on Defence constituted the largest chunk of expenditure on public goods and services. There was an allocation of Rs 2.09 lakh crore in Demand No. 19, Defence Services, though this is essentially revenue expenditure to cover salaries and other establishment expenditure of the Armed Forces. The demand head, Capital Outlay on Defence (No. 20), also had a substantial allocation of Rs 1.33 lakh crore, which also falls in the public goods category. Police (No. 48) had an allocation of Rs 1.05 lakh crore. The Ministry of Health's allocation of Rs 65,000 crore also comes into this category.

Redistribution expenditure at Rs 5.33 lakh crore was about one-fifth of the Budget. Including off-budget redistribution expenditure of Rs 1.13 lakh crore, total allocation for redistribution in Budget 2020–21 was Rs 6.46 lakh crore.

The Central government implements its redistribution function through hundreds of schemes delivering benefits in cash (direct cash transfer or wages) or in kind (education, skill development and so on) to households falling in the categories of destitute and poor.

The analysis of all the 100 demands revealed that the 2020–21 Budget allocated expenditures of Rs 5.33 lakh crore to various schemes and programmes that served the objective of redistribution. A big chunk of redistribution expenditure, like food subsidy payment through NSSF, had been shifted off-budget in Budget 2020–21.

Three demands with the largest redistribution allocations were Food and Public Distribution (No. 15; Rs 1.22 lakh crore), Rural Development (No. 85; Rs 1.2 lakh crore) and Agriculture (No. 1; Rs 0.77 lakh crore). Other significant demands include Women and Children's Development (No. 100; Rs 0.30 lakh crore), Petroleum and Natural Gas (No. 75; Rs 0.37 lakh crore; basically LPG subsidy) and School Education (No. 59; Rs 0.59 lakh crore).

An expenditure of Rs 6.06 lakh crore of the total budgeted expenditure of Rs 30.42 lakh crore, or about 20 per cent, can be considered growth-oriented.

The budgetary allocation of Rs 5.49 lakh crore for 2020–21 for what essentially amounted to private goods and services exceeded the total redistribution expenditure budget. A big part of off-budget expenditure— Rs 1.90 lakh crore—also comes into this category, making total public expenditure on provision of private goods and services Rs 7.39 lakh crore for 2020–21.

The largest allocations are in the transportation sector for Roads and Highways (No. 84; Rs 0.92 lakh crore), Railways (No. 83; Rs 0.72 lakh crore), and Housing and Urban Affairs (Rs 0.25 lakh crore; essentially for metros). There are also significant allocations under Fertilizers (No. 6; Rs 0.71 lakh crore), Telecommunications (No. 13; Rs 0.66 lakh crore) and Higher Education (No. 59; Rs 0.40 lakh crore).

Total budgeted expenditures of Rs 18.27 lakh crore (about 60 per cent of the budgeted expenditure of Rs 30.4 lakh crore) was thus policy-oriented in Budget 2020–21.

Growth-Oriented Expenditure in Budget 2020–21 Was Quite Small

The government can best support growth by maintaining macroeconomic stability and encouraging economic agents to build productive and competitive businesses to grow the GDP of the country. The government is not the best contributor to growth when it tries to engage in production of private goods and services itself.

The government currently runs hundreds of programmes to support the production of goods and services, which can broadly be considered growth-stimulating. One can consider government expenditures on agriculture, industries and services, investment in equity of public enterprises and development of backward and rural areas as growth-oriented expenditures, disregarding their effectiveness and productivity.

There should be a way for the government to classify its budget expenditures in four broad categories: stimulating growth, provision of public goods and services, redistribution and maintenance expenditure. All expenditures meant to cover past liabilities like interest and pensions should be classified as maintenance expenditure. The government Budgets, however, do not classify expenditures in such a manner. As a result, one has to sift through the maze of Budget papers and accounts to identify growth-oriented expenditures.

Expenditure on Infrastructure Made Up Bulk of Growth Expenditures but was Quite Static and Small

The Central government's total estimated expenditure on infrastructure for 2020–21 adds up to Rs 3,63,000 crore (roads Rs 1,46,975 crore; railways Rs 1,60,792 crore; metros and NCR suburban railways Rs 19,571 crore; Rs 22,050 crore lumpsum for the infrastructure pipeline;

and the rest on other smaller infrastructure heads). A striking feature is the preponderance of expenditure on physical transport infrastructure.

The budgeted expenditure on infrastructure for 2020–21 did not increase, even in nominal terms, over the budget expenditure of 2019–20. Railway capital expenditure was budgeted at Rs 1.60 lakh crore in 2019–20; in 2020–21, the amount was Rs 1.61 lakh crore, almost static. NHAI's internal and extra-budgetary capital expenditures (IEBR) were budgeted at Rs 75,000 crore in 2019–20. In 2020–21, they were scaled down to Rs 65,000 crore, effectively a reduction of Rs 10,000 crore. There was an increase from Rs 36,691 crore to Rs 42,500 crore in the budgeted expenditure for NHAI, which did not compensate for the lower IEBR. Together, NHAI's capital expenditure was budgeted to come down from Rs 1,11,691 crore budgeted in 2019–20 to Rs 1,07,500 crore in 2020–21, a net reduction of about Rs 4,200 crore. Non-NHAI roadwork expenditure was slated to go up moderately from Rs 45,880 crore in 2019–20 to Rs 48,759 crore in 2020–21. All considered, capital expenditure on roadworks was almost static, seeing no growth even in nominal terms. Expenditure on metro projects was also static in nominal terms, falling from Rs 17,714 crore in 2019–20 to Rs 17,482 crore in 2020–21.

Static or reduced budgets for all the heads of infrastructure, even in nominal terms, indicated that the government was not banking on any growth stimulus through infrastructure spending while formulating the Budget for 2020–21. The low level of budgeting for infrastructure expenditure appeared even more ironic when seen against the hype of the National Infrastructure Pipeline (NIP) of over Rs 111 lakh crore presented as a game changer to kickstart the economy. The proof of the pudding, as they say, is in the eating.

There are also major issues regarding the productivity of budgeted infrastructure expenditures. Budget-funded infrastructure projects take very long to complete and until these projects are commissioned and put to use, the cumulative expenditures incurred remain unproductive as they do not result in assisting in any production of goods or services. Despite spending so much on railway infrastructure (over Rs 1.5 lakh crore a year), the Railways is not able to complete projects as there are at least fifteen times larger unfinished projects. The value of finished projects in a year in case of the Railways has almost always been much lower than the capital expenditure incurred in that year. The Railways has doggedly refused to privatize its infrastructure operations. Consequently, there is no real investment in infrastructure by either foreign or domestic investors. Further, major freight infrastructure projects like the Delhi–Mumbai Industrial Corridor have been limping along for years.

There were no proposals and allocations in Budget 2020–21 for the troubled infrastructure sectors of the economy. Real estate, especially the residential segment, was suffering its worst slump—new projects were not being launched and older projects under construction for quite some years remained stalled in many cases. The real-estate sector is extremely important from the perspective of employment (surplus agricultural labour gets absorbed in construction work) and spin-off impact on several industries (cement, steel, etc.). The Budget did not have a single proposal to address the residential real-estate sector. No specific provision was made for even the Rs 10,000 crore to be provided to the Real Estate AIF, which was announced by the government a few months earlier to put stalled real-estate projects on track.

The roads sector had played a large supportive role in generating economic growth from 2015–2019, albeit using unsustainable financing models. This sector can be revived only after the issues pertaining to excessive cost of construction are addressed. The private sector will only come in after that. The Budget had no such reform proposal. As noted above, public-sector investment through NHAI and other government outfits for 2020–21 was at a slightly lower level, even in nominal terms. As a good part of the borrowing is now required to service debt already accumulated by NHAI, it appeared that actual government expenditure on roads in 2020–21 were about 25 per cent less than in 2019–20.

There was no proposal in Budget 2020–21 for other struggling infrastructure sectors like telecommunications and power either. For power, there was only an announcement regarding smart metering being pushed. The fundamental problem of the power sector is the gap between the cost of power to the state distribution companies and the revenues they collect. This gap is too large: over Rs 2 lakh crore a year. It has crippled state government finances as they provide over Rs 1 lakh crore of subsidies every year and is responsible for the DISCOMs not paying power generators regularly—an outstanding amount of over Rs 80,000 crore had accumulated on this account (this crossed Rs 1.4 lakh crore by the end of financial year 2020–21). Smart metering addresses a small part of the gap. But even for that, there was no additional provision in the Budget.

Agriculture Expenditure Continued the Old
Package of Interventions

The Government of India runs dozens of agriculture and food security-related programmes with an approximate budgeted outlay of Rs 3,50,000 crore. In addition, food subsidy expenditure of Rs 68,200 crore and irrigation works of Rs 5000 crore were proposed to be funded through NSSF. Total expenditure on agriculture-related programmes in Budget 2020–21 came to about Rs 4.23 lakh crore, about 24 per cent of the total discretionary expenditure of the government.

A large part of this expenditure, including Rs 75,000 crore of PM-Kisan and Rs 1,83,770 crore of food subsidy totalling Rs 3.29 lakh crore, essentially relates to redistribution. The remaining Rs 94,000 crore (including fertilizer subsidy) can be considered to be intended to stimulate agricultural growth. This expenditure is incurred through numerous (exceeding fifty) production and productivity-enhancing programmes, which are largely input-driven (seeds, fertilizer, loan, insurance, pesticides). There was no change in this large number of thinly funded agriculture development programmes for the year 2020–21.

Almost all these supposedly growth-stimulating programmes in the agriculture sector were designed in the 1970s and 1980s (they have been repackaged with different names over the past fifty years) to popularize the use of agriculture inputs and training and visit the technologies of the green revolution era. The job of popularizing these inputs was over a long time ago. In fact, there is now a problem of overuse of many inputs, like nitrogenous fertilizer (urea). These programmes have no real impact on productivity now.

As the Budget proposals for agriculture made no course correction, they were not expected to make any real difference to stimulating growth.

Expenditure for Promoting Industries and Services
Small and Thinly Spread

The Central government undertakes over 100 different programmes to promote industry and service businesses. Over seventy-five of these have a Budget provision exceeding Rs 100 crore for 2020–21. These programmes target a large spectrum of industries and services. The estimated cost works out to approximately Rs 55,000 crore, or 3.2 per cent of the government's total discretionary spend. These outlays did not see any notable increase in 2020–21 over 2019–20.

Most of these programmes focus on some kind of subsidization to small businesses and exporters to reduce cost of debt and incentivize employment. Indian industry faces the triple cost disadvantage of interest, tax and power tariff. Interest rates have to fall in general. Some minor interest cost subsidization is neither efficient nor easily administrable. The tax regime for service enterprises and existing manufacturing industries continues to be disadvantageous; though for new manufacturing it is now comparable to the best. More value added (in excess of 60 per cent) comes from services. There was no proposal to provide power to industries at competitive rates.

There does not appear to be any strategy to fire up the growth engines of the future. Through there are a few programmes to support sunrise sectors like start-ups, these are too few and far between. There is recognition that service enterprises will be the champions of the future and small allocations (mostly a token Rs 5 crore) were made in the budgets of quite a few ministries and departments. But these seem to be more lip service than a real effort to provide a launching pad for champion services.

Investments in Public Enterprises are Directed towards Loss-Making Entities

The equity investments proposed in Budget 2020–21 added up to a little over Rs 45,000 crore or 2.57 per cent of total discretionary expenditure. Loans of Rs 3237 crore were also proposed to be given to the Nuclear Power Corporation from the Budget.

A notable feature of equity investment proposals in public enterprises was the fact that much of it was meant for investing in sick and loss-making enterprises of the government. Equity infusion was proposed for weak financial enterprises of the government (IIFCL, EXIM Bank, insurance companies), sick service enterprises (BSNL and MTNL) and assistance-disbursing organizations like the SC and ST Corporations. Over Rs 23,500 crore was proposed to be invested in the equity of public-sector financial enterprises over and above the investment of over Rs 2,50,000 crore in the equity of PSBs in the previous three years.

All the financial enterprises of the government—banks, general insurance companies, infrastructure-financing bodies like IIFCL, export-promoting organizations like EXIM Bank—have been performing relatively poorly. Sinking such enormous equity in these companies, which are increasingly losing market share and proving unable to compete with private enterprises, amounted to throwing good money after bad.

The government's proposal to provide equity funding to BSNL and MTNL to pay for the cost of 4G licence was another instance of debasement of equity as a risk capital investment. There was no likelihood of BSNL and MTNL adding any significant number of customers, adding value or making profits. It made no sense for BSNL and MTNL to go in for a 4G licence and create a network in a super-competitive field.

It is time the government expeditiously exits areas where the private sector has already acquired more than 75 per cent market share (e.g., airlines, telecom) and plans a phased exit (may be over the next five to seven years) from businesses where the private sector has crossed or is steadily moving towards acquiring a 50 per cent market share (general insurance, banks), desisting from investing fresh capital in any such enterprise in the meantime.

The Budget proposals of investing Rs 45,000 crore in the equity of these enterprises appeared unlikely to give any noteworthy boost to growth.

The Centre Played Miser for Growth Expenditures after COVID-19 Struck

There were three main planks of the Centre's expenditure strategy after COVID-19 and the lockdown.

First, the government decided to offer food and cash assistance to the poor and most vulnerable. This strategic choice was reflected in the composition of the Garib Kalyan package announced by the finance minister on 26 March 2020, with 5 kg of free cereal and 1 kg of free pulses to all ration card holders (later extended to the migrant population without ration cards), free gas cylinder to the beneficiaries of the Ujjwala LPG scheme and Rs 500 in cash assistance per month to all Jan Dhan account holders. The package will cost the government about Rs 80,000 crore in additional expenditures for financial year 2020–21.

Second, the government undertook no fiscal-financed supply side or demand-side growth stimulus package in the first sixth months. The Atmanirbhar Bharat package announced in May 2020 reflected this grim reality. The principal component of this package was a credit provision to small businesses through banks that were directed to provide 'additional' credit of Rs 3 lakh crore to MSMEs, supported by a government guarantee. The government relied on RBI to do the heavy lifting by providing liquidity. RBI did announce a number of programmes to infuse additional liquidity of over Rs 12 lakh crore to enable banks, NBFCs and others to lend; the government to get more Ways and Means Advance (WMA), and the like. The government did announce increasing the size of existing funds and new funds for infrastructure, amounting to over Rs 2–3 lakh crore, for agriculture and allied sectors. However, these were not to have any immediate or even short-term impact as they were expected to be operationalized over many years. None of these measures cost the government anything in current expenditures.

Third, in fact, the government unwittingly took measures to curtail growth-oriented expenditures budgeted for 2020–21. Beginning with the order issued on 8 April 2020 asking several ministries and departments to limit their first quarter expenditure at 20 per cent and 15 per cent (as against the previous year's average of about 25 per cent), cuts were applied to growth-oriented expenditures as all other expenditures (interest, salaries and pensions, mandatory transfers) offered very little scope for reduction.

Contraction in GVA is Partly Owing to Effective Reduction in Government Expenditure on Growth

The sector of Public Administration, Defence and Other Services captures the contribution coming from the government budgets on growth. The GVA from this segment contributes about one-eighth of total GVA.

The GVA contribution of this group, as estimated by NSO, will be Rs 16.87 lakh crore (at constant 2011–12 prices) in financial year 2020–21 as against a contribution of Rs 17.59 lakh crore in the previous year, 2019–20. There is reduction of as much as Rs 0.74 lakh crore, which is 4.1 per cent in the GVA contribution of the year.

Even in a year of great contraction when governments are expected to play a large counter-cyclical role to restore macroeconomic stability and put the country back on the growth path, government expenditure effectively contracted in India with the government deciding not to play an expansionary role during the year.

Chapter Forty-Two

State of Tax and Non-Tax Revenues

State of Taxes

2019–20: Tax Revenue Estimates were Presented Twice

For financial year 2019–20, the Budget was presented twice. First, the interim Budget was presented on 1 February 2019. Later, when the NDA government had returned to power in the May 2019 elections, the regular Budget was presented on 5 July 2019.

Net tax revenues to the Centre (both direct and indirect taxes together after removing the share of states in the gross tax revenues) for 2019–20 were estimated at Rs 16.50 lakh crore in the regular Budget. Net tax revenues to the Centre were estimated to be Rs 17.05 lakh crore. The estimated net tax revenue to the Centre was thus reduced by Rs 0.55 lakh crore in the regular Budget.

There were revisions in the gross tax revenue estimates as well. The Budget paper presents gross estimates of individual tax revenues and makes a single deduction for the share of states in the gross tax revenues. For 2019–20, gross tax revenues were estimated at Rs 25.5 lakh crore, which were Rs 24.6 lakh crore in the regular Budget. The details of states in each of the central taxes is presented in a separate annexure.

Both the interim Budget and regular Budget presented revised estimates of gross and net tax receipts at Rs 22.47 lakh crore and Rs 14.84 lakh crore. The Budget net tax revenues of the Centre (Rs 16.50 lakh crore) were thus estimated to grow over the revised estimates of 2018–19 (Rs 14.84 lakh crore) by 11.18 per cent.

When the interim Budget was presented on 1 February 2019, only the revised estimates of net tax revenues of financial year 2018–19 were available. However, when the regular Budget 2019–20 was presented in July, the actual/provisional tax receipts of 2018–19 had become available. As it turned out, net tax revenues of the Centre for 2019–20 came in much lower than the revised estimates projected at the time of the interim Budget.

As against projected revised estimates of Rs 14.84 lakh crore, provisional/actual net tax receipts for 2018–19 came to only Rs 13.17 lakh crore. Thus, there was a difference of Rs 1.67 lakh crore between the two numbers. Compared to the provisional/actual tax revenues of the Centre for 2018–19, estimated tax revenues for financial year 2019–20 were Rs 3.33 lakh crore higher (whereas in comparison to revised estimates, the increase projected in net tax revenues of 2019–10 was only half or Rs 1.66 lakh crore higher). Thus, there were two growth estimates. One, which projected tax revenue growth rate for 2019–20 over the provisional/actual tax revenues of 2018–19. This growth estimate was quite high at 25.26 per cent. The other estimate was estimated growth of tax revenues over the revised estimates of 2018–19, which was only 11.18 per cent higher. The two estimates generated a difference of Rs 1.67 lakh crore, which along with higher assumed underlying growth of 25.26 per cent stoked a controversy.

Both the interim Budget and regular Budget were presented for the year 2019–20. The constitutional requirement and budgetary convention is to present revised estimates only of the preceding year. Availability of provisional/actuals by the time of presentation of the regular Budget in July did not change that.

Actual Net Tax Revenues were Lower by a Massive Rs 3 Lakh Crore

Actual net tax revenues for the year 2019–20 turned out to be only Rs 13.57 lakh crore. This was Rs 2.93 lakh crore less than the budgeted net tax revenues of Rs 16.50 lakh crore. This was only Rs 0.4 lakh crore more than the actual net tax revenues of Rs 13.17 lakh crore in 2018–19, a growth of only 3 per cent.

The year 2017–18 was the first year of the big reform of the Goods and Services Tax (GST). That year had yielded net tax revenues of Rs 12.42 lakh crore. Tax revenues grew by Rs 75,000 crore in 2018–19 (about 6 per cent). In the next year, 2019–20, tax revenues of the Centre grew by only 3 per cent. 2019–20 was a normal year except in the last month of March 2020, when the government imposed a total lockdown in the last week of the month. But the tax growth of 6 per cent in 2018–19 and only 3 per cent in 2019–20 did substantiate the charge that there was a taxation crisis in the country.

Income Taxes Performed Quite Poorly

There are two principal taxes on incomes, also identified as direct tax revenues. The taxes on income of companies are collected under a separate account—corporation income tax (CIT). The tax on income of all non-corporate bodies, primarily individuals, are collected as personal income tax (PIT).

These two taxes together were budgeted to contribute gross tax revenues of Rs 13.35 lakh crore (Rs 7.66 lakh crore CIT and Rs 5.69 lakh crore PIT) in 2019–20. The government had collected Rs 11.37 lakh crore from these two income taxes in 2018–19. Therefore, direct taxes were expected to grow by about Rs 2 lakh crore or 15 per cent over the tax collected in 2018–19.

Actual CIT collection was Rs 5.57 lakh crore and PIT was Rs 4.93 lakh crore. Both the direct income taxes together contributed Rs 10.50 crore. There was a massive shortfall of Rs 2.85 lakh crore, a drop of 21.3 per cent. CIT alone was down by Rs 2.09 lakh crore, whereas PIT had a smaller contraction of Rs 0.76 lakh crore.

Value-Added Taxes Performed Somewhat Better

The Central government has three principal sources of taxes on value added, usually referred to as indirect taxes. These are Central GST (CGST), excise duties, essentially on petroleum products, and customs duty. The Centre also gets its share from the Integrated GST (IGST) levied on imports, interstate transactions, etc.

Total customs revenues were budgeted to bring in gross receipts of Rs 1.56 lakh crore (provisional/actual 2018–19 Rs 1.18 lakh crore; growth of over 32 per cent). Excise duties were budgeted at Rs 3.0 lakh crore for 2019–20 (actual 2018–19 Rs 2.31 lakh crore; growth of 29.87 per cent).

For 2019–20, the total amount budgeted as receipts for GST was Rs 6.63 lakh crore. This comprised Rs 5.26 lakh crore of CGST receipts, Rs 28,000 crore of IGST undistributed balance at the end of the year, Rs 1.09 lakh crore of Compensation Cess and a small amount of Union Territories GST. The undistributed IGST balance in the CFI at the end of the year (in 2019–20 Budget Rs 28,000 crore) and the Compensation Cess (budgeted balance Rs 1.09 lakh crore) did not belong to the Centre.

Budgeted CGST receipts of Rs 5.26 lakh crore, compared to actuals/provisional of Rs 4.58 lakh crore for 2018–19, provided growth of only 14.96 per cent year on year.

Excise duties had a steep budgeted target of Rs 3 lakh crore. The government finally collected Rs 2.41 lakh crore of excise duties in 2019–20, generating a shortfall of Rs 0.59 lakh crore. There was shortfall in collections under customs as well. The government collected only Rs 1.09 lakh crore of customs revenue against estimated receipts of Rs 1.56 lakh crore in financial year 2019–20 with a shortfall of Rs 0.47 lakh crore.

The year 2019–20 turned out to be the year of shortfall of GST compensation. The government, therefore, distributed all the IGST balances and there was no IGST balance left. It also drew upon balances of the GST Compensation Cess. Finally, the gross collections under CGST turned out to be Rs 5.99 lakh crore. In addition, the GST of union territories was about Rs 5800 crore. Compared to the total amount of Rs 6.63 lakh crore budgeted under different heads of GST, the government got Rs 6 lakh crore, a shortfall of about Rs 0.63 lakh crore.

All the indirect taxes put together yielded a shortfall of about Rs 1.69 lakh crore.

Lockdown Disrupted Tax Performance in the First Half of 2020–21 but It Improved Later

Tax revenue performance in financial year 2020–21 was quite poor until September.

Net tax revenues suffered a big jolt in the first quarter, falling short by Rs 1.16 lakh crore (46 per cent less than the previous year). As the government delivered the states' tax share instalment on the basis of estimated budgeted tax revenues, the three months of April to June 2020 bore the brunt. Tax revenues (net to Centre) came down from Rs 71,637 crore to Rs 21,412 crore in April 2020, from Rs 43,703 crore to Rs 12,438 crore in May and from Rs 1,36,071 crore to Rs 1,00,972 crore in the month of June. Quarterly net tax revenues for the Centre came down from Rs 2,51,411 crore to Rs 1,34,822 crore.

Tax revenues improved in the second quarter. Overall, tax revenue shortfall in the second quarter was only Rs 0.32 lakh crore compared to the previous year. This brought down the first half shortfall to only Rs 1.48 lakh crore, which was less than 25 per cent compared to the previous year.

In the third quarter of financial year 2020–21, the government received net tax revenues of Rs 5,03,891 crore. This was much higher than the Rs 2.97 lakh crore received in the third quarter of 2019–20. At the end of December 2020, net tax receipts were at Rs 9.62 lakh crore, compared to the net tax revenues of Rs 9.05 lakh crore received in the previous fiscal. In the third quarter, not only did the government make up for the entire shortfall for the first two quarters but also recorded an increase of Rs 0.57 lakh crore over the previous year (6.35 per cent).

Having burnt its fingers the previous two years, the government played it safe while projecting tax revenues in the revised estimates. The revised estimate of financial year 2020–21 at Rs 13.45 lakh crore was much lower than the budgeted estimate of Rs 16.36 lakh crore. This assumed that the government would receive only Rs 3.83 lakh crore of net tax revenues (Rs 13.45 lakh crore minus Rs 9.62 lakh crore). These estimated revenues were far less than the net tax revenues of Rs 5.04 lakh crore collected in the third quarter of financial year 2020–21 and Rs 4.51 lakh crore collected in the last quarter of 2019–20.

The government's net tax revenues for financial year 2020–21 are likely to exceed Rs 15 lakh crore, about Rs 1.5 lakh crore higher than the revised estimates.

Excise Duties were the Saviour of the Government's Tax Performance

The contrast of the revised estimates of financial year 2020–21 with budgeted estimates tells an interesting story.

The government projected excessively lower gross tax receipts from CIT (down from Rs 6.81 lakh crore to Rs 4.46 lakh crore) and PIT (from Rs 6.38 lakh crore to Rs 4.59 lakh crore). These estimates were much lower than the actual CIT collected in 2019–20 (Rs 5.57 lakh crore) and PIT (Rs 4.92 lakh crore).

Customs revenues were also revised downwards from Rs 1.38 lakh crore in the budget estimates to Rs 1.12 lakh crore in the revised estimates. GST revenues were reduced from Rs 6.91 lakh crore to Rs 5.15 lakh crore. The only tax revenue source of consequence receiving a leg-up was excise revenues. Gross tax receipts from excise duties (including road and infrastructure cess and the newly introduced agriculture development and infrastructure cess) rose from budget estimates of Rs 2.67 lakh crore to Rs 3.61 lakh crore. Compared to the previous year, the revised estimates of gross tax revenues from excise duties would be much higher than the actual receipts of Rs 2.41 lakh crore.

2021–22: Government Continues to be Quite Cautious

Tax revenue receipts for the Centre have been estimated at Rs 15.45 lakh crore for financial year 2021–22 as against the budget estimate of Rs 16.36 lakh crore. Tax revenue estimates for financial year 2021–22 are only Rs 1.88 lakh crore higher than the actual net tax revenues of the Centre for financial year 2019–20. The Central government, in a way, is estimating its tax revenue to go up by only 13.85 per cent compared to the actual tax revenue collected two years before. As the underestimated revised estimates of financial year 2020–21 are somewhat lower (Rs 2.01 lakh crore) than the actual tax revenues collected in 2019–20 (Rs 1.88 lakh crore), estimated tax revenues for financial year 2021–22 are expected to grow by 14.94 per cent over the revised estimates. If the Centre's actual tax revenues were to come to Rs 15 lakh crore for 2020–21, the asking rate of growth for the year would be only 3 per cent.

The government expects gross tax revenues from CGST to bounce back in financial year 2021–22 (an estimated Rs 6.66 lakh crore against RE of Rs 5.15 lakh crore). It also expects customs tax revenues to rise (from Rs 1.12 lakh crore in RE to Rs 1.36 lakh crore). Excise revenue estimates have been moderated somewhat (Rs 3.35 lakh crore compared to

Rs 3.61 lakh crore) but still continue to be much higher than the revenues of Rs 2.41 lakh crore collected in 2019–20.

On the other hand, estimates of CIT continue to be quite subdued (Rs 5.47 lakh crore compared to the actual Rs 5.57 lakh crore collected two years before in 2019–20). PIT is estimated to be better than revised estimates and also better than the revenues collected in 2019–20.

State of Non-Tax Revenues

The Government of India records all revenues of a non-tax nature, divided into revenue receipts and capital receipts. Dividends from public-sector entities are illustrative of non-tax revenue receipts and proceeds of sale of shares in public-sector entities are non-tax capital receipts. The Budget groups all non-tax revenues, excluding capital receipts, as non-tax revenues and non-debt creating capital receipts, basically receipts from disinvestments and repayment receipts of loans, like housing loans advanced to employees, as non-debt receipts.

Non-tax receipts are broadly accounted for in three categories: interest receipts, dividends and profits, and other non-tax receipts. The interest received on the loans extended by the Central government counts as interest receipts. Though this has notably reduced, the Centre still extends numerous types of loans—to state governments, PSUs, its employees, and others. The equity invested in PSUs and investments made in statutory bodies result in the inflow of dividends and share in profits for the Government of India. Dividends and transfers of surplus get accounted for in this broad category. Surplus transfers from RBI and authorities like AAI get accounted for here. The government receives a lot of payments for granting rights in natural resources like spectrum, collecting tolls, imposing fines, and so on. All these revenues are accounted for as other non-tax revenues.

There are two kinds of receipts of a capital nature that the government receives which are not in the nature of borrowings. These are repayments of loans and advances by loanees of the government and receipts from sale of investments in public sector and other entities. These are accounted for under the broad head of non-debt receipts.

2019–20: RBI Dividend Led to Better than Budgeted Non-Tax Revenue Performance

The Union government budgeted Rs 3.13 lakh crore as non-tax revenues for financial year 2019–20. Interest receipts were estimated to yield Rs 13,711 crore, dividend and profits Rs 1,63,528 crore and other tax receipts Rs 1,33,790 crore. All these estimates were higher than the actual revenues received in financial year 2018–19 at Rs 2.35 lakh crore. Aggregated, non-tax revenues were expected to grow by over 33 per cent in the year.

Actual non-tax revenues came in higher. The government received Rs 3.27 lakh crore as non-tax revenues. Dividends and surpluses received at Rs 1,86,133 crore beat the budget estimates of Rs 1,63,528 crore by a good margin. There was some shortfall in both interest receipts and other non-tax revenues.

There are two broad groups of entities from which dividends and share in profits flow to the government. The Budget recognizes these as dividends from public-sector enterprises and other investments, and dividend/surplus of RBI, nationalized banks and financial institutions. Like the broad division of the economy in the financial sector and non-financial sector, the first group receives dividends from all the real sector public-sector companies like NTPC, Indian Oil and so on while the second group receives surplus transfers and dividends from RBI and other financial enterprises of the Government of India like banks, insurance companies and the like.

Budgeted receipt for 2019–20 from the financial entities group (dividend/surplus of RBI, nationalized banks and financial institutions) was Rs 1,06,042 crore; from the non-financial group (dividend from public-sector enterprises and other investments), it was Rs 57,487 crore.

The actual performance was quite different. Despite most PSBs suffering from losses on account of provisions made for NPAs, the dividend and surplus transfers from the financial entities group was much higher at Rs 1,50,589 crore, whereas the non-financial public-sector enterprises and entities contributed only Rs 35,543 crore.

RBI contributed a sum of Rs 1,47,987 crore out of the dividend and surpluses of Rs 1,50,589 crore received from the financial entities group. This surplus transfer excluded the interim surplus amount of Rs 28,000 crore transferred in March 2019 from the surpluses of 2018–19. All other

PSBs, LIC and general insurance companies contributed a meagre amount of Rs 2602 crore; in fact, this was almost entirely from LIC.

In 2017–18, transfers from RBI were only Rs 40,659 crore, inclusive of Rs 10,000 crore interim dividend. In the following year (2018–19), transfer from RBI rose to Rs 68,000 crore, inclusive of Rs 28,000 crore interim dividend. RBI had transferred Rs 52,679 crore, Rs 65,896 crore and Rs 65,876 crore in the previous three years of 2014–15, 2015–16 and 2016–17. What led to this massive jump in surplus transfer in 2020–21?

RBI earned income of Rs 1,93,000 crore in 2018–19 as against Rs 78,000 crore in 2017–18, an increase of Rs 1,15,000 crore. This was largely on account of massive movement in its four heads of income. First, RBI booked extraordinary profits by selling foreign exchange securities/ reserves. In 2018–19, net foreign exchange reserves of over $25 billion were sold. As these securities are valued at average cost of acquisition, RBI booked a gain of Rs 28,998 crore under 'exchange gain/loss from foreign exchange transactions' as against a loss of Rs 4067 crore in 2017–18. Second, the central bank undertook a one-time revaluation of its foreign exchange assets and took Rs 52,618 crore to its income statement under the head 'provision no longer required and miscellaneous income'. Third, RBI expanded its rupee securities portfolio in 2018–19 by undertaking several Open Market Operations (OMOs) in excess of Rs 3,20,000 crore between July 2018 and June 2019. This led to an increase in the interest income from 'interest on holding of rupee securities' from Rs 47,968 crore in 2017–18 to Rs 58,343 crore in 2018–19. Finally, as it kept liquidity tight for several months (at least until January 2019), RBI earned Rs 1046 crore on its repo operations as against paying Rs 9541 crore on reverse repos in 2017–18, booked under the head 'net interest on Liquidity Adjustment Facility (LAF) operations'. The differences in these four heads amounted to generating an additional income of a little over Rs 1,03,000 crore, which explains the bulk of the difference in the available income of two years (Rs 64,200 crore in 2017–18 and Rs 1,75,991 crore in 2018–19).

The largest contribution in other non-tax revenues comes from the economic services provided by the government. Under this category, a total of Rs 1.05 lakh crore was budgeted for 2019–20 out of total estimated other non-tax revenues of Rs 1.34 lakh crore. This includes a share in petroleum profit and other receipts of the Ministry of Petroleum;

toll and other revenues, including Toll, Operate and Transfer (TOT) receipts from MoRTH, and spectrum auction, licence fee and spectrum fees from adjusted gross revenues under the Ministry of Telecom. The actual revenues from economic services turned out to be Rs 1.02 lakh crore, quite close to the target of Rs 1.34 lakh crore. The other services contributed somewhat less, resulting in overall other non-tax revenues of Rs 1.27 lakh crore.

Disinvestment Programme

An amount of Rs 1.05 lakh crore was budgeted as disinvestment receipts under non-debt receipts for financial year 2019–20. Along with recoveries of loans and advances budgeted at Rs 14,828 crore, total capital receipts budgeted under the non-debt receipts category were Rs 1,19,828 crore.

Actual disinvestment capital receipts came to only Rs 50,304 crore, resulting in a shortfall of Rs 65,000 crore. The disinvestment programme simply flopped in 2019–20, turning out one of its worst performances in many years.

The government had successfully achieved projected targets of disinvestment receipts in financial years 2017–18 and 2018–19. An amount of Rs 1,00,045 crore was received in 2017–18 and Rs 85,045 crore in 2018–19 against a target of Rs 1 lakh crore and Rs 80,000 crore, respectively. Encouraged by this performance in the previous two years, the government had projected an all-time high disinvestment receipt target of Rs 1.05 lakh crore for 2019–20.

The government received an amount of Rs 88,970 crore in 2017–18 from disinvestment comprising Rs 2802 crore of the face value of shares sold and Rs 86,168 crore of premium received on disinvestment of government equity holdings. An amount of Rs 11,075 crore was also received from other miscellaneous assets like evacuee property and treated as disinvestment receipts. In total, disinvestment proceeds at Rs 1,00,005 crore exceeded Rs 1 lakh crore for the first time in India's history.

The Department of Investment and Public Asset Management (DIPAM), which is responsible for disinvestment and strategic disinvestment, made a total of thirty transactions during 2017–18, generating a disinvestment receipt of Rs 40,231 crore in the process. The largest proceeds accrued when CPSE shares of Rs 14,500 crore were sold as part of the Bharat 22 Exchange Traded Fund (ETF). NTPC's 6.63 per cent equity stake was sold in the single biggest individual disinvestment at Rs 9117 crore. Other major transactions included 10 per cent stake sale in the Initial Public Offer (IPO) of Hindustan Aeronautics Ltd which generated Rs 4055 crore, 2.52 per cent of sale of National Mineral Development Corporation, now NMDC Ltd equity at Rs 1223 crore and 9.2 per cent stake sale of NALCO at Rs 1192 crore. The IPO of HUDCO yielded Rs 1207 crore. A few buyback transactions by the government were also done, such as 5.6 per cent stake in Oil India at Rs 1135 crore and 6.64 per cent stake in Engineers India at Rs 658 crore. A few transactions were meant only for employees of CPSEs. The strategic sale of HPCL to ONGC yielded the government Rs 36,915 crore. Sale of equity stakes held in the Specified Undertaking of the Unit Trust of India (SUUTI) contributed Rs 4154 crore.

The disinvestment target for 2018–19 was initially pegged lower at Rs 80,000 crore. The government finally realized Rs 84,972 crore. A total of twenty-two disinvestment transactions were carried out, yielding Rs 62,900 crore. Further, four strategic disinvestments were carried out. The largest was a sale to another CPSE: the entire government stake in REC was sold to power major PFC at Rs 14,500 crore. The other three transactions were also stake sales to other CPSEs. Dredging Corporation was sold at Rs 1049 crore to a joint venture of CPSEs of the Ministry of Shipping. HSCC Ltd and NPCC Ltd were also sold. These were more in the nature of consolidation of similar businesses under one CPSE rather than many small companies doing the same thing. SUUTI holds a significant stake in major companies like ITC, L&T and Axis Bank. In 2018–19, a good chunk of shares held by SUUTI in Axis Bank were sold for Rs 5379 crore.

Buoyed by the success of the previous two years, the government decided to enhance the disinvestment target for 2019–20 to Rs 1.05 lakh crore. It also made a few strategic moves, including putting companies on a disinvestment route. Still, actual performance turned out to be so poor, missing the target by more than half. What went wrong?

For reasons analysed in detail in the chapter on public-sector enterprises, the market kept selling pressure on CPSE share prices, resulting in CPSE market prices declining continuously during the year. Sensing that the minority stake sale through the offer for sale (OFS) and exchange traded fund (ETF) routes would not yield good prices, the government cut down the sale through these routes. Very few IPOs happened in the year.

The government moved over to the new policy of real strategic disinvestment. On 20 November 2019, the Cabinet approved the strategic sale of three major companies: BPCL, SCI and CONCOR. The entire government stake (53.29 per cent) in BPCL, a 63.75 per cent stake in SCI and 30.8 per cent out of a 54.8 per cent stake in CONCOR were decided to be sold to a 'strategic buyer'. These transactions would have been the first real stake sales after 2003–04.

These stake sales, if carried out, could have provided the government, at market valuation prevailing in November–December 2019, about Rs 55,000 crore from BPCL, about Rs 1850 crore from SCI and about Rs 5000 crore from CONCOR, in all about Rs 62,000 crore. It was reasonable to expect a control premium of 20–25 per cent, which could have brought additional Rs 13,000–14,000 crore, in all generating about Rs 75,000 crore.

Unfortunately, the government could not deliver on these stake sales for various reasons. It had not carried out a genuine strategic sale in the previous fifteen years. The administrative ministries and departments are not genuinely on board. The process of selling is tedious and time-consuming. Numerous valuation and other issues put the transactions off track.

2020–21: Government Fixes Sky-High Targets in Budget; Revises Downward in RE

The government fixed the non-tax revenue income target at Rs 3.85 lakh crore for financial year 2020–21. It also fixed a target of Rs 2.10 lakh crore for disinvestment capital receipts. These targets were extraordinary for disinvestment revenues considering the fact that the government was struggling to meet even half the target of Rs 1.05 lakh crore for financial year 2019–20 at the time of presenting the 2020–21 Budget.

For non-tax revenues, the government had hiked the target of other non-tax revenues (revenues from concessioning natural resources, imposing fines and collecting fees, etc.) to Rs 2.16 lakh crore as against the actuals of Rs 1.27 lakh crore in 2019–20.

Every component of non-tax revenues and non-debt capital receipts underperformed during the year. The government reduced the targets massively in the revised estimates.

Estimated revenues from dividends and surpluses were reduced from Rs 1,55,395 crore to Rs 96,544 crore. Budgeted revenues of Rs 2,16,277 crore for other non-tax receipts were revised to just Rs 98,024 crore. Non-tax revenues as such were scaled down from Rs 3,85,017 crore to Rs 2,10,653 crore, a reduction of 46 per cent.

Likewise, in non-debt capital receipts, disinvestment revenue estimates were reduced from Rs 2.10 lakh crore to Rs 32,000 crore, a slash of Rs 1.78 lakh crore, or 85 per cent.

Forget 2019–20 when these transactions were supposed to have been carried out, the government could not accomplish a single sale even in 2020–21. Though COVID-19 had a role to play, the markets reached an all-time high and IPO activity in the private sector was at its highest in many years.

Everything That Could Have Gone Wrong Went Wrong in Disinvestment

The government could not complete even a single strategic sale transaction during the year.

Some steps were indeed taken to carry the process of privatization/ strategic sale further. Expressions of Interest (EoIs) were invited for Air India, BPCL and SCI. Some interest was received as well, but lacked enthusiasm.

CPSEs were asked to pay as much dividend as possible. They paid two interim dividends in quite a few cases in 2020–21. Yet, as their profitability had suffered, overall dividend receipts were lower than the previous year.

RBI also decided to retain a major part of the surplus.

2021–22: Government Announces Ambitious Revenue Targets Based on Privatization of Banks and Listing of LIC

In Budget 2021–22, the government did reiterate its firm commitment to privatization and the sale of all the CPSEs that had been put on the block in 2019–20 or earlier: Air India, BPCL, CONCOR, SCI, etc. It also announced the privatization of two PSBs and one general insurance company in the Budget.

Chapter Forty-Three

Two Big Tax Reforms: GST and Corporate Tax Cut

India has seen two big bang tax reforms introduced in the last four years.

The vastly complicated, disjointed, disintegrated and regressive indirect tax system of the country was overhauled massively in 2017 when the country moved to the Goods and Services Tax (GST) regime for all goods and services barring a few, largely petroleum, products. While the GST did create 'one nation one market' in the country and speeded up movement of goods across states, its impact on India's indirect tax performance and on the GDP has remained quite muted. It remains a work in progress.

The government announced a massive reduction in corporate income tax rates in September 2019 which substantially lowered the corporate tax rates for all companies. For new manufacturing companies, the rates were brought to as low as 15 per cent, which made India immensely competitive on the corporate tax front. The corporate rate reduction was also accompanied by removal of quite a few exemptions and favoured treatment, though this was done in quite a complicated manner.

Where does the country stand in 2021 with respect to these two big bang reforms?

GST: Still a Work in Progress

India Moves to GST on 1 July 2017

GST brought massive reforms to the taxation of goods and services in the country.

This single taxation system unified the fragmented taxation authority vested in the Centre and the states earlier. It heralded a 'one nation, one value-added tax system' for the country. It transformed goods and services taxation from an origin-based system (where tax was collected where the goods and services were produced) to a destination-based one (where tax was collected by the state where the consumption of goods and services took place). GST brought about a single rate of taxation on goods or services all over the country, doing away with the complications of determining maximum sale price in different states by debarring the Centre and states from putting any other tax or cess on goods and services covered under the GST. These were massive reforms, which will affect the structure of production and consumption in the country in times to come.

GST replaced and subsumed more than twenty indirect Central and state taxes. The central taxes subsumed included central excise duty (barring a few products), duties of excise on medicinal and toilet preparations, additional duties of excise on goods of special importance (which had disallowed the states to impose tax rates higher than prescribed), additional duties of excise on textiles, additional duties of customs levied as countervailing duties, special additional duty of customs (which existed to countervail the impact of lesser incidence of state VAT on imported goods), service tax and numerous cesses and surcharges the Centre had imposed on a number of commodities. Among the state tax laws, GST replaced state VAT, Central Sales Tax (which was meant to tax interstate transactions but had become an instrument of interstate war to attract investment), taxes on specific services like advertisements, entertainment, luxuries, lotteries and so on as well as numerous cesses and surcharges most states had levied on several commodities. It made the indirect taxation system much less complex.

Some items were left out; petroleum products (crude oil, petrol, diesel, natural gas, aviation turbine fuel) being the most significant, which are heavily taxed by both the Centre and the states. Alcohol for human consumption, which is taxed by the states, has been left out. Electricity, which is also taxed by the states, has also been left out. These exclusions from GST make the transition still incomplete.

There were hundreds of rates and slabs of taxation in the states. GST did not adopt a single rate of tax but simplified the rate structure quite substantially. When it was implemented for the first time in July 2017, it had five rates of 0 per cent, 5 per cent, 12 per cent, 18 per cent and 28 per cent. The 0 per cent slab included basic food items such as milk, salt and fresh vegetables. The 5 per cent slab covered most essential items like kerosene, LPG, edible vegetable oil, footwear of less than Rs 500, apparel of less than Rs 1000, milk food for babies, etc. The 12 per cent slab was meant for goods of desirable consumption like ghee, almonds, umbrellas, preparations of vegetables, etc. The normal rate of GST was 18 per cent and it was imposed on most items. Most services were also in the 18 per cent slab. The 28 per cent slab included items of high value or luxury like cars, motorcycles, air-conditioners and refrigerators. In addition, 'sin' goods like cigarettes and high-end cars attracted a cess as well. The number of items in the 28 per cent slab has been gradually reduced.

GST Did Not Fulfil its Promise of Generating Additional Tax Revenues

The revenue neutral rate (RNR) is a single rate at which collection of GST is expected to be equal to the collections under the indirect taxes collected by the Centre and states, in the same year under reference. A committee headed by Chief Economic Advisor Arvind Subramanian in 2015 recommended 15–15.5 per cent as a good RNR. However, the Centre and the states did not agree to the concept of a single rate of GST. That said, when GST was implemented in July 2017, there were widespread expectations that it would usher in additional GDP growth of about 2 per cent and would also impart buoyancy to the indirect taxation system.

Unfortunately, these hopes have been belied.

For the nine months of financial year 2017–18, total GST revenues amounted to Rs 7.40 lakh crore at an average of Rs 82,294 crore. Though GST was expected to generate gross tax revenues of about Rs 1 lakh crore per month, in no month did revenues cross this mark.

In 2018–19, which was the first full year of the GST system, gross tax revenues generated by all the components of the GST system (CGST, SGST, IGST with its two components of domestic and imports and Compensation Cess with its components of domestic and imports) was Rs 11.77 lakh crore; an average of Rs 98,114 crore per month. In this year, gross GST collections crossed Rs 1 lakh three times in the months of April, January and March with March 2019 recording the highest revenue of Rs 1,06,577 crore.

The year 2019–20 proved as lacklustre as 2018–19 with GST gross revenues at Rs 12.22 lakh crore; an average of Rs 1,01,844 crore. In this year, GST gross revenues crossed the Rs 1 lakh crore mark in seven months out of twelve.

The growth rate of gross GST revenues was 19 per cent in 2018–19 over 2017–18 but only 3.8 per cent in 2019–20 over 2018–19. The growth rate of 2018–19 is also somewhat inaccurate as the collection in July 2017, the first month of GST rollout, was actually a 'no revenue' month as GST, except for imports, etc., is only due in the following month.

Performance in 2020–21 was impacted by the pandemic and lockdown. GST gross collections fell to Rs 32,294 crore in the month of April, then recovered partly to Rs 62,009 crore in May and Rs 90,917 crore in the month of June. GST revenues remained subdued until September 2020, when the gross revenues came to Rs 95,480 crore after two months of sub-Rs 90,000 crore revenues in July and August 2020. GST revenues crossed Rs 1 lakh crore for the first time in financial year 2020–21 in October when gross collections were Rs 1,05,155 crore. In every month since then, collections have exceeded Rs 1 lakh crore, signifying normality of goods and services production and distribution in the economy. Collections were Rs 1,04,963 crore in November and Rs 1,15,174 crore in December 2020. GST collections maintained good growth in January at Rs 1,19,847 crore. In February, they fell a little but still remained at a high rate of Rs 1,13,143 crore.

The shorter collections of tax revenues under the GST system led to the states requiring compensation as they were guaranteed compounded revenue growth of 14 per cent over their base revenues of financial year 2016–17. The underperformance of the GST system is best illustrated by the experience of 2019–20, which was otherwise a normal year. All the twenty-eight states and the union territory of Delhi required compensation with the shortfall in some states being higher than 10 per cent: Delhi 16 per cent, Haryana 10 per cent, Karnataka 11 per cent, Punjab 20 per cent and Uttarakhand 11 per cent. Total shortfall was as high as Rs 1.65 lakh crore.

GST Budgeting and Accounting in the Central Government

GST budgeting in government accounts is quite complicated.

GST receipts are primarily in four accounts: State GST (SGST) and Union Territories GST (UTGST), Central GST (CGST), Integrated GST over Inter-State and Import Transactions (IGST) and Compensation Cess (to pay for the shortfall in the assured compounded growth of 14 per cent for the states). CGST, IGST (year-end balance), Compensation Cess and Union Territories GST are budgeted by the Central government. SGST revenue is budgeted only by the states as this receipt is directly credited to their respective Consolidated Funds.

IGST is first credited in the Consolidated Fund of India (CFI) and then distributed as per the IGST rules of allocation. An ad hoc approach has been followed towards treating the balance of IGST in the CFI at the end of the financial year. In 2017–18, the IGST balance, a large amount of Rs 1.77 lakh crore, was treated as the Centre's receipt and a share of 42 per cent was transferred to the states on the pattern of transfer of the share of states in central taxes. In 2018–19, most of the IGST was divided between the Centre and the states during the course of the year and only a small amount of Rs 28,947 crore remained as balance in the CFI. This amount was neither divided between the Centre and the states nor was a 42 per cent share transferred to the states.

The Compensation Cess balance at the end of the year is required to be transferred to the Public Account as per the provisions of the Compensation Cess Act and rules made thereunder. As far as budgeting/accounting of the GST Compensation Cess is concerned, the entire gross receipt of the cess is treated as tax revenue receipt in the budgets/accounts of the Government of India. The amount to be transferred to the states to pay the Compensation Cess is budgeted on the expenditure side as 'Other Transfers'.

After the CAG objected to this system of accounting and distribution of IGST revenue, the entire IGST revenues are distributed every month. There was no balance of IGST revenues in the Government of India outstanding on 31 March 2020.

The complications in the accounting of Compensation Cess got resolved by the fact that the availability of GST Compensation Cess turned out to be much lower than required in financial year 2019–20. All the unspent balances of the previous two years got used in paying compensation for the shortfall of 2019–20. In fact, the government used part of the Compensation Cess revenues accrued in 2020–21 to pay for the compensation dues of 2019–20.

Handling IGST and Compensation Cess

The GST Council took some ad hoc decisions to deal with the initial period of stabilization. It decided that IGST, not apportioned to the Centre or states/UTs, may be distributed to the Centre and the states/UTs at 50 per cent each. Likewise, surplus available in a year in the GST Compensation Fund was to be divided among the Centre and states/UTs at 50 per cent each. In the first year of GST implementation, the Centre retained all 100 per cent of IGST surplus in the CFI, thereby treating it as the revenue of the Central government and transferred 42 per cent of this to the states as their share of devolution. The surplus available under the GST Compensation Fund was transferred to the Public Account in 2017–18. In 2018–19, not only was the surplus of 2018–19 not transferred to the Public Account, the amount transferred in 2017–18 was also reversed and brought in the CFI.

There is a complex system of cross-utilization of input credits. IGST credit is allowed to be used for payment of all taxes: IGST, CGST and SGST. CGST credit can be used only for IGST or CGST. SGST credit can be availed only for paying SGST or IGST. There is also a sequencing or order of using input credits. CGST input credit is allowed to be used for payment of CGST and IGST in that order. Input tax credit (ITC) of SGST is allowed for payment of SGST and IGST in that order, and ITC of IGST is allowed for payment of IGST, CGST and SGST in that order. Further, IGST credit balances have to be used before utilization of CGST or SGST.

The GST Compensation Cess became a matter of dispute and contention between the Centre and the states. The Compensation Cess is levied on supply of certain goods and services as recommended by the GST Council, and on goods and services included in the Schedule of the GST (Compensation to States) Act, 2017 (coal, tobacco, motorcars, etc.), to finance the compensation needed. As per the constitutional provision and as provided in the GST Compensation Act, states will get compensation for a period of five years in case any state's GST revenues fall short of the 14 per cent guaranteed increase over the base tax revenue (state VAT + CST + entry tax + octroi + local body tax + luxury tax + advertisement tax) in 2015–16. The Act further provides that all GST Cess collected will be credited to a non-lapsable fund—the GST Compensation Fund—in the Public Account of the Union of India. Amounts in the fund remaining unutilized at the end of the transition period (five years) are to be shared between the Union (50 per cent) and the states (in the ratio of SGST).

An amount of Rs 62,612 crore was collected as GST Cess in financial year 2017–18. However, only Rs 56,146 crore was transferred to the GST Fund Account, leaving Rs 6466 crore in the CFI. An amount of Rs 41,146 crore was released in four instalments to the states as compensation (Rs 10,806 crore, Rs 13,694 crore, Rs 3898 crore and Rs 12,749 crore for a bi-monthly period beginning July 2017). This left a total of Rs 21,466 crore unutilized (Rs 15,000 crore in the fund and Rs 6466 crore not transferred to the fund). In 2018–19, an amount of Rs 95,081 crore was collected as GST Cess (provisional numbers from CGA). Only Rs 69,275 crore was transferred to the states for compensation. In 2019–20, too, the GST Cess yielded a surplus of Rs 25,806 crore. The Central government did not transfer any of this amount in the GST Fund. Instead, it re-transferred Rs 15,000 crore from the fund (left unspent in the previous year) to the CFI. Taken together, a surplus of Rs 47,272 crore of GST Compensation Cess was with the Central government at the beginning of 2019–20.

The year 2019–20 was quite bad for the GST collections of the states. Consequently, the Government of India remained under pressure to release more Compensation Cess than collected. The government delayed the release of GST Compensation Cess for the August–September and October–November periods. It finally relented on 15 December to release Rs 35,298 crore, drawing from the amounts retained during 2017–18 and 2018–19. Finally, the entire shortfall of Rs 1.65 lakh crore for the year 2019–20 in the states' entitled revenues of SGST was paid off using collections of Rs 95,444 crore during the year, previous unspent balance of year 2017–18 and 2018–19 and part of the collections of 2020–21.

The year 2020–21 presented a real challenge and tested the resilience of the GST system to pay off the shortfall in SGST revenues to the states. In the immediate aftermath of collapse of growth and GST tax revenues, the Centre first anticipated a shortfall of Rs 2.35 lakh crore in GST compensation demand and the GST Compensation Cess revenues of year 2020–21. Unwilling to give this hefty compensation, the Centre divided the shortfall in available resources in two parts by attributing the collapse in revenues on account of economic shutdown caused by COVID-19 to an 'Act of God'. The Centre indicated that only Rs 97,000 crore of the anticipated shortfall of Rs 2.35 lakh crore was attributable to GST implementation.

Later, the government enhanced the compensation payable to the states to Rs 1.10 lakh crore and promised to borrow from the market and give it to them on a back-to-back basis according to their projected shortfall. Though the states were reluctant to accept loans for the grants initially, they all finally fell in line as they could not afford the situation of cash out in their treasuries. These loans are expected to be paid off after 2022 from the Compensation Cess accruing thereafter as the current Compensation Cess collection arrangements have been extended until 2025, though the states would not be paid compensation after 2022.

E-Invoicing for Invoice Matching

The success of GST lies in the ability of the system of automatically match the invoices of seller and buyer for verifying the GST paid and GST claimed as input tax. This requires GST invoices to be uploaded to the GST system and the system's technical ability/programming to do the matching.

E-invoicing has been made applicable to all businesses whose aggregate turnover exceeded Rs 500 crore in any of the financial years 2017–18 to 2019–20, from 1 October 2020. From 1 January 2021, the system of e-invoicing has been extended to businesses with a turnover of more than Rs 100 crore.

The government is moving progressively to bring more businesses under the e-invoicing system. From 1 April 2021, the e-invoicing system has been extended to businesses with an annual turnover of more than Rs 50 crore.

Most businesses in India have a turnover under Rs 50 crore. Like the compulsory electronic filing of income tax returns, compulsory uploading of invoices should be made mandatory for all businesses in a year's time.

Considerable Business Still Remains outside the GST System

Besides petroleum products, there are two categories of businesses that either remain out of the GST system or interact with it in a form and manner different than required under GST design.

There is an exemption from the obligation to register under GST and make GST payment if a supplier of service has an aggregate turnover under Rs 20 lakh a year. This is applicable to service providers through e-commerce or in the course of interstate services. For goods, this minimum threshold has been raised to Rs 40 lakh with effect from 1 April 2019. Businesses have the option to obtain multiple registrations in a state if they have more than one place of business.

Businesses with turnover under Rs 1.5 crore of goods or Rs 0.5 crore of services are allowed to be assessed under a 'composition scheme'. Tax rates applicable for goods turnover is 1 per cent to 5 per cent; for services turnover, it is 6 per cent. This facility is provided to small traders with turnover under Rs 5 crore. These businesses can file quarterly returns. Two types of such traders (B2C or B2C+B2B) file their returns in a simpler form (Sahaj and Sugam) quarterly.

The reverse-charge mechanism is a method to get sales reported on the GST system for goods and services supplied by businesses not required to be registered under GST or operating under the composition scheme. However, the mechanism has been implemented only marginally so far. Only goods and services purchased by specified promoters of projects notified under two notifications to the extent that these constitute shortfall from the minimum value of goods/services are currently required to be taxed on the reverse-charge mechanism.

Certain transactions have been subjected to tax deducted at source (TDS) and tax collection at source (TCS) under the GST system. These provisions, with certain exemptions, have been implemented with effect from 1 October 2018. Obligated persons for TDS include government departments, local authorities and government agencies who are recipients of supply under a contract that exceeds Rs 2,50,000. TCS obligation is on e-commerce platform operators, who are required to collect tax at source at rates that are below 2 per cent of net value of taxable supplies out of payments to suppliers supplying goods or services through their portals.

GST on real estate has also been going through changes. As decided in the GST Council meetings held on 24 February and 19 March 2019, GST rate on residential properties was made 5 per cent, with affordable housing properties attracting only 1 per cent GST. This was subject to certain conditions relating to percentage of inputs required to be purchased from registered dealers and GST at higher rates being payable on cement purchased from unregistered dealers and capital goods, etc. This system of lower GST rates, without input tax credit, replaced the original system of 8 per cent GST rate or 12 per cent without input rebate. Rates on electric automobiles were also tweaked on 27 July 2019 by reducing applicable duty from 12 per cent to 5 per cent and bringing down the GST applicable on chargers or charging stations for electric vehicles from 18 per cent to 5 per cent.

Inverted Duty Structure under GST

An inverted duty structure is currently in evidence in quite a few products. Mobile phones have GST of 12 per cent, whereas batteries and phone parts have 18 per cent. Fabric carries GST duty of 5 per cent whereas yarn has duty of 12 per cent. Tractors have duty of 12 per cent, whereas parts have 18 per cent. Desktops are charged 12 per cent, whereas monitors, printers, etc., have a GST rate of 28 per cent.

Corporate Tax Cut 2019

The Government Announced Mega Cuts in Corporate Tax Rates

The government announced massive cuts in corporate taxes on 20 September 2019 though it did not have an impact on CIT collections of the first half of financial year 2019–20 as the advance corporate taxes had been deposited before the deadline of 15 September. Actual CIT collected during the first half of 2019–20 was Rs 2,49,327 crore, 2.29 per cent higher than the Rs 2,43,742 crore collected in the first half of financial year 2018–19.

The government reduced the basic corporate tax rate from 30 per cent to 22 per cent for all companies and 15 per cent for new manufacturing companies. The Taxation Laws (Amendment) Bill, 2019, passed by the Parliament on 5 December 2019, which operationalized the 20 September announcements, brought significant changes.

Domestic companies with an annual turnover over Rs 250 crore were required to pay CIT at 30 per cent (the remaining companies were assessed at 25 per cent) until 2018–19 (assessment year 2019–20). This limit had been raised to Rs 400 crore in July 2019 when the main Budget was presented. By this Amendment Law, all domestic companies (irrespective of turnover) were given an option to pay tax at only 22 per cent if they did not avail certain specified deductions. The health surcharge of 15 per cent continued to apply. Effective rate of CIT for companies opting for this option, therefore, became 25.17 per cent.

For domestic manufacturing companies registered after 30 September 2019 and setting up and starting a new manufacturing facility before 1 April 2023, and not availing the specified deductions, the CIT rate was brought down to 15 per cent. With health surcharge, the effective CIT rate for companies opting not to avail specified deductions would be subject to a very low rate of 17.25 per cent only for the profits arising out of new manufacturing facilities set up after 30 September 2019.

Major deductions to be disallowed to companies opting for lower CIT rates included deduction for new units in SEZ; investment in new plant and machinery in notified backward areas; expenditure on scientific research, agriculture extension, etc., and depreciation of new plant and machinery in certain cases.

The existing companies could exercise the option to move to the lower tax rate regime in any year of their choosing, which would be irreversible after it was exercised.

Significant changes were also made in the Minimum Alternate Tax (MAT) applicable on companies. No MAT was leviable on companies opting for lower corporate income tax rates of 22 per cent and 15 per cent. For other companies, MAT rates were reduced from 18.5 per cent to 15 per cent.

Status of Corporate Tax Incidence on Manufacturing and Non-Manufacturing Corporates

In a press statement issued on 20 September 2019, the government cited promotion of growth and investments as the justification for slashing the normal corporate tax rate to 22 per cent, and attracting fresh investment in manufacturing to boost Make in India for offering an even lower corporate tax rate of 15 per cent for new manufacturing companies. The government estimated 'total revenue foregone for the reduction in corporate tax rate and other relief at Rs 1,45,000 crore'. However, it did not provide any basis for this estimate.

The government publishes a 'Statement of Revenue Impact of Tax Incentives under the Central System' with every Budget. For the financial year, the statement is at Annex-7 of Revenue Receipts 2019–20. The analysis in this statement related basically to financial year 2017–18.

The Statement reported that there were 1,30,676 manufacturing companies (15.53 per cent) out of total return filing companies of 8,41,687 for financial year 2017–18. These manufacturing companies had a share of 38.92 per cent in total profits and 36.74 per cent share in total tax liability. Their effective tax liability was 27.83 per cent.

These companies would not get the benefit of lower tax rate of 15 per cent available to new manufacturing companies, though all these companies would get the benefit of lower CIT rates. Out of these 1,30,676 manufacturing companies, those with turnover of more than Rs 400 crore would get the benefit of lower taxation rate of 22 per cent compared to earlier incidence of 30 per cent and those with turnover less than Rs 400 crore would pay a lower rate of 22 per cent in place of the 25 per cent to which they were subjected earlier.

As these companies would be tax-disadvantaged compared to new manufacturing companies, they may also be incentivized to set up new manufacturing plants, or convert existing manufacturing facilities or those at the work-in-progress stage to new manufacturing facilities in new companies to avail the lower corporate tax rates.

A total of 7.11 lakh non-manufacturing companies, with a share of 61 per cent in profits and 63 per cent in tax liability, had a higher effective tax rate of 30.55 per cent. These companies would also opt for the new scheme, sooner or later, after factoring in the impact of their existing un-availed tax benefit (which would not be available if they shift) as they also stand to take advantage of lower effective corporate tax rate of 22 per cent.

The Statement also shares details on businesses, including manufacturing businesses, organized as partnership firms and Association of Persons (AoPs) or some other non-corporate forms. There were 14.38 lakh such entities that filed returns for income of financial year 2017–18. These firms reported Rs 1,95,669 crore as profit before taxes, declared a taxable income of Rs 1,76,905 crore and paid tax of Rs 52,737 crore. These firms suffered the highest rates of income tax applicable to individuals. The lowering of corporate tax rates to 22 per cent/15 per cent was likely to encourage many of these firms to convert into companies to avail the benefit of lower applicable tax rates.

Impact Assessment

The actual CIT collections for financial year 2019–20 came to Rs 5,56,876 crore, which was lower by Rs 1,06,696 crore compared to the CIT collections of Rs 6,63,572 crore for the previous year 2018–19.

The Statement of Revenue Impact of Tax Incentives under the Central Tax System placed along with the Budget 2021–22 was expected to bring the analysis of the impact of major corporate rate cuts announced in September 2019. However, this Statement does not even mention these cuts. The government has not provided any other analysis bringing out the impact of these corporate cuts on economic growth, new manufacturing facilities established, conversion of non-corporate businesses in the corporate form or the impact of these measures on the government's tax revenues.

The Statement only provides information on the effective tax rate for 8.85 lakh companies that filed returns for financial year 2018–19 (the year before the corporate tax cuts were announced), which was higher than the number of 8.41 lakh that had filed returns the year before. The total number of manufacturing companies filing returns in the year 2018–19 also went up to 1,33,691 compared to 1,30,672 companies that had filed returns for 2017–18.

Data from the Ministry of Corporate Affairs (MCA) indicates that 10,004 companies were registered in the month of August 2019. In September 2019, this number went down to 9,171. It started growing significantly from December 2019 when it went up to 12,057 companies. In January 2020, the highest number of companies were registered in financial year 2019–20 at 12,429. From February 2020, however, the impact of COVID-19 started and the registration of new companies went down to 10,429. It collapsed to 5788 in March 2020 when lockdown was imposed. The month of April 2020 saw the lowest registrations in many years at 3209. Registration activity resumed from June 2020 and flourished from July 2020 onwards when as many as 16,487 companies were registered. Registrations remained quite high, in excess of 16,000 per month, from July to October with registration peaking at 16,707 in October 2020. There was somewhat subdued activity thereafter, though still much higher than in these months in previous years. As economic activity has not picked up much during 2020–21, high registrations since June 2020 seem to indicate that the conversion of non-corporate businesses into companies is taking place.

There were 2,27,260 active manufacturing companies in India at the end of March 2019 as per the MCA data. This number had reached 2,32,932 at the end of August 2019 and 2,34,356 at the end of September 2019, the month when corporate tax rates were slashed to only 15 per cent for new manufacturing companies. As 7096 companies were registered in six months, the average increase in active manufacturing companies can be taken at about 1,150 per month.

The number of active manufacturing companies increased to 2,39,681 by March 2020, recording an increase of only 5325 in six months after the corporate cut announcement, which was in fact much lower than the increase in the first six months of financial year 2019–20. In September 2020, the number of active manufacturing companies reached 2,53,801, recording an increase of 14,120 in six months. This was an impressive increase considering the fact that the first quarter of 2020–21 was practically lost to COVID-19 and the lockdown. The number of active manufacturing companies reached 2,68,069 by the end of February 2021, an increase of 14,268 in five months. More than 30,000 active manufacturing companies were added in financial year 2020–21, which confirms either registration of new manufacturing facilities or conversion of existing non-corporate companies into manufacturing companies.

The medium-term impact of the corporate tax cuts is likely to be a clear loss in revenues. There would also be pressure to extend the lower rate of 15 per cent to new non-manufacturing companies, thereby regressing the corporate tax rate to 15 per cent for all. The impact on advancing manufacturing in the country will have to be assessed in the next few years.

A possible alternative could have been to extend the concessional corporate tax rate of 15 per cent effectively to manufacturing businesses relocating from outside India and the new manufacturing facilities established for exporting the bulk of their product. It would have made the tax giveaway targeted and offered a real competitive advantage. As a broad-based general measure, it may still attract some companies to shift their manufacturing base to India. However, much more advantage is likely to be taken by existing companies shifting their manufacturing to new companies and non-corporate firms to convert into companies to claim lower corporate tax rates.

There is no possible way to estimate the tax loss as no one knows how many companies (with what profitability and tax profile) would opt for this new taxation regime in the financial years from 2019–20 to 2022–23. This will only become clearer with time. One consequence has, however, been quite obvious. Most of the tax forgone has been availed by existing companies as their profits were taxed at lower rates in 2019–20 and 2020–21. This was immediately realized by the stock markets, which reset equity prices based on newly expected corporate profits. The increase in corporate profits net of taxes during the year 2020–21, despite the pandemic, reflects the cost cutting corporates have been able to effect as well as lower incidence of corporate taxes.

Chapter Forty-Four

Cooperative Fiscal Federalism to Fiscal Union

Near Perfect Fiscal Federal System at Inception

The founding fathers of the Indian Constitution opted for a balanced federal fiscal system making the states the pivot of development expenditure on agriculture, health, education, nutrition, infrastructure, and virtually any area concerning public welfare. The people of India reside in states and there is a direct relationship between people and the state governments.

The Constitution, as adopted by the people in 1949 and which came into force on 26 January 1950, conferred substantial taxation sovereignty on states by including several taxation powers in List II of the Seventh Schedule on which states have exclusive right to make laws and exercise executive power. These exclusive taxation powers included taxes on sale of goods, excise duty on alcohol, transportation taxes, tax on agricultural income, octroi, stamp duties on sale of land and other properties, and a few other taxes. These taxation powers were not adequate to meet the states' expenditure but were truly independent and sovereign—states did not need any licence or support from the Union government to decide their taxation policy and administration.

To make sure states were fiscally able to discharge their expenditure responsibilities on their own authority and not remain dependent on the Centre, the Constitution provided for a Finance Commission to be constituted every five years. The Finance Commission was conferred with independent jurisdiction and the right to determine how much of the receipt of the central taxes would be taken out of the CFI (which houses all the receipts of the Government of India) autonomously and devolve to the states and be divided among them, without any interference of the Central government. The Constitution further provided for some central taxes like stamp duties on financial instruments to be collected and appropriated by states even though the rates of levy are decided by the Centre. It is noteworthy that there was no provision for any state tax to be collected by the Centre and distributed to the states in the 1950 Constitution.

This intergovernmental fiscal system was a perfect fiscal federal system with sovereign, independent and self-reliant states.

Loans and grants from the national fiscal authority, or the Central government in India's case, to subnational entities (or states) corrode the strength of their fiscal authority. The Indian Constitution, which devolved taxation powers between the Centre and states so neatly, made provisions relating to loans and grants that were susceptible to be misused by the Centre.

Article 292 (2) permitted the Government of India to make loans to any state and to give guarantees with respect to loans raised by any state. Article 293 (3) subjected loan-raising powers of the state(s) to the consent of the Government of India if there was a central loan outstanding towards that particular state or there was an outstanding central guarantee for a state's loan.

The Constitution debarred states, with very good reason, from borrowing abroad. Their borrowing powers [Article 293 (1)] extended only to borrowing 'within the territory of India'. This provision would soon open another channel of indebtedness to the Centre as all loans from multilateral and bilateral agencies taken by the Centre for states' projects would automatically result in them taking loans from the Centre.

These lending and borrowing arrangements sowed the seeds of states' dependence on the Centre and, over time, corroded fiscal federalism in India.

There was one more Achilles heel in the fiscal federal arrangements in India: the system of making grants by the Centre to the states.

The makers of the Constitution did make an honest attempt to ensure states do not become dependent on the Centre for receiving discretionary fiscal grants. Article 275 (1) permitted the Parliament only to make, by law, grants-in-aid of revenues of such states that it determined in need of assistance.

Further, Article 275 (2) and Article 280 (2), read together, made a provision that until the Parliament makes such a law providing for grant-in-aid to the revenues of states, such grants can be made by the President, only after considering the recommendations of the Finance Commission. The responsibility to frame 'the principles which should govern the grants-in-aid of the revenues of the States out of the Consolidated Fund of India' was conferred on an independent and fair arbiter, the Finance Commission. Constitutionally, it appeared the provisions relating to making grants by the Centre to states were well safeguarded to ensure they received these grants only as non-discretionary, without any strings, much like tax devolution.

The trojan horse was, however, Article 282. Tugged under the broad heading of 'Miscellaneous Financial Provisions', it allowed the Union or a state to 'make any grants for any public purpose, *notwithstanding that the purpose is not one with respect to which the Parliament or the Legislature of the State, as the case may be, may make laws*'.

This provision is worded in the broadest terms. Such grants can be made by any of the fiscal authorities. Such grants can be made for any purpose, including one for which the legislative and executive power of the fiscal authority does not extend. Such grants can be made to the fiscal authority that has the legislative and executive power to deal with such a subject.

Over the next seven decades of India's fiscal policymaking, Article 282 would allow the Centre to virtually take over the expenditure responsibilities of the states and make them subservient. Theoretically, states could also make grants to the Centre for any of the Union subjects—defence, currency, foreign policy—though no state had the fiscal resources or political authority to even consider it.

In a nutshell, though the intergovernmental fiscal relationship instituted by the Constitution in 1950 envisaged a perfect fiscal federation, the seeds of its being undermined were also sown therein.

First Two Decades: Constitutional Fiscal Federalism in Operation

In the 1950s, both the Centre and the states were ruled by the same political party. The states did not assert their independent fiscal sub-sovereign status. They were not required to do so either as the intergovernmental fiscal system operated in line with the constitutional scheme of things and practices of the pre-Independence period.

The constitutional provisions of fiscal federalism were put into practice faithfully. Finance Commissions were constituted at regular intervals and recommended division of central taxes; the President accepted these recommendations almost to a fault; and states got their share of central taxes fully and in time. The CAG audited the receipts of taxes and amounts transferred to states and certified independently whether these were in line with the recommendations of the Finance Commissions. If there was any shortfall, it was pointed out in the CAG reports and made good in time.

The Finance Commissions established their reputation as a fair arbiter between the states and Centre. The government also faithfully implemented the recommendations of the Finance Commissions.

Project-based loans and grants continued on the lines of pre-Independence practice, albeit at a higher scale as states took up a number of flood-control, irrigation, industrial and other developmental projects.

The Government of India decided to establish the Planning Commission in 1951 to make development plans for the Centre and the states.

Along with the Planning Commission came the concept of Plan expenditure, a unique contribution of India to governmental financial management. Both on the capital and revenue accounts, expenditures were bifurcated into Plan and non-Plan expenditures. New developmental expenditure was Plan expenditure and the rest non-Plan.

The Constitution of India did not recognize this classification of expenditure. Nor was it ever amended to provide for it. The terms of reference of the Finance Commission enumerated in Article 280 did not mention such expenditure either.

The Planning Commission was made in charge of Plan expenditure. If the entire developmental expenditure of the government were to be lorded over by the Planning Commission, it had serious implications for distribution of central tax revenues between the Centre and states.

Soon, the matter engaged the attention of the Finance Commissions. The second and third Finance Commissions debated and expressed their resentment but finally accepted that Plan expenditure was outside their scope of work.

The Planning Commission assumed leadership in recommending loans and grants from the Centre for states' development projects, which continued to be formally administered by the respective ministries and departments. It also assumed the role of approving states' Plans, which integrated central loans and grants with states' expenditures on such projects.

In the 1950s and 1960s, though the unintended undermining of the Finance Commission had begun with the establishment of the Planning Commission and system of Plan expenditure, intergovernmental fiscal relations operated without much deviation from the constitutional arrangement.

Next Three Decades: CSSs Make State Finances Subservient to Centre

The 1970s witnessed a massive transformation of fiscal relations between the Centre and the states.

To reform the transfer of developmental/plan resources to the states, it was decided in 1969 to establish a formula (which came to be known as the Gadgil Formula) in place of making individual project-based grants and loans from the Centre. There were thousands of individual budget lines in operation at the end of the Third Plan. The system of intergovernmental development resource transfers was truly in a mess.

Finance Commission transfers, which governed non-Plan transfers, were basically formula-driven. With the adoption of the Gadgil Formula, the distribution/allocation of Plan resources was also made formula-driven. It was a good set of fiscal reforms designed and recommended by technocrats led by D.R. Gadgil, deputy chairman of the Planning Commission. It brought a lot of objectivity, transparency and non-discretion to the system of transferring fiscal resources from the Centre to the states.

However, there was a large side-effect of the new system of Plan transfers that undermined states' finances in ensuing decades.

The Gadgil Formula stipulated the transfer of a state's share (for all states except some minor special category states), termed normal central assistance (NCA), as 30 per cent grant and 70 per cent loan. This instituted a systemic lending-borrowing relationship between the Centre and the states. The same formula (70 per cent loan and 30 per cent grant) was used to transfer multilateral and bilateral loans and grants. The loans provided under NCA arrangements became the primary means of borrowing for states over the years.

In addition to these two sources of loan financing (Plan transfers in the form of NCA and funds under externally aided projects), the Central government continued with another mode of loan financing. Savings from people were mobilized as small savings by post offices acting as agents of the Government of India and then transferred to the states (on the basis of origin of savings) as small savings loans.

These loans became the dominant source of financing for states, so dominant that by the 1990s more than 80 per cent of the borrowings by states came to be raised in the form of central loans. Loans from the market, raised in the form of state development loans, played second fiddle, making up under 20 per cent of overall annual borrowing in the 1990s.

The central planning system of India during this period treated debt like any other revenue resource. Debt raised by the Centre and states was considered par for the course and welcome.

The Constitution has a provision for the Parliament to fix limits of debt for the Centre by law (Article 292) and for state legislatures to fix limits of debt by law (Article 293). No such laws were passed by either the Parliament or state legislatures.

In fact, the Planning Commission encouraged the states to borrow as much as they could to raise their Plan size. The size of the annual Plan came to acquire a trophy status. It became a symbol of political achievement for the party in power in the state, which, in turn, gave governments the justification to pile up an increasing amount of debt while ignoring its adverse consequences.

The three decades from the start of new resource planning for funding Plans in 1969 to the turn of the century in 2000 saw an aggressive build-up of debt by states. Much of it came from the Central government. This overwhelming debt financing allowed the Centre to assume considerable control over the finances of states.

The Constitution made a clean division of taxation powers. However, there was no such clean division of expenditure powers between the Centre and states. The Concurrent List provided a big overlap, with precedence to the Centre, on subjects like economic and social planning, population control and family planning, social security and social insurance, employment and unemployment, welfare of labour, shipping and navigation on inland waterways, and so on. Education and health were added later.

There was a large state list over which states had complete and exclusive authority to make laws and exercise executive jurisdiction. This list included important development and public welfare subjects like local government, public health and sanitation, relief of the disabled and unemployable, agriculture, water, land, fisheries, industries, markets and fairs. The Central government has no constitutional authority to make development schemes to incur expenditures on these subjects.

Attempts were made to modify the state list to confer powers to the Centre from time to time. For example, development and regulation of industries was brought under central control by amending the entry in 1956. However, major inroads were made in the domain of the states by engineering the CSSs, which effectively came into existence after the development financing system was modified in 1969. The Centre used the space provided by Article 282 to get its foot in the domain of state subjects.

The predominant feature of CSSs was to provide the lure of grant resources (though there was a loan component attached for many schemes until the 1990s) for states to adopt the central scheme and fund a part of the cost of the scheme from their own resources. States, especially functional departments, found the temptation too difficult to resist and joined the bandwagon enthusiastically. Gradually, the Centre could build a large number of schemes in almost all development subjects in the state list.

The National Development Council (NDC) clearly stipulated in 1968 that CSSs would not have total outlays larger than one-sixth of total central assistance to state Plans. This stipulation was, unfortunately, observed more in the breach.

Pushed by the Centre, CSSs bloomed. The Central government came up with new schemes but CSSs were mostly successful nationalized development schemes of states. With the Centre acting as a virtual clearing house of good state development schemes, states fell trapped to a one-size-fits-all concept. Gradually, they became implementers of only CSSs.

CSSs required considerable counterpart funding from the budgets of state governments, which consumed an increasingly larger proportion of their Plan resources. There was another practice that made deeper inroads in their fiscal independence. After every five years, the Plan expenditure liabilities of CSSs were transferred to the non-Plan expenditure budget of state governments. Together, past and present CSS-related expenditures took away a big part of the development spending of states.

The debt financing of states by the Centre, by way of granting loans as part of NCA, transferring multilateral and bilateral loans and grants on the pattern of NCA and small savings loans, made states indebted to the Centre. The dominance of these loans and the systemic need to raise more loans in the race to increase Plan size to be approved by the Planning Commission made states the subordinates of the Centre. CSSs enabled the Centre to take over the development functions allocated to states as per the state list of the Seventh Schedule. By the turn of the millennium, the fiscal relationship between the Centre and the states had changed fundamentally. India had predominantly become a fiscal union.

NDA Initiates Process of Restoring Fiscal Federalism

The finances of states had deteriorated immensely by the year 2000. Excessive borrowings had made their debt servicing obligations go up sharply. The interest payment-to-revenue ratio routinely exceeded 20 per cent. Large expansion of state employees, especially in the education and health sectors (largely reflecting expenditures of previous Plans), bloated salary and pension bills. The Pay Commission award in 1997 was turned into a large giveaway by a weak Central government. This modified award dealt a crippling blow to state finances. The expenditure of states on salaries, interest and pensions exceeded 100 per cent of revenues in many cases. Burgeoning deficits in the power sector contributed their mite to the fiscal misery.

States were in a major debt trap.

It was very common for states to avail ways and means advance (WMA) from RBI to remain afloat. Several states were using WMA for more than 200–250 days a year. For quite a few states, WMA was not sufficient to keep their treasuries open. Many states routinely resorted to overdrafts from RBI. Overdrafts came at a higher rate of interest and with stricter conditionalities. If the overdraft was not cleared in a certain number of days, RBI would cut off the payment service. Though RBI is the banker to the states, in such situations it did not honour their bills and cheques. Simply put, the treasury of the state was closed and all payments stopped.

The fiscal stress of the states was so acute in the first few years of the new millennium that closing of the treasury had become a routine event. The treasury of one major state—Assam—remained closed for over 200 days in 2003.

The situation was bordering on hopelessness in the initial years of the new millennium. Something drastic had to be done.

The NDA government led by Atal Bihari Vajpayee decided to take the bull by the horns and took several policy initiatives, beginning in 2003, which successfully remedied the situation by 2006.

First, the government decided to control raising of excessive debt. The FRBM Act for the Union was legislated in the year 2003. The FRBM Act and Rules placed a limit on the overall fiscal deficit of the Centre.

The default resource policy until 2000 of 'raising as much debt as you can' was given up in favour of 'borrowing only this much'. This altered the basic objective and process of budget making. The game changed from raising debt to fill the balance between expenditure and revenues to planning expenditures keeping in mind the extent of resources, revenues and debt. This brought about a paradigm shift.

The Centre adopted this discipline for itself and there was a shift in the policy stance with respect to states as well. They were subjected to a 'golden rule': limit revenue expenditures to non-debt tax and non-tax revenues and borrow only up to the prudent limit decided by the FRBM law to invest in capital expenditures. The states soon adopted FRBM laws. This effectively brought in a ceiling on debt, though indirectly, which had been envisaged by the Constitution but not implemented in the first fifty years after Independence.

Second, the government decided to deal with burgeoning pension liabilities, which effected a fundamental change in the management of fiscal expenditure. The civil service pension (which by extension was applicable for most public-sector employees) was based on the 'defined benefit' principle. The pension benefit was prescribed in legal rules— generally 50 per cent of last pay as pension upon completion of thirty-three years of service. Pension benefits were changed quite frequently to make them more attractive to employees and pensioners at the will of the political masters. No funds were set aside by the government to meet pension liabilities. These were paid from general revenues.

In 2004, the government decided to switch over to a pension system based on 'defined contribution'. This envisaged opening an individual retirement account for every new employee to which the government made a specific contribution (as a proportion of pay). Employees also made their contribution to the account. The corpus of retirement accounts was to be invested by professional asset management agencies keeping in mind the investment pattern preferred by each individual. The government's pension liability to a specific employee was over after contribution to their account. All state governments, over a period of time, also switched over to this defined contribution pension scheme, or NPS.

Third, in 2005, the government decided to discontinue the system of central plan loans (NCA loans) to states upon the recommendation of the Twelfth Finance Commission. This was a major step in restructuring the fiscal relationship between the Centre and states. States were provided only the grant (equivalent to 30 per cent of normal entitlement of funds) and were free to borrow the remaining from the market as state development loans.

This marked a big break from the entrenched practice of the past fifty-five years. For the first time since Independence, the Centre was signalling that it would stop lending to the states.

This decision, implemented in 2005, altered the fundamental fiscal equation between the Centre and the states and the character of states' borrowing. In the next ten to twelve years, states were meeting more than 80 per cent of their borrowing requirement by raising debt from the market.

Fourth, the government, seizing the opportunity offered by low interest rates prevailing during 2003–05, generously urged the states to get their costlier loans from the Centre (past Plan assistance, small savings and loans given as part of transferring multilateral and bilateral loans) refinanced by raising cheaper loans from the market. This debt swap facility worked wonders. A good part of the Centre's loans to the states were refinanced using this facility, bringing down the debt servicing liability of states materially.

Fifth, the Twelfth Finance Commission recommended restructuring of older higher cost loans from the Central government to the states and granted relief on interest payments if they agreed to adopt some fiscal reforms: adoption of a fiscal transition path, enactment/amendment of the Fiscal Responsibility and Budget Management (FRBM) law to limit borrowings to the level specified by the Finance Commission/Central government (3 per cent of gross state domestic product in most cases), and limiting revenue deficits.

The Central government converted these recommendations into a Debt Consolidation and Relief Facility (DCRF). The DCRF helped states to undertake notable debt consolidation and reduce their interest liabilities.

Sixth, the Twelfth Finance Commission also recommended reforms in the system of financing states' projects with the use of multilateral and bilateral funds. It recommended that funds flowing from these institutions should go to states on original terms. Described as the back-to-back system, it literally established a direct financing relationship between multilateral and bilateral agencies on the one hand and the states on the other with the Central government only acting as a conduit.

This meant states could get funds for the original long tenure of the loan (thirty-five years in case of the International Development Association, or IDA, for example), and loans as loans and grants as grants. As multilateral and bilateral loans are usually priced at relatively very low rates, reflecting the AAA credit rating of lending organizations like the World Bank, states' debt servicing liabilities reduced drastically. States were expected to make provisions for the foreign exchange risk using part of the savings resulting from lower interest rate payments.

These reforms fundamentally changed the fiscal relationship between the Centre and the states with respect to debt financing. Over the years, beginning in 2005–06, the flow of loans from the Centre stopped almost entirely. Refinancing, restructuring and debt swap schemes helped reduce states' cost of borrowing and servicing liabilities substantially.

The reforms initiated by the NDA government were continued in the same spirit by the UPA government that came to power in 2004. By 2006 or so, the phenomenon of overdrafts disappeared almost completely in all the states. WMAs became few and far between. The hitherto regular visits of state chief ministers and finance ministers to the Union finance minister to get funds or some accommodation from the Centre became rare.

The years from 2003 to 2007 saw a restoration of balance in the fiscal relationship between the Centre and the states, most prominently in the matter of debt financing and managing debts.

Marching Towards Fiscal Unionism Again

Tax, grants and debt are the principal elements around which the fiscal relationship between the Centre and the states is built. The broad thrust of these relationships defines whether we have a true fiscal federalism (the Centre and the states functioning in balance, with no one dominating the other), a fiscal unionism (one level, usually the Centre, dominating the other), or fiscal competitiveness (both remaining in competition for resources).

Developments in the past few years, most notably in the last two years, indicate that the fiscal relationship is headed towards fiscal unionism again.

The GST reforms in 2017 transformed the fiscal relationship between the Centre and the states substantively in the matter of taxation power-sharing. The basic structure of separate taxation powers has been effectively substituted by a shared taxation system for the bulk of indirect taxes. The power to tax a good or service and decide the rate of tax for each item was transferred to the GST Council. A common tax collection and transfer system—the GST Network (GSTN)—has been created.

In the new architecture of GST tax, the states gave up the right to levy tax, determine the rate of tax, collect tax and grant concessions on taxes. The states accepted this big change in the larger national interest to create 'one nation with one tax system'.

The GST system was expected to have a different impact on different states. Many states stared at the face of losing the revenues they were earning under the VAT system. Rising above narrow state-specific interests, they signed up for a common GST taxation system on the solemn assurance of the Centre, which was constitutionally and legislatively backed, that, for five years, states would be compensated fully if GST revenues fell short of a compounded annual growth of 14 per cent. A mechanism of GST Compensation Cess was devised to cater for any anticipated shortfall in GST revenues to meet the 14 per cent objective.

There was no shortfall in the first two years, 2017–18 and 2018–19. The Centre collected more Compensation Cess than required. In fact, it literally appropriated additional receipts as its revenue in 2018–19 whereas excess funds were to be kept in a GST compensation account in the Public Account of India. The first year of significant shortfall was 2019–20. The Centre did not deliver the due compensation on time and GST compensation was delayed. The shortfall of 2019–20 was finally paid only by July 2020.

In financial year 2020–21, the pandemic created a very difficult situation for both the Centre and states. In the initial months, the Central government anticipated a gross shortfall of about Rs 3 lakh crore in GST revenues and a net shortfall of Rs 2.35 lakh crore (accounting for Compensation Cess receipts of only Rs 65,000 crore). This was a crunch situation and the Centre decided not to honour its commitment to pay full compensation to the states to give them 14 per cent annual compounded growth. The 'Act of God' argument was invoked to argue that the situation was beyond the control of the Central government and accordingly the shortfall on account of loss of GST revenue attributable to COVID-19 would not be compensated.

Despite many differences and contentious meetings, the Centre stood its ground. It is borrowing for the shortfall attributable to the non-

COVID revenue growth trajectory and passing on the same to states on a back-to-back arrangement. The states have to borrow on their own for the remaining shortfall.

The way the GST compensation issue has been handled illustrates the fiscal domination of the Centre.

Another tax matter where the Central government has acted in its interest at the cost of the states relates to appropriating additional tax revenues on petrol and diesel by imposing non-shareable cesses and surcharges. International crude prices in the first half of 2020–21 averaged less than two-third the prices prevalent the previous year. The space created for consumer price reduction by this fall in international prices was used for imposing non-shareable infrastructure cess on diesel and petrol. The effective incidence of excise duty and cesses appropriated by the Centre makes up about 40 per cent of the final consumer price of diesel and petrol. Expanding non-shareable taxes hits at the root of fiscal federalism.

In the matter of grants from the Centre to the states, the juggernaut of CSSs rolls on. In addition, a number of new schemes of the same nature have been introduced. As noted above, as per Budget 2020–21, the size of CSSs is over 40 per cent of total shareable central taxes.

A more significant change is taking place in the matter of delivery of CSSs. CSSs have traditionally always been implemented by states through their budgets or agencies. The Centre never implemented them directly or through its agencies. With increased interest in direct delivery to the end beneficiary, the Central government has now put in place a direct benefit delivery system, using the banking system, under its control. In this system, the central ministries and departments are able to transfer funds directly into the accounts of beneficiaries with states having no real presence or say in the matter.

For the first time in India, the general public has started recognizing which benefits are being provided by the Centre and the state government. As the Centre runs and funds the larger part of CSSs, even though the subject might be in the constitutional domain of the states, there is increasing evidence of people attributing these schemes to the Centre. Even where schemes are implemented through state governments and they contribute a good share of the cost, there is rivalry between the state and the Centre to take the credit.

The unemployment and misery induced by COVID-19 and the subsequent lockdown provided the Centre an opportunity to launch highly publicized programmes to benefit a large part of the population. Additional foodgrains and pulses were provided to over 75 crore ration card holders. Cash assistance of Rs 500 was deposited in over 20 crore bank accounts of women. Financial benefits were delivered directly to people in their bank accounts. The Centre definitely won the battle of perception in delivering benefits.

The debt part of the equation has also undergone important changes. States don't have authority to borrow as much as they like and need. In fact, they need the approval of the Centre to borrow as they are indebted to it, as central loans to the states have come down substantially.

The Central government has started imposing conditionalities on states while granting permission to make extra borrowings to deal with falling tax revenues. The permission granted in May 2020 to allow raising of additional 1.5 per cent of Gross State Domestic Product (GSDP) as borrowing was subject to several conditions. This was an unprecedented development.

Another measure worth noting is the offer to provide a total of Rs 12,000 crore ($1.6 billion) as interest-free loans for fifty years to the states to maintain the pace of capital expenditure. Not only is the amount quite small, it has the potential to keep states indebted to Centre for five decades!

All these changes have again made the states subordinate. The fiscal dominance of the Centre is back with a vengeance.

For the past six years, centripetal forces have gathered strength again. This has been most visible in the way the matter of Compensation Cess for GST was handled; the expansion and administration of CSSs, especially the expansion of direct benefit transfers (DBT); the Disaster Management Act was administered to deal with COVID-19, the renewed expansion of flow of debt resources from the Centre to the states; and the conditionalities being imposed on raising of market borrowing by states. India is closer to a fiscal union today than ever before.

Part B: Policy Reforms for Building A $10 Trillion Economy

Section IX: State of Policy: A Retrospect

Chapter Forty-Five

Fundamental Economic Policy
since Independence

India became the master of its own destiny on 15 August 1947 after gaining independence from British rule. From that day, the country and its policy leaders could decide its economic goals and objectives, adopt the economic model considered most suitable for growth, development, employment and other economic goals and objectives, and make the fundamental policy choices to achieve these goals and implement the economic model.

India decided to adopt the socialist pattern of society and entrusted the 'commanding heights of the economy', which encompassed basic industries, manufacture of capital goods, plant and machinery, utilities and exploitation and processing of natural resources, to the public sector. It also decided to rein in the private sector by reserving several sectors of the economy exclusively for the public sector, debarring the entry of the private sector in these reserved sectors, and subjecting private industry to the licence and control of the government for the rest of the economy. India also later opted to nationalize almost the entire financial sector by taking over the insurance and banking business from the private sector besides nationalizing many real sector companies as well.

The fundamental economic policy choice India made was to build an economy in which the private sector had limited space to make investment in production of goods and services, that too subject to government control and licence. Economic, financial and fiscal policies were built around this fundamental choice. All subsidiary policies were also formulated within the contours of this socialist economic policy, which permeated all sectors of the economy in the next two decades.

In a nutshell, India's fundamental socialist economic model post-Independence comprised the following major components.

First, private enterprise and capital were excluded from the principal drivers of economic activity and growth in the industrial age—manufacturing, mining and quarrying, utilities and infrastructure—which were to be primarily reserved for and developed in the public sector.

Second, agriculture was made into a smallholder sector with no leasing and contracting. Intermediary and absentee landlords were eliminated. Direct relationship of tenants/farmers was established with the state, which freed the farmers from the responsibility to pay any taxes; instead, the state started subsidizing the agriculture inputs and prices.

Third, India's economy was closed to foreign investment and technology. The foreign trade policy centred on import substitution, which ended up neutralizing the objective of containing trade deficit with export promotion.

Fourth, the financial sector—banks, insurance, pensions—was gradually nationalized and brought into the public sector.

Fifth, India went in for debt and fiscal deficit monetization funded public-sector investment and government expenditure, accompanied by highly regressive tax policies.

These formed the core construct of India's economic policy framework for four decades after Independence. This was India Economic Policy 1.0.

India Economic Policy 1.0 Did Not Deliver

The fundamental economic policy framework adopted by India translated into sectoral policies in agriculture, industry and services. It also deeply impacted the traditional factors of production: land, labour and capital. The financial sector, external sector, public sector and the government's own fiscal finances were also impacted severely.

These policies were pursued most vigorously during the four decades of the 1950s, 1960, 1970s and 1980s. The country suffered because of these policy choices. Growth suffered. India's poor growth record was derided as the 'Hindu rate of growth'. While many other developing countries, especially in East Asia, broke out of the circle of low growth and high poverty, India remained largely stuck as a poor country.

India remained hooked on to the socialist bandwagon for four decades and created a planned economy with public-sector dominance and a controlled private sector in a very limited sphere of economic activity. The world, however, changed in the decades from the 1960s to the 1980s. The USSR, the fountainhead of communism and socialism, with a planned economy and all-pervasive public sector, started slowing down and eventually imploded in the 1980s. China, the other centre of communism and centralized planned economy, was a pygmy economy in the 1970s. On the other hand, the market economies of the industrialized world in Europe and Northern America, East Asian countries, like Japan and South Korea, grew spectacularly and became global economic growth engines. China, from the 1980s, and South-east Asian countries from a little earlier, started growing impressively as well.

India, however, persisted with the socialist path. Our governments continued to hold down the private sector, which kept shrinking and was present only in a few consumer sectors. The government held the private sector responsible for the ills of the economy and socially bad, while the public sector, though loss-making and producing shoddy goods, was projected to be good and socially responsible. Unable to operate freely and competitively to make profits by legitimate means, many in the private sector resorted to all means (legitimate and illegitimate) to avoid taxes, take loans from PSBs without the intention to repay or misuse them for other purposes, and defalcate funds from government programmes and projects, mostly in collusion with politicians, government servants and bank officials. The licence permit raj ensured that those in the good books of the government got licences and import permits while others simply cooled their heels. Instead of a socialist pattern, India got a crony-capitalist pattern of society.

India was politically an open and democratic country. However, instead of changing gear in the 1950s when the Germanys, Taiwans and

Japans of the world were rising, or in the 1960s, when South Korea and other East Asian countries were rising, or even in the 1970s, when even a hardcore communist country like China started changing, the country persisted with failing policies and started taking baby steps only in the 1980s towards the rehabilitation of the private sector in the economy. India also wrongly opted for short-term, debt-funded growth in the public sector.

It took considerable time for the country to realize its tryst with destiny—finally, in 1991, India took a decisive turn. The economic policies adopted and persisted with, from 1947 to 1991—the era of Indian Economic Policy 1.0—have been described and analysed in greater detail in Part A of this book.

Indian Economic Policy 2.0

India passed through a very unstable phase politically in the second half of the 1980s with all sorts of patchwork political formations assuming power. The combination of unstable political leadership and floundering economic fortunes brought the country to a pass when it was on the verge of defaulting on its international debt obligation in 1991. The 1991 crisis is commonly dubbed as the foreign exchange crisis as India did not have enough foreign exchange reserves left to pay its due debt. The underlying crisis was, however, the result of an all-pervasive sub-optimally performing economic policy 1.0 framework. With its back to the wall, the country started changing in 1991.

This was in 1991 when massive economic reforms were ushered in. The year 1991 was a landmark for Indian economic policymaking with new industrial, trade and FDI policies being formulated and massive liberalization of licencing and control over industries being brought about. This was the second turning point in India's economic life and journey post-Independence. This was the point when the ghost of socialism began to be exorcised and left behind.

This was the 1991 moment. This was the year when India entered the era of Economic Reforms 2.0.

The Economic Policy 2.0 has been characterized by readmitting the private sector in all economic spheres though the public sector continued to trudge along. The fundamental Economic Policy 2.0 is reflected in material change brought in all the five principal policies of Economic Policy 1.0 framework.

First, private enterprise and capital was permitted in all the principal sectors and drivers of economic activity and growth in the industrial age—manufacturing, mining and quarrying, utilities and infrastructure—by gradually de-reserving all these sectors with the big bang opening up initiated in the 1991 Industrial Policy Resolution. Though it has been a gradual process, there is almost no sector of economic activity completely excluded from the private sector today.

Second, agriculture has seen more informal policy liberalization. Agriculture has continued to be a small-holder sector without the farmers being allowed to officially lease out or contract in almost all states. Agricultural land has become further fragmented, bringing down average operational holding. There is widespread informal leasing by the smaller farmers who have principally shifted to non-agriculture jobs and contract farming in partnership with the corporates and start-ups. The relationship of the state and tenants/farmers has changed from the state collecting some land revenue to the state heavily subsidizing agriculture inputs and buying out crops, most specifically wheat and rice, at off-market prices.

Third, India's economy has been substantially opened to foreign investment and technology. The dominance of the policy of import substitution has been dispensed with substantially though there have been some attempts to bring it back in the name of Atmanirbhar Bharat in the past year. While India has continued to face trade deficit and current account deficit, substantial flow of capital—FDI (predominantly equity) and FPI (both equity and debt)—has resulted in a substantial capital account surplus, large enough to offset the current account deficits in most years.

Fourth, the financial sector—banks, insurance, pensions—has been gradually opened up to the private sector. The private sector has also established itself in the wider financial industry, such as non-banks, mutual funds, the money market and infrastructure financing. It has also raised considerable funds from abroad to invest and lend to the domestic industry. The private sector is again the more dominant player in almost all segments of the financial sector.

Fifth, government finances continued to remain under pressure with India facing high levels of public debt. There is no direct monetization of fiscal deficit, though RBI continues to hold a large amount of government securities.

These policies and their consequential impact on the Indian economy have also been discussed comprehensively in Part A of the book.

Chapter Forty-Six

Seventy-Five Years of Economic Policymaking: Major Lessons Learnt

India has nearly seventy-five years of experience in economic policymaking and execution as an independent nation. The country has come a long way from being a predominantly poor, largely agricultural and rural, almost entirely illiterate and pathetically malnourished nation to become a food surplus, agriculturally self-reliant, rapidly urbanizing, highly literate and globally integrated $3 trillion economy, now the sixth largest economy in the world. We have certainly come a long way.

But there are still miles to go. India has the second largest number of poor. Agriculture still supports about 50 per cent of the population. Manufacturing has not really taken off. The economy is still quite inward-looking and has missed the opportunity of achieving sustained export-led industrial growth. About one-fifth of our children are stunted and malnourished. The economy is still only $3 trillion strong, whereas the Chinese economy is five times larger at $15 trillion. We must not forget that India and China were almost at the same level in the 1970s.

Evidently, we could have done better. We possibly got our democratic model of governance right but the economic model of socialist pattern of society proved wrong. There were several other policy choices that proved to be wrong or suboptimal. We can draw valuable lessons from our economic policymaking experience by placing it in the context of global economic policymaking and performance.

Here is my pick of ten major policy lessons.

No Nation Remains an Economic Growth Leader Forever

No people, economies or geographies have remained leaders of economic growth forever. Different geographies and people have assumed leadership from time to time based on a critical mix of entrepreneurial innovation, technology development, capital and human skills.

India, China and the Golden Crescent Zone of the olden times in the Middle East domesticated wild crops and animals and created a resplendent and rich agricultural economic revolution. The geography and climate were suitable and the land, rich in water, minerals and other nutrients, provided the right 'capital' to bring vast areas under agriculture, produce crops and create income and wealth. This confluence of circumstances and advantages lasted for many millennia.

About 300–500 years ago, the discovery of new American lands by Europeans, development of agricultural technologies that could produce better crops under controlled conditions despite extreme climates and storage and processing of crops that optimized their use neutralized the natural advantage of Asia. The invention of the steam engine and machines brought the Industrial Revolution to Europe and the Americas, which stymied the agricultural revolution by producing higher incomes and wealth from processing of non-agricultural materials. China, India and the Middle East, dependent on agricultural income and wealth, started declining relatively.

In the industrial era, economic leadership, along with income and wealth, shifted to Europe and later to the Americas and Japan once the Industrial Revolution took root. The ability to use coal and other fossil fuels to power increasingly bigger and better machines (machines, in fact, built additional stock of human physical strength besides building additional organs and muscles to perform many functions the human body was not capable of or comfortable performing) provided enormous comparative advantage in producing numerous products from minerals and metals available in nature besides producing richer and better products from agricultural, animal and forest produce. The countries and people that transitioned from the agricultural economy or built a new economy based on industrial products prospered in the industrial age, which started sometime in the late eighteenth century and blossomed in the twentieth century.

For much of the nineteenth and twentieth century, India and China resisted industrial adoption and fell behind. Colonization worsened the matter. By the middle of the twentieth century, they were among the poorest countries in the world. China jumped on the industrial bandwagon in the late 1970s and soon became the factory of the world. India was not as enterprising and aggressive in industrializing the country. As a result, the Industrial Revolution generated only mediocre returns for the country.

Europe, North America and Japan, who were the leaders in the Industrial Revolution, slowed down from the second half of the twentieth century and industrial leadership passed on to China, South Korea, South-east Asia and a few other countries. Europe and Japan, the industrial powers of the twentieth century, are in decline now. North America has moved on to the next economic revolution: the digital revolution.

Using digital technologies and artificial intelligence (AI), the digital revolution has expanded the capability of the human mind and ability to deliver services. People and nations who are mastering and producing digital technologies are forging ahead and, in times to come, will be leaders and winners in the economic sweepstakes. The US, China, Taiwan and a few other countries seem to have forged ahead in the digital era as well. India has a chance to be at the forefront of the full-scale digital revolution, instead of only being a leader in IT services.

Historical performance is no guarantee or even a necessary guide for future prosperity. Countries that master the digital revolution and build their economies using this comparative advantage will lead the next major spurt of economic growth, not those who remain stuck in the agricultural or even industrial era.

Strong Leaders Do Not Necessarily Make Good Economic Policy Choices

India has had three extremely strong and popular prime ministers: Jawaharlal Nehru, Indira Gandhi and Narendra Modi. All three won comfortable majorities in the Lok Sabha on the strength of their sway over the people of the country. All three leaders have been more than presidential in their ability to take decisions. While we have the benefit of hindsight for evaluating the impact of economic policy decisions made by Jawaharlal Nehru and Indira Gandhi, the verdict on economic policy choices which are still being made by Narendra Modi would have to wait for some more time for a more complete assessment.

Jawaharlal Nehru opted for the socialist pattern of society, with the public sector becoming almost the exclusive investor and operator in most industrial areas that required high investment, operated as utilities or processed critical and natural resources.

The most fundamental economic policy choice made by Nehru led to transferring the mantle of producing private goods and services to the public sector by excluding the private sector from many industrial sectors and nationalizing the private sector. The public sector is nothing but the corporatized government sector. This governmentalization of industrial production had massive consequences for the Indian economy.

Government, by its very nature, is not an efficient agency for production of private goods and services. As a result, almost the entire savings of the country got directed to building inefficient high-cost assets in the public sector with poor economic and financial returns. The exclusion of the dynamic part of the economy—the private sector—by reserving most industries for the public sector, institutionalizing the licence and permit raj and cutting off access to new technologies and innovations from abroad led to India achieving what has been derisively called the 'Hindu rate of growth'. Nehru was a global leader with very sound democratic credentials. He built the institutions of democracy and higher education and landmark projects like the Bhakra Nangal dam. However, after seventeen years of his leadership, India plunged into one of its worst food crises. Low economic growth had turned the country non-competitive, largely insular and highly indebted.

Indira Gandhi enjoyed tremendous popular appeal and support, especially after the creation of Bangladesh, which broke Pakistan. She won more than 350 seats in the Lok Sabha in 1972. She remained prime minister for about fifteen years. When she spoke, the country listened, mesmerized.

Her choice of economic policies, however, proved worse than those of Jawaharlal Nehru. She killed private financial industry by nationalizing banks. She subjugated private industry by making the licence permit raj at its most stringent. She raised marginal income tax rates to 97 per cent which ensured there was no interest and enthusiasm left to establish and operate profitable enterprises. She brought in several laws to control enterprise and animal spirits in the name of monopolies control, rent control and serving the poor. She nationalized the wholesale grain trade as well though it was a short-lived misadventure. As a consequence, India became a closed economy, producing substandard goods at high costs that people were forced to consume having no choice. There were endless waits for even such shoddy products. Scooters were delivered ten years after you booked them. The same was the case with telephone connections. The cement you booked after paying an advance was allotted to you well after your house had been constructed. The slogan of 'Garibi Hatao' proved vacuous. The nation became far poorer under her rule.

The Indian Republic has completed seventy-four years by now. Half this time—thirty-seven years—had passed when Indira Gandhi was assassinated in 1984. The economic policies during this period (1947–1984) have been described earlier in the book. This was the period of botched up de-privatization, enormous expansion of the inefficient and capital-guzzling public sector, nationalization of banks and insurance companies, India closing itself off foreign investments and technologies and consequential low growth and perpetuation of poverty. The economic performance of this period should be adequate to convince us that the economic policies followed were not in the larger national interest.

It takes much effort to correct policy wrongs. Vested interests acquire enormous power and clout for continuation of such suboptimal policies. Part of the wrong was corrected by the second fundamental policy shift in India, which took place in 1991. The policy of de-privatization of industrial production was reversed in this year. However, while most sectors of the Indian economy are now open to the private sector, the rollback of the public sector is still to take place.

Narendra Modi, the first non-Congress leader who secured a clear majority in the Lok Sabha after twenty-five years, not once but twice, comes from the economically advanced state of Gujarat. His record as chief minister of the state inspired confidence that he would pursue the liberal and private sector oriented economic policies to make India shed the legacy of the public sector and inspire the world to invest in the country, building a thriving private sector-led economy of India.

The Narendra Modi government completed a landmark transformation of the indirect taxation system of the country by getting Goods and Services Tax (GST) laws passed by the Parliament and all the states and implemented the same. To resolve non-performing loans of the banking system decisively and effectively, the Insolvency and Bankruptcy Code was crafted and implemented. There were notable reforms in the real estate, insurance and space sector. Unfortunately, the fundamental economic policies pursued in the first seven years of his rule have amounted to no more than a continuation of the policy regime established in 1991.

Some significant departure in the economic policy was signalled by the government in 2021. Privatization of the public sector, including banks and an insurance company, has been proposed as a policy choice. Not much privatization has, however, actually taken place. Only one major public sector entity—Air India—has been privatized.

Freeing up agricultural markets was also proposed by dismantling agricultural produce marketing committees. Ending the public sector monopolies in some sectors like coal has also been initiated. However, there has not been good follow-up. There have been some rollbacks as well such as repealing the farm trade liberalization law. We need more time to assess whether the government under Narendra Modi walks the talk on the measures initiated.

Some decisions were taken in a huff, which had very bad economic consequences. 85 per cent of currency in circulation—all the banknotes of Rs 500 and Rs 1000—were demonetized dramatically in November 2016 to sweep down the black money. However, all the banknotes in circulation ended up being deposited with the RBI. In another dramatic decision, all the country was locked down in March 2020 to nip the COVID-19 virus in the bud and prevent it from spreading in the country. The decision did not stop the virus but caused the Indian economy to lose 25 per cent of its GDP in the first quarter of 2020–21. None of these two decisions could have been taken by a less formidable and popular leader.

Curiously, governments led by non-charismatic and less stronger leaders have been able to make decisive shifts in economic policymaking. The 1991 reforms were undertaken by a minority government led by P.V. Narasimha Rao, who was not even the leader of his party in the 1991 election campaign. In fact, he was denied a ticket to contest the Lok Sabha elections! The economic reforms unleashed in 1991 unshackled the Indian economy, rejuvenated the private sector and made the economy grow at one of the highest rates globally for about twenty-five years.

Earlier, Lal Bahadur Shastri initiated fundamental reforms in agriculture by ushering in the green revolution, institutionalizing the Minimum Support Price (MSP) regime and establishing a grain purchase and storage system that helped India overcome its persistent food shortage problem and made it food-sufficient and self-reliant.

Evidently, strong leaders do not necessarily make sound economic policy decisions. And when poor economic policy choices get implemented on account of the stature and strength of these mass leaders, the risk to growth becomes even greater.

The Government is a Poor Entrepreneur and Businessman

Production and distribution of private goods (all goods except classic public or common goods like defence, internal security, currency, some type of infrastructure, macroeconomic stability, etc.) require business acumen, risking of capital for higher returns and flexibility of operations. These qualities are essential for efficient production and distribution of private goods, maximization of value addition at the lowest cost, faster adoption of technology for better quality and competitive cost, and vesting decision-making in managers to take on-the-spot decisions.

The government is not designed to have these abilities. Government managers are selected as generalists, not best suited for technical operations of any enterprise. Government processes are based on layers of decision-makers who are expected to take calls in a manner where the integrity of process, rather than the commercial value of the decision, is more important. The system of incentives and disincentives is differently designed for civil servants who can run excellent public services, but are grossly ill-equipped for operations of business entities.

There have been exceptional managers with tremendous business acumen in the public sector who could turn around loss-making enterprises and compete with the best in the private sector. But they have been few and far between. Most civil servants do not make excellent business managers. Their talents are best utilized in delivering public goods.

The technology and traits of government functioning get imbibed and internalized in the public sector. The Courts have held public-sector enterprises as an instrumentality of the state under Article 12 of the Constitution. The procedural rigidities of government recruitment, procurement and disposal have got built into public-sector processes, subjecting it to a huge handicap compared to private-sector competitors.

The public sector gets stuck with old technology as most entities have been built with import of some technology at some point, whether it was for steel plants, power plants or heavy engineering. As new technologies evolve and other competing companies surge ahead, the public sector falls behind. The public sector has not been able to finalize even technology procurement tenders in time; 4G technology for BSNL and MTNL is a case in point. Several other considerations also enter the equation, such as domestic procurement, public-sector reservation or preference and small-sector reservation or preference. The reservations for certain castes and classes led to crucial positions remaining unfilled or filled with poorer quality managers. Disputes among staff in the public sector relating to seniority, promotion and grant of scale are enormous, leading to human resource management becoming a major casualty.

The government and the public sector are not entrepreneurs and businessmen. Commercial entities established by the government, either as departmental undertakings or public-sector enterprises, do not serve the national interest of making India a globally competitive economy.

Technology and Innovation Provide a Real Competitive Advantage

Fundamentally, every economic good or service is produced using some technology or process. There is no single or permanent technology or process for producing any particular good and service. Humans keep innovating and developing newer technologies for producing the same good or service at a lower cost, producing better-quality products servicing the same need, or producing new products and services that meet some unserved or underserved need.

Transportation by foot was the principal means of transporting goods and persons for centuries. It had its limitations. Harnessing animal power and later the invention of machine power made the production of animal-driven carts and subsequently automobiles possible. The bullock cart out-competed transportation by foot and led to expansion of transportation services in terms of availability of means of transportation and the distances that could be covered. The arrival of automobiles made transportation using animal power relatively inefficient and inadequate. There was no way animal-driven carts and rickshaws could have withstood the competition of automobiles for carrying passengers and freight. Likewise, there was no way hand-spinning could have competed with machine-made textiles. There was no way postal communications would have thrived in the age of instant email and digital communications.

Indian policies of small-scale reservations, public-sector reservations, protection of sick industry, protection of PSBs and other enterprises, subsidization of older technology-based businesses, shielding domestic enterprises from foreign competition and restrictions of technology imports effectively institutionalized inefficiencies and kept Indian industry stunted. On account of these policies, Indian industry did not build real competitiveness based on the use of the most efficient technologies and processes, and has generally lost out.

You cannot run ahead of your competitors in a race while looking behind, with your hands or legs tied, or for that matter using poor quality shoes. Creating the right ecosystem for new technology to be adopted as quickly as possible and building competitiveness are keys to making the Indian economy grow faster and better.

Overuse of Land and Water for Agriculture is Wasteful

About 140 million hectares of India's land is used for agriculture. Only about 3 million hectares of land is used for non-agricultural purposes: residential, industry and infrastructure. This 140 million hectares of land produces 15 per cent of GDP, equal to about $0.5 trillion; 3 million hectares produces 85 per cent of GDP, or $2.5 trillion. Non-agricultural use is about 200 times more productive than agricultural use. Yet, there is so much hue and cry when land is proposed to be diverted from agricultural to non-agricultural use.

India has 4 per cent of global water for 18 per cent of global population; 80 per cent of this water is used for agriculture and the balance 20 per cent for non-agricultural, industrial and residential use. Thus, 80 per cent of water produces 15 per cent of GDP, while 20 per cent produces 85 per cent. Water is used unconscionably inefficiently in agriculture. One kilo of rice consumes 2500 litre of water, sufficient for the drinking needs of ten families for a day. Yet so much is invested to harvest and divert the water for agricultural irrigation and so little to provide tapped safe water to every family in the country.

India's land and water policies have been terribly unproductive in the past seventy-five years.

Land in India has been presumed to exist only for agriculture. Some land was diverted from agriculture use for *abadi* or residential purpose. However, land records treat and classify all lands from the point of view of agriculture. All non-arable land is noted in land records in large chunks/parcels as such. The agriculture use land is surveyed in detail and land records provide owner-wise details for all operational holdings. The abadi land is also classified in one chunky plot with no individual details about each house plot.

In short, the entire land classification and management system exists for management of land as agricultural. There are excessively stringent rules for transfer of land for non-agricultural use. Owing to the policy framework in the past seventy-five years, land availability is scarce for residential, industrial, infrastructure and other non-agricultural use. This has led to the price of land for these uses to become extraordinarily high, making many residential, industrial, infrastructure and other projects unviable and non-competitive. India's road construction programme has become a government-funded programme because of excessively high land costs that give private enterprise no chance to make profits.

Despite certain negative consequences, harnessing India's water by constructing dams and barrages was absolutely necessary to prevent flooding of plains and runoff of precious rainwater to the seas. That investment was necessary. India has still not been able to stop all water run-off, most notably in the North-east.

However, water dammed with massive investments and cost to people has been primarily reserved for use in agriculture. The government made unusually liberal water allowances for irrigation in the leaking lands of Punjab, Haryana, Rajasthan and Gujarat from the dams built in the Himalayas and Vindhyas. The water allowance in Stage 1 Phase 1 of the Indira Gandhi Canal in the districts of Ganganagar, Hanumangarh and Bikaner in Rajasthan was 5.23 cusecs per chak of 404.7 hectares. This was many times over the efficient requirement. It was reduced in the second stage to 3.05 cusecs per chak. In Phase 2, the water allowance has been less than 2 cusecs per chak. The vested interests created in receiving about three times the water required in Stage 1 of Phase 1 have not allowed the water allowance to be reduced even after it has been demonstrated down the same canal system that productivity does not get adversely affected even when water allowance is reduced to less wasteful levels. This surfeit of water created lakes of brackish water in the desert as the gypsum layers did not allow the water to seep down.

Large irrigation projects are still being undertaken in several states. The Accelerated Irrigation Benefit Programme (AIBP) later brought under the umbrella scheme of 'Har Khet Ko Paani' has been going on for decades to provide central funds and loans to states to complete 100-odd major irrigation projects.

The focus on providing drinking water to India's 30 crore households has been less sharp, until recently when the scheme to provide piped water to every family was launched under the Jal Jeevan Mission.

Again, India's lopsided water policies have done great disservice to the nation's economy. Hearteningly, there is now some recognition of this and a move to correct the unproductive waste of the country's limited land and water resources.

India Has Wasted the Economic Potential of Women

The modelled estimates of the International Labour Organization (ILO) put India's female labour participation rate at a measly 20.3 per cent in 2020. The global female work participation rate is 46.9 per cent. India's female labour participation rate is one of the lowest in the world. More worryingly, the rate is falling continuously after 2005, when it was 31.8

per cent. It fell precipitously to 22.9 per cent in 2012. Thereafter, too, it has fallen every year, though more gradually.

When only one in five of India's potential female labour force works to produce economic goods and services for the market, a large potential of generating economic value and growth gets lost. Why have we let the situation come to such a pass and why has the policy framework not done anything to encourage greater participation of women in the country's economic life?

At Independence, India's female workforce was almost entirely uneducated and illiterate. Women worked primarily in homes, in their own agricultural fields or in traditional occupations like beedi-making. After Independence, India provided women the right to vote but did little to encourage their participation in the economic space. This, despite the fact that education for women became a focus area; by the turn of the century, elementary schooling of girls was virtually on a par with boys. In the past thirty years, an increasing number of women have gone to college and their tertiary education status has also improved substantially. Women are as economically productive as men are.

Two developments are primarily responsible for shrinking women's labour participation rates in the past fifteen years. One, as farms have become more mechanized, the need for manual work in fields has gone down. This has led to the displacement of female farm workers. Two, urban women, despite being much better educated and economically productive, have tended to be homemakers rather than working in factories, offices and establishments. This could be owing to implicit division of labour in the family, lack of appropriate jobs or the perception of risk to safety in urban areas or simply backward societal preference.

Policymakers seem to be quite unconcerned with this phenomenon. Nothing has been done to create incentives for establishment of labour-intensive factories in textile and other industries and encouraging participation of female workers. Bangladesh has created a far better framework for participation of women in the textile industry.

Certain decisions have been taken to increase benefits for working women. Paid maternity leave has been increased. Other benefits have also been improved. However, these measures do not seem to have encouraged greater employment of women.

Overprotective Import Policies Hurt the Economy

Before the gold currency standard was junked in the 1970s, the excess of imports over exports was essentially settled by paying in gold or silver or foreign currency reserves that were benchmarked to gold or silver. India ran a trade surplus in much of the twentieth century before Independence. On balance, the country received gold and sterling reserves.

There was a mindset prevalent all over the world that imports were bad and therefore avoidable as they would require exporting the country's gold or silver to pay for them. In the post gold standard era also, this mindset has continued to determine policy in India. The fact that the country has been a net importer of gold for domestic jewellery and investment purposes and ran down its sterling reserves very soon added to the necessity of controlling imports. Further, as industrialization required imports of capital goods, the case for curbing imports of consumer goods became still stronger in the minds of policymakers.

This led to India building an anti-import policy framework in the post-Independence period.

The country introduced a heavy-handed licencing regime for imports. Every item required a licence. The open general licence (OGL) list remained practically abolished for more than twenty-five years until the mid-1970s. Licences were granted after protracted procedural torture. The government agencies came up with so many conditions, forms and procedures that compliance became a nightmare. The licence regime was hugely discretionary. This led to the development of crony-capitalism in the import space.

India also raised big tariff walls. Our peak tariff rate was 300 per cent for over forty years. The country's average tariffs in 1970s exceeded 125 per cent. Consumer goods suffered the highest tariffs. Only after 1991 and India joining WTO did the rollback of high tariff walls commence. Still, the country had the heaviest tariffs in the world at the turn of the millennium. The process of steady reduction of import tariffs or customs duty has been reversed from 2015. Import tariffs on about one-third of tariff lines have been raised in the past five years.

One instrument of controlling imports, however, kept moving in the opposite direction during the first forty years. India's currency was kept overvalued, making imports cheaper and neutralizing the impact of high tariffs to a great extent. Importing cheap foreign goods and avoiding customs duty became a cottage industry as a consequence.

A severe import licencing regime coupled with high tariff walls shielded the public sector and domestic private industry from foreign competition. Availability of captive and protected markets made both the public and private sectors produce shoddy goods. Aided and abetted by the strangulating licence raj system of discouraging expansion of manufacturing capacities, the restrictions on imports led to severe supply disruptions, making Indians wait even for simple products like a telephone, scooter and steel for years. Secured domestic markets for substandard products at high prices generating profits made the Indian industry totally inward-looking. The Indian industry could not and did not try to enter export markets even though demand was expanding phenomenally in developed countries.

India's policy stance in the forty years until 1991 for trading with the world has been described as an import substitution regime. The country opted to encourage production of all industrial goods in the country and keep away the threat of imports. It also opted to give up potential exports to substitute imports with domestically produced goods. This was the policy of 'self-reliance'.

India learnt the consequences of pursuing this emotionally appealing but economically devastating policy at a heavy cost. The crisis of 1991, when the country was on the brink of defaulting its international obligations, was the culmination of this flawed policy that deprived Indians of good quality products and becoming rich by export-led growth.

An Overvalued Rupee is Not a Strong Currency

The paper rupee, like most other currencies globally, began its journey as being fully convertible in silver and gold. The government initially kept the amount equal to the nominal value of paper currency in gold, silver, gold coin and silver coin in reserves to credibly carry out its assurance of being ready to give a silver coin in exchange of a paper rupee.

This process created the notion that paper currency was as valuable and strong as gold or silver currency. However, governments started diluting the gold and silver reserves that backed the issuance of the paper rupee, underwritten by the belief that no one, or at worst only a few, would ever ask for replacement of a paper rupee with a gold or silver rupee. Gradually, a disconnect developed between the gold or silver contained in a one rupee coin and the price of gold or silver in terms of paper rupee notes.

The relative value of the rupee as a currency with other currencies of the world was fairly easy to discern when all currencies were on the gold or silver standard or convertible in gold or silver as long the world had a fixed ratio of 1:15 between gold and silver prices. When the world moved to the Bretton Woods system after World War II, the US dollar became the reference currency. As a fixed ratio of conversion was agreed upon between the US dollar and gold, it became possible for every country to declare its relative value to the US dollar by undertaking to make its paper currency convertible into gold at a fixed ratio.

All this determination of relative value with reference to underlying gold convertibility made policymakers and the public believe that one's currency becomes weak when its nominal value goes down with reference to another currency. If a dollar was fetched by Rs 4 on a day in 1966 and if you needed Rs 5 to get a dollar the next day, everyone perceived that the rupee had become weaker.

The real value of a currency, when it is not backed by 100 per cent reserves in gold and silver, is measurable in relative value of goods and services produced in an economy relative to the nominal value of the currency. If, say, India produced $100 million worth of total goods and services in a year and its stock of currency issued was Rs 1000 crore and the next year it again produced $100 million worth of total goods and services but its stock of currency went up to Rs 1250 crore, the real value of currency depreciated by 25 per cent. If there was no change in this period in the value of all the goods and services produced and the dollar currency issued, the rupee would be equally strong even if its nominal value depreciated by 25 per cent vis-à-vis the dollar.

Unfortunately, in the perception of policymakers, Indian currency would have become weaker in the example cited above if the country were to devalue its currency by 25 per cent. This optical difference between the nominal value and real value of the currency has had an enormous negative impact on policymaking in the country.

India loosened its monetary policy after Independence to raise resources to finance the development and construction of industries. However, this did not raise the production of goods in proportion of additional currency issued, altering the relative ratio of total goods and services produced or GDP vis-à-vis other countries, especially industrially advanced countries. Policymakers kept resisting calls to readjust the value of the rupee in terms of the underlying rupee-gold ratio. This situation had major implications for imports, exports and foreign exchange reserves.

The artificially overvalued rupee led to pressures on imports as imports became cheaper. More imports led to running down of reserves. The overvalued rupee discouraged exports, further depressing foreign exchange reserves. This vicious cycle of larger demand for imports, lower exports and consequential pressure on foreign exchange reserves kept India highly vulnerable. The country resisted as long as it could under the mistaken belief that maintaining the nominal international value of the rupee meant a strong rupee. However, the pressure became unbearable at a certain stage and India had to heavily devalue its currency in 1966.

This misconceived policy of maintaining the strength of the rupee by keeping its nominal value higher than the underlying real value worked to India's disadvantage. Policymakers started acting rationally only after 1991. The Indian rupee finally became fully floating by 1995, following several intermediate steps of devaluation and maintaining dual values for different types of imports over a period of three to four years. The exchange value of the rupee started getting determined in terms of demand and supply of foreign exchange.

The policy of market-determined value of the rupee helped India regain export competitiveness, neutralized the demand for imports on account of an artificially overvalued rupee and helped build foreign exchange reserves. The lesson that an artificially overvalued rupee is not really a strong rupee was learnt the hard way and at a massive cost to the public, industry and government.

Perpetuating a Sick Industry and Vacuous Jobs Does Not Create Employment

Production of goods and services, which are bought and consumed by residents, businesses, governments and foreigners, create value and income. It also creates jobs. The work done in jobs to produce goods and services is real employment.

There is no permanent way or technology to produce any particular good or service. There are many goods and services whose demand disappears or gets replaced by other goods and services. Therefore, there is no permanent work or job. Jobs created/maintained to produce any particular good or service whose demand has disappeared are sick or no jobs. Jobs created/maintained to pay wages without production of any goods or services are vacuous jobs. Sick and vacuous jobs are not employment.

Under the mistaken notion that it was protecting jobs and employment, the government adopted and persisted with several policies after Independence to protect sick and vacuous jobs.

The public sector was presented as a model employer. Millions of unskilled, low-skilled and inappropriately skilled people were employed in departmental undertakings and the public sector, at both the Central and state level, without really producing any marketable goods and services. The pay and allowance systems were designed and distorted with no link to value created. Even after a PSU became sick or was closed, payment to workers continued with borrowing or the government providing funds from taxpayers' money to keep up the charade of continuing employment. The public sector bled and eventually became sick. A major reason for the spectacular failure of the dream of handing over 'the commanding heights of the economy' to the public sector was the false sense of creating jobs despite the fact that the people employed did, in many cases, no work, or did work that constituted only a fraction of what they were paid.

The private sector was not spared either. The industrial laws and labour laws that were framed did not allow sick and failed businesses to close. Industry had to continue with the employment of square pegs in round holes. Industrialists were made to pay bonuses even when the company generated losses. There was no freedom to start a business when someone saw an opportunity and there was no freedom to close a business when it was no longer producing goods that had a demand or generated enough value addition to pay for the labour.

These policies of artificially creating and sustaining sick and vacuous jobs cost the country dearly. They discouraged labour from upgrading skills for newer job opportunities and discouraged capital from hiring labour. They encouraged industry to substitute labour jobs with machines wherever possible and allowed. They perpetuated the climate of sickness in industry. These policies and practices cost India dearly by making industry non-competitive. They also contributed to making Indian industry default on loans taken from banks, thus making the banks also sick.

There was some rethinking on this sorry state of affairs after 1991. Schemes of voluntary retirement were put in place in the public sector and were also permitted in the private sector. The National Renewal Fund was set up to pay for the cost of retraining labour. However, by and large, the basic framework of overprotection of labour stayed in place. In the past five years, there have been further reforms undertaken in this area. The system of fixed-term contract appointments, initiated for a few industries in 2016, has been extended to all enterprises. This allows industry to hire skilled labour for the period it requires. In the recent process of consolidation of labour laws, more liberalization has been given to industry to close enterprises employing less than 300 workers. IBC permits the resolution and liquidation of companies unhindered by the issue of labour.

India Prefers Risk-Free Debt to Risk-Capital Equity

India was a low-income, low-savings country at the time of Independence. Low savings meant low investment, both in debt and equity, hurting the chance of ramping up growth rapidly. The decision to discourage foreign investment further hurt capital creation. Low savings also meant low intermediation by the banks and low credit creation as the credit multiplier worked on a smaller deposit base. In a nutshell, India faced the vicious circle of low income, low savings, low investment and low growth.

This inherently sad state of affairs was further complicated by the government pursuing policies of transforming the country's savings into debt, not equity. As explained earlier in the book, there was no difference in equity and debt capital for the government. The ever-constant capital output ratio was expected to produce the same output even when the capital invested was entirely made up of debt.

The government launched an aggressive small savings programme to mobilize savings to use as capital. The life insurance industry was nationalized and LIC was mandated to invest virtually all its net premiums in government bonds. Private industry was subjected to the EPF scheme, which mobilized workers' savings into the accounts maintained by EPFO with the mandate to invest all net accumulations in government bonds and other public-sector entities. In the 1960s and 1980s, private-sector banks were nationalized and mandated to invest a large part of the savings placed as deposits by people in government bonds under statutory liquidity ratio obligations. Almost the entire financial system worked to channel a major part of people's savings to the government as debt.

Business, or the production and distribution of goods and services to make profits, is inherently risky. There may not be enough demand for the goods and services produced. A competitor may offer better products at a cheaper price. The technology might change, as may consumer preferences. A business may, on the contrary, generate super profits if the product catches the fancy of consumers and the technology choices made allow entrepreneurs to produce goods and services at much lower costs. Thus, any business may make good profits or lose money. Therefore, businessmen need to deploy risk capital. Equity is that risk capital.

A part of capital can be relatively risk-free. Risk-free capital, usually called debt, obligates businessmen to pay a certain fixed rate of interest or an interest rate linked to some measure of inflation. Depending upon the cost of such debt capital and the profit generated on capital, businessmen may make or lose money on the debt undertaken. This leverage enhances the riskiness of equity capital. No business can be incubated and established unless the entrepreneur is able to raise and deploy risk capital.

Surprisingly, Indian policymakers did not consider equity as very necessary capital for enterprises. This was partly because most investments were expected to be made by the public sector and there was no difference between equity and debt as far as the public sector was concerned, at least until 1991. As most of the capital was required for the government and public-sector enterprises, all the institutions to mobilize savings were designed and developed to convert savings into debt. The Indian public also felt more secure in the thought that their savings were protected with no likelihood of default by the government and the government-owned public sector and became unenterprising.

The Indian government established quite a few institutions to provide debt to the industry. Beginning with IFCI in 1949 and later IDBI, SIDBI, IDFC, IIFCL and the like, a number of financial institutions or DFIs were established. These institutions primarily provided debt capital to industry. A very small fraction of total funds lent was provided as equity by IDBI and IFCI. The government established the first institution providing equity, the National Infrastructure Investment Fund (NIIF), only in 2017, about seventy years after Independence. There is a proposal to establish another debt-financing DFI for infrastructure debt, as announced in Budget 2021–22.

As a consequence of this lopsided policy and virtual elimination of equity financing in the country, dubious practices developed in the industry on a large scale. Loans were raised from banks and development finance institutions in holding or sister companies to be provided as equity to new enterprises. Businessmen over-invoiced capital expenditure and used the payments received on the side as equity in other enterprises. A number of cases in the National Company Law Tribunal (NCLT) disclose the sordid practice of manipulating bank loans to generate equity.

India paid heavily for this big policy mistake. The financial system is still debt-oriented. The country still lacks availability of equity. Old habits die hard.

Section X: Policy Reform Agenda

Chapter Forty-Seven

Fundamental Economic Policy Reforms for a $10 Trillion Economy

Economic reforms are all about choosing the right economic policy framework to create the right incentives and institutions for the factors of production to create value by producing goods and services that are expected to have demand in times to come at cost and with quality to make them competitive domestically and internationally. The government's economic policy has the strongest influence on productive forces—businesses and labour—as it affects their incentives and disincentives and shapes their animal spirits, behaviour, actions, investments and participation.

Metamorphic changes are taking place in technology. Digitalization is spreading fast in production of goods and services and fundamentally altering their productivity, competitiveness and quality. Environmental considerations have become extremely important and are having a huge impact on manufacturing and energy systems. Social and governance considerations are also becoming critical.

The private sector and foreign investments have been allowed in India but a large inefficient public sector still exists. Government finances are also quite fragile.

The fundamental economic policy framework (Economic Policy Framework 3.0) to build India's conducive economic, financial and fiscal system to grow India's economy to $10 trillion by 2035 would have to be built around following five fundamental reforms.

First, get the government out of the business of producing private goods and services. This will entail privatization of all commercial public-sector undertakings.

Second, direct all government investments and expenditures to production and delivery of public and merit goods and redistribution. Commons are the concern of the government whereas personal products are best produced and distributed in the private sector. This requires the government to be focused on production of common/public goods and services. This would require fundamental reforms of the taxation system to raise the share of tax in the value added and wealth and also in the system of subsidies, support and transfers to deserving sections of people.

Third, making the Indian economy digital will primarily drive growth by transforming services. Policies to digitalize the economy quickly and fully will make all the difference.

Fourth, the future economy will be environmentally sustainable. This requires all pollutants—carbon and others, in the gaseous, liquid or solid form—to be controlled or recycled to maintain the balance in the natural state. There is also a large infrastructure gap in the country. Corporates informed in environmental, social and governance (ESG) norms will create most value in future. Policies to seize the potential of an ESG-informed economy and ESG-compliant infrastructure will be critical.

Fifth, there is an enormous mismatch between the value agriculture creates and the households it supports for their income and consumption. This mismatch can only be addressed by removing a large proportion of farmers and labourers from agriculture. Industry is witnessing lower growth for some time now. Fundamental restructuring of agriculture and industry will be essential for the Indian economy.

Privatizing the Commercial Public Sector

The rise of communism and socialism made governments in many parts of the world producers of private goods, often replacing the private sector. Almost invariably, the world over, governments have been poor producers of private goods and services. In most countries in the world today, the state is taking a backseat in the production of private goods and services.

In India, too, the state had de-privatized industrial production and created a very large public sector following the first fundamental economic policy reset after Independence (IPR-1948, IDRA-1951, IPR-1956 and the licencing policies, bank nationalization and MRTP Act). The second fundamental policy reset in 1991 has succeeded in stopping the public-sector juggernaut and bringing the private sector into almost every sector of the economy in the production and distribution of private goods.

Unfortunately, the government still spends enormous amounts of public resources on sustaining the inefficient public sector, which continues to be present in the production of private goods. The public sector also distorts economy in several areas. The government needs to completely get out of the production of private goods and services. This would necessitate privatization of the commercial public sector (PSUs that produce and distribute private goods like steel, cement, fertilizers, seeds, electrical machines, power plants and consumer goods).

Reforming Government Expenditures

The rightful function of the state is to produce and deliver public goods and services to people and to redistribute income and wealth to afford a minimum standard of quality life to all and to invest in human capital. This would require expenditure systems to be overhauled and reformed.

Growth is good and wholesome if the national income it generates is fairly distributed such that the animal spirits of entrepreneurs remain high while ensuring every resident enjoys quality of life. Faster growth and fair distribution comprise this dual-track goal.

The right redistribution policies and right amount of expenditure on provision of public goods are needed to attain the objective of banishing poverty and malnutrition and enabling every Indian to lead a quality life with dignity. India's current redistribution and public expenditure policies are confused. A fundamental reset of the policy framework needs to be built around three aspects: discontinuation of all public expenditure on provision of private goods and services, redesigning the redistribution framework to shift to direct income transfers and transforming current public works programmes to make our air, water, skies, earth, rivers and lakes pure and free from pollution.

Making the Indian Economy Digital

Enabled by the three key technological innovations of the chip, the code and the Internet, the digital revolution is transforming every business in the world. The digital revolution is also transforming the production and consumption of many agricultural and industrial goods. There is an increasing use of chips and code in the manufacture of physical goods. With the Internet of Things (IoT) also a reality now, the connectedness of physical machines and equipment is the next game changer in building the digital economy of the future. Economies that advance beyond industrial-age technologies to digital-age technologies will clearly be winners while economies that ignore digital technologies or are inefficient converters will lose out.

India has not been very forward-looking and successful in technological advancement based on two of the three critical technologies: chip-making and code-writing. This needs to change. India will have to invest massively in building and acquiring critical digital technologies to digitalize its entire economic production system across the entire agricultural, industrial and services value chain.

India has been flirting with very restrictive data control and management policies, as seen in the draft Data Protection Law and draft E-Commerce Policy which is in the mindset of the licence permit raj which made India miss the Industrial Revolution. To digitalize the economy and wrest the best advantage in the digital transformation of the world, the country must build data laws that allow it to seize the opportunity offered by the digitalization sweepstakes. That will be the difference between missing the digital revolution or capturing it.

The government's industrial and economic growth policy framework needs to be built around constructing the digital economy of the future. Industrial policies are passé now. India needs to frame a Digital Economy Policy to propel it to the forefront of digital technology innovation, production of digital technology chips and other products, and programming solutions on the cloud and crypto platforms, enabling the country to emerge as a net digital products and services exporter.

Building an Environmentally Sustainable
Economy and Infrastructure

As economies graduate towards middle income status, massive expansion of infrastructure is needed to put the economy on a higher growth trajectory. India has an enormous infrastructure deficit. Massive investments are needed in building transportation networks, communication networks, real estate, digital real estate, electricity generation systems and infrastructure for education, health, irrigation, drinking water, and so on.

Climate change caused by massive expansion of greenhouse gases (GHGs) in the environment is making the world sit up and make fundamental changes in the system of production of goods and services and use of fossil fuels for energy. Likewise, lopsided distribution of income and wealth has made the world quite unequal among and within nations. There are also large governance concerns, especially in the way corporations, which generate more than 50 per cent of global value added, are governed. These concerns are getting increasingly reflected in what has come to be known as the ESG agenda.

Infrastructure and production systems need to facilitate movement of countries towards the goal of contributing net zero emissions. This is ushering in vast investments in producing electricity by renewables, by making infrastructure, manufacturing and mining emit less or no carbon. ESG concerns are going to influence economic decision-making, exports and investments. India has additional responsibility and opportunity to invest in and tap investible funds for an environmental clean-up (sequestering pollutants and carbon emissions).

The policy framework needs to make new investments ESG-compliant to take advantage of the massive investment likely to flow in for retrofitting and rebuilding the economy and infrastructure under initiatives like 'Building Back Better'. A policy framework that creatively leverages the government's fiscal resources and international resources to build ESG-compliant and ESG asset class infrastructure will make a considerable difference to India's aim of building a $10 trillion economy.

Restructuring India's Agriculture and Industry

India's agriculture production systems have three huge problems today. First, agriculture adds too little value compared to the human, land and other resources it uses. More than 50 per cent of the labour force, over 90 per cent of the land under economic production systems and over 80 per cent of usable water resources are employed for only 15 per cent of the value added. Second, agriculture production systems and farmers are massively dependent on government for support at all ends—inputs, agriculture operations and marketing of produce—which has made agriculture a non-business function. Third, agriculture is subject to so many restrictive laws—ceiling, leasing, contracting, marketing, essential commodities and so on—which no other economic activity is subject to, resulting in a total loss of enterprise.

India can neither build a $10 trillion economy nor achieve the goal of fair distribution of incomes and wealth unless agriculture is freed from these emasculating legislative controls, released from the yoke of all pervasive government support and its resource use (labour, land and water) made more proportional to the value it adds. This calls for a comprehensive reform and restructuring agenda.

India was late to join the bandwagon of industry. Today, we lag behind massively in manufacturing on account of this late acceptance of industrialization. The world seems to be getting adequately industrialized on the whole. This is making global supply of industrial goods meet global demand. Reduced growth rates of population, maturing of consumption of industrial goods in advanced economies and productivity introduced by digitalization (Industry 4.0) and global value chains seem to indicate that the opportunity of adding growth and jobs by investing in manufacturing will be much less attractive than in the digitalization of economies. Our industry has lot of obsolescence as well.

An appropriate policy framework to make India industrially competitive and focus industrialization on sectors and niches where we can be global leaders would make the real difference in building India's $10 trillion economy.

These fundamental reforms are developed into specific sectoral reform packages in the ensuing chapters.

Chapter Forty-Eight

Agriculture Policy Reforms

There are quite a few facts apparent when one scans the agriculture situation of India today.

First, land under agriculture has reached saturation point. About 140 million hectares of land is currently under cultivation. Land under cultivation grew from about 116 million hectares at the time of Independence to about 143 million hectares at its peak twenty-five years ago. For many years, it has remained around 140 million hectares. It is unlikely to increase further.

Second, agriculture is primarily land-based. However, productivity of land—value added divided by land use—is 200 times more in non-agricultural use than agricultural use.

Third, much of the land under crops is used for foodgrains. As land is sown more than once in a year, the gross cropped area is higher than 140 million hectares. Total cropped area under foodgrains is around 125 million hectares (45 million hectares under paddy, 30 million hectares under wheat, 20 million under coarse cereals, currently called nutri-cereals, and about 30 million hectares under pulses). Oilseeds are grown on another 25 million hectares of land, cotton takes about 12 million hectares and sugarcane another 5 million hectares. Total area under horticultural crops (vegetables, fruits, flowers, including plantations) is only around 25 million hectares. Field crops (foodgrains, edible oilseeds, cotton and sugarcane) use about 160 million hectares of gross cropped area, whereas horticultural crops use only about 25 million hectares. No land is specifically counted as being under animal husbandry. In any case, animal husbandry either co-uses land under crops or is undertaken on non-cultivated common land or fallow/barren land. Crops contribute about 50 per cent of agricultural GVA, horticultural crops another 20 per cent and animal husbandry the remaining 30 per cent. This makes land productivity quite different within the agricultural group as well. Field crops use 85 per cent of land to produce 50 per cent of output value added, horticultural crops use 15 per cent of land to produce 20 per cent of output value added and animal husbandry uses almost no land to produce 30 per cent of output value added.

Fourth, agriculture uses 80 per cent of India's available water to produce 15 per cent of GDP. Water use in agriculture is grossly inefficient whereas a lot of people in the country do not have adequate drinking water and industry is starved of water to produce higher value addition.

Fifth, renowned demographer and economist Malthus was a false god who surmised that food supply would not be able to expand in the ratio of the expansion of population. The world has shown that food supply can expand to take care of expanding population. In fact, global food supply is now expanding faster than the expansion in population. In India, too, while agriculture has grown on average at over 3 per cent per annum for many years, the population is now growing at less than 1.1 per cent per annum; it is expected to fall below 1 per cent soon.

Sixth, there are too many workers (farmers and landless workers) 'employed' in agriculture. The same level of output can be easily achieved by one-fifth of workers. Overemployment of workers in farming leads to very low wages and income for workers and farmers, which explains the perpetuation of poverty in agricultural and rural areas.

Agriculture policy reforms have to be built around these critical facts.

Reorganize India's Agriculture in 125 Million Hectares

The non-agricultural part of the Indian economy needs more land at lower prices to build industrial areas, set up cities, develop infrastructure and increase India's green spaces. Agriculture has a lot of slack. The ratio of gross cropped area to net cropped area is only around 1.5. Gross cropped area can be increased to twice that of net cropped area with better management. Further, productivity of agriculture can also be raised significantly. The government should actively take up the policy of transferring about 10–15 million hectares of agricultural land to non-agricultural use—preferably the marginal agricultural lands. This will bring down excessively high land prices for residential, factory and infrastructure projects to reasonable levels.

The government should also bring about a transformation of land use within the agriculture field. Land productivity of horticulture is much more than field crops. Output of foodgrain crops has also risen to a reasonably comfortable level whereas demand is not growing that fast. On the other hand, demand for horticultural crops is increasing impressively. Land productivity is the highest in case of animal husbandry and demand for animal husbandry products is also witnessing good growth. Thus, there is good reason to shift part of the land from foodgrain crops to horticultural and animal husbandry products. The shifting of land *inter se* in agriculture will not hurt foodgrains as there is enormous scope to increase productivity of foodgrain crops as well.

Replace Input Subsidy Programmes with Direct Cash Support for Farmers

The green revolution was built on popularization of agriculture inputs: seeds, fertilizers, insecticides, agriculture equipment, electricity and so on. To provide farmers these subsidized inputs, subsidized farm loans were also provided. These more productive inputs helped India transform from being a food-deficit country to a food exporter. The efficacy of input subsidization is now over. Farmers have learnt the advantage of using high-yielding seeds, fertilizers, farm equipment and other inputs. In fact, there is evidence of overuse of these inputs on account of their being highly subsidized. Subsidized inputs do not really help farmers. They end up reducing farmers' income under the MSP system where farmers get a margin of over 50 per cent over the cost of cultivation, which gets lowered when subsidized inputs are used.

India has built a massive system of agriculture input subsidization since Independence. There was some rationale to subsidize inputs like fertilizer, seeds, electricity and water in the initial years to popularize their use to increase productivity of crops. These objectives have now been achieved. In fact, there is now overuse of fertilizers, electricity and water, which is proving counterproductive.

Input subsidy programmes have distorted markets. Many inefficient fertilizer-producing entities continue to exist, putting an undue burden on government finances. The Government of India foots a bill of over Rs 70,000 crore in fertilizer subsidies a year. Most states provide subsidized or free electricity to farmers to the tune of about Rs 1,00,000 crore a year. The Centre and states virtually underwrite payment of all interest on farm loans. The Government of India incurs an annual expenditure of about Rs 20,000 crore annually while state governments are estimated to provide another Rs 30,000 crore in interest subsidies. Water subsidies are not directly computable. India needs to replace input subsidies with direct cash transfer to farmers. Besides providing good income support, it would free farmers from the obligations of raising only certain crops and using the inputs provided through a highly convoluted system. In fact, farmers could have the freedom to raise whatever agricultural produce they wish to: field crops, horticultural products or animal husbandry. This would bring them true independence and much better incomes.

Do Away with the MSP Programme

India needed to nudge farmers to produce foodgrains owing to the perennial food deficit in the 1950s and 1960s.

Farmers tend to switch to the crop that gives them the best assured price. They also tend to invest in land improvement and use of inputs in case they see the benefit in the form of higher realization of price than the cost of inputs. That was the mindset and setting in which India's MSP policy was designed in the middle of the 1960s. The policy worked. Large swathes of land in Punjab, Haryana, Uttar Pradesh and north-western Rajasthan took up cultivation of wheat and rice in the late 1960s and 1970s. The green revolution took flight on the wings of MSPs for wheat and rice.

The success of a policy begets many clones and, often, its perpetuation beyond the rightful date of expiry. The MSP policy was extended to all other crops in the hope that the same magic would be repeated. This was done without applying one's mind to the situation on ground in which other crops are raised and also without ensuring that these crops would be bought by government agencies in sufficient quantities such that their market prices remain anchored at a level higher than MSPs. Most of these programmes flopped on the ground. Crops were not purchased by government agencies and market prices remained lower than MSPs in many cases.

At present, India does not need to support the growth of foodgrains by instituting any MSP. In fact, 'minimum' support prices for foodgrains have degenerated into 'maximum' support prices, making the government the presumptive sole buyer of the crops. Indian MSPs are also higher than international prices, making export impossible without subsidization.

It's time to liberate agriculture from the yoke of MSPs. Let there be a free market for agricultural produce. The fact that there is limited land that can be put to agriculture would make the invisible hand of the free market a better guide for farmers to choose the crop that fetches them the best returns and encourage dynamism among them. The expenditure incurred by the government in providing underlying production subsidies in the MSP system can be provided to farmers as direct income support. These measures will help free farmers from the low-income trap.

The botched attempt to 'reform' three farm laws has ricocheted on the government. Some sections of farmers are now demanding a legally guaranteed MSP. This would, if granted, mean that the government could be sued by any farmer, or any trader in the name of the farmer, if his crop, good or bad, was not purchased by the government irrespective of the prevailing market price. The courts, not the best agency to decide such commercial matters, would get flooded by the suits. The farmers need to be convinced about what is in their larger economic and financial interest. Direct income support in place of MSP, larger than what gets delivered in the MSP system, should convince the farmers. The government has also to be firm in introducing these necessary reforms.

Initiate Major Transition of Labour Away from Agriculture

Currently worth $450 billion, agriculture in India does not need 50 per cent of the workforce, or 200 million agriculture farmers and workers, engaged in it. The world over, farmers and labour have migrated to non-agricultural jobs and enterprises as farms have also become mechanized and better organized. In India, this migration has been very slow. That said, there is increasing evidence that the younger generation is not interested in working in farms and India's agriculture workers and farmers are rapidly ageing.

The government has traditionally pursued policies that are anti-migration. Programmes like MGNREGA, with their stated preference for providing 100-day jobs near homes and not where the public work is, slow this transition. Likewise, massive input subsidization and creation of micro-enterprises in myriad schemes like the Integrated Rural Development Programme (IRDP) and National Rural Livelihood Mission are all intended to provide some survival level of income support in addition to income from agriculture. The fact that the government ends up selling the foodgrains produced by farmers and agricultural labour to rural residents at highly subsidized prices is also meant to retain rural workers in their homes and villages.

These policies and programmes have to drastically change to provide proactive support for migration away from agriculture. A massive skill development programme needs to be launched with the express objective of preparing farmers and agriculture workers for the industrial and services sector—to work in mines, quarries, construction, manufacturing, sports, travel, entertainment and other services. The government must incentivize the creation of decent transitional rental arrangements in cities for rural people to come and look for jobs. It also needs to encourage labour-intensive industries to specifically absorb transitioning workers.

A policy framework that can deliver $1 trillion output from agriculture and allied services with only 10 per cent of India's workforce working in agriculture is the ticket to build a $10 trillion economy by 2035 and eliminate poverty.

Shift Focus from Production and Productivity to Farmers' Income

Today, India is not only self-sufficient in food production but has become a significant exporter of agricultural products. While Indian agriculture has become atmanirbhar, the Indian farmer has not—this is the irony in the story of the turnaround of agriculture in India. Indian farmers have not seen much change in their fortunes. Farmers and agricultural labourers, who still comprise over 50 per cent of India's workforce, continue to be the poorest income earners.

Ever since Independence, India's agriculture programme strategy focused only on increasing production and productivity. The income of farmers was not a real policy goal. Only in 2014 did the government specifically mention the doubling of farmers' income by 2022 as a policy goal. However, programmes and policies did not change much to attain this goal.

Farmers' income is the net sales price farmers get of their agricultural produce minus the cost of cultivation incurred to produce the same. As their operational holdings are small—less than a hectare on average—they end up earning very low profits/income as such small landholdings only deliver a very small agri output for sales. Farmers' incomes in India on average are about one-fifth of other workers and about 30 per cent of the national average income.

The goal of doubling farmers' income has not been very well defined. Nor has a coherent policy and strategy been spelt out to achieve this. Farmers' income needs to be raised at least five times to bring about a worthwhile change in their lives. This requires a multipronged strategy. Primarily, it requires agriculture to be made into a business for farmers to make decent profits out of their hard work and enterprise.

There are five critical planks of the policy, strategy and programmes to achieve the goal of making farming a business enterprise. First, an average farmer's operational landholding needs to become large enough to support earning a decent income. At the minimum, the average operational holding of a farming family needs to become five times of what he cultivates presently. This will raise turnover at least five times to make profit/income five times of the average income today. Second, farmers need to get stable and predictable prices for their agricultural produce from the market, including by locking in output prices before taking up cultivation. Third, farmers should be able to choose the right amount and quality of the inputs to economize/reduce/optimize the cost of cultivation. Fourth, land should become an operating asset, instead of an illiquid liability; farmers should be completely free to use all the properties in the land to get the best out of their land asset. Fifth, the skill sets of farming families need to expand beyond traditional agriculture for them to use their collective labour most productively.

Operational holdings can become five times only by removing all restrictions and prohibitions on land leasing and removing restrictions and impractical provisions in the contract farming laws.

The core objective of the MSP system is to provide farmers a minimum return/income. PM-Kisan operates as an income transfer scheme for the farmer. The element of income in actual procurement undertaken by the government in a year, which should be in the range of about Rs 50,000–60,000 crore, can be added to the actual outgo of PM-Kisan (about Rs 54,000 crore). Taking it to an outlay of Rs 1 lakh crore, PM-Kisan can operate as a genuine income/profit transfer scheme; Rs 1 lakh crore transferred to about 10 crore farmers would imply a transfer of Rs 10,000 per farmer irrespective of crop or the area. A better variation would be to pay an amount per hectare rather than per farmer. As India cultivates about 14 crore hectares of land, an amount of Rs 7000–7500 per hectare would provide requisite support. This will give farmers a minimum assured income.

Fertilizer, electricity and interest subsidies cost the Centre and states more than Rs 2 lakh crore annually. These subsidies should also be replaced by a system of direct cash benefit transfer to farmers. In this system, farmers would get cash support that otherwise accrues to inefficient industries and electricity boards. The industry would become efficient and competitive and farmers would also get a real choice and flexibility in deciding which crops to grow, water and electricity use and how much loan to take.

The direct income support on account of cessation of input subsidies added to the direct income transfer on account of PM-Kisan and dismantling of the MSP system should be able to provide about Rs 5 lakh crore of direct income support for 140 million hectares of land, which is under the plough in the country. This should be able to provide Rs 35,000 per hectare to farmers every year, more than what they can theoretically earn today even if MSP is implemented all over the country for all crops.

Agriculture cannot provide an adequate income to the millions of farmers in India. At the time of Independence, about 70 per cent of workers were farmers and agricultural labourers. Now a little more than 50 per cent of workers are farmers. In absolute numbers, there are about three times more cultivators and agricultural labourers in 2011 compared to 1951, 26.3 crore as against 9.7 crore. Agricultural land has increased only by 15 per cent in this period.

This requires a lot of farmers to move into non-agricultural occupations. While this has been a work in progress, the pace has been quite slow. Government policies have discouraged the migration of agricultural labour to non-agriculture. However, migration of farmers to non-agricultural professions would have no adverse impact on agricultural productivity. Rather, it would be raised as it would lead to more mechanization and efficient operation of farm holdings.

Focused skill development programmes for farmers to equip them to work in construction, manufacturing and services would help this transition. Migrant-friendly policies, ample rental housing in urban areas and industry-led skilling programmes would make a vital difference.

Chapter Forty-Nine

Industrial Policy Reforms

After 1951 and 1991, It Could Be the 2021 Moment for
Industrial Policy Reforms

The government has been talking about a new industrial policy for the past three to four years. It was expected to get finalized in 2021, but has not. The new Industrial Policy should aim at building industry and infrastructure for India's $10 trillion economy by 2035. Manufacturing is industry primarily, though important contributions also come from mining, utilities and construction. The new industrial policy would have to address five major general issues (there are many sector specific issues as well) that have held back industrial growth in India.

First, the country is still not technologically advanced in quite a few industries and there is considerable technological obsolescence in many Indian industries, which has caused widespread sickness. Technological obsolescence and industrial sickness need to be addressed effectively.

Second, Indian industry suffers from high costs of doing business. Higher cost of land, loans and power, among others, makes Indian industry non-competitive and discourages the flow of equity and capital investment. General cost non-competitiveness leads to policymakers bringing industry/ class-specific cost-neutralizing incentive packages. These packages do not address general cost non-competitiveness. In addition to the ease of doing business, the cost of doing business needs to be effectively addressed.

Third, there is still a lot of government and public-sector presence in several industries, distorting policy and competition. The time has come to undo the legacy of the industrial policies of the 1950s and roll back the public sector. This would require Industrial Policy 2021 to take up the agenda of privatizing the public sector.

Fourth, exclusive monopolies, distribution controls and reservations excessively raise the cost of raw materials and other input services unduly in many cases, making private sector and industry stunted and uncompetitive. All anti-competitiveness issues, in addition to cost of doing business, need to be addressed.

Fifth, misplaced preference for excessively protecting organized labour not only hurts industry, but hurts the cause of jobs and employment. The right labour reforms are necessary for industry to flourish in India.

The evolution of industrial policy evolution in India can be captured in two moments when the epoch-bending first big bang changes took place. 1951 saw the IDRA being enacted, which laid the legal and administrative path for de-privatization of industry by translating two major policies adopted by the government of the day: excluding private enterprise from large swathes of Indian industry and handing over industrial development to the public sector. This was the 1951 moment in India's industrial policy development.

The path-breaking new Industrial Policy adopted in 1991 corrected one of these two policy stances by doing away with the reservation of major industries for the public sector. The private sector was re-permitted in almost every industrial space in the country. This policy also rolled back the industry stunting licence and permit raj.

This was the 1991 moment in India's industrial policy development.

In the past thirty years, Indian and foreign industry has, by and large, entered all industrial spaces and acquired dominant status in most industries. The new Industrial Policy can initiate the agenda of re-privatizing the public sector producing private goods and services, opening up Indian industry fully for global investment and technology, and doing away with all governmental controls and interference in establishing and closing industry. Adoption of such an industrial policy in 2021 could have been the 2021 moment of industrial policy development. This policy is necessary to get India completely out of the rut of low manufacturing and industrial growth and put the nation on course to build a $10 trillion economy in the next fifteen years, by 2035.

Bringing Technological Renaissance in Indian Industry

Technology keeps evolving, which makes machines perform better in terms of cost and quality of product. A machine is not a permanent asset in itself. It is only an asset as long as it produces goods competitively; when another machine produces better goods in a more cost-effective manner, the old machine becomes obsolete.

In the planned era, this truth evaded our policymakers, planners and the public sector. The planned economy was based on the mechanical assumption that capital formation drives growth in the incremental capital output mode. Most cutting-edge technology did not evolve in India as there was no private-sector incentive in operation. In fact, the licencing system dissuaded the replacement of obsolete technology with new technology. As a result, Indian industry, in both the public and private sectors, kept becoming increasingly inefficient and non-competitive.

The absurd policy of persisting with a technology/machinery even after it became redundant led to the spread of sickness in industry. Instead of accepting the business logic of creative destruction—a new technology makes the underlying asset more valuable by producing goods and services cheaper—we decided to perpetuate the sickness by following policies and creating institutions to 'revive' sick units by offering financial concessions, which only shifted the cost of sickness to the government and banks.

The technology-related policy framework improved in Industry 2.0. The Sick Industrial Companies Act (SICA) was abolished. Competition, both domestic and international, was allowed in the production of goods and services. This brought in new technologies, including in some PSUs. Finally, the decision to bring in the Insolvency and Bankruptcy Code (IBC) put the last nail in the coffin of industrial sickness. The inefficient entrepreneur running sick and outdated businesses could be booted out using IBC.

As the Indian scientific establishment and enterprise have not been very good at developing technologies, it makes eminent business sense for Indian entrepreneurs to have complete freedom to buy or lease technology from abroad. Instead of importing final products, this allows a lot of value addition to take place in India. There have been sporadic attempts to put caps on royalties and other technical fees. Such attempts must be totally nixed. Most future technologies to produce goods are and will be based on digital technologies, what is widely known as Industry 4.0. We should allow entrepreneurs a free run to import the best technologies to produce products in India.

Industry Policy 2.0 should now yield space to Industry Policy 3.0. In terms of technological renaissance, India should be audacious enough not to provide any subsidies or other support to perpetuate sickness. IBC should be allowed to operate normally for all industrial sick/non-competitive units—small or large—by removing the artificial props of moratorium and suspension of IBC. The government should also enact the FRDI Bill. The government should place no fetters on technology imports from anywhere with payment of royalties or technical fees commercially agreed upon by the private entrepreneur.

Taking Care of Cost of Doing Business

Land was the most critical asset for the agricultural system of production. Machines became the most critical asset for the industrial system of production. Land was required basically to house machines and factories and became secondary to machines in the industrial age.

Much less land is needed to produce one unit of value added in the industrial system compared to agriculture. Even in India, the value added per acre of land is 200 times in the industrial system than the agricultural system. This should have led to freer transfer of land to industry, which made eminent business sense.

Even the communist regime in China that was founded on the hatred of enterprise understood this basic entrepreneurial and business truth. China turned agricultural land into a very cheap industrial asset and equity. As required, land was allowed to be transferred from agriculture to industry and infrastructure at very reasonable (firm and fixed) prices. The profit on conversion of land from agriculture to industry was leveraged multiple times by local bodies and provinces to construct requisite support infrastructure: industrial estates, highways, railways and cities with educational and other facilities. China became the factory of the world in a space of twenty years from 1980 to 2000. It exports goods worth over

$2 trillion every year and has built the largest foreign exchange reserves largely on its manufacturing strength developed in the past thirty years.

In India, we took a different route. Land was primarily reserved for agriculture in Industry 1.0. Conversion of agricultural land for industry was frowned upon. This policy continues unchanged in Industry 2.0. As a result, there is very little land available for industrialization, transport and distribution infrastructure and urbanization. Land has not been a factor of production for manufacturing in India but an inhibitor.

This needs to change. We should free up land markets. The default classification of land as agricultural should be given up. There should be no need to get land converted from agricultural to non-agricultural use from the revenue administration. Factories would, of course, be built keeping environmental considerations in mind. This would unleash creative energies in developing the most appropriate kind of estates for manufacturing and services production.

Governments, both at the Centre and the states, along with their public-sector entities, are sitting on a lot of land, which is used most unimaginatively. Each government should create a single land management corporation. All the land owned by the government and the public sector should be transferred to these land management corporations. They can manage the land as an asset management company to deploy land assets in the most productive manner. This will not only give better returns to the government but make land available for industrialization, urbanization and infrastructure creation at very economical prices to build competitiveness.

Besides land, interest on debt and cost of power are two other major factors affecting financial competitiveness of Indian industry. Industry is the productive sector of the economy. Yet, it pays the highest cost of electricity to the monopoly state power distribution companies. There are so many fetters on industry on generation of captive power and buying power from the cheapest source available. Likewise, there is no bond market for most of the industry in the country and the banking system, dominated by the risk-averse PSBs, lends too little and at too high a cost to most of industry.

Industrial Policy 2021 must adopt policies that make land availability very convenient and cost-effective. Industry should be allowed to source power at the cheapest rate available and the financial ecosystem should develop to enable industry to raise much-needed capital at globally competitive rates.

Introduce Policies to Make Industry Competitive

Reservation of basic industries, heavy industries and utilities for the public sector and nationalization of private enterprises during Industry Policy 1.0 created public-sector monopolies in several industrial sectors. SAIL, NMDC, NTPC, Air India, ONGC, Coal India, DoT/BSNL and many others represented virtual monopolies during the period from 1950 to 1990. There were quite a few monopolies in the financial sector: LIC, General Insurance Corporation (GIC) and the PSBs put together. These monopolies were protected not only from domestic competition but also international competition by raising tariff walls to astronomical levels. They produced shoddy products at much higher costs compared to global costs.

Reservation of over 900 products for SSI, or small-scale industry, had the same effect. SSI is constrained by capital, both financial and human. India lagged behind in heavily labour-oriented industries like textiles on account of the inability of Indian industry to operate at scale. Likewise, many industries, fertilizer and sugar, for example, were subjected to an enormous amount of distribution control.

These monopolies and SSI reservations were abolished in Industry Policy 2.0. Gradually, private industry has come up in many areas earlier reserved for the public sector and some larger industries have also come to operate in areas earlier reserved for the small-scale sector. Much work in specific industries still remains to be done to obviate the inefficiencies and lack of competitiveness of the remaining public-sector monopolies.

Power distribution is still effectively a public-sector monopoly. While the states might have created fifty to sixty-odd companies in the power distribution business and some areas might have seen privatization of power, over 90 per cent of power is still supplied through state entities. The fertilizer industry also operates on concessional/cheaper gas being supplied to public-sector fertilizer entities. The government is still using budgetary resources to prop up high-cost fertilizer producing units. The distribution of petroleum products—diesel and petrol—is also a virtual monopoly leading to a strange pricing policy being followed in the country. Railways at the central level and bus transport at the state level, in many states, still operate as monopolies.

The government should reorganize all remaining industries and businesses that operate as monopolies or virtual monopolies to bring in effective private enterprises and enable them to run as competitive businesses.

Overprotection of Labour Hurts Both Industry and Labour

Labour working with technology—tools, machines and equipment—produces goods. Even the most automatic industrial processes have some workmen and supervisory personnel for control. The mix of labour and machines differs from industry to industry. In highly technology- and machine-intensive production processes (usually referred to as capital-intensive), the proportion of labour employed is much smaller. In distribution and highly customized processes, the proportion of labour is much higher.

No technology confers a permanent advantage. No industry can hope to remain a leader in perpetuity. The evolution of new technologies and products can make highly successful businesses go bust. Lifelong employment and post-retirement pensions run counter to these business realities. The factory has also evolved and modernized over the past two centuries of the industrial era. Working conditions, most notably in large industry where most labour laws apply, have greatly improved.

The relationship of industry and labour has to be developed taking note of these realities and be fair to both the enterprise and workers. The Factories Act needs to be modernized and most labour laws need to be reviewed. Industry must get the freedom to hire and retain workers most suited for the technology used for production.

The government is the arbiter between industry and labour as per the laws enacted for protection of labour. The understanding of the government of business and technology is subpar. The failure of the public sector in many cases is testament to this. Provisions, like the one contained in the Industrial Disputes Act to seek the government's approval before closing a factory if more than 100 workers are employed, are simply unworkable and overestimate the government's understanding of the business. More often than not, this becomes a political football. As the number of workers are larger, either the government refuses permission or keeps the matter pending for ages.

Besides amending labour laws taking more realities on board, it is also necessary for the government to stop being the arbiter between industry and labour. The crux of the relationship between the employer and labour should be left to be determined by the two concerned parties. Aspects of safety and working conditions should be left to expert supervisory bodies. If there are contractual disputes, the courts can adjudicate.

The Right Policies to Be Truly Self-Reliant

Dependence on the world for food was a deep concern for India in the 1950s and 1960s. This is no longer the case.

Imports of pulses and edible oils cost India $11.1 billion in 2019–20. Exports of rice, cereal preparations, other cereals and edible oilseeds fetched $9.4 billion. On cereal, pulses and edible oil, India had a trade deficit of $1.7 billion. On the overall food front, India had a larger surplus of over $16 billion.

Should India go for becoming atmanirbhar in edible oils and pulses where it is significantly dependent on imports? On edible oils, the trade deficit exceeded $8.4 billion, quite a sizeable amount. On pulses, our deficit was $1.4 billion.

If India decides to be atmanirbhar in edible oils and pulses, it will require the country to shift a considerable amount of agricultural land from other crops to production of edible oils and pulses. India's net sown area of 140 million hectares is occupied by some crop or the other. There is no real vacant land. If you shift land from existing crops, it might lead to substitution of rice, wheat or maize and might also lead to reduction in exports of these commodities. If the value of the edible oil and pulses crop so grown turns out to be less than the rice, wheat or maize crop, it might hurt both the farmer and the country. India does not have a comparative advantage in growing edible oilseeds over cereals. Therefore, if the policy of becoming atmanirbhar is stretched to every crop, it might end up adversely affecting the country.

The case of considering comparative advantage in manufactured products is more complicated as technology and innovation have become more powerful factors than labour and land in case of manufactured products.

The lessons from the last seventy-five years of India's experience of fiddling with the policy of import substitution and self-reliance have taught us much.

First, the policy of import substitution and self-reliance is self-defeating. It ends up making agriculture inefficient and manufacturing obsolete.

Second, product by product self-reliance is not a good policy. It puts you in a vicious circle where you might end up achieving self-reliance in a targeted product but something else would give in or come at a greater overall cost.

Third, the policy of import substitution and self-reliance leads to the adoption of inefficient policies of creating tariff walls, imposing physical controls on imports of certain products and using instruments like anti-dumping too frequently. All these lead to trapping the economy in non-competitiveness and unproductive manufacturing.

Fourth, there is a much better option of increasing competitive advantage in select products to make overall balance of payments more favourable to India, which is actually true self-reliance.

Sectoral Policy Imperatives

Mining and Quarrying Needs a New Policy Approach

Mining and quarrying by nature involves disturbing the existing state of stability in the biomass balance. Mines in mountains and forests disturb the ecology and add to the fragility of the terrain. However, minerals and metals are necessary to meet the needs of fuel for producing energy or transportation and to produce goods and machines for consumption.

Balancing the benefits from mining of minerals and metals and the costs to the ecosystem and environment is a delicate task. The policy framework has to get this balance right.

A possible policy framework for developing and exploiting mineral and metal potential with the least possible costs to the environment might evolve on the following lines.

First, cap the coal production of India at 750 million tonnes a year from the current production level of about 600 million tonnes. Fast-track the allocation of coal mines to the private sector without any end-use restrictions and permissions to get them to work within two years maximum—it currently takes five to six years.

Second, small-scale mining and quarrying is inefficient and polluting. Develop mining and quarrying only in large enterprises, mandating the use of technology, minimizing surface disturbance and generating zero or near zero overburden.

Third, mandate the use of technologies to eliminate generation of pollutants and release of CO_2 or equivalent from power generation, even if it makes it costlier. Coal-based thermal power generation can be reduced over a period of time. Undertake a major programme to upgrade coal-based thermal power plants using subcritical and critical technology to superior technology in order to minimize the use of coal.

Fourth, Coal India is a holding company with seven subsidiaries. The holding company should be disbanded by merging it with a sovereign asset management company (SAMC). The nationalization of coal mines in 1973 needs to be undone with the SAMC privatizing all seven subsidiaries over a period of seven to ten years.

Fifth, SAIL has about 15 per cent share in steel production in the country. This share is steadily going down. There are a few other steel plants, directly and indirectly owned by the Government of India. NMDC is setting up a 3 million tonne steel plant in Nagarnar, Bastar. Over Rs 17,000 crore of the estimated cost of Rs 23,000 crore has been invested by NMDC in building this small-capacity plant. The plant has been under construction for over seven years with completion and commissioning nowhere in sight. MMTC, already sick itself, has built a small 1.1 million tonne plant housed in its subsidiary Neelanchal Ispat Nigam Ltd. There is another small steel plant constructed and operated by another Government of India company, Rashtriya Ispat Nigam Limited (RINL). Steelmaking has been very competitively and qualitatively established in the private sector in India. There is absolutely no need for the government to continue running steel plants. SAIL and all other directly and indirectly owned steel companies of the Government of India should be privatized. The Ministry of Steel should simply be wound up.

Sixth, the government is heavily present in the oil and gas space. ONGC and OIL are in exploration as well as oil and gas refining and marketing. The government has initiated consolidation and privatization in these businesses. HPCL was sold to ONGC to make the ONGC-HPCL combine have an interest from the upstream to downstream in the oil and gas sector, from exploration of oil to marketing of petroleum products. BPCL has been put on the block. The process of privatizing oil and gas refining and marketing must be taken to its logical end. Perhaps one integrated entity of merged ONGC and HPCL could remain in the public sector and every other company, including OIL and IOC, sold over the next five years.

Seventh, all the mineral wealth of India belongs to the government. The Centre and states have divided it between them. To get the minerals and metals out of the womb of the earth, the government first set up the public sector and gave it mining licences at throwaway costs and royalties. When the private sector was brought into steel, oil and gas, aluminium, coal and other mineral sectors, the regime of concessions and cess, royalties and other multiple charges levied became a highly complex one. All these policies, laws and practices need to be drastically reformed to make it an efficient regime.

These reforms are absolutely necessary to make mining and quarrying contribute about 10 per cent of industrial GDP of India, or about 2.5 per cent of the $10 trillion, in 2035. These reforms will also be positive from an environmental perspective.

Unleashing the Dynamism of Manufacturing in India

The industrial policy reforms of 1991 brought private industry back into manufacturing. Indian industry could produce a number of products, including machinery and chemicals, which could also be exported successfully. The financial sector, especially banks, and the power sector, especially the critical distribution end, remained in the public sector, making the cost of doing business relatively much higher in India. Over the years, the competitive forces set in motion by the 1991 policy have got blunted and the manufacturing growth story has got into a low-growth rut.

Manufacturing growth, particularly after 2010, has been quite timid. Ten-year industrial growth has been under 4 per cent on average. Obviously, the present policy framework is not delivering. A fit-for-purpose policy framework to enable manufacturing to contribute about 60 per cent of the industrial GDP in 2035 would have to drastically alter the incentives and disincentives for manufacturing in India. It will need to build around the following themes:

First, manufacturing of digital technology products is the future of manufacturing. India has an almost negligible share of digital hardware manufacturing. While silicone or semiconductor manufacturing is the fundamental base of all digital manufacturing, the country need not focus on manufacturing of semiconductors. All efforts made in this direction over the past decade have not succeeded as India does not have the technology and cost advantage. The focus should instead be on value-added chip manufacturing on semiconductors. That is where we might

have an intellectual and efficiency advantage. The Production Linked
Incentive (PLI) scheme does alter incentives correctly in this direction,
but it has focused more on manufacturing products with a relatively small
digital element and also on products which are not digital technology
products. If PLI incentives are channelled to manufacturing of chips
and other digital components, India might attain competitiveness in
much larger product ranges than current PLI. There is another category
of industrial products which would have enormous demand in times to
come—the environmental products—the products which save on energy
consumption, eliminate waste, recycle product and control/eliminate
discharge of pollutants, including greenhouse gases. PLI targets one or two
such products though the possibilities are immense. PLI should be focused
on manufacturing digital and environmental products only.

Second, the principal disadvantage India has faced in the manufacturing
space is lack of technological innovations and advancements. Technology
for most industrial products manufactured in India, whether it is
automobiles, white goods, electrical or electronic machinery, chemicals or
other products, has been largely purchased from abroad or developed over
the imported foreign technology. There is no harm in buying technology
from abroad and then manufacturing products that can compete on
quality and cost using India's other advantages. However, we have been
less than smart in permitting a very welcoming and open regime for
importing technology and paying for it in royalties. Software purchased
from abroad has been subjected to royalty payments that the Supreme
Court has recently quashed after a twenty-year legal battle. Likewise, there
have been sporadic attempts to cap royalties on technology imports, brand
use and the like. India's gain in manufacturing products should be viewed
from the perspective of value addition instead of royalty paid. The country
needs to institute an open and liberal technology import regime.

Third, schemes like PLI or sector-specific subsidies primarily seek to
offset the cost disadvantage of manufacturing in India relative to other
countries. This relative disadvantage is deeper and affects all manufacturing.
Industry is the productive sector of the economy, yet it pays the highest cost
of electricity to the monopoly state power distribution companies. There
are numerous fetters on generation of captive power and buying power
from the cheapest source available. Likewise, there is no bond market for
most companies in the country and the banking system, dominated by

risk-averse PSBs, lends too little and at too high a cost. Power should be sold at the average cost of power plus a margin of profit to industry. Industry should be allowed to source power at the cheapest rate available and the financial ecosystem should develop to enable industry to raise much-needed capital at globally competitive rates. The industrial policy for 2035 must also make land availability convenient and cost-effective. The government need not provide any fiscal support; adoption of the right package of policies to dismantle the power distribution companies, privatization of public sector banks and liberalizing the land markets would do what's necessary.

Fourth, the Government of India has hundreds of PSUs making heavy machines, machines, industrial products and consumer goods. Most of these undertakings are either loss-making or barely keeping their heads above water by supplying manufactured goods to other PSUs or the government. BHEL exists to supply power plants—even government undertakings no longer wish to buy from it. ITI manufactures telephone handsets and some telephonic switching gear using old technologies. There are undertakings manufacturing steel, aluminium and other metals. SAIL is an almost monopoly supplier of rails to Indian Railways. There is absolutely no reason for any of these PSUs manufacturing common industrial goods using and losing scarce public funds. The state governments started a plethora of manufacturing undertakings—almost all of them are losing money and producing shoddy products. The governments must adopt a no-nonsense policy of selling off each of these PSUs, at whatever price a competitive bid yields.

Utilities Sector is Crying for Reforms

Gas, water and electricity are the principal utilities. India's GDP number-crunchers count their value addition together under one broad head. Utilities contribute about 2.5 per cent of India's GDP. These were almost entirely in the government/public sector until 1991. Now, gas and electricity distribution has been opened up albeit in a very limited manner. We have seen the entry of the private sector in the establishment of gas grids and supply of city gas though the public sector still has the lion's share. The private sector is also slowly and steadily gaining a foothold in interstate electricity transmission. Electricity distribution and supply, however, still remains predominantly in the hands of the public sector. Only in a few cities have electricity distribution and supply networks been given to the private sector on a concession basis. Water remains an exclusive state business primarily because of social considerations.

There is enormous unmet demand for most of these utilities. India's electricity consumption is still one of the lowest in the world. Piped gas has reached only a handful of cities. Decent water supply on a 24/7 basis is still a far cry even in the capital cities of the country. Taking these ground realities into consideration, the policy reform agenda for utilities would need to be built around the following elements:

First, the private sector has been permitted to participate in the construction of new interstate transmission lines, although the government still tends to hold back many such projects. While PowerGrid may continue to exist as a public-sector enterprise, it has to be placed at arm's length from the Ministry of Power. This can be done by transferring the equity of the government in PowerGrid to the SAMC. There has been almost no opening of the intrastate transmission business for the private sector except recent privatization of a transmission utility in eastern UP. State governments should be incentivized/mandated to sell all state transmission utilities to PowerGrid and the private sector. New intrastate transmission lines should be awarded on a purely competitive basis.

Second, there is enough evidence in India that privatization of electricity distribution reduces transmission, distribution and collection losses as the private sector is more efficient at modernizing and maintaining networks and collecting bills. Consumers in Delhi, Kolkata and quite a few other cities have been saved an increase in the cost of electricity supply and have experienced better quality of service since privatization. The national policy should be to privatize distribution and supply of all cities by 2025. Rural areas can be bundled in appropriate territorial sizes and should also be privatized. The government can subsidize preferred customers like farmers and rural residential customers, if it chooses to do so, by paying subsidies directly in their bank accounts. With these reforms, the private sector would turn around the rural electricity businesses as well while employing modern technologies of electronic metering, prepaid billing and other necessary practices. To ensure that privatized electricity distribution businesses do not become exploitative monopolies, a strong regulatory system needs to be put in place besides making the electricity distribution and supply business open to anyone—by simply doing away with the requirement of a licence to set up such a business. The government has proposed to do away with distribution licencing in the new Electricity Bill. However, a collateral casualty of three farm laws is postponement of this Bill till its provisions affecting agricultural power supply are discussed with farmers' representatives. The government should use this opportunity to bring a comprehensive reform bill addressing all the needed policy measures outlined above.

Third, piped natural gas supply, in whatever possible variants, is not only efficient and clean but quite competitive, even considering international prices. India is deficient in not just oil but also gas. Oil is our largest item of imports. Gas imports are relatively small at present. However, if the country were to aggressively go in for a national piped natural gas system for residential cooking and transportation fuel, this import bill would go up. That should, however, be fine. It will partly substitute import of oil. And as oil prices are on a decline given the global demand-and-supply situation, gas imports are likely to remain relatively benign in times to come. India should, therefore, opt for a piped natural gas supply system. The government has awarded concessions for city gas supply. Many of these concessions have gone to the private sector but there is still a large number of concessions bagged by PSUs or companies like Indraprastha Gas and Mahanagar Gas, which are private sector only in name. In the gas transmission and supply sector, the policy reform agenda needs to be built around separating the gas grid and gas supply business of GAIL on the lines of the separation of the power generation and transmission business of NTPC, strengthening the Petroleum and Natural Gas Regulatory Authority for regulating the gas grid business, aggressive concessioning of city gas and other natural gas supply networks and ultimate privatization of gas supply businesses housed in GAIL and joint-sector companies like Indraprastha Gas.

Fourth, water has to remain with the government as water is a merit good with many externalities. However, the private sector should be roped in to construct pipelines to bring water to residential and industrial areas. Likewise, the government can use the private sector to operate city and village supply networks as a concessionaire. Moreover, it should start recovering some part of the cost of water supply to ensure there is no wastage and so that it can make investments in maintaining the networks.

The utilities sector can improve upon its current share of 2.5 per cent of GDP to go up to 3–4 per cent by 2035. This would have considerable positive spin-offs.

Construction Could Be the Best Bet for 2035

The construction sector gave the largest fillip to India's growth in the first decade of the current century. It was also a major contributor to the slowdown of growth in the second decade of the current century. Construction of housing, dwellings, office buildings, factories, infrastructure and other structures has an enormous role to play in raising the GDP to $10 trillion by 2035.

The construction sector is often known as the real-estate sector. India's policy framework has not viewed the construction sector positively. Until the 1990s, even residential housing was considered unproductive and discouraged. The banking sector was prohibited from lending to the real-estate sector. It is still prohibited from lending for land purchase and for most types of real-estate projects. ECBs, or external commercial borrowings, cannot be availed for the real-estate sector.

Over the years, the policy has changed somewhat. Residential housing was upgraded to a productive sector. Banks were permitted to lend to individuals for buying and constructing houses. Banks were subsequently permitted to lend to affordable housing projects. Non-banking institutions were allowed to fund builders for construction. The government also aligned tax incentives to promote borrowing for housing.

There is a big risk in the real-estate business. The valuation of housing and other properties can rise without any connection with the value delivered for housing or maintaining a business. The disconnect between valuation and underlying utility has given rise to valuation bubbles in several parts of the world, including India. Such bubbles have also burst, leading to crises in banking and the larger economy.

The policy for the construction and real-estate sector has to be developed keeping these ground realities in mind, as follows:

First, construction has to grow at very high rates of 10–12 per cent per annum as India has enormously high unmet needs of almost every segment of real estate: housing, factories, offices, warehouses, data centres, logistics hubs and other infrastructure. Land is the most essential asset for the construction business. As argued earlier in this chapter, the country has to increase supply of non-agricultural land. It needs to adopt easy and functional policies and legal frameworks to enable conversion/transfer of agricultural lands for non-agricultural use.

Second, the real-estate and construction industry requires a large amount of finances during the construction phase, which may remain stuck for long periods of time unless there is a system of monetizing construction investments. The banking and non-banking system needs to be allowed to provide finance during the construction phase. This would require tweaking in the current policy treating land and construction as a no-go for banking. India needs to develop and scale up monetization mechanisms like Infrastructure Investment Trusts (INVITs) and Real Estate Investment Trusts (REITs) to permit construction and real-estate companies to recover the costs of construction by transferring built assets to INVITs and REITs. A good beginning has been made in developing these instruments in the past few years. However, this needs faster traction.

Third, there is a policy preference for own housing compared to rental housing. There are large tax incentives for own housing. The government also provides substantial subsidy support to affordable housing. This leads real-estate and construction companies to construct residential housing projects to be sold on an owned basis. Real-estate companies do construct office buildings, warehouses and other buildings for use on a rental basis. The innovation of REITs and INVITs has further helped rentable properties to be monetized. However, tax and other incentives for own housing have distorted the valuation of housing, further accentuated by irrational valuations of owned residential houses. We need a sharp policy correction to bring equality of incentives for construction of rental and owned housing schemes. The proof of such a balanced policy regime would be whether the real-estate industry constructs as many residential housing complexes to be owned by companies/REITs for income from rentals. If rental incomes can sustain residential investments, the industry would become financially attractive and boom. If India were to have such a sensible housing policy, about half the houses to be built till 2035 should be for rental housing.

The construction sector should be contributing about 10 per cent of India's GDP in 2035, which will contribute GDP equal to the GDP of the agricultural sector in 2035. In other words, 40 per cent of India's industrial GDP in 2035 should come from the construction sector.

Reforming and Revitalizing the Small Sector

India formally divides small businesses in three categories of micro, small and medium based on capital investment in plant and machinery.

Mass production and distribution or customized production and distribution are the real differentiators between large and small businesses. The unique selling preposition of these small businesses is more customization, localization and personal delivery to the consumer.

Unfortunately, many policymakers treat large and small businesses as competitors, which is problematic. When both small and large businesses compete to produce the same product, the small business will suffer because of cost and scale disadvantages. Providing financial support to small businesses to compete with large businesses is not a good policy. An auto-rickshaw (a small business) cannot compete with a railway or bus business (a large business) for long-distance transportation, but it certainly beats these businesses in local transportation, which is the right business for it (customized service).

No real purpose is served by classifying small businesses into micro, small and medium. This is a totally artificial construct. The fact that the government has been changing the investment and turnover criteria for classifying the small businesses into micro, small and medium businesses quite arbitrarily supports the contention. There is no real distinguishing factor between small, smaller and the smallest.

The primary imperative of production at scale and customized production leads to the deployment of two principal factors of production—capital and labour—in different proportions. Large capital is required for investing in machines, automation and technology for creating large businesses while more labour is required to deliver more customized, personalized and niche goods and services.

In the new digital age, plenty of opportunity will come the way of small businesses as technology can be used effectively to produce customized goods and services. The critical advantage of machine and technology use in the industrial age is likely to be less advantageous in the production of a lot of goods and services.

Building a System for Registering and Serving MSMEs

This would require the creation of a new institution. The MSME Ministry or the Ministry of Corporate Affairs should create an authority, let us say, the Registrar of Unincorporated Small Businesses, under the Small Enterprises Act. Just like all incorporated businesses, small or large, have a unique business identity under the Companies Act, all unincorporated small businesses should have a unique business identity under the MSME Act.

The government and the Registrar of Unincorporated Small Businesses should undertake a mission to register every small business of the country, obtain critical entity-related information for all the small businesses in the country and assign a Unique Small Business ID (USBID) to every small business. Keeping in mind the smallness of resources of small businesses, this system of collection of information should be digital and require only a minimum set of critical business information to be obtained, preferably once a year.

As unincorporated small businesses are organized on the unlimited liability of their owners, it therefore becomes necessary to register the details of every owner of such businesses, including their individual Aadhaar numbers. The USBID should have all its owners mapped to it.

The Registrar of Unincorporated Small Businesses can be organized from the bottom up; from the municipality/panchayat to the tehsil, district and state, and finally combined in a single national digital register. In the present digital age, it should be quite easy and costless to construct a register of 7 crore small businesses in a decentralized-centralized mode.

Mapping All Services to the USBID

The USBID should be made mandatory to transact with every public and financial entity. Banks should consider providing credit to the small businesses recording their USBID and link all their loans and deposit accounts with it.

All other authorities that need an identity distinguisher for small businesses can create and link their identifier with the USBID of a small business. Banks can link their account number with the USBID. Taxation authorities, direct and indirect, can link their PAN and GST numbers to the USBID. Likewise, many other authorities, like the authorities under the Shops and Establishment Acts or the Factories Act, should also link their identifiers with the USBID of small businesses.

Such a system would be able to create a comprehensive database of small businesses and their needs and performance. Using the fintech revolution underway in the country, such databases and identity can be gainfully used to determine and meet their credit requirements, link their markets with production, and provide a whole host of other services.

Reconfiguring Government Support for Small Businesses

The total allocation in the 2020–21 Budget of the Central government for the MSME Ministry was around Rs 7500 crore. For 7 crore small businesses, this amounts to only Rs 1000 per small business. The Budget is spread over about forty schemes. Most programmes have tiny allocations and there is a lot of duplication in the mandate and interventions of various schemes. It is delivered through multiple agencies.

Crores of small businesses faced an existential crisis after the lockdown. However, the MSME Ministry could not assess what losses and misery small businesses suffered, how many simply shuttered forever and what these millions of businesses needed to survive and revive their businesses. The MSME Ministry or, for that matter, the government had no means to reach out to them.

The ability to understand small businesses and reach out to them would come with the Registrar of Unincorporated Small Businesses and the Authority of Small Businesses. Numerous programmes of the MSME Ministry and other ministries can be reorganized into two focused programmes to serve the MSME world better.

One, a registration and recognition grant can be provided to incentivize every small business to register and file its annual return with the Authority of Unincorporated Small Businesses. A grant of Rs 5000 can be paid at the time of registration of every unique small business by its owners. On filing an annual return, an amount of Rs 500 can be paid per business entity. Assuming there are 8 crore unincorporated small businesses in India and all of them register, it would involve a one-time expenditure of Rs 40,000 crore.

The incentive expenditure on filing annual returns would cost the government only about Rs 4000 crore, which is only about 50 per cent of the annual budget of the MSME Ministry. By spending this meagre amount, the government would not only get all the requisite data for policymaking but would be able to get better estimates of the industrial and services profile of the small enterprises, employment of labour and the value addition/contribution to GDP made by them.

Second, we need a workplace equity support programme to assist small businesses and help them hire a place to set up business. In its simplest construct, the programme would provide equity support equivalent to the rental of the working place (subject to a normative limit) to micro-entrepreneurs for the first three to five years after setting up a new business. This programme would encourage the construction of plug-and-play workplaces for small businesses and build an equity base for micro-entrepreneurs. It would obviate the need for small businesses to spend their limited capital in buying a place of work. The remaining allocation of Rs 4000 crore can be kept for this programme.

All other programmes to extend myriad forms of support, such as credit-linked subsidy and technology and marketing support, should simply be closed. The basic assumption that a small business is unviable is wrong; it is only different to a large business. Small businesses should be taken up only when entrepreneurs believe they would be able to earn profits higher than what they would earn as employees. A small business should be able to avail credit on its strength without any interest subsidy and buy whatever technology best fits its business plan.

State governments should also reshape their support for small businesses on these lines. They can provide support based on the extent to which the wages make up a value add weighted by the number of employees to encourage labour orientation.

Chapter Fifty

Services Policy Reforms

As we saw in an earlier chapter, services have been the largest growing segment of India's GDP for many years now. Services contribute about 55 per cent of total GVA. They also deliver a higher share of GVA to workers when we consider all forms of employee compensation together as part of the total value added. Services are more labour-intensive and thus help in better distribution of income. These primary growth engines see the most equitable distribution of value added among the three groups of stakeholders receiving income from GVA: workers, capital and the government. Services require much less capital and are most efficient in the use of capital. Services are increasingly using digital technologies, where India seems to have a better advantage compared to industrial-era machine technologies.

In the National Accounts, in terms of groups of services, data is available for as many as thirteen different groups: trade and repairs; hotels and restaurants; railways; road transport; water transport; air transport; services incidental to transport; storage; communications and services related to broadcasting; financial services; real-estate, dwellings and professional services; public administration and defence; and other services.

Among these thirteen broad groups of services, the trade and repairs group adds the largest contribution to India's GDP (about 11 per cent). Financial services (about 5–6 per cent), ownership of dwellings (a little over 6 per cent) and the public services account (about 6 per cent) are the next three large services contributing to GDP. Information and computer-related services (4.5 per cent), road transport (about 3 per cent), other professional services (about 3.5 per cent) and education services (3.5 per cent) are other significant service groups contributing to the national output and GVA.

Any policy aiming for a much higher proportional GDP from services of about 65–70 per cent of GDP would have to take into account the current policy matrix for these services in India and the policy reset that could enhance their potential for contributing higher growth in future. Human resources and technology are the two most important factors which determine the quantity, quality and value of services. Government policy plays a very significant role in nurturing the ecosystem for human resources and technology to work best. Therefore, policy reforms relating to the services sector can contribute best to India's quest for a $10 trillion economy fifteen years from now.

Policy Reforms for Maximizing the Opportunity of Trade Transformation

With trade and repairs contributing 10–11 per cent of GDP, the value addition in the trade and repairs services group exceeds Rs 20 lakh crore. The trade and repair group is also the largest employer of labour, after agriculture.

Digitalization of distribution is upending the trade group. E-commerce is fast making significant inroads in all segments of trade: wholesale, storage, distribution and retail. The nature of the e-commerce business—large fulfilling centres employing labour largely in managing stores and delivering packets—is threatening the viability and sustenance of traditional wholesaling and retailing through fixed warehouses and retail shops. The e-commerce model uses IT extensively on omnipresent mobile networks and is far more cost-effective and efficient. Though e-commerce appears to be in the control of large e-commerce companies like Amazon and Flipkart, it is also enabling manufacturers to establish a direct relationship with the consumer. E-commerce has become an existential threat to middlemen and all available evidence suggests that its onward march cannot be stopped. The traditional model of distribution and retailing will have to yield space to e-commerce sooner or later.

India has adopted a policy stance of providing only limited space to foreign e-commerce companies in trade services; the most restrictive is the retailing regime. Indian companies like Flipkart also suffer the same treatment when they receive FDI. Domestic organized retail gets more favourable treatment. E-commerce rules recently proposed under the Consumer Protection Act bring domestic e-commerce companies within the policy regime, providing more restrictive and differential treatment to protect the small traditional traders.

Traditional retail has been in the business of retailing goods. Retailing of services has been totally disorganized. Traditional retail stores did not provide services. The e-commerce revolution is bringing order in retailing of services. Repair and maintenance services are getting better organized through several start-ups in this space. There is no reason why traditional goods retail stores cannot also retail services.

With the inevitable transition of agricultural labour and farmers from agriculture, the retail segment, for both goods and services, offers a very promising field of occupation for transitioning labour. It needs to be better organized and supported. Accordingly, a supportive policy framework for building further momentum in trade and repair services, potentially to raise its share to 12.5 per cent of GDP by 2035, is required, as follows:

First, support extensive training of transitioning agricultural labour and farmers for myriad services that urbanizing India and developing rural India need: delivery persons, security persons, vehicle repairers, home workers, drivers, construction workers, plumbers, electricians, IT device carers and painters, to name a few.

Besides imparting the right training and skilling, the employment of these workers needs to be optimized through two major interventions: converting goods retailers into retailers of goods and services; and

'Uberizing' service providers by linking demand and supply of these services. This programme has the potential for doubling the people in retail. The transformation of goods-only retail stores into goods and services retail stores and their digitalization has a much better chance of making them competitive businesses to e-commerce companies. E-commerce platforms like Meesho seek to make home workers small retailers, leveraging the power and ease of digital technology. Several start-ups have come up which are retailing urban services. These platforms need to be provided a supportive policy framework.

Second, the government must actively pursue digitalization of trade services providers. The proposal to register and recognize every unincorporated business (traders are the largest such businesses outside farms) and improving their access to financiers, the taxman and people in general would help immensely. The government should support creation of appropriate networks to help retailers manage their suppliers, customers, staff, accounting, tax filing, and all other tasks.

Third, a lot of policy capital is being wasted in trying to make artificial constructs like the inventory model versus platform model, prohibiting collection of necessary data on the buyer and payment mechanism in the name of privacy of data, and permitting FDI in single-brand retail but not in multi-brand retail. These policies will only make India non-competitive.

All these restrictive policies should be replaced with regulation where no one has a conflict of interest in selling products and discouraging the sale of competing products.

Fintechization of Financial Services the Best Bet

There are three main segments of financial services businesses: payments, investments and credit. While Fintech is fast becoming mainstream in the financial business in India, it needs a lot of policy support.

The UPI (Unified Payments Interface) platform created by the NPCI (National Payments Corporation of India) revolutionized the payment space. All the accounts in banks became digital accounts after every bank had computerized and brought in core banking solutions to put every bank account in cyberspace. NPCI linked all these 40 crore plus accounts into one single database—as if all the bank accounts of hundreds of banks were in the digital ledger of one single bank. UPI succeeded because technology companies created an interface between smartphones/computers with bank accounts using appropriate application programming interfaces (APIs), compatible with NPCI and the banks' technology system. The technology interface has made deposits in bank accounts mobile, capable of dancing down from one account to another at the behest of the deposit holder. While digital payments, largely enabled with the introduction of technology, have grown spectacularly and are expected to maintain this breakneck speed of growth, more than 80 per cent payments still remain non-digital or cash payments. This is because currency is not digital.

The first policy imperative in the payment space is to digitize currency. Most central banks are mulling over the creation of blockchain and cryptography-based central bank digital currency in retail and wholesale currency formats. However, these moves/experimentations are unlikely to succeed in replacing physical currency. Small currency users are unlikely to be interested to come on the blockchain-based retail cryptocurrency platforms. Nor would they find it cost- and time-effective. For large players, even otherwise, it makes no difference. These players already make their payments digitally using the deposits in their bank accounts. The most feasible solution to transform the bulk of physical currency into digital currency would be to dematerialize (demat) currency notes and allow people to hold demat currency in digital wallets. A technological system can be developed with appropriate interfaces with own, suppliers', third-party phones', computers' and other digital media where payments can be authorized by typing a code, touching a finger or batting an eyelid.

The second major policy agenda is for RBI to combine the three payment platforms—Immediate Payment System (IMPS), National Electronic Funds Transfer (NEFT) and Real Time Gross Settlement (RTGS)—into a single platform that functions 24/7 and processes payments instantaneously instead of batch processing, which the present NEFT system currently does. The three platforms may remain only in name for categorizing accountholders. This platform can compete with NPCI as a public-sector platform.

The other major reform agenda is to introduce competition to NPCI. RBI has already started the process of licencing a few more National Umbrella Entities (NUEs) to establish platforms like UPI. These entities were to be primarily non-bank entities while banks could also be among their promoters. RBI has put this proposal on hold for the time being, which is not a good move. These five to six NUEs are necessary to make India's payment system most efficient, competitive and the best in the world. Customers would be the real winners.

The investment universe is very large.

Digital technologies are transforming investments. While large equity and debt investment securities have got dematerialized and the entire space has been consequently digitalized, both equity and debt investment instruments are tightly regulated and not opened to fintech by the respective regulators, RBI and SEBI. Investment in mutual funds (MFs) and small investments in new pension products have seen limited opening to fintech in terms of some intermediary services provided. Some start-ups have come up in the field, though the bulk of the investment business is still routed through traditional banking channels, albeit in digital format. Fixed deposits, insurance products and retirement funds like EPFO and NPS still remain in the physical ecosystem although electronic copies of fixed deposits, insurance policies and retirement accounts are available to investors for information purposes. Government investment products like government securities and small-saving products or government-guaranteed investment products like EPFO, Shram Yogi Maandhan and Karam Yogi Maandhan are completely traditional products in an electronic environment. Technology has found no real application in managing these investments.

The fintech policy agenda in the investment space is massive.

All investment products—fixed deposits, small savings products, retirement savings and pension products, insurance policies, government securities, MF units—should be turned into digital products by dematerializing them or creating a crypto blockchain.

Banks can issue fixed deposits in the specific amounts for a specific period at a specified rate of interest without specifying any particular deposit holder. These are akin to certificates of deposit currently in use in the non-retail/ commercial space. Investors can buy these fixed deposits and keep them till maturity, sell them to others in between or raise loans against them. These fixed deposits virtually acquire the character of bonds. Banks can also issue deposit holders specific fixed deposits that the depositors may not be able to sell but can raise a loan against. Such deposits can be provided with a facility of premature encashment with a penalty. Similarly, all other investment products can be reengineered as digital securities or securities-like products.

Once this is done, fintech companies can join the party as technology intermediators, much the same way as they do in the payment space today. Fintech companies will bring millions of investors in the investment universe and free banks, insurance companies and governments of the need for a direct retail interface. These financial companies will become lean and mean and would focus on their core business of banking, insurance or debt management.

Of the three key financial functions—payments, investments and credit—credit is the most complex. It is not simply a transaction. For credit, a decision has to be made in each individual case about the credit risk faced by the lender. This assessment of credit risk leads to certain other decisions regarding the time for which credit can be made, the interest to be charged, collateral to be taken and the like. These decisions require a lot of supporting data, information and security.

Digitalization of businesses, cash flows, assets and registration of charges has made it much easier to assess the credit, secure the security and take control on cash flows when necessary. Digitalization makes such assessments and decisions even for the smallest of businesses, like single-account or single-person businesses.

Digitalization of businesses and digitization of data has made it possible to break down credit businesses in specific discrete actions. It is possible to make credit assessment a discrete activity, which is facilitated by the credit information bureaus, to ascertain the credit worthiness, which is facilitated by credit rating agencies, doing KYC ('know your customer'), which is facilitated by the central KYC agencies, Aadhaar system and others, registration of charges, which is facilitated by central charge registration systems and taking control of cash flows, which is facilitated by the banks holding the bank account of the business concerned, including by way of creating escrow mechanisms.

Digitalization has also enabled decentralization and disintermediation of lenders. It is now possible to undertake direct lending through small lenders instead of depositing savings with banks.

This has created the right conditions for credit and loans businesses to thrive. Major businesses were able to get credit earlier in the non-digital system as well. Small businesses (let us define every unincorporated business that employs even a single person as a small business) are now in the process of getting connected to the credit system thanks to a number of lending platforms (peer to peer), digital non-banking companies and other upcoming structures. E-commerce and card companies and others have also joined the game. Still, only a fraction of small businesses have been mainstreamed in the formal credit system. Increasing digitalization of small businesses is the key to ensuring credit delivery to small businesses. There is no credit regulator in the country. RBI is a bank regulator and, as such, it regulates credit by banks. We need a simple digital regulatory system for credit to small businesses.

Emerging decentralized finance or DeFi solutions in the crypto-blockchain technology platforms also have enormous potential to make an entire menu of financial services—credit, investments, insurance, pensions and so on—much more efficient, less cost-intensive and secure. This is alternative digital resolution brewing. India should develop a conducive policy framework to support the DeFi-delivered financial services.

With successful transformation of payments, investment and credit services, Indian firms can look to capture the global payments, investment and credit services businesses.

Education Services Require Deeper Policy Reforms

Education essentially serves two major societal and personal needs: first, it brings every individual familiarity, knowledge and understanding of self, society and the geophysical world (me, we and the universe) to develop as a healthy, happy and responsible human being; second, it equips every individual to work productively and contribute to the economy. The first type of education is a pure 'merit good' with enormous externalities, while the second type is essentially skills and deeper knowledge, which is largely a private good with limited externalities. Let's call the first type general education and the second, technical education. A clearer understanding of these two different forms of education has enormous implications for designing the correct policies. As a classic merit good, general education is a community responsibility and should be delivered and funded as a community/state enterprise. On the other hand, as a private good, technical education should be delivered and funded as a private enterprise.

In India, all educational institutions can be established only as a 'society', 'trust' or 'not-for-profit' company. Educational institutions, including technical education institutions, cannot be established legally as proprietary or partnership companies or any other 'for-profit' entity. This policy is incorporated in all the education-related laws of the Centre and states. The mindset of all educationists is informed by the requirements of general education and it makes no distinction between general and technical education. The courts, including the Supreme Court, have upheld this. NEP-2020 also carries forward the same idea.

India needs to abandon the policy of keeping technical education institutions as not-for-profit institutions. All fit-for-purpose private entrepreneurs and companies should be free to establish technical institutions without the requirement of a licence or approval and charge any fees. When buying and selling of goods and most services require no licence and they can be bought and sold with the mutual consent and agreement of the buyer and seller for the consideration, why should learning and imparting skills not be so? A regulator of technical education in the states and one central technical education regulator for technical institutions in more than one state can at best lay down standards in terms of physical and digital facilities, teachers, and other relevant matters. Just like credit-rating agencies in the assets field, technical education rating agencies should be established to rate these institutions. Let students decide on institutions they consider appropriate and pay for their education through appropriate finance.

The policy proposed for technical institutions should also be made applicable to HEIs, or higher educational institutions. All graduate and postgraduate colleges should be governed by the same policy. Only school education, minus the technical/vocational component, should be governed by the present policy of not-for-profit education.

Educational institutions of leading countries in the field receive students from abroad for onsite teaching and also establish branches in different forms abroad to set up education facilities in host countries. In WTO parlance, there are four modes of trading in services. The provision of education service in the first case (where a student goes to the teaching institution in another country) is considered trading of services in Mode 2 (i.e., consumption abroad). Provision of education service in the second case is considered trading in services in Mode 3 (i.e., commercial establishment abroad).

According to a background note prepared by the WTO Secretariat in 2010, South Asia recorded the largest growth in sending students to study abroad between 1999 and 2007, an increase of 150 per cent in this period. It further listed India as the fourth largest importer of education services in 2007 with a share of 9.1 per cent in total global expenditure on import of education services. Curiously, India did not figure even in the top twenty exporters of education services—Slovenia was the twentieth largest exporter with a share of only 0.1 per cent in global education exports. The situation has only worsened since 2009. In 2019, India had over 3.75 lakh students studying abroad. We also had the second largest number of foreign students studying in the US.

We need to encourage foreign universities and technical institutions to establish their branches in India or set up universities in the country. This would lead to three significant advantages. First, Indian students would not need to go to foreign universities as they would get the same quality of education at home. Second, these foreign universities would collaborate with Indian corporates and educational institutions to establish Indian branches/universities that, in due course, would grow to be able to establish branches/institutions abroad. This has happened in many other industries and services. Third, foreign universities employ a lot of Indian faculty today. More Indian faculty would get the opportunity to work with foreign universities/institutions when they establish their branches here. This would help grow Indian academia.

India should permit 100 per cent FDI through automatic route (subject, of course, to technical affiliation, etc.) in the entire for-profit education space. We have a tremendous comparative advantage in education. Most of these foreign educational institutions are likely to be staffed by Indian teachers, researchers and technologists. Very quickly, foreign educational institutions and their competing Indian counterparts will make the country a global hub of education. From being a large importer of educational services, India can become a major exporter.

A Three-Pronged Policy Strategy in Health Will Work Wonders

Publicly funded, universal, good quality and easily accessible primary healthcare, a publicly funded health insurance programme to pay for secondary and tertiary healthcare services for the poor and a world-class private secondary and tertiary healthcare system for serving the better-off and global patients would make an ideal three-pronged strategy for India.

The Budget of the Department of Health and Family Welfare has fifty-one 'heads' of schemes.

These thinly spread micro-interventions do not serve India well. They should all be combined into two broad programmes to strengthen the primary healthcare system, and fund secondary and tertiary treatment for the poor. The objective of the first programme should be to establish, within five years, a comprehensive, good quality, functional, easily accessible and free primary healthcare system in the country. The objective of the second should be to pay for all the hospitalization needs of the poor and the vulnerable (not exceeding 10 crore genuinely poor families).

The private sector should rapidly expand in the country—going to districts, sub-districts and tehsils—to provide quality secondary and tertiary health services as close to people as economically justifiable. There is enormous health entrepreneurial talent in the country. The government can support it by taking the following measures:

First, bring in a good regulatory framework to obligate private hospitals to provide health and medical services benchmarked to established standards. The country does not have a good regulatory framework for hospitals or service standards. The regulatory framework need not adopt the licencing route, which can be extortionary and rent-seeking. The regulator must lay down standards to design and implement a system of reporting on adherence to standards and enforce compliance.

Second, sustain demand for the services of private-sector hospitals. This should primarily be achieved by expanding services available for the poor under Ayushman Bharat and empanelling as many private hospitals as possible that meet regulatory and quality standards.

Third, increase the supply of quality medical doctors and paramedics by liberalizing the establishment of medical colleges. India has only one doctor for about 1450 people; the WHO norm is one doctor for 1000 people. Most well-served countries have a much better ratio—China 670, the US 400, Australia 300 and Germany 250. India needs to aim for one doctor for 500 people. This would require the number of doctors to be tripled in the country.

Fourth, bring down the cost and time in establishing hospitals. There is no fast-track method of allocating land for hospitals. It is difficult for doctors to go through the maze of land conversion and other required processes. The cost of land is disproportionately high for non-agricultural use as there are enormous constraints on the supply of such lands. It is difficult to obtain loans and equity for non-established or single-doctor units. It might make sense to establish medical industrial parks in the country—the size depending on plots available to establish health and related facilities for doctors (after obtaining all approvals), with the government providing equity/grant support to meet part of the cost, akin to what we do to establish mobile manufacturing facilities.

Exporting Services and Trained Indian Personnel Abroad Can Solve Our External Account Deficit

India would continue to be massively dependent on energy, electronics, technology and gold imports for many decades. It is also not in the interest of the country to try to artificially minimize these imports. Let there be full freedom to import these goods to build the economy of the country.

Our human resources are the best solution to pay for these imports. Even today, India's services export performance is much better than our goods export. The Indian diaspora and workers working abroad remit more than $80 billion every year to India which serves majorly to keep our financial external account in surplus.

By adopting the right kind of policies for Indian professionals and workers to capture the services business across a wide spectrum of services—information technology, finance, education, health, legal, accounting, data processing, e-commerce services and the like—India can capture much more of the services market globally. We will need to dare to adopt free and liberal policies in permitting import and export of these services to really gain big ground.

Likewise, it makes tremendous sense to train Indian workers to serve health, construction, transportation and many other businesses all over the world capitalizing on their hard work, strong work ethic and preference to save.

A major chunk of services can be delivered by the foreigners visiting India and consuming services—travel, health and others—here.

The services export and export of serving personnel can be a real clincher to raise the share of services to 60-65 per cent of GDP and reach $10 trillion by 2035.

Chapter Fifty-One

Reforms of Land and Labour

Land Reforms

Requisites of a Post-Agricultural Economy

The non-agricultural economy has been expanding faster.

Industry requires only a fraction of land to produce the same amount of value addition. Services require even less land to produce an equal amount of value addition. The services economy, however, runs on large infrastructure. It also requires a lot of social infrastructure, such as houses, schools, hospitals and numerous other facilities. Urbanization is the result of the services economy.

Land is required for the construction of infrastructure and urban facilities to meet housing and other requirements of managers and workers of the non-agricultural economy.

All this, however, requires much less land than agriculture. Even today, as noted earlier, less than 1 per cent of land in India is occupied for non-agricultural economic use, while it produces over 80 per cent of GDP and provides infrastructure and housing for more than one-third of the people. The productivity of land use in industry, infrastructure, services and urbanization is 200 times the productivity in agriculture.

It should be a no-brainer that we liberally allow the transfer of land from agricultural to non-agricultural use. Unfortunately, there are massive misgivings about the land required for non-agricultural use. There is a widely shared, though completely unfounded, feeling that such a transfer would hurt agriculture and farmers. Thus, the transfer of agricultural land has become an extremely difficult proposition. Transfer to non-agricultural use is permissible only exceptionally. Land transfer is mired in so many procedural hassles that direct purchase of agricultural land for non-agricultural use and its conversion for such a purpose is rarely executed successfully.

As a result, the state stepped in and used the Land Acquisition Law to acquire land, in the name of public purpose, for industrial, housing and infrastructural use. The Law, passed in 2013, made it necessary to pay about four to five times the market cost to acquire land for non-agricultural purposes. Indeed, land acquisition through the state for non-agricultural purposes has become a casualty of the law.

All this has resulted in the extreme shortage of non-agricultural land, sending land prices through the roof. Prices have risen to unjustifiably high levels and are outpricing manufacturing in India now. Infrastructure creation is suffering and the residential housing sector is also in deep trouble.

For faster growth and employment creation, India needs five basic land reforms urgently.

Creation of a National Land Record Registry

The land record system in India has evolved over centuries, principally to record data relating to ownership and tilling of agricultural land.

India has been trying to digitize its land records for quite some time. Currently, a programme named the Digital India Land Records Modernization Programme (DILRMP) is under implementation. The data available on the DILRMP-MIS 2.0 dashboard of the Department of Land Resources informs us that computerization of the key land record—the Record of Rights—has been completed in 5.99 lakh villages of a total 6.58 lakh villages, over 91 per cent of villages. The dashboard further shares that there are, in all, 301.46 million records of rights in the country; there are about two-and-a-half records of rights for each operational holding.

There are three major deficiencies in DILRMP. First, it computerizes the record of rights as it exists in the states. There is no national template. These records are also only available in the local language. As a result, there is no national registry. Second, the records essentially state the status of tenancy/ownership of a person over the surveyed plot of land. It is also a static record; assignment of different rights in the land, such as leasing, mortgage, etc., are either not recorded or updated. Thus, it is not a comprehensive record of ownership and other attributes of ownership over land. It is not a live record of 'ownership rights' in the land. Third, the record is maintained basically for agricultural land. Urban areas or abadi areas usually get clubbed into one or a few survey numbers. The responsibility of maintaining a record of buildings is entrusted to urban bodies. In practice, there is no system of recognizing land in non-agricultural areas (residential, industrial and infrastructure). The record thus accounts for only a part of the land parcels in the country.

It is extremely important for India to evolve an integrated system of land survey and record, covering both rural and urban areas. There should be a national template that can provide additional information. We need to move beyond recording ownership and other rights only from an agricultural standpoint. A National System of Land Records is necessary. We must embark on a ten-year mission to survey all land—agricultural, residential, businesses, housing, infrastructure—recording the type of activity the land is subject to, ownership and other attributes. This national record should be managed by a depository institution. The register should be dynamic, with every change relating to ownership or rights in land being recorded as part of the transaction itself. It should also be available in the public domain.

Comprehensive Reform of Land and Property Leasing

Restrictions on land leasing led to the development of informal sharecropping arrangements. As self-cultivation was considered nobler in the socialistic mindset and the exploitative absentee landlord the archetypal villain, policymakers decided to outlaw agriculture land leasing in India. Almost all land reform laws either completely disallowed land leasing or made it so conditional that formal land leasing just could not have taken place.

Such statutory bans and restrictions, however, could not overcome the real economic necessity of leasing land. There were several reasons why agricultural lands had to be given to other farmers for cultivation. The landowner might not be in a physical state to undertake cultivation. The landowner might have taken up different work or might have migrated to a city or town. A land parcel might be too small to be cultivated. A little larger scale of operations is likely to yield better crops. Another farmer might be more skilful. These factors operated equally on the demand side. Unsurprisingly, an informal leasing system has developed and become widespread. It operates on commercial principles. The lessor and the lessee enter into an informal agreement, commonly described as *batai* or a sharecropping arrangement. The informal lessee cultivates the land and shares a part of the crop or its proceeds with the lessor, the actual share depending upon several factors relating to who bears the input costs, type of land, etc.

Thus, land leasing has become rampant over the past few decades.

Land leasing restrictions have been relaxed in some states over the years. The Andhra Pradesh Licenced Cultivators Act was passed in 2011. Some other states brought in contract farming through amendment in other laws. Yet, there are millions of landowners who still cannot formally lease land.

NITI Aayog constituted an Expert Committee on Land Leasing in 2015 which recommended negating all the provisions in the land laws of the states banning and restricting land leasing. It also proposed a new Model Agricultural Land Leasing Act, 2016. The Model Act is quite business-like in nature and protects the legitimate interests of both the lessor and lessee. It also recommended a standard land leasing agreement.

The draft model law was circulated to the states. A few states, like Madhya Pradesh, Maharashtra, Uttar Pradesh and Uttarakhand, either passed new laws or amended their existing legislation in line with the model law. The Central government seems to have become lukewarm towards this idea though, in her 2020–21 Budget speech, Finance Minister Sitharaman announced that the government will 'encourage those state governments who undertake implementation of . . . Model Agriculture Land Leasing Act, 2016 . . .' No action has been taken to implement the Budget announcement.

The enactment of the Model Agriculture Land Leasing Act is an absolute must for the welfare of farmers, and the growth of agriculture and the Indian economy. It would be in India's interest if the leasing reforms proposed in the Model Agricultural Land Leasing Act are extended to allow leasing of agricultural land for non-agricultural purposes as well.

Free Conversion of Agricultural Land into Non-Agricultural Use

Agricultural land operates under severe restrictions. The biggest constraint is that it can be used only for agricultural purposes. Unfortunately, on account of larger economic forces at work, agriculture has become a very low-income yielding business over the years. As a result, the asset value of land as agricultural property remains hugely depressed. Whatever multiple you use to value agricultural land, it would throw up a small valuation as the basic profit emanating from agricultural operations is quite small.

The situation changes dramatically whenever agricultural land becomes non-agricultural. There is an enormous demand-supply gap of non-agricultural land. The income generated from non-agricultural use of land is manifold.

The states have opted for little or no conversion as a default policy. Conversion of land is an exception. For instance, the Andhra Pradesh Agricultural Land (Conversion for Non-Agricultural Purposes) Act, 2006, states: 'No agricultural land in the state shall be put to non-agricultural purposes, without the prior payment of Conversion Tax to government.'

States want to capture as much of the exaggerated value increment upon conversion as possible for themselves. Rules for conversion offer the authorities too much discretion as well. For example, the Odisha Land Reforms Act, 1960, provides that only a *raiyat* (someone who has the right to hold land for cultivation) can apply for conversion of agricultural land for non-agricultural purposes.

Non-agricultural use of land is more productive and is essential to meet India's residential, commercial and infrastructure demands. If only 2 per cent of the 140 million hectares of agricultural land were converted into non-agricultural use, the entire demand-supply scenario would probably disappear. Land for non-agricultural use would not be as costly as it is today. Industry, infrastructure and housing would become affordable and promote businesses and growth. Farmers would get a little more money without land availability for agriculture being affected.

Therefore, the reform of the land conversion regime is absolutely justified. Conversion should be freely permitted without the requirement of a state officer passing a conversion order. In fact, the distinction between agricultural and non-agricultural land should disappear. Whatever the use, land will anyway remain subject to laws that govern environmental, health, safety and other legitimate common concerns.

Compulsory Acquisition Should Only Become an Exception

In legal parlance, agricultural land usually belongs to the state. However, for all practical purposes ownership vests in the person recorded as a tenant. In this sense, agricultural land is the private property of the landholder. Private property is normally transferable by sale and purchase contracts. A lot of agricultural land also gets purchased and sold by such private contracts.

The normal system of free sale and purchase collapses in two situations. First, when the state needs land for a public purpose. The state is powerful and its relationship with small landholders is grossly unequal. Further, it is generally difficult for state authorities to accept the price demanded by the seller and determine, in an accountable and objective manner, the right price. Consequently, barring exceptions, the state does not enter into purchase and sale contracts. Second, whenever private enterprises require large chunks of land for an industrial, infrastructure or residential project, dealing with numerous small holders subjected to restrictive provisions under various laws makes private purchase and sale a messy affair. As a result, larger procurement of land for non-agricultural purposes has been made under the land acquisition laws.

There was another practical problem. Until converted for non-agricultural use, agricultural land purchased remained agricultural and subject to ceilings. The ceilings were small. Consequently, industry or entrepreneurs could not procure agricultural land for their purpose. The Land Acquisition Act, 1894, became the principal instrument of land acquisition for public and private projects after Independence.

As development required a good amount of land to be used for non-agricultural purposes, the Act came to be used quite frequently.

Both by design and operation, the Land Acquisition Act worked against the landholder farmer. Land could be acquired for almost any purpose as 'public purpose' was widely interpreted in practice. Compensation payable was the market value of similar land. This value, as recorded in the Registrar's record, was quite depressed on account of agriculture being a poor value creator and real transaction prices not being disclosed in registration documents. A solatium was offered, but it was a meagre 30 per cent. For the first thirty to forty years, farmers literally received a pittance as compensation and not only became poorer but in many cases rootless. As land was usually possessed much before compensation was provided, lakhs of farmers were rendered destitute.

Lands acquired by the private sector produced enormous profits as the value of non-agricultural uses such lands were put to was much higher. Many intermediaries also saw an opportunity. Whenever there was a proposal of land acquisition, some functionaries would get wind of it, buy the land, record it at high rates and rip the cream off.

The Right to Fair Compensation and Transparency in Land Acquisition, Rehabilitation and Resettlement Act, 2013, moved the pendulum to the other extreme. Compensation was made four times in rural areas and twice in urban areas. Such multiples hurt more as the base price recorded was also rigged/manipulated to be much higher than the normal market price. Further, compensation and assistance were mandated to be provided to not only landowners but various other affected persons. Provisions of social assessment and obtaining the free consent of a large number of people (70–80 per cent) in case of projects with private participation were made stringent. The process became impossible to navigate.

The result was obvious. The private sector stopped acquiring land under the 2013 Act. And the government is making payments that are way above anything justifiable.

The NDA government tried to roll back some provisions (prior consent and social impact assessment) in five specified types of acquisition: projects vital for national security or defence; rural infrastructure projects; affordable housing and housing for the poor; industrial corridors; and infrastructure, including social infrastructure projects.

However, the 2015 Amendment Bill, brought for this purpose, could not get through the Rajya Sabha and the government abandoned the effort. A lot of irreparable damage has already been done. Urbanization, industrialization and infrastructure building have collapsed. Capital expenditure is constantly coming down and infrastructure in the private sector has become a casualty.

The situation has to change. A balance between the interests of landowners and purchasers has to be restored. Land has to become freely available for industrialization and infrastructure building. This is necessary to build a $10 trillion economy.

Two fundamental reforms are required in the 2013 Law:

First, the applicability of the law needs to be severely limited. It should only be used for projects that require land for the government to produce public goods and services. Defence, policing, health, regulation, etc., should be the purposes for which land could be 'acquired'. The 2013 Law extends the liability to provide for a relief and rehabilitation package even for purely private purchase of land through private negotiations if the land involved is more than the limit prescribed by the government. These provisions need to be dropped. For private projects, the acquisition law should be used only where the private entrepreneur is able to buy more than 80 per cent of the land by private negotiations but some minority landowners are unjustifiably holding up the remaining land. In such a situation, the Law should be used just to determine a reasonable price.

Second, all the confusions and contradictions of the 2013 Law should be sorted out. The environmental and social impact consideration should be made applicable to the project, not the land acquisition. The price paid for land should be related to the market price plus compensation. If the underlying market price is not reflective of true price, the same should be objectively determined by the acquisition officer. Other interests in the land property should be recognized and compensated in a fair manner. Requirements of giving jobs and annuities should be done away with.

Land for industrialization, infrastructure, housing and other private non-agricultural purposes should become a private transaction. The law should be used only for limited purposes.

Land Reforms for Slum Development

There are no good and reliable official estimates available for the urban slum population in India. The World Bank estimates that 35 per cent of India's urban population lives in slums, which puts the number at about 13–14 crore now.

No good estimates of land area occupied by slums are available as these are not recorded in any official system.

Two basic facts need to be noted. First, most slums are built invariably on land belonging to government and local authorities. A survey estimated that 60 per cent of slum land is government land; the balance belongs to local bodies. Second, slums are almost always inhabited by migrants. Those migrants who come to cities in search of work and are unable to find an affordable rental to live and work from end up finding shelter in slums.

The economic policies pursued by India are responsible for creating slums. The fact that elite urban planning did not envisage the need to build affordable housing and rental places where such supply was needed is reflected in the location of slums. Renting as a policy for housing was totally decimated by a misconceived policy of rent control and the almost impossible ejection of the tenant.

The private sector did not build affordable rentable apartments for migrants in cities. Government planners did not allow any such housing to come up as well. The result was an absolute shortage of affordable housing, leading to slums mushrooming on government lands. While the programmes undertaken by the Centre and states would somewhat improve living conditions, at least in some slums, the solution has to be found in the roots of the problem.

First, the government and local bodies must recognize that clearance of slums is neither feasible nor necessary. Second, the entire land of the government and local bodies occupied under slums, minus what is required to create minimum infrastructure for utilities, should be, as a policy, used to create affordable housing, mostly rental housing, for migrants. Third, slum lands, excluding the utilities infrastructure land, should be auctioned to cooperatives of slumdwellers and private developers to primarily develop rental housing for migrants. As rental housing would be developed in higher rise buildings, which a liberal policy should allow, existing inhabitants should be able to get rental housing. The proceeds of the auction can be used for infrastructure creation and providing cash support for slumdwellers.

Slums cannot be wished away. They are the result of a particular set of policies followed. However, a different set of polices can convert slums into inhabitable and healthier places to live and work. Slumdwellers provide significant services to the inhabitants of cities. They can serve the cities better if they live in comfortable and hygienic conditions.

Labour Reforms

Labour Reforms Should Address the Real Labour Issues of the Day and Times to Come

The labour laws in force and the policies the Indian government pursues today are based on the industrial situation prevalent in the early stages of industrialization. These laws and policies have not taken into account the massive changes in the situation of labour that have been taking place over the past couple of decades.

There are three mega trends impacting labour as a factor of production:

First, labour supply is outpacing demand, making the share of labour go down steadily in value addition.

Labour supply jumped big in the twentieth century with the global population increasing from 1.6 billion in 1900 to 6 billion in 2000. Improvement in life expectancy also added to the longevity of life, increasing labour supply.

The big increase in population and rising global incomes (rose from $1.1 trillion in 1900 to $41 trillion in 2000 in equivalent 1990 dollars) increased consumption demand for goods and services. This led to large labour demand in new mines to extract raw materials and fuel; the expansion and modernization of agriculture to produce more foods and fibres; the establishment of manufacturing factories to convert raw materials from mines and agriculture and produce industrial goods; and the setting up of innumerable shops and establishments to take goods and services to over a billion households and workplaces. Labour employed globally increased from an estimated 0.6 billion in 1900 to about 2.8 billion in 2000.

The situation, however, began to change in the last quarter of the twentieth century and has intensified in the twenty-first century. Advancement in technology, establishment of global value chains, setting up of more factories to produce goods and establishments to produce services have enormously increased the supply of goods and services. Digitalization has made the production of services easier, virtually eliminating supply constraint.

This transformation has impacted the terms and conditions and the bargaining power of labour and has also resulted in reduction of share of labour in value addition. The share of labour in total income started peaking in the 1980s in advanced countries and has been declining ever since, which has been confirmed by several studies by the OECD and ILO. This trend is likely to get accentuated with IoT and widespread digitalization. This is resulting in declining labour participation rate.

Second, the workplace has been transformed significantly.

Workplaces, specifically factories, which employ the most workers in organized establishments, have changed a great deal over the past two centuries with increasing automation. With steam technology being replaced by electricity, there is literally no soot, excessive humidity and heat in most factories. With improvement in mechanical and electrical engineering, machine safety is no longer a major issue.

The larger value addition in the economy now takes places in services. Service establishments using IT, the Internet and sleeker gadgetry are relatively more comfortable places to work. This has been clearly demonstrated after the pandemic, when such a large amount of work shifted from offices to homes, or for that matter anyplace.

In many cases, the necessity of the workplace has become redundant with the advent of the digital economy. Labour in the gig economy does not provide services to a fixed employer or at a fixed workplace. New studies are indicating that, globally, there will be reduced growth of office space and, soon, no net additions might be needed.

Third, the nature of work itself is changing very fast.

From the physical and manual world of the early days, we have come a long way. While mechanization and robotics reduced the requirement of physical labour, digitalization is changing the very nature of brainy work. Wholesalers and retailers are being replaced by e-commerce companies.

Banks and financial services companies are being replaced by fintech and mobile app-based banking and financial services companies.

The changing work and engagement of labour is changing the traditional employer-employee relationship and the need for fixed workplaces.

This transformation is making labour virtually a 'labour capitalist', using skills and knowledge as intellectual capital to contribute to the production of goods and services. Even sophisticated services can now be delivered using digital knowledge and skills.

All these profound changes necessitate a rethink in government policies, programmes and legislations for protection and welfare of labour.

Enact a Single Modern Workplaces Legislation

India enacted several legislations to provide for safe and healthy workplaces. For instance, the Factories Act, 1948, took care of the safety, health and working conditions in manufacturing factories, while the Mines Act, 1952 and the Plantation Labour Act, 1951, did the same for mines and plantations respectively. The Motor Transport Workers Act, 1961, sought to take care of workers engaged in the operation of vehicles. There were different laws for cine workers, dockworkers, construction workers, beedi and cigar workers, and so on. Similar laws were enacted for interstate migrant workers, working journalists and other newspaper employees.

The Occupational Safety, Health and Working Conditions Code, 2020, consolidates the safety, health and working conditions provisions of these thirteen laws in one Code. It neither recognizes the fundamental change in workplaces and nor does it create a modern law to appropriately address these concerns. It also does not simplify the administration of and compliance with the right working condition requirements.

Labour laws relating to safety, health and working conditions are still caught up in the time warp of the nineteenth and twentieth centuries. The consolidated Code of Occupational Safety, Health and Working Conditions displays the same outdated mindset. It essentially groups together different occupational laws in a single code, building on a dividing line of ten workers or less. All occupations employing ten or more workers need to follow certain standards and regulations for safety, health and working conditions. This does not help much, nor does it change much.

The hazardous nature of workplaces, including factories, has substantially reduced. There are some specific industries, such as mines, where working conditions are still hazardous but a great majority of workplaces are non-hazardous.

Recognizing this, the Occupational Safety, Health and Working Conditions Code, 2020, should be replaced by a simple Hazardous Workplaces Code.

This law should define workplaces comprehensively to include all factories, mines, plantations, office establishments, mobile vending carts, working homes and virtual workplaces, etc. The law should thereafter strictly define what constitutes a hazardous workplace. It should require all workplaces to file a declaration whether they are hazardous or non-hazardous. Non-hazardous workplaces may be required to file only an annual declaration about their status. No other compliances should be required from them. If there are about 8 crore workplaces in the country today, more than 99 per cent of them would be relieved of any compliances.

The Hazardous Workplaces Code should classify hazardous workplaces into appropriate classes. For each such class, the Code should designate an authority to prescribe the safety and other measures the occupiers should take. The hazardous workplaces could be subjected to periodic reporting, which should be made exclusively digitally. All periodic inspections should be abolished. An inspection should be carried out, with full transparency, only in case of a complaint or when there is reasonable suspicion.

A Labour Management Law in Place of Wage Code and Industrial Relations Code

The Code on Wages (Wage Code) and the Industrial Relations Code are based on the basic concept of 'employer-employee' as the only or at least predominant form of engagement in the production process. In the industrial economy, the employer was essentially the controller of capital who engaged labour as the employee. In today's world, the intellectual property (IP) creator or owner is the principal 'employer' of skilled labour. But, in many situations, the employee is not labour, but a contractor or vendor. Laws and regulations need to be amended to reflect this change.

This can be done by bringing a single Workmen Management Act by replacing the Wage Code and Industrial Relations Law. The minimum age of labour should be revised from fifteen to twenty—neither is there a requirement of so much labour that children below the age of twenty should work nor is fourteen years adequate enough a period for children to acquire requisite education and skills for modern jobs/work. Until the age of twenty, everyone should be expected to study, play and learn skills, paid for by family and wherever needed by the state.

This law should provide for compulsory single-point national registration of every person as a working age person/labour upon completion of twenty years of age. This system should have all the basic details about the skills and experience possessed by every such person. This portal should enable matching of skills needed by establishments and offered by the labour, wherever needed. The labour should file changes in its employment status, including statistically important information. The government should also reform the complex compensation structure embodied in the Wage Code in myriad forms—wages, overtime, bonus, gratuity and other job-related benefits— by adopting a simple cost-to-company/cost-to-employer compensation system. By abolishing the occupation-wise minimum wage system, the cost-to-company/cost-to-employer compensation should be left to be agreed between the employer and employee by the Workmen Management law. The government should only declare a national minimum wage and create enforcement machinery only to deal with the exploitation of labour in the form of non-payment of national minimum wage.

Make the Minimum Wage Work by an Employment Guarantee Programme

The government should redesign all employment-oriented programmes by merging them into and expanding MGNREGA into a work programme to provide work on national minimum wages, fixed on the basis of the consumption expenditure requirement of a healthy person, to every person of twenty years or more on demand, to be utilized for creation of public infrastructure and provision of public goods and services to the community.

The programme would convert labour into public goods and would help both labour to get the means for sustenance and the government to get public works done using people's skill sets.

The success of the programme could be measured by the fact that there is no unemployment and no one in the workforce gets paid less than the national minimum wage.

A Comprehensive Social Security Code for Households, Not Labour

India's workers' participation rate has fallen below 40 per cent. This means 60 per cent of the population in the working age of fifteen to sixty-five does not even want to work. More than 90 per cent of the workforce works in the unorganized sector or informally. Even the 4 per cent of working-age people who work in the organized/formal sectors are witnessing the change in the employer-employee relationship and the mode of compensation. No social security code based on the concept of worker or labour is likely to provide a safety net to all households.

The Social Security Code enacted by the government, based on the notion of worker, will be as big an administrative failure as many legislations previously enacted to address the welfare of informal and unorganized sector workers. The government also ends up bringing up several schemes for unorganized workers like PM SYM, Old Age Pension Scheme, Handicapped Pension Scheme, and so on.

The government should promulgate a comprehensive social security code for households, not for labour. Productively employed workers can take care of their social and household responsibilities. Temporary joblessness can be ameliorated by the revamped employment guarantee programme.

Only three kinds of people will need government support. First, children until the age of twenty to pursue their education and acquire requisite skills. The government must offer to meet this cost for any child whose parents cannot afford it. Second, all less than able-bodied persons, who cannot earn their livelihood either working as part of the main economy or under public works, should be provided financial assistance equivalent to the national minimum wage for sustaining them and their families. Third, the government must take care of the aged who don't have adequate savings/means to support their normal and medical expenditures. Other than these three, all other social security programmes can be simply shut down.

Chapter Fifty-Two

Public-Sector Reforms

The 1951 turn towards the socialist pattern of society had two fundamental outcomes, as noted earlier. First, the private sector was excluded from a large economic and business space in the country by means of several policy actions: reserving most strategic, capital-intensive, natural resource, utilities and other major businesses for the public sector; putting in place a strangulating system of licence and permits to control private-sector investments in the areas permissible for it; and nationalizing private enterprises in both the real and financial sectors. Second, spinning off a large public sector to produce goods and services, most of which were of the nature of private goods with, at one point in time, almost 90 per cent of large industry investments and banking assets being in the public sector.

India took at decisive turn again in 1991 and embarked on the path of re-privatization of the economy. The exclusion of the private sector brought about by the Industrial Development and Regulation Act (IDRA) 1951, Industrial Policy Resolutions of 1948 and 1956 and Industrial Licencing Policies has been largely rolled back by now. The private sector has entered almost every real and financial sector space. The public sector still remains largely intact though in almost every industrial and financial space, its share has shrunk to less than 50 per cent. In many sectors, it has shrunk to less than 10 per cent. The re-privatization agenda initiated in 1991 is still a work in progress.

The re-privatization agenda of 2021 has two main components. One is simple and the other more complex. The second one, however, is more necessary. First, to consign the IDRA-1951 to the history books and end the remaining reservation for the public sector. Second, to privatize the public sector which still makes and distributes private goods and services.

Perform the Last Rites of IDRA-1951

The strangulating IDRA-1951, which brought in the infamous licence permit raj, was mostly undone by the liberalization policies followed after IP-1991. However, IDRA-1951 is still on the statute book, though its sting has been removed. At present, IDRA-1991 is essentially used for two purposes. First, it prevents the states from instituting licence and control systems though the states are largely unaware of these provisions. Second, there are still five industries (electronic aerospace and defence equipment, specified hazardous chemicals, industrial explosives, tobacco products like cigars, cigarettes and distillation and brewing of alcoholic drinks) for which licencing is still mandatory under the law.

There is no justifiable reason to prescribe the requirement of an industrial licence for any of these remaining five industries.

Defence equipment manufacturing is thriving all over the world—except in communist countries—in the private sector. There is no licencing for making aero-space sector investments in India. The government has recently issued a clarification in this regard as well. But, the private sector has not really come in, in a big way. We need to encourage the private sector to freely invest in defence and aerospace to wipe out the dubious distinction of being the largest importer of defence equipment in the world.

The remaining four other products, such as hazardous substances and tobacco products, are better regulated under environmental and workplace laws than under IDRA-1951. The manufacture of alcoholic drinks is excessively regulated by the states under their excise laws. There is no need for the Centre to provide a licence. Therefore, licencing can be easily done away with for all the five industries.

Two industries are still reserved for the public sector: railway operations and atomic energy. Public-sector monopoly of railway operations has stunted the growth of the Railways in the country. They only carry about 7 per cent of passenger traffic now with the number of passengers declining in absolute numbers. Railways are also losing freight traffic steadily as the bulk of freight traffic has shifted to roads despite their relative inefficiency for bulk traffic. There is no longer any justification to reserve railway operations for the public sector. This monopoly should be disbanded.

Atomic energy is a high-technology sector. In the absence of development of cost-effective, indigenous commercial atomic power generation technology, India has opted to find global technologies to generate atomic power. While some success has been seen in building atomic power reactors with Russian technology, there has not been much headway in joint ventures contemplated with the Americans and French. Collaboration with the Russians has also been downscaled. Incidentally, the American and French companies approached are in the private sector. There is no technological and commercial gain in keeping atomic energy reserved for the public sector. It should also be deleted from the reserved list.

Indeed, it is time to close the chapter of reservation for the public sector in India fully and formally.

The most appropriate thing left to do is to simply repeal IDRA-1951.

Public-Sector Enterprises Require Massive Reforms of their Governance

The normal mode of doing business in corporations is to entrust management to their boards of directors for policy and strategy and to chief executives for operations. The owners remain either pure investors without interfering in the operations and management of the company or, if they intend to partake in the management of the company, they join the board of directors and assume operational roles as well. The Government of India, as the owner of public-sector companies, does not allow conduct of the business of public-sector undertakings by their boards and management. Every public-sector company is placed under the policy and investment control of one administrative ministry/department of the government. The officers of the concerned ministries/departments join the board of directors. This arrangement results in strategic, investment and operational control of public-sector undertakings being effectively passed to the hands of the administrative ministries/departments.

The Government of India has quite a few big ministries and departments to dabble in at the industry level despite ending the reservation for the public sector and abolishing the licence permit raj. These include the Ministry of Steel, Ministry of Heavy Industries, Ministry of Fertilizers and Department of Chemicals and Petrochemicals, to name a few. As they do not have much of a policymaking role, they essentially end up controlling and managing public-sector enterprises under their administrative control including their investments, appointment of senior managerial personnel and foreign travel, besides heavily influencing operational matters of CPSEs.

For re-privatization of public-sector undertakings, the Government of India would have to bring fundamental change in their governance arrangement. The best way would be to delink public-sector enterprises from their administrative ministries. If such a delinking takes places, a number of industry-specific ministries/departments may also not be required. Industry-specific ministries and departments should therefore be disbanded.

Complete the Privatization Programme Initiated in Budget 2021–22

After selling small stakes in public-sector undertakings for many years and some pseudo-privatization (HPCL sold to ONGC, two power companies sold to NTPC, etc.), the government announced its decision to privatize two PSBs and one general insurance company in Budget 2021–22 in addition to privatization announced earlier of BPCL, CONCOR, SCI, IDBI Bank and Air India.

In Budget 2021–22, the finance minister also announced a policy for delineating strategic sectors and privatization of public-sector enterprises. Its principal elements are minimizing the number of CPSEs, including financial institutions; strategic sectors to include atomic energy, space and defence; transport and telecommunications; power, petroleum, coal and other minerals; and banking, insurance and financial services; retaining 'bare minimum presence of CPSEs with the rest of CPSEs to be privatized, merged or subsidiarized with other CPSEs or closed' in strategic sectors; and CPSEs to be privatized, else closed, in non-strategic sectors.

These announcements clearly indicate acceptance of the fact that it is time to let the public-sector undertakings go. Though still somewhat timid, the policy is clear on acceptance of privatization of CPSEs as policy. Now, the government must demonstrate the administrative ability to carry out this agenda. If it does so, it might be laying the foundations of Economic Policy 3.0. It will be the 2021 moment.

Consolidating CPSEs Land and Managing it Professionally Will Be Key

Land is the Achilles heel in case of privatization of CPSEs and closure of loss-making CPSEs. The government, despite permitting several CPSEs in the past (IDPL, Air India, BSNL, for example) to sell their land parcels to wipe out/reduce their losses, has not seen any significant sale of land. In fact, most such land sales programmes have come a cropper.

In Budget 2021–22, the government announced monetizing CPSEs' lands by way of direct sale, concession or similar means and to form an SPV with special abilities for this purpose. Formation of a Land Monetization Corporation or Trust would bring twin advantages. CPSEs divested of surplus land parcels would be easier and less controversial to sell. Further, the SPV, managed by real-estate industry professionals, can get the best value for the land as it would be able to use the right monetization strategy/ option for each specific parcel of land: outright sale, development of land with capital cost met by creating REIT or leasing of land with or without development.

The record of the government in carrying out economic reforms and privatization transactions has been quite poor (there has not been a single privatization in India after 2003). It would have to deliver an extraordinary performance to achieve the goals of completing the announced privatization of the CPSEs and setting up a functional SPV for land management.

An Alternative Way for Disinvestment and Privatization—Creating a Sovereign Wealth Asset Management Company

The divestment strategy of CPSEs has not been successful for three primary reasons. First, the stock markets do not perceive good value in

CPSEs and the market sees oversupply coming from the government as part of the minority stake sale as a big drag. Second, the biggest drag on the performance of CPSEs is administrative control by the concerned ministries that pass on all kinds of directions and instructions of a non-commercial nature. The way PSBs have been micromanaged and directed is the prime reason for their non-professional and non-commercial functioning. This applies to power and many other PSEs. Third, there is no professional management overseeing and directing the functioning of PSEs and PSBs and creation of value in their stocks.

All these shortcomings can be addressed if the Government of India were to create an Indian Sovereign Wealth Fund (ISWF) or a Sovereign Asset Management Company (SAMC). This Fund/SAMC can be created by transferring the government's stakes in all listed companies as well as commercially valuable unlisted companies. There are over eighty real sector PSUs like IOC, GAIL and NTPC and financial entities like PSBs and insurance companies with market capitalization of over Rs 20 lakh crore. The stake of the government in these companies is around Rs 14–16 lakh crore. Market capitalization of unlisted entities, including companies like LIC, should also be about Rs 13–15 lakh crore. With a combined potential capital valuation of about Rs 30 lakh crore, or $450 billion, an ISWF/SAMC, if created, would have enormous market heft. These valuations have gone up further in 2021.

The ISWF/SMAC can serve the objective of implementing the structural reform of privatization and raising disinvestment revenues for the government much better than the present arrangement of government-managed minority stake sale and privatization.

First, this will increase the valuation of the CPSEs. The ISWF/SMAC as a holding company of CPSEs can model itself on the lines of assets managed by professionally run sovereign wealth funds (SWFs) like TAMASEC or private equity firms like Blackstone. To become such a vehicle, it would have to be professionally run and its management handed over to real investment professionals. Second, the SMAC/ISWF would be able to significantly increase its assets base as well. Such a powerful and well-capitalized fund would easily be able to borrow large amounts from the market, in excess of Rs 10–15 lakh crore, which can be used to buy equities and assets of long-term interest to the country domestically and abroad. Such a vehicle can also be used to support the market during major crises like the one witnessed in March 2020 on account of COVID-19. Such investments can be expected to generate excellent returns for the ISWF. Third, the ISWF/SMAC would continue to serve the two financial objectives the CPSEs currently serve for the government: payment of dividends and realization of capital proceeds upon disinvestments. The government gets about Rs 50,000 crore as dividends and has averaged about Rs 80,000 crore in the three years as disinvestment capital receipts (excluding the COVID-19 impacted 2020–21). With better management, the ISWF would be expected to earn more dividends for the government, which will get routed through the fund instead of coming from CPSEs. The objective of generating disinvestment revenues can be served by either selling a part of the stake in ISWF or by privatizing companies in the portfolio of ISWF/SMAC and receiving the proceeds as special dividends. Assuming the Fund could create a valuation even equal to the value of equities transferred to it, by selling a 5 per cent stake, the government can generate more than Rs 1.5–2 lakh crore every year as disinvestment resources.

The government must aim at privatizing all commercial CPSEs by 2030, barring a few (ten to fifteen) that can perform as market leaders, managed by a professionally run SWF, and create value generating total returns of not less than 15 per cent a year. India should be free of public-sector undertakings both at the Central and state level.

Chapter Fifty-Three

Infrastructure Reforms

Infrastructure is an asset—physical or digital—providing a service.

Infrastructure contributes to GDP in two ways. First, by consuming goods and services at the construction stage and, second, by delivering vital services. The consumption of goods and services in the construction of infrastructure gets counted in the form of value add coming from those goods and services. Steel and equipment used in putting together telecommunication networks get counted in manufacturing value added, programming gets counted as IT/professional services, and so on. Services delivered by telecommunication networks get counted as part of the GDP under the group relating to broadcasting.

Creation of efficient, adequate and profitable infrastructure facilities will be the most critical element in building India's $10 trillion economy by 2035. It is necessary to increase the productivity of natural resources, humans, machines and intelligence in every sector of the economy. It is critical for establishing the most competitive manufacturing base in the country. It is vital for the most efficient, competitive and productive generation and delivery of services.

India should develop and articulate an infrastructure vision for 2035. Considering the fact that 30 per cent of GDP contribution comes from fixed capital formation (this should actually go up to 40 per cent in the run up to 2035) and that infrastructure constitutes an important part of fixed capital formation, it is important that all policy issues for realizing infrastructure targets are addressed.

Major Policy Proposals for Building Infrastructure for 2035

First, infrastructure has a long life. Most investment is made upfront whereas services and returns flow over a long period of time. There is a considerable amount of uncertainty in long-term projections of returns. A 100 km road project with a life of twenty-five years requires an upfront investment of Rs 2500 crore, whereas toll collections cannot be estimated with any degree of certainty. India has given concessions of six airports for fifty years, which means investment in constructing city-side and airport terminal facilities incurred upfront would be recoverable over this long period. Several infrastructure projects have had problems as estimated traffic or revenues turned out to be very different from projections. Renegotiation of contracts is generally, and correctly, frowned upon, post-award events lead to disruption in operation of facilities and unproductive litigation.

All profitable infrastructure projects should be concessioned only on design, build, operate and transfer (DBOT) basis. All non-profitable infrastructure projects (which by their very nature would require the government to subsidize them) should be split in two packages: constructing the facility and monetizing it. The construction phase should be designed and built by the private sector at the public cost. The infrastructure facility can thereafter be monetized by using any of the models: INVIT, sale or any other appropriate mode.

In 2019, the government announced an NIP (National Infrastructure Pipeline). The NIP is a completely disappointing document with almost 75 per cent of envisaged investments of over Rs 100 lakh crore expected to come from the Centre and states. The government announced a National Monetization Pipeline (NMP) in the 2021–22 Budget.

The NIP has not moved an inch as it is only a listing of infrastructure projects and nothing more than that. Likewise, the existence of NMP merely will not make any monetization plan move. The NIP and NMP are not needed for building India's infrastructure. It is the ability to envision the infrastructure of India for 2035 and then go about it by structuring infrastructure projects and auctioning and building these using the policy of DBOT for profitable infrastructure and public-funded construction followed by monetization for unprofitable but desirable infrastructure projects.

Second, road infrastructure policy needs to be revamped completely. BOT (build, own, operate) projects in the Indian roads sector have completely dried up as the cost of construction turned out to be much more than anticipated (also on account of policy change relating to land acquisition compensation after award of concessions) and the traffic projection too low (sometimes, alternative roads were also operated free of toll by the government). The government is keeping roads sector investment going by spending all the funds required at government cost on an EPC (engineering, procurement and construction) basis or annuities.

In the process, the National Highways Authority of India (NHAI), which has responsibility for specifically assigned national highways, and National Highways and Infrastructure Development Corporation Ltd (NHIDCL), which has the responsibility for the remaining highways, have accumulated an enormous amount of debt. The losses embedded in most of their road projects require the two entities to internalize large capital losses whenever these assets are given away on toll, operate and transfer (TOT) basis. These entities are trying, and NHAI has been able to create the first INVIT and to transfer some of the road assets through INVITs. But the INVIT structure, on account of higher embedded returns on units, would increase the capital losses.

All new highways should be given away on DBOT (if assessed profitable). All non-profitable new road assets should be constructed on public funds followed by monetization. All existing road projects, bundled into appropriately sized and structured SPVs, should be given away on TOT basis.

Third, power-sector policy needs complete overhauling. Four principal policy reforms would be needed. First, create a national power market with bulk power purchase and sales taking place only in the power market. Second, stop building power plants in the public sector. All new power-sector projects, most specifically renewables, should come up only in the private sector. Third, the distribution end of power infrastructure should be completely privatized. Fourth, the generation and transmission business in the central and state public sector should be consolidated and handed over to the national and state sovereign asset management companies to manage or be privatized.

These policies would require considerable action. All state power distribution companies should be disbanded by creating 250 city-based private power distribution companies. The system of long-term power purchase agreements should be liquidated by a statute and a free exchange-based power market created. No state government should have any power generation, transmission or distribution company under its belt. The central power business should be organized in three central government entities: NTPC, PowerGrid and one more company that can competitively build a city-based power distribution and supply business. All other Central government power companies should be sold to private enterprises or at best be transferred to NTPC and the distribution company.

Fourth, the present departmental undertaking of the Railways should be restructured in four verticals: passenger tracks and railway infrastructure; freight tracks and related railway infrastructure, along with the incoming dedicated freight corridor infrastructure; the passenger traffic business, along with all wagons and engines; and all the remaining businesses, including manufacturing facilities, residential colonies, catering and ticketing. Passenger tracks and related infrastructure can be organized in an appropriate number of subsidiaries under one holding company, say, IndRail Tracks and Stations. Freight carrying lines that connect ports, mines and major plants should be separated from passenger tracks and be merged with the Dedicated Freight Corridor Corporation, which as a company already exists. The passenger business should also be organized into one holding company with an appropriate number of subsidiaries. Finally, the rest of the business should be brought under one holding company.

The reorganized four holding companies should be entrusted to four different professional boards. Existing railway staff should be asked to choose to go to any of the four companies or their subsidiaries. The government can grant them pensionary benefits for services rendered until the date of transfer, which can be paid from existing budgets/funds. The services in the new companies should be organized on the basis of a defined benefit system with the staff and the companies contributing 10 per cent of salary in the new pension account. The current structure of the Railway Board needs to be revamped and below board formations should be disbanded. The holding companies may take up a privatization programme to sell appropriate subsidiaries, concession infrastructure facilities to be constructed and/or operated and take the subsidiaries to list and raise capital from the market. The government should not be expected to provide any capital support from the Budget. It should also do away with all passenger and freight subsidization programmes. However, if it wishes to continue some of these, it should create arrangements to pay the support directly to intended beneficiaries rather than distorting railway operations and commercial arrangements.

Fifth, the state roadways corporations have outlived their utility. Likewise, the system of notifying nationalized routes for state carriage purposes has no relevance any more.

The government should repeal the State Road Transport Act completely and allow Central government equity in state roadways corporations to be written down to zero. Thereafter, states should simply sell the state roadways corporations in the appropriate number of subsidiaries. Roadway bus stands can be organized as one holding company and developed, in partnership with the private sector, much the same way as railway stations are proposed to be dealt with.

Sixth, the government should get out of the airline business. It has succeeded in selling Air India. It will be a task to sell Air India's assets retained by the government but that is fine. Land and buildings can be transferred to a sovereign land management corporation. The government, of course, would be expected to discharge the debt of Air India and its subsidiaries, which can be managed by transferring and refinancing the same in the Air India Asset Management Company already created.

The Airports Authority of India (AAI) has made an excellent beginning by concessioning six airports in 2019–2020. It should be organized as a holding company with all airports transferred into separate subsidiaries. The holding company should operate as an asset management company, with all the airports in the subsidiary companies being concessioned over the next five years. The airports that are not commercially viable, even with development and use of city-side land, can be either given away on concession with viability gap funding or sold as real estate.

Seventh, other infrastructure—metros, ports, urbanization, irrigation—should also be reorganized on the policy of a holding company with all distinct facilities organized as subsidiaries of the holding company. The holding company should work primarily as an asset management company and all infrastructure businesses in subsidiaries be given away to the private sector on appropriate concessions. All these sectoral holding companies should also be transferred to the sovereign asset management authority.

Auction 5G by Reducing Reserve Price to What the Market Can Bear

The Telecom Regulatory Authority of India (TRAI) has recommended reserve prices for 5G spectrum. Various estimates are floating about the kind of funds the industry will have to come up with to take all the spectrum on offer. Some estimates place the amount in excess of a couple of lakh crore.

Considering the potential revenue 5G telecom spectrum can generate and the morass the telecom industry finds itself in, only one of the three players seems to have indicated an interest. If the auction attracts just one bidder, it is no auction at all. This has been the situation until February 2021 with no auction of 5G telecom spectrum. In February 2021, the TRAI Chairman expressed his willingness to look at the reserve prices if the government were to make a request to that effect. Some work has been initiated in this regard, but there is no definitive movement.

The principal advantage of 5G spectrum would be the expansion of the digital economy. 5G telecom spectrum will build digital expressways/superhighways and connect machines and equipment in the form of the Internet of Things. The future economy will be built on these digital superhighways like the analogue economy was built on roads and highways in the last century. The best way to protect revenue in the current circumstances is to link spectrum charges to the revenues that 5G spectrum and licence would generate for telecom companies. In view of the massive infrastructural role that 5G spectrum will play, it might be worthwhile to allocate 5G spectrum at a very low capital/one-time cost, somewhere close to one-tenth/one-fourth of the reserve price recommended by TRAI. Such an arrangement would serve the national interest and Indian economy well.

Policy Reforms to Make Power Supply to Industry Competitive

To make Indian industry competitive and manufacturing to take off, electricity pricing for industry has to be rationalized.

First, distorting and debilitating measures need to be done away with. These include abolishing cross-subsidy surcharge on open-access purchases; removing all restrictions on sale of power on captive power-generating units and allowing them to sell their surplus power; and removing all restrictions on open access regarding purchase of power from exchanges, bilaterally or otherwise.

Second, distributing companies (DISCOMs) should start treating industry as good, if not preferred, customers. There is no need to provide them subsidized power. But rates for industrial and commercial consumers should be bearable—most likely, the market will clear at prices higher than the average cost of purchase but below the 20 per cent upper corridor the tariff policy has laid down.

Third, India has now become a stable surplus power generator. On quite a few days in 2020, India used less than 25 per cent of its capacity to generate power. It is not unusual now to see the power load factor of thermal power plants remain at less than 60 per cent; some of these plants are forced to back down on some days. In such a situation, DISCOMs should assure reliable, uninterrupted power supply to industry. It is a shame that India still has about 15,000 MW of diesel-generating capacity in the country, though it is not used as much these days. Just like inverters have practically become a thing of the past in Delhi and most cities with assured power supply becoming a norm, industry would be incentivized to dismantle diesel power-generating capacity by providing assured uninterrupted power. This would also have a positive impact on the environment.

These measures would boost power consumption. DISCOMs would get good customers back, which will add to their volumes. In fact, they might actually benefit from higher sales realization in this distortion-free pricing regime.

The policy of overcharging industrial consumers and keeping them captive has not really helped the DISCOMs as these 'good customers' have managed to escape their clutches, wherever possible, albeit at a very high cost to them. Both DISCOMs and industrial customers have suffered. India has also suffered as DISCOMs generate enormous losses (in excess of Rs 1.5 lakh crore a year before subsidies provided by states and not counting interest liabilities taken over under Ujwal DISCOM Assurance Yojana [UDAY] and other schemes)—and Indian industry struggles to be competitive as it is chained by such high electricity costs.

Every unit of electricity does the same work, whether used in industry, agriculture or homes. Pricing it differently based on the user is a cardinal error. The electricity tariff policy of the Government of India, which is supposedly binding on the State Electricity Commissions that set the tariffs, recognizes this policy principle. For many years, this policy mandates tariffs to be set for customers not exceeding 20 per cent of the average cost of supply. This policy directive has, however, been mostly honoured in the breach.

Setting tariffs has also been made unduly complex. In some states, there are over sixty kinds of electricity consumers. A unit of electricity does the same work but it has over sixty different prices. Reading the tariff schedule of any DISCOM reveals how chaotic and complex the system is, resulting in unnecessary disputes and unhappiness all around.

States also try to achieve their social goals through pricing power differently. Agriculture tariffs and residential tariffs are set at lower rates; industrial and commercial tariffs at higher rates. Then, state subsidies come into play, which are also delivered through tariffs. Effective tariffs are reduced factoring in these subsidies, making the tariff structure even more complex.

Railway Reforms Urgently Needed

Low railways fares do not guarantee passenger traffic when alternatives are emerging. This is evident considering the massive loss of traffic by Indian Railways consistently over the past seventy years. Good quality and timely service are needed by passengers and they don't mind paying for it. Quality service can be provided by rationalizing railway fares to be commercially competitive in order to raise resources for investments. Railway passenger fares for non-AC classes could be raised in periodic small doses to compete with non-AC bus fares in a period of two years. Fares of suburban and local trains in cities should also be raised in small doses gradually to achieve two-thirds of full cost recovery over a three-year period. Fares of AC services should be made competitive to AC bus fares over a period of two to three years raised in quarterly instalments. Freight traffic should be competitively priced to the road sector, even 5–10 per cent lower on routes where there is spare capacity. Dependence of the Railways on freight income from coal transportation needs to be reduced by diversifying its freight business.

The Station Development Programme needs to be accelerated. The Railways should identify 100 stations, out of a total of about 8000-odd stations, where the real-estate value of the building and the land appurtenant thereto offers a good possibility of monetization by improving customer experience. These stations should thereafter be developed on the pattern of the model of AAI for giving six airports on concession, which has unlocked the potential value of cityside development.

Ad hoc commercialization of passenger services done by transferring a few trains to the Indian Railway Catering and Ticketing Corporation (IRCTC) will not work. Railway passenger services should be reorganized by offering these on a twenty to twenty-five-year concession basis for the private sector to invest in refurbishing existing train sets and invest in new ones. The privatization process can begin with specialized train services like Vande Bharat, Rajdhani, Shatabdi and Duronto being offered first. The Railways/regulator should specify minimum service standards and set a formula for fare fixation. Non-premium services can be privatized on a regional/state/sub-state basis with improved standards of services being specified. This can be done in the second phase. Running trains by handing them over to the IRCTC is not privatization. After ten years, the Railways should not be operating any passenger trains on its own.

The country should aim to develop 10,000 km of high-speed and semi high-speed passenger rail corridors by 2030. These corridors should be constructed on PPP basis with the Railways bidding them out for forty to fifty-year concession on a viability-gap basis. The viability gap costs, borne by the Railways and supported by the government, can be partly recovered by concessioning passenger services on these tracks. The Railways would earn an income by charging for use of tracks and stations.

India should develop a 10,000 km dedicated freight corridor rail network by 2030. These corridors, concessioning the freight movement, should be constructed by bidding them out on a PPP concession and viability-gap basis. Alternatively, these can be constructed on the hybrid annuity model (HAM) of the roads sector or a mix of HAM and EPC modes.

The Railways should identify all its residential land parcels and housing complexes and select land parcels and existing housing complexes for redevelopment on the basis of an agreed criterion relating to size and the necessity of having a railways residential/office space. These identified places should be offered on fifty to sixty-year concessions to the private sector on a modified NBCC model to get redeveloped space and cash monetization. Over a ten-year period till 2030, the Railways should modernize and redevelop all such identified land parcels/residential complexes. It can create one or more land monetization and management corporations for this purpose.

The Railways should hive off/privatize most non-core (other than passenger and freight transportation) activities. After making the terms and conditions of license/concession between CONCOR and private players similar, there should be a sale of the majority or complete stake in CONCOR. The manufacturing rolling stock of departmental undertakings should be corporatized and hived off from the Railways. These can be either privatized or best technology partners inducted with majority equity stake and technology transfer for manufacturing—and exporting—rolling stock on competitive terms. The Research Design and Standards Organization (RDSO) can be hived off into an independent organization with no mandatory testing work from the Railways. RDSO can also work for other railways of the world. Catering should be completely privatized with popular brands being allowed to set up their kitchens in appropriate places (including outside railways premises wherever appropriate) and supply to consumers on demand. Prices should be also deregulated with competition ensuring that there will be no artificial hike. Ticketing, like airline ticketing, should be allowed to be done by agents, initially for AC service. IRCTC should be disinvested. Hospitals need to be hived off in a separate entity.

In short, the government should open up all segments of railway operations for private investment; appoint an independent regulator to determine fares and quality of service; separate railway tracks into one national trunk public utility and a few regional utilities; gradually privatize all passenger and goods operations; and create a competitive railway business in the country.

State Roadways and Bus-Stands are Past Their Due Dates

Two major reforms needed in the roadways sector are denationalization of routes and selling state roadways undertakings. The practice of state governments notifying various routes and reserving them for STUs for stage carriage traffic has been hampering the legal establishment of passenger road transport businesses. Over the past three decades, many road operators have built competing businesses by misusing contract carriage provisions. The policy and practice of nationalizing routes needs to be junked. Routes should be allotted or auctioned to private operators with stringent quality conditions and under a regulated fare regime.

This policy of permitting legal private operations in the stage carriage business will bring in strong players and help upgrade the quality and frequency of services. This would also sound the formal death knell of STUs. As state roadways have several assets—buses, workshops, domain knowledge and the like—it would be prudent to separate bus operations and bus stations management businesses. The bus operations businesses can be sold off. The bus stations businesses can be converted into a bus stations asset management company state-wise, owned by the government (this will also take care of ownership-related disputes over bus station lands), which can use the best land and building asset management concepts to develop and manage the bus-port business and assets.

Policy Solution to Revitalize Real-Estate Sector

The residential real-estate business will have to be fundamentally restructured. Like their counterparts in other businesses, existing insolvent developers need to be ousted from their projects and lenders should take required haircuts to make projects financially viable.

In India, we have an individual ownership model of residential real estate. All our incentives, tax and non-tax, are designed to basically serve this model. At the same time, we have totally irrational rent control laws, which discourage corporates and non-corporates from building and managing houses/apartments for rent. As capital gains have disappeared, the individual ownership model has become quite unattractive, even to individuals. Deterred by rent control laws and lack of tax and non-tax incentives, corporates have not gone into residential housing with leasing as a business model. The policy solution has to be built around the fundamental structural reforms in the real estate sector.

First, simply abolish rent control laws. Vested interests have thwarted this for long. They need to be told to stay out. Owners, corporates or individuals, should have all rights to repossess their property on the date of conclusion of contract or on default of payment of rent. No court intervention should be needed.

Second, seed the corporate residential housing business in the country. Corporates have carried on very successful commercial real-estate businesses. Millions of square feet of commercial real estate have been constructed in the country and numerous projects are currently going on. A great majority of these are doing very well financially, earning decent returns to service their lenders. These corporates have also been able to monetize their investments by setting up REITs to release their capital to invest in new projects. Corporates, especially large established players, now need to be encouraged to take up residential real-estate projects to be managed on a leasing basis, not selling to individual owners. This also synchs with the requirement of housing by millennials and many workers who change their jobs or move to different cities for work, and increasingly find owning homes in a city a liability rather than asset. As the economic model is still not very established, these projects need to be provided tax incentives. There is no harm if they are given income-tax exemption for ten to fifteen years and receive full GST refunds for all taxes paid on inputs, including capital machinery. Simultaneously, liberal tax incentives should be provided to households and individuals renting these houses, much like individual homeowners are provided. If the entire rent paid is allowed as deduction from salary, it would provide a fillip to corporate residential real-estate projects.

Third, landowners should be encouraged to provide their land, at least a good part of it, to corporate developers as equity to the project. This will help landowners get steady returns over a period of time rather than getting the bulk of the money upfront. It will also reduce the borrowing requirements for undertaking such projects. This has started happening and needs to be scaled up.

Fourth, all stressed real-estate projects should be put on an expeditious resolution path in the IBC process. Failed owners should be thrown out and replaced with good and established ones and lenders should take due haircuts. The resolved entities would then fast-track investment and complete projects. This will kickstart the stalled economy.

Such fundamental restructuring of the residential real-estate business would put the economy on a higher growth path again.

Chapter Fifty-Four

Building India's Digital Economy

Spurred by the three key technological innovations of the chip, the code and the Internet, the digital revolution is in the process of transforming every business in the world. These three building blocks of the digital revolution are getting stronger, becoming more powerful and efficient, and increasingly reaching the unreached every day. Chips are packing more transistors. Blockchain-crypto coding is competing harder with centralized database technology on which most of the digital economy has been built so far. The Internet is becoming faster, bigger and reaching everywhere with digital devices becoming commonplace.

Most services, whether it is trade and commerce, accounting, banking, outsourced processing, entertainment or banking, have already seen a massive digitalization shift. The coronavirus has given a further disruptive push to digitalization in the delivery and consumption of services.

The digital revolution is also transforming the production and consumption of most agricultural and industrial goods. There is an increasing use of chips and code in the manufacture of physical goods. With IoT also a reality now, the connectedness of physical machines and equipment will further digitalize the economy. The Industrial Revolution transformed muscles into machines creating giant factories for production of goods on a big scale. The digital revolution is transforming humans and products into data and bringing intelligence to machines. The cocktail of data and artificial intelligence (AI) will enable the digital revolution to permeate every product and service.

The countries, companies and human beings who adopt and adapt to this transformation will prosper. Economies that advance beyond industrial-age technologies to digital-age technologies will clearly be winners while economies that ignore digital technologies or are inefficient converters will lose out.

India's Digital Transformation Imperatives

Digital technologies are transforming economies the world over. The global digital economy is estimated to be worth about $5 trillion now, or about 5–6 per cent of global GDP. Indian technology entrepreneurs did well in starting and establishing IT services in India beginning in the 1990s and India today has a share of over one-third in global GDP of IT services of about $500 billion. However, India did not do well in electronics manufacturing and building software and the new-age businesses of cloud computing, IT-enabled services and services based on AI.

New digital start-ups have begun building India as a global force in software as a service (SaaS) and some major corporates have signalled their intention to get into semiconductors and chip making.

India's digital transformation agenda is fourfold.

First, the unique differentiating factor between digitally advanced and digitally backward economies is the ability to produce chips. The production of chips requires semiconductors and the ability to design chips. India is literally bereft of the capacity to produce semiconductors and has acquired very limited capacity to design and produce chips. This needs to change and India should aim at becoming a major semiconductors and chip-making and designing power.

Second, digital technology and infrastructure are developing and changing rapidly. With the advancement of machine learning and machine communications (IoT), the digital technology and infrastructure of computer networks, data storage, including cloud and data analytics, are providing amazing productivity, user experience and competitiveness to digitally advanced economies. While data storage and spectrum-based telecommunication infrastructure have made a promising beginning in India, the country has enormous ground to cover in the digital technology and infrastructure sweepstakes. The ability to create artificial intelligence and harness it for production and distribution of goods and services, including newer digital goods and services, will make a critical difference going forward.

Third, the code is the heart of digital transformation. It makes everything digital—chips, technology, cloud, platforms, applications—work. India has created excellent companies and there are many start-ups that are leading development of codes—the software. Indian companies and start-ups are also catching up with the development of SaaS and software-defined infrastructure (SDI), though our share of the global software market is still minuscule, at less than 2 per cent. Like one-third share India could command in information technology services, India can legitimately aim at garnering one-third share in global software writing and deployment.

Fourth, digitalization of services was massively encouraged by the development of data transfer networks. India was in the forefront of this segment of digital economy capitalizing on its quality labour processing the raw data into usable data/information. The country still commands a very large share of global IT services. IT services comprise over 60 per cent of India's export of services. There are two major challenges emerging in this area: other processing destinations have come up and data generation and use is becoming transactional. Both these challenges are likely to cause the IT market to slowly taper off in future. India would need to train and prepare its youth and manpower as global digital workers.

India's digital policy framework must address all the four imperatives.

India's Best Bet Lies in Software and Digital Services

Development of software for digitalization of existing businesses, creating and running digital platforms, applications, networks and machines using human and AI will remain a major growth opportunity for many years. Indian human resources are best suited for writing software and delivering SaaS. The software writing and service businesses will best develop in the private sector, with the right kind of policy support from the government. The policy reforms and support need to be built around three broad areas. The government should provide the policy support bigger than the support provided to the IT services in the last twenty-five years.

First, software and SaaS will increasingly be delivered as part of cloud-based services on digital platforms. The cloud resides in data storage parks. The government should bring for data storage parks and cloud services a new scheme of Data Storage Infrastructure Parks. Development of Data Storage Infrastructure Parks should be declared as the most promising infrastructure and environment-friendly activity to enable quick purchase/allotment and conversion of land, and provide all clearance expeditiously, if not given a free pass for all clearance. Likewise, making of digital hardware, establishing digital technology services parks, etc., should also receive most favourable infrastructure creation treatment. The digital infrastructure should be given income tax treatment better than that given to new manufacturing companies in the taxation policy of 2019. This policy will give the requisite push to make India the hub of data storage parks and digital manufacturing.

Second, IT services enjoyed income tax free treatment for many years. The BPO (business process outsourcing) and KPO (knowledge process outsourcing) of the past, which flourished under the tax-free regime, contributed to the faster economic growth India witnessed since the 1990s and has also been one of the best employment generators. It is now time to make IT services more nuanced from the tax viewpoint. Incomes from software development and SaaS should be made tax-free for fifteen years as they would be the primary engines of India's digital services growth story.

Third, start-ups essentially leverage digital technologies for providing more efficient, convenient and better production and delivery of goods and services to businesses and consumers. For most start-ups, '—to C or consumers' is the real game. For building these businesses, start-ups spend big chunk of their capital in acquiring these consumers. Conventionally, these expenditures are treated as revenue or current expenditures, not capital expenditures. In this conventional accounting sense, most start-ups therefore lose an enormous amount of capital while building their businesses. The world has learnt to treat brand building and other goodwill expenditures as capital expenditures. India should figure out treating genuine customer acquisition expenditures as capital expenditure; treat it as such for accounting and tax purposes, and allow writing down of such expenditures as 'depreciation' over many years. This accounting and tax treatment would help start-ups in raising capital, both equity and debt, from conventional investment markets.

Focusing PLI on Digital Chip-Making Would Bring Best Rewards

India has a couple of policies that focus on electronic manufacturing. Electronics Policy 2018 aims at electronics production of $400 billion by the end of 2025. India also promotes the establishment of electronics hardware parks and provides some capital subsidies. More recently, the government has come up with a number of PLI (production-linked incentive) schemes, which provide a pre-fixed percentage of incremental turnover as incentive. There are a slew of PLI schemes for electronics manufacturing. The Scheme for Promotion of Manufacturing of Electronic Components and Semiconductors (SPECS), PLI for Electronics Manufacturing (the first one of a set of fourteen PLI schemes), Modified Electronics Manufacturing Clusters Scheme (EMC 2.0) and Production-Linked Incentive Scheme for IT Hardware are four schemes that specifically target electronics manufacturing in India.

The National Digital Communications Policy (NDCP-2018) also seeks to encourage investment in and manufacturing of telecom and IT hardware products. Further, PLI schemes in non-electronic sectors—like medical devices, telecom and networking products, air-conditioners—also heavily rely on digital chips and other electronic components.

There are two major strategies to develop digital manufacturing. First, develop new and competitive digital technologies for digital devices and the digitalization of non-digital products and devices to be the leading supplier of such products globally. Second, encourage global technology majors to come and set up their manufacturing facilities in India. Of course, there can be a combination of both strategies as well.

Currently, Indian firms are not frontrunners in development of new digital technologies. India also does not have a good digital manufacturing base. The National Electronics Policy and PLIs are trying to encourage global companies to establish a manufacturing base for digital hardware products.

The PLI Policy can definitely be used creatively and decisively to help India establish a digital products manufacturing base in India if properly crafted and implemented recognizing our limitations and objectives. Two major strategies will work:

First, it will help to restructure all the PLI schemes that focus on products using semiconductor products as their ultimate competitive proposition into one PLI focused on manufacturing of semiconductor chips, modules or other needed forms of digital products. This would require discontinuation of separate schemes for renewables, air-conditioners, medical devices and so on. To achieve this objective, it would be necessary to invite the global enterprises that have developed and own digital technologies and Indian corporates that can get these digital technologies in joint ventures or otherwise to India. The policy should focus on getting these technology majors and Indian firms to bring their technologies to India by investing in building the most advanced, globally competitive and functional digital chips, cells, modules, products, etc. The PLI currently committed to several product-based small schemes can be combined (and enhanced) to get these digital components, and not the final consumer products, manufactured in India. If India can really incentivize the design and manufacture of chips, cells, modules, etc., for use in all goods and products, we can seize the initiative in the digital economy space in a big way.

Second, semiconductors remain the pivot of digitalizing the global economy for many years. India does not have any semiconductor manufacturing facility. The government of India has been keen to get a semiconductor FAB (fabrication plant) set up in India for over fifteen years. All attempts to invite investors have been unsuccessful so far. Another notice inviting Expression of Interest (EoI) was issued in December 2020 for 'setting up/expansion of existing Semiconductor wafer/device fabrication (FAB) facilities in India or acquisition of Semiconductor FABs outside India.' Indian firms do not own semiconductor FAB technology while global players have set up FABs at several places in the world.

Global semiconductor firms will come and set up such a FAB only if they see profits. Digital manufacturing suffers from the same ills that held back India's industrialization. There are land, labour and many other issues as well. The non-competitiveness of India's financial sector is sought to be tackled by setting up a foreign enclave in the Gujarat International Finance Tec-City (GIFT city), a business district near Ahmedabad. The semiconductor industry will most likely come to India only if one can create a Taiwan, China or Vietnam on our territory. India should establish a foreign territory in a relatively business-friendly Indian state with laws, financial system, tariff structure and freedom of engaging labour applicable in the model foreign country chosen for the purpose. This proposal is not same as an SEZs; this is SEZ plus +.

Data Laws and Regime Would Be Critical for Creating the Digital Economy of India

India has been flirting with very restrictive data control and management policies, as seen in the draft Data Protection Law and draft E-Commerce Policy proposed by DPIIT. India's current evolving policy on protection of personal data is not in the best interests of economic growth by building a digital economy. It leans too much towards protection of personal data and pays no consideration to its effect on legitimate businesses. Likewise, the attempt to provide the government access to a lot of business data will create large disincentives to businesses in the country.

The proposals to deny access to important business data in the name of personal data and share a lot of data with the government will create a regime worse than the licence permit raj, which destroyed private enterprise in the country's industrialization process. Personal data should be defined very strictly. Further, there should be a more liberal and easier process of obtaining the consent of the person concerned for use of personal data. Willingly provided information while filling up an application or interacting otherwise should suffice and there should be a requirement to obtain consent that is 'free, informed, specific, clear and capable of being withdrawn'. Misuse of personal data can be akin to breach of privacy.

Technology itself seems to be evolving the right way to balance the interest of individuals to own their data and capitalize on it. It is going to be possible for each individual to keep all her data in a protected mode under her control. Such data can be shared and accessed by any businesses she is willing to do business with. This kind of arrangement would obviate the need for creating a regulated system of data fiduciaries to collect, hold and share data.

To digitalize the economy and wrest the best advantage in the digital transformation of the world, India must scrap both these proposals and bring in a modern, liberal and facilitative law for data management and use, including personal data with both centralized and personal data storage and sharing options. That will be the difference between missing the digital revolution or capturing it. The country missed the Industrial Revolution by getting on board very late after opposing it for many decades. The same mistake should not be repeated with the digital revolution.

Chapter Fifty-Five

Seizing the Environmental, Social and Governance Agenda

Roots of ESG Concerns and Issues

In the pre-agriculture era, humans lived as part of the natural eco-system. The food was sourced from the trees and plants and also animals growing and living in the natural state of planet. Everyone could consume whatever was available and necessary for maintenance of body. The natural age was the African age. In the later part of the natural age, humans learnt to make stone tools to secure food better, control fire to make better food and banded together in small numbers to begin living early community life. There was no environmental, social or governance issues in the natural age.

In the agricultural age, humans grew and reared their food. Over the years, human settlements developed and created rich and mighty Chinese, Indian, Sumerian, Egyptian and Greek civilizations. The agriculture surplus birthed kings, princes and the state. Property in land and property in goods and services took shape. The environmental issues created by development of land for agriculture and human settlements did interfere with mother nature, but the issues it spewed were all local and the impacts minimal. Environmental, Social and Governance or the ESG issues began to emerge but were too small and too local to make any difference to the natural state of the planet.

The machine is the principal producer and distributor of goods and services in the industrial economy. Machines, however, are not auto-propelled. Machines need artificial power to make them do work. The artificial power comes from energy. Steam engines came into being first to provide the requisite energy to drive machines. These engines used coal to generate steam. Coal became the principal source of energy for the industrial era. Oil became the principal energy source for transportation machines. Coal, oil and gas, all fossil fuels, fired and drove billions of machines in the world to produce goods and services which have made the global economy reach very close of $100 trillion in value today. For this, humanity mines the bosom of our planet to take out about 20 billion tonnes of material, 90 per cent of which are fossil fuels.

While machines driven by fossil fuels did a lot of good to raise living standards and make humanity grow and become rich (poverty has been banished in most of the industrial and emerging market world), the use of fossil fuels had massive side-effects. Coal produced greenhouse gases like CO_2 and polluting gases like NOx and SOx and materials like mercury. Oil produced lot of CO_2. The world produces more than 50 billion tonnes of CO_2 equivalent every year presently. The environmental issues of concern are mostly on account of the use of energy for running machines in the industrial age. Some environmental issues are caused by disturbing the natural state of the planet in carrying out agriculture operations and building infrastructure for the industrial economy.

This is the big, fat 'environmental' challenge for humanity.

Factories could be owned by a few and with machines working to produce goods and services, social inequality is the product of the industrial era. The increasing supply of labour (because of cheaper and universal availability of food and other industrial products) and decreasing demand of labour (because of machines increasingly taking over more and more of physical labour work) made the terms of trade weaker for labour. While the industrial economy generated considerable income and wealth, which lifted living and health standards all over the world for most people, the wealth got massively concentrated in fewer hands in the industrial economy as the income and property became more and more privately owned. The rich managed most of the income and wealth in corporations with limited liability for them.

The inequality of income and wealth in the world and the inability of a large chunk of people to earn enough to live a life better than what is described as living below the poverty line, at the minimum, and a life of human dignity beyond what is now recognized as multidimensional poverty is the social challenge.

The corporations today control more than 60 per cent of global GDP and wealth. They have also become convenient vehicles for tax evasion or lower taxation liabilities. The corporations also socialize pollution and carbon discharges to save costs for them at the cost of people at large.

This is the core of the governance challenge today.

The ESG issues that exist today are primarily because of the nature of the industrial economy, the heavy mechanization and fuels used, unequal control of value created and concentration of wealth in the hands of a few.

The industrial age is past its prime. It is now the age of digital technology. Digital technologies are making agriculture and factories more efficient with less fuel consumption. Semiconductor chips are the machines of the digital economy. While industrial-era machines built artificial muscles, digital era technologies built data that creates AI. While machines and energy power took care of production of goods in the industrial era, data and AI are increasingly taking over the production and distribution of services in the digital era.

Digital-era technologies and machines consume less energy. Digital-era energy is also increasingly generated by semiconductors that harness the sun's natural energy. Wind-power generation, green-hydrogen and other technologies are emerging as better substitutes for fossil fuel energy generation. The digital era has enormous potential to reduce fossil fuel energy consumption. Thus, the digital era is much less worrisome from an environmental viewpoint.

That said, digital-era technologies are even more amenable to centralization of ownership in fewer hands with their efficiency in the use of intelligence in production and delivery of services. What the world is witnessing today in the form of dominance of social media by a few digital technology companies is the testimony of that centralization and concentration power. As a consequence, the digital revolution is likely to further accentuate social and governance issues.

There are fewer environmental issues with the digital economy but the social and governance issues are likely to get more accentuated.

The World Adopts a Sustainable Development Agenda

In September 2015, all countries, under the aegis of the United Nations, adopted seventeen Sustainable Development Goals (SDGs) as the 'plan of action for people, planet and prosperity'. These seventeen goals, which came into force in January 2016, represent the global ESG agenda.

All countries and stakeholders, acting in collaborative partnership, are expected to implement this plan. The social agenda is most eloquently captured in the resolve 'to free the human race from the tyranny of poverty and want' and the goal 'to realize the human rights of all and to achieve gender equality and the empowerment of all women and girls'. The environmental agenda is captured in the commitment 'to heal and secure our planet'. The governance agenda, in a way, is encapsulated in the determination 'to take the bold and transformative steps which are urgently needed to shift the world on to a sustainable and resilient path'. The SDGs 'are integrated and indivisible and balance the three dimensions of sustainable development'.

The seventeen goals detail different dimensions of the social, environmental and governance agenda.

While the SDG agenda is quite ambitious, though unduly verbose and detailed (there are 189 targets as well), it does not deal directly with the real cause of the unsustainable state of the planet and grossly unequal distribution of income and wealth on account of the 'profit' chased and generated by the corporations by socializing all environmental and social costs to the people.

The real ESG agenda is to balance the interests of people, planet and profit.

ESG Agenda is Still Not Well Defined

There are three key components of the ESG agenda: environmental, social and governance. All three dimensions have seen lot of action in the past fifty years but are still to be defined clearly and fully.

The environmental agenda has two parts: climate change and pollution.

The climate change ambition is quite well articulated by now: the net-zero carbon addition to the atmosphere by 2050 to restrict the rise in global temperatures to less than 2 per cent over pre-industrial era average global temperatures. Climate change is a global issue and has rightly become a global concern. However, what it would take to become a net-zero carbon emission world is not fully understood and agreed upon.

The pollution issue is both global and local. Pollution of oceans has turned out to be a global issue. Air pollution is more local, but there are trans-boundary flows of air pollution as well. Likewise, pollution of rivers and water systems has a more regional element. In many countries, pollution is a more pressing issue than climate change. The global agenda on pollution, which was the principal focus of the Stockholm Conference, is losing international play. Carbon has taken over the global pollution agenda. Most of the world still has massive pollution problems on its hands. Pollution needs to regain prominence in the environmental agenda.

On a macro level, the social agenda is moving in the opposite direction. The digital technology revolution has reduced the need for labour and replaced many labour-driven services. There is much more inequality in the world now. There is also a big difference in the digital capabilities of advanced nations and technically lagging nations. The advent of digital technologies has crushed the right of labour to unite and replaced traditional employer-employee relationships with gig and contract work. The social agenda in the SDGs is defined more in terms of what human beings deserve to get, not how they should earn or get resource transfers. The social agenda requires clearer definition and understanding.

Corporations had introduced enormous governance problems. These have been increased manifold by technological takeover of the governance system. Governance would need to be thought through quite differently.

In its meeting on 7 June 2021, the G-7 accorded primacy to the climate standards agenda to become part of the mainstream financial statement. It emphasized 'the need to green the global financial system so that financial decisions take climate considerations into account'.

The G-7 tasked the International Financial Reporting Standards Foundation (IFRS) 'to develop the baseline standard under robust governance and public oversight'.

IFRS has set up an International Sustainability Standards Board (ISSB) to take care of the expected standards on climate change.

Developing Key Environmental Standards in Financial Terms

There are two key environmental concerns embedded in the ESG agenda: bring down carbon emissions to net zero; and stop pollution of air, water and other natural resources.

When translated in the context of businesses, they can be legitimately expected and bound to make no net carbon emissions and discharge no pollutants in the process of production and distribution of goods and services.

From a carbon perspective, there can be three potential situations that a business can find itself in. First, it generates no carbon emission or reduces existing carbon load. Second, it generates emissions but offsets this by capturing an equivalent amount of carbon, thereby being a net zero contributor of carbon. Third, it generates more emissions than it offsets, thereby being a net contributor of carbon.

The regulatory environmental standards can be established to make a measurement of carbon, both emissions and its capture/reduction, mandatory for every business. With the rapid evolution of digital technology, such measurement can be a continuous 24/7 process. The regulatory system can also determine a price per kg of carbon.

With the carbon price so determined and carbon emissions/capture measured continuously, businesses can be expected to determine in financial terms their net priced carbon emissions/capture. They can be mandated to pay for their net emissions to society/government and be rewarded for their net emissions capture. There is a case for instituting a carbon levy for neutralizing the cost such businesses impose on society and economy. Net emitting businesses should have complete freedom to make investments to bring their net emissions to zero or purchase emission credits from the market equal to their net emissions. They can also be given the option to deposit an equivalent carbon cost with the government concerned to discharge their carbon liability; it can use such proceeds to pay for carbon capture investments. This whole arrangement would lead to net-zero national contribution and development of a carbon market.

The present state of carbon emissions and pollutant discharges in almost all countries is above net zero. In fact, in many economies, emissions and discharges are still rising. Many of these countries justify these increasing carbon emissions as necessary to support their growth. They have a right to do so. In such countries, the governments could provide an arrangement to socialize such costs according to some standards on a tapering basis for a specified period of time. Governments can also provide financial incentives to mainstream adoption of technologies that capture carbon or produce the same product at a lower carbon cost.

Such arrangements would clarify corporate responsibility for carbon emissions in a manner and terms where they are integrated into businesses.

They also provide the right financial incentives to low carbon technologies and businesses.

Similar arrangements for determination of standards, measurement and pricing should be developed for the discharge of all pollutants.

Developing Social Standards in Financial Terms Is More Difficult

The social agenda of the ESG is more complex. It also applies more to governments than corporates. However, many elements like equal pay for equal work, elimination of gender discrimination, right to freely associate and creation of safe working conditions concern businesses as acutely.

There is a larger economic and financial agenda embedded in the social part of ESG—preventing falling share of wages in the value added by businesses; rather, increasing this share is the best way to take care of the social agenda. Over the years, the share of profits is going up and the share of wages falling in value added. This happened in the industrial age for physical (blue collar) workers. The onset of technology in the digital age is aggravating the matter for white collar or intellectual workers as well.

The social agenda of ESG, as far as businesses are concerned, needs to be divided into two parts. First, a fair labour code agenda that makes businesses adhere to the right standards set in fair labour codes. Second, a positive financial agenda that pegs the share of wages at a minimum specified level in the value added created by the organization concerned.

Minimum share of wages for every corporate business, for example, can be set at 60 per cent of total value added. Companies must hire enough workers/work time to ensure that not less than 60 per cent of the total value added goes to workers as salaries, compensation, bonuses or in any other appropriate form. The companies that expense less than 60 per cent of value added as wages could be subjected to a wage tax, which would require them to pay the differential to the government. The government, in turn, can use such proceeds to undertake public works to serve the ESG agenda or redistribute this to help labour households to live a life better than the multidimensional poor.

Such a labour wage agenda would also reduce inequality in society. The regulatory social agenda can be in the form of obligatory compliances.

Governance Agenda

The governance agenda for corporates is, in key terms, essentially twofold. First, companies should be run in accordance with the highest standards of corporate governance to ensure that the legitimate interests of *all* stakeholders—not the controlling shareholders or CEO—should get a fair deal. Second, corporates must discharge their social and national responsibility well.

The first is more of a quality issue and therefore very difficult to quantify. A system of corporate governance rating can be instituted based on standards developed by the corporate regulator or the concerned corporate governance rating agency. A credit system of corporate governance rating can instil due confidence in all stakeholders.

The national and social responsibility governance agenda could be proxied by the tax paid by companies. A minimum standard of taxation—based on value addition by the company—can be institutionalized. For example, 20 per cent of the value added can be assessed as total tax liability of the company without getting into the numerous types of taxes companies are currently subject to. This can be a flat value added tax of 20 per cent on the value added by the company.

A 60 per cent:20 per cent:20 per cent split of the entire value added by a corporate entity between the workers, government and owners would serve the social and governance agenda.

India Should Set Her Environmental Goals Clearly

India does not have any specific law to combat climate change though it has a comprehensive and intrusive environmental protection law that deals with environmental pollution. The environmental problems of India are so massive that it would be impossible for the government to deal with every polluting element. However, climate change and environmental pollution can be handled more effectively if we were to focus on some specific pollutants.

There are five such major pollutants:

First, CO_2, which makes up more than two-third of GHGs. If CO_2 emissions can be reduced significantly, there is a likelihood that the world can achieve a net-zero carbon emissions goal.

Second, particulate matter 2.5 ($PM_{2.5}$), which is the largest and most damaging pollutant today. If $PM_{2.5}$ can be reduced substantially, the problem of environmental pollution would largely disappear.

Third, ozone (O). Surface ozone, the result of nitrogen oxides chemically reacting with organic matter, is a major health hazard. Ozone that escapes to the ozonosphere causes a hole in the ozone layer. To tackle ozone, one has to fix the problem of nitrogen oxides as well.

Fourth, burning solid fuels in households is the primary reason for indoor pollution and also contributes to release of CO_2.

Fifth, discharge of untreated sewage in the commons: water bodies or land.

If India can manage these five polluting elements without compromising on the production of goods and services, GDP or national income, the quality of life of residents will improve tremendously and the country will also play its rightful role in solving the problem of climate change.

For this to happen, some serious reforms will need to be undertaken.

Establish an Independent Environment Ministry

Climate change is global. India cannot act alone to bring GHGs under requisite levels to contain global warming. The lead in this matter domestically and internationally has to be taken by the Government of India. States will need to work with the Centre on this front more as implementation agencies. Tackling climate change will necessitate reforms in economic policies and regulation of CO_2 and other GHG emissions. This can be done only under the leadership of the Government of India. Therefore, the subject of 'Climate Change and Control of Greenhouse Gases' should be included as a separate entry in the Union List or be interpreted as part of the Residual Entry in the Union List.

The primary way to control pollution of air, land and water is to control the use of polluting chemicals and fuels in workplaces, factories, vehicles and households; fix emission/discharge standards; and develop means to ensure observance of these standards. There are millions of workplaces and households. The control of actions of these millions of agents has to take place at the local level: in villages and cities, workplaces and households, and vehicles of all types. This can only be done by state governments and their agencies.

There is no specific entry in the Seventh Schedule relating to pollution control. However, various places where pollution originates (agriculture, industry, power generation) are mentioned in the lists. Likewise, impacts of pollution, like public health, are also specifically mentioned.

Pollution control has assumed extraordinary importance over the past three to four decades. It is as important as public health or industrial development. Therefore, it is advisable to include 'Pollution Control' in the Concurrent List to enable both the Centre and the states to act.

Environment was neither an international nor a national issue when the Indian Constitution was written. Consequently, it is not mentioned as a subject in any of the three lists of the Seventh Schedule allocating business of the government to the Union, the states or as Concurrent Subjects. The environment became an international concern and, thereafter, a national concern only in the 1970s. The government tagged the environment with forests (as if the environment were an adjunct of forests) and established the Ministry of Environment and Forests (MOEF). Later, 'Climate Change' was formally added to MOEF and it became MOEF&CC.

Forests do act as carbon sinks and are a good way to convert atmospheric carbon in the woods. However, they are not responsible for or directly concerned with the pollution of air, water and non-forest lands. Diversion and increase of forest lands is one of the many ways to manage CO_2. However, managing pollution of air, water and non-forest lands requires a much broader sweep of action that is more related to agriculture, industrialization and urbanization. The environmental agenda is wide—forests constitute just one set of interventions as part of that agenda.

The state of environmental pollution in India has reached gargantuan scales despite MOEF&CC having been entrusted with the most sweeping authority and powers for the past thirty-five years. The ministry has adopted a gatekeeper approach for most economic activities involving large investments. It is necessary to obtain the consent of the ministry or its authorized delegates before any serious industry or infrastructure can be started in the country. It is tortuous to go through the processes, which consume years before consent is granted—that, too, usually with unimplementable conditions. There is very little connect between the process of obtaining consent and the significance of the impact of such consent on the state of air, water and land pollution.

The basic orientation and purpose of the ministry needs to be changed. The MOEF&CC does not have separate departments for handling the issues of forest and wildlife on the one hand and environmental issues, including climate change, on the other. The ministry is divided into three broad sets of divisions: establishment divisions, environmental divisions, and forest and wildlife divisions.

The environment part of the MOEF&CC needs to be entrusted with clear goals with respect to the five key determinants of environmental pollution in India, as explained in the previous section. It should be held accountable for making progress and achieving those goals. Forest management is also more akin to land management. The Government of India is not the best agency to manage forests, except setting the policy of protecting and growing forest area, as part of the larger environment policy. The management of forest land, forests and wildlife needs to be handed over fully to the states. The MOEF&CC should be made a pure play environment ministry to focus on environmental issues and to help India achieve its environmental goals.

Revamped Environment Ministry Will Need to Reinvent Itself

MOEF&CC should identify major sources of pollution and carbon emissions and take requisite measures to eliminate the root causes. India has taken such initiatives. In Delhi, emissions of CO_2, particulate pollution and nitrogen oxides, besides other pollutants, were majorly contributed by buses using diesel. The replacement of diesel engines with engines based on compressed natural gas (CNG) in buses reduced the pollution and carbon emission load significantly in the national capital.

The environmental regulatory system in the country needs to move from dictate-based regulation to a participation-based technology upgrade system. In 2015, MOEF&CC passed orders fixing emission standards for nitrogen oxides (NOx) and sulphur oxides (SOx) for all power plants in the country. For example, for power plants established between 2003 and 2016, NOx emissions were to be brought down to 300 mg/Nm3. Several other standards were fixed depending upon the year of inception of the plant and other factors. Unfortunately, the ministry had no idea whether appropriate technology exists and how costly it would be if imported. There was also no consideration of how the additional cost would get factored in. In such situations, dictates often remain unimplemented. This is what happened in case of NOx and SOx. The deadline has come and gone but compliance is hardly 5–10 per cent.

Environmental courts like the National Green Tribunal have also adopted the dictate methodology. Every now and then, orders are passed to stop production or take a particular step with a threatened penalty of jail. A case in point is the burning of stubble by farmers in Punjab and Haryana. There are several solutions to the problem but instead of coming up with an appropriate one, including the use of public funds for a cause like this, only farmers are being targeted. Despite the spectre of criminal punishment, farmers are not heeding these dictates as the economic logic of preparing the field for sowing wheat in the quickest turnaround time prevails.

There have been efforts of late to de-clog the system and expedite environmental clearances. The Environment Impact Assessment Draft Rules, 2020, are a small step in this direction. Unfortunately, people who are overly concerned with non-environmental issues—mostly of a social nature—and who have used parts of the process like consultation to put a spoke in the wheel of industrialization, urbanization and infrastructure creation are objecting to these reforms. These reforms should be expedited, though they would have only a limited effect.

The real solution lies in the ministry focusing on a significant reduction of carbon and pollution emissions without adversely affecting economic growth and employment.

Replace Process Orientation of Environmental Laws with Outcome Orientation

Environmental protection has become a prisoner of process. The entire focus of attention is the consent required to start a new specified industry or infrastructure work or modify an existing one. Processes have become more draconian than the industrial licencing processes in the 1970s.

Elaborate environmental impact assessment processes are convoluted. There is no clarity on what is intended to be achieved. Instead of quantifying the climate change and pollution impact of the project, these processes get into impacts on income, employment and livelihood of people living in the catchment area, impact on wildlife, and diversion of forest lands and natural habitats. These are important aspects but the whole purpose of assessing the impact on the environment, which is defined as environmental pollution in the Environment Act, is lost and the process degenerates into finding real and imaginable negative impacts on anything and everything.

An elaborate and hugely entangled process is not required for every project. Environmental impacts depend upon the technology, fuel chosen and the pollutants generated as by-products. For instance, a 500 MW thermal power project using coal as fuel and a specific technology and different machines to control/reuse steam, waste heat and trap effluents can be expected to generate a certain quantum of CO_2, particulate matter (ash), nitrogen oxide, sulphur oxide, etc. Such an assessment needs expertise on power plant technology and engineering, not a wildlife or forest expert. It also does not require any consultation with the tribals or villagers affected. If power generation is based on renewable technology, there is hardly any generation of CO_2 and other polluting gases.

The process orientation of environmental approval clearly needs a rethink.

Policymakers and regulators must not get lost in the maze of the clearance process. Rather, they should focus on getting the right kind of technology and production processes that minimize the consumption of chemicals, fossil fuels and other materials that impact climate change or cause pollution without sacrificing national output or income.

The Environmental Impact Assessment Rules, 2006, which are currently in place, confer so much discretion on authorities granting consent that they often become tools in the hands of the minister and other officials to extract bribes by simply sitting on approvals. The average time taken to get one Category A project approval exceeds years.

These rules are under revision, with the government having notified the Draft Rules, 2020. As these rules clarify and simplify concepts and processes and set time limits on various stages, the environmental protection lobby, which has vested interests in perpetuating existing rent-generating processes, have cried themselves hoarse. The government has been flooded with thousands of suggestions and it remains to be seen what emerges. In fact, the government should be more adventurous in the interest of growth and well-being of people to enhance industrial and infrastructure activities where environmental impacts can be easily absorbed or neutralized.

The construct should be simpler. If you intend to establish a thermal power plant based on coal, you need technology that ensures that, say, the carbon used per unit of power generated will not exceed 'x' kg. If you use such technology, no clearance should be required. Or, if you want to be aggressive on carbon control, one could take the decision to establish no coal-based plants in the country. These are policy choices that should be exercised with due caution and clarity. None of these policy decisions require the arduous process of assessment by 'experts' and consultations with people.

The process needs to be replaced by the correct policy choices and robust technological regulation.

Not Only Net Zero CO_2 but Also Net Zero SOx, NOx and Other Pollutants

India also declared net zero CO_2 by 2070 as India's carbon commitment in the Conference of Parties (CoP-26) held in Glasgow in November 2021. This declaration seeks to balance India's obligations to contribute to the global goal of building a net zero carbon emission world by 2050 and also asserts India's claim to continue to use fossil fuels longer than the industrialized world as part of climate justice where the industrialized world, which pumped most of the CO_2 to achieve net zero much sooner than 2050.

This balancing declaration is fine but the real action India needs is to get on the task of inventing and developing technologies for building a high growth economy which generates less or no carbon emissions and the other four main pollutants mentioned above. Solar and wind technologies will help transform most of the energy required into electrical energy, which will not only be less polluting but also more efficient. Digitalization of industry and services using more and more of semiconductors and software would also contribute to controlling all these pollutants. Investment in carbon and other pollutants measuring and capturing technologies would help in neutralizing pollutants which the industries and services would still generate without becoming non-competitive.

There is going to tremendous demand for the pollutant controlling/eliminating technologies and capturing technologies the world over for the next twenty to thirty years. If we can get our act together to emerge as the creator and supplier of these technologies and equipment, India will end up making up for our delayed industrialization. India can become a net negative CO_2 and other pollutants much before 2050 if we can get this act together.

Chapter Fifty-Six

Financial Sector Reforms

The Indian financial system, as shaped by policies over the years, is a mixed economy type of financial system, a mix of the public and private sectors.

Reforms of the Financial Sector since 1990s have Partially Undone the Damage

India started liberalizing the financial sector in the 1990s after industrial policy and trade policies reforms were initiated in 1991.

The banking sector was opened up in 1993 when ten private banks (PVBs) were given licences. These licences gave birth to today's private-sector banking giants like HDFC Bank, ICICI Bank and Axis Bank, though some of these ten licencees got waylaid on the way. As time went by, some more banking licences were given. Today, about 40 per cent of outstanding banking credit has been given by PVBs. In the past six years, more than 70 per cent of new credit flow has come from them.

The insurance industry was opened to the private sector in 1999 with the constitution of an insurance regulator and appropriate amendments in the Insurance Act. Foreign ownership was also permitted to the extent of 26 per cent in 2000, which was raised to 49 per cent in 2015. There are now twenty-three private life insurance companies and twenty-eight private general insurance companies out of twenty-four life insurance companies and thirty-three general insurance companies. Private non-life insurance companies have about 55 per cent share of the market and private life insurance companies a little over 30 per cent.

Both the industrial DFIs set up in the public sector after Independence—IFCI and IDBI—are now either totally sick (IFCI) or closed and merged in a bank (IDBI merged in IDBI Bank). There are some specialized DFIs (NABARD for agriculture and rural development, PFC and REC for power, SIDBI for small-scale industry and IIFCL for infrastructure finance) that still exist. There is no DFI in the private sector (ICICI got merged in ICICI Bank) as such although there is a significant number of NBFCs and HFCs that have assumed leadership position in sectoral development finance, such as HDFC in housing finance.

The asset management industry, which began to emerge from the 1970s, has been established by PSBs, PVBs and other financial institutions. The majority of MF assets are in the hands of asset management companies promoted by private-sector banking companies and financial institutions.

There has been notable opening of the financial sector since 1992. However, significant stakes still remain in the public sector: PSBs control more than 70 per cent of deposits and 60 per cent of credit; LIC has around 70 per cent of life insurance assets; the general reinsurance business is the monopoly of public-sector GIC and infrastructure finance is still largely in the hands of government-controlled companies.

Barring LIC and SBI, most of the public-sector financial industry is financially sick, capital-constrained and inefficient. The government has to use scarce taxpayer resources to constantly capitalize these corporations. In the past three years, it has pumped in more than Rs 3 lakh crore of equity in banks, general insurance companies and infrastructure finance companies. There is hidden sickness in power-sector finance companies. A large bill might be awaiting the government.

Reforming the Financial Sector is Critical for a $10 Trillion Economy

In 2035, India will need a private-sector economy with the government focusing only on delivering public goods and services, including macroeconomic management, regulation of markets and redistribution. Such an economy would need to have a dominant private financial sector as well.

The state-owned financial sector misallocates and directs credit, finance and asset management away from the productive sectors of the economy and has become the handmaiden of the government to serve social objectives, effectively turning credit and finance into grants. Social objectives are better served by the government channelizing support to economically weaker sections of people as grants and cheaper loans. The state-owned financial sector, staffed by officers with a government mindset and skills, is also not the right assessor of risk involved in commercial lending and thus usually ends up providing credit to the wrong entrepreneurs. Banking and financing is best done by private sector enterprise putting its own capital at risk. Depositors' interests are best taken care of by the right regulation.

The transformation of the public-sector financial system into a private-sector one will be the biggest driver of the financial reforms agenda and essential to achieve the $10 trillion target.

The financial sector reforms would need to take place across the entire spectrum of finance beginning with currency and money markets, extending to credit and capital markets and to insurance, asset and wealth management.

Rupee as a Digital Currency

Several central banks are working on a potential digital currency. China's central bank has been experimenting with digital renminbi and trials of such a digital currency have been conducted in a number of identified cities in the country. The use of this digital currency has been limited only to domestic use and not for international payments.

In India, a committee set up by the Ministry of Finance recommended a draft legislation for dealing with private cryptocurrencies in 2019. It also recommended exploration of the idea of a 'digital rupee'. The government, despite notifying Parliament of its intention to bring a bill for laying down the framework for digital currency twice in 2021, has not done so until December 2021.

While digital currency has not seen the light of day in India, digital payments have become quite mainstream. Let's be clear, however, that that we are discussing a digital rupee, not digital payments in this section. A digital rupee would replace the physical paper rupee as currency. That would happen gradually over decades. Still, just as coins continue to be used for making some payments, the paper rupee would continue to be used to make some payments and all payments by some. And like coins are convertible into paper rupees, the paper rupees should be and would be convertible into digital rupees and vice-versa.

Digital currency is indeed the future as the paper rupee system has innumerable problems.

Transactions require parties to come into contact. Rupee notes cannot be carried in large value as the largest note still in circulation is Rs 2000. You have to keep notes of several denominations to make exact payments. For making a payment of Rs 156, you need a Rs 100, Rs 50, Rs 5 and Re 1 note. As Re 1 notes are not commonly available, you have to use a coin. Carrying fifteen to twenty notes and a few coins in your wallet or pocket is irksome.

Currency also acts as a store of value. Large denomination notes are more amenable to shove under the mattress to hide ill-gotten money or make payments of unaccounted transactions. Paper currency notes are also prone to be counterfeited.

Digital payments have shown the way. Digital currency can do the rest of the work.

It's time for India to move on to digital currency.

Crypto-Blockchain Technology Options Not Best Choice for Digital Rupee

Digital payments are fast becoming commonplace in India. Yet, digital payments are not the same as digital currency. If cash or the Indian rupee can become digital and cash payments are made digitally, i.e., by exchange of digital notes, cash payments would also become digital and all payments will become digital. For this to happen, paper currency will have to get a makeover to digital currency.

There are two competing options for converting the rupee into digital currency. We could call it the crypto-rupee or, in the dematerialized form, the demat-rupee. The crypto-rupee also has two options: the wholesale crypto-rupee or retail crypto-rupee with some hybrids. The World Economic Forum published a Central Bank Digital Currency (CBDC) Policy-Maker Toolkit. The Indian rupee is a Central Bank Paper Currency (CBPC). The difference in CBPC and CBDC is that the currency is digital in the case of CBDC and it is physical in the case of CBPC.

The wholesale CBDC is meant for wholesale transactions and retail CBDC is designed for retail or common cash transactions. The wholesale CBDC is issued by the central banks to commercial banks and potentially other financial institutions, as proposed in the Toolkit, for use in interbank payments and securities transactions. The wholesale CBDC is primarily a currency of settlement and not for common use of cash as currency. In retail CBDC, the proposal is to create an account of everyone in the central bank and use the balance in this account to make digital payments, as in the case of UPI, by using balances in bank accounts.

Both the wholesale and retail CBDCs essentially create digital currency using blockchain technology in permissioned mode. Basically, the cryptocurrency so created would be used to make payments as digital wallets do today. There is no likelihood of everyone holding all the data blocks in everyone's computers or private miners and others discovering transactions. The CBDCs as envisaged are not cryptocurrencies like bitcoins or others created using blockchain and crypto-graphic technology in the decentralized mode. Wholesale and retail CBDCs are cryptocurrencies largely in name.

Dematerialization of Rupee Banknotes Offers a Good Solution for the Digital Rupee

In the securities system, dematerialized recordkeeping has replaced the physical system. Share or bond certificates are no longer issued or held in physical form. A depository keeps all shares and bonds in its ledger. Holders only have a statement noting their beneficial ownership of the number of shares and bonds of different companies and governments. But they can buy, sell and transfer these securities with total ease and at a much lower cost compared to physical transfers of securities.

In India, stamps to be affixed on registration documents are now being increasingly issued in dematerialized form. It is more user-friendly and governments are also able to collect their revenues more efficiently.

Recently, the Centre and state governments have agreed to collect stamp duty on securities in a seamless manner digitally using a centralized collection system.

It is possible to dematerialize currency notes as well. The central bank can issue currency in dematerialized form instead of releasing new notes or by converting issued banknotes into dematerialized banknotes progressively. People can get dematerialized rupees from banks by exchanging paper notes or by withdrawing from their deposits dematerialized rupee banknotes on their digital wallets.

All the Rs 30 lakh crore-odd of rupee currency—in notes of Rs 2000, Rs 500, Rs 200, Rs 100 and so on—can be replaced by dematerialized notes. This will place rupee notes in a digital wallet in place of a physical wallet. Everything else moves as normal. As every transaction involves moving from one wallet to another wallet, all transactions undertaken leave an audit trail.

It is far more easier, convenient and efficient to switch over to the dematerialized rupee as digital rupee in place of the crypto-rupee.

The dematerialized rupee would be able to replace the existing physical rupee system without any major technological switchover or modifications in the current institutional system.

Global Payments Would Also Be Revolutionized by Digital Currency

Three major policy and structural changes are likely to make the transformation to digital payment systems complete all over the world: conversion of paper currency into dematerialized digital currency; popularization of digital payment systems in domestic markets; and integration of global banking and payment networks for seamless international payments and transfers.

Global payment networks use a complex system to transfer money based on compulsions of the pre-digital era. Money transfer requires banks to be in a correspondent relationship with each other, payment messages to be transferred in a secure way and settlement to take place through a central bank or third system. All this takes time, while introducing another complication of currency exchange value. This complex system leads to the high cost of transfers and needs to change.

One possible way is to take the concept and technology of UPI to other countries. A beginning can be made with the Middle East by, say, NPCI integrating Indian bank accounts with the bank accounts of countries in the region. It could be a partial integration, with only those banks interested in payment and transfer. Once this integration takes place, you just need to use a reference exchange rate, which can be mutually agreed upon by the central banks or a reference rate agency like Financial Benchmark India Pvt. Ltd (FBIL). This will almost eliminate the cost of international transfers and payments.

There can also be a global currency; for example, making electronic SDRs, a global reserve currency created by IMF, into a global currency or creating official stable-coins or even integrating private stable-coins into the global payment system with sovereign digital currency made convertible into such global currency or stable-coins.

Managing Foreign Currency Reserves

As foreign exchange assets are kept in liquid investments with the Bank of International Settlements (BIS), the central banks of hard currency countries or invested in liquid treasury bonds, etc., the returns on foreign exchange assets kept as reserves in liquid form are very poor.

Most foreign exchange reserves accumulated by RBI have originated as ECBs, foreign investment (FDI and FPI) or deposits made by NRIs. These are all high-cost inflows received by India. The fact that the country pays over $30 billion as interest or other returns on foreign currency investments and deposits stock we currently hold must always be kept in mind.

If the same funds are invested at a fraction of the cost paid as foreign currency reserves, India pays a huge cost. There is, therefore, an indisputable need to determine the amount of foreign currency assets we should keep as liquid reserves. The difference on the cost of these foreign currency assets and earning on these reserves invested as liquid assets can be worked out and explained as the cost of insurance against speculative attacks and keeping the economy and markets protected.

The reserves in excess of this limit should not be invested in liquid assets and certainly not by RBI as it is not a great investment manager. This part of India's foreign exchange reserves is the country's sovereign wealth, which should be invested by a professional sovereign wealth management fund on the lines of Temasek and GIC of Singapore. The Singapore institutions are not unique. Today, a number of countries with official foreign currency reserves or reserves created by earnings from natural resources entrust professional managers to manage their sovereign wealth funds.

It would require a professional study to determine the appropriate level of foreign currency assets of India to be kept and managed as foreign currency reserves for exchange management. However, if one goes by the simple yardstick of four months of import requirement being adequate for foreign exchange management, India would need about $200 billion as reserves. The rest, about $400 billion, can then be managed as sovereign wealth funds. If we want to be more conservative, 25 per cent of foreign currency debt liabilities can also be kept as additional reserves. This would require another $150 billion. There does not appear to be any justification to hold beyond $350 billion in the present low-yield investments and lose about 2–3 per cent at the minimum as cost, as India currently does.

Creation of an Equity-Financing Development Finance Institution (DFI)

To promote equity culture and tackle the equity deficit, the government should promote an equity-financing DFI in the country. Though it should not own majority stake in such a company, it should have a substantial stake, say 49 per cent. The management control of such an entity must be in the hands of real professionals who understand businesses and the market.

Such a DFI, the India Equity Development and Finance Corporation, should be listed right in the beginning by offering 10 per cent of equity to the general public. The rest can be with financial institutions, both domestic and international, public and private. This institution should aim to provide equity support of about Rs 10 lakh crore in the next ten years. It should not take over management control or majority stake in any company it invests in.

Banking Reforms

Four Necessary Reforms in the Banking Sector

Four major banking sector reforms are necessary to make banks play their rightful role in powering India's growth and development:

First, while the government can undertake redistribution and subsidization, it cannot undertake banking. It was a blunder to nationalize PVBs. The officials of banks, treated as public servants, and the system of incentives aligned to make PSBs risk-averse. They either did not lend or did so incorrectly, with their non-performing loans ballooning to double digits every ten to fifteen years. PSBs need to be re-privatized. SBI can remain in government control; the rest should be brought under the control of a sovereign asset management company and then sold in the next three to five years.

Second, we should encourage the consolidation of private banks and establishment of greenfield banks owned by financial corporate houses. The urban cooperative banks, district cooperative banks and land development banks in the cooperative sector are, in principle, PVBs organized on cooperative principles. Banking based on cooperative principles has proved to be a failure in India. These banks should be allowed to become small finance banks or converted into non-banks. The payment banks experiment has also proved to be quite unsuccessful as the model is fundamentally flawed. There is not much income in the payments only business and the establishment expenditure of maintaining a brick-and-mortar payments bank (like the Postal Payment Bank) is too high. They should be converted into small finance banks or digital payment non-bank companies. The government and RBI should provide banking licences on tap to financial corporate companies like NBFCs, insurance companies, housing companies and other financial powerhouses. It is not advisable to give banking licences to industrial houses as it would lead to a conflict of interest with the same people being on both sides of the business.

Third, banking laws and regulations need to be streamlined. The two Bank Nationalization Acts the Banking Companies (Acquisition and Transfer of Undertakings) Act 1970 and 1980—should be repealed. Likewise, the SBI Act, 1955, should be repealed and SBI, like all other banks, should be corporatized under the Companies Act and face a similar regulatory regime as private banks. Depositors should have the opportunity to seek insurance of their deposits beyond the limits covered by the Deposit Insurance and Guarantee Corporation by paying an additional premium. The government should cease to have any power of licencing and terminating a bank. Banks should be solely supervised and regulated by RBI and any resolution, including liquidation, should be entrusted to a specialized agency like the one proposed in the Financial Resolution and Deposit Insurance Bill, though there is no need to merge the deposit insurance function with the financial resolution authority. IBC is entirely unsuitable for resolving financial entities, including banks.

Fourth, banks should cease to be vehicles for directed lending programmes and implementation of the government's subsidy programmes. The whole premise of directed lending programmes, like priority-sector reservations of credit, is based on the foundation that these are not normally credit-worthy businesses. This premise is wrong. Farmers, small businesses and affordable housing are all legitimate businesses. Small finance banks, microfinance institutions and specialized NBFCs would serve these credits very well. The announcement of targets for crop lending by banks by the finance minister should make us realize that this is not a banking service but an unsuitable bargain being forced upon banks and farmers. Likewise, governments have a number of subsidy programmes. The government should not link subsidy with credit. Credit should be availed only if the beneficiaries concerned need credit and it should be left to them to take credit from where they are comfortable. The government can deliver the requisite assistance through the direct benefit transfer mechanism. There are about 25 crore borrowers from banks today. Over 20 crore are linked with government-directed credit or subsidy-linked programmes in some way. Banks would be able to focus on lending for growth and development if they were not asked to manage such a large clientele.

Undo Nationalization by Privatizing all PSBs except SBI

By the 1980s, 90 per cent of banking credit in India was under the umbrella of government control. However, the error of this policy soon became apparent and new private banks were licenced in 1994. PSBs have lost 29 per cent of share in credit in the past thirty years. Even if it remains business as usual, it seems certain that by 2025, the share of PSBs (including SBI Group) in outstanding credit will fall below 50 per cent in India.

The government has been consolidating the PSBs by merging them. Vijaya Bank and Dena Bank were merged with Bank of Baroda in 2019. In 2020, Oriental Bank of Commerce and United Bank of India were merged with Punjab National Bank. Allahabad Bank was merged with Indian Bank. Syndicate Bank was merged with Canara Bank. Andhra Bank and Corporation Bank were merged with Union Bank of India. Thirteen PSBs thus stand consolidated in five PSBs: Bank of Baroda, Punjab National Bank, Canara Bank, Union Bank and Indian Bank. Besides SBI, these five are relatively bigger banks. There are also six smaller PSBs: Central Bank of India, Indian Overseas Bank, Punjab and Sind Bank, UCO Bank, Bank of Maharashtra and Bank of India.

The government announced in Budget 2020–21 that IDBI would be privatized. It had been technically privatized in 2018–19 when the government transferred majority shareholding to LIC and the government shareholding fell below 50 per cent. The 2020–21 Budget announcement meant that the government stake would be sold to private parties. This announcement, however, is still to be implemented.

In the 2021–22 Budget, the government announced privatization of two more PSBs though they are yet to be identified. In the same Budget, the government also announced a public-sector enterprises policy. It said that public-sector enterprises in non-strategic sectors would be privatized; and in strategic sectors, it would retain a maximum of four public-sector enterprises. Banks were included in the strategic sector. Therefore, the current policy is that up to four of the eleven PSBs can be retained. There was another important announcement in Budget 2021–22 that the government could consolidate or close public-sector enterprises as well.

The government has not been able to walk the talk on bank privatization until December 2021. The government has not identified two PSBs for privatization and could not initiate the legislative process for privatization by introducing the promised bill for amending two nationalization laws of 1970 and 1980. Neither was the process initiated for selling the government's large controlling interest in IDBI Bank. After seeing the fate of farm laws, it looks increasingly doubtful that the government might not persist with this agenda.

On the contrary, in the national interest and to serve the cause of building a $10 trillion economy, the government should take up the following measures to put privatization of PSBs on a clear and unambiguous path:

First, scrap the 'strategic sector' element from the public-sector enterprises policy announced in Budget 2021–22. PSBs have no 'strategic' value and should not be held back from privatization on this flimsy ground.

Second, consolidation of banks serves no purpose. Therefore, stop the exercise of further consolidating PSBs. Likewise, there is no need to close down any of the PSBs.

Third, put all the ten PSBs (SBI excluded) on the block for privatization. Have a three-year programme to complete this privatization before December 2023, well before the next general elections in 2024.

Open Up Banking to Financial-sector 'Corporate Houses'

A technical group set up by RBI recently recommended banking licences to be given to private-sector industrial houses. This created a lot of flutter as it amounted to a total reversal of government and RBI policy thus far. In fact, the policy has been to cap the voting rights of any person in banks to a maximum of 10 per cent, thereby ensuring that no person—individual or corporate—has a controlling voice in any of the scheduled banks in India.

India's banks were owned and managed by industrial houses before nationalization. However, since then, no banks have been controlled by industrial houses. The development of private-sector banking in the country suggests that the absence of ownership by industrial houses has not hindered the development of banks. Ironically, PSBs have ended up giving much larger credit to industrial houses than PVBs. In reality, quite a few major PVBs are controlled by corporate groups. HDFC Bank, the largest PVB in India, is effectively controlled by HDFC Group. Kotak Mahindra Bank is effectively controlled by the Uday Kotak Group. Several small finance banks are owned and controlled by individuals.

There is no evidence to suggest that the growth and financing of these PVBs have been adversely affected by corporate groups or individuals controlling the banks. Rather, the success of these banks can be attributed to the business acumen and commitment of these corporate houses/individuals.

The relationship of a banker and a borrower is actually the relationship of the financial sector with the real sector. The real sector needs credit and other financial support. The financial sector provides this credit and financial support. The two interests—the real-sector borrower and the financial-sector lender—are constructive but in inherent conflict.

Both parties on the table have to be completely independent to ensure any deal struck is in the best interest of both. Therefore, there is considerable merit in the case that industrial houses are not allowed to be bankers. The equation between the two sides on the table becomes healthier and more professional if the banker is also equally competent to evaluate the risk and reward of lending to the real sector. This competence has to be moulded by real financial interest.

The financial interest of managers does not coincide with the banks' interest in the case of the public sector, but the managers' financial interest in PVBs coincides with the owners' interests.

Thus, there is enormous merit in allowing non-industrial corporate houses, individuals or financial corporate houses and professionals to be granted banking licences preferentially.

Establish Technology or Digital Banks, Including by Converting Payment Banks

Technology has upended payments and banking. IT programmes, conveniently placed on smartphones as apps, allow payments to be made instantly and even credit to be granted almost instantaneously. With deposits also becoming increasingly digital, the core functions of banks (savings, credit and payments) are being carried out instantaneously, conveniently and cost-effectively. If these core functions of a bank can be fulfilled on smartphones, the rationale for brick-and-mortar banks disappears.

This is precisely what is happening to banking the world over, including India. Most bank customers do not visit their branch any longer. They make their payments using their bank's app on their phones. Increasingly, credit is also being delivered digitally. The government/ RBI created the institution of a payment bank to help digitalization of payments. However, innovation in the payments field has made payments using mainstream banks also equally efficient. Further, digital wallets and innovations like UPI that have created a one-touch payment mechanism have cut at the root of the logic of separate and specialized banks. As payment banks, barring some owned by mobile technology companies, have not been able to gain traction, many of the original eleven payment banks have surrendered their licences. Payment banks owned by technology banks are in the best position to establish truly digital banks if they are allowed to offer credit services as well.

RBI should therefore allow payment banks to be converted into full-fledged banks/small finance banks with the condition that these would be predominantly or fully digital banks with very few or no brick-and-mortar branches. India Post Payments Bank, set up by the government under the administrative control of the Department of Posts, is a payment bank. It is losing money heavily and is on the completely wrong track of establishing branches despite only being allowed to offer payment and limited deposit services. It should be closed or privatized.

Globally, fully digital banks are being licensed in some countries. In others, 'neo-banks' using digital technologies have set up businesses, integrating them with the licenced banks' digital systems to offer many banking-related services. RBI has not been open to the idea of licensing digital banks. It is time India adopts digital banking and starts licensing digital banks.

End the Charade of Cooperative and Regional Rural Banking

India saw the establishment of lakhs of primary credit societies at the base of the cooperative banking system in the 1950s and 1960s. These societies were not banks. They existed to collect equity from borrowing members, collect deposits and get finance from the cooperative banking network to lend to members. Barring one or two states, these primary agriculture cooperative societies or PACS were unable to collect enough equity and deposits. Their loans also usually defaulted. The structure became sick soon enough. The government stepped in and provided equity and cheaper credit support, occasionally writing off defaulted loans and paying off the interest. The district-level cooperative structure was organized into a bank but with the restriction to lend only for crops. These district cooperative banks had some branches that worked more like intermediaries between them and PACS, which probably made some sense in the days of physical communication and transfer of money and credit.

Simultaneously, some cooperative banks developed in urban areas. As private banking was nationalized in the 1970s and 1980s, some private-sector entrepreneurs saw an opportunity in setting up private local banks in the name of urban cooperative banks. While the essence of a cooperative bank's governance structure is 'one member, one vote' irrespective of capital contribution, these banks were de facto managed in such a way that the real sponsor could exercise effective control despite formally having only one vote. Another class of cooperative banking arose in the form of primary land development banks or PLDBs, with a state structure as well. These PLDBs, again with a cooperative governance structure, were meant to provide land development and agriculture equipment financing. The Centre and states contributed to their equity capital by subscribing to their bonds as PLDBs could not collect any worthwhile equity from members. As the demand for such loans was far lower and default much higher, these banks effectively folded quickly.

There is also dual control of the state governments and RBI over cooperative banks. This has been a recipe for disaster. The Government of India recently passed a law in the Parliament that confers powers on RBI to initiate a scheme for reconstruction and amalgamation of these cooperative banks without placing them under moratorium. This has been done to empower RBI to deal with situations like the one regarding the Punjab and Maharashtra Cooperative Bank. The Amendment Law, however, does not change the governance structure and the division of powers between the state governments and RBI. It is unlikely to bring any fundamental change to the moribund status of cooperative banking in the country.

The Government of India made PSBs set up several regional development banks in states to accelerate provision of credit for rural development and financing individual beneficiaries of development schemes. These banks had the participation of state governments though the sponsor invariably was a PSB. They were intended to be cost-effective with staff being paid lower than those of PSBs and lower cost of operations as they were localized. None of these intentions held up and a process is in motion for the past few years to consolidate and merge these regional rural development banks with their sponsors. There are still over forty of them in the country.

Banking on a cooperative basis has proved unworkable. However, if certain groups of cohesive shareholders—such as farmers, labour, teachers—intend to set up a bank on the cooperative governance basis, it should be fine. However, the government must exit the governance structure and need not support such banks with grants or equity. Let these banks be set up, licenced and regulated like other banks.

There is a class of banks in the country called small finance banks. These banks are also local and finance poor borrowers. Regional rural banks, district cooperative banks and urban cooperative banks should be allowed to convert into small finance banks with the option to use a normal or cooperative governance structure. Banks that cannot convert should be allowed to close. RBI should be the only regulator of these banks.

Delving deeper, the multiplicity of banking licensing types creates unnecessary regulatory issues and comes in the way of growth of banks. Limiting payment banks to only payments and not permitting these to provide credit is leading to payment banks getting into partnerships with other banks to become originators of loans for their account holders. Restricting small finance banks to offer loans of only a specified ticket size creates complications for the growing-business clients. There is a case to consider overhauling the entire banking licensing regime in two broad categories of large commercial banks and small commercial banks.

Non-Bank Reforms

Non-Banks are Not Banks and Should Be Regulated as Such

There is a clear movement in the country to treat non-banks as banks. Regulatory and supervisory systems are being developed accordingly. The requirement of capital, liquidity, ownership and other key regulatory parameters are being redefined to bring non-banks closer to the system applicable to banks.

Non-banks do not accept deposits (the only class of deposit-taking NBFCs is shrinking and may be considered for conversion into either small banks or non-deposit taking non-banks). They also do not create credit (they can only lend equal to their borrowed funds and equity). There is no risk of a run on a non-bank as there are no demand deposits. Therefore, non-banks should not be treated as banks at all.

The capital adequacy, liquidity, leverage and other regulatory considerations applied to banks need not be applied to non-banks as the risk of run-off on these institutions does not apply.

Currently, RBI is extending more and more of the banking sector regulations to non-banks (finance companies). The non-banks do not have the four privileges of banks: accepting vast deposits resources, especially low cost savings and current account deposits; large capital-raising ability, especially by the public sector banks; being central to the digital payment system as all digital payment transactions have to be routed through bank accounts; and the enormously beneficial privilege of creating credit.

Unavailability of these privileges make non-banks hugely different than banks. RBI, the regulator of banks and non-banks, tend to increasingly treat non-banks as banks. There is a very good case for licencing and regulation of non-banks/ finance companies by a regulator other than RBI.

Develop Private-Sector DFIs As Non-Banks

Private enterprise is the best judge of credit and other risks involved in long-term financing. RBI is too focused on banks and depositors' interest, which is not the case with long-term infrastructure and asset financing.

The government should develop a new regulatory architecture for long-term infrastructure and asset financing. This law should provide for the creation of a new infrastructure and long-term asset regulator. HFCs, infrastructure debt non-finance companies and government-owned infrastructure companies like PFC, REC, IRFC and SIDBI should also be brought under the purview of this regulator.

The new law should help develop long-term corporate bond financing as the principal instrument of raising finance for these private-sector DFIs. The law should also create appropriate credit rating and other arrangements to assess the creditworthiness of these private-sector DFIs and pave the way for the long-term savings institutions of the country (LIC, other life insurance companies, NPS, EPFO, etc.) to invest in the bonds of these DFIs and contribute some equity. Foreign ownership of these institutions should be freely permitted.

India has created a successful regulatory structure for insurance companies. It should now create a robust and successful regulatory structure for private-sector infrastructure and DFIs.

These institutions could be game changers for building India's $10 trillion economy.

The government announced the establishment of a government-owned DFI in Budget 2021–22. This was quite surprising considering that almost all government-owned DFIs have ended in failure after being engulfed with non-performing loans. Moreover, with the economy fast privatizing, long-term lending by a government-owned institution to private players is neither desirable nor efficient.

The National Bank for Financing Infrastructure and Development Act, 2021 (NABFID Act) has been enacted to establish the National Bank for Financing Infrastructure and Development to support the development of long-term non-recourse infrastructure financing in India, including development of bonds and derivatives markets necessary for infrastructure financing and to carry on the business of financing infrastructure and matters connected therewith. The NABFID Act ends up creating a framework for establishing a government-owned infrastructure financing institute to carry out development and financial functions for infrastructure financing. The idea of a government-owned DFI is quite wasteful and should be junked altogether.

Instead, the Act should be comprehensively overhauled to consolidate licensing and regulation of all infrastructure financing institutions, whether in housing finance or established as non-bank infrastructure financing companies or debt funds, under licence from RBI, or legacy sectoral infrastructure financing institutions like REC, PFC and others. This Act should lay down the framework for development, licencing and regulation of infrastructure financing in the private sector. Government owned and funded infrastructure financing institutions, to be regulated by the authority under the NABFID Act, should be made commercial in nature first (by stopping further infusion of government equity and handing over the management to a professional board) and eventually privatized.

Reform of Pension Funds

Starved of yields in government securities, the pension funds of developed countries have made significant changes in their investment strategies and assets.

The global pension fund industry is estimated to be about $50 trillion. According to an OECD report titled *Pension Markets in Focus 2020*, total pension assets under management in retirement savings plans were $49.2 trillion in the OECD countries at the end of 2019. The total corpus of retirement savings assets in the rest of the world was only $1.7 trillion.

With the yields of treasury and other corporate bonds going down substantially in OECD countries, there has been a massive change in the investment pattern of pension funds for the past twenty to twenty-five years. In 2009, according to the report, asset allocation for bonds and bills (debt) was 52.4 per cent, equities 19.6 per cent, cash and cash equivalents 8.3 per cent, and the balance 19.7 per cent in alternative assets like exchange-traded funds, emerging market assets, real estate, etc. In 2019, the proportion of assets invested in bonds and bills went down further to 43.6 per cent while investment in equities went up to 26.8 per cent. With cash and cash equivalents constituting about 6.9 per cent of the corpus, the remaining 22.7 per cent was invested in alternative assets.

In the past thirty years, declining yields on debt investments have been augmented by an increase in mark to market valuation realized by selling debt assets. With bond yields providing negative or close to zero returns in most OECD markets and capital appreciation stopping on account of the yields not declining much any longer, pension investment in bonds and bills is likely to see a further drop.

The emergence of alternative assets in the portfolio of pension funds is transforming the way pension funds are managed and returns generated on the asset portfolio. A number of large pension funds have built up considerable investment capability inhouse to make investment in infrastructure and real-estate assets.

Global pension funds are branching out to emerging markets in search of yields. India has also received investments from American and Canadian pension funds.

India is at the tipping point as far as the pension industry is concerned. With NPS close to reaching the Rs 7 lakh crore mark in investible funds and EPFO crossing Rs 15 lakh crore, the size of the pension fund industry investible corpus is nearing 10 per cent of GDP.

As explained above, at present, almost all the pension fund corpus is invested in government securities. While the global pension industry has moved more than 50 per cent of its investible corpus to equity markets, private equity, real-estate assets and infrastructure financing, the Indian pension industry hardly has any exposure to equity and alternate assets. This is a waste of opportunity. Further, as India is also bound to get into a low interest yield economy on bond and other debt assets, pension funds will find it difficult to earn a decent return for their members if they remain focused only on government securities.

India's financial regulators—RBI, IRDA and PFRDA—are too conservative. The investment pattern they prescribe almost rules out equity investment. There is no recognition of the role their regulated entities can play in the development of infrastructure, a manufacturing base, service enterprises and start-ups in the country. PFRDA is as conservative as IRDA. The pension regulatory system and pension fund administration need to be professionalized to enable funds to invest in assets that meet the country's infrastructure and economic needs by providing equity support and generate better returns for the subscriber. There is a lot to learn from the way the global pension fund industry has evolved.

We have had a bad precedent in the way exempt funds— establishments that manage their own provident funds—have been treated in the provident fund administration. The focus of the administration is to generate an annual return from investment in debt securities. Exempt funds are subject to the same investment pattern and have to match the returns generated by EPFO. This leaves them no flexibility and long-term/alternate investment choices.

The pension regulator needs to encourage the development of pension fund investment desks in large organizations and a class of professional asset managers that can serve the twin objectives of making good investments in equity and alternative assets and generate decent returns in the medium and long term. This would require reforms in the PFRD Act.

Reforms of the Insurance Industry

The four general insurers in the public sector—one listed and three unlisted—don't serve any great public purpose. These were created by nationalizing private general insurers in the early 1970s. Over twenty-five new private general insurers are in operation now. Private insurers have already taken away about 60 per cent of market share. The government is pumping in more than Rs 12,000 crore of equity in the three general insurance companies—Oriental Insurance, National Insurance and United Insurance—to help them meet their 'solvency ratio'. The total equity invested in these three companies before this decision was taken in financial year 2020–21 was not even Rs 500 crore. Such a large waste of public money needs to be avoided. The solution is simple: privatize these three general insurance companies.

The reinsurance company, General Insurance Company (GIC), is owned by the government. Despite its near monopoly business, it is making losses for quite a few quarters now. To compete with global reinsurance companies, which are taking away Indian reinsurance business, GIC needs nimbleness, deep financial pockets and the ability of a private reinsurance company. It is time to privatize GIC as well.

LIC is doing a decent job and is able to hold its ground by improving its technology and services. Being a government-owned entity, it also enjoys a higher degree of implicit trust among people about the safety of their long-term savings. A lot of the government's wealth is locked in LIC. It should be transferred to a sovereign asset management company and its value gradually unlocked. The decision taken by the government to disinvest about 10 per cent of the equity of LIC and list it should definitely be carried out; the transfer to a sovereign asset management company can take place thereafter.

For much of the history of business in India, business families have provided equity for their ventures. As most entrepreneurs lacked equity, including established family businesses many a time, businesses were either forced to borrow or launder bank loans as equity. The stock exchanges in India have also singularly failed to help enterprises raise greenfield equity.

Private equity is now emerging as a major financing source. There are a lot of savings in the world, and in India, which, if properly developed, can provide valuable equity to businesses, including start-ups and ventures. SEBI regulates private equity too rigidly. A more conducive regulatory regime to allow high-net-worth individuals to participate in private equity ventures would help address the equity deficit. The country also needs to adopt a more liberal attitude towards private equity and venture capital funding from abroad—not only is there a much larger pool of savings out there, these equity funds can also bring cutting-edge technology to India.

Reforming the FDI Regime

India had a very myopic view of FDI until 1991. Despite being hugely deficient in technology and capital, the country had virtually shut its doors to foreign investment in the first forty years after Independence. The liberalization of FDI began with industrial and trade liberalization in 1991.

In the past thirty years, successive governments have opened the door increasingly wider to FDI. By 2020, India had adopted a liberal and open FDI policy.

FDI has been defined to mean 'investment through capital investments by a person resident outside India in an unlisted Indian company' or in

10 per cent or more of post-issue paid-up capital on a fully diluted basis of a listed Indian company. Any investment in an unlisted Indian company is FDI as is investment in excess of 10 per cent of equity capital in a listed company. However, if an existing investment of 10 per cent or more of the equity capital were to fall to a level below 10 per cent, the investment would continue to be treated as FDI.

The 10 per cent rule is a significant feature of the Indian system. Investment lower than 10 per cent has been deliberately considered not to confer significant ownership stake or decision-making powers to be considered a direct investment. Such smaller investments are financial investments and considered portfolio investments.

India's FDI regime liberalization has proceeded essentially based on four questions. First, is any sector 'prohibited' for FDI? Second, how much ownership can be taken by foreigners? 100 per cent ownership by non-residents is most liberal. There are shades of liberalization depending upon how much less than 100 per cent can be taken by non-residents. Third, how easily can foreign investment be brought in? There are primarily two routes: automatic (requires no prior approval) and government approval (one of the twelve departments among whom sectors have been assigned for granting FDI approval). Four, how many conditions are permissions made subject to?

There are almost no investment activities under the prohibited category now. Section 5.1 of the FDI Master Circular prohibits only speculative businesses like lottery, gambling and betting; weaker financial vehicles like chit funds and 'Nidhi' companies; speculative real-estate activities like trading in Transferable Development Rights (TDRs) and 'real-estate business' excluding the development of townships, construction of residential/commercial premises, roads or bridges and REITs; products injurious to human health like manufacturing of cigars, cheroots, cigarillos and cigarettes; tobacco or tobacco substitutes; and specified sensitive sectors like atomic energy and certain railway operations. The cobwebs of policy prohibition for the real-estate business, railways and atomic energy should be cleared up as there is no real justification to keep these sectors outside the reach of foreign investment.

There is a system of sectoral cap in the country. All kinds of foreign investments, whether direct, portfolio or in some other permissible manner, are pooled together for the purpose of sectoral cap. The government liberalized rules relating to the operation of sectoral cap in 2019–20. Earlier, companies had the option to decide the permissible FDI subject to the ceiling of the sectoral cap. After the amendment, the sectoral cap is the default applicable FDI limit. If a company decides to fix FDI limit at a level lower than the sectoral cap, it can do so by passing an appropriate resolution to that effect.

There are subsectors of many sectors that still remain out of bounds for FDI. For example, in agriculture, FDI is not permitted in case of field crops. It is only permissible in specified high-technology areas like floriculture, horticulture, cultivation of vegetables and mushrooms under controlled conditions, production of seed and planting material. In plantations, it is only permissible for tea, coffee, rubber, cardamom, palm oil and olive oil.

The second type of restriction is when only a certain amount of FDI is permissible. In the pension sector, infrastructure company in the securities market and the insurance sector, for instance, permissible FDI is 49 per cent. In the case of PSBs, permissible FDI is only 20 per cent. In PVBs, permissible FDI is limited to 74 per cent. In multi-brand retail, permissible FDI is 51 per cent, that too only if the concerned state agrees to allow the operation of multi-brand retail.

FDI in most sectors is subject to laws and conditions. In e-commerce, it is only permissible in the business to business (B2B) segment but not in the business to consumer (B2C) segment. Further, it is permissible only in the inventory-based model of e-commerce. In the telecom sector, FDI is subject to observance of licencing and security conditions notified by the DoT. Only registered airline companies that have their principal place of business within India, whose chairman and at least two-thirds of directors are Indian citizens and whose substantial ownership and effective control is vested in Indian nationals are eligible for FDI.

The biggest restriction on FDI still in operation is the government-approval route. FDI in scheduled air transport service/domestic scheduled passenger airline beyond 49 per cent is possible only with the approval of the government. In print media, permissible FDI of 26 per cent is with government approval, while in broadcasting all permissible FDI is with government approval. Mining and mineral separation of titanium-bearing materials and multi-brand retail FDI are permissible only with the approval of the government. Likewise, FDI in several other sectors, such as private banking beyond 49 per cent, PSBs and pharmaceuticals beyond 74 per cent, also need government approval.

For some sectors, very detailed conditionalities have been laid in the FDI Master Circular.

The financial sector reform agenda is vast. Transformation of India's financial sector and its massive growth is absolutely essential for India to realize the dream of being a $10 trillion economy by the middle of the 2030s. The agenda spelt out in this chapter provides a template to transform the finance sector and put it on an accelerated growth path.

Chapter Fifty-Seven

Expenditure Reforms

Fundamental Construct of Public Finances

The government in India—the Centre and states together—is the sovereign. The theory of social contract postulates that the sovereign or government is created by the people to take care of the common good. This includes providing public goods and services to people paid for by them in the form of taxation and other revenues from natural and common resources. The expenditure on public goods and services incurred by the government paid for by its revenue from taxes and exploitation of common resources is the basic structure and construct of public finances. Soundness of public finances requires the expenditure incurred by the government and revenues raised for making these expenditures equal. There may, however, be intertemporal differences in the revenues received and expenditure required. The same may be met by keeping revenues in funds if the revenues exceed normal expenditure or by borrowing to meet the deficit in case expenditure exceeds revenues.

This fundamental construct of public finances, therefore, comprises three parts:

First, the government incurs public expenditure on providing common or public goods and services to people.

Second, the scale of public expenditure should and is limited by the normal revenues the government can collect from taxes and exploiting natural/common resources.

Third, intertemporal mismatches in normal expenditure and normal revenues can be met by raising debt or keeping excess revenue in funds for future use.

In the past 200 years, governments have tended to enlarge the scope of this fundamental construct beyond common goods. In welfare states, governments have chosen to redistribute incomes and wealth, taking from the rich and better-off and giving to the poor and worse-off in various forms, from cash handouts to delivering food and specific goods and services like education, health, etc. In socialist states, governments have taken over private property and private businesses to run and manage themselves or through the instrumentalities they control. This has expanded the scope of public finances to take on many other kinds of expenditure, which could be primarily classified in three additional broad categories:

First, redistribution. governments may provide food, water, health, education and other services considered minimally necessary for the well-being of citizens. This redistribution may be carried out by handing out cash support or providing goods and services in kind.

Second, business investments. Governments may set up different businesses: steel plants, cement factories, telecommunication services, banks or other real sector or financial businesses. To set these up, the government invests in the capital of the enterprises. These enterprises may turn in profits, which may be channelled to the government as dividends; if they turn in losses, the government may even have to provide support from public finances to cover these losses.

Third, governments may choose individuals and businesses to provide capital support or subsidize the prices of their inputs or outputs. Farmers, labour and small businesses are among those selected to provide this kind of business support.

The Centre and states of India have taken upon themselves the responsibility for the basic function of the state as sovereigns to provide public goods and services as well as redistribution and business support to select sections of people. They have also adopted elements of the socialist pattern of society as their policy and have established and are running several enterprises in the purely private goods and services space.

The additional responsibility of redistribution is expected to be financed from revenue collected from taxes and working of natural/common resources. However, additional expenditure on public enterprises and economic support to preferred groups of people, as it is expected to be paid back, is usually met by raising public debt. As these responsibilities have widened quite a bit and these investments have not yielded returns to pay off the debt taken, governments have tended to take more debt to meet the resource shortfall.

Central Government Expenditures Reflect the Biases, Priorities and Structure of the Planned Era

The Constitution of India speaks of the division of Central government expenditure in two broad categories of revenue expenditure and capital expenditure. It also has a small set of expenditures classified as charged expenditure on which the Parliament has no right to vote to recognize the obligatory nature of such expenditures. The Constitution gives complete latitude to the government to plan expenditures according to its priorities and present these as grants for approval of Parliament. In practice, the Parliament has never disagreed with the expenditure proposals presented by the government.

Deeply influenced by the Soviet model of planned development, in the 1950s, the government decided to classify expenditures in two principal categories of 'development expenditure' and 'non-development expenditure'. While development expenditure was given priority, considered as 'good' expenditure, and was accorded ever-increasing allocations, non-development expenditure, considered not so good, was muzzled.

Principal sovereign functions like defence, police, jails, administration of justice, district administration, etc., were adjudged non-developmental. These services and expenditures were clubbed under 'general services' for planning, budgeting, presentational, allocation and accounting purposes.

It was also decided that expenditures of a social and economic nature, without a distinction of whether these constituted public goods and services or not, would be considered and classified as expenditures of a developmental nature.

Provision for health, education and development of SCs, STs and OBCs, for example, were categorized as development expenditure under a broad class of 'social services' expenditure. Expenditure on establishment of steel mills, power plants, nationalization of private industries and expansion of financial services, being of an economic nature, also got classified as developmental and accounted as 'economic services' expenditures.

India also classified all its expenditures as 'plan' and 'non-plan' expenditures. Again, plan was considered good and desirable and non-plan something of a non-desirable and bad expenditure. Curiously, only new developmental expenditure was recognized as plan expenditure. This required development expenditure incurred in the previous plan period to be shifted to the non-plan category.

The government accorded the highest priority to plan expenditure. The development expenditure of the previous plan came second in terms of priority. Non-development expenditure, which basically was the core sovereign function of government, was relegated to being non-priority expenditure.

The distinction between plan and non-plan was finally abolished in 2017. The Central government now approves, without any formal classification, schemes for development with a longer term (typically five to seven years) expenditures horizon. These schemes are budgeted under the heads of concerned line ministries and departments as line items like other non-development services. However, the schematic expenditures of the Central government still mimic plan schemes. A few schemes focused on sovereign or other public goods functions of the government, see the light of day, even today.

Real Expenditure Responsibilities of the Central Government

To reform the current structure of expenditures, it is necessary to look at the real expenditure functions and role of the Central government. It has two primary functions:

One, the provision of public goods and services. Defence, internal security, environmental well-being like control of pollution, law and justice, macroeconomic stability, regulation of markets, currency are some of these public goods and services. Other legitimate government functions include provision of primary education, supplementary nutrition to women and children and primary health, which have positive spillovers or externalities and functions like control of beggary, vagrancy, consumption of narcotics, etc., which have substantial negative spillovers and externalities. While provision of many of these goods and services are within the domain of the states in our constitution, the Centre is duty-bound to deliver and support such services and incur expenditures thereon.

Two, redistribution. There are many unfortunate citizens who, on account of physical and mental inadequacies, are not able to earn income for their living. Working of the economic system also leaves a large number of people unable to earn enough to meet their multidimensional minimum needs. These people have to be provided resources to meet their minimum needs. The rich have to be taxed or the government has to borrow from the future to redistribute resources to reduce/eliminate social income inequality.

It is helpful to recognize and classify these people in three groups of the poor to design the programmes of support from the government:

First, the poorest of the poor or literally destitutes. The poorest of the poor/destitute are the people who cannot work to earn a living, like the old, infirm and physically challenged. The redistribution programme for such people need to have both financial (cash transfers/pensions) and non-financial (health, housing, access to roads) support.

Second, the economically poor. These persons can and do earn but not enough to lead a healthy and productive life (such people are classified economically poor on the multidimensional poverty template; India has about 25 per cent of its population considered multidimensionally poor). They need support for meeting their basic necessities, like electricity, gas, toilets and a house, as well as for acquiring education, health facilities, skills and financial support to be able to raise their income to get out of the multi-dimensional poverty levels.

Third, the vulnerable non-poor. These people ordinarily earn an adequate income to lead a healthy and productive life but may fall back in poverty or become economically poor during natural or manmade crises/catastrophes. They need support to meet their needs during such adversities only, like the labour who lost their jobs during the lockdown imposed after COVID-19 spread.

Expenditures the Centre Should Not Undertake

There are two broad types of expenditures the Centre must not undertake, as such expenditures amount to gross misallocation of otherwise scarce public resources. In addition, the Central government is not the best agency to deliver the services such expenditures seek to provide.

First, provision of private goods and services. The 1991 reforms have created an economy in which most of what can be termed 'private goods' are best provided by the private sector, such as production of food and clothing, bus transport, hotels, travel and bus services, telecom, power, steel and engineering goods. These are provided more efficiently and at a lower capital cost by the private sector than the public sector. The government still spends a considerable amount of budgetary resources to subsidize or cover the losses of public enterprises providing such services. For example, providing budgetary resources to cover the losses of telephone services (MTNL and BSNL), transport services (Air India and Indian Railways), electricity services (DISCOMs), or several other goods the so-called 'public enterprises' are delivering today is not the correct use of scarce budgetary resources.

Second, excessive subsidies for private goods and overgenerous post-retirement benefits. Such excessive subsidies, like the ones for food, fertilizers, petroleum products, housing and crop loans, have led to unnecessary borrowings, which in turn have led to an unsustainable burden of debt and interest payments. Similarly, liberal and excessive post-retirement benefits to public servants cost a lot. These expenditures are generally incurred without focusing on those who are the poorest of the poor or the economically poor, and do not benefit the public in general.

Reforming the Basic Framework of Expenditures

India's expenditure framework, when examined against the basic framework stated above, is found to be riddled with numerous expenditures which the government should not be incurring and absence or inadequacies of many expenditures which the government should be incurring. India's expenditure framework urgently requires five basic reforms:

First, budget allocations for production of private goods and services in the public sector need to be thoroughly reviewed and downsized or eliminated. This should lead to the closure of loss-making and shuttered public enterprises and stoppage of budgetary support to cover losses in public-sector enterprises. This should also reduce capital investment in such enterprises and undertakings.

Second, there are numerous programmes and schemes operated by the Government of India which support production of private goods and services in the private sector. Such programmes include the provision of inputs to agriculture and animal husbandry sectors and cheaper credit to MSMEs and private enterprises. These have led to the perpetuation of inefficiencies in private enterprises and loss of competitiveness in agriculture and industry of India. Such expenditures also need to be thoroughly reviewed and streamlined.

Third, redistribution programmes need to be reviewed for being better designed and targeted. This should lead to a major overhaul of the hundreds of redistribution programmes currently run by the government. The redistribution schemes which do not target and reach the three classes of deserving poor people: the poorest of the poor/destitute, the economically poor and the vulnerable poor should be discontinued and those that reach these sections should be appropriately redesigned, focused and delivered.

Fourth, the government has not been spending enough on public goods and services like control of pollution and provision of primary health services. These needs should be properly identified and appropriate schemes for delivering an adequate level of these services need to be better designed, started and expanded.

Fifth, expenditure on personnel hired to implement public expenditure programmes has acquired a character of redistribution rather than being a fair compensation of services rendered by them. No wonder such expenditures have become very large. These expenditures require careful scrutiny and management.

Roll Back the Public Sector and Stop Funding from Budgets

India's public expenditure objectives, structure and mode of implementation are steeped in the socialist era. In a period of about forty years (1947–1990) lasting until serious industrial, financial and trade reforms were initiated in the 1990s, the Central government made a lot of investments from the Budget in public-sector enterprises to produce heavy machinery, basic goods, electricity, etc. Public resources were also spent on nationalizing a number of consumer industries and services like textiles, airlines, insurance, banking and so on.

The Central government stopped fresh investments and new nationalizations after 1990. However, many of these public-sector industries and financial institutions undertake expansions or have become loss-making, requiring constant provision of capital and survival support. The Centre's Budget bears the heavy burden of such recapitalization and loans and grants to pay salaries and maintenance costs. Such expenditure on sustaining an unsustainable public sector must be stopped.

There were seventy loss-making public-sector enterprises that incurred aggregate losses of over Rs 31,000 crore in 2018–19. There were also more than fifteen closed public-sector enterprises. Most of these loss-making and closed enterprises are in heavy industry and consumer goods. Every year, the government has to come up with budgetary support (revival) packages to keep some of the public enterprises afloat, to pay salaries to the persons employed or to offer them a voluntary retirement package. Sometimes, a lot of capital is injected to undertake modernization, expansion and adoption of new technology. In 2019–20, the government decided to spend over Rs 70,000 crore for the revival of BSNL and MTNL. Much of this cost was budgeted and spent in 2020–21.

Loss-making enterprises need to be wound up with their land and buildings transferred to a sovereign land management agency. This agency can monetize them in the best possible manner, from outright sale to REIT or lease. These reforms can easily save the government Rs 2–3 lakh crore a year without any loss to public welfare.

There are financial-sector enterprises in which the government is forced to pump in capital year after year. In the past three years, it has pumped in over Rs 3 lakh crore as capital in PSBs. In 2020–21, the government budgeted considerable sums of money to provide solvency capital to insurance companies and growth capital to IIFCL. While the private sector banks and insurance companies were generating large profits and raising capital from the market, the government had to pump large capital into public sector banks and insurance companies to help them meet their minimum capital requirements at the expense of constrained budgets.

The government should stop making further capital contribution to these enterprises. All the equity investment of the government in profit-making financial and non-financial public-sector enterprises can be transferred to a sovereign assets management company. It can take the appropriate call to capitalize further, sell or disinvest a further minority stake in each of these companies. The government can get capital receipts against disinvestment proceeds by selling stakes in the sovereign asset management company.

Reforming Models of Assistance to Agriculture and Small Industry

There is a very intrusive and wasteful model of schematic development assistance in several areas like agriculture and MSMEs, which are essentially private-sector activities.

There were thirty-three schemes listed in the budget of the Department of Agriculture, Cooperation and Farmers' Welfare (other than PM Kisan and Annadata schemes, which are direct benefit delivery schemes) to deliver free or subsidize all kinds of agriculture inputs, extension services, interest subvention, insurance cover, mechanization support and water management, at a total cost of over Rs 57,000 crore in the Budget 2020–21.

Two dozen schemes have outlays of less than Rs 1000 crore. In terms of implementation on ground, while some farmers get some support, the rest continue to live with unmodernized farms, distorted input prices and rationed supplies.

Indian agriculture and MSMEs would be much better served and develop into genuine businesses if such intrusive programmes with thinly delivered support were stopped and the savings gained transferred to farmers as direct cash benefits.

The expenditure allocations for such schemes exceed Rs 2 lakh crore. Most of these schemes can be converted into direct cash grant support to the concerned class. The allocations meant for agriculture input schemes can be delivered as direct cash transfer to farmers with decontrol of input prices. This will improve choices for farmers and make agriculture input markets competitive.

These reforms should be aimed at improving the competitiveness of industry and agriculture, not saving any budgetary allocation.

Reforming the Redistribution Framework

Redistribution is a legitimate function of the government. However, the mode of delivery is still schematic, micromanaged and indirect. There are hundreds of Central government schemes to deliver redistribution in India.

There are numerous wage employment schemes. There are multiple skill acquisition financing schemes. There are several small capital/grant support schemes for the poor to undertake livelihood enterprises. There are schemes to deliver education. There are numerous scholarship and funding support schemes. There are also cash transfer schemes aimed at specific groups. There are retirement savings support schemes. There are subsidization schemes for specific products and services. You name it and there is a Central government scheme for it!

All these schemes, after going through so many pipes of bureaucratic organizations, ultimately reach (minus the amount lost in the leaks) the same poor households. Poor households may get five, ten, fifteen or twenty kinds of 'benefits' over a period of time, but such supplied benefits don't respect their judgement. They rarely have a say in determining what 'benefit' they want. They are passive recipients only.

A few schemes have been started by the Central government to deliver direct benefit or cash to the 'beneficiary'. Multiple ministries and departments implement such direct benefit schemes. The government still does not focus on individual households and deliver a package of direct benefits suiting their needs and aspirations.

This redistribution mechanism needs to be transformed.

For this, as proposed above, we must identify and categorize the economically poor households of India into three groups: poorest of the poor/destitute (who cannot earn a living), economically poor (with deficiency between their objectively determined standard needs and the income they earn) and economically vulnerable (who are economically fine normally but tend to fall back in poverty during times of emergency).

The redistribution package for each of these three groups should be restructured.

The destitute can be provided only cash income support, directly delivered.

The poor can be served by providing mostly cash support along with a few products in kind (largely delivered through vouchers).

Contingency support programmes for the vulnerable should kick in only during emergencies and disasters.

It is not very difficult to identify about 20 crore of destitute, poor and vulnerable households of India. The Economic and Caste Census did a lot of groundwork for this. A slightly refined methodology can deliver these lists. It will save much of the waste, delay and leakage that the present system entails.

Reforming Redistribution—Non-Cash Benefits

The economic cost of wheat purchased, stored and distributed in FCI for 2019–20 was Rs 26.8 per kg. The MSP for wheat for the year was Rs 18.40 per kg. The average price in most mandis was around Rs 19–20 per kg. Actual prices received by farmers (net of transportation) would be around Rs 15–16.

Wheat produced in villages comes back to villages through public distribution shops after doing the rounds of the mandi and FCI storage. Many Indians who don't prefer wheat as a cereal crop end up getting wheat in ration.

Poor and non-poor households get wheat at a hugely subsidized price of Rs 2. For the 35 kg of wheat a household gets, at the economic cost of FCI, they receive a benefit of about Rs 875 per month. At actual market prices, it is around Rs 450 per month or about Rs 5400 a year.

The country ends up footing a food subsidy bill of about Rs 2 lakh crore a year or about Rs 10,000 per household (there are about 20 crore households receiving subsidized grain). About 50 per cent is wasted. Only about 50 per cent of this subsidy reaches poor households.

Transformation of the system by providing a food coupon of Rs 5000 per household, restricted to destitute and poor households (estimated to be about 10 crore; 40 per cent of households), will bring down the food subsidy bill to Rs 50,000 crore. The government can save Rs 1.5 lakh crore and poor households would get their choice of food.

There are several programmes where the Centre delivers services to poor households at government cost. School education has a budget of Rs 60,000 crore (state governments spend another Rs 3 lakh crore a year). Higher education has another Rs 40,000 crore of budgeted expenditure. The skills department has a budget of Rs 3000 crore. There are several other demands with a budget to meet the expenses of indirect delivery of a service to people.

A comprehensive service-by-service examination is needed of budget provisions, service delivered and the right mode of delivering the benefit—in cash or kind, or by voucher. Broad estimates would suggest that most benefits delivered by the Central government can be restructured—with some phased over a long period—for efficient delivery.

There are quite a few subsidy schemes, like LPG subsidy to the non-poor, which have no real reason to exist. Such subsidies can be limited to the destitute and economically poor.

It is also quite reasonable to expect that the government can save over Rs 50,000 crore of expenditure from the non-food sector as well in a short time.

Indeed, redistribution reforms can yield an annual savings of about Rs 2 lakh crore.

Reforming Redistribution—Cash Benefit Schemes

Another reform in redistribution services is to deliver cash benefits from the household perspective, not the departmental perspective. All the cash benefits delivered today—PM-Kisan, payments to labour, scholarships and so on—can be pooled in three specific groups of funds: one for the destitute, another for the economically poor and the third for the economically vulnerable. Depending upon a conditionality framework (health status, number of children, type of dwelling, etc.), an appropriate cash transfer can be made to the concerned household per month.

This reform can be implemented quickly. It will serve poor households much better and save a lot of money, at least Rs 50,000 crore a year.

Augmenting Allocations for Public Goods and Services

Most ministries and departments concerned with providing public goods and services have relatively smaller allocations. This reflects the old mindset of giving priority to 'development expenditure' and squeezing sovereign and public goods functions, which were earlier consigned to the dustbin of the so-called 'non-Plan' category.

The inadequacy of these allocations gets exposed during challenging situations—for instance, the lack of adequate defence equipment during war; the inefficacy of response teams during national disasters; and poor health infrastructure during the pandemic. It is also not unusual to see overloaded hospitals, hugely deficient pollution control apparatus or overcrowded courts.

There is a case to improve the productivity of some public expenditure, but in general the gross inadequacy of allocations for these services has to be remedied for better governance and public welfare.

Chapter Fifty-Eight

Taxation Reforms

Tax Revenues Are the Principal Source of Government Revenues

The revenues to the government as sovereign come from primarily three sources. First, tax revenues—from income tax, corporation tax, central GST, customs, excise, wealth tax, etc. Second, from the sale or concessioning of natural and sovereign resources like minerals, spectrum, etc. Third, revenue from minting of coins and printing of notes; seigniorage in the form of dividends/transfer of surplus from RBI or penalty and fines received in exercise of sovereign powers. Taxation revenues are the principal source of government revenues.

Other non-tax revenues like dividends from commercial enterprises and capital receipts from sale of equity stake in PSUs are actually not 'revenues' of the government as sovereign. Such receipts are against investments made in business enterprises established by the government and should be basically treated as returns on business investments made. Unfortunately, government revenues as sovereign and from its commercial enterprises get mixed up and hide the poor comparator returns from the commercial investments made by the government.

India's current tax system is complicated and dysfunctional. It yields less revenue for the government to pay for public goods and services.

Yet, it taxes the productive forces of the economy excessively and in a manner that it disincentivizes productivity. Economic agents have to spend far too much time contriving to avoid payment of taxes. The current system also taxes workers too much and profits relatively lightly, but in a complicated manner. Wealth is taxed too little.

There Are Essentially Three Tax Bases

First is the output produced by the economic agents—farms, factories, service establishments and so on. The output produced, mostly measured in the form of value added now, has become the basis of all output taxes almost everywhere. These output/value added taxes, usually known as indirect taxation, whether called excise, customs, VAT or GST or by any other name, forms the bedrock of tax revenues.

Second is the income accruing to workers and entrepreneurs, which is taxed as income taxes, corporation tax or in some other name. Physical assets like land and buildings and financial assets like bonds and equity also generate a considerable amount of income in the form of rent, interest, or dividend, etc., in today's increasingly wealthier world. The income taxes form the second largest tax-bases all over the world.

Third, the wealth in the form of personal assets like houses, business assets like farms, factories and digital networks and financial assets in the form of bonds, equities, derivatives and now in cryptocurrencies, has been growing in the world. Wealth has been taxed in the form of wealth taxes, property taxes, estate duties, etc., but relatively sparingly. Wealth grows besides generating income. Wealth is largely in the control of the rich and super-rich. These groups have managed to avoid taxation of valuation gains and income from wealth. The tax on wealth and income generated from wealth is underexplored in the world, and in India.

A Basic Reset of Taxation System Is Urgently Needed

A basic reset of the taxation system would not only institute a fair system of taxation across all segments of economic agents but yield a much larger and steadily increasing source of revenue for the government. This can be achieved with fundamental reforms in our taxation system in three major ways:

First, by bringing taxation of all 'incomes' (capital gains, which is a valuation gain on an asset, which should be treated as part of wealth taxation) under one system of direct or income taxation—whether these incomes are from businesses, wages or wealth. Incomes earned or accruing to businesses in the form of profits generated or incomes earned or accruing to workers as salaries or wages or in any form (allowances, bonuses, ESOPs), which are essentially a variant of salary or wages or arising from wealth or assets (rent, dividend), should be taxed under this single income tax law. Indian income tax law does have all the three basic forms of income—wages, profits and income from wealth—under the law but it also deals with taxation of capital gains and other benefits from the assets.

Second, by bringing a fragmented system of taxation of value added (customs, excise, value added, GST) under a single law of indirect or value-added taxation. Value is added in the production of goods, services and assets. While the system of value addition taxation for goods and services has been consolidated in the form of GST (there are still many parts outside), creation and construction of real assets, whether a house, factory, warehouse or any other physical asset, still lacks a good value-added taxation system. The indirect or value-added taxation system should also be applicable to all businesses, small or big, producing goods, services or assets.

Third, by bringing all assets (or 'wealth'), whether physical or financial, visible or invisible (goodwill, brands), under one wealth taxation system. The wealth taxation system is most fragmented and non-existent for many assets. Creation of one single system of wealth taxation would require drastic reforms of the existing taxation system on property (property taxes, stamp duties), capital gains (currently done in a fragmented form as part of income taxes) and many other taxes (royalties, premium on sale of land, etc.).

The system of income taxation bases tax on income generated. The system of value-add taxation bases tax on value added created. The system of wealth taxation would require to be based on the change in the valuation of assets and capital gains made in transfer of assets.

Income Taxation

Indian Income Tax Law

The Constitution divides the authority to tax incomes between the Union and the States. Entry 82 of the Constitution allocates the subject of taxes on income other than agricultural income to the Union. There is a separate Entry 85 for Corporation Tax. The state list in the Seventh Schedule of the Constitution allocates land revenue to the states (Entry 45). Entry 46 allocates taxes on agricultural income to the states. Taxes on lands and buildings are also given to states (Entry 49).

The British introduced income tax in India as soon as the Queen of England took over the administration of India. The Indian Income Tax Act 1860 was introduced along with the first Budget of India in 1860. This made four kinds of income taxable: income from landed property, income from professions and trades, income from securities and income from salaries and pensions.

The law was abolished for some time, came back and trudged along before a more comprehensive Income Tax Act was enacted in 1886. It replaced income from landed property and income from professions and trades with net profits of companies and other sources of income. Salaries, pensions and gratuities continued to be taxed as such and income from securities was made more specific—interest on securities of the Government of India.

The next major edition came in 1922, which is the law that was in force when India became independent in 1947.

The Indian Income Tax Act, 1961, was promulgated to tax personal incomes, corporate incomes and certain wealth-related incomes. This Act continues to remain in force today although there have been attempts to replace it by an Income Tax Code twice between 2010 and 2020.

Kaldor Proposed a Basic Overhaul of the System in the 1950s

American economist Nicholas Kaldor proposed a basic restructuring of income taxation in India in 1950s. Arguing that the system in force taxed savings, he proposed an expenditure tax-based system that spared savings from tax. As the prevalent system taxed entire income irrespective of it being spent on consumption or retained for savings, he argued that the system discouraged savings and consequently investment. He proposed that income tax should not be levied on entire income but only on the income spent on consumption.

The government accepted his proposals in principle but transformed the same materially while enacting the Expenditure Tax

Act in 1957. Kaldor had suggested that expenditure tax be levied on all income taxpayers but the highest income tax slab be reduced from the 80 per cent then prevalent to 45 per cent. In addition, there was a super-tax in vogue those days, which he proposed to be abolished as well.

His proposals would have had the effect of transforming the tax on income at higher income slabs (including super-tax that higher income slabs attracted) from income tax to an expenditure tax. And in case the assessee spent less than the income that attracted tax at a higher rate (i.e., in case expenditure was lesser than the income in the concerned tax slabs), his actual incidence of tax would have come down (as expenditure tax would be lesser than the income tax and super-tax otherwise payable on such income).

The government, instead, chose a different structure. It did not change the higher rates of income tax. It also retained the super-tax by and large and only reduced its rate marginally. The government chose to exempt all assessees who earned income of less than Rs 36,000 a year from the expenditure tax. This reduced the applicability of the tax to only a minority of taxpayers—about 8000 people in all!

The effect of not reducing the marginal rate of income tax and super-tax meant that expenditure tax was effectively an additional tax, not a tax replacing income tax. The complex regime of exempting certain expenditures and assessment of expenditure also created massive administrative problems and intrusion in the lives of people. In fact, the total tax paid by many of the people on whom expenditure tax became applicable exceeded 100 per cent of income and people had to pay tax from their capital.

As a result, the expenditure tax neither resulted in incentivizing savings nor in earning any meaningful revenues for the government. It only resulted in massive taxpayer harassment.

None shed a tear when the expenditure tax law was abolished in 1966.

Income Tax Rate Structure Was Gradually Made Non-Extortionary

The marginal rate of income tax was 97.75 per cent in 1974 and had been so high for many years in India. In addition, there was wealth tax.

This worked as the strongest disincentive to expand business income. This also worked as the strongest incentive to make taxpayers tax-evaders.

This was recognized in 1974, albeit after it had done a lot of harm to India's growth and enterprise. In his Budget speech for the year 1974–75, Finance Minister Y.B. Chavan said:

'One of the important recommendations of the Direct Taxes Enquiry Committee relates to reduction in the rates of taxes. The Committee has expressed the view that prevalence of high rates is the first and foremost reason for tax evasion, because this is what makes the evasion, in spite of attendant risks, profitable and attractive. The Committee has, accordingly, recommended that the maximum marginal rate of income-tax, including surcharge, should be brought down from its present level of 97.75 per cent to 75 per cent.'

The finance minister went on to reduce the marginal rate of basic income tax to 70 per cent on income in the slab over Rs 70,000. Rate of surcharge was also reduced to a uniform level of 10 per cent. Accordingly, the marginal rate of income tax was brought down to 77 per cent in the highest slab of taxation.

The effect of high rates of income tax was that direct tax collections in the country remained relatively much smaller than indirect taxes. A 77 per cent marginal rate of tax was better than 97.75 per cent but still hugely unattractive to unleash the animal spirits of businessmen and individuals to earn more profits and income.

In 1980–81, the share of direct taxes in total tax collections was quite low, at about 22 per cent.

Marginal income tax was brought down to 50 per cent in 1985–86, to 40 per cent in 1992–93 and to the lowest rate to date of 30 per cent in 1997–98.

The movement towards reasonableness started making a difference. The share of direct taxes was very low at 19 per cent in 1990–91, but increased to about 30 per cent by 1995–96 and crossed 35 per cent at the turn of the century. It crossed 50 per cent of total tax collections for the first time in 2007–08 and was at the highest level of over 55 per cent in 2008–09.

It remained in excess of 50 per cent thereafter until 2015–16. It fell to 48.6 per cent in 2016–17 when excise duties were hiked on petroleum products, but returned to being higher than 50 per cent from 2017–18 onward, not because of any higher buoyancy in direct taxes but because indirect tax revenues suffered badly after the introduction of GST.

Restoration of Simpler Personal Tax Rate Structure is the Easiest Reform

The personal income tax (PIT) structure was made very simple and streamlined in 1996–97 when tax rates were fixed at 10 per cent, 20 per cent and 30 per cent by dividing the total income on which tax was payable in four slabs of income (there has been an exempt tax slab). In addition, no surcharges were levied.

While one or two surcharges were levied from 1996–97 to 2013–14 for some time as temporary measures, the tax rate structure remained by and large unchanged for about twenty-five years.

The government abolished wealth tax in 2014–15 but imposed a 2 per cent surcharge on income higher than Rs 1 crore in lieu thereof. This was intended to be permanent. This effectively introduced one more tax slab of 30.6 per cent for income higher than Rs 1 crore. The surcharge regime was continuously fiddled with in the next few years. Surcharge was made applicable to incomes between Rs 50 lakh and Rs 1 crore as well.

The surcharge regime became most complicated in the 2019–20 Budget when higher surcharges on income tax were made applicable on assessees with taxable income between Rs 2 crore and Rs 5 crore and those with over Rs 5 crore to tax the super-rich.

With the introduction of these enhanced surcharges, there were effectively eight taxation slabs in the personal income tax in 2020-21: Nil up to Rs 2.5 lakh; 5 per cent for income from Rs 2.5 lakh to Rs 5 lakh; 20 per cent for income from Rs 5 lakh to Rs 10 lakh; 30 per cent for income between Rs 10 lakh and Rs 50 lakh; 33 per cent (30 per cent plus 10 per cent surcharge) for income from Rs 50 lakh to Rs 1 crore; 34.5 per cent (30 per cent plus 15 per cent surcharge) for income between Rs 1 crore and Rs 2 crore; 37.5 per cent (30 per cent plus 25 per cent surcharge) for income between Rs 2 crore and Rs 5 crore; and 41.1 per cent (30 per cent plus 37 per cent surcharge) for income over Rs 5 crore.

There is an additional Health and Education Cess chargeable at 4 per cent of income tax payable on tax plus surcharge.

In the budget 2020–21, the government introduced further complication.

A lower taxation rate structure was offered by splitting the slab of Rs 5–10 lakh into two slabs of Rs 5–7.5 lakh and Rs 7.5–10 lakh and introducing two more slabs, Rs 10–12.5 lakh and Rs 12.5–15 lakh, in the Rs 10–20 lakh slab for assessees who opt not to avail of the exemptions which were otherwise available.

There are more than ten effective income tax slabs and rates for those who opt for the new regime introduced in 2020–21 (for those taxpayers who decide not to avail specified exemptions) and more than eight rates (for those taxpayers who decide to avail specified exemptions). The rate structure has indeed become the most complicated ever.

The effective marginal rate of tax has also gone well beyond 40 per cent.

Besides making the PIT structure unnecessarily complicated, the use of the surcharge mechanism to transform the rate structure of income taxes is unfair to states as surcharge revenues are not shared with state governments under the Constitution as these do not form part of the devolution pool shared with the states in accordance with share recommended by the Finance Commissions.

The following reforms in the personal tax structure appear quite necessary, to be carried out almost immediately:

First, India's lowest slab of tax (Rs 2.5 lakh to Rs 5 lakh) is too low considering even the average income levels in the economy. It also carries a nominal rate of tax of 5 per cent. Recognizing this, the government had exempted all taxpayers with taxable income under Rs 5 lakh from payment. India's per capita GDP income in current prices in 2019–20 was Rs 1.5 lakh and in 2020–21, Rs 1.46 lakh. The minimum income exempt from personal income tax can be linked to average per capita GDP of the country for once and then automatically revised every year for the average general inflation in the country. If we take 200 per cent of the average per capita GDP as the reasonable exemption limit, the lowest slab of income tax can be determined at Rs 3 lakh and made exempt from taxation.

Second, surcharges and cesses should be abolished in the interest of a simple tax structure and for fair sharing of income tax revenues with the states. There is also no merit in complicating the tax structure by giving options for lower tax rates if one does not avail specified exemptions.

Third, a simple five-rate tax structure introduced: no tax for taxable income less than Rs 3 lakh, 5 per cent from Rs 3–10 lakh, 15 per cent from Rs 10–25 lakh, 25 per cent from Rs 25–100 lakh and 35 per cent for income over Rs 100 lakh. The minimum exempt tax slab of Rs 5 lakh should be adjusted every two years to retail price inflation.

Elimination/Rationalization of Deductions

Most income tax deductions look sensible on the face of it. However, they end up introducing unnecessary complications and distortions.

Take, for example, the deductions for construction of a house. This appears to be a good thing as it encourages people to construct their homes by availing loans. It encourages construction activity, which in turn gives a push to the infrastructure industry and also spreads banking and credit. However, the deduction for interest on loans taken for one's personal house ends up discouraging construction of rental housing in the country. While lakhs of personal houses get constructed every year, the rental housing industry in the country is completely non-existent. Deductions and exemptions of interest from Public Provident Fund (PPF) and other small saving products discriminate against fixed deposits and other saving investment products in the banks and other financial institutions.

Likewise, deductions permitted for investments—backward area, technology parks, start-ups—may all be intended to encourage industrial development. However, these incentives end up making manufacturing costlier and non-competitive in the country.

The tax instruments are too complicated and blunt to achieve the objectives stated for their introduction.

Therefore, first, most if not all personal deductions should be abolished from the income tax laws. At best, if the government intends to encourage savings over consumption, it could provide one single incentive for long-term savings, irrespective of whether it is small savings, bank deposits, government bonds or corporate bonds. Second, the government should switch over to expenditure-side support to industry by formulating appropriate incentive schemes like PLI.

Fundamental Reforms of Income Taxation

As noted above, essentially, there are three fundamental sources of income—income from labour, profits from businesses and incomes which assets yield. The income taxation law should be built around identifying these three classes of incomes, assessing the same and taxing it. A major foundational reform would be to treat income coming in the hands of individuals/households only as taxable income. The undistributed income of corporate entities raise the capital value and should therefore be considered as part of wealth taxation. Income received in any corporate structure meant for holding income of any individual(s) can and should be taxed as that individual's income.

To sum it up, three income classes would be:

First, income by use of labour—use of physical and mental skills and abilities in any of the myriad ways in which these are employed to earn income. Labour incomes can be received in different forms: salary, wages, bonuses, pensions, superannuation contributions, employee stock options (ESOPs), and the like. Irrespective of the form in which labour income is received, it remains income and should be taxed as such.

There are millions of own-account one person or household businesses in India. The surplus of such businesses (excess of income receipts over costs) will constitute labour income for such own account enterprises.

Second, income from profits. Profits are earned in businesses. Businesses (other than own-account enterprises noted above) can be of any form and scale: proprietary, partnership, companies, limited liability partnership or any other form. For non-corporate entities, the income from businesses—small or large—will equal the profits earned (after payment of salaries to non-owning labour of such firms). Salaries or any other payment made to owners which is in the nature of income to the individual concerned should also be treated as part of his income. The profits earned by corporate entities are either distributed or retained or partly retained and partly distributed. Profits distributed by such business entities and received by the individuals/households/income holding corporate entities (which have a business interest in such corporate entities) should be treated as profit income and taxed accordingly. The law can define what holding in a corporate entity can be considered as business interest.

Third, incomes resulting from assets/wealth. Interest earned on loans given, rent earned on land or house property leased or for that matter dividend earned on equity investments (other than those who have a business interest) will all come under this category.

Capital gains, whether realized or unrealized, are not necessarily an 'income' from wealth. There could be an element of inflation in capital gains. The realized capital gains and also unrealized capital appreciation should be treated as taxation of wealth, which we will discuss subsequently.

The Income Tax Act of India should therefore be reorganized to tax these three types of incomes.

The government should not have preference for any one type of income. All should be taxed at the same rate structure; the equity element taken care of by different tax rates for different scales or slabs of income. The individuals, households and small businesses would suffer no or lower taxes depending upon the level of their incomes.

Taxation of Non-Resident Incomes

In principle, there should be no differentiation in taxation of income earned in India by a resident or by a non-resident. Profits made by a foreign direct investor in an Indian company should be taxed at the same rate as the profits made by a domestic investor instead of treating dividends distributed to foreign investors at lower rates. The reverse—the domestic investor getting better treatment—is also not desirable as the foreign capital serves India's economic interests equally well. The same logic applies to bond investments by domestic and foreign investors or, for that matter, by portfolio investment investors of both equity and debt.

Like many other countries, India has also entered into a number of double taxation avoidance agreements (DTAA). DTAA provisions are built on the fundamental rationale of residents being taxed for their global incomes. This leads to the creation of all kinds of fake residences in countries that levy very low or no tax. It also leads to roundtripping of funds from the residents to other countries. If this logic is fundamentally upended by taxing everyone (resident or non-resident) on the same basis by taxing all domestic income, all the incentives to set up fake residences in tax havens will go away. Likewise, there would remain no incentive for roundtripping.

The only disadvantage would be that India would not be able to tax foreign income of residents. That should be fine. This income is earned in the foreign country. That foreign country should be the one to tax this income.

There is an important ongoing debate in the world about the taxation of profits earned by digital companies like Google and Netflix on the services streamed in a country without establishing any permanent establishment in that country. Profits are earned by such companies in the country of delivery of the digital service. Therefore, there is a legitimate justification to find a way to tax such companies. India has levied equalization levy, which is an income tax. However, this has still not got established as a direct tax. Rather, this is being passed on to the consumer like an indirect tax.

The recent international agreement (two-pillar solution to address the tax challenges arising from the Digitalization of the Economy Agreement signed in Washington DC in October 2021) to treat such incomes of foreign entities taxable in the country of users of services is a step in the right direction. However, this deal is applicable to a very small number of companies (those with annual global profits of €20 billion and profitability above 10 per cent). When this Agreement comes into force, India would have to abolish the equalization levy. India might not really be a net gainer under the deal and would have to work to bring more multinational digital companies within the scope of this taxation agreement.

Reform Agenda for Indirect Tax System

The taxation system of goods evolved from a tax imposed on the value of the good at the time it passed from a manufacturer or seller to another manufacturer, seller or consumer. Later the system evolved to capture the value added at each stage of manufacture or sale and tax was collected at the net value added. This change, however, does not change the basic nature of taxation of goods and services, which is the taxation of goods and services produced and sold.

The production and distribution of goods and services may take place domestically or abroad. The goods and services brought in the territory of a country for being used in production or consumption usually suffer taxation known as customs duty. The production and distribution of goods and services domestically suffers taxation known as excise duties and value-added tax (VAT). When the taxation of goods and services gets merged into one single system of taxation, it becomes goods and services tax (GST).

Allocation of Taxation Powers on Goods and Services

Taxation of goods or commodities goes back in history. Salt was taxed even during Mauryan and Mughal times. British also started taxing salt very early. Salt taxation became the foundation of excise taxation on commodities. Excise duty on silver was imposed in 1930. More commodities like iron and steel, matches and sugar were brought under excise tax sometime in 1934. The legislative framework for commodities taxation took more concrete shape around this time. The Provisional Collection of Taxes Act was enacted in 1931, the Tariff Act was legislated in 1934 and the Central Board of Revenue was constituted the same year.

The Central Excises and Salt Act was enacted in 1944. Excise duty on salt was removed in 1946. However, the word salt was removed from the Act only in 1996 by the Finance Act, 1996, and the Act became known as the Central Excise Act, 1944. Customs duties were collected under the Provisional Collection of Taxes Act, 1931, until the Customs Act was enacted in 1962. The Government of India Act, 1935, made sales tax the subject of provincial jurisdiction.

When the Indian Constitution divided the subjects of taxation between the Union and the states, the duties of excise on tobacco and other goods manufactured or produced in India, except duties on alcohol for human consumption and opium, Indian hemp and other narcotic drugs and narcotics, but including medicinal and toilet preparations containing alcohol or any of these other substances mentioned, were allocated to the Union of India. Tax on the sale or purchase of newspapers was also placed in the Central government's domain. Duties of customs, including export duties, were also allocated to the Union.

While no omnibus concept of services taxation existed at the time the Constitution was promulgated, certain specific services were identified for the Union List. Terminal taxes on goods and passengers carried by rail, sea or air, taxes on railway fares and freight, and on advertisements published in newspapers were specifically mentioned in the Union List for taxation by the Centre.

The states' mandate in terms of taxation of goods extended to duties of excise on alcohol for human consumption, opium, Indian hemp and other narcotic drugs and narcotics, excluding medicinal and toilet preparations. States got major indirect tax powers by inclusion of entry taxes on the sale or purchase of goods other than newspapers (subject to some exclusions). States also had powers with respect to taxation on entry of goods into a local area for consumption, use or sale therein and taxes on consumption or sale of electricity.

The list of specific services included in the domain of states was much larger. It included taxes on advertisements other than advertisements published in newspapers (later, advertisements broadcast by radio or television were also excluded from the state list); taxes on goods and passengers carried by road or on inland waterways, taxes on vehicles, whether mechanically propelled or not, suitable for use on roads, including tramcars (subject to some exclusion); taxes on animals and boats; tolls, taxes on professions, trades, callings and employments; capitation taxes; and taxes on luxuries, including taxes on entertainment, amusements, betting and gambling.

Concept of VAT Got Introduced in the 1980s

India's indirect taxation system was cascading. At every stage of manufacture and sale, excise tax, sales tax or both were leviable on the value of goods, inclusive of taxes paid previously. If an item is manufactured and sold at Rs 100, which included inputs purchased of Rs 75, inclusive of Rs 10 of excise duties paid thereon, excise duties would be levied on goods of Rs 100 without giving any credit for excise duties paid earlier. If goods of Rs 100 suffer excise duties of, say, Rs 20, the wholesaler would pay Rs 120, which would have a total element of excise duties of Rs 30. If the wholesaler were to sell these goods at Rs 150 to the retailer, which attracts sales tax of Rs 15, the cumulative excise and sales tax element in goods of Rs 165 will be Rs 45. The cascading of excise duties would go on with further imposition of sales tax when the retailer sells it to the final consumer. No wonder there was a rampant tendency to avoid billing in the country.

In the 1970s, the L.K. Jha Committee on Indirect Taxation first recommended a value-added taxation system in the country. In the value-added system, the manufacturer/seller at every subsequent stage pays duty on the entire value of goods sold but gets credit for the input excise duties paid. In our example above, the first manufacturer would get credit of Rs 10 when he sold his goods of Rs 100. As he paid excise duties of Rs 20 and got credit of Rs 10, his net incidence of excise would reduce to Rs 10 and the goods would be sold at Rs 110, instead of Rs 120.

The 1986 Budget introduced the value-added concept in the system of indirect taxation in India, albeit in a modest form. The 1986–87 Budget speech dealt with this subject extensively. To quote:

'In excise taxation a vexatious question which has been often encountered is the taxation of inputs and the cascading effect of this on the value of the final product. The Long Term Fiscal Policy had stated that the best solution would be to extend the present system of proforma credit to all excisable commodities with the exception of a few sectors with special problems like petroleum, tobacco and textiles. The scheme, which has been referred as Modified Value Added Tax (MODVAT) scheme—I shall stress MODVAT, not MADVAT—allows the manufacturer to obtain instant and complete reimbursement of the excise duty paid on the components and raw materials.'

The MODVAT scheme was applied on all goods covered by thirty-seven specified chapters of the Central Excise Tariff Act, 1985. The scheme allowed all the final products covered by the specified twenty-seven chapters credit for the inputs used in manufacture thereof, which are also covered by the same thirty-seven chapters.

With this, the journey of the value-added taxation system in the country began, which was finally completed with the introduction of GST in 2017.

VAT Replaces State Sales Taxes

The Government of India, after gradually extending the value-added concept to most excises and also rationalizing the VAT structure of excise duties, took the initiative to introduce it to state sales taxes. To ensure fuller involvement of the states, an Empowered Committee of State Finance Ministers was set up in July 2000, which, among other terms of reference, intended 'to decide milestones and methods of States to switch over to VAT'.

The committee, after considerable deliberations, agreed on the draft of a model state VAT law. States started enacting their VAT laws from 2003, when Haryana became the first state to enact the law, though very few had actually done so by the time the new UPA government took over at the Centre in May 2004.

The new government pushed the introduction of VAT laws and offered to compensate the states if they suffered loss in the growth of state sales tax/VAT revenues.

To quote from the Budget speech of 2004–05:

'Value-added tax is a tax that has been tested and tried, and found beneficial throughout the world. The country needs a modern and efficient trade tax system that incorporates the international best practices. At the 18 June 2004 meeting of the Empowered Committee of State Finance Ministers, . . . there was a broad consensus among the States to implement VAT. 1 April 2005 has been set as the date for implementation. I welcome the decision and warmly congratulate the state governments. I urge all States that have not yet passed the relevant VAT legislation to do so before the end of 2004. International experience, as well as the experience of the State of Haryana, suggests that VAT will lead to an increase in revenue and not a loss in revenue. Nevertheless, in order to give comfort to the States, I propose to evolve a formula for determining the compensation for the loss of revenue, if any.'

The good work done in the Empowered Committee of the Finance Ministers and the Centre's encouragement sweetened by the compensation for loss, made over 80 per cent of the states enact the VAT laws and made them applicable in financial year 2004–05. The remaining five states did so in 2005–06. By the end of financial year 2005–06, the entire country had switched over to the VAT system for goods in place of states' sales taxes.

Services Taxation Introduced in the 1990s Integrated the VAT Concept Gradually

Services taxation was quite fragmented until the 1980s. While some services mentioned in the Union and state lists like entertainment, luxuries and passenger travel did have incidence of taxation under respective central and state legislations, there was no concept of taxing services generically. Most services were outside the indirect tax net in the 1980s.

Services got recognized as an area of taxation in the 1990s and the first steps to build a comprehensive system of taxing value added in services began with the Government of India imposing service tax on three services that were hitherto untaxed. To quote Finance Minister Manmohan Singh from the 1994–95 Budget speech:

'Over the years, while attempts have been made to widen the base for domestic indirect taxes, the services sector has not been subjected to taxation. Yet the sector accounts for about 40 per cent of our GDP and is showing strong growth. There is no sound reason for exempting services from taxation, when goods are taxed and many countries treat goods and services alike for tax purposes. The Tax Reforms Committee has also recommended imposition of tax on services as a measure for broadening the base of indirect taxes. I, therefore, propose to make a modest effort in this direction by imposing a tax on services of telephones, non-life insurance and stock brokers. The tax will be charged at 5 per cent on the amount of telephone bills, the net premium charged by the insurance companies, and the brokerage or commission charged by the stock brokers in relation to their services.'

Gradually, the list of services subjected to service tax increased. There were more than 100 services that were subjected to service tax by the end of the first decade of the twenty-first century. The government moved the system of taxing all services, except services placed in a negative list. The policy shift was announced in the 2012–13 Budget. To quote Finance Minister (later President) Pranab Mukherjee:

'Last year, I had initiated a public debate on the desirability of moving towards taxation of services based on a negative list. In the debate that continued for the better part of the year, we received overwhelming support for this new concept. It has been perceived both as sound economics and a prudent fiscal arrangement. Thus, I propose to tax all services except those in the negative list. The list comprises seventeen heads and has been carefully drawn up, keeping in view the federal nature of our polity, the best international practices and our socioeconomic requirements.'

The services in the negative list included services provided by the government or local bodies, education services, renting of residential dwellings, entertainment and amusement services and public transportation. There was also a list of exemptions, including healthcare, services provided by charities, religious persons, sportspersons, etc.

Over the years, the negative list and the exemptions have shrunk. In the GST system, there is a very small negative list of services. This includes services by employee to employer in the course of employment, services by any court or tribunal, functions performed by MPs, MLAs, etc.

GST Integrates the System of Value-Added Taxation on Goods and Services

Once the excise system of the Central government and the sales tax system of the states had adopted the value-added system and services had emerged as an important source of indirect/value added taxation, the movement towards integrating the entire indirect tax system into a comprehensive GST system appeared logical and essential. The government started announcing this goal from the 2009–10 Budget. However, this proved to be quite tough as it involved virtually restructuring the basic constitutional scheme of taxation, sharing of taxation powers, potential loss of sovereignty for both the states and Centre on taxation of goods and services and creation of new constitutional bodies like the GST Council. There were also serious implications for the tax revenues of manufacturing states as GST was a destination-based taxation concept. While there were clear advantages, including introduction of a 'one nation, one indirect taxation' system, the unknowns of the GST system and loss of authority over such an important and comprehensive taxation system as the state VAT and many other indirect taxes were daunting challenges. Finally, Finance Minister Arun Jaitley was able to build consensus on the matter, offering a very liberal compensation scheme in the process.

His Budget speech in 2017–18 captured the challenge and final movement towards GST:

'There has been substantial progress towards ushering in GST, by far, the biggest tax reform since Independence. Since the enactment of the Constitution (One Hundred and First Amendment) Act, 2016, the preparatory work for this path-breaking reform has been a top priority for the government. In this context, several teams of officers both from the States and Central Board of Excise and Customs have been working tirelessly to give the finishing touch to the Model GST law and rules and other details. Government on its part has promptly given effect to various provisions of the Constitutional Amendment Act, including constitution of the GST Council. Since then, the GST Council held nine meetings to discuss various issues relating to GST, including broad contours of the GST rate structure, threshold exemption and parameters for composition scheme, details for compensation to States due to implementation of GST, examination of draft model GST law, draft IGST law and the Compensation

Law and administrative mechanism for GST. It is my privilege to inform this august house that the GST Council has finalized its recommendations on almost all the issues based on consensus and after spirited debate and discussions. The preparation of IT system for GST is also on schedule. The extensive reach-out efforts to trade and industry for GST will start from 1 April 2017 to make them aware of the new taxation system.'

The Central Goods and Services Tax Act 2017 was notified on 12 April. All the states passed their respective state GST Acts in time for India to implement the GST system from 1 July 2017. The country moved to a very comprehensive and integrated national system of taxation of goods and services on the basis of value-added principles.

Bringing Remaining Products into the GST System

There are three commodities/classes of commodities out of the GST system: petroleum products, alcohol for human consumption and electricity duty.

There is no good economic reason to keep petroleum products out of GST. Petroleum products, electricity and alcohol are also commodities like other commodities. Alcohol may have an element of sin tax, but so do cigarettes. The only reason why petroleum products are outside the GST system is the vested interest of the Central government and states to protect the excessively high revenues they get from the VAT/excise/cesses collected from their sale. Likewise, keeping electricity out of GST only serves to complicate the system of commodity and service taxation and give undue leverage to states to manipulate revenues from electricity duty.

All these products should be brought under the GST system. To ensure that the legitimate interests of the Centre and states in collecting high but reasonable taxes from these products are protected to a reasonable extent, the following proposals might strike the right balance:

First, take the base cost of $60 per barrel as the reference price for calculating what the Centre and states would collect at the existing rates of taxation. This should be the targeted revenue from the reformed system of taxation. Thereafter, applying the GST rate of 28 per cent (20 per cent in case the rates are reformed), the revenues that will flow to the Centre and states can be worked out. Finally, the remaining incidence of tax can be collected by way of fixed rate of excise duties.

The excise duties so collected should be divided between the Centre and states as per the share of tax determined by the Finance Commission. This reform will address the issue of volatility in crude oil prices. If crude goes beyond $60 a barrel, the GST tax incidence would increase only to the extent of the price increase in crude price. Similarly, in downward revision, the tax incidence would fall proportionally. The tax revenues of the Centre and states would remain unaffected to the extent of fixed rate excise duties.

Second, excise revenues on alcohol for human consumption accrues entirely to the states and they have different policies for levying excise duties on alcohol. An exercise similar to petroleum product taxes can be done in the case of alcohol, which should be brought under GST.

Third, electricity can be simply brought under the GST system without much of a problem placing it in an appropriate slab.

GST Rates Reform

It is the value added by a business that pays wages to the workers, profits to the businessmen and taxes to the governments. The share of value added in the turnover of goods and services sold differs from goods to goods and services to services. Many are high turnover, low value added goods/ services, while others are low turnover, high value added goods/services. There are some high turnover high value added goods and services as well. The value added margins and quantum of value added created differs for the businessmen massively.

From the consumers' perspective, there are certain goods and services that individuals/households have to consume to live a normal life. These are generally considered essential goods/services. The household incomes have to be used first to get these essentials. There are many goods and services that individuals/households would consume if they had incomes over and above for meeting their essential needs. These goods and services might increase their comfort/enjoyment of life or might be of the nature of luxuries. A great proportion of households are income constrained and therefore, if there is a higher incidence of GST on essential goods and services, they might not be able to maintain their normal standard of life.

The rates of GST applied on individual or class of goods and services need to be conscious of this economic and consumption reality.

Most economists tend to favour a single uniform rate of GST on account of its efficiency in tax management treating all the goods and services of the same utility nature. This, however, is not the right approach. The basic structure of indirect taxation or GST rates should be to tax low value added margin and essential goods at low rates. Goods and services which have reasonable value added margins or which are of the nature of comfort goods should be taxed at medium rates. The goods and services that have high value added margins or are of the nature of luxury should be taxed at relatively high rates of GST. Finally, a limited number of goods which are of the nature of sin or are of undesirable consumption from a social point of view, should be taxed at the highest rates of GST.

India's GST rate structure is riddled with considerable misapplication of GST rates. Further, the highest rate of 28 per cent is too high and 0/1 per cent and 5 per cent is quite low. Some goods are subject to a high rate of cess as well, making the real incidence of GST on these goods unconscionably high.

There is need to rationalize the GST tax structure. It might be advisable to design a three- rate tax structure—8 per cent, 14 per cent and 20 per cent—and to subject all goods and services by classifying these in these three categories taking into consideration the nature of margins and consumption.

Reforming Customs Taxation

Customs duties should essentially be viewed as similar to value-added tax on goods and services produced abroad. The goods and services imported should therefore suffer the same rate of goods and service tax as similar goods and services when produced domestically suffer. After the introduction of GST, these duties are levied on all imported goods (earlier as countervailing or additional customs duties)

In addition, basic customs duties are charged on most imported items at rates prescribed in the Customs Tariff Act. In principle, these customs duties act like additional excise duties/GST imposed. These basic customs duties end up effectively raising the level of GST imposed on imported goods. In that sense, these provide extra protection to the domestic producers of the goods and services.

For Indian industry and service providers to become internationally competitive, the whole scheme of customs duty should be reviewed to place basic customs duties only on three kinds of items: sin goods like alcohol and cigarettes; items where India has a natural comparative disadvantage, e.g., palm oil, gold, coal, etc.; and commodities and services susceptible to dumping.

For the rest of the items, customs duties should either be abolished or reduced to very low levels.

Reforming State-Level Remaining Indirect Taxes

Most indirect taxes levied at the state level have been subsumed in GST. However, some goods and services still remain outside the GST system. Alcoholic drinks, narcotic substances, entertainment taxes and electricity duty are a few prominent sets of goods and services that are outside the GST system still.

There is a need to reform the system of taxation of these goods and services. As the revenues of these taxes accrue entirely to the states and the states would be reluctant to cede their control over taxation of these goods and services after experiencing the GST system, it would be advisable to reform the taxation of these goods and services on the pattern of GST but outside the GST system.

On the pattern of taxation of petroleum products proposed above, the states can do an exercise to divide their current total revenues from excise duties and narcotics substances into GST-like revenue which would accrue to them at the maximum rate of GST and the remaining revenue. The states can impose GST at the maximum applicable rate and the rest of the revenue collected can be converted into a fixed rate excise duty. With this, the system of administration of excise duties on alcoholic products and narcotics substances can be aligned with the GST system.

Entertainment taxes and electricity duties can be similarly administered as a GST-like duty choosing an applicable rate of GST as charge.

Taxing Wealth

A portfolio of assets is wealth. Wealth usually comprises three types of assets.

First, financial wealth, which can be in numerous forms: stocks, bonds, deposits, currency, insurance policies, MF units, REITs and many others.

Second, physical wealth, which can also be in many forms: land, buildings, apartments, shops, rights in mines, furniture, machines, artworks and numerous others.

Third, intellectual and invisible assets, which, again, can be in myriad forms: brands, goodwill, copyrights and crypto-assets, for example.

There is negative wealth as well, which we call debt or liabilities.

GDP is the measure of goods and services produced and consumed in a year and also the capital formed during the year. Goods and services produced and consumed do not constitute wealth. It is the capital—physical, financial and intellectual—created during the year that gets added to wealth.

Global wealth grew massively in the twentieth century and continues to grow rapidly in the twenty-first century.

Taxation of wealth has been mixed up broadly as taxation of income or aggregated income thus far. It needs to be treated and taxed as wealth now.

Taxation of Wealth in India

Elements of wealth have been recognized in the Indian Constitution and allocated to the Centre and the states in their respective lists.

Taxes on capital value of the assets, exclusive of agricultural land, of individuals and companies and taxes on the capital of companies have been allocated to the Centre (Entry 86).

Estate duty, which is the taxation of wealth upon death of the wealth holder, with respect to property other than agricultural land is also with the Centre (Entry 87).

Duties with respect to succession to property other than agricultural land is also in the central domain (Entry 88).

Rates of stamp duty on transactions in stock exchanges and future markets (Entry 91) is within Central jurisdiction. These duties are collected and appropriated by the states.

Duties with respect to succession to agricultural land (Entry 47) and estate duty with respect to agricultural land (Entry 48), taxes on lands and buildings (Entry 49), taxes on mineral rights subject to any limitations imposed by the Parliament by law relating to mineral development (Entry

50) and rates of stamp duty with respect to documents other than those specified in the provisions of list one with respect to rates of duty (Entry 63) are all assigned to the states.

There is quite a fragmented and disjointed system of wealth taxation in the country.

After abolition of the Wealth Tax Act, 1957, in 2014, there is no assessment of wealth in the hands of an individual or household in the country. There is no tax on wealth as such in the country currently. However, transfer of wealth results in incidence of taxes. The Government of India imposes tax on the capital gains made at the time of transfer of assets. There are different rates of taxes on different types of assets and on the same assets held from different dates and for a different time. Capital gains are taxed more like income taxation and taxed under income tax laws. The states tax the transfer value of assets as such by collecting stamp duty on most of them. Mineral assets and many other natural resources suffer taxes differently: one time or periodic.

The surfeit of global savings, easy credit and monetary policies have contributed to asset valuations rising massively, lowering underlying interest rates. This in turn has raised valuation of financial assets as well. The global wealth is many times of global GDP now and there are millions of millionaires and billionaires in the world now. Unfortunately, there is no tax on valuation gains over assets at all. The wealth, which should pay good tax, pays no tax on uncashed valuation gains and low tax or no tax on cashing of valuation gains.

The taxation of wealth needs a complete makeover.

Wealth Tax Act, 1957

The Wealth Tax Act, 1957, as originally enacted, was a simpler construct, though it had excluded several assets from its scope. Wealth was defined as 'assets' which included property of every description, movable or immovable, except agricultural land, agricultural building, livestock and the right to any annuity or any interest in property where such annuity or interest was for a period not exceeding five years. The tax was leviable on 'net wealth' (the amount by which the aggregate value computed in accordance with the provisions of the Act on the valuation date exceeded the aggregate value of all the debts owned by the assessee on the valuation date).

Wealth tax was not payable with respect to property held under trust or other legal obligation for religious or charitable purposes within India, interest in the coparcenary property of any Hindu Undivided Family, any works of art, archaeological, scientific or art collections, books, manuscripts or heirlooms, the right of the assessee to receive a pension or other life annuity, rights under any patent or copyright, domestic animals and furniture, household utensils, jewellery (subject to a maximum value), the right or interest of the assessee in any policy of insurance, tools and instruments necessary for carrying on profession or vocation, ten-year treasury savings deposit certificates, postal savings certificates and deposits, any deposit made by the assessee with the government or in any security of the government or of a local authority and amount in the credit to the provident fund. Property outside India was also excluded.

The definition of assets kept getting modified. Major amendments were carried out in 1969, 1970, 1981 and 1993. With these amendments, the definition kept getting increasingly complicated and the net of exemptions wider. Building was included but a house meant exclusively for residential purposes and one allotted by a company to an employee or an officer in whole-time employment with a gross annual salary of less than Rs 5 lakh was excluded. Any house for residential or commercial purposes that forms part of stock in trade and any house the assessee may occupy for the purposes of any business or profession carried on and residential property that had been let out for a minimum period of 300 days in the previous year and any property in the nature of commercial establishments or complexes was excluded. It is easy to imagine the kind of complexities wealth tax had gotten into. There were numerous other complications relating to other assets.

Wealth tax yielded a meagre amount of Rs 154 crore in 1993–94 (CIT, or corporate income tax, Rs 10,060 crore, PIT Rs 9123 crore). It declined rapidly for the next four years (Rs 105 crore in 1994–95, Rs 74 crore in 1995–96 and Rs 78 crore in 1996–97). It received a leg-up in 1998–99 when it reached Rs 162 crore and then again declined and remained static in the range of Rs 120–150 crore until 2004–05. In 2005–06, it increased somewhat to Rs 250 crore but its share had fallen very low in direct taxes (CIT Rs 1,01,277 crore and PIT Rs 63,629 crore). It increased steadily thereafter and grew to Rs 950 crore in 2013–14 and 2014–15. Its share in gross tax revenues was, however, less than 0.1 per cent. It had become completely insignificant.

The government abolished wealth tax in 2014–15 and replaced it with 2 per cent surcharge that yielded thirty times more revenue.

Fundamental Issues with the Present System of Taxation of Wealth

There is need for a fundamental rethink on taxation of wealth. Let us begin by understanding wealth and its taxation in India. There are five stylized characteristics/facts.

First, there are two primary kinds of income or gains that accrue to the holder from wealth. First, the assets when given to others for use yield income for the holder. Financial savings given as loans yield interest and those invested as equity yield dividend. Likewise, a house given on lease yields rent and intellectual property given out for use yields royalties. The assets retained by the holder for self-use do not result in an income (though it might save expenditure, but that is not income earned) but might appreciate in value.

Second, the assets when sold or rights transferred therein may result in realized or cashed capital gains.

Third, there are three kinds of income and gains that accrue from the asset/wealth: income from use of the asset by others, valuation gains and capital gains on transfer.

Fourth, the present system of wealth taxation is very convoluted and complex on account of its historical evolution. Rent from leasing of land or building is rightly assessed as income for tax purposes. However, capital value of the land and building suffers two taxes at the time of its transfer. State governments collect stamp duty on the entire value of the asset and the Central government taxes the capital gains. The interest earned on bonds kept for less than three years suffers income tax but kept for more than three years is treated as capital gains and subjected to a lower rate of interest. Royalties earned on allowing the use of technological innovation suffer royalty as well as income tax. There is no depreciation permitted either.

Fifth, valuation gains suffer no tax on holding but suffer massive taxation on transfer.

Reforming the Wealth Taxation System

Taking into consideration the key characteristics of wealth, basic reforms are required in the system of taxation of wealth.

Income from the use of wealth should be taxed only as income. All types of incomes from all kinds of assets should be recognized as a separate part in the income tax code and taxed. This we have discussed in taxation of income.

The system of taxing gains/profit on transfer should be streamlined and integrated. Stamp duties on transfer of assets should be abolished. Only the capital gains on the transfer of assets should be taxed.

All assets, physical, financial or intellectual, should be subjected to wealth transfer tax at a uniform rate, which can be equal to the modal rate of tax on value added, say 20 per cent. The system of price indexation should be built in as price increase on account of inflation cannot be considered a capital gain or profit.

Wealth transfer tax should be considered on a par with the GST system and divided in two parts, like SGST and CGST. This will also take care of the loss of capital gains taxation by the Centre and stamp duty taxation loss by the states besides simplifying the entire taxation of assets transfer. The GST Council can be renamed the Wealth and GST Council.

For assessing the valuation gains made on wealth, an annual return of wealth should be introduced on the lines of an annual return of income. All assets should be included in this return with the valuation done by the owner (certified by a chartered accountant or other valuers) on the basis of general valuation principles determined by the government. No exemption of any kind whether financial assets or one house or whatever needs to be provided in terms of listing and valuation of assets.

There should be no need to get valuation verified by the departmental officers, except on the basis of scrutiny of only about 0.5 per cent of returns.

A small tax on the valuation gains made during the year on the total portfolio of assets should be imposed—say at the rate of 2 per cent assessed and payable every year. The government can also create a class of extraordinary or super valuation gains, say, exceeding Rs 10 crore in a year, which should be subjected to a higher wealth tax of 5 per cent on the valuation gains made over Rs 10 crore.

The tax on valuation gains so assessed can be paid either in cash or transferring a part of the financial asset.

Introduction of a New Pollution and Carbon Tax

The businesses create positive value added. They also contribute negative value added. All the pollutants, including carbon, emitted or discharged in the air, water and soil, affect the quality of air, water and soil and, in turn, the quality of life. Positive value added in goods and services contribute to the maintenance of humans and their quality of life, whereas the negative value added adversely impacts them and their quality of life.

Businesses have gotten away with discharging the pollutants, including carbon, imposing these costs on people and planet without being asked to pay for the same. The time has come to make the businesses internalize these costs. This can be done by imposing a new Pollution and Carbon Tax linked to the negative value added to the environment.

India's Efforts at Imposing Carbon Tax

Coal and other fossil fuels contribute considerable negative value added in the form of CO_2, NOx, SOx and other pollutants like mercury, etc. India imposed a cess on coal in the year 2010 as additional excise duty, which was like a carbon tax. The government amended the law to take authority to impose this cess at the rate of Rs 100 per tonne, but started with a cess of Rs 50 per ton on coal. The cess was raised from time to time. In 2014–15, it was raised to Rs 100 per ton, in 2015–16 to Rs 200 per ton and finally to Rs 400 per ton. The cess on coal, also known as clean energy cess, was abolished in 2017 when GST was introduced and the same amount was collected as GST Compensation Cess to pay the shortfall on projected GST revenues of states. The cess on coal still operates as GST Compensation Cess.

India Needs a Comprehensive Pollution and Carbon Tax

Carbon emergency has acquired real international crisis proportion. The movement to get to net zero emissions globally by 2050 has gathered considerable traction. There is a definite need for India to also contribute imaginatively and meaningfully to the international efforts to get to net zero by 2050.

India also suffers the more immediate problem of high pollution. Life in Delhi gets disrupted in November–December every year with the quality of life as measured by the air quality index (AQI) going down to the very poor and severe category—sometimes getting into the unfit to live grade of more than 500 AQI. More than seventeen of the top twenty most polluted cities in the world are Indian. We need to sort out the pollution problem as well.

A good and equitable measure in this regard is to impose a Pollution and Carbon Tax linked to the negative value added by businesses measured in terms of CO_2 equivalent for carbon emissions and a robust pollutant equivalent for all other pollutants (let us call it PO_2 equivalent for the present). Businesses can be subjected to preparing an account of the CO_2 and PO_2 contributed by them during the year while producing their goods and services. Businesses can be given credit for the CO_2 and PO_2 embedded in the inputs bought by them from their suppliers.

A scale of taxation can be designed to pay pollution and carbon tax for the net CO_2 and PO_2 (or the negative value added) contributed by a business at the rates specified by the government. The rates can be determined and applied to the industries/businesses over a period of time for the businesses to get time to adjust.

This tax will make every business/industry completely conscious of the negative contribution their businesses make to society. This sensitization would also help the businesses look for solutions to reduce and eliminate the carbon and pollution footprint of their activities.

The government can also introduce a positive incentive to the businesses whose pollution and carbon account turns out to be in the negative, meaning that they actually emitted less carbon and pollution than what was contained in the inputs they used.

Reforming System of Natural Resources Taxation

Democracies work on a system of private property. Most physical properties like lands and buildings have been privatized over a period of time. Earlier, land used to be the property of the king/state and the revenues of governments primarily came from land revenues collected from the use of lands for raising crops. In India, land revenues do not contribute anything meaningful to the resources of the state governments to which land is assigned as a subject.

The resources underneath the land, however, belong to the state. As the womb of the earth has enormously valuable natural resources—crude oil, gas, coal, iron ore, other minerals and metals—governments do get significant revenues by auctioning, concessioning or otherwise permitting the use of these natural resources. Natural invisible resources over the land—spectrum, etc.—also belong to the state. As the development of technology allows these electromagnetic sounds and other waves to be harnessed, these resources have emerged as valuable contributors to the revenue of the state. There are also valuable resources in the seas and oceans where governments have rights, as well as in space. These resources can also contribute to the revenue of governments.

There are various modes in which governments can collect revenues on these resources. These resources can be simply auctioned off to the highest bidder for one-time or staggered payments. They can be auctioned with the government share linked to revenues generated from the use of the resources. They can also be placed under PSUs with the profit generated accruing to the government. There can be other structures as well. In essence, the government gets a share of the value added generated from the natural resource used.

There is no organized system of inventory of natural and other common resources of the government and designing the most appropriate manner of making the most productive use of these resources for society and the economy and generating optimum revenues in the process. The system gets more complicated and confused when governments decide to reserve such mineral, metal and other natural resource rights for public-sector enterprises.

The system of managing sovereign natural resources needs to be streamlined along the following lines:

First, create a Ministry of Natural Resources to inventorize all natural resources, make a policy for their exploration and exploitation, and for selling or granting rights and concessions. This ministry may not control actual management of natural resources, which may remain with existing or reorganized ministries and departments dealing with minerals, coal, petroleum products, spectrum, etc.

Second, a separate ledger head should be created in the financial and budgetary accounting system to capture revenues from natural resources recorded and analysed with as much detail and precision as is done for tax revenues.

Third, the system of giving away these natural resources should be simplified and designed such that these are given away by means of simple leases and concession agreements that are comparable and understandable, and promote optimal use of resources from the viewpoints of society and the economy.

Fourth, the share of the government in the revenues generated by the use of these natural resources and rights should be so designed that the revenue it gets is relatable to value added created from using the resources. This will maximize the revenues of the government as well as the value added for the economy.

Such a system would put the natural resources of the country to best service and contribute a growing share of revenues for the government. It would also contribute to achieving the $10 trillion goal.

Chapter Fifty-Nine

Debt Reforms

FRBM Act is Dead

Ever since the Fiscal Responsibility and Budget Management Act (FRBM Act) was enacted in 2003–04, India has revised and reaffirmed its commitment to the elusive fiscal deficit target of 3 per cent of GDP three times. The last restatement was made in 2018–19. The Act was amended by the Finance Bill, 2018, to specifically state two commitments: to reduce fiscal deficit to 3 per cent by 2020–21 and maintain it, or go lower thereafter; and to bring the government's debt and liabilities to less than 40 per cent of GDP by 2024–25.

Fiscal developments after 2018–19 did not ensure adherence to these two statutory commitments.

India revised its fiscal deficit from 3.5 per cent in financial year 2017–18 and announced its headline fiscal deficit (the number in the Budget papers representing the fiscal deficit in the CFI) at 3.3 per cent for financial year 2018–19 (some expenditures/investments were pushed off-budget). Some further compression was expected in 2019–20 to finally achieve the 3 per cent target in 2020–21. However, budget management for the financial year 2018–19 and thereafter turned out to be more difficult than planned. The headline fiscal deficit came to Rs 9.34 lakh crore in 2019–20, which was as high as 4.6 per cent of the GDP. The fiscal deficit math went out of any consolidation arc completely in 2020–21. This fiscal deficit was projected, in the revised estimates, to be 9.5 per cent of GDP. The budget estimates of 2021–22 pegged it at 6.8 per cent.

Likewise, the debt and liabilities trajectory moved in the opposite direction than expected while fixing the deadline of 2024–25 to achieve a 40 per cent debt to GDP ratio.

The Economic Survey 2020–21 argued for debt-funded growth, singing the virtues of growth, however funded, over the irritants of fiscal deficits, debts and credit ratings. While the finance minister talked about introducing an amendment to the FRBM Act in the Budget speech, in effect the Act has been given a literal burial. With the government talking of continuing 'with our path of fiscal consolidation' and intention 'to reach a fiscal deficit level below 4.5 per cent of GDP by 2025–2026', the FRBM Act is as good as dead.

Eliminate All Non-Market Borrowings?

India's Central Government Market Loans Were a Little Less than 60 Per Cent in 2019–20

Taking Budget numbers into consideration, India's market loans (these are made up of government securities issued for terms higher than one year, that may also go up to forty to fifty years) were Rs 59.86 lakh crore in 2019–20. In addition, the outstanding amount of treasury bills (short-term government securities of less than one year; usually for three months) were for Rs 6.14 lakh crore. Together, these market borrowings constituted Rs 66 lakh crore of liabilities. As total liabilities were Rs 102.47 lakh crore, the longer-term market borrowings were a little higher than 58 per cent of total liabilities, whereas total market borrowings were 64.4 per cent.

The rest of borrowings were made up of myriad sources of funding. These borrowings included Rs 2.51 lakh crore worth of special securities issued to PSBs to fund their recapitalization, and securities issued to NSSF against borrowing of small savings of Rs 8.49 lakh crore.

There were a few other types of special securities and bonds issued, including securities issued to international financial institutions like IMF, World Bank and ADB of Rs 1.02 lakh crore and special security issued against securitization balance under the Postal Life Insurance Fund

(POLIF) of Rs 0.21 lakh crore. External debt was, at historical values, of Rs 2.99 lakh crore. Borrowings from NSSF, other than the securities issued to the Central government, were Rs 9.33 lakh crore. The liabilities of the provident fund balances of Central government employees, recorded as State Provident Fund, myriad sources were to the tune of Rs 2.28 lakh crore. The special securities issued through the Public Account for paying dues to oil and fertilizer companies were worth Rs 1.63 lakh crore and other items Rs 2.71 lakh crore. Together, these other accounts liabilities made up Rs 4.34 lakh crore. Lastly, reserve funds and deposits had a balance of Rs 3.32 lakh crore.

Non-Market Special Securities, Including FSBs, Need to Be Eliminated

All the special securities issued, other than those to international financial institutions and banks/domestic financial institutions for recapitalization, are carry-overs of the past.

The special securities issued to PSBs, EXIM Bank, IIFCL and IDBI Bank were used to provide equity capital investment to these public-sector entities. These banks and institutions were required to invest in these special securities, which they got back as equity. Equity infusion is a legitimate capital expenditure/investment of the government as long as these entities remain in the public sector and require capital. The government should have provided equity support by borrowing from the market. This would have led to proper accounting of the investment made and depicted the correct fiscal deficit.

Special securities issued to POLIF are also a relic of the past. Earlier, many retirement and long-term savings institutions like EPFO and POLIF were allowed to invest in special government securities. EPFO has moved to investing in government securities through the market mechanism. This also gives EPFO the full flexibility to make investments at the market-determined rate and sell government securities when considered appropriate. POLIF special securities should also be paid off and POLIF asked to make appropriate investments through the market.

Special securities in the form of oil bonds and fertilizer bonds have not been issued after 2009. The oil bonds and fertilizer bonds would get paid off at the beginning of financial year 2021–22. No special action needed to be taken for the same.

The two kinds of special securities issued by the NDA government needed to be dealt with. FSBs, or fully serviced bonds, which began to be issued from financial year 2016–17 have not been proposed to be issued for financial year 2021–22. The last bunch of such securities were issued in 2020–21. While there is nothing that stops the Government of India from issuing FSBs again as these were not subject to Parliamentary approvals, it is expected that these would not be issued. The government is now quite comfortable in enlarging the fiscal deficit.

The special securities issued to banks and other financial institutions for financing their capitalization are a drag on the Government of India and also constrain the ability of banks to manage their treasury. It will be advisable if these special securities are swapped with regular market securities by the Government of India. This will lead to a nominal increase in fiscal deficit one time, which should not matter as there would be no increase in the outstanding debt and liabilities of the Government of India.

NSSF and Small Savings Reforms

People's Access to Savings Investment Instruments Have Changed Materially

The small savings system evolved in the country from the 1950s to the 1980s, when the government had the widest reach to people through the network of field functionaries and post offices. Banks were present only in cities, and that too in much smaller numbers. Funds were needed for government schemes and capital investment. Small savings schemes served both purposes: to raise funds for the government and provide an avenue of savings for people, especially agricultural and rural people.

Much has changed. The banking network has expanded all over the country, including in very small villages, and is accessible to every individual and household in the country with the digital footprint expanding massively.

In this day and age of widespread banking and digital banking enabled by omnipresent mobile phone networks, there is no need for the government to provide an avenue for people to park their savings. With almost universal Jan Dhan accounts in the banking system (we need to convert these zero minimum deposit accounts into normal savings accounts to enable poor people to use the entire set of banking services), there is absolutely no necessity for savings bank account services to be provided by post offices.

The inability of the government to adjust small savings schemes rates from time to time to align with the market rates of savings for the same maturity, including in the banking system, results in the effective cost of small savings instruments remaining higher. The government also uses these instruments to serve its social objectives like paying off-market rates to senior citizens and the girl child. These may be desirable objectives but they make the small savings instrument distort the financial savings market. The government ends up getting excessive flows in small savings schemes. The cost of administration of these schemes is also relatively much higher as the administrative cost of post offices is far higher.

As these cost elements make the effective interest cost of small savings much higher than the interest rates state governments pay on their market loans, states have stopped taking loans from the NSSF. Even in the year of COVID-19, states have not taken loans from small savings despite their finances coming under heavy strain.

RBI has introduced reforms to enable the participation of small savers in government securities. Recently, RBI created a facility for direct bond subscription for retailers (RBI Retail Direct) by allowing retail buyers to open and maintain an account (Retail Direct Gilt Account) with RBI. This platform and account will give retail subscribers access to primary issuance of government securities and access to Negotiated Dealing System-Order Matching or NDS OM for selling and buying government securities.

Some corporates like PFC have come up with retail corporate bond issues.

The government has also introduced Exchange Traded Bond Funds. Retail investors can participate in all these avenues. The smallest savers in rural areas can participate in the banking system through their Jan Dhan accounts and using digital channels.

Investment Avenues for NSSF Funds Have Also Dried Up

Aggregate deposits/balances in these small savings accounts at the end of financial year 2019–20 were Rs 17.82 lakh crore. These are estimated to be Rs 20.92 lakh crore at the end of 2020–21 as per the revised estimates presented at the time of Budget 2021–22. These are expected to further rise to Rs 24.33 lakh crore at the end of financial year 2021–22 as per estimates in Budget 2021–22. Small savings outstanding balances have grown at a much higher rate in the years 2019–20 and 2020 on account of non-revision of higher than market interest rates on small savings instruments.

The savings of people invested in NSSF, like savings invested in MFs, are in a way assets under management (AUM) of the government. AUMs with all the MFs were about Rs 32 lakh crore at the end of 2020–21. AUMs under NSSF were about Rs 21 lakh crore at this time.

Until financial year 2020–21, there were primarily four investment avenues for small savings flows: investment in special securities issued by the Centre; investment in special securities issued by state governments; loans to the public enterprises and authorities of the Government of India; and, finally, partly meeting the fiscal deficit with cash balances lying uninvested. In addition, the Central government has liability towards accumulated losses in NSSF.

The Central government issues three kinds of special securities to the NSSF: against balances on 31 March 1999, the day the NSSF arrangement came into being (earlier the Centre used to provide small savings loans against accruals of small savings in the states from the CFI); against fresh accumulations in NSSF from 1 April 1999; and against redemption of special securities by the Centre and states.

On 31 March 2020, net investment in these three types of securities was Rs 64,567 crore, Rs 3,86,897 crore and Rs 3,97,453 crore respectively, amounting to Rs 8,48,917 crore in total. Outstanding balance of securities issued by the states as on 31 March 2020 amounted to Rs 4,40,438 crore.

The Centre started using funds in NSSF to provide loans to Central government entities from financial year 2016–17. The first such loan was made to FCI when a Rs 70,000 crore loan was extended (repayable in five annual instalments) in lieu of food subsidy claims for 2016–17. In

2017–18, this practice was extended to other PSUs and authorities for both investment and subsidy support. In 2020–21, NSSF loans to FCI were cleared up and the practice of food subsidy paid through NSSF loans stopped. Other investment avenues for investing NSSF AUM also dried up.

Almost the entire net inflow in NSSF in 2021–22 had to be taken by the Government of India. NSSF has become a government financing vehicle only and the government ends up accepting these inflows at costs much higher than the market borrowings.

Government Introduces a New Saving Instrument

In June 2020, the government introduced a new small savings instrument: a variable interest rate bond. This new savings bond is a floating rate taxable savings bond. The first and initial coupon was fixed at 7.15 per cent. The coupon would be reset half yearly from 1 January 2021. The coupon rate, in principle, will be pegged with the prevailing National Savings Certificate (NSC) rate with a spread of 35 basis points over the respective NSC rate.

The variable bond replaced the savings bonds (commonly known as RBI bonds) offered by the government that had a fixed interest rate of 7.75 per cent. The RBI bonds stopped selling from 28 May 2020. The key difference is that the earlier one was fixed and this will be floating, and can thus work as an inflation hedge while saving the government from higher cost when rates are low. However, much will depend upon the ability and willingness of the government to adjust the interest rates of the NSC. If these are not adjusted, the variable saving bond rates will also remain unchanged.

It Is Time to Wind-Up

It is time the Government of India starts winding up the small savings schemes beginning with discontinuing the certificates like National Small Savings Certificates and Kisan Vikas Patras immediately. New fixed and recurring deposits should also be stopped. Post office savings bank accounts should stop accepting deposits from the next financial year.

PPF deposits should be allowed to be transferred to NPS accounts. This would leave only certain special deposits like those for senior citizens, the girl child, etc. These deposit accounts should be transferred to SBI with the interest rate difference being provided by the government as fiscal subsidy.

Sovereign Bonds or Special Securities?

Government Has Shied Away from Issuing Foreign Currency Sovereign Bonds

The Government of India raises debt by issuing government securities (g-secs). These sovereign bonds are issued in the Indian domestic market and are denominated in Indian rupees. If g-secs are issued in foreign markets and denominated in specified foreign currency, they would acquire the character of foreign currency-denominated sovereign bonds. Countries with complete capital account convertibility issue foreign currency-denominated debt securities or sovereign bonds even in the domestic market. India does not have capital account convertibility to this extent and the government has not issued any foreign currency-denominated sovereign bonds in external markets since Independence.

As per the data available on the site of the Bank of International Settlements (BIS), a total of $24.86 trillion (India's GDP is less than $3 trillion dollars currently) international debt securities were outstanding at the end of March 2020. International debt securities issued by governments exceeded $2 trillion. India is the only G-20 country that has not issued a government bond in foreign markets.

In Budget 2019–20, the government announced its intention to issue sovereign bonds. Para 103 of the Budget speech expressed the same in clear terms:

'India's sovereign external debt to GDP is among the lowest globally at less than 5 per cent. The government would start raising a part of its gross borrowing programme in external markets in external currencies. This will also have beneficial impact on demand situation for government securities in the domestic market.'

The finance secretary had indicated that 10 per cent of the annual bond-raising programme, or about Rs 70,000 crore ($10 billion), might be raised in the form of sovereign bonds. The announcement led to a protest by RBI, a number of economists including former RBI governors, and traditionalist outfits like the Swadeshi Jagran Manch. The issue was quietly buried in the latter part of financial year 2019–20.

Special Government Securities for Increasing Foreign Currency Flows

Budget 2020–21 sang a different tune. Arguing that it was necessary to encourage flow of external capital in India's financial system to achieve aspirational growth, in para 100 (1) it announced that 'certain specified categories of government securities would be opened fully for non-resident investors, apart from being available to domestic investors as well'.

RBI implemented this announcement on 30 March 2020, opening a 'Fully Accessible Route' (FAR) for investment by non-residents in government securities. FAR permitted any 'person resident outside India' to invest in 'government securities as periodically notified by the Reserve Bank for investment under the FAR route' (specified securities) without being subject to the limits for foreigners' investment specified under the FPI route currently in operation. Essentially, new investments by FPIs in specified securities are subject to no caps. Even if 100 per cent of a specified security is subscribed to or purchased by non-residents, RBI would be fine with it.

The rationale provided by the government for FAR was India's inclusion in international bond indices, which is likely to result in flow of extra debt resources. The authorities are working with prominent international bond indices like JP Morgan Emerging Market Bond Index and Bloomberg Barclays Global Aggregate Bond Index. However, inclusion in any of the bond indices is still to take place at the end of calendar year 2021.

Difference between FC Sovereign Bond Issuance and Rupee-Specified Securities

There are significant differences in the implications of FC sovereign bonds and specified securities issued under FAR (rupee-specified securities) for fiscal operations, monetary policy, foreign exchange management, interest rate in the system, and so on.

First, the issuer, the Government of India, receives debt subscriptions in different currencies. In case of US dollar-denominated sovereign bonds issued and listed abroad, it receives US dollars in its account. The government can, of course, sell the US dollars so received to RBI for rupees. In case of rupee-specified securities, the subscription to the government is in rupees. Foreign subscribers would usually bring US dollars or other foreign currencies to India to subscribe to such securities. However, they might also borrow or use other funds available in India to subscribe to such bonds in rupees.

Second, the net inflow of foreign currency desired and in which the bonds are denominated would be different in the two cases as far as the economy is concerned. In case of dollar-denominated sovereign bonds, the government would receive only dollars. In case of rupee-specified securities, the real subscriptions from foreigners/non-residents can be in dollars, other foreign currencies or even in rupees. FC sovereign bonds could be better in terms of targeting the inflow of any specific foreign currency.

Third, foreign holders of bonds desiring to encash would be able to sell their holdings on the exchange where such bonds are listed. Other non-residents would normally buy such securities offered for sale. Flows to the Indian economy remain unaffected as the entire trade gets settled abroad. In case of rupee-specified securities, there is outflow of foreign currency from India. Rupee securities held by a non-resident would be sold on an Indian exchange or in the over-the-counter (OTC) market to another non-resident or resident. In either case, the seller wishing to redeem the securities would take the money back by taking US dollars for the rupee proceeds of the securities sold. There is a higher likelihood of foreign currency invested in rupee securities resulting in the outflow of foreign currency for bonds sold by non-residents in case of rupee-specified securities than FC sovereign bonds.

Fourth, demand for Indian securities improves equally in both cases, though the manner of improvement is different. In case of FC sovereign bonds, the supply of rupee-denominated securities reduces by the amount of foreign currency-denominated sovereign bonds issued, which is good for the demand-supply situation. In case of rupee-specified securities, the demand for government securities improves, which has a favourable impact on the demand-supply situation of government securities.

Fifth, there are different implications when the rupee is under pressure on account of factors like sharply rising oil prices, the Indian government running heavy deficits or the economy faring badly. In such situations, there is a clear tendency among FPIs to sell at least part of their rupee securities and repatriate the proceeds. Such behaviour puts additional pressure on the rupee. In case of FC sovereign bonds, the buy-and-sell action can take place only among foreign holders. Their actions cannot put any additional pressure on the Indian rupee as the demand-supply situation is not adversely affected.

Sixth, the possibility of manipulating the rupee exchange rate is theoretically higher in case of FC sovereign bonds than rupee-specified securities. In case speculators decide to mount an assault on the rupee, they can drive down prices on FC sovereign bonds by aggressively selling them. This is not even theoretically possible in the case of rupee-specified securities. The likelihood of any speculative attack on Indian currency is as good as non-existent as India is a large economy, has large foreign exchange reserves, low foreign exchange liability and, at present, has no foreign currency bonds issued. For even such a possibility to emerge, India has to have a large stock of foreign currency-denominated bonds outstanding in the market.

Seventh, there are good savings on the interest payment liability of the government in case of FC sovereign bonds compared to rupee-specified securities. Rate of interest payable on rupee securities is far higher than in the case of foreign currency sovereign bonds. There would be some offset in savings on account of the likely depreciation of the rupee over the period of the bond while repaying the principal proceeds. On the whole, however, the likelihood of significant net interest savings is much higher and will remain so for a long time in view of the massive savings glut and quantitative easing policies of advanced countries.

Eighth, sovereign bonds create a good external currency-financing yield curve for India whereas specified securities under FAR fragment the government securities market. On account of different rules applicable to foreign participation in specified securities and other securities issued by the Government of India, which are otherwise the same in every other respect, the demand-supply situation for these two sets of securities become different, which will have an impact on their yields and liquidity.

Issue of Foreign Currency Sovereign Bonds Would Be a Good Policy

Indian companies and financial institutions have been raising foreign currency bonds for quite some time, though the government has not issued such bonds yet. At the end of June 2020, total outstanding external currency bonds issued by Indian corporates amounted to Rs 3.3 lakh crore or about $44.63 billion (at Rs 74 to a dollar).

There is a very strong case for India to initiate the issue of foreign currency-denominated sovereign bonds in external markets. If the government were to raise 10 per cent of annual borrowing, or about Rs 70,000–1,00,000 crore a year, in foreign currency bonds, the country would be able to build a portfolio of about $50–60 billion sovereign bonds in about five years and a $100 billion portfolio over ten years. Thereafter, there would be only incremental addition as there will also be repayments of the bonds issued. Assuming India's GDP to be about Rs 5 trillion after five years, such a bond portfolio would be only about 1 per cent of GDP. It might still be lower than even 10 per cent of India's foreign exchange reserves and smaller than the portfolio of foreign currency bonds issued by the private and public-sector financial and non-financial corporations.

First, the interest cost of government borrowing can be minimized, taking advantage of lower interest rates prevalent abroad, especially in advanced markets. India can borrow at good rates applicable to advanced countries.

Second, the sovereign bonds raised abroad would correspondingly reduce the supply of government bonds in domestic markets. As the government's general fiscal deficit is very high (over 7 per cent of GDP on average a year) and financial savings in the economy are very low (less than 10 per cent of GDP a year), the reduction in supply of government borrowing on account of foreign currency bonds would have a favourable impact on government bond rates, which also feeds into lowering of corporate borrowing rates.

Third, sovereign bond rates have a bearing on bond rates available to private and public-sector financial and non-financial companies when they raise bonds abroad. Sovereign bond rates also work as a benchmark. The availability of a sovereign bond rate curve considerably aids borrowings by Indian companies.

Fourth, India is still a capital-deficient country. Growth will require considerable financing from abroad, equity and debt. Sovereign bonds will help bring this capital to India.

Fifth, sovereign bonds are issued by all major countries, including developing countries. Such bonds are standard practice. Therefore, there is no artificiality or novelty about sovereign bonds as a means of raising external debt. Specified securities under FAR are artificial devices that are not easily understood by everyone. This is likely to confuse foreign investors as well as debt index creator institutions.

In view of the above, there is a lot of merit in the government overcoming its shyness and initiating a well-crafted, long-term sovereign bond issuance programme.

Chapter Sixty

Destination 2035

Real Economy Today

Today, India, seventy-five years young as an independent country, is a diversified $3 trillion real economy, with roughly one-sixth of goods and services each produced in agriculture, manufacturing and government. The services sector exceeds half of the real economy. There are two relatively minor sectors of mining and quarrying, and utilities. The construction sector has grown into a significant size of the economy.

India's growth rate has been quite low in the second decade of the twenty-first century, with a slowing economy turning out poor growth in the 2010–2013 and 2017–2019 periods with unprecedented contraction of over 7 per cent in 2020–21, though followed by recovery of 9 per cent in 2021–22.

On the consumption side, roughly 70 per cent is accounted for by private and government consumption and 30 per cent of GDP income gets invested in capital formation. Consumption had been a major growth support from 2014–2018 but started flagging from 2018. Investments/ capital formation have considerably weakened with domestic savings rates and investments falling from the peak of 35–36 per cent in the first decade to the bottom of 28–30 per cent in the second decade (ignoring the exceptionally bad year of 2020).

The government's taxation revenues have stagnated (there are some signs of the tide turning in 2021–22 but that may not last long as fundamental revenue dynamism is still lacking). GST, introduced in 2017, was expected to give a boost to indirect tax revenues but has performed poorly with indirect tax revenues declining as a proportion of GDP in 2018–2020. There has also been a noticeable reduction in the share of value added going to workers. Growth of profits for businesses has been positive but somewhat lower. However, the share of profits in the distribution of GDP income has gone up somewhat.

The Indian economy has seen a definite slowdown in growth in the last few years and a big contraction in 2020–21. These setbacks would have to be left behind and the task of building the $10 trillion economy by 2035 taken up in right earnestness.

Sectoral Composition of the $10 Trillion Economy

India's current $3 trillion economy is approximately 15 per cent agricultural, 30 per cent industrial (including mining and quarrying, manufacturing, utilities and construction) and 55 per cent services (trade, hotels, transport, communication, broadcasting, financial, real estate, professional services, public administration, defence and other services). Agriculture value added is $450 billion, industrial value added $900 billion and services $1650 billion.

Raising the $450 billion dollar agricultural value added to $1 trillion in fifteen years would require value added to grow by a little over 5 per cent per annum. Considering the current nature, composition, price levels and exportability of the agriculture sector, a growth of over 5 per cent looks ambitious. However, if agriculture were to get commercialized, the handicaps of input subsidies and MSP-induced price depressions removed and a system of future price hedging built in, a growth of over 5 per cent is possible. The reorientation of agricultural production from crops to proteins and horticultural products would also help. This transformation would require considerable policy and programme reforms.

Increasing the current $900 billion industrial economy to $2.5 trillion by 2035 would require industry to grow from 7–8 per cent on average over the next fifteen years. This is eminently doable if India were to get its manufacturing, mining, utilities and real-estate policy framework right. Refocusing the government on production of public goods and services and aggressive privatization of the public sector would also help.

The services economy, which is about $1.65 trillion, would need to grow at 9 per cent per annum on average to get to $6.5 trillion by 2035. This is eminently achievable. However, significant reforms would be required in trade policies, the financial system, strengthening of IT, hospitality, transportation and broadcasting. Important policy reforms would also be needed in the health and education sectors.

Infrastructure 2035

An enormous amount of investment and reforms in policies is required to build the infrastructure of India for the $10 trillion economy. These investments and reforms have been described extensively in this book. If these investments and reforms are realized, India's infrastructure in 2035 should look something like this:

First, total power-generation capacity at 1,000 GW, approximately three times present capacity, with thermal power-generation capacity not exceeding 250 GW. More than 60 per cent of power-generation capacity should be from renewables, especially solar.

Second, 1 lakh km of national highways, mostly six lane, with 10 per cent minimum expressways, to connect business centres and large urban agglomerations, along with 4 lakh km of state highways (two to four lanes) as a functional grid of roads with interconnections to national highways.

Third, 1 lakh km of primarily passenger railway network, with about 10,000 km of high-speed railway network with average speed of 250 km per hour. Another 10,000 km of dedicated freight corridors to connect ports and major manufacturing and mineral-producing areas.

Fourth, port capacity at about 2.5 billion tonnes with about twenty major ports with modern facilities capable of receiving all kinds of cargo.

Fifth, about fifty international airports and 100 major domestic airports capable of handling 1.5 billion passengers a year.

Sixth, 100 million hectares of irrigated cropped area, with all distributaries of canal waters from the main canals until the delivery of water to individual fields is piped.

Seventh, more than fifty metropolitan cities and over 250 cities with population between 5 lakh and 10 lakh providing pollution-free, smart, efficient and wholesome urban living to an expected 50 per cent of urban population. Simultaneously, a distributed living model leveraging IT.

Eighth, 100 per cent of Indian population living in decent and *pucca* houses with water, sanitation, power and fuel supply.

Ninth, 100 per cent of homes, businesses and buildings connected to high-speed Internet and almost all communication, entertainment and information delivered digitally.

Tenth, digital infrastructure to ensure that the Centre and state governments are working completely in digital mode.

Indeed, a clear goal focuses the attention of everyone. If the Indian government clearly and unambiguously declares the goal to make India a $10 trillion economy by 2035, it will act like a lodestar to guide and inspire all participants in the economy—governments, businesses and people—to plan, coordinate and achieve the goal in time.

Set of Policy Reforms Proposed in This Book Can Alter the Arc of India's Future

Fundamental reforms of reorganizing the production and distribution system in the country have been proposed in this book. The production and distribution of private goods and services would need to be organized entirely in the private sector. This would require the commercial public sector, both in real and financial sectors, to be privatized fully within the next few years. The government would need to be focused on production and delivery of public goods and services to secure a good and healthy people and environment and also on redistribution to eliminate multidimensional poverty from the country.

Sectoral reforms, which have been described extensively in this book, across all the sectors—agriculture, industry and services—and also for infrastructure, the digital economy and environmental economy, would lead to prepare the country, its people, its businesses and the government to secure the kind of high economic growth described above.

India has been a slow and reluctant reformer. This has delayed reaping of the advantages of new and emerging technologies and production shifts. We cannot afford to commit the same mistakes again in mainstreaming the digital and environmental economy. The world is becoming one large market and production system. We need to be able to conquer world markets to earn incomes for raising the standard of living of all Indians and create the wealth to become a high-middle-income country by 2035.

A very bold set of reforms has been proposed in this book. Many of these reforms might appear quite non-doable at first sight. However, these reforms form a coherent whole for fundamental reformation of the Indian economy by 2035. These reforms would unleash the full force of the energy and enthusiasm of the people of India, the government in India and the businesses of India.

Let us all work to make India a $10 trillion economy by 2035 and realize this goal.

Data Sources and Other Notes

Data Sources

This book actually has three books built into it. The first is about the state of the Indian economy, which seeks to carry readers through the macroeconomic and sectoral performance of the country since Independence in 1947. The second is about India's economic policy journey during this period, including the fundamental reset of economic policies in the 1950s and 1990s. The third is about the country's policy options in the emerging digital and environmentally sustained global economy taking shape in the twenty-first century.

The landscape of the book is very wide. Using an enormous amount of data, it covers all macroeconomic dimensions, factors of production, sectoral performance of the economy, and India's economic and financial linkages with the rest of the world through trade, commerce, flow of investments and technology, and human migration.

I have attempted to write this book as a narrative. Therefore, I chose to weave the data into the book without any tables, graphs and footnotes or endnotes. While I have used exact data in a lot of places, I have approximated the same at most places to fit into the narrative. The whole idea is to use the meaning and significance of the data, rather than writing precise numbers. Thus, the texture of the book does not require citation of specific data sources.

Most of the macroeconomic data has been sourced from the publications of the Central Statistical Organization (CSO) and National Statistical Organization (NSO) and their press releases. RBI publications have also come in handy for macroeconomic, monetary and financial sector data. Reports relating to the Census of 1951 and the subsequent one, Plan documents, annual reports of the ministries and departments of the Government of India and publications of the CAG have been useful sources of the data used in different chapters of Part A.

Budget documents, which are publicly available since Independence, and Finance Ministry publications on debt and liabilities have been rich sources of data for the macroeconomic and fiscal chapters of the book.

The policy chapters in the book, especially in Part A, carry specific quotes in many places. I have referred to the specific report or document I have used to source these quotes or phrases. Almost everywhere, the extracts are from official government documents. Part B of the book also has some historical policy context. Wherever needed, I have referred to the source if I have quoted from any document.

I have not used any private copyrighted book, document or other publication in the book.

A Note of Thanks

This book presents my understanding, assessment and insights of the state of India's economy. It also documents and attempts a critical analysis of the formulation and implementation of economic, financial and fiscal policies and programmes since Independence. I have observed and participated in this journey for a long time, most closely in the last fifteen years. Learning from and building on this long participation and interaction with different parts and facets of the Indian economy, I present a comprehensive policy reform agenda for building a $10 trillion Indian economy by the middle of next decade.

This book has been possible only because of the enormous support and help I have received from a number of people over this long period. This moment is, to my mind, the right occasion to express my gratitude to these exceptional and extraordinarily considerate, helpful and empathetic people in my life.

I must begin by thanking my parents, Sita Ram Garg and Satyawati Devi, who bestowed upon me genes and a value system of honest and sincere work ethics. They, despite their hard financial conditions, allowed me to pursue my education and to realize my potential. They created conditions which made me practice that the real economic and public service opportunities can be seized only by raising your standards equal to the underlying asks.

I have always been fortunate to have numerous friends right from my school days who showered their love and affection on me and also assisted in smoothening financial and operational constraints in my path. In the acute financially struggling years of my college years, several friends, in particular Sunil Saxena, helped me to earn and get the minimum required financial resources to meet my expenditures and family commitments.

The experience of implementing numerous programmes of poverty alleviation, promoting industrial and infrastructure enterprises in cooperative and public sectors, designing and monitoring redistribution programmes in education, health and renewables sectors, dealing with policy issues in agriculture, power, transport and finance sectors in the first fifteen years of my service in Rajasthan provided an immensely valuable foundation for my understanding of the vast Indian economy. During this period, several officers gave me opportunity and space, consciously or subconsciously, to try out unconventional approaches and make innovations. In particular, I would like to acknowledge contributions of C.S. Rajan, Priyadarshi Thakur, Rajiv Mehrishi, the late Dr Adarsh Kishore, the late M.L. Mehta and the late V.B.L. Mathur.

Dr E.A.S. Sarma initiated me to the Government of India in the year 2000 by inducting me as a director in the department of economic affairs. This proved to be a stepping stone for providing me the real opportunity to get into the economic and financial policymaking of the country. In the Government of India, I had an incredibly productive and satisfying time in a variety of departments—economic affairs, expenditure, agriculture, cabinet secretariat and Ministry of Power. Working in the Ministry of Finance gave me excellent access to understanding the policies and programmes of almost every department and organization of the government. I benefited from working with many secretaries and other senior officers. Many talented young officers and colleagues worked with me in these departments as well. Their notes, briefings and valuable contributions are gratefully acknowledged. My heartfelt thanks to all of them.

I returned twice to my cadre, Rajasthan, in 2006–2009 and 2014. Both times Vasundhara Raje used my services in the finance department. She entrusted me with the responsibility of heading and managing state finances in 2008 when I was virtually one of the junior-most principal secretary level officers in the cadre. She trusted my judgement and opted for the digitally advanced and remarkably prescient Bhamashah programme (which was a precursor of the JAM trinity later) in place of populist programmes like free power, free rations, etc. She called for my services again to head the finance department when she returned to power in 2013. I am thankful to her for the responsibilities she entrusted me with and the freedom she accorded for managing the finance department professionally.

Prime Minister Narendra Modi chose me, in a very unconventional manner, to go to the World Bank as India's executive director while I was still in the service at the level of additional secretary. The experience I gained there of the inner workings of the global financial system, in particular, international developmental financing, was quite extraordinary.

I am thankful to Srimulyani Indrawati and Kristalina Georgieva, two chief executive officers who chaired most of the board meetings for their deft handling of the board. I express my appreciation for the board practice of four minutes' intervention, which equipped me to present my case on any complex policy matter within the time limit and without referring to any notes.

Prime Minister Narendra Modi and Dr P.K. Mishra brought me to the department of economic affairs as secretary—the place where my understanding and assessment of the Indian economy got more clarified and deepened. I must thank both Prime Minister Modi and Dr Mishra for giving me this extraordinary opportunity to participate in national economic policymaking, budget-making and interacting with world leaders in multilateral fora.

The late Arun Jaitley was quite a remarkable finance minister and human being. His ability to get to the nub of the issues and trust his officers to run the departments was simply extraordinary. This provided me unprecedented opportunity to make the best of my two-year time in the finance ministry. I will always remain grateful to him. The arrival of Nirmala Sitharaman in the ministry created the right conditions for me to think of widening my sphere of work—from the government to society at large. The last two years, since October 2019 when I left the government after taking voluntary retirement, have been most satisfying, enriching and productive despite COVID-19 disruptions. I thank Nirmala Sitharaman for making me harness enough strength to break out from the gravitational pull of the government service.

I began writing blogs on economic, financial and fiscal matters after I left the government, which attracted the attention of a lot of people. I am deeply thankful to Penguin Random House India who agreed to publish a book authored by me. Manish from Penguin has been with me in this journey—from conceptualizing this book to now publishing it. I am thankful to Manish, Ralph and the team of editors and associates at Penguin for making this maiden venture of writing a book a great learning, enjoyable and rewarding experience.

Arati Menon, at my request, did the first editing of this book. She has the uncanny ability to reconstruct sentences, making these read well without any loss of content and meaning. I cannot thank her enough for making this long book an eminently readable book.

I want to thank you, the reader as well, for the time spent on going through this book or some parts of it. I hope this was worth your time.

Makar Sakranti, 14 January 2022   Subhash Chandra Garg
New Delhi